An Historical Geography of

IRELAND

Edited by

B J Graham

Department of Environmental Studies, University of Ulster at Coleraine

L J Proudfoot

School of Geosciences, The Queen's University of Belfast

ACADEMIC PRESS
Harcourt Brace, Jovanovich, Publishers
London   San Diego   New York   Boston
Sydney   Tokyo   Toronto

ACADEMIC PRESS LIMITED
24–28 Oval Road
London NW1 7DX

United States Edition published by
ACADEMIC PRESS, INC.
San Diego, CA 92101

This book is printed on acid-free paper.

A catalogue record for this book is available from
the British Library

ISBN 0–12–294881–5

Typeset by Fakenham Photosetting Limited, Fakenham, Norfolk
Printed in Great Britain by the University Press, Cambridge

Acknowledgements

We are most grateful to the technical and secretarial staff in the Department of Environmental Studies, University of Ulster at Coleraine, and the School of Geosciences, Queen's University, Belfast, for their help in cartography, photography and word-processing—especially Killian McDaid, Gillian Alexander, Maura Pringle, Nigel McDowell, Shirley Morrow and Mary McCamphill. Valerie Graham has typed (and re-typed) considerable portions of the text and we are indebted to her patience and good humour. The following figures have been adapted from various originals in *A New History of Ireland* by permission of Oxford University Press: 3.4, 3.5, 4.1, 4.2, 4.3, 4.5, 6.1, 7.3, 7.4, 12.4. Figure 7.1 is reproduced from the Ordnance Survey map with the sanction of the Controller of H.M.S.O., Crown Copyright reserved, Permit No. 519.

Contributors

T. B. BARRY, *Department of Medieval History, Trinity College, Dublin 2, Ireland.*

L. A. CLARKSON, *Department of Economic and Social History, The Queen's University of Belfast, Belfast BT7 1NN, Northern Ireland.*

B. COLLINS, *Institute of Irish Studies, The Queen's University of Belfast, Belfast BT7 1NN, Northern Ireland.*

R. GILLESPIE, *Department of Modern History, St Patrick's College, Maynooth, County Kildare, Ireland.*

B. J. GRAHAM, *Department of Environmental Studies, University of Ulster at Coleraine, Coleraine BT52 1SA, Northern Ireland.*

C. J. HOUSTON, *Department of Geography, University of Toronto, Erindale College, Mississauga L5L 1C6, Ontario, Canada.*

L. KENNEDY, *Department of Economic and Social History, The Queen's University of Belfast, Belfast BT7 1NN, Northern Ireland.*

L. J. PROUDFOOT, *School of Geosciences, The Queen's University of Belfast, Belfast BT7 1NN, Northern Ireland.*

S. A. ROYLE, *School of Geosciences, The Queen's University of Belfast, Belfast BT7 1NN, Northern Ireland.*

W. J. SMYTH, *Department of Geography, St Patrick's College, Maynooth, County Kildare, Ireland.*

WILLIAM J. SMYTH, *Department of Geography, University College, Cork, Ireland.*

M. TURNER, *Department of Economic and Social History, School of Economic Studies, University of Hull, Hull HU6 7RX, England.*

Contents

2
The High Middle Ages: *c.* 1100 to *c.* 1350
B. J. GRAHAM

3
Late Medieval Ireland: The Debate on Social and Economic Transformation, 1350–1550
T. B. BARRY

4
Explorers, Exploiters and Entrepreneurs: Early Modern Ireland and its Context, 1500–1700
R. GILLESPIE

10

The Irish Diaspora: Emigration to the New World, 1720–1920
C. J. HOUSTON and W. J. SMYTH 338

11

The Irish in Britain, 1780–1921
B. COLLINS 366

12
The Making of Ireland: Agendas and Perspectives in Cultural Geography
WILLIAM J. SMYTH 399

List of Illustrations

List of Tables

Introduction

A Perspective on the Nature of Irish Historical Geography

B. J. Graham and L. J. Proudfoot

During the past twenty years, the themes and methodology of Irish historical geography have changed radically. In many ways, these developments have taken place in a context almost entirely divorced from the contemporary development of the subject in Britain. The sequential paradigm shifts that occurred in Britain, ranging from H. C. Darby's 'experimental and pragmatic scholarship' through flirtations with logical positivism and a more enduring relationship with the 'Grand Theory' of Marxists and structuralists, to today's postmodern eclecticism, have no parallel in Ireland.[1] There are occasional echoes perhaps but the heritage of Irish historical geography is very different to, and rarely convergent with, that of Britain.

Although inevitably doubly iniquitous in that it appears to deny the numerous contributions of others, and conversely, heap their many sins upon a few, we can identify two individuals as symbolizing this divergence. The first was E. Estyn Evans, Lecturer and later Professor of Geography at Queen's University, Belfast, between 1928 and 1968. Intellectually, Evans did not regard himself as an historical geographer, holding the adjective redundant in a world which he saw defined by the theme of man and his environment. To Evans, geography was 'the common ground between the natural world and cultural history'.[2] He regarded the essential unity of Ireland as lying within the traditions and folkways of the countryside and Irish historians as being 'document-bound', constrained by their innate source-dominated caution. Evans advocated a broadening into what he called 'unrecorded history', that of archaeology, anthropology and ethnology. His own mentors were men who have had relatively little influence on the development of British histori-cal geography. From H. J. Fleure, he followed the maxim that 'geography, history and anthropology are a trilogy to be broken only with a severe loss of truth'. He applauded the work of the French geographers, Vidal de la Blache, Jean Brunhes and later the historians of the *Annales* school, Marc Bloch, Lucien Febvre and, perhaps above all, Fernand Braudel.[3] The other major influence on his ideas was the landscape paradigm formulated by the American geographer, Carl Sauer. Like Sauer, Evans emphasized the French genius for synthesis, endorsing Bloch's idea that the framework of institutions within which a society lives can be understood only in the light of the whole human environment.[4] This dimension of synthesis is amongst the most important and enduring characteristics which Evans bequeathed to the subsequent development of Irish historical geography, and it constitutes an important thread of this text. Nevertheless, Andrews argues that Evans' vision of Ireland possessed a major limitation, observing that one of his earlier and most famous books, *Irish Heritage*, consciously excluded the 'controversial realms' of religion and politics.[5] While this criticism is less true of some of Evans' later work in which these issues were addressed in a generalized way, they were never to be systematically incorporated into his arguments. While this is an important flaw, nevertheless, there remains a curious but pronounced contemporaneity to many of Evans' ideas. A key premise of postmodernism is our need to contemplate the human world less in the context of 'grand theories' and more in terms of 'humble eclectic and empirically grounded materials'.[6] Paradoxically, that is precisely what constitutes the *tradition* of Irish historical geography, the legacy which—to a very considerable extent—the re-evaluations of the past twenty years have sought to question.

If Evans sought to define the 'common ground' both between the natural world and cultural history and between the rump of Ulster and the remainder of Ireland, then—in a neat touch of symmetry—the same phrase was used as the title of a book of essays in honour of our second symbolic figure, T. Jones Hughes, former Professor of Geography at University College, Dublin. Again we can see a similarity of content, the self-same belief that the central concern of geography was with the relatively humble and eclectic. Jones Hughes' common ground was that of the ordinary, country people; 'his concerns and sympathies were with (their) lives, pains and aspirations'.[7] Again, like Evans, there is the intellectual connection with France rather than Britain, particularly in Jones Hughes' case, the influence of Pierre Flatrès, who brought continental insights to the study of the villages of Ireland and the impact of 'landlordism' on Irish settlement and culture.[8] In comparison to Evans' world, sensitivity to place carries a less privileged status. Jones Hughes' vision of a landlord-created landscape built upon the backs of the common people was not assembled from intensive field study but through an analysis of documentary sources and, in particular, the Griffith Valuation. In an appreciation of Jones Hughes' career, John Andrews credits him with a more fundamental role than that of Evans in the development of Irish historical geography, 'for his mission was to socialise and thereby revolutionise the Irish past'. Andrews sees Jones Hughes as a progressively radical academic, increasingly an exponent of a colonial axis of explanation of the Irish past. By this he meant the assumption of rights by planters and the natives' denials of those rights.[9] However, this is very much the stuff of the traditional and no longer widely accepted nationalist historiography of O'Brien, Pomfret and the like,[10] and Jones Hughes never made any attempt to define or justify the limited and loose ideas which he derived from them and which appear in his work as a simple binary classification— the 'Anglo-colonizer' and the 'Gaelic-colonized'. Consequently, in his vision of Ireland, 'geography is made social by the involvement of two parties in every geographical fact'.[11] To qualify Andrews' statement, it is the actual attempt to socialize the past through an intensive analysis of a particular source, rather than its theoretical content, which might lead one to describe this geographical perspective as radical.

Thus, there was no past consensus as to the nature of Irish historical geography. There were dominant figures and those they influenced but also numerous individuals, themselves the product of a disparate array of intellectual backgrounds. F. H. A. Aalen's *Man and the Landscape in Ireland* provides a convenient watershed, presenting an interpretation of much of this work, couched within what we might call the several traditional perspectives of Irish historical geography.[12] Since its publication, there has been a re-evaluation of almost every aspect of that synthesis. In part, this has been driven by intellectual dissatisfaction with the assumptions upon which these traditional perspectives are based, and also with their research methodologies. First, whatever their internal dialogue, they share several 'common grounds'. As MacDonagh has observed, one of the most compelling of all Irish images is of sea-made isolation conferring the island's identity.[13] As Evans himself put it, the diversity of Ireland comes from its very insularity which attracted intrusive cultures from the earliest times.[14] 'Insular' is a word often applied to traditional perspectives in Irish history, archaeology and geography. Despite the influence of intellectual ideas drawn from France and the United States, both Evans and Jones Hughes internalized those, allowing them to be consumed within this 'compelling image' of insular integrity. Therefore, their work shares the notion that particularity of place—especially conferred by surrounding water—provides a sufficient explanatory structure for geographical phenomena. This perspective is dependent upon assumptions drawn, perhaps subconsciously, from traditional perspectives on Irish nationalism. There is, for example, an implicit contradiction in Evans' ideas between his acceptance of insularity and particularity and his condemnations of the 'racialist' nature of that ideology.[15]

A second area of 'common ground' is the emphasis on morphogenesis which runs through all Irish historical geography. Neither Evans nor Jones Hughes was guilty of contemplating artefacts for their own sakes but both shared a consuming interest in their empirical distribution in the landscape. These are not the Darby-type landscapes criticized, perhaps rather unfairly, as 'Whiggish, materialist and bourgeois in orientation'. Rather, a characteristic trait in Irish historical geography is the notion that the visible scene is a 'manifestation of a given culture', an idea which, as Williams states, goes back to Sauer.[16] Evans' theme, for example, was the common people and the land itself, the land that they had helped to make.[17] The concept, currently fashionable with some British historical geographers, that landscape is a reflection of the society that produces it, and that representative landscapes are symbolic and part of the very iconography of a nation, constitutes another curious example of the modernity—in the British sense—of traditional perspectives in Irish historical geography.[18] The difficulty here is therefore not the idea, which is presented in this text as one of the strengths of contemporary Irish historical geography, but the constraints which both Evans and Jones Hughes applied to their definitions of characteristically Irish landscapes. The world as defined by Evans was entirely rural and for Jones Hughes, towns and villages were no more than symbolic of the simplified duality of his ill-defined colonialism.

Third, while both Evans and Jones Hughes were thus well aware of the metaphorical function of settlement and landscape, such ideas remain subterranean in their work, implicitly rather than explicitly expressed for neither was given to overt theorizing. Thus, perhaps the single most important deficiency of the traditional perspectives is the absence of a clearly-constituted recognition that all academic studies, and hence every result of those endeavours, are theory-structured, and further that those theories are themselves dependent on ideological perspectives. To deny that—as some in Ireland might do—is itself an ideological statement. One example of the lack of certainty about theory is provided by Jones Hughes' use of complex conceptual terms such as 'colonial' and 'colonialism' without even the most limited attempt at definition. It is an example of an ambivalence which sadly has had a deleterious effect on the discipline. Much Irish historical geography is underpinned by quite simplistic and unacknowledged assumptions, derivative of one particular nationalist identity and by an overt antipathy to the concept that the empirical world is a succession of ideological representations, constituted by ever-changing forms of social order. Consequently, the symbolism of the landscape and its role as a repository of evidence for the large-scale forces of past social and ideological change which in part created it are too often ignored in the effort to measure and describe it through the medium of simplified stereotyped represen-tations. As we discuss below, the problem for geographers is that an idealized landscape is a necessary environment for the political concept of a nation.[19]

Therefore, while on one hand there is much to be admired in and retained from Irish historical geography's own pasts, there is also much that is paradoxical. The several perspectives were open to a diversity of intellectual influences but simul-taneously developed a marked insularity of explanation. They were receptive to the common people and have produced profound interpretations of the creation and further symbolism of particular representations of what might constitute an Irish landscape. They were open to the regional variations which characterize Ireland although less than even-handed in their interpretation of the fusion of internal and external socio-ideological forces which have created those. Often, they were careless too, even insular, in accepting particular nationalist posturings. Because of the somewhat dismissive attitude adopted to the theory-construction of all explanation, it is less than clear if particular ideological perspectives were incor-porated wittingly or inadvertently. In fairness, historical geography was not alone amongst academic disciplines in these shortcomings. The revisionist synthesis presented in this text attempts to address these particular problems, drawing negatively but positively too on what has gone before. Before turning to consider the nature of this re-evaluation, it has to be placed within a wider debate concerned with nationalism and the meaning of Irishness.

Revisionism and the Irish Past

The importance of the past and the way in which it is used to validate and legitimize contemporary beliefs and actions can be seen with unusual clarity in Ireland. It is self-evident that the past is not an optional extra but part of the living present. However, if we see particular competing pasts as being created to provide and enhance specific visions of communal and national identity, it follows that any resolution to Ireland's contemporary political and moral dilemmas requires the formulation of a different past.[20] That has to triumph over those historiographies written to underpin both the demand for independence from Britain, and the

Unionists' position that partition and the foundation of the northern state was a legitimate expression of their right to self-determination and territory within the island of Ireland.[21] Arguably, any nationalist ideology is the work of the imagination and a nation as an 'imagined community' requires a representative landscape as one crucial component in the achievement of an actual communality. Nationalism aspires to provide social and political identity through the creation of a set of shared ideas, drawing upon the historic unity of a people and a particular image of an historic past to develop a sense of mutual belonging.[22] As we shall see, Irish historical geography has contributed to a very particular image of the past, one which is vested within a representation of landscape derived from the Gaelic historiography developed in the nineteenth century to underpin the demand for Home Rule and eventual independence from Britain. One of the fundamental weaknesses of the Unionist position is that it has never developed a representative northern landscape to underpin both its separatist ideology within Ireland and its British connection. Curiously, as Evans, the north's most important contributor to the development of historical geography, argued, Ulster, the six counties of Northern Ireland together with Donegal, Cavan and Monaghan, is perhaps the most Irish of all the four provinces (Fig. I.1). It is different from the rest of Ireland but that too is characterized by regionalization. Out of that diversity and even dissension emerges what Evans called Irish heritage, something he saw as a total inheritance. The paradox is that while, as we shall see, this emphasis is congruent with contemporary reinterpretations of the meaning of Irishness, Evans' geographical ideology led him to identify instead with the transmitted landscape of traditional Gaelic nationalism.

The re-evaluations characteristic of recent Irish historical geography cannot be divorced from the rather wider debate amongst historians and social scientists generally. Broadly, this is what has become known as revisionism. As Brady states, the notion that there is a school of historical revisionists bent on replacing the old nationalist orthodoxies with an alternative framework, is overly simplistic.[23] There is a range of differing interpretations; to quote Bradshaw's polemical defence of the *status quo*, the revisionist claim is that:

> the holistic interpretation of Irish history stands exposed as a myth designed to validate the aspirations of modern nationalism and to provide an origin-legend for the twentieth-century nation-state.[24]

As we have argued, the role of any nationalism is to forge a communal sense of identity and to validate that, it must stress stability, or to put it another way, continuity. In essence, at the heart of the debate over Irish nationalism is the definition of the limits of 'Irishness'. It is not a new debate but it is one which has resurfaced with considerable vehemence in recent years. In part, it has been driven by the intractable issue of the North, but also—and perhaps more important to the mainstream of contemporary society—by the pressing need to redefine a new Irish identity suitable for a context of European integration.

Foster has described traditional Gaelic-Irish nationalism as 'a curious compound of radicalism, conservatism and reaction'.[25] It was radical in the sense that it linked the question of the land to the fundamentally long-standing aspirations of the Irish

Fig. I.1. The provinces and counties of Ireland.

people.[26] To the Young Ireland movement of the 1840s, for example, nationalism had to be directed exclusively at the attainment of a secure, independent agricultural peasantry.[27] Crucial to this was the classification of the propertied classes as alien. As the Marxist historian, V. G. Kiernan, puts it, because the bulk of the rent-devouring class was foreign, patriots were spared part of the awkwardness of linking classes. Nationalism had to rest itself in the soil to grow strong.[28] Somewhat paradoxically, it was radical too in that it linked Irishness with the conservatism of Catholicism. Hutchinson argues that the seventeenth-century conquest and plantations had the effect of forcing ethnic identities in Ireland into a religious framework, the Catholic Church being depicted as a last native bastion against the alien state.[29] While this oversimplifies the nature of Catholicism, which was by no means monolithic, and overlooks the divergent character of the plantations, the linkage that was achieved between this perspective of nationalism and a particular religion had the further effect of separating the majority of the Irish population from the Protestant peasant and working class in the north of the island. Coakley is but one commentator who has argued that the failure of class conflict to achieve a clear political articulation is perhaps the most strikingly unique factor in Ireland's nationalisms.[30]

Gaelic nationalism sought its historical justification for the definition of Irishness and the Irish people in a particular origin-myth. In this context, a mythology is a set of ideas derived from ancient legend which is used to justify political demands, and aspirations and justify contemporary events.[31] The origin-myth of traditional nationalism was concerned to establish that the genesis of Irish identity and nation-hood predated the colonizations of the Anglo-Normans in the twelfth century and the Vikings before them. It centred on sources such as the *Lebor Gabála, The Book of Invasions*, a composite text of the twelfth century, the core of which probably dates back to the seventh, and which details the successive invasions of Ireland after the time of the Flood.[32] In the first instance, this and similar texts were used to establish a myth of national integration that Ireland could be a melting-pot of different cultures, but combined with a further myth of racial superiority which held that the other inhabitants of the country had to Gaelicize themselves to become Irish. Rather perversely, some Northern Protestants are now seeking their own origin-legends in similar texts, in particular the *Táin Bó Cúailgne*, 'The Cattle Raid of Cooley', which depicts a prehistoric Ulster with its capital at Emain Macha (Navan Fort near Armagh), in confrontation with the forces of Connacht and Leinster.[33] MacDonagh uses the phrase, 'foreshortening of time', in referring to this use of pseudo-histories of Celtic origin to validate nineteenth- and now twen-tieth-century political and social aspirations and order.[34] Another example of the historical myth is provided by the concept of the late-medieval 'Gaelic Revival' which, it has been argued, provided the fledgling Irish Free State with respectable antecedents in the Middle Ages.[35] Bradshaw prefers to emphasize the 'beneficient legacy' or, as he puts it, 'the positive dynamic of this mythology', its 'wrongness not withstanding'.[36] Consequently, the Irish nationalism formulated in the nine-teenth century was defined by three characteristics. It was Gaelic in the sense that it looked to this distant past, Catholic and, because the peasantry defined it, rural. Exclusive on all counts, it was incorporated by De Valera into the 1937 constitution as the definitive ideology of the Irish state where it remains as a fundamentalist barrier to a resolution of the problem of the North. Gaelic nationalism defines Ireland by its insular boundary but in a notable paradox, denies—indeed pro-scribes—the plurality entailed by such a claim.[37] It is the complexity of that plura-lity which constitutes the central theme of this book.

Inevitably, the exclusivity of this nationalism was bound up with reaction against subordination and dependency. The debate over Ireland's relationship to Britain is central to this text. As we shall see, there is no consensual resolution to offer because of the often conflicting ideological perspectives involved. Nor is there even an agreed chronology of colonialism. However, the Gaelic nationalism of the late nineteenth century was exclusive in that it identified the Anglo-Irish and the descendants of the seventeenth-century planters as representative of that subordination and dependence. The Anglo-Irish and the Anglo-Normans long before them, were alien in the sense that they were 'inserted elites'. Yet the eighteenth-century Anglo-Irish, while self-consciously *arriviste*, also proclaimed an identity derived from Ireland's sea-made isolation.[38] To the Anglo-Irish of the Middle Ages, the successors of the Anglo-Normans, the same may well have been true. It is a refusal to accept this exclusion of diversity from amongst those who can be included within the definition of Irishness which lies at the core of the revisionist critique. Cullen, for example, sees the whole concept of a history represented in these traditional terms as impoverishing Irish nationality and its sense of identity. Rather than being couched in terms of oppression, Irish identity should be framed within 'the rich, complex and varied stream of identity and racial (sic) consciousness, heightened in the course of centuries of Anglo-Irish relations'.[39] Evans made an analogous if different point when he argued that Ulster was one strong regional variant within Ireland's habitat, heritage and history. As he observed, most of the nations of Europe had evolved 'through a fusion of regional loyalties'.[40]

It is this word—fusion—which is crucial and which has to be distinguished from the acculturation or assimilation of the Gaelic 'melting-pot'. In his attack on revisionism, Bradshaw decries it as a Whig view of history—the idea of history as progress—and one invalidated by its claim for value-freedom. In turn, it could be argued that Bradshaw's own position constitutes little more than a claim for the value-freedom of his own perspective in a world in which every interpretation is value-laden. In essence he argues that national consciousness is a recurring cultural phenomenon in Ireland for 'perhaps a millennium before the onset of modernity'. To identify a national consciousness within medieval Irish society is a perfectly respectable academic argument, so long as it is recognized that like all other such contentions, it rests upon a set of assumptions, themselves reflective of a particular ideological construct.[41] Bradshaw's critique—which falls into the category known rather awkwardly as re-revisionism—is fallacious too in its understanding of the revisionist position (if there is such a thing). The crucial point is not the longevity *per se* of Irish identity but rather its nature—'assimilative' melting-pot or 'fusion'. On the one hand there is the seamless integration of virtually all exogenous influences within a stable and continuous Gaelic identity, on the other a society constantly renewed (in the non-Whiggish sense) by a plurality of influences, conflict, invasion, trade, social contacts and ideas. This is what we mean by fusion. What is specifically Irish is the precise delineation of those inputs. It is vital to remember that revisionism does not set out to destroy Irish nationalism; rather it seeks to redefine a new origin-myth, one dependent on the idea that Irish identity stems from that particular fusion of a disparate array of cultural elements drawn from all over Europe rather than the stereotyped notion of eternal Gaelic triumph. That latter notion is scarcely congruent with the country's role in the late twentieth century and is divisive within Ireland. Because of its sectarianism and exclusivity, the Unionists do not have to face and define their own identity and relationship to place. Rather, they continue to derive their justifications from the essential negativity of Gaelic nationalism because that remains as the intellectual basis of the constitution of the Irish state.

Theoretical Structuring of the Past

Before we can draw out the implications of this debate for the historical geography of Ireland, consideration has to be given to the influence of a parallel set of ideas. All social and economic phenomena are created and defined by a set of *a priori* (pre-existing) assumptions, derived implicitly (subconsciously) or explicitly (deliberately) from a set of ideological principles. But it is a characteristic of Irish historical geography to have ignored the ideological construction of society. Demonstrably, however, past approaches were theory-led; the difficulty is that the particular set of guiding principles was rarely made clear. Nor is this merely an arcane academic issue because the results, conclusions and outcomes of that research—its 'reality'—were determined by those principles. Essentially, the research of the last 20 years demonstrates the simple maxim that a change of principles leads to a different set of results and, therefore, to a different representative Irish identity, landscape and history.

Implicit within almost all traditional Irish historical geography is the underlying mythology of a Gaelic and rural society—Catholicism is less overt. By this we mean that the representative landscapes produced by traditional perspectives of historical geography are congruent with what Corkery called the 'Hidden Ireland'. This was the Gaelic side, 'stretching back unbroken and productive to pre-Christian' times.[42] As Cullen has shown, its central tenet was that the eighteenth-century Gaelic environment was one of economic, political and religious oppression.[43] The conscious, or possibly subconscious, incorporation of this type of historiography meshed with particular sets of geographical ideas to produce a discipline with a very particular dichotomy of subject content. On one hand, it sought to elucidate the landscape of the Hidden Ireland—the Gaelic side. For all his recognition of the diverse fusion of elements and regional identities which constituted Ireland, it was Estyn Evans who was primarily responsible for creating this representative Gaelic and rural landscape, characterized by the sort of 'time-collapse' referred to by MacDonagh.[44] For example, contemporary settlement patterns were explained as traditions extending as far back as the Iron Age, a remarkable testament to the importance of implicit assumptions of the foreshortening of time and inherent stability of Gaelic society. There was no place in this landscape for the Anglo-Norman traditions in the south and east of the island nor for towns. There was no urban society in the Hidden Ireland, no contradiction between town and country society because the towns themselves were overwhelmingly rural.[45] On the other hand, it was Jones Hughes, in his many studies of the estates and estate towns of the Anglo-Irish landlords, who set out to establish the landscape of oppression, his results a teleological repercussion of the latent assumptions of Gaelic nationalism implicit but never explicit in his work.[46] As we noted earlier, some emphasis was placed on ideas of subordination and dependency but this was done in an entirely commonsense fashion. There was little or no definition of terms nor any attempt to integrate Ireland into the extensive literature on colonialism or underdevelopment.[47] Thus, we had a geographical reality—or several realities—which stemmed from particular sets of ideas, the wider theoretical provenance of which was rarely if ever acknowledged. This can be seen as a further example of insularity, an expression of the assumption that the surrounding sea was itself a sufficient explanation of Ireland's particularity. The traditional perspectives of Irish historical geography failed to address the influence of the successive waves of immigrants who crossed that sea except through their depiction in the essentially negative role of destroying the purity of that Gaelic and rural society. The only external analogies generally invoked were with other Celtic areas—Brittany, Wales, Scotland and Cornwall.

If these comments sound unduly critical, it has to be recognized that as historical geographers of Ireland, these perspectives constitute our intellectual heritage. It is the nature of academic enquiry that new ideas feed off the deficiencies and strengths of their predecessors. It would be entirely wrong to depict this book as characterized by theoretical agreement, but there is a virtual consensus that empiricism and description are no longer sufficient. It is recognized that the topics and artefacts which historical geographers—together with economic historians and archaeologists—investigate, must be placed within the context of the large-scale forces of change and continuity which operate within and between societies. The outcomes may be particular to Ireland, but these are explicable only within a wider geographical framework and also as reflections of particular methods of organizing societies. Obviously, there are intimations here of the debate on structuration which extends far beyond the realms of geography.[48] In summary, this perspective holds that individuals and groups are studied in a context of interaction with social and economic structures, upon which they effect transformation, while themselves expressing changes in view, action and reaction.[49] Perhaps, the clearest elucidation of such ideas is to be found in the work of some economic geographers who argue that the particularity of places is the result of the fusion or integration of individual or local forces with global or general process. The result is the spectrum of myriad differences which characterize the geography of any locality and indeed there are substantial regional variations within Ireland.[50] Such ideas shade into the contemporary concept of postmodernism 'as object', the retention of a belief in social order but the recognition of a multiplicity of outcomes.[51] Very much the same sort of debate is taking place in archaeology.[52]

Before considering the repercussions of all this for Irish historical geography, we need also to examine one aspect of the concept of economic and social transformation in more detail. Ostensibly, continuity and change seem relatively easy terms to define, but in actuality, their meanings can be multi-faceted. At its most straightforward, continuity is a descriptive physical process which occurs when existing features such as settlements or units of landownership display a continuing usefulness and are retained by an incoming group. Thus, they are incorporated into some new landscape and social matrix which, if changed, is not necessarily completely divergent from what had gone before. All societies—in any epoch—are characterized by the simultaneous presence of elements of continuity and change, the specific balance of those elements in any one locale being the definitive essence of the particularity of that place. However, continuity and change also possess deeper underlying ideological meanings and thus we must be extremely cautious in our use and interpretation of the terms. Continuity can be equated with essentially endogenous forces—which may be equated with stability—whereas change can be exogenous or indigenous or both simultaneously but is more likely to be linked to external—alien—influences.

In its ideological sense, continuity and change can possess a radical meaning in that their duality constitutes the basis of the concept that any one society is a fusion of a 'rich, complex and varied stream of identity', a mix of internal and external forces in a state of constant mutation. In Ireland, this means a rejection of a stereotyped past, 'couched in terms of a simplified context of land resettlement, oppression and resentment'.[53] In its radical sense, continuity and change is an ideological force for enrichment; it defines the specific, exclusive nature of place but this particularity is seen to emerge from a mix of heterogeneous influences rather than the continuity through foreshortened time of a set of ideas designed to underpin a sectarian and chauvinistic separateness. In this latter guise, we can identify the conservative manifestation of continuity and change. If the balance is set towards the former, change can be integrated within a continuing stability of the *status quo*. Thus the traditional nationalist idea of Ireland as a 'melting-pot', in which Gaelicism remains eternally assimilative and essentially unchanged, constitutes a reactionary but commonplace concept of continuity. As Canny points out in a review, it is expressed in the notion that the Irish environment and society prevailed over the best endeavours of settlers to dominate it.[54] In this regard, the social stability offered by the particular representative mythology of Gaelic, rural nationalism remains embedded in some Irish historical geography. We argue that it is inappropriate and ambivalent, part of a concept which defines national identity by assimilation, exclusivity and a misconceived notion of ethnic purity, rather than by a fusion of multiple influences and the consequent particularity of place. Thus we need to be very clear about the context in which ideas of social continuity and change are being used.

The Repercussions of Revisionism and Theoretical Debate for Irish Historical Geography

Demonstrably, the model of continuity and change can be applied to Irish historical geography itself. From its own heritage, many ideas—occasionally ill-defined— can be retained. But the discipline has been influenced too by forces for change, particularly with regard to redefining the limits of its subject matter and placing these within wider geographical and theoretical frameworks. It is through this fusion of internal and external forces that the subject itself can define its particular distinctiveness. It is our purpose here to identify the themes of this book and attempt to relate them to this wider context. Three sets of ideas, linked by a common thread of re-evaluation, are apparent.

Theme One

As we have already discussed, first, there is the plurality of Irish identity, landscape and history, a concept inherently incompatible with the traditional model of nationalism. Theoretically, this notion of plurality is linked to the concepts of continuity and change and the need for historical geographers to address the nature of underlying social order and the ways in which that mutates through time. At almost every point in the text, it is seen that traditional modes of explanation are vested—explicitly or implicitly, knowingly or otherwise—within that traditional nationalist model. By contrast, the book addresses changing ideas on the diversity of Ireland, the rich tapestry of culture and regional identity which inspired Estyn Evans. Therefore, the debate over acculturation and assimilation as opposed to transformation is a recurring theme throughout the book. For example, the meaning and importance of continuity and change is fundamental to the debate on the historical geography of Ireland in the high and later Middle Ages (Chapters 2 and 3), and it resurfaces again when the ability of landlords to transform eighteenth-century landscapes is considered (Chapter 7). In turn, that analysis is firmly linked to the broader discussion of revisionist nationalism considered above. It should be reiterated that the purpose of revisionism is not to dispose of a national identity but rather to re-align it along a less disruptive and exclusive axis of interpretation, one mature enough to admit to an Irish diversity without recourse to a set of convenient and ambivalent assimilations dependent on myths of continuity and stability. As Smyth demonstrates in his exploration of the making of Ireland (Chapter 12), there is a wonderful but specific complexity to Ireland's cultural location.

Theme Two

These concerns mesh with the second theme, which combines a retention of the traditional strengths of Ireland's historical geography, particularly in morphological analysis, with the illumination to be gained from exposing them to wider perspectives. This can be achieved in a relatively superficial fashion through the sort of empirical or chronological analogy which can be found in virtually any chapter in this book. At another and more profound level, however, insularity has to be obviated by the unambiguous recognition that all reality is theory-structured and therefore, that explicit recognition must be given to the ideological constructs which underlie and construct our ostensible subject matter. By extension, as Proudfoot demonstrates in Chapter 6, it must be emphasized that explanation at the island-wide scale, small though it is, can be unduly monolithic. Every country is a fusion of regions and Ireland is no exception. As our understanding of its past becomes more sophisticated, then so too does our awareness of the ways in which general and local processes combine to produce myriad regional differentiations within it.

As we have seen, the traditions of Irish historical geography are vested in the study of landscape and the human artefacts found therein. Ireland's more distant past is not particularly well documented and one important theme in this book is that we are working towards defining a position where those artefacts are a primary, diagnostic clue to the relative balances of continuity and change, the latter reflective of the fusion of internal and external social, economic and political forces upon Ireland's societal development. Therefore, the morphogenesis of settlement is no longer seen as being something worth contemplating for its own sake but, instead, indicative of rather more profound forces, a discriminating and sensitive indicator of that social transformation. If society is in a constant state of mutation, through an interaction of internal and external forces, classification schemes can no longer depend upon morphological details. People, their settlements and other material artefacts, have to be placed within that context of continuous transformation. The plethora of humble, eclectic and empirically grounded material artefacts which constituted the medieval Irish landscape is seen to rest upon a retained belief in social order. Therefore, as Graham and Barry argue in their discussion of medieval Ireland (Chapters 1–3), it is those objects and materials, studied in the field and classified by their physical parameters, which can provide illuminating insights into that social order and the mechanisms of transformation therein. As we have indicated, the debate on the nature of that transformation is of major significance in an island with divergent nationalities and one of the most resolutely unsolved dilemmas of identity in western Europe.

Obviously, this approach owes much to the traditions of Evans if set within a different ideological context and willing to exploit the available documentary sources. As we have observed, however, Evans specifically eschewed a methodology based on documentary or archival research. In contrast, much of the historical geography of the last twenty years has used such evidence, which is relatively extensive from the seventeenth century onwards. This approach reflects Jones Hughes' own methodological contribution to the subject, and in common with much of his work, has been characterized by a sensitivity to the particularities of place. Thus, Smyth has used various national censuses and surveys to reconstruct the fine detail of the changing settlement structures in Counties Kilkenny and Tipperary in the seventeenth century.[55] On a more local scale, Horner, Duffy and Smyth, for example, have explored disparate collections of eighteenth- and nineteenth-century estate papers, to reconstruct the geography of agrarian and demesne landscapes in Counties Kildare, Tipperary and Waterford.[56] In Chapter 4, Gillespie presents a broader documentary analysis of Ireland's place within the expanding colonial world of the sixteenth and seventeenth centuries, which reconstructs contemporary perceptions of Ireland's regional identity. Proudfoot explores the limitations as well as the strengths of documentary and archival sources in Chapters 6 and 7. His discussion of revisionist interpretations of the Penal Legislation, for example, stresses the hermeneutic and thus value-laden nature of all such historical analyses. Nevertheless, as Chapter 7 demonstrates, archival sources can add significant social meaning to the geographical analysis of spatial structures and morphological outcomes.

Our attempts to understand the ceaseless mutations of Irish society are hopefully enlightened too by the adoption of wider intellectual perspectives. As observed above, Irish historical geography has often been described as insular in the sense of being exclusive or inward-looking. Again, one of the major factors driving revisionist nationalism has been the necessary integration of Ireland, politically and economically, into a wider world, following the enforced rejection during the 1950s and 1960s of what Brunt has referred to as De Valera's policies of 'almost claustrophobic insularity'.[57] Consequently, no matter which period is being discussed, we can see scholars incorporating theoretical ideas and drawing upon analogous circumstances from the wider world of Europe and North America to help explain the social and economic transformation of Ireland. In Chapter 4, for example, Gillespie examines the ways in which social and economic change in sixteenth- and seventeenth-century Ireland was related to the wider context of the British Empire. In this context, it has to be remembered too that the number of people of Irish descent living abroad (perhaps as many as 70 million) is far greater than the contemporary population of the island (slightly over five million). In Chapter 10, Houston and Smyth examine the diaspora to the New World, while in Chapter 11, Collins presents a detailed examination of the Irish experience in Britain. Plainly, Irish historical geography can no longer be seen as insular. But there does remain a negative side to this. Firstly, external influences can be acknowledged but thereafter depicted as having been assimilated without effectively altering the status quo of Irish society—the traditional model. Secondly, a marked ambivalence can remain about Britain as a source of potential analogical comparison and contrast.

Theme Three

In terms of the subject matter of re-evaluation, virtually every aspect of Ireland's historical geography has been re-examined in some way. However, there is no doubt that one aspect of study—Ireland's urbanization—sums up the positive outcome of the incorporation of revisionist concepts into historical geography. Essentially an area of research proscribed by the assumptions of the former orthodoxy, there has been a veritable explosion in our understanding of the origins and subsequent development of towns in Ireland. Two decades ago, there were scarcely any studies of Irish urban history. Towns were regarded as alien institutions, the last symbolically negative vestiges of the island's history of subordination. The very destruction of their built fabric was sometimes presented as an act of national self-purification.[58] While traces of these attitudes may remain, Ireland now possesses urban historical studies of real substance. The town is no longer seen as some imposed colonial adjunct to the rural landscape but as the principal geographical centre through which the articulation of society is organized. There can be no better illustration of how a redefined landscape becomes part of the redefinition of the iconography of a nation. Thus we have the debate on urban origins (Chapters 1 and 2), the ambivalence of our knowledge of urbanization in late medieval Ireland (Chapter 3), the role of landowners in the promotion of urban settlement in the eighteenth century (Chapter 7), and finally, the complex pattern of urbanization which developed in the nineteenth century (Chapter 8). Indicative perhaps of a maturation of nationality, the creation of this knowledge owes much to the explicit incorporation of theory into Irish historical geography, the illumination of analogy, the recognition that any country's social and economic structure is a fusion of external and internal forces locked in ever-changing motion, and finally, the argument that a country's landscape is in itself one of the most potent indicators of the history of that transformation. The approaches to urbanization discussed here are also symbolic of the way in which Irish historical geography has moved away from its former concentration on landscape artefacts towards a methodology which is very much more document-orientated. As we have noted, the resultant fusion of written and field evidence is very much a distinctive feature of the discipline.

The Structure of the Text

While we have been referring to Irish historical geography, clearly that discipline does not stand alone. The revisionist and indeed re-revisionist debate is character-istic of contemporary studies in history, economic and social history and political science, as well as geography's traditional collaborator, archaeology. While it would be an exaggeration to describe this revision of the Irish past as inter-disci-plinary, certainly it has been and remains multi-disciplinary. We have consciously sought to incorporate that characteristic here by seeking contributions from an archaeologist and several economic and social historians. The relative strength of the archival tradition within recent Irish historical geography is reflected in the subject's increasingly close alignment with Irish economic history. Just as Irish historical geographers are increasingly aware of the 'internalizations' inevitably involved in any reconstruction of the particularities of place from written sources, so too Irish economic historians are becoming increasingly spatially aware. The frequent commonality of purpose but also the differences in approach between the two disciplines are reflected in Chapters 5 and 9. Kennedy and Clarkson's analysis of Irish demographic change is firmly grounded in the traditional concern of social and economic historians with the mechanisms of change over time, but it is also sensitive to the regional variations within this. Turner's analysis of the post-Famine 'agricultural geographies' of Ireland, similarly considers the process of change in terms of its inherent spatiality. Inevitably, this disciplinary diversification militates against an agreed perspective on Irish historical geography. But even amongst the geographers, it would be unrealistic to claim that there is a consensus of approach or attitude.

The contributors were asked to select and develop the themes which they con-sidered most pertinent to their particular periods. It is fashionable to decry the customary divisions of the Irish past, defined as they often are by the character-istics of the latest in a succession of colonizers—or immigrants to use the language of the new Ireland. The periodization of the book tends to follow the traditional lines, partially because the efficacy of chronology is part of the actual revisionist debate. In a sense, the only logical starting point would have been *c.* 7000 B.C. with the first evidence of the peopling of Ireland (the datings are a question of dispute) but we felt that it was unnecessary to duplicate any part of Harbison's masterly synthesis of the archaeology of Pre-Christian Ireland.[59] The contributors to this book were encouraged to approach their selected themes through the perspective of personal research experiences. Consequently, at one level, the book operates as a synthesis. The bulk of the research material referred to dates from within the last two decades and we have made no attempt to expand that synthesis to incorporate the work of the more traditional schools of thought. This remains readily access-ible.[60] At another level, however, the text is dealing with the most contemporary of research issues—as defined by the perspectives of the contributors. Thus the topics are of course specific to those people but demonstrate, nevertheless, the generality of re-evaluation, whichever period is being considered. Revisionist approaches have been around sufficiently long that there are now re-revisionist ideas in some areas (see, for example, Turner's argument in Chapter 9 which questions the revisionist stance that tenant farmers achieved a relatively favourable position in late nineteenth-century Irish agriculture); in others the old certainties have been barely questioned.

Another factor militating against any mythical consensus in Irish historical geography generally is that not only do we have differing personal perspectives but further, each period tends to have a differing approach, a product of the history of its own traditional historiography and the particular type of evidence available to it. In the earlier periods, partly because of the deficiencies and difficulties of the documentation, the study of settlement landscape tends to be predominant. But increasingly, that is seen as an ideological construct, a means of analysing the rationale of past social and economic structures. In the later periods, we can see a far greater dependence on documentation, but there remains that self-same integration of landscape iconography and ideological forces. But as the text makes clear, its real unity comes from the spirit of re-evaluation around the three sets of themes outlined above rather than from its methodology. Of course the outcome is a collage of the eclectic, the humble and the myriad possibilities of any place but then, that is the postmodern condition. One final point: with reference to the most vexed place-name in contemporary Irish society, the editors have made no attempt to standardize upon Doire, Derry or Londonderry. Perhaps in the best traditions of Irish historical geography's attempts to define the 'common ground', the compromise is to refer to the city by its original name of Derry, retaining Londonderry for the county. As that was delimited after the plantation, there never actually was a County Derry.

References

1. R. A. Butlin, 'Theory and methodology in historical geography', in M. Pacione (ed.), *Historical Geography: Progress and Prospect*, (London, 1987), pp. 16–37.
2. Robin E. Glasscock, 'Obituary: E. Estyn Evans, 1905–1989', *Journal of Historical Geography*, **17** (1991), pp. 87–91.
3. E. Estyn Evans, *The Personality of Ireland: Habitat, Heritage and History*, (revised ed., Belfast, 1981), pp. 10–11. See also, A. R. H. Baker, 'Reflections on the relations of historical geography and the *Annales* school of history', in A. R. H. Baker and D. Gregory (eds.), *Explorations in Historical Geography*, (Cambridge, 1984), pp. 1–27.
4. Evans, *Personality of Ireland*, p. 11. See R. H. Buchanan, Emrys Jones and Desmond McCourt (eds.), *Man and His Habitat: Essays Presented to Emyr Estyn Evans*, (London, 1971), for the best thematic discussion of the ideas and influences upon Evans' work.
5. E. Estyn Evans, *Irish Heritage: The Landscape, the People and Their Work*, (Dundalk, 1942), p. 2. See J. H. Andrews, 'Jones Hughes' Ireland: a literary quest', in William J. Smyth and Kevin Whelan (eds.), *Common Ground: Essays on the Historical Geography of Ireland*, (Cork, 1988), pp. 1–21; see p. 11.
6. Paul Cloke, Chris Philo and David Sadler, *Approaching Human Geography: An Introduction to Contemporary Theoretical Debates*, (London, 1991), p. 171.
7. William J. Smyth and Kevin Whelan, 'Professor T. Jones Hughes', in *idem*, (eds.), *Common Ground*, pp. xiii–xvi.
8. See, for example, W. J. Smyth, 'The dynamic quality of Irish village life—a reassessment', in *Compagnes et Littoraux D'Europe: Mélanges Offerts à Pierre Flatrès*, (no editor given, Lille, 1988), pp. 109–113; P. Flatrès, *Géographie Rurale de Quatre Contrees Celtiques*, (Rennes, 1957).
9. Andrews, 'Jones Hughes' Ireland', p. 18.
10. See, for example: G. O'Brien, *The Economic History of Ireland from the Union to the Famine*,

(London, 1921); J. E. Pomfret, *The Struggle for Land in Ireland, 1800–1923*, (Princeton, 1930).

11. Andrews, 'Jones Hughes Ireland', p. 18.
12. F. H. A. Aalen, *Man and the Landscape in Ireland*, (London, 1978).
13. Oliver MacDonagh, *States of Mind: A Study of Anglo-Irish Conflict, 1780–1980*, (London, 1983), p. 15.
14. Evans, *Personality of Ireland*, p. xii.
15. *Ibid.*, p. 80.
16. Michael Williams, 'Historical geography and the concept of landscape', *Journal of Historical Geography*, **15** (1989), pp. 92–104.
17. E. Estyn Evans, *Ulster: The Common Ground*, (Mullingar, 1984); *idem, Personality of Ireland*, p. 10.
18. D. E. Cosgrove, *Social Formation and Symbolic Landscape*, (London, 1984); Denis Cosgrove and Stephen Daniels (eds.), *The Iconography of Landscape*, (Cambridge, 1988).
19. James Loughlin, 'Some comparative aspects of Irish and English nationalism in the late nineteenth century', in Myrtle Hill and Sarah Baker (eds.), *Aspects of Irish Studies*, (Belfast, 1990), pp. 9–15; see p. 13.
20. For example, see David Lowenthal, *The Past is a Foreign Country*, (Cambridge, 1985), esp. chapters 1 and 2.
21. Jennifer Todd, 'The conflict in Northern Ireland: institutional and constitutional dimensions', in Hill and Baker (eds.), *Aspects of Irish Studies*, pp. 3–8.
22. For a general argument, see D. George Boyce, *Nationalism in Ireland*, (London, 1982).
23. Ciaran Brady, 'Introduction: historians and losers', in Ciaran Brady (ed.), *Worsted in the Game: Losers in Irish History*, (Dublin, 1989), pp. 1–8; see p. 3.
24. Brendan Bradshaw, 'Nationalism and historical scholarship in modern Ireland', *Irish Historical Studies*, **XXIV**, no. 104 (Nov. 1989), pp. 329–51.
25. R. F. Foster, 'Introduction', in C. H. E. Philpin (ed.), *Nationalism and Popular Protest in Ireland*, (Cambridge, 1987), pp. 1–15.
26. L. M. Cullen, 'The cultural basis of modern Irish nationalism', in Rosalind Mitchison (ed.), *The Roots of Nationalism: Studies in Northern Europe*, (Edinburgh, 1980), pp. 91–106.
27. Graham Walker, 'Irish nationalism and the uses of history', *Past and Present*, no. 126 (1990), pp. 203–14.
28. V. G. Kiernan, 'The emergence of a nation', in Philpin (ed.), *Nationalism in Ireland*, pp. 16–49.
29. John Hutchinson, *The Dynamics of Cultural Nationalism: The Gaelic Revival and the Creation of the Irish Nation State*, (London, 1987), p. 213.
30. John Coakley, 'Typical case or deviant? Nationalism in Ireland in a European perspective', in Hill and Barber (eds.), *Aspects of Irish Studies*, pp. 29–38.
31. Hiram Morgan, 'Milesians, Ulstermen and Fenians', *Linen Hall Review*, **8**, no. 4 (Winter 1991), pp. 14–16.
32. Charles Doherty, 'Ulster before the Normans: ancient myth and early history', in Ciaran Brady, Mary O'Dowd and Brian Walker (eds.), *Ulster: An Illustrated History*, (London, 1989), pp. 13–43; see p. 26.
33. *Ibid.*, p. 15: Morgan, 'Milesians'.
34. MacDonagh, *States of Mind*, p. 2.
35. Steven G. Ellis, 'Nationalist historiography and the English and Gaelic worlds in the late Middle Ages', *Irish Historical Studies*, **XXV**, no. 97 (May 1986), pp. 1–18; *idem*, 'Representations of the past in Ireland: whose past and whose present?', *Irish Historical Studies*, **XXVII**, no. 108 (Nov. 1991), pp. 289–308.
36. Bradshaw, 'Nationalism and historical scholarship', p. 348.
37. For an alternative view, see Joseph Lee, 'The Irish constitution of 1937', in Seán Hutton and Paul Stewart (eds.), *Ireland's Histories: Aspects of State, Society and Ideology*, (London, 1991), pp. 80–93.
38. MacDonagh, *States of Mind, passim*.
39. Louis M. Cullen, *The Hidden Ireland: Reassessment of a Concept*, (revised edn, Mullingar, 1988), p. 37.

40. Evans, *Ulster: The Common Ground*; see also, *idem, Personality of Ireland*, p. 77.
41. Bradshaw, 'Nationalism and historical scholarship', p. 345; see D. Ó Corráin, 'National-ity and kingship in pre-Norman Ireland', in T. W. Moody (ed.), *Nationality and the Pursuit of National Independence, Historical Studies*, **XI** (Belfast, 1978), pp. 1–36.
42. Daniel Corkery, *The Hidden Ireland*, (4th impression, Dublin, 1956).
43. Cullen, *Hidden Ireland, passim*.
44. MacDonagh, *States of Mind*.
45. Joseph Lee, *The Modernization of Irish Society, 1848–1935*, (Dublin, 1973), pp. 97–8.
46. Although a review article, many of Jones Hughes' ideas are apparent in, 'Village and town in nineteenth-century Ireland', *Irish Geography*, **14** (1981), pp. 99–106.
47. For example, see Raymond Crotty, *Ireland in Crisis: A Study in Capitalist Colonial Underde-velopment*, (Dingle, 1986).
48. A. Giddens, *The Constitution of Society: Outline of the Theory of Structuration*, (Cambridge, 1984); Derek Gregory, *Regional Transformation and Industrial Revolution: A Geography of the Yorkshire Woollen Industry*, (London, 1982).
49. Butlin, 'Theory and methodology in historical geography', p. 32.
50. See, for example, Doreen Massey, 'New directions in space', in Derek Gregory and John Urry (eds.), *Spatial Relations and Spatial Structures*, (London, 1985), pp. 9–19.
51. Cloke, Philo and Sadler, *Approaching Human Geography*, chapter 6; David Harvey, *The Condition of Postmodernity*, (Oxford, 1989).
52. For example, see Harold Mytum, *The Origins of Early Christian Ireland*, (London, 1992).
53. Cullen, *Hidden Ireland*, p. 37.
54. Nicholas Canny, in a review of Smyth and Whelan (eds.), *Common Ground*, in *Irish Economic and Social History*, **XVI** (1989), pp. 116–17.
55. See, for example, William J. Smyth, 'Society and settlement in seventeenth-century Ireland: the evidence of the 1659 Census', in Smyth and Whelan (eds.), *Common Ground*, pp. 55–83.
56. For example, A. A. Horner, 'The scope and limitations of the landlord contribution to changing the Irish landscape', in V. Hansen (ed.), *Collected Papers Presented at the Perma-nent European Conference for the Study of the Rural Landscape*, (Copenhagen, 1981), pp. 71–8; P. J. Duffy, 'The evolution of estate properties in south Ulster, 1600–1900', in Smyth and Whelan (eds.), *Common Ground*, pp. 84–109; W. J. Smyth, 'Estate records and the making of the Irish landscape: an example from Co. Tipperary', *Irish Geography*, **9** (1976), pp. 29–49.
57. Barry Brunt, *The Republic of Ireland*, (London, 1988), p. 3.
58. Kevin Corrigan Kearns, *Ireland's Imperilled Architectural Heritage*, (Newton Abbot, 1983), p. 28.
59. Peter Harbison, *Pre-Christian Ireland: From the First Settlers to the Early Celts*, (London, 1988).
60. Aalen, *Man and the Landscape in Ireland*.

1

Early Medieval Ireland: Settlement as an Indicator of Economic and Social Transformation, *c.* 500–1100

B. J. Graham

Introduction

In company with many other periods in Irish history, there has been a recent and intensive re-evaluation or revision of the accepted explanations of the nature of Irish society during the period *c.* 500–1100 A.D. The 'Early Christian' label traditionally applied to this period, is rejected here in favour of the more neutral 'early medieval'. The reasons will be developed more fully in the ensuing discussion, but three general points can be made at this stage. In the first instance, the use of 'Early Christian' as a ubiquitous signifier carries with it the now discredited connotation that the structure of society during this period can be defined solely by the characteristics of a particular variant of Christianity. Further, the implication that the explanation of social and economic change between *c.* 500 and *c.* 1100 is also to be found exclusively within those constraints, can no longer be sustained. Finally, the term is redolent of a romanticized charter-myth of some 'golden age' of Irish history, untrammelled by foreign interference (except of course the spiritual). Again, that is contrary to the ethos of much contemporary research which seeks to analyse Ireland from rather wider theoretical and, indeed, geographical perspectives.

Although the periodization of the book has been referred to in the *Introduction*, some further reference must be made to the chronology adopted in the chapter. It has been argued that there is little to mark out the period between the fifth and seventh centuries from previous ages. For example, Warner emphasizes the degree of continuity which existed between the late Iron Age and the early medieval period, and again, it has been observed that the changes apparent in the sparse historical records are not substantiated to any significant extent in the material remains.[1] However, in terms of the interpretation offered here, the economic, political and social transformations which are more readily apparent after *c.* 800 A.D., demonstrably have their origins between the fifth and seventh centuries. The introduction of a new religion was accompanied by a whole suite of technological advances and substantial external influences upon the development of indigenous societal structuring.[2]

The chapter pursues the idea that settlement can be one of the most potent and discriminating indices of such transformation. In this epoch, it reflects the evolution of new means of articulating early medieval Irish society, and also contributes significantly to an assessment of the balance between endogenous–indigenous and imported–exogenous ideas and influences upon those developments. Nevertheless, as we shall see, major difficulties remain in applying our contemporary understanding of the settlement of the period to such a purpose. In this approach, the methodology of the discussion owes much to Irish historical geography's traditional interests in morphology and origins, but it is argued that these must be analysed within a wider spatial perspective than the island alone. Further, morphogenesis must be placed within a theoretical context which locates the gestation of settlement forms within a 'nexus of social, political and economic transformation'.[3] The potential contribution of morphological studies is emphasized by the ambiguity and sparseness of documentary and material evidence available to articulate that 'nexus'. Thus, as Mytum argues in his elaboration of the archaeological case for structural explanations of Irish settlement morphologies and distributions in this period, 'many scholars are now confident that real progress can be made in analysing past . . . ideological systems through material culture'.[4]

The Organization of Economy and Society in Early Medieval Ireland

Economy and Society

Consequently, a distinctive trend is discernible in much recent scholarship concerned with this period. Increasingly, the interpretation of documentary sources and material remains is being placed within a theoretical and analogical context which stresses the interrelationship of economy and society. Although this is a welcome development and one which is a timely response to numerous descriptive and insular perspectives on the period, its implementation is constrained by a number of problems. First, the defining trait of much of the documentary sources, including the Annals and the various hagiographies, is their ecclesiastical provenance, one of the reasons indeed for describing this as the 'Early Christian' period. It is all too easy to place undue stress upon the church as the principal agent of social change, and in turn ascribe a pre-eminence to its monuments. Second, and to an unknown degree, such evidence can be apocryphal rather than literal and further, it is often substantially later in origin than the events which it purports to describe. Third, much of that written evidence which is not of ecclesiastical origin takes the form of the law tracts of the seventh and perhaps early eighth centuries.[5] But again, there is the recurring problem of assessing how far the literal meaning of these sources was ever translated into reality. Fourth, in terms of the analysis of economic and social transformation and consequent developments in settlement, the documentary evidence—almost without exception—is tangential, if not hypothetical. In particular, there is virtually no substantive fiscal and juridical material of the sort characteristic of the high Middle Ages. Finally, in the context of the material evidence, sometimes there appears to have been very little change in either morphology or artefacts throughout the early medieval period. Crucially, it was function which seems to have altered and that may be less than apparent in the extant monuments upon which our studies depend.

If there is a dominant theoretical idea amongst scholars currently working on the period, it is that the economy was constructed within and constrained by the existing social system and the norms which that system defined.[6] As Mytum argues, the documentary sources suggest that the principal objectives in early medieval Ireland were the acquisition of power or social status on the one hand, and salvation in the world hereafter on the other.[7] But the methods by which these objectives were attained changed during the period. In essence, the critical transformation which has been identified was the evolution, from an earlier system defined by reciprocity and kinship, of a redistributive rank society, based on clientship. Ó Corráin dates this to the ninth and tenth centuries by which time, dependence of men upon lords seems to have grown greatly.[8] Mytum depicts a rising sense of individuality as opposed to community, clientship being the inevitable corollary.[9] A redistributive system—one in which there are flows of goods towards a dominant centre—differs from a reciprocal—one in which the consumption of goods is defined by symmetrical kinship relations—in that the former demands a social hierarchy based upon the power to control production. Thus, it requires both central places and central people unlike the reciprocal system which required only the latter. Consequently, the shift from reciprocity to redistribution is seen as fundamental in the evolution of urbanization.[10] The system of clientship which emerged in early medieval Ireland was hierarchical in this way, each individual being bound to another more powerful individual by ties of protection and obligation. As Mallory and McNeill argue, if society was structured in this way then, so too, must have been its archaeology.[11]

Demonstrably, such transformations point to the gestation of a feudal mode of social and economic organization, one in which surplus production was transferred from a subordinated majority to a social elite, a nobility both secular and ecclesiastical. Consequently, Ó Corráin, for example, sees the concept of dynastic overlordship, already apparent by 800, evolving into the characteristic eleventh- and twelfth-century Irish lordships, polities which bore 'striking resemblance to the feudal kingdoms of Europe' (Fig. 12.3).[12] Doherty also depicts an early evolution of feudal characteristics, pointing to evidence of vassalage and serfdom occurring as early as the eighth century. By the ninth century, the documentary evidence points to the emergence of a mass of peasant rent-payers. He too agrees that embryonic states can be detected in the lordships of the eleventh and twelfth centuries.[13]

Such arguments firmly locate the transformation of early medieval Ireland within a north-west European context. Feudalism can be seen as a social and economic structure which developed to control incipient or actual anarchy in the absence of centralized power. In its earliest manifestation, the characteristic spatial unit was relatively large, but during the period between the eleventh and thirteenth centuries, hierarchical relationships intensified in their complexity, and feudalism became more and more intensely localized.[14] All this is reflected in the forms and functions of settlement, both in Ireland and elsewhere. As the feudal hierarchy evolved in its complexity, there was a concomitant proliferation of castles, villages and towns, the central places through which the system functioned. An instructive analogy to events in early medieval Ireland between the tenth and eleventh centuries is to be found in the contemporary ducal domination of Normandy. Here, the crucial period for the proliferation of seigneurial (or 'private') castles—perhaps the most potent symbols of feudalism and by far the most prolific settlement nuclei—was the later eleventh century onwards. Prior to 1066, there were comparatively few castles or towns, those that did exist being ducal nuclei such as Falaise and Caen, or episcopal centres like Sées and Evreux.[15]

Similarly, there is little evidence in early medieval Ireland of the proliferation of 'private castles' and towns characteristic of the period of seigneurial initiative which followed the onset of the Anglo-Norman colonization in the late twelfth and thirteenth centuries. The earliest indications of systematic incastellation in the island comes from the very late tenth century when a succession of fortresses was begun in Munster by Brian Bóruma. As in Normandy, these castles, and those constructed by other kings such as Toirrdelbach and Muirchertach Ua Briain in Thomond and Toirrdelbach Ua Conchobair in Connacht, were symptomatic of the earliest stages of feudalism.[16] So too was a whole raft of social and economic changes occurring between 900 and 1150—including the growth of trade, beginnings of urbanism and use of coinage.[17]

The politico-geographic expression of this transformation was the consolidation of lordships, controlled from central points. This system of polities arose out of the *tuatha*, the 150 or so tribal kingdoms which were the basis of the kinship system (see Chapter 12). In that, every free man belonged to the kindred group or joint-family, the *fine*, each of which owed loyalty to the small rural community of the *tuath*. Byrne sees this unit as having been incapable of evolving 'into even the embryo of a state'. It was too limited in area, the king had insufficient power and above all, no army.[18] The emergence of the feudal polity in the eleventh and twelfth centuries demanded a new model of monarchy and system of administration to supersede the old intensely local tribal kinships.[19] To a considerable extent, this seems to have occurred because *tuatha* became linked in federations, and implicit within that system were the origins of hierarchical clientship from which lordship evolved. The corollary was the centralization of power and that had enormous implications for settlement, not least for the origins of urbanization. The ritual inauguration sites of the old order such as Rathcroghan, Co. Roscommon, and Tara, Co. Meath, appear to have been abandoned before the ninth century.[20] While this may have been due to the church suppressing pagan rites, the shift in power from the ritual to the ceremonially more prosaic but socially far more complex urban, is deeply symbolic of the profound social changes occurring in early medieval Ireland.

The Church in Early Medieval Ireland

To reject 'Early Christian' as the definitive nomenclature for this period is not to ignore the role of the church in early medieval Ireland. Nonetheless, that has been subject to intense historical revisionism. The essence of the traditional interpretation is encapsulated in the argument that the church was an institution in a way that early medieval kinship could never be, offering stability and continuity amidst secular anarchy.[21] However, the concept of the church, from which such ideas emanate, is now partly discredited. This held that the early church was character-ized by a diocesan system of tribal bishoprics, each of which corresponded to the *tuath* of a petty king. During the sixth and seventh centuries, this system was succeeded by an alternative, predominantly monastic, structure which, by the eighth century, had evolved into a system of monastic federations or *paruchiae*, jurisdictional authority resting in the hands of abbots who were not necessarily bishops.[22] Geographically, there was no territorial contiguity involved in the feder-ations; as Hughes notes, 'the monastic *paruchiae* consisted of scattered houses'.[23] In the most sustained critique of this interpretation, Sharpe argues that there is no direct evidence for the early existence of dioceses, nor is there more reason to suppose that these were replaced by monastic federations.[24] Bishops existed beside abbots throughout the early medieval period, partly because many abbots were not even clerics. A common arrangement was for one branch of a ruling family to hold the kinship, while another controlled the abbacy of the most important local monastery.[25]

Therefore, by no means all early medieval churches were monastic; many were proprietary foundations and a wide range of church sites fulfilled different func-tions.[26] Thus, some were monastic, some were founded by bishops, while yet other churches were local centres for clergy administering to a lay population.[27] Argu-ably, a separation of clerical and lay society cannot be justified. The two had become so intermeshed as early as the eighth century that any attempt to 'distinguish the traditional categories of church and state does some violence to the evidence'.[28] The monasteries were essentially secular and, for the most part, monks were laymen. Abbots, often secular figures, controlled lands and revenue and thus 'the church in (early medieval) Ireland should not be treated as purely an ecclesiastical structure'. Indeed, Sharpe believes that the real particularity of the Irish church between the seventh and eleventh centuries lay in its secular function, a characteristic developed to a degree not found elsewhere in western Europe.[29] The morphological reper-cussion was a continuum in which great monasteries defined one extreme and small graveyards and a church served by a single priest, the other.[30] As we shall see, the interlinked revisionist arguments that a church structure, characterized by diversity, was fully integrated into secular society, are of fundamental importance to the reinterpretation of early medieval Irish settlement.

Early Medieval Ireland in its European Context

Despite the particularity of its ecclesiastical and political structures, this was not a closed society, obviously Christianity itself being amongst the most significant of numerous external influences. Reaching Ireland in the fifth century, it was an undoubted force for change but one largely contained within the existing social and economic framework.[31] A possible mechanism for the transmission of such ideas was provided by the existence of Irish communities in Wales and perhaps, Cornwall. Further, the cultural absorption of Irish migrants into the late Roman fabric of this society also probably led to the transfer of ideas concerning industrial techniques across the Irish Sea. One such example was the change in Ireland by the sixth century, to larger-scale production of less ornate artefacts.[32]

But the exchange of goods and the potential for an interchange of ideas extended far beyond the Irish Sea. Ireland was involved in long-distance trade—for example with Gaul, Aquitaine and even the Mediterranean—in the seventh and eighth centuries. If trade is an index of influences, this was a two-way movement but James believes that, on balance, western Gaul, for example, was likely to have had a far greater influence on Ireland than vice versa.[33] The balance of trade seems to have been from Europe to Ireland, perhaps connected to the demand for wine for the mass. Hodges suggests that Dalkey Island in Dublin Bay was a sixth- or seventh-century port-of-trade for luxury goods coming from abroad. He also argues that coastal monasteries, such as Nendrum, Co. Down, and even promontory fortresses like Knockdhu, Co. Antrim, fulfilled similar functions.[34] The subsequent development of an enhanced trading network is suggested by an increase in the number of royal ordinances to protect traders which are characteristic of the ninth century.[35] As Ó Corráin observes, this is further evidence of the growth in the power of kings, because their interests extended to promoting trade. It suggests too that there was an established network for the distribution of imported goods, perhaps operated by travelling merchants.[36]

Undoubtedly, the most significant exogenous influence upon early medieval Ireland, after the profound changes of the fifth and sixth centuries, was the appearance of the Vikings during the ninth century. There were two phases to their subsequent settlement in Ireland. In the first, a number of bases were established around the coasts during the second half of the ninth century. These included Larne (Ulfreksfiord), Co. Antrim,[37] Strangford, Co. Down, Annagassan, Co. Louth and the *longphort* at Dublin. It is not clear if any of these survived the destruction of Dublin in 902 and the subsequent emigration of its population. Dublin was refounded in 917, together with new or enlarged settlements at Waterford and Limerick (Fig. 1.1). Once seen as having what Binchy referred to as a 'profound, one might say, shattering effect on Irish society', it is now widely accepted that the Vikings were not responsible for 'the passing of the old order'.[38] Evolving social, economic and political change is now held to have been well in train prior to their arrival. Thus, as Holm observes, a trend of some recent scholarship has been to marginalize the Vikings, analysing them instead as an integral part of the Irish social fabric.[39]

While this could be construed as an example of the conservative view of continuity outlined in the *Introduction*, in which the emphasis of explanation is placed upon the assimilative capacity of an indigenous society, it is perhaps overstating the point. Few recent commentators deny the irrevocable changes in Irish society brought about by the fusion of these external influences with the essentially indigenous transformations already occurring. For example, Bradley argues that the extent of Viking settlement in Ireland has been seriously underestimated and compares their transformation of the Irish economy to that of the Scandinavians in Normandy during the tenth century.[40] However, in contrast to the latter area where economic change went hand-in-hand with accession to political control, the Viking success in Ireland—as shown by the material wealth uncovered by the excavations in Dublin—was primarily economic. By the eleventh century, Irish kings were establishing political suzerainty over the Hiberno-Norse towns. Clearly, this is evidence of partial assimilation despite the usually hostile relations between Irish and Vikings. But then as Lucas has shown, relations were hostile

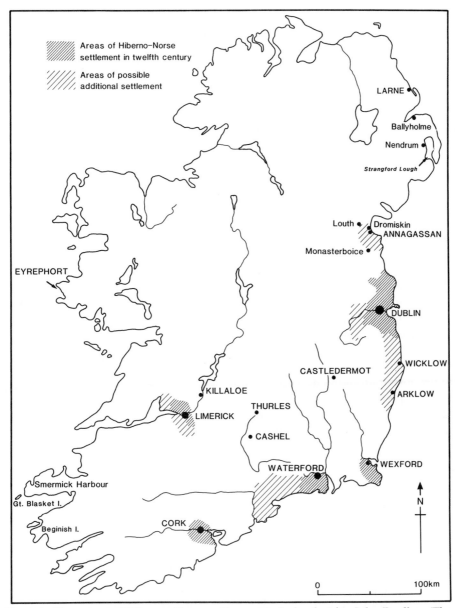

Fig. 1.1. The extent of Hiberno-Norse settlement in Ireland. After John Bradley, 'The interpretation of Scandinavian settlement in Ireland', in John Bradley (ed.), *Settlement and Society in Medieval Ireland*, (Kilkenny, 1988), pp. 49–78; see p. 63.

between many of the Irish too.[41] Sawyer argues that twelfth-century and later Irish writers exaggerated the contrast between brutal and ferocious Viking warriors opposed by idealistic Irish kings.[42] As Ó Corráin has pointed out, contemporary annalists made no such distinction.[43] What we must guard against is assuming that partial assimilation is in turn evidence of the capacity of indigenous society to absorb external influences; inevitably those were part and parcel of the former's transformation.

While pre-Viking trade appears to have been primarily with Britain and north-west Europe, it does seem that Ireland became part of a northern trading network during the ninth and tenth centuries.[44] But all the evidence of the Dublin excavations points to a rapid restoration after *c.* 980 of the routes to south-west England and France, as the Vikings became partially assimilated into Irish society. As Wallace states, the material artefacts found at Dublin are neither Viking nor Celtic nor Anglo-Saxon, but relate rather to a common north-west European *milieu*.[45] Thus, Ireland was integrated into that world long before the Anglo-Norman colonization of the late twelfth century.[46]

Early Medieval Urbanization

As we have seen, a number of scholars now see the church in Ireland becoming fully integrated into secular society between the eighth and tenth centuries. Further, Doherty contends that this fusion of monastic and secular power was resulting in the simultaneous emergence of some major monasteries, including Kildare and Clonmacnoise, Co. Offaly, as the capitals of particular kingdoms.[47] This argument justifies and underpins the principal explanation of the emergence of urbanization in early medieval Ireland. Undoubtedly, the development of a theory proposing an indigenous origin for Irish urbanization is amongst the most significant repercussions to emerge from the re-evaluation of the early medieval period in Ireland. The previous orthodoxy that the island 'possessed no native urban tradition ... largely attributable, as elsewhere in the moist cool fringe of Atlantic Europe, to the pastoral nature of society', can no longer be sustained.[48] Because the issue of urban genesis has become inextricably linked with monastic settlement, it is necessary to consider the latter first.

The Monastery as Urban Core

Eremitic foundations, such as the monastery on Skellig Michael off the coast of County Kerry, were not typical of monastic location.[49] Rather, the majority of sites were positively chosen for their accessibility by river or land.[50] As a consequence, many monasteries were to be found at coastal or riverine sites, in the optimum zones for settlement, with ample natural resources and existing concentrations of population.[51] Sometimes, monasteries were associated with ancient seats of power, the most potent example being the juxtaposition of Armagh with the late Bronze Age Emain Macha (or Navan Fort), chief residence of the kings of Ulster.[52] There is archaeological evidence that the earliest settlement on Cathedral Hill in Armagh, the central focus of the subsequent medieval town, was a hill-fort of some kind and it is possible that this site was a successor to Navan Fort.[53] Occasionally, there was a close geographical juxtaposition of monastic foundations with centres of royal power as at Slane, Co. Meath, close to the palace of the kings of the northern Brega at Knowth, or the proximity of the eleventh-century house at Killaloe, Co. Clare, to the royal fortress built there initially by Brian Bóruma *c.* 1012.[54] Smyth considers that locational characteristics of this type suggest that the direction of power could be from the local aristocracy to the monasteries, the latter acting as the royal chapels of ruling provincial overlords.[55] A further essentially secular characteristic is noted by Ó Riain (1972) who has compared the sites of many important monasteries to the Iron Age *oppida* of western Europe, which similarly, he argues, were often located close to territorial boundaries, favoured as places of refuge, assembly and commerce.[56] However, as Hurley observes, it is very difficult to assess the validity of this hypothesis, given the vagaries of those boundaries.[57]

It is within this consensual context of an increasingly profound integration of monasteries into the secular world that the morphology of the sites has to be considered. To some extent, however, a marked ambiguity exists within the literature. Although the notion of increasing secularity and royal dominance is now widely accepted, often it remains the case that monastic morphology continues to be described and explained in largely spiritual terms. In part, this is due to a uniformity of form, although not scale, throughout the early medieval period, but that should not be equated to a continuity of function. Again, only a minority of the most important monasteries evolved into secular centres of power. Nonetheless, arguments that the monks arranged spaces and buildings according to their spiritual importance do require qualification.[58] It has to be recognized that such a context is valid only for the seventh and eighth centuries for as structural transformation occurred, a concept of the separation of sacred and the profane was—to a large extent—negated by the increasing secularization of some sites. A demarcation or enclosure of the *termonn*—the most sacred area—appears to have been a feature of the earliest monasteries. Herity suggests that high crosses may have been used as the boundary markers, symbolically enclosing sacred space and separating it from the *platea* or open area beyond.[59] Eventually, the church site came to occupy the centre of the *platea*. The concept of enclosure is of particular significance in attempting to understand the evolution of these sites and will be considered in more detail below.

Both Bitel and Hurley agree that as the monasteries grew, lay people were excluded from the sacred space and that their huts were to be found beyond the enclosure wall or *vallum*.[60] In addition to the churches, high crosses and round towers were also located within the enclosure. It is possible that the latter, now thought to date to the tenth and eleventh centuries, were constructed to emphasize the status of the monasteries and even to act as indicators to pilgrims.[61] The presence of such features contributes to the belief that there was a difference in quality of space inside and outside the enclosure (Fig. 1.2). Bitel argues that in the eighth century, all the space within was sacred, 'consecrated by the remains of the saintly dead.'[62] Consequently, it is assumed that this layout was intimately connected with the notion of spiritual sanctuary, a form of defence characterized by moral deterrence which held that persons or property within the church or its ritual boundary were immune from attack.[63] Therefore, in summary, we have a model of monastic sites divided into areas of sanctuary, the most holy space and artefacts at the core of the *platea*, separated by a *vallum* from the lay *suburbana* which lay

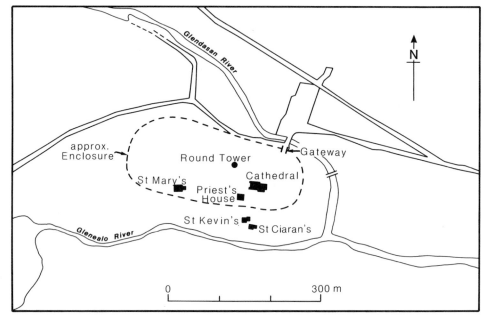

Fig. 1.2. The monastic site at Glendalough, Co. Wicklow. After John Bradley, 'Recent archaeological research on the Irish town', in H. Jäger (ed.), *Stadtkernforschung*, (Köln, 1987), pp. 321–70; see p. 331. L. Swan, 'Monastic proto-towns in early medieval Ireland', in H. B. Clarke and A. Simms (eds.), *Comparative Urban Origins in Non-Roman Europe*, (Oxford, 1985), pp. 70–102, suggests that the arcs of the streams acted as the outer enclosure.

beyond.[64] It is this morphological complex which, it has been argued, evolved into the characteristic early medieval Irish town.

The Argument for Early Medieval Urbanization

In the revisionist dismissal of an entirely exogenous imposition of urban origins, Ireland has much in common with other parts of Europe, especially those beyond the frontiers of the Roman Empire. Here too urban genesis has traditionally been attributed to colonization. Thus, it has been argued that the most convincing parallel to the early development of the town in Ireland is to be found in the Slav lands east of the Elbe and Saale, where the orthodox explanation, attributing urban genesis to the Germanic colonizations between the tenth and twelfth centuries, is no longer acceptable.[65] However, a very fine line has to be drawn here between the radical notion of an indigenous derivation of urbanization and the perhaps unintentional but nonetheless real connotations of chauvinistic nationalism that can accompany such arguments. It is a commonplace perception that an urban heritage can be equated with civilization. Thus, it is unacceptable that the former be imposed upon a society by exogenous and, thus, by inference, culturally superior peoples.

Further, it is an unnecessarily limiting notion that an appropriate analogy for early medieval Irish urbanization need be restricted to non-Romanic Europe. Irrespective of the very difficult issues attending the assessment of the degree of urban continuity between the Roman epoch and the early Middle Ages, the period between the ninth and eleventh centuries witnessed a revival and intensification of urbanization throughout western Europe.[66] In essence, this was consequent upon structural changes in economy and society, specifically the emergence of feudalism, and the ever-increasing degree of localization which followed the collapse of the Carolingian empire in the early ninth century. In north-west Europe, fortified towns, such as the Anglo-Saxon *burh*, began to develop around what Pirenne described as the 'crystallization points' of commercial activity, monasteries, abbeys, palaces, but particularly, an increasingly large number of fortresses.[67] At first, as we have seen, these were comparatively few, associated with only the most powerful. However, after *c.* 1000, castles began to proliferate as the feudal hierarchy deepened and localism intensified. In essence, structural change in Europe was both creating a need for urbanization and, through the rapid expansion in the number of cores, multiplying the number of possible sites with potential for urban growth. As observed earlier, Ó Corráin and others have argued cogently that a political system not dissimilar to that of Europe was evolving in Ireland by the eleventh and twelfth centuries. It can be argued that this process was accompanied by the same proliferation of potential urban cores, amongst which monasteries were prominent but not ubiquitous. In this context, it is perhaps unfortunate that the early development of urbanization in Ireland has been so inextricably linked with the issue of monasticism.

It is exceptionally difficult to define 'urban' and further, it is impossible to specify a point at which a settlement definitively becomes a town. Thus, the literature on urban origins is peppered with qualifications such as 'proto-towns', 'pre-urban cores' and 'incipient towns'. The difficulty is that urbanization is a 'multi-functional phenomenon' and as such is not amenable to precise measurement.[68] The clearest exposition of this argument was worked out by Max Weber in *Economy and Society*. Historically, according to Weber, in order to constitute a full urban community, a settlement had to possess the following features: fortification, market, court and a degree of autonomous law, a related form of administration, and at least partial autonomy and autocephaly.[69] The best known attempt to operationalize this definition specified a *kriterienbündel* of urban characteristics against which particular settlements could be assessed (Table 1.1).[70]

In terms of the constraints of this epistomological scheme, the validity of the notion of an early medieval Irish urbanization, centred upon rapidly-secularizing monastic cores, depends initially upon an assessment of evidence pointing to the generation and expansion of economic functions at these sites. Further, corroboration of the existence of social differentiation is required, together with evidence of institutional and morphological complexity.[71] Although it has been claimed that early medieval Ireland has one of the richest documentations for the period in Europe, the written evidence for such characteristics is both deficient and problematical. Doherty's work provides the most sustained analysis, demonstrating the difficulties of interpretation and the problems of reconciling literal descriptions with theory and chronology.[72] As Byrne, for example, warns in the context of Tara, when the eleventh- and twelfth-century writers came to ascribe imaginary glories

Table 1.1: A *kriterienbündel* of urban characteristics.

1. Economic characteristics	Market
	Central place roles
2. Social criteria	Relatively large and
	differentiated population in
	diversified employment
3. Morphological features	Planned street systems
	House plots
	Defences
4. Institutional phenomena	Complex religious organization
	Juridical functions
	Mechanism of administration

Source: Adapted from C. M. Heighway (ed.), *The Erosion of History: Archaeology and Planning in Towns*, (London, 1972).

to that site, they may have had Hiberno-Norse Dublin in mind, especially when assigning quarters to craftsmen like cobblers and comb-makers.[73]

According to Doherty, a key step in urban genesis in Ireland was the relocation to monasteries of the traditional tribal *óenach*, simultaneously a political assembly, market-fair and an occasion for jollification.[74] Out of this process, fixed markets and redistributive centres emerged at major church sites, sometime between the tenth and early twelfth centuries. It was this economic transformation which was crucial to the emergence of urban centres. Frequently, as at Armagh, Glendalough, Co. Wicklow, and Kells, Co. Meath, the market-place lay to the south-east of the ecclesiastical core, often being marked with a special cross.[75] Numerous coin hoards, found in the vicinity of monastic houses, attest to the argument that they had become centres of exchange.[76] However, it should be observed that evidence of this type cannot be equated axiomatically with economic activity because the concept of sanctuary extended to property as well as people. Additionally, however, there are intimations that monastic sites began to display other indications of urbanization.[77] The evidence points to a possible development of social differentiation and, perhaps, an increasingly complex division of labour, with the expansion, particularly, of craft industries. As Ryan observes, for example, the evidence for metal-working at monastic sites 'now constitutes an impressive body of data'.[78] Craft industries would have been encouraged by the expansion which occurred in pilgrimage, especially after 1000.[79] Again, some sites appear to have become institutionally more complex with the juxtaposition of governmental and religious functions. Indeed, at Kildare, for example, Sharpe argues that the governmental role preceded the sacremental.[80]

Nonetheless, it has to be stressed that despite a body of documentary evidence pointing to economic, social and institutional complexity, no *one* site demonstrates all of the urban criteria listed in Table 1.1, although a number possess evidence of some (Fig. 1.3).[81] Thus it remains an essentially intuitive argument, based upon a reinterpretation of societal structuring and the application of analogy, to accept the documentary evidence as indicative of urbanization. There is a general fragility to the concept and care must be taken not to exaggerate either the scale of urbanization in general, or that of any one site in particular. There are no indications of hierarchical sophistication, and the evolution of an urban *network* was to be the achievement of the Anglo-Normans in the thirteenth century.[82]

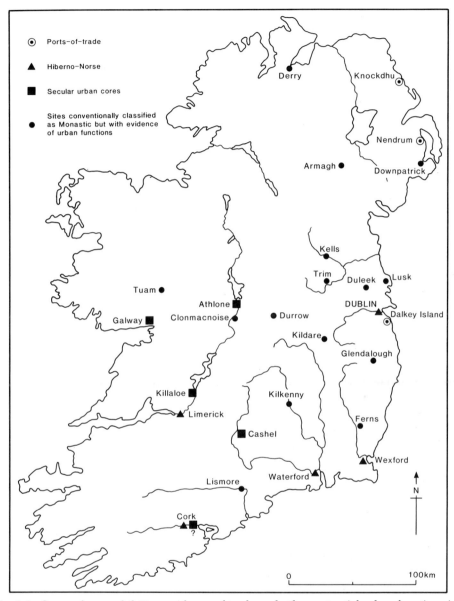

Fig. 1.3. Some places exhibiting evidence of trade and other potential urban functions in early medieval Ireland.

The Morphological Evidence

No matter how sensitive and discriminating the analysis, it is unlikely that the enigmatic and deficient documentary evidence of economic activity, social differentiation and even institutional complexity can ever unambiguously substantiate the theory of the early medieval Irish town. Consequently, one central theme in recent research has been that deductions made from morphological analysis offer some possibility of compensation. An issue of particular concern is the apparent absence of evidence which could be equated with defences at those sites offering the possibility of urbanization, one reason why particular attention has been paid to the surrounding enclosure. In its original form, the *vallum* was probably a relatively insignificant feature, a circular wall or bank of stone or earth, even a wooden fence or thorny hedge.[83] The concept of monastic enclosure was not specific to Ireland. Ryan suggests that the monasteries of the Merovingian world, powerful economic entities with large estates and many lay dependants, provide the best analogies for the developed Irish examples.[84] Merovingian—and Anglo-Saxon—monasteries were always sited within a ward or enclosure, which was not defensive but rather a definition of the sacred bounds of the monastery before the development of the cloister. This enclosure was 'the architectural embodiment of the monastic renunci-ation of the world'.[85] In an eighth-century life of St Philibert, the stone-built enclos-ure was the first feature mentioned in a description of the great monastery of Jumièges in Normandy. As James remarks, this could have been a Roman *castrum*, a fortified enclosure, or even the idealized image of the *Castrum Dei*.[86] However, the degree of separation should not be exaggerated for in urban monasteries like Centula-St Riquier, near Abbeville, spiritual solitude *within* society was stressed rather than physical separation from it. McKitterick makes the very important point that it was the interdependent relationship between town and monastery which had developed by the ninth century.[87]

Enclosures—actual or symbolic—appear to have been ubiquitous within early medieval Irish monastic morphology. Swan estimates that their diameters ranged from 30 to 400 metres, but most commonly from 90 to 120 metres.[88] Considerable areas could be enclosed, more than 10 acres at Clonmacnoise and an astounding 30 acres at Seirkieran, Co. Offaly. Most enclosures were elliptical but some, most notably at Clonmacnoise, rectilinear (Fig. 1.4).[89] It may be that as Bitel and Lucas suggest, monks sometimes used abandoned ring-forts or other secular enclosures for their churches.[90] A royal settlement, surrounded by a rampart, preceded the Columban settlement at Kells, Co. Meath, in the very early years of the ninth century.[91] But the very ubiquity of enclosures suggests a more fundamental reason for their occurrence and Doherty has suggested that the feature has its origins in cosmological symbolism.[92]

However, the issue is rather more complex than might initially appear. Although enclosures—symbolic or actual—date from the foundation of the earliest monas-teries (for example, Adomnan's seventh-century life of Columba makes several references to the *valla* at Clonmacnoise and Iona)[93], and appear to have been a characteristic feature until the twelfth century, it is probable that their functions and morphologies altered as some monastic cores became secularized and the separation of the sacred and profane worlds less and less relevant. Further, to recognize that enclosures date from the initial foundation of monasteries is not to claim that all extant examples are of such antiquity. Nevertheless, several writers do make the assumption that the spiritual and legal enclosures of the seventh and eighth century were functionally similar to those of the eleventh and twelfth.[94] Further, extant features are often equated with those built during the early devel-opment of the monastery. But as Simms writes of Kells—and the same point applies elsewhere—Columba's monastery, established within its royal stronghold,

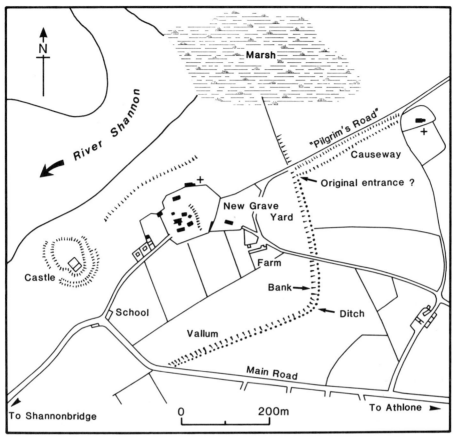

Fig. 1.4. Clonmacnoise, Co. Offaly, showing the line of the rectilinear enclosure. After C. Thomas, *The Early Christian Archaeology of North Britain*, (Oxford, 1971), p. 29.

was essentially secularized by the eleventh century.[95] Again, it is the problem of morphological uniformity obscuring functional transformation.

Swan's work on these features has been immensely valuable in extending our knowledge of the potential morphology of the early medieval town in Ireland. Perhaps rather more important than the inner *valla* enclosing the more important ecclesiastical buildings and burial grounds, many sites, if not most, also possessed an outer enclosure which—in a remarkable display of morphological continuity—can still be identified in the street plans of contemporary towns, including Armagh, Kells (Fig. 1.5) and Duleek, Co. Meath. Clearly, the secular town must have occupied the space between the enclosures, with possible *suburbana* lying beyond the outer *vallum*. As observed earlier, the location of the market-place at a south-eastern entrance to the inner enclosure does appear to be a consistent feature. Swan sees this as the principal element of continuity in those cases such as Kildare and Kells where an Anglo-Norman town succeeded the early medieval development.[96] A shift such as this in the centre of gravity of the settlement, followed by the continuing centrality of the market-place, might be seen as symbolic of the secularization of the early medieval town.

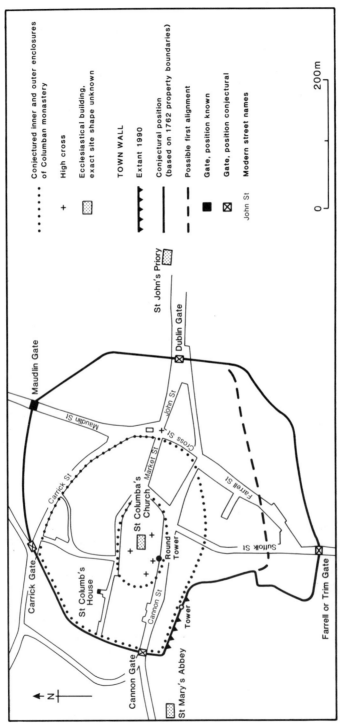

Fig. 1.5. The morphology of Kells, Co. Meath, showing the projected lines of the enclosures and their relationship to the later medieval wall. Note the location of the market-place in relation to the inner enclosure. After A. Simms, 'Kells', *Irish Historic Towns Atlas*, **4** (Dublin, 1990), p. 3.

In its ground plan, this morphological complex does no more than replicate that of innumerable medieval European towns, pointing to the possibility that, by the eleventh century at least, some enclosures were primarily defensive in intent. However, there is a paradox here. Although warfare may have been the most significant form of socio-economic interaction in early medieval Ireland,[97] and despite the various Annals containing innumerable instances of the forces of one monastery fighting those of another, conversely, there is not a solitary documentary example of a monastery being successfully defended against raids.[98] But as Coulson remarks in the context of medieval monastic and cathedral precinct walls, this enclosure was a form of defence characterized by moral deterrence, seconded by a measure of physical power, a response to everyday threat rather than open warfare.[99] Further, some extant enclosures are quite massive affairs, that at Glendalough, for example, having an apparently fortified gateway—possibly of eleventh- or early-twelfth-century date—set within what Henry described as a rampart of 'stone, wattle and earth'.[100] Again there is an analogical context for this because in Europe, the fortified *enceinte* became much more common as a result of the collapse of the Carolingian empire and the Viking invasions of Normandy in the tenth century.[101]

Therefore, one inference which might be drawn from the morphological evidence is that the function of enclosures at major sites could have changed through time. Certainly, the idea of such features separating the sacred from the profane is incompatible with the essentially secular settlement form which apparently had evolved by perhaps the tenth century. Most of the other extant features which can be observed at these sites, including churches and round towers, are also relatively late, pointing to continual rebuilding as the towns evolved. However, while outer enclosures may define the defensive limits of settlements—allowing for the possibility of *suburbana* beyond—it has to be admitted that other morphological evidence of early medieval towns is extremely poor. There are occasional annalistic references citing the number of houses at a few sites, including Clonmacnoise, Armagh and Downpatrick, Co. Down (often in the context of them being burned). But there is virtually no evidence alluding to the methods by which these settlements might have been administered. Nor is there any evidence to suggest that they had formal property layouts, precursors of those characteristic of high medieval towns, and also of Hiberno-Norse Dublin in the eleventh and twelfth centuries.[102] Simms observes that charters, copied onto blank pages in the Book of Kells, record grants and purchases of land there between 1033 and 1161.[103] But such evidence appears to be extremely rare.

Of the towns which evolved around monastic cores, Armagh is the example best documented in the Annals. Clearly, it was divided into three sub-sections or thirds—known as Trian Mór, Trian Masain and Trian Saxon—with the church occupying its own separate enclosure or *ráth* (Fig. 1.6). However, the only evidence of the internal layout of the various areas is to be found in a very late source, Richard Bartlett's early-seventeenth-century map of Armagh (Fig. 1.7).[104] Demonstrably, however, the interiors of many other enclosures are subdivided by earthworks too, and it has been suggested that these might denote areas of differing sanctity.[105] However, excavations at a number of sites, including Inishcaltra, Co. Clare, Clonard, Co. Meath, and Moyne, Co. Mayo, have all shown these earth-

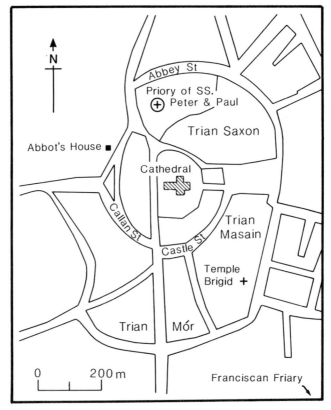

Fig. 1.6. A simplified contemporary street plan of Armagh showing the survival of the lines of the enclosures. After Bradley, 'Recent Archaeological Research', p. 327.

works to be post-abandonment additions—the reasons not necessarily readily explicable.[106]

Therefore, while Swan is correct in stating that enclosures are a markedly consistent feature of Irish monastic sites, the features themselves may not be consistent in function or dating. Such a claim can be no more than supposition because, despite their importance, scarcely any major early medieval settlement complexes have been archaeologically investigated (the principal exception is Nendrum but that was excavated between 1922 and 1924). Most archaeology has been confined to the ecclesiastical features rather than the enclosures. In terms of urbanization, the most important area would be that beyond the inner enclosure. Given this most unfortunate deficiency in the evidence, morphological analysis does advance the case of early medieval urbanization but only if it is admitted that there are grounds for clarifying and reassessing the evidence on enclosures. Clearly the problems associated with early medieval Irish urbanization, outlined earlier, are not resolved by morphological enquiry, nor does this do away with the essentially intuitive basis of the concept. But if it can be shown that some enclosures were remodelled in the eleventh and twelfth centuries as urban defences, then a major difficulty in establishing the concept of the early medieval Irish town is circumvented. As things now stand, one crucial element in what Carter called the medieval urbaniz-

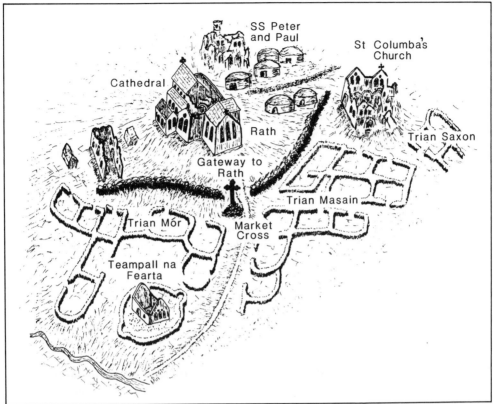

Fig. 1.7. Armagh in the seventeenth century, showing the subdivisions of the enclosed area. Adapted from Bartlett's map, in G. A. Hayes-McCoy, *Ulster and Other Irish Maps, c. 1600*, (Dublin, 1964).

ing catalyst of temple, market and fortress was apparently absent.[107] Additionally, the case is further strengthened by other evidence which points to a possible plurality of potential urban cores—which in turn might indicate institutional complexity—and by the contemporary analogy of the Hiberno-Norse towns in Ireland, in particular, Dublin.

Secular Urban Cores

While a reassessment of the evidence on monastic *valla* offers some possibility of resolving the enigma of an apparent absence of urban defences in a war-riven society, morphological interpretation also points to a concept more flexible, and less characterized by contradiction, than the 'monastic town'. Given an analogical context which stresses a plurality of urban cores, it is perhaps unfortunate that this term, with its inherent implication that monasticism was somehow the principal causative process in the genesis of such a complex socio-economic phenomenon as urbanism, has entered common usage. 'Town at monastery' might be a rather more accurate, if semantically less attractive term. Further, the usage, 'monastic town', implies that early medieval Irish urbanization evolved ubiquitously around ecclesiastical cores and, that further, the monastery was the dominant institution at these settlements. This is unfortunate as there is evidence of both secular and dual cores. Returning to the context of urban definition, this is indicative of settlements which were institutionally complex.

Several writers have pointed to the possibility of non-monastic towns. Ó Corráin argues that 'some permanently fortified places seem to have been secular towns in embryo', and Wallace too believes that pre-Anglo-Norman secular towns developed through increased centralization of authority.[108] The argument for secular towns is a corollary to the exposition that feudal polities were evolving in eleventh- and twelfth-century Ireland. As Smyth observes, one of the difficulties in tracing this process lies in the problems of identifying the fortresses of the secular elite.[109] The most convincing evidence comes from Connacht where the Ua Conchobair kings erected a number of fortresses in the twelfth century.[110] Several of these, notably Athlone, Co. Westmeath, Galway and Dunmore, Co. Galway, appear to have been nuclei for more extensive settlements. Other places at which essentially secular towns may have emerged include Cashel, Co. Tipperary, and Killaloe (Fig. 1.3); although both developed important ecclesiastical functions in the twelfth century, these were consequent upon the political pre-eminence of the sites.

Additionally, there is some evidence that town genesis in Ireland originated from the morphogenesis of monasteries into secular settlements in which the church fulfilled *one* but not necessarily *the* definitive function, a process symbolized morphologically by the juxtaposition of royal fortresses and monasteries. In turn this infers institutional complexity and, perhaps, the pre-eminence of the governmental over the spiritual role. A good example is provided by the juxtaposition of the church at Ferns, Co. Wexford, with the palace-fortress of Diarmait Mac Murchada, king of Leinster. According to Byrne, the general demeanour of brutality which attends the history of the Mac Murchadas reflected their determination to create a modern kingship, a process reflected, perhaps, in the physical morphology of their capital.[111] A similar juxtaposition of church and fortress occurred at other major sites including Tuam, Co. Galway, Durrow, Co. Offaly, Derry, and perhaps Clonmacnoise, where there is some evidence to suggest a pre-Anglo-Norman origin for the castle (Fig. 1.4).[112] Thus, there is an argument for a plurality of urban cores and for the existence of nuclei made up of the fusion of several such 'generating cells'. However, the validity of this evidence has to be assessed in concert with that relating to the Viking towns in Ireland.

The Viking or Hiberno-Norse Towns

As with many other aspects of Irish settlement history, a difficulty of terminology has to be addressed here. The Viking settlements began in the early ninth century but, ethnically, the twelfth-century towns which formed the bridgeheads for the Anglo-Norman colonization were something else. Thus, it has been suggested, at least in the case of Dublin, that the Viking period extended until the end of the tenth century, after which Hiberno-Norse becomes a more accurate label.[113] Traditionally, five of the Viking settlements established from the ninth century onwards—Dublin, Wexford, Waterford, Cork and Limerick—were regarded as the earliest Irish towns. Despite the enormous increase in our knowledge of these settlements, particularly from the excavations in Dublin, their relationship to the coeval evolution of an indigenous Irish urbanization remains unclear. There has been a movement away from the idea that 'monastic town life' was a response to the Viking settlement, and that Dublin was no more than a parasitic *emporium*, possessing scarcely any organized interaction with an Irish economy and society.[114] As Doherty puts it somewhat more circumspectly, the Norse and 'monastic settlements each thrived as a result of the existence of the other'.[115]

There is some evidence that the interaction was relatively well organized. Holm argues that the Vikings brought with them a practice of warfare which had a profound effect on Irish society.[116] As the internal struggle for over-lordship escalated and powerful provincial kings attempted to create stable feudal polities, the centres of population, including monasteries, became involved in the endemic warfare that resulted.[117] By the eleventh century, the taking of prisoners for the international slave-market seems to have been a widespread phenomenon. Dublin was the centre of this activity. Again, Bradley, remarking on the close similarity of material culture between Dublin and that of royal sites such as Knowth, Co. Meath, and Beal Boru, Co. Clare, argues that this shows a high degree of interaction, indeed a common Hiberno-Norse culture.[118]

This evidence points to what is perhaps the most important conclusion to emerge from the re-evaluation of the role of the Vikings in Ireland. Their settlements are no longer seen as parasitic; by the eleventh century, Dublin and the other towns—if ruled by Norsemen—were subject to over-kings who were always Irish. Dublin was founded twice over by the Vikings, first in 841 as a *longphort* on the banks of the Liffey. It is more or less agreed that this settlement, abandoned in 902 when there was a mass emigration of the Dublin Norse, was not so much 'a town as a complex pre-urban core or proto-town'.[119] However, the settlement refounded *c.* 915–17 was very different. Continuously rebuilt, it was an 'organized planned town' with a series of fortifications and a complex morphology, complete with evidence of organized urban property boundaries. A succession of nine waterfronts was unearthed by excavation, although not all of these were defensive. However, during the tenth century, a defensive embankment of refuse, mud and gravel was built up around a pre-existing post-and-wattle fence, to be replaced *c.* 1000 by an even more substantial affair. Both these embankments which probably encircled the whole town were replaced *c.* 1100 by a stone wall (Fig. 1.8).[120] It is possible that the Vikings derived the idea of the original embankments from the ubiquity of the enclosure in Irish society, but as Wallace observes, the idea of encircling towns within banks was so widespread in late-ninth- and early-tenth-century England that the lesson can hardly have gone unnoticed by the Hiberno-Norse.[121] For example, the Dublin exiles were involved in a siege of the fortified Anglo-Saxon *burh* of Chester *c.* 911.[122]

However, in other ways, Hiberno-Norse Dublin was apparently influenced by the development of Irish settlement. Wallace observes that its high-street layout—with a free accommodation to a natural crest—owed little to the orthogonal layout of the Anglo-Saxon *burhs*.[123] York was the only English town which bore morphological similarities to Dublin, not surprising perhaps, given the close political links

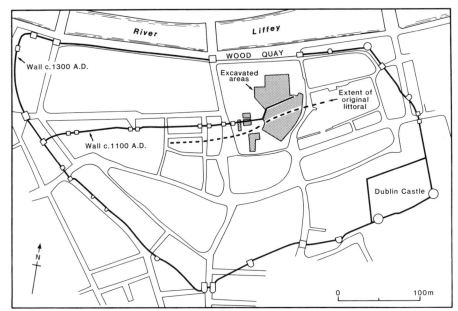

Fig. 1.8. Medieval Dublin showing the relationship of the Hiberno-Norse and Anglo-Norman towns. After P. F. Wallace, 'The archaeology of Viking Dublin', in Clarke and Simms (eds.), *Comparative Urban Origins*, pp. 103–45. See p. 104.

between the two dynasties in the tenth century.[124] As Wallace remarks, it is the artefacts found at Dublin, rather than the morphology of the settlement, which are indicative of the contact with England.[125] But more important than street layout or defences, the Dublin excavations uncovered a row of 14 tenements or plots repeated over 13 building levels. Trapezoidal in shape, and possible surviving into the Anglo-Norman era, they provide evidence of an 'ordered urbanized society in which property was respected and its regulation possibly controlled by an urban authority'.[126] This is precisely the sort of evidence which is lacking for the Irish towns.

Bradley believes that Dublin should not be seen as a stronghold or colonial way station but rather as the hub of a settled area containing both the town and its rural hinterland which was known as Dyflinarskiri or Dyflinarskidi. By the twelfth century this encompassed much of the modern county of Dublin as well as parts of Wicklow, North Wexford and Kildare (Fig. 1.1).[127] Far less is known archaeologically about the other Hiberno-Norse towns in Ireland; indeed the site of Cork, for example, has yet to be established.[128] Further, Wallace warns against using Dublin as an exemplar.[129] But what does seem clear is that by the eleventh century, none of these towns could be described as Viking, given that they had fallen under the suzerainty of Irish kings. The integration of Dublin into the socio-political structure of Ireland became regular and definitive, no longer intermittent and tentative, during the high-kingship of Máel Sechnaill mac Domnaill, king of Mide, in the late tenth and early eleventh century.[130] Elsewhere, the Ua Briain kings of Munster essentially abandoned their royal seat at Cashel in favour of the walled Hiberno-Norse town of Limerick. Jefferies suggests that in the early twelfth century, it was actually the castle of the Mac Cárrthaig kings of Desmond, rather than the Hiberno-Norse settlement, which was the core feature at Cork.[131]

Synthesis

In terms of the discussion of the origins of Irish urbanization, the significance of all this is that by *c.* 1000, long before the Anglo-Norman invasion, Irish kings were well aware of the practical and conceptual importance of having a defended urban capital. Throughout Europe, as Wallace points out, such a settlement was an accompaniment to the growth within territories of centralized authority.[132] Thus, in turn it is difficult to believe that those self-same Irish leaders were not stimulating secular urban development, at least around their principal seats of power. With regard to the criticism voiced above of the term 'monastic town', the confusion may have arisen because often those seats were located next to monasteries, or at sites where the monastery now appears as the more readily identifiable artefact. Arguably, many extant ecclesiastical monuments of this period reflect the exercise of royal patronage rather than the centrality within early medieval Irish society of religious ceremonial centres.

Thus the example of the Hiberno-Norse towns, perhaps influenced at least in terms of defence and urban administration by the coeval Anglo-Saxon *burhs* of England, may in turn have influenced the progressive development of the Irish town, particularly in the eleventh and twelfth centuries. It is probable that these influences interacted with others which were essentially indigenous because there is no evidence that the origins of Irish urbanization were primarily imitative. If we know nothing of the urban administration of these places, it is inconceivable in such a context that massive enclosures were designed to do no more than delimit sanctuary. If early medieval Ireland is held to have undergone such a profound economic and social transformation, then a more discriminating analysis and classification of these archaeological artefacts is required. Once again, it cannot be assumed that continuity of form—if not scale—is indicative of uniformity of function.

Other Types of Settlement in Early Medieval Ireland

In parallel to their hypothesized array of ecclesiastical sites, Mallory and McNeill have proposed that the secular settlements of the early medieval period were arranged along a second continuum of status in which, again, enclosure was a key morphological element. At one extreme they place settlements of the elite including *crannógs* and promontory forts, at the other the unenclosed sites of servile communities. The centre of the continuum comprises a range of enclosed sites, including various forms of ring-fort and larger enclosures.[133] An obvious deficiency in this model is that there is no place for the concept of status being conferred by height, either as an alternative or addition to enclosure. In contrast to the currently very limited excavation evidence relating to early medieval towns, a reasonable corpus of archaeological scholarship relates to the various elements of this continuum. However, as the ensuing discussion will make clear, this is somewhat limited in scope, being biased in particular towards the various forms of ring-fort. A further and intractable problem is that despite the revolutionary structural changes in early medieval society, it appears that an enduring and ubiquitous settlement structure often became modified, but without substantive morphological change. Thus, it is exceptionally difficult to erect a settlement chronology which could be matched with and help substantiate the consensus of understanding on the nature, if not dating, of social and economic transformation.

Crannógs

In being merely controversial, the *crannóg* ranks as perhaps the least contentious of all the early medieval Irish settlement forms. Strictly it takes the form of an artificial island and, as a settlement type, almost certainly evolved between the fifth and seventh centuries A.D. Although the *crannóg* may have been an indigenous development, it has been argued that its origins are associated with the introduction of new farming methods and improved iron technology which together constitute one of the primary factors defining the beginnings of the early medieval period. Lynn attributes these to a spread of people and influences from Roman Britain.[134] However, it now seems more likely that the means of dissemination of such ideas, together with Christianity, might have been through the Irish migrants who had settled in Britain, particularly in Wales. There is no evidence of migration to Ireland at the very beginning of the early medieval period. Another possibility, suggested by Edwards, is that the *crannóg* was introduced through contact with south-west Scotland.[135] Whether exogenous, endogenous or both, Lynn's chronology of origin is strongly supported by Baillie's dendrochronology dates for timber from *crannóg* sites.[136] Without exception, the origins of six Ulster examples have been dated to the late sixth or early seventh centuries.

Edwards estimates that there may be as many as 1200 extant *crannógs*, obviously most densely distributed in areas with a high preponderance of lakes. In terms of function, recent archaeological syntheses display a marked consensus, agreeing that they were defended homesteads, occupied by the wealthy and prestigious in Irish society.[137] Indeed, some were royal sites. The occupation of *crannógs* seems to have continued into the high Middle Ages when several were actually occupied by Anglo-Norman lords.[138] There can be no better example of the problem of morphological insensitivity to large-scale social and economic change. Demonstrably, the longevity of *crannógs* implies that functional change, dictated by social and economic transformation, was accommodated within a continuity of morphological form. The conventional concept of the *crannóg* precludes this possibility because it is but one example of a settlement artefact which has been defined primarily by its physical form. The justification for studying morphology rests upon the allied assumptions that settlement can be used as a profound indicator of change in society, because, in turn, it is often one of the most sensitive indicators of those transformations. Therefore, the *crannóg* is uncontroversial, simply because the concept depends upon an as yet insufficiently discriminating mode of classification.

Early Medieval Fortresses

Despite their frequency and apparent morphological continuity throughout the entire period, *crannógs* do not exhaust the possibilities for elite settlements. If early

medieval Irish society was undergoing the profound transformation which historians have proposed and the evidence on urban origins supports, then there
must have been a concomitant evolution of secular centres of power, and in particular of castles. The essence of that transformation was the replacement of the
former foci of power—the communal ritual centres—with permanent fortresses
which could be used to defend the territories which constituted the basis of embryonic feudal order. As we have seen, the juxtaposition of fortress and town as the
ultimate centre of power should also have been characteristic. Documentary evidence dates such a change to *c.* 1000 although there are very great difficulties in
equating this with specific morphological forms or even field monuments. It is
entirely possible that specific classes of medieval timber and earthen fortifications
in Ireland may be polygenetic. It is a traditional characteristic of Irish settlement
studies to ally earthwork classifications to rigid ethnic attributions, but recent
research demonstrates how this may obscure understanding of settlement function.[139] Elsewhere in Europe, two specific forms of timber and earthwork castle
formed the basis of feudal incastellation. By the eleventh century, a relatively
simple tradition of defence by ramparts and ditches—*enceinte circulaire* or
ringwork—seems to have been the dominant form. By mid-century, it was being
replaced, or complemented, by an earthwork using height as its mode of defence—
the motte. While the ringwork and motte are dissimilar morphologically, the
consensus is that both forms fulfilled the same societal function as feudal fortresses.[140] If the changes in social structure in Ireland during the early medieval
period reflected those occurring elsewhere in western Europe, these ideas on
fortifications must have been reaching Ireland. As Richter argues, the appearance
of castles in Ireland was 'most likely, as a result of the international dimension of
Irish society in general and the aristocracy in particular'. While he dates castles too
late and precludes indigenous developments, the point remains valid. Conceivably, there was an international *esprit de corps* amongst the aristocracy, links which
Richter calls 'horizontal loyalties'.[141]

Monuments using height, either to display status or for defence, do occur in
Ireland. They are known as platform ring-forts (or *ráths*) and are especially
common in Ulster, although the significance of this has never been explained
satisfactorily (Fig. 1.9). Formerly, it was thought that height was an attribute
introduced with the Anglo-Norman motte, and that the platform ring-fort was an
indigenous copy of this form. However, a number of excavations, notably by Lynn
at Rathmullan, Co. Down, Big Glebe, Co. Londonderry, Gransha, Co. Down, and
Deer Park Farms, Co. Antrim, have shown that 'some of the physical if not conceptual attributes of the motte had been adopted in Ireland several centuries before the
coming of the Normans'.[142] Although these sites may have originated within a
continuum of status, it is entirely possible that as the structural transformation of
society occurred, a change from social to socio-military function was accommodated by adapting existing structures through successive heightening.[143] Further,
it is probable that earthworks were constructed or adapted as ringworks although it
is extremely difficult, without documentary corroboration, to identify such features
because of their morphological similarity to ring-forts. A possible example may be
provided by Duneight, Co. Down, where the original earthwork was incorporated
into the bailey of the Anglo-Norman motte.[144] Again, the English Mount at Down-

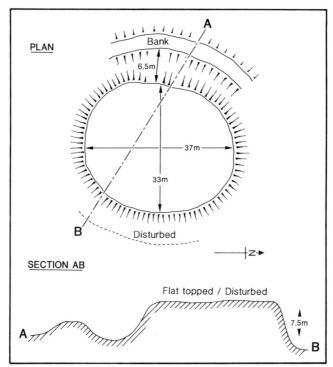

Fig. 1.9. A platform ring-fort at Bohola, Co. Mayo.

patrick appears to be a motte set within a pre-existing and massively defended enclosure; Mallory and McNeill regard the latter feature as the Dál Fiatach centre of the eleventh and twelfth centuries.[145] Just as the *crannóg* could have functioned as a water-defended ringwork, sometimes promontory forts—although not peculiar to this period—were either built or adapted as another particular form of this defensive feature. Usually but not necessarily coastal, these required only the construction of a ditch and rampart across the neck of the promontory. Dunbeg, Co. Kerry, is one example where excavation has shown early medieval occupation within substantial defences, although the site was first constructed very much earlier.[146]

In summary, if the gestation of lordship, vassalage and the emergence of feudal polities were all characteristic features of Irish society in the period after *c.* 800, the evolution of the fortress was an inevitable corollary. There must have been many more castles apart from the few known from the documents or tentatively identified through field-work. Some may have been ringworks—distinguished conceptually but not necessarily morphologically from ring-forts—*crannógs* and promontory forts, while others may have been platform ring-forts which were either built or adapted to act socially and economically as mottes.

Ring-forts

Paradoxically, although the most commonly occurring, widely distributed and heavily researched settlement artefact dating from the early medieval period in

Ireland, the ring-fort (or *ráth*) largely remains an enigma. There is some agreement on its chronology but a succession of researchers have advanced a conflicting range of theories on its origins, distributional characteristics, functions and general role in articulating the operations of society. The classic definition of a ring-fort is of 'a space most frequently circular, surrounded by a bank and fosse' (Fig. 1.10).[147] The

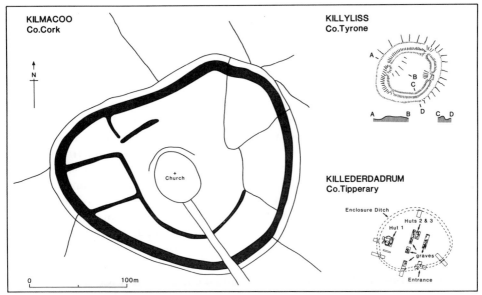

Fig. 1.10. A range of enclosed sites. Killyliss is a uni-vallate ring-fort; after R. J. Ivens, 'Killyliss rath, Co. Tyrone', *Ulster Journal of Archaeology*, **47** (1984), pp. 9–35. Killederdadrum is described as an Early Christian enclosure; no evidence was found of a church. After Conleth Manning, 'The excavation of the Early Christian enclosure of Killederdadrum in Lackenavorna, C. Tipperary', *Proceedings of the Royal Irish Academy*, **84C** (1984), pp. 237–68. Kilmacoo has an inner enclosure not dissimilar in size to Killederdadrum, although in this case it contains a church. There is a much larger outer enclosure, subdivided in a rather haphazard fashion. After V. Hurley, 'The early church in the south-west of Ireland: settlement and origin', in S. Pearce (ed.), *The Early Church in Britain and Ireland*, BAR British Series 102, (Oxford, 1982), pp. 297–332.

enclosed area of extant examples varies considerably in size from a diameter of around 15 metres to a few sites as large as 80 metres. The median is somewhere around 30 metres.[148] Traditionally, the settlement form was assumed to be a dispersed farmstead, the home of a free-man and his family, the centre of a mixed agricultural economy in which the dominant element was cattle-rearing.[149] In this argument, the enclosure was seen as defensive in the sense that its purpose was to cordon domestic animals in a place of safety, and to keep cattle raiders and, more especially, wild animals out. The ring-fort was the first of two key elements in Evans' argument that dispersed and nucleated settlement forms coexisted in Ireland from as early as the Iron Age. The latter was represented by the cluster of farmsteads and associated outhouses which became known as the clachan.[150]

Turning first to origins, Caulfield sees the ring-fort as the culmination of long-term indigenous development, beginning in the Bronze Age, whereas Proudfoot argues that the settlement form was not an insular development but one which fitted in with general trends of European social development in the late Bronze and early Iron Ages.[151] Conversely, more recent surveys of the evidence incline towards a third hypothesis which attributes the origin of ring-forts to the same period—the fifth and sixth centuries A.D.—which probably witnessed the first construction of *crannógs*.[152] In other words, ring-forts may also represent part of that wave of technological, economic and social change which marks off the early medieval period from the Iron Age.

Amongst archaeologists, it remains an article of faith that ring-forts were abandoned before *c.* 1200.[153] Conversely, it has been suggested that the arrival of the Anglo-Normans in the twelfth century led to a spatial dichotomy with ring-fort construction ceasing in those areas which they controlled but continuing into the high Middle Ages beyond their frontier.[154] While a more recent elaboration of the archaeological chronology—heavily biased towards Ulster—does not appear to support this proposition, archaeologists have failed to develop any credible alternative theory which might explain the abandonment of ring-fort construction prior to *c.* 1100–1200. If this change occurred, apparently so precipitately, the reasons must lie within the realm of fundamental change in Irish society. Some relatively superficial factors, including a 'breakdown of public morality' and internecine warfare, have been put forward, but adequate and fundamental propositions are still awaited.[155] Irrespective of the question of *construction*, a number of finds of pottery and other artefacts show that many ring-forts were *inhabited* during the high Middle Ages—and later.

While excavation results are of course indispensable, most ideas on the social and economic functions of the ring-fort actually originate from distributional studies, principally of the 30,000 or so sites recorded on the First Edition Ordnance Survey Six Inch Maps of *c.* 1840 (Fig. 12.2).[156] It is now apparent that three sets of factors—apart from inaccurate recording—have combined to make that total a serious underestimate. First, as Barrett points out, there is the crucial question as to how far that distribution is an accurate reflection of the density of the settlement form during the early medieval period. Her own studies, using the results of aerial reconnaissance, point unequivocally to the conclusion that, in this respect, the distribution derived from the Ordnance Survey is markedly inaccurate. Aerial photography reveals what she calls a 'cropmark landscape' with a widespread incidence of large but destroyed curvilinear enclosures, identifiable only from the air. However, Barrett believes that the additional sites identified in this way essentially 'infill' the distribution recorded *c.* 1840. In Louth, a broad dichotomy between areas of high ring-fort density in the north of the county and lower densities elsewhere remained apparent.[157]

The second distributional issue concerns the dating of the destruction revealed by such methods. Undoubtedly, some of it is recent. In Donegal, for example, an archaeological survey of the county recorded well over 400 surviving ring-forts and cashels—the latter the variant in which the earthen enclosing bank is replaced by a stone wall. But almost 250 destroyed enclosures were identified as well, the majority recorded on the first or second editions of the Ordnance Survey Six Inch Maps.[158] Again, in the Barony of Ikerrin, Co. Tipperary, another survey identified almost 80 sites destroyed since the compilation of either the 1840 or 1904 editions.[159] In County Kerry, it has been estimated that in excess of 40 per cent of ring-forts marked on the Ordnance Survey maps may have been destroyed.[160] Additionally, there is further evidence of removal prior to the mid-nineteenth century. For example, a survey of the maps of the Devonshire estates in Waterford and east Cork showed considerably more ring-forts in 1774 compared with 1841. The inference is that farming intensification and estate improvements were leading to destruction.[161] Barrett has suggested that one reason for the distributional dichotomy in County Louth might be that ring-forts have been removed more readily in more fertile and thus intensively farmed areas.[162] Further, in both Louth and Meath, surviving ring-forts appear to be more prolific in areas less intensively settled by the Anglo-Normans in the twelfth and thirteenth centuries; the areas of low ring-fort density on the enhanced Louth distribution do appear to correlate with zones of intensive Anglo-Norman settlement.[163] Conversely, it has been observed that there are areas of low ring-fort density which were not occupied by the Anglo-Normans, suggesting other forces must be at work.[164] However, this does not negate the argument that the Anglo-Norman colonization may have been one factor in the distributional characteristics of the ring-fort; rather, it points to multiple influences upon the spatial incidence of the settlement form.

The third dilemma is even more complex because it calls into question the entire basis of distributional analysis. As has been remarked, the traditional estimate placed the total number of ring-forts at around 30,000. The most recent synthesis of the evidence suggests a doubling to around 60,000 examples 'as a working figure'.[165] But the difficulty does not lie in this previous underestimation alone. Rather, as Mallory and McNeill argue, it is apparent that 'some of the individual sites cannot have been contemporary with others'.[166] Mytum goes further, pointing out that the long-lived chronology of the settlement form imposes severe limitations on the social implications of regional distributions. Excavation has produced results which range from ring-forts which were not occupied at all to examples with long complex sequences. He believes that on average, ring-forts were each occupied for a century.[167]

In addition to distributional characteristics, a further factor appears to be of relevance in attempting to understand the function of ring-forts. Most—for example, 84 per cent in southern County Donegal, 81 per cent in Ikerrin, Co. Tipperary—are uni-vallate but a minority have two or even three enclosing banks.[168] The obvious explanation is that the latter were higher-status sites although this is a hypothesis which is proving very difficult to substantiate. However, the question of status brooks large in recent attempts to explain the function of ring-forts. Rather than serving material purposes such as defence or livestock containment, a social explanation for enclosure is stressed in contemporary analyses. The most developed hypothesis argues that bank and ditch had a social message, one way of indicating that the ring-fort inhabitants had base clients. The morphological features of enclosure were not so much a question of straightforward status, but instead, representative of the social obligation of base clients to build nobles' forts. Crucial to this argument is the evidence that ring-fort banks were 'generally insubstantial and constructed only once'; afterwards, they were often allowed to fall into decay.[169]

Thus we have a subtle rather than radical redefinition of the function of ring-forts. Retained is the idea that the settlement was characteristic of a free class. Conversely, the notion that primarily it fulfilled the role of a defended farmstead is rejected. There does not appear to be any easy resolution to the several paradoxes of aggregate distribution and, in particular, the absence of contemporaneity in that distribution. Aerial reconnaissance has provided more accurate depictions of density but the reasons for these patternings remain obscure. Mallory and McNeill paint a picture of an early medieval countryside in which individual sites, ring-forts in particular, were the nuclei of a greater number of buildings and the dwelling places of free farmers, themselves clients of aristocrats.[170] On the basis of some mathematical assumptions which require a little too much precision to escape controversy, Mytum argues that ring-forts actually represented the aristocratic settlements within each *tuath*.[171] In both arguments, the status of the ring-fort dwellers was marked socially by physical enclosure. Whatever the resolution of these ideas, it follows that the key distributional question relates not to the general location of ring-forts but to their siting in relation to each other. But paradoxically, clusters of ring-forts are relatively rare.[172] Ultimately, perhaps the only common ground in all this is that studies of the ring-fort continue to produce as many questions as answers.

Enclosures

It was analysis of the First Edition Ordnance Survey Six Inch Maps which also revealed the widespread occurrence of the house-clusters to which the generic term, 'clachan', was once applied. As observed earlier, these became the traditional distributional and social corollary to ring-forts, being regarded as the homes of kin-groups who constituted the base of the social hierarchy. In many ways, this has always been an unsatisfactory concept, not least because there is no excavation evidence to mesh with the conclusions drawn from distributional studies. The concept that a nucleated settlement form persisted from the Iron Age to be recorded in the nineteenth century is now largely discredited. The clusters revealed in the Ordnance Survey were polygenetic in origin, many dating from the late Middle Ages and subsequent social and economic change in the seventeenth and eighteenth centuries.[173] Thus, it is perhaps best that the term 'clachan' be expunged from our collective geographical consciousness. Nonetheless, the notion that there were settlement forms in the early medieval Irish landscape associated with social groups lower down the status hierarchy than the ring-fort dwellers retains a considerable validity. Indeed, this is particularly so if ring-forts are equated with an elite class.

Again, the clues come from aerial survey. Some hundreds of large enclosures, with an average diameter of 90–120 metres, have been identified (Fig. 1.10). They are found all over the island, although the current distribution shows a tendency towards the midlands. However, the discussion of these features has been obscured by the self-same problem of recurring and ubiquitous morphological forms throughout the entire early medieval period. In ground plan and diameter, an enclosure of this size is akin to a monastic *vallum*. Further, the defining features listed by Swan are seen as being primarily ecclesiastical—a church, burial ground, curving wall of the enclosure, place-name which often has an ecclesiastical element, holy well, ballaun stones, crosses and cross slabs.[174] Although he states categorically that these features are not synonymous with 'monastic', they are sufficient to have led to the application of the term, 'ecclesiastical enclosure', to these settlements.

Edwards, writing of the site at Killederdadrum, Co. Tipperary, isolates the difficulty which ensues: 'the problem is that there is no evidence to identify the early medieval settlement as ecclesiastical rather than secular'.[175] Arguably, the supposedly ecclesiastical features listed by Swan are no more than relict artefacts of nucleated human habitation. After all, thousands of villages and hamlets throughout Europe are named for the patron saints of the churches around which they cluster; they are not commonly known as 'ecclesiastical villages or hamlets'. In terms of constructing an early medieval settlement typology, the real value of Swan's work is more likely to be found in his own statement that these enclosures represent secular settlements of small communities.[176] The minimal excavation evidence dates the sites generally to the early medieval period.[177]

It is possible that the enclosures were meant to provide some elementary form of communal defence, but following the logic of the contemporary analyses of the ring-fort which equate encirclement with status, the inhabitants of these settlements were not at the bottom of the social hierarchy. Precisely how they and their settlement form related chronologically, functionally or socially to the ring-fort dwellers, has yet to be worked out, even hypothetically. As the example of Millockstown, Co. Louth, shows, larger enclosures could evolve from ring-forts, but we have no idea how common this process was.[178] The difficulties with the settlement form are exacerbated by its lack of documentation. Hurley suggests that it probably declined in importance prior to the twelfth century but there is no evidence to show this.[179] Indeed, there is rather more to the contrary. In an argument yet to be fully worked out, Swan observes that the churches within the enclosures became the centres of at least some of the parishes defined in the ecclesiastical reforms of the early twelfth century. Further, many enclosures also contain Anglo-Norman mottes. Thus it is possible that these settlement features are relatively late and, indeed, may play a key role in the processes of continuity following the onset of Anglo-Norman colonization in the late twelfth century (see Chapter 2).[180]

Unenclosed Settlements

The base of the social hierarchy comprised the unfree or servile communities. If enclosure was a social entitlement as well as an obligation, these people lived in open or unenclosed settlements.[181] As enclosure is by far the most potent of the methods by which early medieval settlements can be identified on maps, aerial photographs or in the field, it is very hard to isolate locations of unenclosed sites.[182] As Mytum puts it, 'archaeologically, low status individuals are undetectable'.[183] This is perhaps something of an exaggeration but the uncovering of their habitation sites is very much due to the chance discovery of hearths, pottery or upland house-field sites. Another clue is provided by the occurrence of souterrains, often quite complex underground passages which also are found associated with ring-forts. A point worth noting here is that open sites with souterrains attached seem to have had square houses.[184] As Lynn has shown, a change from round to rectangular buildings occurred in the eighth or ninth centuries, which could make these unenclosed sites fairly late.[185] The evidence, however, is very tentative. One final problem of settlements associated with the servile class is that many may have been no more than temporary encampments.[186]

Synthesis

The idea of an array of sites arranged along a continuum of status, one extreme defined by *crannógs* and other elite forms, the other by the unenclosed settlements of servile communities, possesses a very considerable validity if due allowance is made for height as well. As the discussion has shown, current thinking subdivides this continuum on the basis that enclosure was the primary morphological representation of status. However, what is very much less clear is precisely how status can be subsumed within the rather larger questions surrounding the emergence of a redistributive rank society, essentially feudal in nature. Partially, this is because we do not as yet possess a chronology for the continuum. Certain components—in particular *crannógs* and ring-forts—were in use throughout the early medieval period, although given the argument for fundamental shifts in societal ordering, it is unlikely (indeed illogical) to suppose that they fulfilled identical functional and social roles throughout that time. To reiterate, longevity of morphological form is not in itself evidence of functional and social continuity. Other components of the continuum, particularly the large and arguably entirely secular enclosures, are much harder to date. If these were settlements clustered around a church core, they may be comparatively late, representing the communality of feudal ordering at local level. One spatial correlation which needs to be resolved is that between these secular enclosures and early medieval fortifications. Finally, one section of the continuum is definitely late, feudal fortresses—unfortunately not well defined morphologically—dating from the final two centuries of the period.

Conclusions

By the end of the early medieval period, *c.* 1100, very substantial changes had been wrought in the nature of Irish society and economy. Those changes, while occurring within a framework particular to Ireland, can be seen as part of the rather greater structural shifts occurring throughout early medieval western Europe. Richter argues that it is 'understandable that Irish historiography should reflect . . . the national aspirations of Irish society in our own century', a process which resulted in the emphasis being placed 'on a national political history of the past'.[187] The summation of modern scholarship underscores the unduly constraining nature of such an ideology. Early medieval Irish society was a product of the fusion of external and internal forces. Physical linkages with Britain and Europe must have resulted in the interchange of ideas as well as trade. If the assumption of isolation is removed, the role of the church can be reduced to its proper perspective. Christianity was the dominant and unifying social ideology of medieval Europe; but the church itself functioned as a secular institution, one arm, with the nobility, of a dual elite. The interpretation of early medieval Irish history has at last moved away from a dependence on explanation of social change through the church alone. Unfortunately, the echoes of that traditional perspective have survived in the terminology of 'monastic towns' and 'ecclesiastical enclosures'. In part, this is conditioning from the traditional nationalist historiography; again, it is a repercussion of the imbalance of sources.

Because a revised historiography is being created for the early medieval period, our understanding of settlement is in a period of flux. It is plagued by the apparent uniformity of morphological form which disguises the changes in the economic and social functions of particular settlement forms as society itself was restructured. Clearly, historical geographers and archaeologists need to develop rather more discriminating classification systems which can attempt to match settlements with structural change, albeit still inadequately understood. But the chronology of the latter is crucial to that of the former. It is essential too to refine our understanding of early medieval urbanization although the deficiencies of the evidence remain a crucial barrier. But the most encouraging characteristic of much contemporary research is that whichever settlement artefact is being analysed, it is now commonplace to relate its interpretation to the fundamental theoretical notion that particular settlement forms are created by certain configurations of societal ordering. In turn, and despite the difficulties, they can provide one of our most discriminating indicators of the progression of that ordering.

Acknowledgements

I am grateful to the Twenty Seven Foundation for their financial support of some aspects of the research which is included in this chapter.

References

1. R. B. Warner, 'The archaeology of early historic Irish kingship', in S. T. Driscoll and M. R. Nieke (eds.), *Power and Politics in Early Medieval Britain and Ireland*, (Edinburgh, 1988), pp. 47–68; Lloyd and Jennifer Laing, *Celtic Britain and Ireland, AD 200–800: The Myth of the Dark Ages*, (Dublin, 1990).
2. Harold Mytum, *The Origins of Early Christian Ireland*, (London, 1992).
3. P. Wheatley, *The Pivot of the Four Quarters*, (Edinburgh, 1971), p. 318.
4. Mytum, *Early Christian Ireland*, p. 20.
5. For a brief summary and introduction to the sources, see D. Ó Corráin, *Ireland Before the Normans*, (Dublin, 1972), Chapter 2 and pp. 196–7.
6. C. Doherty, 'Exchange and trade in early medieval Ireland', *Journal of the Royal Society of Antiquaries of Ireland*, **110** (1980), pp. 67–89.
7. Mytum, *Early Christian Ireland*, p. 10.
8. Ó Corráin, *Ireland Before the Normans*, p. 37.
9. Mytum, *Early Christian Ireland*, p. 105.
10. For a fuller discussion, see B. J. Graham, 'Urban genesis in early medieval Ireland', *Journal of Historical Geography*, **13** (1987), pp. 3–16; R. Hodges, *Dark Age Economics: The Origins of Towns and Trade AD 600–1000*, (London, 1982), pp. 6–28.
11. J. P. Mallory and T. E. McNeill, *The Archaeology of Ulster From Colonisation to Plantation*, (Belfast, 1991), pp. 220–1.
12. Ó Corráin, *Ireland Before the Normans*, p. 32.
13. C. Doherty, 'Some aspects of hagiography as a source for Irish economic history', *Peritia*, **1** (1982), pp. 300–28; *idem*, 'Exchange and trade', pp. 84–85.
14. Marc Bloch, *Feudal Society*, (2nd edn, London, 1962).

15. D. Bates, *Normandy Before 1066*, (London, 1982); see pp. 99–146.
16. B. J. Graham, 'Medieval timber and earthwork fortifications in medieval Ireland', *Medieval Archaeology*, **XXXII** (1988), pp. 110–29; *idem*, 'Medieval settlement in County Roscommon', *Proceedings of the Royal Irish Academy*, **88C** (1988), pp. 19–38; D. Ó Corráin, 'Aspects of early Irish history', in B. G. Scott (ed.), *Perspectives in Irish Archaeology*, (Belfast, 1974), pp. 64–75.
17. Doherty, 'Exchange and trade', p. 72.
18. F. J. Byrne, *Irish Kings and High Kings*, (London, 1973), p. 31.
19. *Ibid.*, p. 12.
20. M. Herity, 'A survey of the royal site of Cruachain in Connacht, I: introduction, the monuments and typography', *Journal of the Royal Society of Antiquaries of Ireland*, **113** (1983), pp. 121–42; J. Waddell, 'Rathcroghan—a royal site in Connacht', *Journal of Irish Archaeology*, **1** (1983), pp. 21–46.
21. C. Doherty, 'Monastic towns in Ireland', in H. B. Clarke and Anngret Simms (eds.), *The Comparative History of Urban Origins in Non-Roman Europe*, BAR International Series 255, (Oxford, 1985), pp. 45–76. See pp. 55 and 67.
22. K. Hughes, *The Church in Early Irish Society*, (London, 1966).
23. *Ibid.*, p. 63.
24. R. Sharpe, 'Some problems concerning the organisation of the church in early medieval Ireland', *Peritia*, **3** (1984), pp. 230–70.
25. V. Hurley, 'The early church in the south-west of Ireland: settlement and organisation', in S. Pearce (ed.), *The Early Church in Britain and Ireland*, BAR British Series 102, (Oxford, 1982), pp. 297–332.
26. *Ibid.*, pp. 300–5; D. Ó Corráin, 'The early Irish churches: some aspects of organisation', in D. Ó Corráin (ed.), *Irish Antiquity: Essays and Studies Presented to Professor M. J. O'Kelly*, (Cork, 1981), pp. 327–41.
27. Nancy Edwards, *The Archaeology of Early Medieval Ireland*, (London, 1990), p. 100.
28. Ó Corráin, 'Early churches', p. 327.
29. Sharpe, 'Organisation of church', pp. 265–8.
30. Mallory and McNeill, *Ulster*, p. 221.
31. Mytum, *Early Christian Ireland*, p. 38.
32. *Ibid.*, p. 34. The same stress on the relationship between the introduction of Christianity and new technological methods can be found in, C. J. Lynn, 'Some early ring-forts and *crannógs*', *Journal of Irish Archaeology*, **1** (1983), pp. 47–58.
33. E. James, 'Ireland and western Gaul in the Merovingian period', in Dorothy Whitelock, Rosamond McKitterick and David Dumville (eds.), *Ireland in Early Mediaeval Europe: Studies in Memory of Kathleen Hughes*, (Cambridge, 1982), pp. 362–86.
34. R. Hodges, 'Ports of trade in early medieval Europe', *Norwegian Archaeological Review*, **II** (1978), pp. 97–117; *idem*, 'Knochdhu promontory fortress', *Ulster Journal of Archaeology*, **38** (1975), 19–24.
35. Doherty, 'Exchange and trade', p. 76.
36. D. Ó Corráin, 'Nationality and kingship in pre-Norman Ireland', in T. W. Moody (ed.), *Nationality and the Pursuit of Irish Independence*, Historical Studies 11, (Belfast, 1978), pp. 1–35; see p. 23 *idem*, *Ireland under the Normans*, p. 71.
37. C. Doherty, 'Ulster before the Normans: ancient myth and early history', in Ciaran Brady, Mary O'Dowd and Brian Walker (eds.), *Ulster: An Illustrated History*, (London, 1989), pp. 13–43; see p. 32.
38. D. A. Binchy, 'The passing of the old order', in Brian Ó Cuív (ed.), *Proceedings of the Dublin Congress of Celtic Studies*, (Dublin, 1962), pp. 119–32.
39. Poul Holm, 'The slave trade of Dublin, ninth to twelfth centuries', *Peritia*, **5** (1986), pp. 317–45.
40. John Bradley, 'The interpretation of Scandinavian settlement in Ireland', in John Bradley (ed.), *Settlement and Society in Early Medieval Ireland: Studies Presented to F. X. Martin, o.s.a.*, (Kilkenny, 1988), pp. 49–78.
41. A. T. Lucas, 'The plundering and burning of churches in Ireland, 7th to 16th century', in E. Rynne (ed.), *North Munster Studies*, (Limerick, 1967), pp. 172–229.

42. Peter Sawyer, 'The Vikings and Ireland', in Whitelock *et al.* (eds.), *Ireland in Early Mediaeval Europe*, pp. 345–61.
43. Ó Corráin, 'Nationality and kingship'.
44. See, for example, H. Jankuhn, 'Trade and settlement in central and northern Europe up to and during the Viking period', *Journal of the Royal Society of Antiquaries of Ireland*, **112** (1982), pp. 18–50.
45. P. F. Wallace, 'The origins of Dublin', in B. G. Scott (ed,), *Studies on Early Ireland: Essays in Honour of M. V. Duignan*, (Belfast, 1981), pp. 129–43; see p. 129. See also, P. F. Wallace, 'Anglo-Norman Dublin: continuity and change', in Ó Corráin (ed.), *Irish Antiquity*, pp. 247–67.
46. P. F. Wallace, 'The archaeology of Viking Dublin' in Clarke and Simms (eds.), *Comparative Urban Origins*, pp. 103–46.
47. Doherty, 'Monastic towns'.
48. T. Jones Hughes, 'The origin and growth of towns in Ireland', *University Review*, **11** (1957–62), pp. 8–15.
49. Mallory and McNeill, *Ulster*, p. 205.
50. Edwards, *Early Medieval Ireland*, p. 104.
51. Hurley, 'Early church in the south-west of Ireland', pp. 306–10; Lisa M. Bitel, *Isle of the Saints: Monastic Settlement and Christian Community in Early Ireland*, (Ithaca, 1990), p. 17.
52. Mytum, *Early Christian Ireland*, p. 165.
53. Peter Harbison, *Pre-Christian Ireland: From the First Settlers to the Early Celts*, (London, 1988), p. 193.
54. Ó Corráin, 'Aspects'; Graham, 'Medieval fortifications', pp. 12–13.
55. A. P. Smyth, *Celtic Leinster: Towards an Historical Geography of Early Irish Civilisation*, (Blackrock, 1982), p. 27.
56. P. Ó Riain, 'Boundary association in early Irish society', *Studia Celtica*, **7** (1972), pp. 12–29.
57. Hurley, 'Early church in the south-west of Ireland'.
58. Bitel, *Isle of the Saints*, pp. 74–6.
59. M. Herity, 'The buildings and layout of early Irish monasteries before the year 1000', *Monastic Studies*, **14** (1983), pp. 247–84; *idem*, 'The layout of Irish Early Christian monasteries', in P. Ní Chatháin and M. Richter (eds.), *Ireland and Europe*, (Stuttgart, 1984), pp. 105–16.
60. Bitel, *Isle of the Saints*, pp. 74–8: Hurley, 'Early church in the south-west of Ireland', p. 326.
61. G. L. Barrow, *The Round Towers of Ireland: A Study and Gazetteer*, (Dublin, 1969); Peter Harbison, *Pilgrimage in Ireland: The Monuments and the People*, (London, 1991), Chapter 13.
62. Bitel, *Isle of the Saints*, p. 66.
63. Lucas, 'Plundering and burning', esp. p. 184.
64. Doherty, 'Hagiography', p. 302.
65. H. B. Clarke, 'The topographical development of early medieval Dublin', *Journal of the Royal Society of Antiquaries of Ireland*, **107** (1977), pp. 29–51.
66. For a recent discussion on these issues, see A. Verhulst, 'The origin of towns in the Low Countries and the Pirenne thesis', *Past and Present*, no. 122 (Feb. 1989), pp. 3–35.
67. H. Pirenne, *Medieval Cities: Their Origins and the Revival of Trade*, (rev. edn, Princeton, 1952), pp. 130–67.
68. H. B. Clarke and A. Simms, 'Towards a Comparative History of Urban Origins', in Clarke and Simms (eds.), *Comparative Urban Origins*, pp. 619–714.
69. Max Weber, *Economy and Society*, (re-issue, Los Angeles, 1978), II, pp. 1212–25.
70. C. M. Heighway (ed.), *The Erosion of History: Archaeology and Planning in Towns*, (London, 1972).
71. Graham, 'Urban genesis', *passim*.
72. See Doherty, 'Exchange and trade', 'Hagiography', and 'Monastic towns'.
73. Quoted in P. F. Wallace, 'Archaeology and the emergence of Dublin as the principal town of Ireland', in Bradley (ed.), *Settlement and Society*, pp. 123–60; see p. 158.

74. Doherty, 'Monastic towns', *passim*; Byrne, *Irish Kings*, p. 30.
75. Anngret Simms, 'Kells', *Irish Historic Towns Atlas*, **4** (Dublin, 1990), p. 2.
76. Michael Kenny, 'The geographical distribution of Irish Viking-age coin hoards', *Proceedings of the Royal Irish Academy*, **87C** (1987), pp. 507–25.
77. Graham, 'Urban genesis', *passim*.
78. Michael Ryan, 'Fine metal-working and early Irish monasteries: the archaeological evidence', in Bradley (ed.), *Settlement and Society*, pp. 33–48.
79. Harbison, *Pilgrimage, passim*.
80. Sharpe, 'Organisation of church', p. 262.
81. Doherty, 'Monastic towns', p. 68; Graham, 'Urban genesis', pp. 12–14.
82. Graham, *ibid.*, p. 14.
83. A. Hamlin, 'The archaeology of early Irish churches in the eighth century', *Peritia*, 4 (1985), pp. 279–99. See p. 282.
84. Ryan, 'Fine metal-working', p. 34.
85. Edward James, 'Archaeology and the Merovingian monastery', in H. B. Clarke and Mary Brennan (eds.), *Columbanus and Merovingian Monasticism*, BAR International series 113, (Oxford, 1981), pp. 33–55.
86. *Ibid.*, p. 40.
87. Rosamond McKitterick, 'Town and monastery in the Carolingian period', in Derek Baker (ed.), *Studies in Church History 16: The Church in Town and Countryside*, (Oxford, 1979), pp. 93–102.
88. Leo Swan, 'Enclosed ecclesiastical sites and their relevance to settlement patterns of the first millenium AD', in Terence Reeves-Smyth and Fred Hamond, *Landscape Archaeology in Ireland*, BAR British Series 116, (Oxford, 1983), pp. 269–94; *idem*, 'Monastic proto-towns in early medieval Ireland', in Clarke and Simms (eds.), *Comparative Urban Origins*, pp. 70–102; *idem*, 'The early Christian ecclesiastical sites of County Westmeath in Bradley (ed.), *Settlement and Society*, pp. 3–32.
89. C. Thomas, *The Early Christian Archaeology of North Britain*, (Oxford, 1971).
90. Bitel, *Isle of the Saints*, p. 38; Lucas, 'Plundering and burning'.
91. Simms, 'Kells', p. 1.
92. Doherty explains his ideas on the 'celestial city' in 'Monastic towns'. These are heavily influenced by Wheatley, *Pivot of the Four Quarters*.
93. A. O. and M. O. Anderson (eds. and trans.), *Adomnan's Life of Columba*, (Edinburgh, 1961); see pp. 109, 183 and 215.
94. For example, Thomas, *Early Christian Archaeology*, pp. 29–38; Kathleen Hughes and Ann Hamlin, *The Modern Traveller to the Early Christian Church*, (London, 1977), p. 51.
95. Simms, 'Kells', p. 1.
96. Swan, 'Monastic proto-towns', pp. 99–101.
97. Hodges, *Dark Age Economics*, p. 194.
98. Thomas, *Early Christian Archaeology*, p. 29.
99. Charles Coulson, 'Hierarchism in conventual crenellation: an essay in the sociology and metaphysics of medieval fortification', *Medieval Archaeology*, **XXVI** (1982), pp. 69–100; see p. 75.
100. F. Henry, *Irish Art During the Viking Ages, 800–1020 AD*, (London, 1967), p. 45.
101. Jacques Le Goff (ed.), *Histoire de la France Urbaine: Tome 2: La Ville Médiévale, Des Carolingians à La Renaissance*, (Paris, 1980), pp. 36–41.
102. Bradley, 'Scandinavian settlement', has an up-to-date summary.
103. Simms, 'Kells', p. 1.
104. G. A. Hayes-McCoy (ed.), *Ulster and Other Irish maps, c. 1600*, (Dublin, 1964).
105. See examples in E. R. Norman and J. K. S. St. Joseph, *The Early Development of Irish Society*, (Cambridge, 1969); see Hamlin, 'Archaeology of early Irish churches', p. 297, for an example of the argument about areas of differing sanctity.
106. See, for example, P. D. Sweetman, 'Excavations of medieval field boundaries at Clonard, Co. Meath', *Journal of the Royal Society of Antiquaries of Ireland*, 108 (1978), pp. 10–22; Conleth Manning, 'Excavation at Moyne graveyard, Shrule, Co. Mayo', *Proceedings of the Royal Irish Academy*, **87C** (1987), pp. 37–70.

107. H. Carter, *An Introduction to Urban Historical Geography*, (London, 1983), p. 9.
108. D. Ó Corráin, 'Nationality and kingship', p. 30; Wallace, 'Origins of Dublin', p. 139; B. J. Graham, 'Secular urban origins in early medieval Ireland', *Irish Economic and Social History*, **XVI** (1989), pp. 5–22.
109. Smyth, *Celtic Leinster*, p. 32.
110. Ó Corráin, 'Aspects', *passim*; Graham, 'Medieval fortifications', pp. 114–18; *idem*, 'Roscommon', pp. 20–2.
111. Byrne, *Irish Kings*, p. 272.
112. F. Henry, *Irish Art in the Romanesque Period, 1020–1170 AD*, (London, 1970), p. 31; Graham, 'Secular urban origins', pp. 17–19.
113. H. B. Clarke, 'Gaelic, Viking and Hiberno-Norse Dublin', in Art Cosgrove (ed.), *Dublin Through the Ages*, (Dublin, 1988), pp. 5–24; see p. 19.
114. A. Simms, 'Medieval Dublin: A topographical analysis', *Irish Geography*, **12** (1979), pp. 25–41; Hodges, *Dark Age Economics*, pp. 194–5.
115. Doherty, 'Monastic towns', p. 116.
116. Holm, 'Slave trade', p. 345.
117. Lucas, 'Plundering and burning', *passim*.
118. Bradley, 'Scandinavian settlement', p. 60.
119. Clarke, 'Topographical development', p. 46; Wallace, 'Origins of Dublin', p. 85.
120. Wallace, 'Archaeology and Dublin', see pp. 130–5.
121. P. F. Wallace, 'The English presence in Viking Dublin', in M. A. S. Blackburn (ed.), *Anglo-Saxon Monetary History: Essays in Memory of Michael Dolley*, (Leicester, 1986), pp. 201–22; see p. 207.
122. Wallace, 'Origins of Dublin', pp. 139–40.
123. Wallace, 'English presence', pp. 207–8.
124. A. P. Smyth, *Scandinavian York and Dublin*, (2 vols, Dublin, 1975–9).
125. Wallace, 'English presence', p. 220.
126. Wallace, 'Archaeology and Dublin', pp. 149–50.
127. Bradley, 'Scandinavian settlement'.
128. T. B. Barry, *The Archaeology of Medieval Ireland*, (London, 1987), pp. 41–5; Henry A. Jefferies, 'The history and topography of Viking Cork', *Journal of the Cork Historical and Archaeological Society*, **XC**, no. 249 (1985), pp. 14–25.
129. Wallace, 'Archaeology and Dublin', p. 126.
130. Clarke, 'Gaelic, Viking and Hiberno-Norse Dublin', p. 19.
131. Jefferies, 'Viking Cork', p. 17.
132. Wallace, 'Archaeology and Dublin', p. 59.
133. Mallory and McNeill, *Ulster*, pp. 220–1.
134. Lynn, 'Early ring-forts and *crannógs*', p. 56.
135. Edwards, *Early Medieval Ireland*, p. 37.
136. Quoted in *ibid.*, p. 37.
137. Edwards, *Early Medieval Ireland*, pp. 34–41; Mallory and McNeill, *Ulster*, pp. 200–2.
138. Graham, 'Medieval fortifications', p. 127.
139. *Ibid.*; *idem*, 'Roscommon'.
140. B. K. Davison, 'Early earthwork castles: A new model', *Château-Gaillard*, **III** (1969), pp. 37–47.
141. Michael Richter, 'The European dimension of Irish history in the eleventh and twelfth centuries', *Peritia*, 4 (1985), pp. 328–45; see pp. 343–4.
142. C. J. Lynn, 'The excavation of Rathmullan, a raised rath and motte in County Down', *Ulster Journal of Archaeology*, **44–5** (1981–2), pp. 65–171. This refers to Big Glebe, pp. 149–50. See also, C. J. Lynn, 'Excavations on a mound at Gransha, County Down, 1972 and 1982: an interim report', *Ulster Journal of Archaeology*, **48** (1985), pp. 81–90. For an interim report on Deer Park Farms, see Ann Hamlin and Chris Lynn (eds.), *Pieces of the Past*, (Belfast, 1988), pp. 44–47; Mallory and McNeill, *Ulster*, esp. pp. 219–20.
143. Graham, 'Medieval fortifications'.
144. *Ibid.*, p. 118: Mallory and McNeill, *Ulster*, p. 241.
145. Mallory and McNeill, *Ulster*, p. 145.

146. T. B. Barry, 'Archaeological excavations at Dunbeg promontory fort, Co. Kerry, 1977', *Proceedings of the Royal Irish Academy*, **81C** (1981), pp. 295–330.
147. S. P. Ó Ríordáin, *Antiquities of the Irish Countryside*, (London, 1953), p. 1.
148. Barry, *Archaeology of Medieval Ireland*, p. 17.
149. V. B. Proudfoot, 'The economy of the Irish rath', *Medieval Archaeology*, **5** (1961), pp. 94–122.
150. For a summary, see V. B. Proudfoot, 'Clachans in Ireland', *Gwerin*, **II** (1959), pp. 110–22.
151. S. Caulfield, 'Some Celtic problems in the Irish Iron Age', in Ó Corráin, *Irish Antiquity*, pp. 205–15. V. B. Proudfoot, Irish raths and cashels: some notes on origins, chronology and survivals', *Ulster Journal of Archaeology*, **33** (1970), pp. 37–48.
152. See Edwards, *Early Medieval Ireland*; Mytum, *Early Christian Ireland*; Mallory and McNeill, *Ulster*; Lynn, 'Early ring-forts and *crannógs'*.
153. Mallory and McNeill, *Ulster*, pp, 202–4; Edwards, *Early Medieval Ireland*, p. 19.
154. G. F. Barrett and B. J. Graham, 'Some considerations concerning the dating and distribution of ring-forts in Ireland', *Ulster Journal of Archaeology*, **38** (1975), pp. 33–45.
155. C. J. Lynn, 'The medieval ring-fort: an archaeological chimera?', *Irish Archaeological Research Forum*, **II** (1975), pp. 29–36.
156. See, for example, D. McCourt, 'The dynamic quality of Irish rural settlement', in R. H. Buchanan, Emrys Jones and Desmond McCourt (eds.), *Man and his Habitat: Essays Presented to Emyr Estyn Evans*, (London, 1971), pp. 126–64.
157. G. F. Barrett, 'Aerial photography and the study of early settlement structures in Ireland', *Aerial Archaeology*, **6** (1980), pp. 27–38; *idem*, 'Ring-fort settlement in County Louth: sources, pattern and landscape', *County Louth Archaeological and Historical Journal*, **XX**, no. 2 (1982), pp. 75–95; *idem*, 'The reconstruction of proto-historic landscapes using aerial photographs: case studies in County Louth', *County Louth Archaeological and Historical Journal*, **XX**, no. 3 (1983), pp. 215–36; *idem*, 'The hidden landscape— the evidence of aerial reconnaissance, July 1989', *Archaeology Ireland*, **4**, no. 3 (1990), pp. 26–8.
158. Brian Lacy *et al.*, *Archaeological Survey of County Donegal*, (Lifford, 1983), pp. 197–217.
159. Geraldine T. Stout, *Archaeological Survey of the Barony of Ikerrin*, (Roscrea, 1984), p. 32.
160. J. Cuppage, *Archaeological Survey of the Dingle Peninsula*, (Ballyferriter, 1986).
161. Patrick O'Flanagan, 'Surveys, maps and the study of rural settlement development', in D. Ó Corráin (ed.), *Irish Antiquity*, pp. 320–6.
162. Barrett, 'Ring-fort settlement in County Louth'.
163. Barrett and Graham, 'Dating and distribution of ring-forts'; G. F. Barrett, 'Problems of spatial and temporal continuity of rural settlement in Ireland, AD 400 to 1169', *Journal of Historical Geography*, **8** (1982), pp. 245–60.
164. Mallory and McNeill, *Ulster*, p. 204.
165. Mytum, *Early Christian Ireland*, pp. 131–2.
166. Mallory and McNeill, *Ulster*, p. 202.
167. Mytum, *Early Christian Ireland*, p. 132.
168. G. F. Barrett, 'A field survey and morphological study of ring-forts in southern County Donegal', *Ulster Journal of Archaeology*, **43** (1980), pp. 39–51; Stout, *Ikerrin*, p. 26.
169. Mytum, *Early Christian Ireland*, p. 123.
170. Mallory and McNeill, *Ulster*, p. 223.
171. Mytum, *Early Christian Ireland*, p. 132.
172. Mallory and McNeill, *Ulster*, p. 204.
173. For some comments on this and related issues, see: B. J. Graham, 'Clachan continuity and distribution in medieval Ireland', in P. Flatrès (ed.), *Paysages Ruraux Européens*, (Rennes, 1979), pp. 147–58; W. J. Smyth, 'The dynamic quality of Irish village life: a reassessment', in *Compagnes et Littoraux D'Europe: Mélanges Offerts à Pierre Flatrès*, (no editor given, Lille, 1988), pp. 109–113; Kevin Whelan, 'Settlement and society in eighteenth-century Ireland', in Gerald Dawe and John Wilson Foster (eds.), *The Poet's Place: Ulster Literature and Society*, (Belfast, 1991), pp. 45–62.
174. Swan, 'Enclosed ecclesiastical sites', p. 88.

175. Edwards, *Early Medieval Ireland*, p. 121. See, Conleth Manning, 'The excavation of the Early Christian enclosure of Killederdadrum in Lackenavorna, Co. Tipperary', *Proceedings of the Royal Irish Academy*, **84C** (1984), pp. 237–68. Somewhat similar comments concerning the difficulty of the ecclesiastical labelling of these sites have been made by T. Fanning, 'Excavations of an Early Christian cemetery and settlement at Reask, Co. Kerry', *Proceedings of the Royal Irish Academy*, **81C** (1981), pp. 3–172.
176. Swan, 'Enclosed ecclesiastical settlements', p. 277.
177. For example, see L. Swan, 'Excavations at Kilpatrick churchyard, Killucan, Co., Westmeath', *Ríocht na Mídhe*, **6** no. 2 (1976), pp. 89–96; Manning, 'Killederdadrum'; Edwards, *Early Medieval Ireland*, pp. 114–21; Maurice F. Hurley, 'Excavations at an early ecclesiastical enclosure at Kilkieran, County Kilkenny', *Journal of the Royal Society of Antiquaries of Ireland*, **118** (1988), pp. 124–34.
178. Conleth Manning, 'Archaeological excavation of a succession of enclosures at Millockstown, Co. Louth', *Proceedings of the Royal Irish Academy*, **86C** (1986), pp. 135–81.
179. Hurley, 'Early church in the south-west of Ireland', p. 314.
180. Swan, 'Ecclesiastical sites of Westmeath', pp. 26–8.
181. Doherty, 'Ulster before the Normans', p. 31.
182. Edwards, *Early Medieval Ireland*, p. 46.
183. Mytum, *Early Christian Ireland*, p. 136.
184. Mallory and McNeill, *Ulster*, pp. 187–8 and 202.
185. C. J. Lynn, 'Early Christian period structures: a change from round to rectangular plans', *Irish Archaeological Research Forum*, **5** (1978), pp. 29–46.
186. Barry, *Archaeology of Medieval Ireland*, p. 18.
187. Richter, 'European dimension', p. 327.

2

The High Middle Ages: *c.* 1100 to *c.* 1350

B. J. Graham

Introduction

A number of themes, several of which have been addressed in the Introduction and Chapter 1, can be identified in the rapidly growing body of research dealing with the historical geography of Ireland during the high Middle Ages. In the first instance, geography is rather too limiting a description. Although malevolent inter-disciplinary jealousies continue to flourish—as the negligent bibliographies of several recent publications indicate—much of the work of the last two decades is methodologically diverse, drawing pragmatically from geography, history and archaeology. In part, this multi-disciplinarity reflects the difficulties and de-ficiencies of the medieval documentary sources, but it is also explicable by the traditions of Irish historical geography.[1] Estyn Evans approached geography through man's artefacts and the way in which he came to terms with his habitat. As we have seen with the approach adopted in Chapter 1, the result was the inte-gration of geography and archaeology, united by their dependence on field obser-vation, while the documentary sources favoured by historians were relegated to a secondary role. Although contemporary historical geographers have become much more dependent on the written sources, many have also retained this traditional interest in settlement morphology.

The resultant fusion of documentary interpretation and field observation gives a particular flavour to much Irish medieval historical geography, and marks it off from the dominant themes characteristic of comparable studies in Britain.[2] But this is not to say that the study of the historical geography of high medieval Ireland has developed in isolation. Much recent research stresses that the processes creating the characteristic artefacts of Irish medieval settlement had analogical parallels elsewhere in the British Isles and more widely, in Europe. A final theme discernible in the literature, is a growing conviction that the Anglo-Norman military coloniz-ation of Ireland, which began in 1169, did not constitute as abrupt a breakpoint in the evolution of Irish society as was once thought. Flanagan is but one historian who sees the pre- and post-Norman twelfth century as being an artificial creation of scholars.[3] Again, Smyth argues that historians have overestimated the impact of the Anglo-Normans on Ireland, pointing out that such interpretations fail to take account of the partial Norman conquest and its limited effects on Gaelic-Irish areas.[4] One of the most important factors which differentiates the high Middle Ages—and our analysis of it—from the early medieval period, is the sudden and substantial increase in documentation after the onset of Anglo-Norman colonization. In particular, for the first time, there is a mass of material, albeit seriously flawed, relating to the fiscal and legal minutiae of everyday government. The existence of this material is the most significant reason why there is a very different flavour to the study of settlement in the high Middle Ages compared with the early medieval period. Our approach to the latter is much more overtly morphological. The availability of this documentation is a major reason why it is very easy to see 1169 as *the* break-point, but we must be careful not to explain social change by an increase in documentation alone. Nevertheless, some diminishment of the importance of the Anglo-Norman colonization as an agent of change is not to detract from its role as the most significant event to occur in Ireland during the high Middle Ages. The same spirit of re-evaluation is characteristic too of the relatively limited research dealing with the end of the period considered here. Traditional explanations of decline, which stressed a Gaelic-Irish resurgence during the late fourteenth and fifteenth centuries, can no longer be regarded as entirely acceptable (see Chapter 3). Thus, the concept of 'continuity' brooks large in the study of both the early and late medieval historical geography of Ireland.

Before addressing this research in more detail, and to emphasize the core of the argument put forward in Chapter 1, the underlying presumption of the discussion should be made clear. Settlement is regarded as rather more than a mere morphological entity. In its physical manifestations, it is seen as reflective of the social and economic structure within which and by which it was created. All settlement landscapes develop within an ideological context and cannot be understood without that being clarified.[5] But equally, when documentation is deficient and those ideological contexts unclear—as is the case where medieval Ireland is concerned—an understanding of the evolution of settlement icons can in turn provide evidence of the gestation of social and economic ideas, and the development by that society of institutional structures to put these into effect.

An Analogical Context for Ireland During the High Middle Ages

Analogies help isolate contrast as well as complementarity. Consequently, placing the assessment of Irish medieval settlement within a wider context somewhat paradoxically helps to isolate and understand its particularity as well as identify the similarities which it shared with other regions. The high medieval colonization of Ireland by the Anglo-Normans was part of a much more extensive movement of peoples throughout Europe during the twelfth and thirteenth centuries. In the first instance, Ireland can be seen as part of an Anglo-Norman British Isles but as Barrow has stated, studies of medieval society in this region tend to have been characterized by a 'malign parochialism' which is not unconnected from the nationalist underpinning of much historical reconstruction.[6] A recent exception attempts to examine the medieval political development of a British Isles within which a feudal aristocracy 'helped to foster not only institutional and cultural uniformity, but also a web of connections that was of great political importance'.[7] This interconnectivity extended to northern France as well. Consequently, 'Ireland was increasingly drawn into a European, specifically a north-west European, Anglo-Norman cultural ambit' (Fig. 2.1).[8] A particular example was the introduction of the chartered borough to the island, an innovation which helped bring medieval Ireland into the mainstream of European urban development.[9] This was but one of the many methods which had evolved in Normandy, England and Wales prior to 1169 to put into practice, or articulate, the set of economic and social obligations which we have come to call feudalism. In addition to the chartered borough, lordship, the manor, various forms of fortresses and the market patent were prominent amongst these devices.

But geographically, an analogical context for Ireland's medieval settlement can be extended beyond the area which Le Patourel termed the 'incipient Anglo-Norman empire'.[10] The Anglo-Norman colonization of the island was but one minor part of a widespread migration of people moving into the wastelands and peripheral regions of Europe—what Marc Bloch called the quest for 'internal Americas'. One of the most significant and enduring of these expansions was that of Germanic peoples into the Slav lands east of the Elbe. While many similarities— such as the use of the chartered borough—can be drawn between this colonization and that of the Anglo-Normans in Ireland, it must be repeated that analogy embraces contrast as well as similarity, pointing to the specific differences between places. Thus, both Simms and Empey suggest that the Germanic migrations were also rather different in that the Anglo-Norman colonization of Ireland was a much less systematic process.[11] Both Otway-Ruthven and Frame have pointed to the immigration of large numbers of peasants into Ireland as one important factor demarcating its experience from that of England a century before;[12] but there is no evidence of the nobility using middlemen—the *locatores* of eastern Europe—to organize the movement of peasants into Ireland.[13] Nor, apparently, was there the same degree of planning in land measurements and settlement morphology. Hence, Empey sees Wales as being the best exemplar for Ireland, the Anglo-Norman colonization of the former being shaped too by the requirements of a military aristocracy rather than the broad-based peasant movement of central and eastern Europe.[14] Nevertheless, the colonization of Ireland was more systematically organized than that of Wales, in that the position of the crown was more sharply defined and the feudal hierarchy better controlled. Irrespective of the detail, however, the Anglo-Norman colonization of Ireland was not an isolated nor even an unusual process in the Europe of the Middle Ages, a point with important repercussions when we consider traditional nationalist attitudes to the history of the island in medieval times.

The Anglo-Norman and Gaelic-Irish Worlds

As Martin writes, one of the major conceptual problems in dealing with the Irish Middle Ages is that the debate and nomenclature used has serious relevance to the politics of the twentieth century.[15] Some historians hold that the prefix, 'Anglo', is

Fig. 2.1. Medieval Ireland in its European context. After G. Holmes (ed.), *The Oxford Illustrated History of Medieval Europe*, (Oxford, 1988), p. 161, and F. J. Byrne, in Art Cosgrove (ed.), *A New History of Ireland: II: Medieval Ireland, 1169–1534*, p. 133.

the defining characteristic of the medieval colonization of Ireland. Richter argues that the national label preferred in the Middle Ages was *lingua* and that the higher echelons amongst the Norman invaders can be classified 'quite confidently' as 'Anglo' because English was the *lingua materna* of the vast majority amongst them.[16] Again, Watt believes that the principal factor distinguishing the Anglo-Norman colonization from the previous Viking settlement was that the former instituted a dependency on England. The administration established in Ireland was a replica of the English governmental system.[17] Davies believes that the colonization was a self-conscious policy, whether the crown initiated it or simply channelled a movement which had already generated its own momentum. He argues that, particularly in those areas effectively settled by the process of colonization, the result was domination, brought about by acculturation, acquisitive kingship and a centralizing church. The concept of systematic conquest was one which developed later during the thirteenth century.[18] Such an interpretation is shared—if for different reasons—by a traditional nationalist history, steeped in 'invasion neurosis' which depicted the Anglo-Normans as the second wave of invaders who attempted to subdue a civilized island by force, while lacking any legitimate claim to be in Ireland.[19] The most recent expression of this viewpoint is by Richter who argues that a 'remarkably vital' Irish society remained basically stable through the Middle Ages, managing to assimilate almost seamlessly the onslaught of the English and of the Vikings before them. These 'encroachments' 'left their traces without . . . crushing the core of Irish life and culture'.[20]

Such nationalistically convenient explications of assimilation are the antithesis of the argument offered here, that it is precisely a particular fusion of diverse cultural elements which provides any one locale with its individuality. Reference has already been made in the Introduction to a traditional nationalism with its defining origin-legend that Ireland could be a melting-pot of different cultures, on condition that to become Irish, the other inhabitants of the country had to Gaelicize themselves. It is argued here that such hypotheses are simply inadequate in accommodating the evidence of the high Middle Ages. The soldiers who came to Ireland in 1169 were not part of a systematic conquest but rather mercenaries enlisted by the deposed king of Leinster, Diarmait Mac Murchada, in an attempt to regain his territories.[21] Ó Corráin speculates that Mac Murchada—'Diarmait na nGall' or 'Dermot of the Foreigners' as the fifteenth- and sixteenth-century Annals describe him—was trying to establish a new type of centralized power over his kingdom.[22] As we have seen in Chapter 1, early medieval society in Ireland was characterized by the absence of an island-wide polity, the ensuing political disunity militating against any effective military resistance to the Anglo-Normans.[23] Their leaders were lords from the Welsh marches, ambitious men such as Robert fitz Stephen and Richard fitz Gilbert de Clare, far better known as Strongbow. Giraldus Cambrensis points to the motivations of such men when he says of Strongbow that 'he had a great name rather than great prospects, ancestral prestige rather than ability, and had succeeded to a name rather than to possessions'.[24] To these freebooters, Ireland, situated beyond the immediate control of the English crown, offered opportunities of power, wealth, land and prestige, likely to be denied to them in their homelands by the feudal laws of primogeniture. They took their chances and thus the initial Anglo-Norman colonization of Ireland was very much a question of individual enterprise. Diarmait's invitation 'inevitably became an invasion, and like most great changes in history it was an accident, unforeseen and unplanned, which opened Ireland to expansive Anglo-French feudalism'.[25]

The institution of a more systematic crown involvement followed Henry II's visit to Ireland in 1171–2. The king's motives have been the subject of some debate. They have been attributed to the fear that some of the barons were becoming too independent and powerful. Strongbow, for example, through his marriage to Mac Murchada's daughter, Aífe, succeeded to the lands of Leinster on Diarmait's death in 1171. Conversely, others are more inclined to believe that following the murder of Thomas Beckett, Henry was motivated by a desire to ingratiate himself with the papacy; in the absence of any central civil power in Ireland, Henry regarded the church as the only effective national institution.[26] In turn, the latter saw their opportunity to impose the full Gregorian reform on Ireland. Whatever the mixture of motives, by the time he departed from Ireland in 1172, Henry had received the homage of the hierarchy of the Irish church as well as that of the Gaelic-Irish kings and Anglo-Norman barons. However, in many ways the subsequent history of the crown's involvement in Ireland can be interpreted as an often unsuccessful attempt to curb the ambitions of these men. By granting major lordships to the barons because it did not itself possess the resources or inclination to conquer Ireland, the crown gave these men powers which often made them remote from the mechanisms of government established in Dublin. However, the barons also needed the rewards and social prestige which the crown could confer and in the long term most magnates were, at least to some extent, 'royalist'.[27] Thus, Flanagan sees the defining characteristic history of Anglo-Norman Ireland as improvisation, Henry and his successors lacking the time, men, resources and control over the adventurer-settlers of Ireland to do anything else.[28] Some commentators see the same trait of improvisation as being the motif of British involvement in Ireland ever since.

The Treaty of Windsor, signed in 1175 by Henry and Ruaidrí Ua Conchobair, the *ard-rí*, was intended to divide the island between Anglo-Norman and Gaelic-Irish interests. Under the terms agreed, Dublin, Meath, Leinster and Waterford as far west as Dungarvan were defined as the region of Anglo-Norman influence— effectively a recognition of the *status quo*—and in general these were the first areas to be colonized. However, Ruaidrí was unable to keep the Gaelic-Irish provincial kings in order and in the ensuing anarchy, Anglo-Norman adventurers such as John de Courcy, who invaded east Ulster in 1177, were able to seize other territories by force.[29] As Lydon says of de Courcy, he began to fight in the Irish way; 'like most of the other adventurers who created lordships . . . in twelfth-century Ireland, he had little choice if he wished to survive'.[30] This instance was very much an act of personal initiative and illustrates the difficulties encountered by the crown in restraining baronial ambitions. It was soon followed during the 1180s by the initial occupation of east Cork and Uriel (modern Louth) so that by 1190, the Anglo-Normans controlled the coast from Dundalk to Cork. Inland their colonization of Meath was beginning to extend in the direction of the Shannon and the early settlement of north Leinster was well advanced.[31] Further advances had been made by 1200 with the consolidation of the initial occupation of Limerick and Tipperary, the final major region to undergo an intensive colonization.[32]

In the early years of the thirteenth century, the impetus of territorial expansion slowed as the Anglo-Normans began speculatively to enter territories which they had neither the settlers nor resources to colonize effectively in their entirety. Amongst these incursions were the first tentative movements across the Shannon and west into Kerry, while a little later *c.* 1220, there was a further penetration into east Clare. The final region to undergo a limited, patchy but sometimes locally, surprisingly long-lived, degree of Anglo-Norman colonization was Connacht, the conquest of which was as complete as was ever to be achieved after Richard de Burgh's campaigns against the Ua Conchobairs between 1221 and 1235.[33] By then, and to varying degrees, the Anglo-Normans controlled about two-thirds of the island (Fig. 2.2).

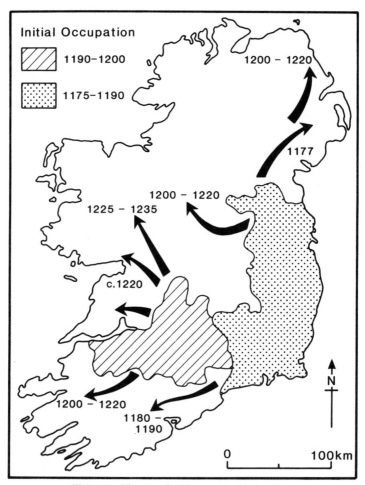

Fig. 2.2. The Anglo-Norman colonization.

In those areas beyond the direct imprint of Anglo-Norman colonization—most of Ulster, much of the west coast, part of the central lowlands and almost all the uplands—some degree of Gaelic-Irish political autonomy was preserved, as was a social and economic system very different to that developed by the Anglo-

Normans.[34] However, as Nicholls remarks, the extant documentation of this society is so deficient and late that for the 150 years following the Anglo-Norman invasion, only 'a few deductions can be hazarded'.[35] When it is combined with a traditional nationalist sentiment, this documentary imbalance can accentuate the divide between Anglo-Norman and Gaelic-Irish worlds and care must be taken to avoid what Empey calls the 'two-nation' school of Irish historiography.[36] It is probably best to visualize the spatial relationship between the two medieval cultures as a complex, ambiguous and dynamic one. Frame observes that there was 'a relentless cacophony of military activity, and of contradictory attitudes that were never fully resolved'.[37] A common thread linking the two cultures was the church, the only institution which operated right across the island but curiously, one which has been little studied. Despite a commonality of ecclesiastical structure, the church was itself divided on national and cultural grounds. However, as Watt argues, it did slowly develop a role as a mediator between Anglo- and Gaelic-Irish.[38]

The perpetual warfare, which was the most persistent means of contact, and the occasional Gaelic-Irish adoption of Anglo-Norman feudal practices or military innovations, show that Gaelic-Irish society was inevitably altered by the Anglo-Norman presence.[39] Simms sees the transformation of the Gaelic-Irish ruling classes as being partially attributable to the Anglo-Norman presence in Ireland, but also connected to wider developments taking place in Europe generally during the later Middle Ages.[40] In turn, although never overwhelmed by the Gaelic-Irish world, Anglo-Norman society in Ireland was irrevocably altered by its presence, an interchange which led to the 'degeneracy' of the colony much referred to in four-teenth-century government sources.[41] Out of this coexistence during the Middle Ages arose what Lydon calls the 'middle nation', the Anglo-Irish, neither one nor the other but by implication, something different again.[42] The question does arise as to the point at which Anglo-Norman became Anglo-Irish. As Martin states, the answer would vary according to individual, institution and the part of the country being described. He tends to attribute Anglo-Norman to the period before 1216, and Anglo-Irish thereafter.[43]

Spatially, this complex array of economic, political and social interrelationships was represented by a shifting frontier. Lydon has claimed that the incastellation of Ireland by the Anglo-Normans produced what was to be one of the first systematically fortified frontiers in Europe and certainly there are intimations of strategic planning, in, for example, the chain of royal castles along the Shannon.[44] But in general the situation seems to have been rather less formal. At the local scale, there were numerous and shifting frontiers with control vested in the hands of the local Anglo-Norman settlers. These were the marches, the tracts of debatable land which some historians have referred to as the 'land of war'.[45] The capacity of the centralized Anglo-Norman authority in Dublin to manage the marches was very limited, but districts where the government rarely intervened directly, such as Uriel on the borders with Ulster, often lay within the orbits of Anglo-Norman magnates who were normally reliable.[46]

The Role of Continuity During the Twelfth Century

In many ways, the inadequacy of a 'two-nations' historiography is paralleled by the debate concerning continuity. As we have explained in the *Introduction*, this can describe the relatively simple idea of continuity of settlement or of site, but in a more profound sense, it refers to the constraints placed upon Anglo-Norman activities in Ireland by the configuration of the extant social and economic structure. The Ireland which the Anglo-Normans invaded in 1169, and which was by no means unknown to them, was a settled, bounded and organized—if divided—society. In his classic work, *Ireland Under the Normans*, G. H. Orpen stressed the revolutionary rather than evolutionary nature of the Anglo-Norman colonization.[47] He tended to attribute social change in medieval Ireland to the achievements of this exogenous and superior group, a viewpoint also readily apparent in A. J. Otway-Ruthven's later *A History of Medieval Ireland*.[48] The radical perspective on continuity which stresses evolution and demonstrates how the Anglo-Normans built upon, or were constrained by, existing political, social and settlement structures, does much to redress this balance. But if overstated—which means placing undue emphasis on assimilation rather than a mutuality of transformation amongst both Anglo-Normans and Gaelic-Irish—a conservative interpretation of continuity can go so far as to deny the concept of social change entirely, thereby running the risk of stopping history. Thus in this context, it can be—but not necessarily is—part of a traditional nationalist ethos which would deny any English contribution to Ireland.[49] Geographically, the radical definition of continuity implies a fusion of Anglo-Norman and Gaelic-Irish cultural, political, economic and settlement phenomena which in turn determined Ireland's particularity of place during the Middle Ages. Identity of place stems from the configuration of that fusion rather than through the predominance of one or other of these cultural entities. As we have seen, the Gaelic-Irish were irrevocably changed by their contact with the Anglo-Normans, but through the same process, the latter mutated into the Anglo-Irish. It is in this regard that the antediluvian hypothesis that Irish society was able to resist external forces must be resisted.

If the settlement landscape is symbolic of the ideological context which created it, its evolution is in turn evidence of the continuous change in those ideologies.[50] Thus, for instance, the evidence concerning early medieval fortifications gives support to those historians who believe that a form of feudalism had developed in the polities of pre-Anglo-Norman Ireland. Arguably, the extant political organization and geographical dimensions of these polities constituted the initial constraint upon Anglo-Norman activities. The basis of Anglo-Norman feudalism was lordship. Empey defines this as the personal ties which mutually bound lord and vassal.[51] As he notes, the institution was also synonymous with a bounded territory within which the lord exercised his prerogatives. In a parallel fashion, the manor—the essential subdivision of the lordship—was simultaneously a military, economic, social and juridical institution, and a geographical unit.[52] The boundaries of lordships were often identical to those of the pre-existing Gaelic-Irish kingdoms. One of the best examples was Henry II's charter of 1172 which granted Meath to Hugh de Lacy to hold as the Ua Máel Sechlainn kings of Mide had before him.[53] The process by which the Liberty of Meath and the other lordships of Anglo-

Norman Ireland were subdivided was known as subinfeudation. The internal boundaries used in this activity often followed earlier divisions as Leister, for example, showed in her study of the colonization of Tipperary.[54] More specifically, Empey demonstrates that in the cantred of Eliogarty in north Tipperary, the Anglo-Norman grantee, Theobald Walter 'had to use the existing pre-Norman divisions as the basis of his enfeoffments'.[55] Again, the initial Anglo-Norman settlements—generally military in form—were often if not always located at existing seats of power.[56] But it is fundamental to the concept that the occurrence of such continuity of site was not axiomatic.

As Walton notes, such sequential development was to some extent no more than simple expediency, reflecting the extant distribution of resources and population and the need to redistribute land rapidly. For example, the association of mottes with earlier churches and the large secular enclosures (see Chapter 1) does suggest that the Anglo-Normans, not surprisingly, were drawn to existing settlement nuclei of the agricultural population. Walton goes on to argue that continuity of this form was also part of a conscious attempt to dislocate the Irish polity by removing the basis of its power.[57] It is possible, however, that the same effect could sometimes have been achieved through deliberate discontinuity, allowing existing mechanisms and seats of power to wither away. Simms is perhaps the most enthusiastic proponent of continuity, seeing the process as being a primary constraint upon the ultimate evolution of settlement on the Anglo-Norman manors.[58] She holds that the townland system which the Anglo-Normans inherited in Ireland was ultimately to prevent the evolution of the large nucleated villages found elsewhere in medieval Europe. In Ireland, she argues, free tenants lived on their own separate pieces of land. There are problems with the lateness of the documentation supporting this idea, and it may be best to remember Leister's caveat that continuity of boundaries did not preclude very considerable reorganization, particularly in the establishment of the seigneurial demesne lands.[59]

Another element of continuity was provided by the church for the imposition of the Gregorian reform upon Ireland predated the arrival of the Anglo-Normans. Gaelic-Irish monastic traditions had already been replaced by the liturgy of the continental orders such as the Cistercians and Augustinians, while the hierarchical institutions of the Roman church were in place as was the diocesan system forged at the Synods of Ráthbreasil (1111) and Kells (1152) (Fig. 12.4).[60] Some of the earlier Gaelic-Irish monasteries had become cathedrals and a number of these, including Kilkenny, Ferns, Co. Wexford, Cashel, Co. Tipperary, and Lismore, Co. Waterford, were to be amongst the earliest centres of Anglo-Norman settlement in their respective regions.[61] However, many major ecclesiastical centres did not flourish as secular centres of any significance after 1169. Most historians have been agreed that an enduring parish system had to await the delimitation of the Anglo-Norman manorial system, the boundaries of which it generally shared. However, recent work by Swan argues that the survival of many churches associated with the large secular enclosures as parish centres may show that this process was well under way prior to the Anglo-Norman colonization.[62]

A further aspect of continuity is provided by the post-1169 development of urbanization. The argument for an indigenous pre-Anglo-Norman urbanization in Ireland has been examined in Chapter 1 where it was concluded that, despite the many difficulties of the evidence, the actual number of early medieval towns must have been very small, and that the elaboration of a hierarchical urban network remained an achievement of the Anglo-Normans.[63] Nevertheless, it is apparent that particular early medieval towns provided some sort of basis for the development of urbanization subsequent to 1169. This has long been recognized—or at least asserted—in the case of the Hiberno-Norse towns. The Dublin excavations have demonstrated the striking degree of morphological continuity from the tenth to thirteenth centuries, while very much more limited investigations in Waterford have shown similar results.[64] By contrast, excavations in Cork, which fell to the Anglo-Normans in 1177, indicate that the Anglo-Norman town was laid out on a virgin site. Indeed, it is possible that the real precursor to Anglo-Norman Cork was not the Hiberno-Norse 'town' at all but the settlement around the Mac Cárrthaig castle.[65] This sharp break in what Aalen calls the centre of gravity of the settlement[66] is replicated at several of the early medieval ecclesiastical or secular sites such as Kildare, Kells, Co. Meath, Kilkenny, and Athlone, Co. Westmeath, where the Anglo-Norman towns were established around or to one side of the pre-existing settlements.[67] As we have seen in Chapter 1, this may reflect no more than a change of emphasis within the settlements as they gravitated more and more around the market-place, often found to the east or south-east of the ecclesiastical enclosure in the pre-Anglo-Norman town. Another clear instance of morphological continuity is provided by the enclosing *enceintes* also discussed in Chapter 1, the outlines of which can still be traced in the morphology of a number of Irish towns including Armagh, Kildare and Kells, Co. Meath.

One final point is that the concern with continuity should not obscure its converse. Only a very few important early medieval ecclesiastical sites such as Kildare and Kells developed into reasonably substantial Anglo-Norman towns. Others, such as Armagh—where there is some documentary if, disappointingly, little archaeological evidence for continued urban development during the twelfth and thirteenth centuries[68]—Derry and Tuam, Co. Galway, remained beyond the Anglo-Norman ambit. As shall be seen, our understanding of their high medieval urban role is frustratingly sketchy. But others—amongst them Glendalough, Co. Wicklow, Clonmacnoise, Co. Offaly, and Clonard, Co. Meath—are major discontinuities, disappearing from the documentary record, apparently because they sank into decline soon after the invasion. It may be that they were poorly located to the colonists' scheme of settlement; conversely, they may have been ignored deliberately, an example perhaps of the Anglo-Normans abandoning settlements in order to consolidate their political control through undermining existing mechanisms and seats of power. Thus, they are illustrative of the point which is well worth reiterating that while continuity played an important role—by no means yet fully understood—in the initial development of the Anglo-Norman colonization of Ireland, it was not an axiomatic process.

The Processes, Functions and Form of Settlement in Anglo-Norman Ireland

Dodgshon contends that the constraints of feudalism demanded a socio-economic structure which was spatially integrated. The system had to reach the ordinary peasant through its institutional structure, while feudal kings sought to weave webs of authority and dependence through all corners of their realms.[69] But as Elias argues, this requirement brought about the central paradox at the heart of feudal structures. It was a system in which power was concentrated in the hands of kings. However, in order to reach their subjects, kings had to devolve power through lordship to vassals, who in turn, could use such autonomy to establish some degree of independence within their territories.[70] Anglo-Norman Ireland has to be seen not as a single polity but as a patchwork of lordships.[71] Within each, the settlement structure created was the means or conduit through which the ordinary peasant was integrated into the wider economy and society. Consequently, central to the argument put forward, both in this chapter and its predecessor, is the notion that any specific means of organizing an economy and society will produce its own characteristic settlement landscape.

As the following discussion makes clear, there is a considerable debate about that settlement landscape and to pretend otherwise in the interests of synthesis would be misleading. In part, such uncertainties in our understanding of the nature of Anglo-Norman settlement reflect the difficulties and uncertainties of the evidence. There is a considerable mass of documentary material, but this is rarely continuous for any one locale, nor is it commonly less than ambiguous about the morphology and function of settlement. Furthermore, the distribution of surviving written sources as they relate to different lordships is very imbalanced, and we know much less about some than others. As this discussion emphasizes, the models of settlement advanced by various researchers tend to depend upon a process which, where possible, integrates field observation and distributional characteristics with the evidence of extant documentary sources. As the latter is often inadequate, an understanding of evolutionary process, dating and function of settlement can often depend on analogical case studies originating from rather better documented regions, or drawn from the relatively limited body of archaeological excavation evidence.

This problem of the imbalanced nature of the sources is compounded by the certainty that there were undoubtedly significant regional variations in the structure of colonization and settlement which in part relate to the density and general effectiveness of that process. Further, environmental variations within Ireland would have reflected primarily upon agricultural production and thus on the relative attractiveness of an area to the Anglo-Normans. Another problem is implicit within the assumption that settlement was controlled by the cognate agencies of lordship and manor. There must have been variations, even within particular regions, in the seigneurial response to the challenge of mounting an effective colonization of these land grants. Again, the enthusiasm and effectiveness with which individual seigneurs obtained peasant migrants would have been instrumental in determining the patterns of settlement which evolved in particular manors. The difficulty remains that because of the piecemeal nature of the sources, it is unlikely that such singularities can ever be isolated and thus we are forced to generalize. But the paradox remains that such generalizations are built upon specific and particular case studies chosen for their extant evidence, but which, nevertheless, may be misleading.

Bearing these several qualifications in mind, four elements of the feudal landscape of Anglo-Norman Ireland can be identified, these being fortifications, manorial settlement, the church, and finally, towns and boroughs. It is not the intention to be even-handed in dealing with these but to devote much of the discussion to town and borough. To some extent, this reflects the balance in the research so far carried out, but more fundamentally, it underscores the particular importance of these institutions in the articulation of the feudal process. In turn, it can be demonstrated that medieval townscape was the product of the feudal ideological ordering of economy and society.

Fortifications

The occurrence of feudal fortifications after c. 1000, and the repercussions of that evidence in understanding the structure of early medieval Irish society, has already been addressed in Chapter 1. After 1169, however, there was a change in the controlling institutions for, as we have seen, all Anglo-Norman settlement took place within the spatial dimensions of lordship, the ideological concept which was to shape the geography of much of the island during the high Middle Ages in exactly the same way as that of kingship had governed that of early medieval Ireland. The traditional view, derived from the work of G. H. Orpen, was that the conical earthen motte castle—sometimes attached to a bailey although in Ireland more often not—was introduced by the Anglo-Normans and that its distribution constituted the best index to their settlement of the island.[72] However, as Glasscock has demonstrated, around 90 per cent of surviving examples are to be found in Ulster and Leinster. In contrast, the motte was apparently absent in more westerly regions such as east Cork, much of Tipperary, Limerick, Kerry and eastern Galway and Mayo, all of which underwent intensive if patchy Anglo-Norman settlement during the first half of the thirteenth century (Fig. 2.3).[73] Undoubtedly, most of those working in the field are guilty of over-enthusiastic recording of mottes. As Mallory and McNeill point out, they are very difficult to identify and any motte list is essentially one of round flat-topped mounds of earth.[74] A particular problem lies in distinguishing mottes from platform ring-forts. Moore suggests that motte-like sites which lack baileys and a church association, and are low in relation to their breadth, are more likely to be platform ring-forts, which we now know can date to well before the Anglo-Norman invasion.[75] Other recent work suggests that in addition to the motte, a second form of Anglo-Norman fortification was commonly built in Ireland. This was the ringwork, essentially a circular earthen enclosure surmounted by a palisade, the dominant feature of which would have been a timber gatehouse (Fig. 2.4).[76] Both variants of the earthen feudal fortress were also to be found in other parts of the Anglo-Norman dominion.[77] For example, in England, no less than 700 mottes and 200 ringworks are known for the period between 1066 and 1215, after which masonry castles became more common.[78]

In Ireland, both mottes and ringworks appear to have been constructed from the onset of the invasion although the former predominated in those parts of Leinster and Ulster settled before the end of the twelfth century. In the early years of the Anglo-Norman colonization, the ringwork appears to have functioned primarily as a campaign fortress.[79] For reasons that are not entirely understood, motte construction seems to have generally ceased in the early thirteenth century and thus, with

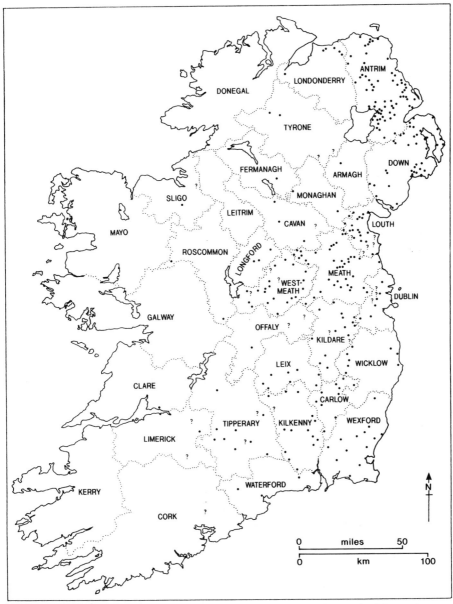

Fig. 2.3. Distribution of surviving mottes in 1973. After R. E. Glasscock, 'Mottes in Ireland', *Château-Gaillard*, **VII** (1975), pp. 95–110.

the exception of Ulster, it is not often to be found in those areas subjected to Anglo-Irish colonization after *c.* 1220. The first castles built by the Anglo-Normans in Munster and Connacht were generally ringwork in form although the earthen banks were often replaced rapidly by masonry castles.[80]

Turning from the morphological and distributional characteristics of these settlements to their actual function in the articulation of the economy and society of

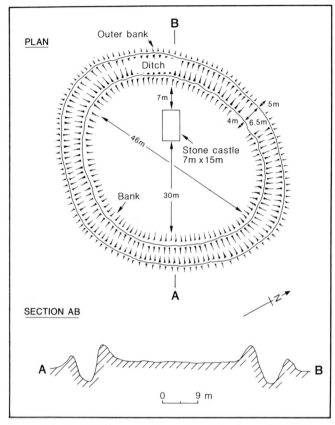

Fig. 2.4. A possible Anglo-Norman ringwork at Dundonnell, Co. Roscommon.

medieval Ireland, fortifications represent the imposition of seigneurial power, their primary function having been to establish initial control over the land grants of the various subinfeudations. As Orpen observed in the first-ever systematic study of Anglo-Norman fortifications in Ireland, there is a direct causative linkage between a seigneur's importance in that process and the scale and importance of his castle.[81] Consequently, large motte-and-baileys or in the west, ringworks, tend to be associated with what Empey has termed the 'capital manors' of a lordship, or with those held by the principal sub-tenants.[82] For instance, in Hugh de Lacy's Liberty of Meath, the most substantial fortresses were those associated with the initial subinfeudation, essentially the process through which de Lacy set out to establish effective control over his territories after 1172. Consequently, they were generally located at strategic points—often existing settlement nuclei—on those land-grants held directly of de Lacy himself and on the manors which he personally retained.[83] Apart from such sites, large motte-and-baileys were built only at defensive locations, for example on the peripheries of lordships where there is some distributional evidence to suggest the construction of defensive screens.[84] Otherwise, the bulk of the Irish mottes, which often lack baileys, tend to be less substantial than their English and Welsh counterparts. Only 20–25 per cent of the extant mottes in

Ulster have baileys, compared with over 80 per cent in Britain; the Ulster examples are also much smaller.[85] As McNeill argues, motte possession seems to have extended relatively far down the social scale in Ireland, and many appear to have been constructed at the centres of the manors which constituted the base of the Anglo-Norman landholding hierarchy for little more than reasons of status.[86]

Many mottes and ringworks would have been used throughout the thirteenth century but in technological terms, they were quickly superseded by stone castles.[87] In the Anglo-Norman colonization, these did not proliferate in a comparable fashion to the tower houses of the fourteenth and fifteenth centuries (see Chapter 3), their ownership being restricted to the more powerful barons or to the crown. The first wave of stone castle building began *c.* 1180, two of the largest examples being the de Lacy headquarters at Trim, Co. Meath, started before 1200 but not permanently occupied until the mid thirteenth century,[88] and the de Courcy (later royal) fortress at Carrickfergus, Co. Antrim.[89] These early castles were usually tower keeps surrounded by curtain walls, a fashion which seems to have died out *c.* 1250 to be replaced by the less defensive hall keeps of the later thirteenth century.[90] At the end of the process came the fortresses of Roscommon, Ballintober, Co. Roscommon, and Ballymote, Co. Sligo, the latter two built in the very late thirteenth century and notably similar in design to the contemporary castles of Edward I in Wales. But these major castles were strategic garrisoned fortresses and as such, a little remote from the actual daily business of settling and cultivating the manors. As Empey rightly observes, our attention is caught by the great men—and their artefacts—but we must not forget that the task of establishing and developing the colonization on the ground was accomplished for the most part by their vassals, the lesser barons and knights.[91]

Manorial Settlement

The establishment of their military hegemony over lordship and especially manor, represented in the landscape by the incidence of mottes and ringworks, underpinned the subsequent development of Anglo-Norman settlement. We know little about the time-span of this process or about the origins and numbers of immigrants who settled on the Irish manors. Eagar shows that, perhaps unsurprisingly, the origins of immigrants into Leinster correlate with the English and Welsh estates held by the two most important magnates, Strongbow and later, William Marshal.[92] Otway-Ruthven suggested that the lure of increased social status and lessened labour services may have been used to encourage migration; interestingly, the same tactics were also common in the Germanic migrations into eastern Europe.[93] The effective colonization of the lordships and manors demarcated in the various subinfeudations was dependent upon this influx of settlers. Settlement took place around the various castle nuclei although its exact nature has been a subject of some debate. As yet, it is impossible to present more than an interim report and one which is very far from consensus.[94] Glasscock was the first to moot the possible existence of manorial villages, now mostly deserted.[95] Following the methodology used by Beresford in England, he argued that the most significant clue to the site of a possible lost village in the contemporary landscape is a ruined medieval church, frequently juxtaposed with an earthwork fortification of the motte or ringwork type.[96] Such a conjunction of features is by no means to be taken as infallible evidence of a former village for churches often appear to have been isolated.[97] Occasionally, however, earthworks which demarcate the footings of abandoned houses may also be visible at such sites. Through field observation, Glasscock was able to identify a number of deserted settlements, particularly in Tipperary and Kilkenny. In a further study of the eastern part of the Liberty of Meath, almost 100 manorial villages were identified.[98] It was apparent, however, that there were other types of settlement to be found on the manors of Meath. In particular, there were a significant number of hamlets, possibly the homes of the feudal base class, the *betagii*, who were generally Gaelic-Irish in origin.

Simms has argued that the designation of 'village' is often inappropriate and that the term, 'manorial centre', would frequently be more apposite.[99] This proposition is derived from McNeill's work in Ulster in which he claims that villages were not a feature of the medieval earldom. Instead, manors were administered from a node which he sees as a fiscal centre, a place where tenants met to pay rents, and the seat of the manorial court.[100] However, it could be argued that Ulster does not provide a convincing analogy as the Anglo-Norman colonization there was very much a military overlordship, existing side-by-side with Gaelic-Irish socio-economic phenomena. Nevertheless (as alluded to in the discussion on continuity), it has been argued that the constraint of the Gaelic-Irish townland system pre-empted the formation of large villages on the Anglo-Norman manors of Ireland. This model holds that the demesne farm—the land retained by the lord of the manor—was run from the manorial centre while major free tenants held land independently in townlands of their own, thereby rendering settlement nucleation inefficient.[101] These hypotheses remain to be thoroughly tested because they are generally based on late medieval sources and as we have seen in the earlier discussion, involve quite formidable assumptions concerning continuity. Nor do their proponents appear to consider the possibility that the arrangements of manorial settlement which they propose might well be accounted for by colonization of marginal lands subsequent to the initial settlement, or by a decline in the later Middle Ages of the communality of life represented by the village.

Evidence that the processes of manorial colonization were characterized by such change as well as continuity comes from another settlement form, the so-called 'medieval moated site'.[102] This was a rectangular earthwork, surrounded by a moat, extant examples occurring most commonly in parts of Wexford, Carlow, Kilkenny, east Cork and east Tipperary (Fig. 2.5). Barry observes that these areas often correspond to Anglo-Irish border regions where the settlers were often under pressure from the Gaelic-Irish, particularly in the later Middle Ages.[103] Thus, moated sites tend to be located at some distance from the centres of manors. This distributional characteristic led Empey to argue that the earthworks represent a secondary colonization which could perhaps be correlated with the rise in agricultural production that occurred in the second half of the thirteenth century.[104]

Pursuing this point, the nature of manorial settlement was dependent on the agricultural economy, the basis of all production in Anglo-Norman Ireland. The organization of agriculture and the associated arrangement of field systems remain seriously under-researched areas. Otway-Ruthven claimed that the manorial lands were laid out in open-fields and that this was true throughout the heartland of the

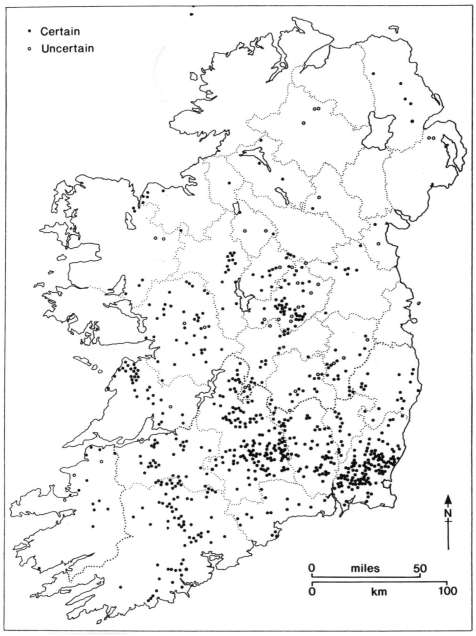

Fig. 2.5. The distribution of moated sites. After R. E. Glasscock, 'Moated sites and deserted villages and boroughs: two neglected aspects of Anglo-Norman settlement in Ireland', in N. Stephens and R. E. Glasscock (eds.), *Irish Geographical Studies in Honour of E. Estyn Evans*, (Belfast, 1970), pp. 162–77; see p. 165.

Anglo-Norman colony. Further, she suggested that each social group amongst the tenants often held land in separate parts of the manor, an idea which we have already encountered in Simms' arguments on manorial settlement.[105] Thus by 1300, some free tenants already had compact holdings, either as a result of agreed exchange of strips or through colonization of peripheral lands.[106] Another example is provided by the *betagii*, the unfree Gaelic-Irish tenants who can be equated with the English villeins. It has been argued that they retained specific areas of the manors which were farmed on an indigenous infield–outfield system similar to the system known later as rundale.[107] In a stimulating critique which evinced almost no response, Butlin argues that the 'native betagh rundale and Norman three-field models have to be relegated to the realms of mythology'. He observes that the analogy with an idealized, midland English field system is outmoded.[108] As Dodgshon has shown in that context, there were no regional models but innumerable variations arising out of the vigour of social and economic change and through environmental differences.[109] Thus both manorial settlement and field systems can be seen as a response to the same basic set of problems within a shifting set of social, economic and environmental constraints upon individual seigneurial initiative. The result, perhaps, was variety of settlement and field pattern, a fluidity of response determined by the particular interaction at any one locale of those extraneous processes with local particularities.

The essential seigneurial problem was to organize agricultural production within an economic structure in which Ireland was subjected to external control. In terms of the actual production, Down believes that the Anglo-Normans brought to Irish agriculture not so much a revolution as an expansion and extension of the existing system.[110] Central to this was an emphasis on arable production, particularly between 1169 and 1300; however, grazing on both permanent pasture and fallow was always important.[111] As Down observes, arable land in medieval conditions was inadequate without pasture for the livestock, which was used in its cultivation and manuring, and meadowland to provide hay for its winter fodder. Oats seem to have been the most important grain crop, followed closely by wheat with barley a poor third.[112] There is some agreement that change began to occur around 1300. Pollen analysis of samples taken from Littleton Bog, Co. Tipperary, and the documentary evidence both suggest that cereal growing began to contract around then.[113] However, the reasons are rather less clear. Environmental factors may have played a role for the early part of the fourteenth century seems to have been exceptionally wet, a factor thought to be important in the famine which characterized the second decade of that century.[114] Lyons has carried out a very detailed analysis of the relationship between population, famine and plague. She estimates that the demographic base was subject to severe erosion in the late thirteenth and early fourteenth centuries. Famine prevailed with increasing frequency after *c.* 1270 and later, the great north European famine coincided with the very considerable political instability and warfare within Ireland, brought about by the Bruce Invasion of 1315–18. Thus, Lyons' major point is that the downturn occurred long before the first visitation of the Black Death in 1348.[115] Finally, external factors may also have been important for production in Ireland was determined to a very considerable extent by the demands of the English market, notably purveyance for the royal armies.[116] Growing resistance by merchants to this system, and especially resentment of the long delays which occurred in payment, combined with the devastation of Irish agriculture to end purveyance in the 1320s.[117]

The Church

Curiously, given the enduring importance of the church in Irish life and the ubiquity of its ideology in medieval Europe, relatively little attention has been given to the role of this institution within Ireland during the high Middle Ages. The Gregorian reforms had been instituted prior to the Anglo-Norman colonization, leading to the establishment of around 70 Cistercian and Augustinian houses by 1169.[118] A further 30 were founded between then and the arrival of the mendicant orders in the 1220s. By 1340, the most important of these, the Dominicans, Franciscans and Carmelites, had established over 80 houses, which, reflecting the functions of the orders, were usually located in towns (Fig. 2.6).[119] Many of these houses of all orders were owners of substantial estates endowed to them by both Gaelic-Irish and Anglo-Norman patrons. As Hennessy shows in his study of the estate of the Augustinian Priory and Hospital of St John the Baptist outside Dublin, benefactors also came from all strata of society, noble and peasant, and from city and countryside.[120] Despite their common involvement in the contemporary reform movement, Empey regards this issue of patronage as being the core of the fundamental difference between the Anglo-Norman church and its predecessor.[121] After the invasion, the scope of patronage expanded from bishops, abbots and nobility to embrace a wide variety of tenants-in-chief and sub-tenants. This was especially true of the houses of the Canons such as the Augustinian house at Kells-in-Ossory, Co. Kilkenny. It was only the tenants-in-chief 'who could afford the luxury of Cistercian houses'.[122] This dichotomy is best symbolized by the frequent and continued construction of royal or seigneurial tombs in the Cistercian houses. Two such examples are the effigies of a thirteenth-century king of Thomond in the beautifully-sited Corcomroe Abbey, Co. Clare, and the elaborate sixteenth-century monument to a Butler lord at Kilcooley, Co. Tipperary.[123]

In theory, the Cistercian and Augustinian houses would have divided their land into granges, independent monastic farms which were worked by lay brethren to yield a surplus for the use and enjoyment of whichever monastic communities owned them.[124] One of the best examples is provided by Mellifont, Co. Louth, which by the mid-thirteenth century possessed extensive estates divided into granges along the lower Boyne valley.[125] But by then, the system was already breaking down. As Stalley argues, the monks increasingly became *rentiers* rather than active farmers, concerned with profit making rather than self-sufficiency.[126] Thus, the thirteenth-century estates of the Priory and Hospital of St John the Baptist were organized into granges but farmed by tenants.[127] As a result there was increasingly little to distinguish the abbeys from the other great landowners of the age. In a similar fashion, as was the norm elsewhere in the feudal societies of western Europe, the magnates of the church were also great secular lords. One of the best examples is provided by the Archbishops of Dublin who held a whole succession of manors around the fringes of the city.

While the Gregorian reformers of the twelfth century had introduced the continental religious orders and established the basis of the Roman church's territorial

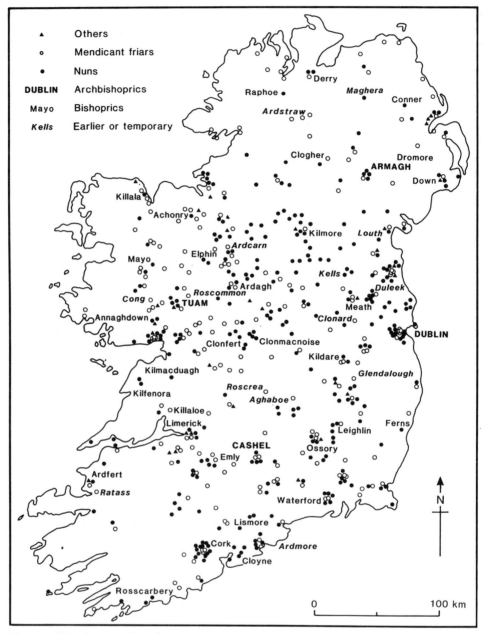

Fig. 2.6. Distribution of medieval monastic houses. After R. A. Butlin, *The Development of the Irish Town*, (London, 1977), p. 23.

order, the diocesan system (Fig. 12.4), the general consensus is that the creation of a functioning parish structure did not occur until after the onset of the Anglo-Norman colonization. Indeed, Empey believes that the diocesan reorganization had not got far either prior to the invasion.[128] Again, the process of 'continentalizing' the monastic church was pushed faster and more vigorously by the Anglo-Norman lords; in County Kilkenny, for example, all the post-1169 foundations were unconnected with the older Irish houses, none of which seems to have survived into the thirteenth century.[129] In her study of the rural deanery of Skreen in County Meath, Otway-Ruthven demonstrated the synonymity of manor and parish, and in general this relationship has been found to hold true.[130] Although the issues raised by Swan concerning possible parish continuity have yet to be addressed—as noted earlier—it may be that the actual element of continuity was not provided by the parish but by the manorial landholding. Thus, in Tipperary, for example, Hennessy observes that the Anglo-Norman colonization 'introduced a laity for whom parishes were an essential part of their culture'.[131] The inception of their manorial structure—which would have owed much to earlier land sub-divisions—allowed the rapid establishment of the parish system. It took a considerable time for the process to be completed; Brand has traced the emergence of the Louth parish of Beaulieu which was only so demarcated in the fourteenth century, probably because the manorial lord felt that his holding was incomplete without its own parish church.[132] The churches themselves were generally very modest by contemporary European standards; there appear to have been no significant architectural differences between Anglo-Norman and Gaelic-Irish areas.[133] Beyond the Anglo-Norman frontier, hereditary ecclesiastical families continued to govern the church,[134] leading Hurley to argue that the twelfth-century reforms changed the organization and structure, but not the nature, of the Gaelic-Irish church.[135]

Boroughs and Towns

Definitions and Classifications

It is in the study of the medieval borough and town that the historical geography of medieval Ireland has perhaps made most progress. Here too, we can develop the idea that the settlement landscape evolves from the requirements of the feudal system and understand Dodgshon's point that all ideologies create their own specific landscape. Again, the study of towns and boroughs demonstrates most clearly the value of analogy in circumstances where the particular evidence is notably deficient. In Anglo-Norman Ireland specifically and medieval Europe generally, arguably the borough and town together constituted the single most crucial element in the geography of lordship. This class of settlement provided the principal means by which the abstraction of feudal ties was translated into an operating reality across space. But again, it was through towns that feudal kings reached out to control their barons and sought to exert centralized control. There is considerable agreement as to the general factors which motivated the involvement of the feudal elite in town foundation throughout Europe, but it needs to be remembered that the elite was itself hierarchically organized. This was highly significant to the elaboration of the developing urban network in post-conquest Ireland, both between and within lordships. As we have seen in the context of manorial settlement generally, the patchwork of landholdings produced by the patterning of lordships constitutes the most convincing spatial framework within which urbanization can be interpreted. But because the Anglo-Norman expansion continued well into the thirteenth century, the evolution of urbanization across the island was—at least to some extent—chronologically staggered. Further, and this remains to be investigated, it is possible that—paralleling the conclusions already advanced about manorial settlement—there were considerable regional variations in the effectiveness of the economic development of particular lordships which, in turn, had repercussions for the promotion and development of towns.

Despite this necessity for rather more detailed comparative research, it seems that the hierarchical ordering of the feudal elite was a potent influence on the development of the urban hierarchy within any specific lordship. Inevitably, the *capita* of the most important and powerful lords were the first Anglo-Norman towns to be founded. Their sites, frequently dominated by motte and, later, by stone castles, were chosen with regard to strategic factors such as control of communications. But just as the boundaries of Anglo-Norman lordships display a strong continuity with those of the earlier Gaelic-Irish polities, a number of these *capita* were adapted from pre-existing settlements. Thus in Meath, while Walter de Lacy gave a charter to the new town of Drogheda in 1194, slightly later he also incorporated his military *caput* at Trim and nearby Kells, both—the latter in particular—important pre-Anglo-Norman settlements. That Trim was preferred to Kells as the military and administrative centre was probably a reflection of its centrality to the lordship as a whole.[136] Again, the first action of Theobald Walter in north Tipperary—where the patterning of subinfeudation was rather different to Meath and Leinster—was to fortify his *caput* of Thurles, and only then did he set about the task of creating a network of dependent fiefs. Thus, it is not surprising that the most significant urban foundations were often identified with the capital manors of the great lords.[137] At the local level, this confirms the conclusion that the *capita* of the most important lords were generally the first towns to be established in the particular lordships and seigneurial manors throughout the Anglo-Norman colony.[138] Further, the subsequent development of a functional urban hierarchy within these political units replicates Beresford's finding that in England, the most significant contribution to urban success was an early arrival.[139] Consequently, as a generalization—to which there were a number of exceptions—the towns which subsequently proved to be most successful were those associated with the most powerful lords, established first within their respective lordships.

However, such towns were relatively few in number, as were great lords. As we have seen, colonization of the lordships and seigneurial manors was the responsibility of the 'immediate lords of the soil'.[140] Thus, the majority of medieval Irish boroughs were founded by Anglo-Norman fiefholders of comparatively minor significance. If we look elsewhere in Europe, the same pattern can be found, the reason being a commonality of motivation within the feudal structure. For example, the work of Beresford and Hilton—amongst others—has established that by the end of the thirteenth century, up to two-thirds of all English boroughs were seigneurial in origin. The remainder comprised what Hilton has termed mercantile towns, places characterized by an urban division of labour in which the surplus raised in the small borough markets was spent. Thus these towns were the centres of trade, industry, administration and, increasingly, banking, and contrasted with the seigneurial boroughs which functioned as the places where peasant surplus production was converted into cash; for the most part, the peasants sold their produce in order to buy other products for consumption. Increasingly, as labour services were commuted to cash payments, the demand of the peasantry for cash expanded in order to pay money rent, fines and taxes, not only to the seigneurs but also to the state as the levies of centralized taxation proliferated.[141] To the feudal lord, the borough provided profit from market tolls, fines, rents and taxes which could be spent on military equipment and the other necessities of a noble life.[142] It was part of the mechanism by which he abstracted the maximum profit from his lands. Therefore both seigneur and peasant needed a market and, consequently, the borough was critical to the mutual dependence of peasantry and aristocracy. This same pattern of interrelationships has been observed in France where Musset, for example, has established that the bulk of boroughs in Normandy were seigneurial in origin.[143] Again, in eastern Europe, the chartered settlement was an integral component of the Germanic colonizations. Thus, in Ireland's analogous regions, the small seigneurial borough was a quintessential expression of the mutual dependence of lord and peasant in feudal society, a diagnostic element of that specifically feudal landscape. To quote the *Histoire de la France Urbaine*, 'le marché urbain est donc indispensable au monde rurale'.[144]

Many such settlements were established throughout Normandy, England and Wales by feudal lords from the eleventh century onwards, the pace of foundation accelerating rapidly after 1100. The seigneur used a charter to give tenants a plot of land—the burgage—within a borough on which to build a house, and usually a small acreage outside the settlement with access, for example, to woodland (for building timber and firewood), peat bog and grazing.[145] The inhabitants of a borough were also granted—at least in theory—a range of economic privileges and monopolies.[146] In Anglo-Norman Ireland, the most common package of borough rights was that modelled on the charter of the small Normandy town of Breteuil-sur-Iton.[147] It is possible that laws such as these were a reflection of colonization in a context in which the customary law was perceived to be radically different from that of the colonists.[148] Thus the borough of the fiefholder—Empey's immediate lord of the soil—was not, as MacNiocaill has argued, an offshoot nor an overflow of an Anglo-Norman agrarian economy; rather it was the settlement form through which that economy operated.[149]

So far, however, I have been circumspect about the equation of borough with town and it is now time to distinguish between these. But first, several problems must be outlined. These relate to the apparent paradox that all towns were boroughs but not all boroughs were towns. One is that a legal grant is insufficient evidence of urban foundation; as Reynolds succinctly states of the English context, the offer of urban life contained in a charter singularly fails as proof that it developed.[150] Again, and perhaps more significantly, there is the question of the division of labour. In his study of Normandy, Musset used the expression, *bourgs ruraux*, to refer to the seigneurial boroughs which proliferated between 1050 and 1300. By this, he meant settlements which, despite possessing the legal attributes of a town, were characterized by a division of labour in which agriculture remained dominant, and by the survival of feudal obligations on the part of *les bourgeois* who still regularly owed labour services.[151] This is very similar to Glasscock's concept of the rural-borough. As he observes, the custom of Breteuil was granted 'apparently freely and without royal authority' in Ireland, resulting in manorial villages—although essentially agricultural in function—being given the inflated status of boroughs, perhaps in order to attract settlers.[152]

Given the detailed studies carried out in Britain and Europe, it is likely that the concept of the rural-borough as defined by Glasscock, is an overly limited one, for the market function alone—with its potential for linking the peasantry to a cash economy—was sufficient to distinguish boroughs from rural settlements.[153] In turn, however, boroughs do need to be distinguished from towns because clearly many were not characterized by an urban division of labour, their inhabitants being primarily cultivators. In part, these difficulties result from no more than the constraints of the English language which does not have a word to interpose between 'town' and 'village'. In this respect, French is much more flexible with its intervening category of *bourg*, still in use today to describe the settlement in the commune where the market is held and around which the agriculturalists' villages are organized.[154] Frequently, the twentieth-century expansion of the tertiary sector has made the *bourg* rather more urban than was true of the Middle Ages, but a town–*bourg*/borough–village classification system has a far greater relevance to understanding the functioning of the feudal economy and society of Anglo-Norman Ireland than a simple town/village dichotomy.

In excess of 330 Anglo-Norman settlements in Ireland, distinguished by some form of urban constitution *c.* 1300, have been identified.[155] Only a very few possess extant charters, the remainder having been identified from various references to the occurrence of burgages and burgesses. It must be allowed that there may have been more. Glasscock states that it was perhaps the aim to establish chartered settlements on almost all the principal manors, although this will never be confirmed from the documentation.[156] Again, as Bradley observes of the 35 identified boroughs in Tipperary, 'it is likely that there were many more'.[157] However, it may be that such statements contain an element of exaggeration for although its precise form is open to debate, there is as we have seen, very considerable evidence for other forms of manorial settlement from which boroughs can be differentiated by their economic and jurisdictional functions within the feudal society. Graham has attempted to classify the identified boroughs through composite definitions which link the settlements to their role in the feudal economy and thus, in the light of the previous discussion, to the status of their founding lord (Fig. 2.7). He argues that no more than 25 can be categorized as mercantile towns, but a further 80 settlements can be identified as having sufficient evidence of urban criteria to be classified as small towns, operating as the principal market centres within which peasant exchange occurred. Testimony to their seigneurial origin, almost 70 per cent developed around a castle core, undoubtedly the most potent symbol in the landscape of the feudal mode of production.[158] A total in excess of 100 towns is rather higher than the 55 produced in an earlier attempt to apply a definitional scheme, based on the survival of morphological criteria such as the presence of walls, castles, bridges, cathedrals, quays and suburbs. In this, a settlement was classified as a town if it was endowed with at least three of these features in addition to holding a market, and possessing a street plan with houses and associated plot.[159] The former scheme is arguably more comprehensive because it attempts to combine a settlement's morphological structure with social criteria such as population, the division of labour and jurisdictional roles which, in turn, relate the borough to its origin as a means of operationalizing feudalism.

Although a number of the remaining settlements identified by Graham were market villages with no further evidence of borough status, the majority were rural-boroughs. This category constitutes almost 50 per cent of the settlements identified, a very similar percentage to Normandy where about half the places listed by Musset were classified as *bourgs ruraux*. In Ireland, the most prolific sub-category again comprised agglomerations around castles. It is assumed that all rural-boroughs were local marketing centres, for the primary motivation of a knight was to ensure that others were excluded from reaping the direct profits of trading with his tenants.[160] There may have been some specialization of labour— we have occasional evidence for bakers and brewers—but almost all rural-borough populations were agriculturalists. Nevertheless, as an analysis of the functions of these settlements would show, it is insufficient to dismiss rural-boroughs as mere agricultural manorial villages because in the Middle Ages, they were differentiated from these, both economically and jurisdictionally. Rural-boroughs fulfilled a specific role in the integration of the peasantry and minor nobility into feudal society, not only in Anglo-Norman Ireland, but throughout Europe generally.

An Example of Feudal Space; the Morphology, Functions and Social Geography of Medieval Irish Boroughs

To a considerable extent, the evidence of the physical structure of the Anglo-Norman towns and boroughs of medieval Ireland is derived by extrapolation from extant urban morphologies, supplemented by various cartographic sources and relatively limited archaeological data.[161] Apart from surviving monuments, par-ticularly castles and churches, three diagnostic physical elements of the medieval town—plan, plot pattern and walls—can be identified. Just as the towns estab-lished during the Germanic migrations into eastern Europe and the internal colon-izations of south-west France were planned, so too were those of Anglo-Norman Ireland. Where the medieval urban layout can be reconstructed, it was predomi-nantly linear. The houses often had their gable ends to the street with burgages behind. The market-place—occasionally marked by a market cross—was either the main street of a linear town or sometimes a triangular extension at one end. A few town plans were more elaborate, the most common such form—as at Clonmel and Carrick-on-Suir, Co. Tipperary, or Drogheda, Co. Louth—being an irregular che-quer (Fig. 2.8).[162] Uniquely, Kells, Co. Meath, developed on a concentric plan, presumably dictated by its pre-Anglo-Norman morphology. Castles were normally located either on the edge of, or outside, the town. That Anglo-Norman morpholo-gies can often be reconstructed in considerable detail emphasizes what is perhaps the most remarkable manifestation of continuity, the links that exist between the medieval and contemporary Irish urban worlds.

Furthermore, such sequential development is not restricted to street layout alone, but is characteristic too of a second major plan element—the property plot. First there was continuity between Hiberno-Norse and Anglo-Norman Dublin, for both excavation and morphological analysis of the city's plan units point to the possible incorporation of individual Hiberno-Norse garths into the layout of the

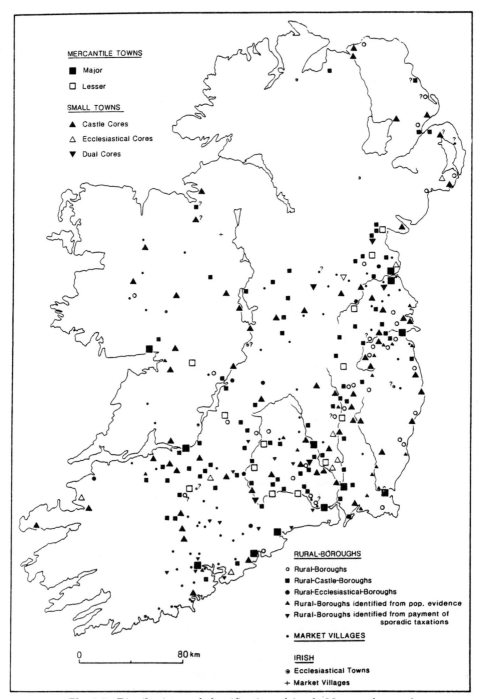

Fig. 2.7. Distribution and classification of Anglo-Norman boroughs.

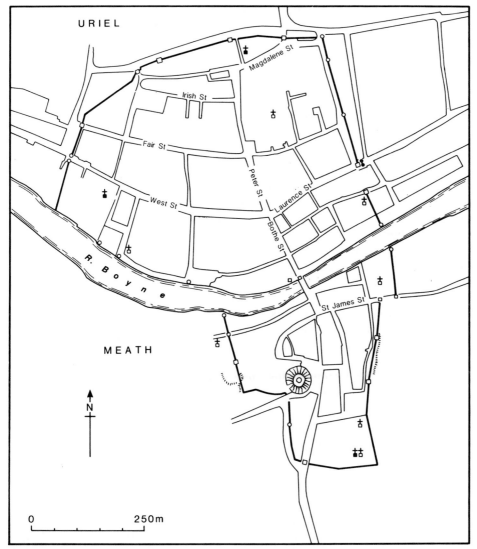

Fig. 2.8. A planned Anglo-Norman town: Drogheda. Until the fourteenth century, Drogheda comprised twin boroughs on the Meath and Uriel sides of the Boyne. After John Bradley, 'Planned Anglo-Norman towns in Ireland', in H. B. Clarke and Anngret Simms (eds.), *The Comparative History of Urban Origins in Non-Roman Europe*, pp. 411–68; see p. 437.

Anglo-Norman town of the late twelfth century.[163] Secondly, despite detailed changes, there is often a marked degree of morphological continuity—as at Drogheda—between the Anglo-Norman plot patterns which evolved after 1169, and those recorded on the mid-nineteenth-century First Edition Ordnance Survey Six Inch Maps.[164] Numerous extant Anglo-Norman charters and many rentals refer to burgesses paying a rent, generally set at 12d per annum, included in which was a burgage, a plot of borough land between 25 and 30 feet wide, and usually having a length:width ratio of about 5:1.[165] While these long thin plots were an important diagnostic physical feature of the medieval town, not only in Anglo-Norman Ireland but also elsewhere in Europe, some caution needs to be expressed about their interpretation, particularly as it relates to continuity. Recent work in England, where studies of medieval urban morphology are much more advanced than in Ireland, and where the documentation is very much better, suggests that complex patterns of continuity and piecemeal change of burgage patterns were characteristic, reflecting centuries of property development.[166] Again, Astill has suggested that burgages were only belatedly or never laid out in many of the smaller English medieval towns. Therefore, what appear ostensibly to be typical medieval patterns may date only from the fourteenth and fifteenth centuries.[167]

A further characteristic medieval morphological element was the town wall. The evidence for walling comes both from the survival of remnants, and through documents in the form of murage charters. Interpretation of the latter is complicated by the doubts which always attend the translation of legal grants into reality, particularly where corroborating physical evidence is lacking. (Similar problems occur in the interpretation of borough and market charters.) Using such sources, Thomas has identified around 50 Irish medieval towns which definitely were walled by 1500; additionally, she lists another 30 doubtful examples, many being places which obtained murage charters but lack reliable morphological evidence. Not all walls were of stone, a number being of suitably reinforced earth. Murage charters were not granted en masse, but as a result of individual requests from the towns; the terms and conditions in relation to taxation tend to become much more complex as time passes. While the earliest places to receive murage charters were the Hiberno-Norse coastal towns plus a few other new Anglo-Norman foundations such as Drogheda, the most intensive period for murage grants was between 1250 and 1320 when about 50 per cent of all those known were granted.[168] The dual role of the walled town—commercial centre and defensive facility—inevitably led to compromise, especially with regard to waterfronts. Here, particularly if the town lay on a navigable river, estuary or shore, the defensive function tended to be undermined to permit access to quays. As many towns were walled after they developed commercially, the lines of the wall circuits and the location of gates could be determined by the pre-existing shape of the town and its communications. Larger towns had between four and six gates. The largest walled areas were at Drogheda and Kilkenny which were both twin boroughs; the largest unitary walled town was New Ross, Co. Waterford, with an enclosed area of 39 hectares.[169]

Partly because of the morphological orientation of much of this research, but also as a by-product of documentary deficiencies, rather more is known about the physical structure of Anglo-Norman towns in Ireland than of their economic and social functions, which, indeed, often have to be assumed. A considerable amount of the extant evidence is collected in MacNiocaill's *Na Buirgéisí*.[170] A great deal of work remains to be done here, and it may be that given the difficulties of the Irish documentary evidence, one of the most profitable ways forward will be through the use of analogous studies. The economic and social functionings of medieval towns in both England and France have been studied intensively, and must have relevance to the imitative settlement structure established by the Anglo-Normans in Ireland.[171] As discussed earlier, the primary economic motivation of the feudal elite in establishing towns and rural-boroughs was to provide markets for their tenants. The peasant surplus had to be converted into cash for which there was a continuous and growing demand in order to pay rent, taxes and fines as labour services were commuted. The evidence is that the latter were always light anyway in Anglo-Norman Ireland,[172] a factor which must have been a considerable stimulus to the intensity of borough foundation. But as we have seen, the evolution of a hierarchical urban system took place at the scale of 'robust, territorially concentrated private lordship', rather than that of Anglo-Norman Ireland as a whole.[173] Thus, within any particular lordship, one might expect to find the network of towns and boroughs acting as the framework for the sort of marketing circuits which have been identified in medieval England.[174] Lords were granted markets on different days in their various boroughs so that middlemen—who collected the tolls—and itinerant traders could travel around from place to place. Although the evidence is extremely poor, Best found some indications to support the contention that such a pattern occurred within particular lordships in Anglo-Norman Ireland.[175] But nowhere can the precise hierarchical relationships of settlements be worked out. Indeed, the primary source of evidence for marketing once again comes from charters and often it can only be assumed that the grants recorded ever became operative. To compound the difficulties of examining the economic functioning of medieval Irish boroughs, there is very little evidence which might enable the reconstruction of their division of labour. It can be assumed that the populations of rural-boroughs were essentially agriculturalists, but even in the small market towns and larger mercantile centres, the degree of non-agricultural employment is unclear. Presumably, most industry took the form of food processing. There must have been craftsmen of various sorts in the towns but we rarely find any evidence of them.

Despite the enduring importance of lordship, even the greatest of barons was not unconstrained by the demands of the crown. In addition to their economic roles, towns and boroughs fulfilled a jurisdictional role in the attempt by the latter—increasingly frustrated—to administer the Anglo-Norman colony as a whole. For example, the Town Subsidy of 1300 not only shows urban centres but also rural-boroughs being used as a framework for the collection of the sort of sporadic taxation characteristic of the Middle Ages, in this case to help support the crown's campaigns in Wales, Scotland and France.[176] Towns and rural-boroughs also acted as the geographical basis for the activities of royal officials such as the escheator and justiciar and as locations for the eyres of justices. Presumably, they also fulfilled a local role in the administration of lordship and manor.

Undoubtedly the best documented settlements are the 25 mercantile towns involved in Ireland's external trade. These were probably characterized by a burgher class—organized in guilds—comprising artisans, traders and merchants. They were either directly in the hands of the crown, or conversely, held by baronial families who ranked at the peak of the feudal hierarchy. In the case of the latter, they were real economic assets. Youghal, Co. Cork, for example, provided over 60 per cent of the income of the estates of the lords of Inchiquin in the late thirteenth century.[177] All were walled and were most commonly located on the various navigable rivers; about half were ports. The latter—places like Dublin, Drogheda, Waterford, New Ross, Youghal and Cork—controlled Ireland's overseas trade, not only with Britain but also directly with continental Europe (Fig. 2.9). They were also the largest towns. The most important inland centre seems to have been Kilkenny, *caput* of one of the greatest of the private lordships.

A further aspect of the medieval Irish town which demands much research attention is its social geography. Theoretically, the Anglo-Normans created a duality of law, one for the colonizer and one for the colonized. But once again, *de facto*, this may have obtained only the most dubious reality. Generally, the urban population, and that of the rural-boroughs too, seems to have been primarily colonial. But that is not to say that the Gaelic-Irish were excluded, for people with Gaelic-Irish names were always present in towns. There may have been some form of segregation because 'Irishtowns' survive in a number of medieval towns—Ardee, Co. Louth, Athlone, Clonmel, Drogheda, Dublin, Enniscorthy, Co. Wexford, and New Ross—while those at Kilkenny and Limerick were both separately walled. Indeed, Irishtown at Kilkenny possessed its own borough constitution.[178] Again, there may have been separate suburbs at Dublin, Waterford, Wexford, Cork and Limerick for the descendants of the Hiberno-Norse—the Ostmen. In practice, it may well be the case that as time passed, the theoretical duality of law foundered but we still lack a sufficiently sustained investigation of the ethnic geography of the medieval Irish town to allow a more detailed summary.

Some attention has been given to urban population, although again, the data available is poor and the calculations controversial.[179] When the number of burgesses is known—usually from some form of rental—some estimate can be made of population size by using a household multiplier of five.[180] However, it is clear that the population of a town or rural-borough was not necessarily composed entirely of burgesses and their families. Again, it is probable that some burgesses were agriculturalists living outside the actual borough. Nor can population be estimated if a burgage rent alone is recorded in the documents. Although each burgess theoretically paid 12d for a plot, total burgage rents for a borough often included the burgesses' share in the common fields. Further, there is some evidence that burgage rents could vary and that often, one individual may have held several burgages. Given these various problems, population estimates are very difficult. It is probable that very few towns had in excess of 2000 inhabitants, and that indeed the majority had well under 1000, and frequently less than 500.[181]

Settlement in Gaelic Ireland During the High Middle Ages

So far, 'Anglo-Norman' or 'Anglo-Irish' have been used carefully as qualifications in describing Ireland's medieval settlement. However, parts of the island, especially in the north and west but also in the midlands, remained beyond both direct control of the English crown and the subinfeudation process of Anglo-Norman lordship. But such areas were subject to Gaelic-Irish social and economic institutions and it is difficult to conceive that these were not modified by the Anglo-Norman presence. The Gaelic-Irish leaders in these regions had contacts with the Anglo-Normans, most obviously because of war but also through intermittent alliances and intermarriage. In turn, some historians have argued that numerous

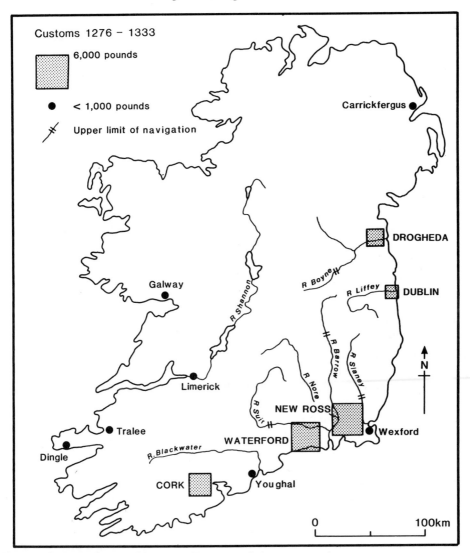

Fig. 2.9. Ports and navigable rivers. Due to under-reporting, the customs returns are certainly inaccurate, especially for the western ports. However, they do show the principal arteries of trade within the heartland of the Anglo-Norman colony.

Anglo-Irish lords became wholly or partially assimilated into Gaelic-Irish society.[182] Accepting this proposition of a considerable frequency of physical and cultural contact, we are faced with what is perhaps the major enigma of medieval Irish settlement. As Simms questions, why apparently did Gaelic-Irish lords not adopt the concept of towns as a means of developing a territory, when in eastern Europe, for example, Slavic princes were enthusiastic sponsors of towns?[183] Further, this apparent disdain of the town during the high Middle Ages presents a significant problem—not yet addressed—to the entire theory of an early medieval indigenous urbanization in Ireland. As Barry discusses in Chapter 3, the only possible exceptions are the settlements at some ecclesiastical centres such as Armagh, Clogher, Co. Tyrone, Clonfert, Co. Galway, and Rosscarbery, Co. Cork. These places, and others like them, may have been towns. One interesting example might be Killaloe, Co. Clare, where the boroughs may have been incorporated by the O Briains prior to the Anglo-Norman settlement of the kingdom of Limerick.[184] But the only other evidence of Gaelic-Irish lords founding chartered settlements either immediately before or after the invasion relates to a solitary attempt—probably abortive—by Cormac MacTomaltach to establish a market at Port-na-Cairge (Rockingham) in County Roscommon in 1231.[185] Nor—with the possible exception of Sligo—does there appear to be any record of an Anglo-Norman borough continuing to exist under a Gaelic-Irish secular lord during the fifteenth and sixteenth centuries.[186] In terms of the evidence, it is not until the sixteenth century that a 'real town' of Gaelic provenance grew up at Cavan.[187]

As Nicholls observes, there are virtually no records for Gaelic Ireland dating to the first 150 years after the invasion.[188] To put this deficiency in perspective, the major part of our knowledge of Anglo-Norman settlement and colonization during the same period—often indeed the very evidence for their occurrence—comes from the documents, fiscal and legal, of the administration in Ireland. Nothing comparable exists for Gaelic Ireland. Thus, the possibility remains that our lack of evidence of high medieval urban settlements outside the Anglo-Norman colony is a function of the absence of documents. Conversely, the few sources that do exist stress the pastoral nature of the economy. Thus, Nicholls believes that agglomerations of buildings were rare, the forms of settlement being for the most part scattered and impermanent.[189] A more enduring element may have been provided by the habitation of ring-forts (see also Chapter 1).[190]

In contrast, there is ample evidence that Gaelic-Irish lords were not adverse to adopting Anglo-Norman innovations. Thus, in north-east Roscommon, for example, there is a group of moated sites, possibly dating to the early fourteenth century, in an area which had no Anglo-Norman connection.[191] Again, the Gaelic-Irish lords were also enthusiastic castle builders and these may have provided nuclei for settlement agglomerations and exchange. That they shared ideas on fortifications with their Anglo-Norman counterparts makes the apparent lack of interest in urbanization even more puzzling. This is particularly so when it is considered that settlements have a conceptual meaning as well as a physical manifestation. McNeill has shown that the distribution of mottes in Ulster cannot be understood without making the assumption that some were built by Gaelic-Irish lords.[192] But this is not necessarily simply evidence of an innovation being copied. As we have seen in Chapter 1, the whole issue of medieval fortifications is one of the most potent clues to the changing structure of society in the eleventh and twelfth centuries. Motte building is suggestive of landholdings being organized along feudal practices. But everywhere else in western Europe, this process was a precursor to a manorial organization based on town and borough. Nicholls argues that Gaelic Ireland differed widely from western Europe in general, not least in its laws of succession. To these he attributes the 'extreme political instability of native Irish society and ... the endemic disorder which afflicted it'.[193] If this interpretation is sustained, and Nicholls makes a convincing case, the corollary is that serious problems remain with the ideas—advanced in Chapter 1—of an indigenous Gaelic-Irish society developing along essentially European lines prior to the Anglo-Norman invasion.

Conclusions

As a result of the research summarized here, we are part way towards an understanding of the historical geography of Anglo-Norman Ireland. Although numerous lacunae remain, substantial work has been completed on the most accessible topics but it is important that some of the more morphologically orientated findings be placed within the much wider context of the changing economic, social and political structures of medieval Ireland. A careful and extensive analogical analysis would be relevant here, one moreover which does not obscure the possibility that substantial differences occurred within Ireland. Again, the issues of continuity, both in the twelfth century and between the fourteenth and late sixteenth centuries, remain to be fully addressed. It is difficult to believe, given the outright absence of documentary evidence, that any real empirical advance can be made in understanding the settlement structure of the Gaelic-Irish. That particular problem can be approached only through the interaction between theory and analogy. If settlement is one of the most potent indicators of social change, then it follows that social change itself is the primary constraint upon the settlement which can evolve.

References

1. The most comprehensive although not well organized account of Evans' ideas is to be found in E. Estyn Evans, *The Personality of Ireland: Habitat, Heritage and History*, (revised edn, Belfast, 1981).
2. For example, see B. M. S. Campbell, 'People and land in the Middle Ages, 1066–1500', in R. A. Dodgshon and R. A. Butlin (eds.), *An Historical Geography of England and Wales*, (London, 1990), pp. 69–122.
3. Marie Therese Flanagan, *Irish Society, Anglo-Norman Settlers, Angevin Kingship*, (Oxford, 1989), p. 2.
4. A. P. Smyth, *Celtic Leinster: Towards An Historical Geography of Early Irish Civilisation, AD 500–1600*, (Blackrock, 1982), p. 106.
5. Robert A. Dodgshon, *The European Past: Social Evolution and Spatial Order*, (London, 1987); *idem*, 'The changing evaluation of space, 1500–1914', in Dodgshon and Butlin (eds.), *England and Wales*, pp. 255–84.
6. G. W. S. Barrow, *The Anglo-Norman Era in Scottish History*, (Oxford, 1980), p. 5.
7. Robin Frame, *The Political Development of the British Isles, 1100–1400*, (Oxford, 1990), p. 53.
8. R. R. Davies, *Domination and Conquest*, (Cambridge, 1990), p. 16.
9. Brian Graham, 'The town in the Norman colonisations of the British Isles', in Dietrich Denecke and Gareth Shaw (eds.), *Urban Historical Geography: Recent Progress in Britain and Germany*, (Cambridge, 1988), pp. 37–52; Anngret Simms, 'Core and periphery in medieval Europe: the Irish experience in a wider context', in William J. Smyth and Kevin Whelan (eds.), *Common Ground: Essays on the Historical Geography of Ireland*. (Cork, 1988), pp. 22–40.
10. J. Le Patourel, *The Norman Empire*, (Oxford, 1976).

11. Simms, 'Core and periphery', p. 9; C. A. Empey, 'Conquest and settlement patterns of Anglo-Norman settlement in North Munster and South Leinster', *Irish Economic and Social History*, **13** (1986), pp. 5–31; see p. 30.
12. A. J. Otway-Ruthven, 'The character of Norman settlement in Ireland', *Historical Studies*, **5** (1965), pp. 75–84; Robin Frame, *Colonial Ireland, 1169–1369*, (Dublin, 1981).
13. Brian Eagar, 'The Cambro-Normans and the Lordship of Leinster', in John Bradley (ed.), *Settlement and Society in Medieval Ireland: Studies Presented to F. X. Martin, o.s.a.*, (Kilkenny, 1988), pp. 193–206.
14. Empey, 'Conquest', *passim*.
15. F. X. Martin, 'Introduction: Medieval Ireland', in Art Cosgrove (ed.), *A New History of Ireland: II: Medieval Ireland, 1169–1534*, (Oxford, 1987), pp. XLIX–LXII.
16. Michael Richter, 'The interpretation of medieval Irish society', *Irish Historical Studies*, **XXIV**, no. 95 (May 1985), pp. 289–98; see esp. pp. 292–4.
17. J. A. Watt, 'Dublin in the thirteenth century: the making of a colonial capital city', in P. R. Coss and S. D. Lloyd (eds.), *Thirteenth Century England: I: Proceedings of the Newcastle Upon Tyne Conference, 1985*, (Woodbridge, 1986), pp. 150–7; see p. 151.
18. For a general discussion, see R. R. Davies, 'Lordship or colony?', in James Lydon (ed.), *The English in Medieval Ireland*, (Dublin, 1984), pp. 142–60; *idem, Domination and Conquest*, pp. 14–16 and 112.
19. The origin-myth of this viewpoint is to be found in: J. H. Todd (ed.), *Cogadh Gáedhel re Gallaibh: The War of the Gaedhil with the Gaill*, (London, 1867).
20. Richter, 'Interpretation of medieval Irish society', p. 298. See also, *idem, Medieval Ireland and the Enduring Tradition*, (Dublin, 1988).
21. F. X. Martin, 'Diarmait Mac Murchada and the coming of the Anglo-Normans', in Cosgrove (ed.), *New History of Ireland: II*, pp. 43–66; see pp. 44–5.
22. Donnchadh Ó Corráin, 'Diarmait MacMurrough (1126–71) and the coming of the Anglo-French', in Ciaran Brady (ed.), *Worsted in the Game: Losers in Irish History*, (Dublin, 1989), pp. 37–48; see p. 31.
23. F. J. Byrne, 'The trembling sod: Ireland in 1169', in Cosgrove (ed.), *New History of Ireland: II*, pp. 1–42.
24. A. B. Scott and F. X. Martin (eds.), Giraldus Cambrensis, *Expugnatio Hibernica: The Conquest of Ireland*, (Dublin, 1978), p. 55.
25. Ó Corráin, 'Diarmait MacMurrough', p. 32.
26. F. X. Martin, 'Allies and an overlord, 1169–72', in Cosgrove (ed.), *New History of Ireland: II*, pp. 67–97; see p. 87. See also, W. L. Warren, 'The interpretation of twelfth-century Irish history', *Historical Studies*, **VII** (1969), pp. 1–17.
27. See the argument in Robin Frame, *English Lordship in Ireland, 1318–1361*, (Oxford, 1982); *idem, Colonial Ireland*.
28. Flanagan, *Irish Society*, p. 304.
29. F. X. Martin, 'Overlord becomes feudal lord, 1172–85', in Cosgrove (ed.), *New History of Ireland: II*, pp. 98–126.
30. James Lydon, 'John de Courcy (*c*. 1150–1219) and the medieval frontier', in Brady (ed.), *Worsted in the Game*, pp. 37–48.
31. B. J. Graham, 'The mottes of the Norman Liberty of Meath', in H. Murtagh (ed.), *Irish Midland Studies: Essays in Commemoration of N. W. English*, (Athlone, 1980), pp. 39–56.
32. George Cunningham, *The Anglo-Norman Advance Into the South West Midlands of Ireland*, (Roscrea, 1987).
33. James Lydon, 'The expansion and consolidation of the colony, 1215–54', in Cosgrove (ed.), *New History of Ireland: II*, pp. 156–78.
34. K. W. Nicholls, *Gaelic and Gaelicised Ireland in the Middle Ages*, (Dublin, 1972).
35. *Idem*, 'Gaelic society and economy in the high Middle Ages', in Cosgrove (ed.), *New History of Ireland: II*, pp. 397–438; see p. 398.
36. C. A. Empey in a review of Lydon (ed.), *English in Medieval Ireland*, in *Irish Economic and Social History*, **XIII** (1986), pp. 145–6.
37. Robin Frame, 'War and peace in the medieval lordship of Ireland', in Lydon (ed.), *English in Medieval Ireland*, pp. 118–41; see p. 140.

38. J. A. Watt, 'Gaelic polity and cultural identity', in Cosgrove (ed.), *New History of Ireland: II*, pp. 314–51; see pp. 306 and 345.
39. See, for example, the influence on fortifications. T. E. McNeill, *Anglo-Norman Ulster*, (Edinburgh, 1980), esp. Chapter 6; K. W. Nicholls, 'Anglo-French Ireland and after', *Peritia*, **1** (1982), pp. 370–403: B. J. Graham, 'Medieval timber and earthwork fortifications in western Ireland, *Medieval Archaeology*, **XXXII** (1988), pp. 110–29; Brendan Smith, 'The medieval border: Anglo-Irish and Gaelic-Irish in late thirteenth and early fourteenth-century Uriel', in Raymond Gillespie and Harold O'Sullivan (eds.), *The Borderlands: Essays on the History of the Ulster–Leinster Border*, (Belfast, 1989), pp. 41–54.
40. Katherine Simms, *From Kings to Warlords*, (Woodbridge, 1987).
41. J. A. Watt, 'Approaches to the history of fourteenth-century Ireland', in Cosgrove (ed.) *New History of Ireland: II*, pp. 303–13; see p. 310.
42. James Lydon, 'The Middle Nation', in Lydon (ed.) *English in Medieval Ireland*, pp. 1–26.
43. Martin, 'Introduction', in Cosgrove (ed.), *New History of Ireland: II*, p. LIII.
44. James Lydon, 'The problem of the frontier in medieval Ireland', *Topic*, **13** (1967), pp. 5–22.
45. See, for example: M. C. Lyons, 'Manorial administration and the manorial economy in Ireland, *c.* 1200 to *c.* 1377', unpublished PhD thesis, University of Dublin (1984); Brendan Smith, 'The concept of the march in medieval Ireland: the case of Uriel', *Proceedings of the Royal Irish Academy*, **88C** (1988), pp. 257–69.
46. Robin Frame, 'Military service in the lordship of Ireland, 1290–1360: institutions and societies on the Anglo-Gaelic border', in Robert Bartlett and Angus MacKay (eds.), *Medieval Frontier Societies*, (Oxford, 1989), pp. 101–26; see p. 102; Smith, 'Medieval border', in Gillespie and O'Sullivan (eds.), *Borderlands*.
47. G. H. Orpen, *Ireland Under the Normans*, 4 vols., (Oxford, 1911–20).
48. A. J. Otway-Ruthven, *A History of Medieval Ireland*, (London, 1968).
49. Nicholas Canny in a review of, Smyth and Whelan (eds.), *Common Ground*, in *Irish Economy and Social History*, **XVI** (1989), pp. 116–17.
50. Dodgshon, *European Past*, passim.
51. See as one example of Empey's approach: 'The Anglo-Norman settlement in the Cantred of Eliogarty', in Bradley (ed.), *Settlement and Society*, pp. 207–28; see p. 208.
52. For a detailed study of a manor, see C. A. Empey, 'Medieval Knocktopher: a study in manorial settlement', Part 1, *Old Kilkenny Review*, 2, no. 4 (1982), pp. 329–42; Part 2, *ibid.*, 2, no. 5 (1983), pp. 441–52.
53. J. Mills and M. McEnery (eds.), *Calendar of the Gormanston Register*, (Dublin, 1916), p. 177.
54. I. Leister, *Peasant Openfield Farming and its Territorial Organisation in Co. Tipperary*, (Marburg/Lahn, 1976).
55. Empey, 'Eliogarty', p. 212.
56. B. J. Graham, 'The medieval settlement of County Roscommon', *Proceedings of the Royal Irish Academy*, **88C**, (1988), pp. 19–38; *idem*, 'Medieval fortifications'.
57. Helen Walton, 'The English in Connacht, 1171–1333', (unpublished PhD thesis, University of Dublin, 1980).
58. A. Simms, 'Rural settlement in medieval Ireland: the example of the royal manors of Newcastle Lyons and Esker in south County Dublin', in B. K. Roberts and R. E. Glasscock (eds.), *Villages, Fields and Frontiers*, BAR International Series 185, (Oxford, 1983), pp. 146–7; K. J. Edwards, F. W. Hamond and A. Simms, 'The medieval settlement of Newcastle Lyons, County Dublin: an interdisciplinary approach', *Proceedings of the Royal Irish Academy*, **83C**, (1983), pp. 351–76; 'The geography of Irish manors: the example of the Llanthony cells of Duleek and Colp, County Meath', in Bradley (ed.), *Settlement and Society*, pp. 291–326.
59. This issue is discussed in B. J. Graham, 'Anglo-Norman manorial settlement in Ireland: an assessment', *Irish Geography*, **18** (1985), pp. 4–15; Leister, *Peasant and Openfield Farming*.
60. J. A. Watt, *The Church in Medieval Ireland*, (Dublin, 1972); Roger Stalley, *The Cistercian Monasteries of Ireland*, (New Haven, 1987), see Chapters 1 and 2.

61. The most detailed source is, A. Gwynn and R. N. Hadcock, *Medieval Religious Houses: Ireland*, (London, 1970).
62. Leo Swan, 'The Early Christian ecclesiastical sites of County Westmeath', in Bradley (ed.), *Settlement and Society*, pp. 3–32; see pp. 26–8.
63. For an early summary, see B. J. Graham, 'The towns of medieval Ireland', in R. A. Butlin (ed.), *The Development of the Irish Town*, (London, 1977), pp. 28–60.
64. For Dublin, see Chapter 1; an accessible summary can be found in T. B. Barry, *The Archaeology of Medieval Ireland*, (London, 1987), Chapter 2.
65. Henry A. Jefferies, 'The history and topography of Viking Cork', *Journal of the Cork Historical and Archaeological Society*, **XC**, no. 249 (1985), pp. 14–25; *idem*, 'The founding of Anglo-Norman Cork, 1177–1185', *Journal of the Cork Historical and Archaeological Society*, **XCI**, no. 250 (1986), pp. 26–48.
66. F. H. A. Aalen, *Man and the Landscape in Ireland*, (London, 1978), p. 105.
67. See J. H. Andrews, 'Kildare', *Irish Historic Towns Atlas*, 1 (Dublin, 1986); Anngret Simms, 'Kells', *Irish Historic Towns Atlas*, 4 (Dublin, 1990); John Bradley, 'The early development of the town of Kilkenny', in W. Nolan and K. Whelan (eds.), *Kilkenny: History and Society*, (Dublin, 1990), pp. 63–73.
68. For example, C. G. Brown and A. E. T. Harper, 'Excavations on Cathedral Hill, Armagh, 1968', *Ulster Journal of Archaeology*, **47** (1984), pp. 109–60: Ann Hamlin and Chris Lynn (eds.), *Pieces of the Past*, (Belfast, 1988), pp. 57–60.
69. Dodgshon, *European Past*, chapters 6–8.
70. N. Elias, *State Formation and Civilisation, Vol. 2: The History of Manners*, (Oxford, 1982), *passim*.
71. Robin Frame, 'Power and society in the Lordship of Ireland, 1272–1377', *Past and Present*, no. 76 (1977), pp. 3–33; *idem*, *Colonial Ireland*, p. 72.
72. See, for example, G. H. Orpen, 'Mote and *bretesche* building in Ireland', *English Historical Review*, **XXI** (1906), pp. 417–44; *idem*, 'Motes and Norman castles in Ireland', *English Historical Review*, **XXII** (1908), pp. 228–54.
73. R. E. Glasscock, 'Mottes in Ireland', *Château-Gaillard*, **VII** (1975), pp. 95–110.
74. J. P. Mallory and T. E. McNeill, *The Archaeology of Ulster: From Colonization to Plantation*, (Belfast, 1991), p. 74.
75. Michael Moore, 'The moat at Castletown Kilberry, Co. Meath', *Ríocht na Mídhe*, **VIII**, no. 2 (1988–9), pp. 21–9.
76. T. B. Barry, 'Anglo-Norman ringwork castles: some evidence', in Trevor Reeves-Smyth and Fred Hamond (eds.), *Landscape Archaeology in Ireland*, BAR British Series 116 (Oxford, 1983), pp. 295–314; see also, Nicholls, 'Anglo-French Ireland'.
77. B. J. Graham, 'Twelfth- and thirteenth-century fortifications in Ireland', *The Irish Sword*, **XVII**, no. 69 (1990), pp. 225–43; *idem*, 'Twelfth- and thirteenth-century earthwork castles in Ireland: an assessment', *Fortress*, **9** (May 1991), pp. 24–34.
78. H. Clarke, *The Archaeology of Medieval England*, (Oxford, 1984), p. 109.
79. McNeill, *Anglo-Norman Ulster*, p. 103; Graham, 'Twelfth- and thirteenth-century fortifications', *passim*.
80. Graham, 'Medieval fortifications'; *idem*, 'Roscommon'; C. J. Lynn, 'Some thirteenth-century castle sites in the west of Ireland', *Journal of the Galway Archaeological and Historical Society*, **LXXI** (1986), pp. 90–113.
81. Orpen, 'Motes in Ireland'.
82. See, for example, T. B. Barry, E. Culleton and C. A. Empey, 'The motte at Kells, Co. Kilkenny', *Proceedings of the Royal Irish Academy*, **84C** (1984), pp. 157–70.
83. B. J. Graham, 'The evolution of the settlement pattern of Anglo-Norman Eastmeath', in R. H. Buchanan, R. A. Butlin and D. McCourt (eds.), *Fields, Farms and Settlement in Europe*, (Belfast, 1976), pp. 38–47.
84. Graham, 'Mottes of Meath'; B. Colfer, 'Anglo-Norman settlement in County Wexford', in K. Whelan (ed.), *Wexford: History and Society* (Dublin, 1987), pp. 65–101; see p. 75.
85. Mallory and McNeill, *Ulster*, p. 262.
86. McNeill, *Anglo-Norman Ulster*, *passim*.
87. For useful recent summaries, see, Barry, *Archaeology of Medieval Ireland*, Chapter 3;

Tadhg O'Keeffe, 'The archaeology of Norman castles in Ireland', *Archaeology in Ireland*, 4, no. 3 (1990), pp. 15–17; *ibid.*, **4**, no. 4 (1990), pp. 20–22.

88. P. D. Sweetman, 'Archaeological excavations at Trim Castle, County Meath', *Proceedings of the Royal Irish Academy*, **78C** (1978), pp. 127–98.

89. T. E. McNeill, *Carrickfergus Castle*, (Belfast, 1981); P. Robinson, 'Carrickfergus'. *Irish Historical Towns Atlas*, **2** (Dublin, 1986).

90. R. E. Glasscock, 'Land and people, *c.* 1300', in Cosgrove (ed.), *New History of Ireland: II*, pp. 205–39; see pp. 217–20; Barry, *Archaeology of Medieval Ireland*.

91. C. A. Empey, 'County Kilkenny in the Anglo-Norman period', in Nolan and Whelan (eds.), *Kilkenny*, pp. 75–95; see p. 76.

92. Eagar, 'Cambro-Normans and Leinster', *passim*.

93. Otway-Ruthven, 'Character of Norman settlement'; Simms, 'Core and periphery'.

94. Graham, 'Manorial settlement', *passim*.

95. R. E. Glasscock, 'Moated sites and deserted villages and boroughs: two neglected aspects of Anglo-Norman settlement in Ireland', in N. Stephens and R. E. Glasscock (eds.), *Irish Geographical Studies in Honour of E. Estyn Evans*, (Belfast, 1970), pp. 162–77; *idem*, 'The study of deserted medieval settlements in Ireland', in M. W. Beresford and J. G. Hurst (eds.), *Deserted Medieval Villages: Studies*, (London, 1971), pp. 279–301.

96. M. W. Beresford, *The Lost Villages of England*, (London, 1954); Beresford and Hurst (eds.), *Deserted Medieval Villages*.

97. Rosanne Meenan, 'Deserted medieval villages of County Westmeath', unpublished M Litt thesis, University of Dublin (1985).

98. B. J. Graham, 'Anglo-Norman settlement in County Meath', *Proceedings of the Royal Irish Academy*, **75C** (1975), pp. 223–48.

99. Simms, 'Rural settlement in medieval Ireland'; Edwards *et al.*, 'Newcastle Lyons'.

100. McNeill, *Anglo-Norman Ulster*, Chapter 5.

101. Simms, 'Rural settlement in medieval Ireland'; *idem*, 'Geography of Irish manors'.

102. Glasscock, 'Moated sites and deserted villages'; T. B. Barry, *Medieval Moated Sites of South-East Ireland*, BAR British Series 35, (Oxford, 1977).

103. Barry, *Archaeology of Medieval Ireland*, p. 84.

104. Empey, 'Knocktopher', p. 335.

105. A. J. Otway-Ruthven, 'The organisation of Anglo-Irish agriculture in the Middle Ages', *Journal of the Royal Society of Antiquaries of Ireland*, **18** (1951), pp. 1–13.

106. Glasscock, 'Land and people', p. 211.

107. R. H. Buchanan, 'Field systems in Ireland', in A. R. H. Baker and R. A. Butlin (eds.), *Studies of Field Systems in the British Isles*, (Cambridge, 1973), pp. 580–618. For a case study, see D. N. Hall, M. Hennessy and T. O'Keeffe, 'Medieval agriculture and settlement in Oughterard and Castlewarden, Co. Kildare', *Irish Geography*, **18** (1985), pp. 16–24.

108. R. A. Butlin, 'Some observations on the field systems of medieval Ireland', *Geographia Polonica*, **38** (1978), pp. 31–6.

109. R. A. Dodgshon, *The Origin of British Field Systems*, (London, 1980).

110. Kevin Down, 'Colonial society and economy in the high Middle Ages', in Cosgrove (ed.), *New History of Ireland: II*, pp. 439–91.

111. H. Jäger, 'Land use in medieval Ireland: a review of the documentary evidence', *Irish Economic and Social History*, **10** (1983), pp. 57–65.

112. Down, 'Colonial society', p. 476.

113. G. F. Mitchell, 'Littleton Bog, Co. Tipperary: an Irish agricultural record', *Journal of the Royal Society of Antiquaries of Ireland*, **95** (1965), pp. 121–32; Jäger, 'Land use'.

114. Glasscock, 'Land and people', pp. 206–7; James Lydon, 'The impact of the Bruce invasion, 1315–27', in Cosgrove (ed.), *New History of Ireland: II*, pp. 275–302; see p. 285.

115. Mary C. Lyons, 'Weather, famine, pestilence and plague in Ireland, 900–1500', in E. M. Crawford (ed.), *Famine: The Irish Experience, 900–1900*, (Edinburgh, 1989), pp. 31–74.

116. See James Lydon, *The Lordship of Ireland in the Middle Ages*, (Dublin, 1972), *passim*; Linda P. Best, 'Trade in Anglo-Norman Ireland'; unpublished DPhil thesis, University of Ulster, 1989.

117. Down, 'Colonial society', pp. 483–4.
118. J. A. Watt, *The Church and the Two Nations in Medieval Ireland*, (Cambridge, 1970); *idem, Church in Medieval Ireland*, see Chapter 3.
119. See Gwynn and Hadcock, *Medieval Religious Houses*, for the most comprehensive listings and details.
120. Mark Hennessy, 'The priory and hospital of New Gate: the evolution and decline of a monastic estate', in Smyth and Whelan (eds.), *Common Ground*, pp. 55–83.
121. C. A. Empey, 'The sacred and the secular: the Augustinian priory of Kells in Ossory, 1193–1541', *Irish Historical Studies*, **XXIV**, no. 94 (Nov. 1984), pp. 131–51.
122. *Ibid.*, p. 139.
123. Stalley, *Cistercian Monasteries*, pp. 208–11.
124. C. Platt, *The Monastic Grange in Medieval England*, (London, 1969), p. 14. See Simms, 'Geography of Irish manors', for an example.
125. Father Colmcille, *The Story of Mellifont*, (Dublin, 1958), *passim*.
126. Stalley, *Cistercian Monasteries*, p. 21.
127. Hennessy, 'New Gate', p. 45.
128. Empey, 'Kells in Ossory', pp. 132–6.
129. Empey, 'Anglo-Norman Kilkenny', p. 81
130. A. J. Otway-Ruthven, 'Parochial development in the rural deanery of Skreen', *Journal of the Royal Society of Antiquaries of Ireland*, **94** (1964), pp. 111–22.
131. Mark Hennessy, 'Parochial organisation in medieval Tipperary', in W. Nolan (ed.), *Tipperary: History and Society*, (Dublin, 1985), pp. 60–70.
132. Paul Briand, 'The formation of a parish: the case of Beaulieu, County Louth', in Bradley (ed.), *Settlement and Society*, pp. 261–75.
133. Mallory and McNeill, *Ulster*, p. 282. H. G. Leask, *Irish Churches and Monastic Buildings*, II and III, (Dundalk, 1966 and 1971).
134. Nicholls, *Gaelic and Gaelicised ireland*, pp. 91–111.
135. Vincent Hurley, 'The early church in the south-west of Ireland', in S. Pearce (ed.), *The Early Church in Western Britain and Ireland*, BAR British Series 102, (Oxford, 1982), pp. 297–332; see p. 329.
136. Graham, 'Settlement pattern of Eastmeath'.
137. Empey, 'Conquest', p. 22.
138. B. J. Graham, 'The evolution of urbanisation in medieval Ireland', *Journal of Historical Geography*, **5** (1979), pp. 111–25; *idem*, 'Anglo-Norman colonisation and the size and spread of the colonial town in medieval Ireland', in Clarke and Simms (eds.), *Comparative Urban Origins*, pp. 355–72; *idem*, 'Urbanization in medieval Ireland, *ca.* AD 900 to *ca.* AD 1300', *Journal of Urban History*, **13** (1987), pp. 169–96.
139. M. W. Beresford, *New Towns of the Middle Ages*, (London, 1967), pp. 55–70.
140. Empey, 'Conquest', p. 27.
141. See, for example, R. H. Hilton,'Towns in English feudal society', *Review*, **iii** (1979), pp. 3–20; *idem*, 'Small town society in England before the Black Death', *Past and Present*, no. 105 (Nov. 1984), pp. 53–78; *idem*, 'Medieval market towns and simple commodity production', *Past and Present*, no. 109 (Nov. 1985), pp. 3–23.
142. Beresford, *New Towns, passim*.
143. L. Musset, 'Peuplement en bourgage et bourgs ruraux en Normandie', *Cahiers de Civilisation Médiévale*, **9** (1966), pp. 177–208.
144. Jacques Le Goff (ed.), *Histoire de La France Urbaine: II: La Ville Médiévale*, (Paris, 1980), p. 241.
145. John Bradley, 'The medieval towns of Tipperary', in Nolan (ed.), *Tipperary*, pp. 34–59; see p. 35.
146. Brian Graham, 'Economy and town in Anglo-Norman Ireland', in Bradley (ed.), *Settlement and Society*, pp. 241–60; see pp. 252–5.
147. G. Mac Niocaill, *Na Buirgéisí*, 2 vols., (Dublin, 1964).
148. H. B. Clarke and Anngret Simms, 'Towards a comparative history of urban origins', in Clarke and Simms (eds.), *Comparative Urban Origins*, pp. 669–714; see p. 703.
149. G. Mac Niocaill, 'The colonial town in Irish documents', in Clarke and Simms (eds.),

Comparative Urban Origins, pp. 273–8. For a counter argument, see Graham, 'Economy and town'; *idem*, 'Town in Norman colonisations'.

150. Susan Reynolds, *An Introduction to the History of English Medieval Towns*, (London, 1977), p. 52.
151. Musset. 'Peuplement et bourgs ruraux', *passim*.
152. Glasscock, 'Moated sites and deserted villages and boroughs', *idem*, 'Land and people', pp. 223–4.
153. P. J. O'Connor, *Exploring Limerick's Past: An Historical Geography of Urban Development in County and City*, (Newcastle West, 1987), p. 14.
154. Fernand Braudel, *The Identity of France: I: History and Environment*, (London, 1988), p. 127; William J. Smyth, 'The dynamic quality of Irish village life—a reassessment', in *Campagnes et Littoraux D'Europe: Mélanges Offerts à Pierre Flatrès*, (no editor given), (Lille, 1988), pp. 109–13.
155. B. J. Graham, 'The definition and classification of medieval Irish towns', *Irish Geography*, **21** (1988), pp. 20–32.
156. Glasscock, 'Land and people', p. 223.
157. Bradley, 'Towns of Tipperary', p. 35.
158. Graham, 'Definition and classification'.
159. John Bradley, 'Planned Anglo-Norman towns in Ireland', in Clarke and Simms (eds.), *Comparative Urban Origins*, pp. 411–67.
160. Empey, 'Conquest', p. 10.
161. For a summary of the archaeological evidence, see Barry, *Archaeology of Medieval Ireland*, Chapter 5; John Bradley, 'Recent archaeological research on the Irish town', in H. Jäger (ed.), *Stadtkernforschung*, (Köln, 1987), pp. 321–70.
162. John Bradley, 'The role of town-plan analysis in the study of the medieval Irish town', in T. R. Slater (ed.), *The Built Form Of Western Cities*, (Leicester, 1990), pp. 39–59; *idem*, 'Planned Anglo-Norman towns', *passim*; *idem*, 'Towns of Tipperary', *passim*.
163. Simms, 'Medieval Dublin'; P. F. Wallace, 'The archaeology of Viking Dublin', in Clarke and Simms (eds.), *Comparative Urban Origins*, pp. 103–46; *idem*, 'The archaeology of Anglo-Norman Dublin', *ibid.*, pp. 379–410.
164. John Bradley, 'The topography and layout of medieval Drogheda', *County Louth Archaeological and Historical Journal*, **XIX** (1978), pp. 98–127.
165. *Idem*, 'Towns of Tipperary', p. 38.
166. T. R. Slater, 'English medieval town planning', in Denecke and Shaw (eds.), *Urban Historical Geography*, pp. 93–108; A. J. Scrase, 'Development and change in burgage plots: the example of Wells', *Journal of Historical Geography*, **15** (1989), pp. 349–65.
167. Scrase, *ibid.*, pp. 362–3; G. C. Astill, 'Archaeology and the smaller medieval town; *Urban History Yearbook* (1985), pp. 47–8.
168. Avril Thomas, 'Financing town walls in Ireland', in C. Thomas (ed.), *Rural Landscapes and Communities: Essays Presented to Desmond McCourt*, (Dublin, 1987), pp. 65–91; see p. 82.
169. *Idem, The Walled Towns of Ireland*, 2 vols., (Dublin, 1992), *passim*.
170. Mac Niocaill, *Na Buirgéisí*, II.
171. Graham, 'Town in Norman colonisations'; *idem*, 'Economy and town'.
172. Frame, *Colonial Ireland*, p. 78.
173. *Idem, English Lordship*, p. 327.
174. T. Unwin, 'Rural marketing in medieval Nottinghamshire', *Journal of Historical Geography*, **7** (1981), pp. 231–51.
175. Best, 'Trade in Anglo-Norman Ireland', pp. 200–6.
176. Glasscock, 'Land and people', p. 239.
177. A. F. O'Brien, 'Medieval Youghal: the development of an Irish seaport trading town, *c.* 1200 to *c.* 1500', *Peritia*, **5** (1986), pp. 346–78.
178. Bradley, 'Kilkenny'.
179. J. C. Russell, 'Late thirteenth-century Ireland as a region', *Demography*, **3** (1966), pp. 500–12.
180. Otway-Ruthven, 'Character of Norman settlement', p. 80.

181. Graham, 'Towns of medieval Ireland', pp. 43–7.
182. See, for example, Alan Bliss, 'Language and literature', in Lydon (ed.), *English in Medieval Ireland*, pp. 27–45.
183. Simms, 'Core and periphery', p. 33.
184. John Bradley, 'The interpretation of Scandinavian settlement in Ireland', in Bradley (ed.), *Settlement and Society*, pp. 49–78; see p. 64.
185. A. W. Freeman (ed.), *Annals of Connacht*, (Dublin, 1944), pp. 40–1.
186. Nicholls, *Gaelic and Gaelicised Ireland*, p. 122.
187. Nicholls, 'Gaelic society and economy', p. 404.
188. *Ibid.*, p. 398.
189. *Ibid.*, p. 397.
190. B. J. Graham, *Medieval Irish Settlement*, Historical Geography Research Series 3, (Norwich, 1980), pp. 34–41.
191. *Idem*, 'Roscommon', pp. 31–2.
192. McNeill, *Anglo-Norman Ulster*, pp. 102–4.
193. Nicholls, 'Gaelic society and economy', pp. 397–8.

3

Late Medieval Ireland: The Debate on Social and Economic Transformation, 1350–1550

T. B. Barry

Introduction

Despite its comparative modernity, the late Middle Ages between *c.* 1350 and *c.* 1550 remains amongst the most elusive of periods in terms of our understanding of the transformation of Irish society and economy. The discussion in this chapter, consciously written from an archaeological perspective, seeks to analyse the characteristics of the physical remains of material artefacts as a contribution towards achieving a wider understanding of both the nature and distribution of social and economic changes which occurred during this period. The methodology falls within the remit of what might be called 'landscape archaeology', the body of relevant excavation evidence being extremely limited. Landscape archaeology depends upon the interpretation of data culled from field survey and from the distributional analysis of those artefacts.[1] In addition to the lack of excavation, most late medieval sites are representative of elitist social groups. There is virtually no record of the settlements of the mass of the population. Thus, in the first instance, it is essential to place the evidence which we have within a socio-economic framework. Because the late medieval period is a contentious one in Irish history, the issues of debate are outlined here. This is followed by a discussion of various material artefacts, particular attention being paid to fortifications, churches and towns.

The Crisis of the Fourteenth Century and its Repercussions

In general, the debate on the nature of late medieval Irish society has proceeded without reference to the wider ideological concerns which are apparent in the English or French historiography dealing with the same period. Orthodox explanations have been framed almost entirely *within* an Irish context, partly because they constitute an important component of, or have been influenced by, the traditional expression of Gaelic nationalism. Thus, it is instructive to examine the contemporary English historiography of the fourteenth century, both in terms of its ideological content and also because relationships with the metropolitan state are part and parcel of the explanation of events in late medieval Ireland.

In England and north-west Europe generally, the fourteenth century was one of crisis. At one level, economic expansion in the late thirteenth century had proved incapable of absorbing a rapid expansion in population, and hence in the workforce.[2] Ireland was further weakened and impoverished by the system of purveyance, through which Edward I financed his campaigns in Wales and especially in Scotland.[3] But everywhere, the imbalance between population and resources became such that the economy was ill-equipped to deal with external events. The first half of the fourteenth century saw a whole succession of these—the Great European Famine of 1315–17 (its effects exacerbated in Ireland by the Bruce Invasion of 1315–18), war and the culminating catastrophe of the Bubonic Plague or Black Death of 1348–9. Even the climate seems to have become cooler and wetter.[4]

As Lyons has shown, Ireland shared in this succession of crises. During the first half of the fourteenth century, there was a succession of severe weather-related famines and climatic changes which weakened the demographic base prior to the Black Death.[5] In Europe it is estimated that the Plague killed between one-third and one-half of the population,[6] although it is difficult to assess fully its effects upon Ireland. Lyons believes that these were regionalized, Leinster being more severely hit than other regions remote from ports and the main urban centres.[7] It is possible that the impact of the Plague on such locales may have been overestimated because of the impact which it had on contemporary chroniclers who, in the main, were Anglo-Irish. There has also been some recent debate about the nature of the disease itself. If it was the case that the pestilence was a form of anthrax rather than bubonic plague, as Twigg has argued, it would have important repercussions regarding the differential death rates among the various population groups of late medieval Ireland. In such a case, the largest urban centres might in fact have been sheltered from its worst impact because they were located furthest away from the probable cause of infection.[8]

In England, a mixed bag of repercussions followed upon this half-century of crisis. The area under cultivation contracted and there was a retreat from marginal land. Conversely, living standards rose while some settlements shrank and many more were abandoned.[9] But the latter effect had less to do with demographic loss than the structural transformation which a number of economic historians have termed the transition from feudalism to capitalism.[10] In the fourteenth century, feudal social and property relationships were gradually dissolving, labour services were commuted to money rents, demesne land was leased and a more mobile peasantry had less need for the network of localized borough and village markets (see Chapter 2).

The Debate on the Gaelic Revival

In Ireland, the late medieval period is rarely discussed in these terms. Mallory and McNeill observe that the regional specialization which was part and parcel of the transition from feudalism to capitalism benefited the natural cattle country of Ireland where much land, which had been maintained but was perhaps not well suited as arable, reverted to pasture. A number of lesser lords advanced from being tenants into effective freeholders, achieving a modest but genuine gain in prosperity.[11] But in general, the debate on Ireland during the late Middle Ages, has been dominated by the notion of the 'Gaelic Revival' or 'Gaelic Resurgence'. As Cosgrove points out, this concept, which refers to a reassertion of Gaelic-Irish hegemony, possesses both cultural and territorial dimensions.[12] More recent interpretations, Cosgrove's amongst them, have placed the concept within generally revisionist terms. For example, Nicholls argues that the Gaelic Reconquest was as much a process of Gaelicization of the Anglo-French elite as a revival of the Gaelic-Irish one. He urges that we beware allowing the notion of a 'static' Gaelic-Irish society leading to an exaggeration of the continuity of its tradition. Much of the latter was the conscious creation of scholars who provided the intellectual justification for the new Gaelic-Irish lords.[13] Frame also condemns the over-neat habit of dividing Ireland into two halves. As he observes, researchers have either been expert in the records of the English administration in Ireland, the latter replete with their references to English degeneracy, or conversely, the literary remains of a self-conscious Gaelic-Irish culture:

> The dichotomy was real enough; but it may be regarded as representing two poles, between which large elements of the population oscillated.[14]

Nevertheless, our attitudes to the period are deeply imbued with the notion of Gaelic Revival and, on the whole, we are loath to see explanations of political, economic or even settlement phenomena within either the wider context of general European decline and subsequent revival during the fourteenth century, or of structural transformation. In part, this can be attributed to the lingering influence of the ideological basis which underpins the concept of the Gaelic Revival. Ellis argues that the orthodox historiography of later medieval Ireland has had an unfortunate influence on modern Irish politics. Its purpose was to provide the fledgling Irish Free State with respectable medieval antecedents, and as he remarks, it is a notion which has remained 'surprisingly resilient'. It means an Ireland which is a political entity, its history shaped by the interaction between its inhabitants, while the impact of outside factors is ignored or dismissed as deleterious.[15]

Although Bradshaw has attacked Ellis's view as an overstatement, it underscores the comparative recency of the concept of a Gaelic revival. Nonetheless, it has to be acknowledged that the terminology can survive despite the modification of emphasis.[16] However, it would be unfair to imply that most contemporary historians see this phenomenon as a simple dichotomy between 'Two Nations'. As Cosgrove has argued, Ireland in the late Middle Ages can be seen as a synthesis of *Saxain, Gaill* and *Gáedhil*, respectively, the English, the English-by-blood but born and usually resident in Ireland, and the Gaelic-Irish. There was no necessary equation between descent and allegiance, nor was there a consistent antagonism between *Gaill*—Lydon's 'Middle Nation'—and *Gáedhil*;[17] even more confusing, there was no consistent territorial demarcation. Indeed, if one phrase encapsulates the attitude of contemporary historiography to the late Middle Ages, it is 'fragmentation of authority'.

The area under the control of the Dublin government contracted during the first half of the fifteenth century, primarily because of its inability to put sufficient forces in the field long enough even to stabilize the frontier.[18] The result was the Pale around Dublin, extending to the four counties of Dublin, Kildare, Meath and Louth. It was first fortified in the mid-fifteenth century and later substantially reinforced. Beyond the Pale, lay a mosaic of autonomous and semi-autonomous Gaelic-Irish and Anglo-Irish lordships. Not even the most dedicated traditional interpretation could claim that a putative Gaelic Revival was a politically unifying or unified force. Struggles for power took place at the local level, without reference to ethnic division.[19] As Quinn has written:

> Apart from the skein of continuity . . . of the Pale and its English associations . . ., it is not possible to write a history of Ireland in this period, only a series of local histories.[20]

It is important, however, not to allow this political fragmentation to lead to an exaggerated sense of decline combined with economic and institutional localism. As we shall see, there is ample evidence that trade and exchange continued in a relatively organized way as did the activities of major ports and other urban centres, despite the apparent political splintering of their hinterlands. The machinery of the church operated on a pan-Irish basis, the diocesan and parish system of the thirteenth century continuing into the sixteenth. Thus the Archbishops of Armagh lived in Louth—where their estates were centred—and after 1346 were English, but went to Armagh—beyond the Pale—without any hindrance.[21] Further, as the ensuing discussion will demonstrate, there was a commonality of material culture, both religious and secular, throughout much of the island. As Lyons has argued, this is demonstrative of a fifteenth-century period of economic recovery, a redistribution of perhaps modest wealth amongst a diminished population. Undoubtedly, the demographic recovery was slower than the economic.[22]

Nevertheless, some idea of the resultant complexity of the territorial fragmentation can be gained from Fig. 4.1. Nicholls' map shows that there was no neat territorial division between *Gaill* and *Gáedhil* beyond the Pale. The principal lordships are summarized on Fig. 3.1. In Ulster, the medieval Earldom had fallen apart into a set of successor lordships or family aristocracies.[23] The only more or less royalist areas were the port of Carrickfergus and south-east County Down. In the far west of Connacht, the Anglo-Norman de Burghs had become the Burkes, while in the south-west, the extent to which a great magnate like Desmond lorded it was an 'index of the ineffectiveness of the central administration'.[24] The most English of the lordships—that of the Butler Earls of Ormond—occupied the rich lands of Kilkenny, Tipperary and Waterford. Empey argues that these constituted a second Pale, retaining a distinctive Anglo-Norman character.[25] From their centre at Maynooth, the Earls of Kildare, to whom royal authority in Ireland was delegated in the first part of the sixteenth century, controlled a huge area stretching from the Wicklow hills to the Midland bogs of Offaly and Laois.[26] The stability of a whole series of Gaelic-Irish lordships was bedevilled by the failure to establish a system of succession. Turlough O'Connor, for example, fought for 42 years to achieve recognition as undisputed king of Connacht, but was frustrated by his failure to capture the key castle of Roscommon from his rivals. After his death in 1426, the competing branches of the royal family 'pursued their vendetta with undiminished zeal' until the 1460s. Cosgrove believes that the pre-eminence of the Burkes in Connacht by the mid-fifteenth century was due to their being less prone to succession disputes.[27] The same sort of dynastic quarrels were true too of the O'Neills in Ulster.[28]

In summary, therefore, before addressing the nature of the material culture, four substantive points can be made. Together, these emphasize the importance of an analysis of that evidence to an understanding of this period. First, the polarization in the documentary sources, on one hand those of an English administration concerned with the decline of its authority, on the other an essentially literary corpus, contributed much to the idea that the late Middle Ages was characterized by a simple 'Two Nations' dichotomy. Second, these sources emphasized decline—or conversely triumph—but concealed the political fragmentation and, conversely, the arguable economic and social continuity that characterized Ireland beyond the Pale. The political geography of the late Middle Ages was a complex mosaic; there was no simple east–west split. Thirdly, the crown, administering its area of shrinking authority—the Pale—was as pre-occupied with the Anglo- as with the Gaelic-Irish, as concerned with the 'English rebels' as with the 'Irish enemies'. As Cosgrove emphasizes, the Wars of the Roses demonstrated how a predominantly Yorkist Anglo-Ireland could be used as a base for counter offensives against the Lancastrian cause.[29] From this we can derive our final and perhaps most important point. Ireland was integrated into wider economic and political structures. The events of the late Middle Ages in Ireland were part of the political retreat from periphery to core characteristic of late fourteenth-century England.[30] But more fundamentally, Ireland was affected by other pan-European processes, particularly the transition within feudalism, including the decline in manorial farming and the changing relationships of lords and peasants. Environmental forces, famine and war were not peculiar to Ireland either, nor should they be ascribed to a 'Gaelic Revival'. As Ellis cogently argues, the adoption of an anachronistic Hiberno-centric perspective, with associated nationalist themes, for late medieval Ireland, is a conceptual trap.[31] (See Chapter 12 for a sustained discussion of the hybrid culture of late medieval Ireland.)

We now turn to address the evidence of landscape archaeology. The themes implied in the above discussion—localism, Gaelic- and Anglo-Irish interaction, the incompatibility of material evidence and political sources—will recur. So too will the discussion on the relative balance of decline and recovery. In essence our question is this: beyond the larger question of political authority in late medieval Ireland, does the material evidence point to a level of localized political and economic stability, combined with a recovery from the events of the late thirteenth and early fourteenth centuries?

Fortifications

This section will consider the evidence for the late medieval construction of fortifications—first, the Pale, and secondly, castles. The former is perhaps the most famous symbol of the concept of a beleaguered Anglo-Irish colony retreating before the Gaelic-Irish onslaught. In one sense, castle construction might be considered evidence of instability and insecurity in society, but conversely, it might also be interpreted as representing a degree of economic recovery through the mobilization and consolidation of resources by an elite within both Anglo- and Gaelic-Irish

Fig. 3.1. The principal lordships in the late fourteenth century. After Art Cosgrove, *Late Medieval Ireland, 1370–1541*, (Dublin, 1981), p. 21.

lordships. Further, while castles are functional buildings, they are also prestige artefacts, reflective of status, social norms and expectations.

The Pale

As we have seen, the period 1350–1550 was characterized by a dramatic decline in the area controlled by the English crown. By the later fifteenth century, royal authority really only extended to the Pale, whereas two centuries before, it had embraced almost two-thirds of the island. The phrase, 'Pale', was first used in the 1440s and the delineation of a fortified barrier in eastern Ireland can be compared with the earlier Pale constructed around the port of Calais, the last area of France still under the control of the English crown.[32] Essentially a ditch and internal earthen bank, the term, Pale, was probably derived from the wooden palisade erected on top of the bank to enhance its defensive characteristics.

As recent revisionist interpretations have indicated, it would be wrong to over-emphasize the differences between the Pale proper and areas contiguous to it, especially those which were under the control of great Anglo-Irish magnates.[33] However, it is indisputable that the Pale ditch and bank, where it was constructed, did constitute a real barrier, if only to prevent the raiding or 'preying' of cattle from the lands controlled by the English crown. The general delineation of the frontier is known from *c.* 1490, when it stretched from Dundalk, Co. Louth, in the north, southwards through Kells, Co. Meath, and Kilcullen, Co. Kildare, then swinging eastwards to join the coast just to the south of Dalkey, Dublin's outport in the Middle Ages (Fig. 3.2). This was the line defined in legislation formulated during the regime of Sir Edward Poynings between 1494 and 1496, the general purpose of which was to reassert the dominance of the king over any Anglo-Irish government.[34] In the event, the Pale shrank even further during the sixteenth century. By 1537, it ran from Drogheda, Co. Louth, through Navan, Co. Meath and Maynooth, Co. Kildare, to Tallaght in south County Dublin.[35]

The Pale was not a notional frontier, nor was it a fixed one, but it possessed a physical manifestation. To some extent, it depended on the walled towns such as Ardee, Co. Louth, and Kells, Co. Meath, and castles, but as noted above, running between these were stretches of substantial earthworks, although there is no evidence that these were continuous. Some linear field boundaries and roads were labelled as 'the Pale' on the First Edition Ordnance Survey Six Inch Maps of *c.* 1840. However, if these identifications are checked with the Name Books of the Ordnance Survey, kept by the surveyors in order to record the original form of a particular name, it becomes apparent that these features were only so labelled because of local tradition. Nevertheless, several possible lengths of the Pale have been identified through field survey north of Siddan, Co. Meath, together with four stretches in County Kildare, including those at Kilteel and Clongowes, and a further short length near Sandyford, Co. Dublin.[36] Some of these surviving portions, especially the Kildare examples, reveal that the earthwork was not always aligned north–south although it may have been planned as such originally. As O'Keeffe argues, the location and orientation of the known sections (of the Pale) indicate that the actual line of the earthworks was dictated by local factors of land ownership.[37] It is not surprising that the pattern of earthwork enclosure was more complicated than the late-fifteenth-century legislation suggests, considering the several references to the construction of local defensive earthworks throughout the period, *c.* 1440 to *c.* 1550.[38] Altogether, O'Keeffe has identified about 12 km of the Pale boundary, but he observes that often it is difficult to isolate possible Pale earthworks from later field boundaries; nor can they be dated. Most of the features identified as being part of the Pale are made up of flat-topped banks raised about one metre above field level with an accompanying ditch, one metre deep.[39]

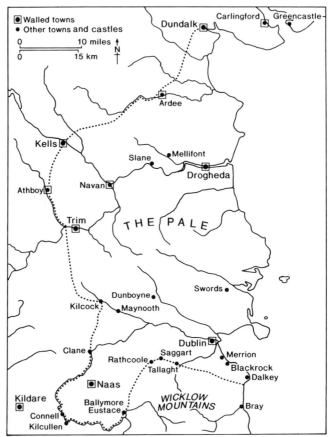

Fig. 3.2. The Pale in the later fifteenth century. After Cosgrove, *Late Medieval Ireland*, p. 70.

It has often been suggested that the line of the Pale was also marked by a concentration of tower houses. These are simple stone towers of three or four storeys, usually between five and eight metres square, sometimes with the remains of an attached defended courtyard or bawn, and ancillary buildings.[40] Their traditional association with the Pale stems from Leask's argument that an origin for the Irish tower might be found in what were called 'the £10 castles'. In 1429, Henry VI granted a subsidy of £10 to each of his 'liege men' in the counties of the English Pale who 'chooses to build a castle or tower sufficiently embattled or fortified within the next ten years to wit twenty feet in length, sixteen feet in width and forty feet in height or more'.[41] However, tower houses were the most common stone defensive structures constructed in Ireland during the later Middle Ages and, inevitably, some do occur along the line of the Pale boundary. An imposing example is the late-fourteenth- or fifteenth-century five-storied tower house and gateway of the preceptory of the Knights Hospitallers at Kilteel, Co. Kildare. This complex of buildings was sited at the vulnerable southernmost corner of the Pale where it turned eastwards to the coast just south of Dalkey, and probably would have functioned as an important strongpoint for the defensive system.[42] However, despite the incidence of such sites, the Archaeological Survey of Ireland had found that there is no significant correlation between the alignment of the Pale and the concentrations of tower houses in Counties Louth, Meath and Kildare.[43]

Castles and Tower Houses

Several ramifications attach to a study of the more general question of the dating, distribution and functions of defensive fortifications in late medieval Ireland. Their chronology provides an effective insight into the recovery from the fourteenth-century crisis. Further, because castles are the settlements of an elite, their distribution is fundamental to any understanding of the political fragmentation of late medieval Ireland. Finally, as potential cores for settlements, they are one of our best clues to the distribution and functioning of the peasant population. It should be emphasized that various types of castles were characteristic of both Anglo- and Gaelic-Irish areas.

There is some limited evidence of large fortresses being built or added to in the later fourteenth and fifteenth centuries. Those constructed at the beginning of the fourteenth century, such as the de Burgh fortresses at Greencastle, Co. Donegal, and Ballymote, Co. Sligo, or Ballymoon and possibly Clonmore, Co. Carlow, represent the end of the castle-building of the high Middle Ages before the full severity of the crisis.[44] There then seems to have been a hiatus in the construction of more elaborate castles although we can point to some examples of late-four-teenth-century date. These include Dunluce, perilously sited on a high sea-eroded rock off the north Antrim coast, and possibly first built by the Gaelic-Irish MacQuil-lans who took over the area in the late fourteenth or early fifteenth century. As Mallory and McNeill remark, Dunluce, together with Harry Avery's Castle, Co. Tyrone, show that there were Gaelic-Irish lords with the resources to erect castles far more elaborate than simple towers.[45] Leask also allocated Carrigogunnell, Co. Limerick, to this period by a documentary citation of 1339, but most of the surviving fabric dates from the later fifteenth or sixteenth century.[46]

Nevertheless, in contrast to the situation in England and France, there appears to have been no revival of large-scale castle construction in the latter half of the fourteenth century in Ireland. This should not really surprise us if we realize that the country, even in the expansionary thirteenth century, was relatively under-populated. The crisis of the fourteenth century combined to ensure that these massive feudal fortresses were often too large to be garrisoned effectively. Nevertheless, there was something of a resurgence of construction and refurbishment in the fifteenth and early sixteenth centuries. As Rae has remarked, this was related to the existence of the multiplicity of autonomous and semi-autonomous lordships. Amongst the more spectacular examples were the Desmond castle at Askeaton, Co. Limerick, and the Butler fortress at Cahir, Co. Tipperary, the largest fifteenth-century castle in Ireland.[47] Again, there was the episcopal palace of the Archbishop of Dublin at Swords, Co. Dublin, which has the feel of a castle because of its high crenellated external walls and towers.[48] Nor should it be thought that all tower houses were relatively modest structures. Amongst the most impressive, were the McCarthy pile at Blarney, Co. Cork, and the mid-sixteenth century rebuilding of Bunratty, Co. Clare, by the Macnamaras.[49]

However, it was the more modest type of tower house which became the characteristic fortified building of late medieval Ireland. Around 7000 examples may have been built between the fourteenth and seventeenth centuries. Local lords with restricted resources looked for more secure and permanent fortifications in stone to replace their much more vulnerable moated sites, often the defended manor houses of the lesser Anglo-Irish nobility, or even their ring-forts, the buildings and defences of which were often composed of wood and earth. O'Conor has suggested that some of the earlier motte-and-bailey earthwork castles initially raised by the Anglo-Normans in the twelfth century to hold down the areas they had conquered, 'continued to be used as castles throughout the fourteenth and fifteenth centuries'. He argues that mottes were constructed in the early fourteenth century in Scotland and Wales while some were inhabited into the late fourteenth century in Denmark and Holland. It is possible that the extant square or angular mottes were the last examples to have been built. These mottes would still have had a role to play, 'especially at the basic level of manorial defence against small raiding parties in the largely minor scale internal wars of late medieval Ireland'.[50]

Although the majority of tower houses date to the fifteenth and sixteenth centuries, it is nevertheless illogical to assume that none were being built late in the preceding century, especially when there are fourteenth-century towers in Scotland. These are the so-called 'pele' houses of the Scottish borders.[51] Some scholars, most recently Ó Danachair, have argued that Irish tower houses were derived from such examples.[52] But, if this were the case, there should be a denser distribution of the features in Ulster which, geographically, is the closest Irish province to Scotland. However, the northern half of the island has far fewer examples than the southern, the only significant concentration of extant examples in Ulster being in south-east County Down. Additionally, the dating of some Irish tower houses to as early as the fourteenth century would make them contemporary to those in Scotland. Thus we should not necessarily look to Scotland or northern England for the origins of the Irish tower house as, arguably, it was a settlement form which evolved independently in those parts of Europe where the breakdown of centralized authority and organization necessitated the provision of protection against local enemies. Thus, towers are found not only in Ireland and the Scottish borders, but also in those parts of France fought over by the English and French.[53] Essentially, they were a compromise between the large stone castles of an earlier period and the undefended Elizabethan and Jacobean manor houses of the sixteenth and seventeenth centuries, such as the sole intact Irish example at Carrick-on-Suir, Co. Tipperary, built about 1568 by Thomas, Earl of Ormond, or those at Jigginstown, Co. Kildare, and Oldbawn, Co. Dublin.

Turning to the distribution of tower houses, they are to be found concentrated in the areas which Jones Hughes termed the 'hybrid zone'.[54] This included much of the centre and south of Ireland, the regions characterized by a complex and intensely localized fusion of Anglo-and Gaelic-Irish influences occasioned by the ebb and flow of the later Middle Ages. Thus the densest distribution of towers is to be found in a swathe across the island from east Clare, through east Galway, Limerick, Tipperary, east and south Cork, Kilkenny, Offaly, Laois, Westmeath, Carlow and south Wexford.[55] In Ulster, for example, the tower houses although far less densely distributed, are commonest in those areas which either remained English or were taken from them. Conversely, they are rare in that part of the north which had remained beyond the Anglo-Irish remit. This pattern holds true of the rest of the island too. It has to be admitted that it is easier to describe this pattern than explain it. The Archaeological Survey of Ireland has recently demonstrated that only between 55 and 65 per cent of archaeological monuments are marked on the Ordnance Survey maps, an under-representation confirmed by Cairns who has doubled the number of tower houses in County Tipperary (Fig. 3.3).[56] However, this in-filling in density does not negate the general dimensions of the distribution described above.

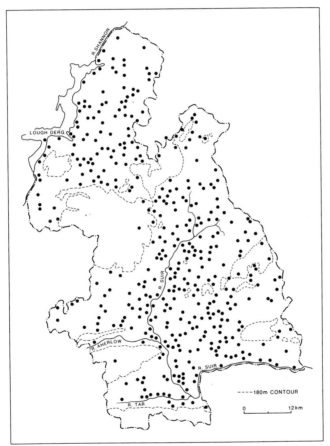

Fig. 3.3. The tower houses of County Tipperary. After C. T. Cairns, *Irish Tower Houses*, (Athlone, 1987).

Moving on from the aggregate pattern to more local scales, the evidence is somewhat mixed. Ó Danachair observes that tower houses were often clustered in 'the fertile heartlands of the great lordships, where settled conditions prevailed, rather than in wild, remote or border districts'.[57] For example, MacCurtain found that the Desmond tower houses around the Shannon estuary were concentrated on 'rich and fertile land holdings'.[58] In County Sligo, O'Dowd observes that towers were most frequently sited along the littoral, especially in the Sligo and Ballysadare areas. She also emphasizes their preferred locations along rivers, at bridges and on the main roads.[59] Elsewhere, at least one defensive line of tower houses has been identified. This was located along the northern boundary of the two most southerly baronies of Forth and Bargy in County Wexford, the most Anglo-Irish part of the county, and may have been set up against the expansionary tendencies of the powerful McMurrough Kavanagh family in the fifteenth century.[60] In Tipperary, towers are to be found clustered around towns such as Nenagh, Thurles, Clonmel, Cashel and Fethard and in the most fertile lowland areas.[61] Many were also located in towns and at ecclesiastical foundations.

To some extent, these somewhat conflicting trends in location were a reflection of function. As in Wexford, tower houses may have acted as local defences but their role in late medieval society was rather more complex. In her study of the Sligo examples, O'Dowd suggests that they 'were the normal residence of the landowning families; two or three members of the family sometimes owning the house together'.[62] Ó Danachair supports this view, writing that in the areas with the greatest concentrations of tower houses, 'every petty gentleman, office holder and small landowner ... rushed to build himself a house in the new fashion'.[63] As in Tipperary and Limerick, towers also acted as the cores of nucleated settlements.[64] Again, in the north-west, O'Dowd found that:

> many of the lords followers or tenants lived in the neighbourhood of the tower house. It thus formed the nucleus of a small settlement with perhaps a church or an abbey in the vicinity. Many tower houses also had a cornmill or tucking mill situated nearby.[65]

We shall return to this issue below.

The urban tower houses sometimes seem to have been used as town residences of wealthy rural families. One example is 'Dowdalls Castle' in Dundalk, its late medieval occupation by the Dowdall family confirmed by documentary sources.[66] Archaeological excavations during the 1970s at Carrickfergus, Co. Antrim, located the foundations of a tower house on High Street subsequently dated by numismatic and dendrochronological evidence to 1560–67. By using contemporary map evidence, the excavators were able to suggest that it was built by Thomas Stephenson, who was Mayor of the town several times in the mid-sixteenth century.[67]

Thus, the occurrence of so many tower houses could suggest that there was a marked instability in Irish life during the late Middle Ages. However, as we have intimated, they also represented the 'standard' dwelling of the more privileged classes, Anglo-Irish and Gaelic-Irish, urban and rural, across much of the country. Their concentration in the hybrid zone might suggest that these areas were particularly insecure, but against this, there is the role of tower houses as the cores of nucleated settlements. Undoubtedly, they do represent the intense localization of control in much of late medieval Ireland but this should not be equated with either decline or cultural hegemony. Tower houses can be interpreted as representing a very local form of stability and even a modest creation and mobilization of resources, as evidence of some recovery from the vicissitudes of the fourteenth century. It may be that they are distributed most densely in those areas where recovery was most marked. In cultural terms, they were simply Irish, neither

Cairns nor Jordan being able to discern any architectural differences between the examples built by the Anglo- and Gaelic-Irish in Tipperary and Wexford.[68]

Religious Settlements

As observed earlier, the church continued to act in a pan-Irish way throughout the later Middle Ages, taking little account of the welter of conflicting political authorities.[69] The church was presumably affected by the crisis of the fourteenth century, and Rae argues that the Cistercians in particular never recovered from the effects of the Black Death.[70] Nevertheless, the Order did undergo a modest revival in the fifteenth century, most ambitiously represented by the rebuilding of Holycross Abbey, Co. Tipperary.[71] However, paralleling the dynamics of tower house construction, the most dramatic manifestation of recovery in so far as church buildings are concerned, was the dramatic increase in the number of new friaries set up, predominantly in the Gaelic-Irish regions of Connacht and Ulster (Fig. 3.4). It has been suggested that these were needed to compensate for the collapse of the parish system caused by the Gaelic Resurgence, following which the Gaelic-Irish pattern of dispersed settlement reasserted itself so that fixed parishes became difficult to maintain.[72] There is little evidence to support this contention. Rather, these new houses were established in the west and north of the island, generally in rural areas, either close to small towns or to the chief settlements of their Gaelic-Irish founders. This was in contrast to older friaries which were generally established in urban locations.

As Watt writes, this new wave of friary building was indicative 'of the increasing self-confidence of Gaelic culture in later medieval Ireland'. He calculates that more than 90 new friaries of the Franciscan, Dominican Augustinian and Carmelite orders were set up in Ireland during the fifteenth century. The Franciscan Third Order was the most active, establishing over 40 houses for both sexes, primarily in Connacht and Ulster.[73] With these later foundations it would appear that construction often proceeded in a piecemeal fashion as funds became available from the nearby communities. Again, this is strong evidence of the ability of a local elite to mobilize probably modest resources. Although this was in direct contrast to the patronage of the Cistercian monasteries of the early Middle Ages which were often founded by rich and powerful lords, the pattern of community subsidy to the houses of other orders was well established in medieval Ireland.[74] In their general layout, the friaries generally followed the Cistercian plan: a rectangular cloister garth was bounded on one side by the church and on the other three sides by ranges of domestic buildings. In many cases there were additional attached structures and a few extra courtyards surrounded by more buildings. One example is Quin, Co. Clare, constructed after 1433 by the Macnamaras on top of the remains of a thirteenth-century de Clare castle which had been captured by the family in the early fourteenth century. The southern curtain wall of the castle was reutilized as the south wall of the nave and chancel church, and the east and west ends of the church were also built on to the corresponding walls of the castle. At the east end the thick castle wall had to be considerably altered to accommodate the triple-light window.[75] However, the buildings of these later friaries were often simple, reflect-

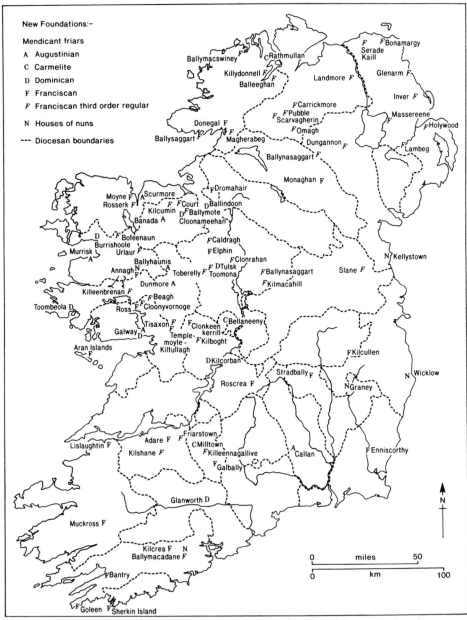

Fig. 3.4. Distribution of religious houses, 1420–1530. After F. X. Martin, in Art Cosgrove (ed.), *A New History of Ireland: II: Medieval Ireland, 1169–1534*, p. 585.

ing the modest economic base upon which they were constructed. For example, Bonamargy, Co. Antrim, apparently only ever had stone structures along two sides of the cloister. Detail was not sophisticated, the amount again reflecting local economic conditions. The most modest buildings and elaborations were in Ulster, perhaps the least developed of the four provinces during the later Middle Ages.[76]

The later Middle Ages also saw the construction of some new parish churches and extensions to others, especially within the Pale. Most of these were of simple nave and chancel design, although they often acquired substantial towers as well, perhaps to serve as the residences for the local priests. In County Meath the important and influential Plunkett family was responsible for the building of churches at Dunsany, Killeen and Rathmore. These buildings reveal architectural influences from England in their window tracery. Outside the Pale, although the friaries made up the greater number of new constructions, there were also some new parish churches, such as those built in Ulster under the patronage of Gaelic-Irish lords such as the O'Flanagans and Maguires in County Fermanagh.[77] In summary, the evidence of religious building confirms that of the pattern of tower house construction. All over the island, during the fifteenth century, there was considerable expenditure at the local level. The results may have been modest in terms of their architectural elaboration, but nevertheless remain indicative of a society with at least some degree of surplus production and the social organization to capitalize upon it.

Urban Settlements

The debate on the repercussions of the early-fourteenth-century crisis for English urbanization offers a useful introductory perspective to our analysis of Irish urbanization in the later Middle Ages. In England, the period 1350–1500 has been described as one of 'urban vigour and demographic decline'. Despite the loss of population, the towns remained essential to the running of the commercial economy.[78] Thus, the largest towns in the later fourteenth century were those associated with agricultural markets, the cloth industry or overseas trade.[79] Further, because of the transition from feudalism to capitalism, the entire marketing structure changed through the fifteenth century. The majority of the small rural markets created by the granting of borough charters disappeared, to be replaced by a marketing system organized around important communications nodes. As the peasantry became freer and mobility increased, the *raison d'être* of the local market, set up by the seigneurial lord, simply vanished. In this context, shrinkage or desertion of such settlements cannot be taken as evidence of decline but rather of structural transformation.

In Ireland, the same pattern of ostensibly conflicting trends is apparent, although our understanding of them has been obfuscated by the emphasis placed on the Gaelic Revival. In general, the larger Anglo-Irish dominated towns, which were also the major ports of the south and east of the country, seem to have survived the socio-economic and political vicissitudes of the fourteenth century and probably started expanding again as the fifteenth-century recovery got under way.[80] Within the Pale, Dublin seems to have weathered the effects of the Black Death, later outbreaks of the plague and the economic recession which followed in their train. Its population *c.* 1550 has been estimated at 8000, which would have made it the sixth largest city in the British Isles. This was probably an increase on the mid-fifteenth century but still only about a third of its probable size of around

25,000 at its high point at the end of the thirteenth century.[81] It was also an important manufacturing centre throughout the later Middle Ages and its port mainly exported raw materials such as wool, hides and skins for luxury goods through the English ports of Bristol and Chester as well as further afield. However, its economic development was made difficult by the restrictions imposed on its hinterland by the Dublin mountains to the south, the Gaelic-Irish often preventing supplies from reaching the city's markets. Although there is documentary evidence of the construction of buildings and mural towers and other material signs of economic activity from the fifteenth century onwards, we lack archaeological evidence because of the destruction of these layers by later building.[82] But these new constructions were often erected only by the wealthy few in the city and were not necessarily representative of the population as a whole.[83]

The comparatively buoyant evidence for fifteenth-century Dublin is supported by Bradley's study of the Louth town of Ardee. Ostensibly in a highly vulnerable position at the northern end of the Pale ditch, Ardee not only survived the late Middle Ages but also apparently prospered. A series of murage grants was made for the repair of its walls in 1376, 1379, 1389, 1399 and 1413. In addition, there are two extant fifteenth-century houses on Market Street, known as 'Pippard's Castle' and 'Hatch's Castle', and Bradley believes that these are survivors of a once-larger number of fortified houses. As we have seen, tower houses were a common form of residence for the urban elite in the fifteenth century and many other Irish towns still retain examples. At Ardee, the parish church of St. Mary, originally founded in the thirteenth century, had a south aisle added in the fifteenth century, while a chantry college had been 'recently built' in 1487. These material artefacts combine to reinforce Bradley's belief that although Ardee may have declined in area before 1400, it was a 'wealthy town in the fifteenth century'.[84]

The same indications that urban vigour continued through the fifteenth century, despite political fragmentation and demographic decline, can be found outside the Pale proper. The area drained by the Barrow, Nore and Suir river system in south-eastern Ireland contained a concentration of urban nodes, including Carrick-on-Suir, Cashel, Clonmel, Callan, and Fethard all in County Tipperary, New Ross, Co. Wexford, and Kilkenny and Waterford, which were among the most prosperous towns of the later Middle Ages. The agricultural surplus of this rich region was easily carried down the rivers to be traded though the inland port of Kilkenny or the coastal ports of New Ross and Waterford. The latter, bitter commercial rivals, dominated the external trade of much of south-eastern Ireland. Politically this economic power was harnessed by the powerful Butler family who controlled this large area from its two administrative centres of Kilkenny and, to a lesser extent, Carrick-on-Suir. Kilkenny was a prosperous town in the fifteenth century, being 'well walled and well replenished of people and wealthy'.[85] The later fourteenth century had seen a significant shift in the power base of the Butlers away from Nenagh in north Tipperary, which was abandoned to the Gaelic-Irish. This resulted in an effective consolidation of their power in south-eastern Tipperary and south County Kilkenny, which was to last into the post-medieval period.

Waterford was not far behind Dublin in terms of the numbers of hides and cloth exported from its extensive quayside. Lydon has shown that despite constant problems of the period, such as pressure by the Powers and other 'rebel' English, troubles with the French over trade, and the heavy cost of maintaining the extensive circuit of walls and towers, the town survived and even extended its thriving export trade. The walls caused continual problems for the mayor and citizens of the city. In 1430, for example, Waterford was granted £30 a year to be spent 'on the repair and defence of the town' as 'the ditches, walls, towers, gates and portcullises are so old and ruinous in many places as to be all but fallen to the ground.'[86] This might lead one to conclude that the city was in decline since the boom days of the thirteenth century, but Lydon suggests that in common with other towns, the citizenry of Waterford often overemphasized its predicament in order to gain more favourable financial treatment from the crown. In this regard it is significant that Waterford was able to hold out against a siege in 1495 and its garrison was also able to participate in the defeat of the army of the supporters of the pretender to the throne, Perkin Warbeck. Although often only a small portion of the murage grant was actually used to maintain the walls of most medieval towns, in Waterford's case, expenditure was obviously sufficient to maintain the extensive circuit of walls and keep the besieging army at bay.[87]

Clearly trade was flourishing between Waterford and its essentially Gaelic-Irish hinterland. As O'Brien remarks and the comment is applicable to a number of other trading towns and not only in the south-east, 'unlike the later fourteenth and earlier fifteenth centuries, in Ireland the later fifteenth century was a period of at least relative political stability and economic buoyancy'[88] (Fig. 3.5). As we have observed, this is precisely the pattern which has been observed in England, notwithstanding the very different political conditions in Ireland. Although the issues remain to be investigated, it does suggest a commonality of structural change, exemplified in particular by the emergence of urban patriciates of merchants and industrialists who controlled urban economies and were no longer subject to the will of feudal lords. As MacNiocaill has shown, Dublin like many other medieval cities was controlled by a tight merchant oligarchy until the latter half of the sixteenth century, which made access to the governing class extremely restricted.[89] Even in the Butler capital of Kilkenny, it appears that the dynamism in the town's economy originated from its urban elite. It should be observed that commercial transactions between the Anglo-Irish towns like Waterford and Galway and their Gaelic-Irish hinterlands were restricted by law but obviously, much commercial interchange took place. As Cosgrove states, 'the profits of trade, like those of warfare, had an attraction that surmounted the ethnic divide'.[90]

As we saw in Chapter 2, it is very difficult to determine either the degree or condition of urbanism in those areas controlled by Gaelic-Irish lords. Extant documentary sources are very few and far between, and relate primarily to places of Anglo-Irish foundation which subsequently came under Gaelic-Irish control. One such example is Sligo, originally an Anglo-Norman borough centred around the castle built *c.* 1245. Both castle and town probably continued to exist under the control of either the Gaelic-Irish O Conors or their overlords, the O Donnells, throughout the later Middle Ages. In 1414 a fire largely destroyed the town and the major structures within it such as the friary, although the latter was extensively rebuilt about 1416. Through the activities of local merchants, Sligo was an important port, with herrings being a major export item.[91] It is possible that there was a town at Cavan, centred around the Franciscan friary founded at some time in the

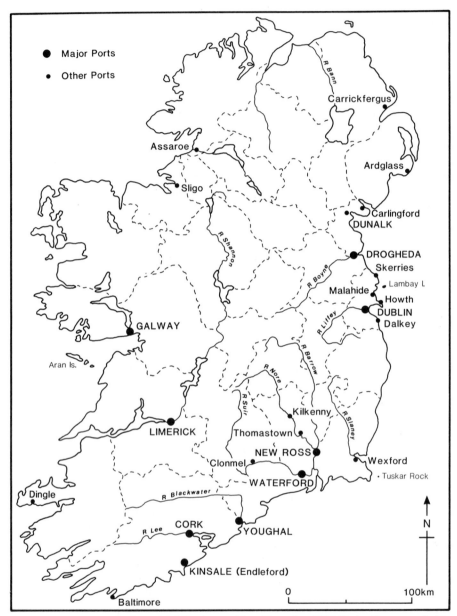

Fig. 3.5. Irish ports in the later Middle Ages. After Timothy O'Neill, in Cosgrove (ed.), *New History of Ireland: II*, p. 499.

fourteenth century by the O Reilly lords of Breifne. Unfortunately, the evidence is essentially sixteenth century. No known portion of the friary now survives as it was burnt in 1451, 1468, and 1576, and no other structures of this period survive, either.[92] Other Gaelic-Irish dominated towns, such as Armagh, show much the same pattern both because of the lack of contemporary Gaelic-Irish sources and the very limited amount of archaeological excavations.[93] Documentary sources dated to 1517 describe Rosscarbery, Co. Cork, now little more than a village, as a walled town with as many as 200 houses.[94]

Conversely, several towns in the midlands and in the west apparently went into steep decline or were completely deserted. Desertion is a difficult issue because there was a multiplicity of possible causes and evidence is usually lacking. Conventionally, it is explained by the Gaelic Revival. Thus, in Connacht, for example, Roscommon town, despite the existence of the powerful castle there, was apparently finally deserted in 1360 after it had been burnt yet again by the Gaelic-Irish. What this actually means is that the settlement disappears from the English documentary records. We know that Roscommon Castle passed into Gaelic-Irish hands and as the medieval borough was probably never any more than an adjunct to that fortress anyway, its disappearance from the English documentary record cannot be accepted as evidence of desertion. If the castle continued—which it did—then so too hypothetically did its dependent settlement. The same could be true of Rindown, Co. Roscommon, where the castle was taken by the Gaelic-Irish in the 1340s.[95] We will return to the issue of desertion in the discussion on rural settlement.

Rural Settlement

When the agricultural system of the period is examined, it is soon apparent that few advances have been made on MacNiocaill's 1979 conclusion that 'the problems of progression or regression in the late medieval period, [have] so far have been even less attractive to historians than the relatively prosperous period of the later thirteenth century'.[96] Within the Pale, it is possible that agriculture was still based upon the holdings in strips of the common field pattern with cereal crops such as wheat and rye mainly being grown in them.[97] But until further research has been completed, it is probably safer to suggest, as with the contemporary situation in England, that there were many different field patterns all determined by varying local conditions. It is a distinct possibility that the agricultural hinterlands of the major east and south coast ports were characterized by a shift away from mainly arable to pastoral farming, reflecting the change in exports in the later Middle Ages.[98] We know, for instance, of large flocks of sheep in County Wexford which brought great profit to the Bigod lords and their successors there.[99] European trading conditions relating to both wool and cloth obviously affected this trade; in the fifteenth century, there was a decline in the export of raw wool from Ireland. This was probably due to a switch to the manufacture of cloth because taxation levels were much lower on the finished product than on the raw wool.[100]

If our present degree of knowledge concerning the status of urbanization in much of late medieval Ireland verges on the enigmatic, the same is true for rural settlement. As Mallory and McNeill point out, the castles, tower houses and various churches and friaries are often sites which are 'sitting alone without their context'.[101] There has been no systematic research into the settlements which might once have been associated with them. The few regional or local studies which have been carried out suggest a wide degree of variation but it is unclear if these can be extrapolated into more widely applicable models. Further, it is impossible to estimate the degree of internal migration taking place as the result of fourteenth-century crisis, fragmentation of authority and the general decline in feudal ties.

One particular local variant of rural settlement, occurring principally in south Kilkenny, was the cluster of farmsteads which Burtchaell has identified as the 'farm village'. Demonstrative of the long-term stability which Ormond paternity gave to this area, these may well represent one post-feudal resolution of the rural settlement pattern, as tenant farmers became the norm and labour ties disappeared. Burtchaell believes that the villages were socially varied and economically prosperous.[102] In parts of Jones Hughes' hybrid zone, the tower house belt, Smyth has emphasized the continuity of rural settlement types, ranging from dispersed settlement through small agglomerated settlement forms to nucleations with more than 10 hearths in the seventeenth century. In County Tipperary, the latter were often clustered around the church and/or castle from the later Middle Ages onwards.[103] The same pattern was observed in Meath where many of the fifteenth-century towers became the cores of small nucleated rural settlements.[104]

The evidence is beginning to suggest that the seventeenth century was the period of greatest desertion of rural settlements, at least in eastern and southern Ireland. This was probably the case in the rural-boroughs at Ardmayle, Buolick and Kiltinan all in County Tipperary, and the once flourishing borough of Newtown Jerpoint, Co. Kilkenny. The latter probably went into decline after the suppression of the nearby Cistercian monastery in 1541 and because of the competition provided by Thomastown, a few kilometres down-river, where there was another important bridging point across the Nore.[105] While the plagues and socio-political uncertainties of the late Middle Ages may have weakened these small settlements, they had outlived the socio-economic structure which had created them.

There is little surviving archaeological or historical evidence relating to the west and north of the island which might indicate where the great majority of Gaelic-Irish lived. As O'Dowd has shown in her study of the Sligo tower houses, small nucleated settlements often grew up around these in much the same way as occurred in Tipperary and Meath.[106] In the Gaelic-Irish areas of County Tipperary, Smyth has identified the existence of 'kin clusters'. These were small agglomerated settlements generally associated with partnership farmers of 'husbandmen' status who were farming the land at a subsistence level.[107] Obviously some ring-forts and *crannógs* were still lived in during the later Middle Ages, but again, without archaeological evidence, it is very difficult to judge the extent to which they were being reutilized.[108] According to Nicholls, however, many of the Gaelic-Irish lived in impermanent agglomerations made up of flimsy houses which could be taken apart quickly when their inhabitants moved between winter and summer pasturage. He also states that the contemporary Elizabethan sources make it quite apparent that the rural population of Gaelic Ireland did not live in settled communities, but moved from place to place.[109] There is also some literary evidence to suggest that there was a growth in the 'permanent state of nomadry', especially in Ulster, during the later Middle Ages at the expense of the temporary displacement of population. Nicholls argues that these dispersed settlements were few and far between and concludes that all the evidence would show that Gaelic Ireland in the later Middle Ages was very underpopulated by contemporary European standards. These very transient settlements are almost impossible to trace by most contemporary archaeological methods. However, a refinement of remote sensing techniques and the use of large-scale phosphate analysis might begin to help identify some examples. It follows that the intensity of land utilization was low, as well, with a concentration upon pastoral farming. Where there was the cultivation of crops such as oats, this took place utilizing the 'long fallow' or shifting system rather than a fixed rotation of crops.[110]

Conclusion

In conclusion, the material evidence of the late Middle Ages confirms that the idea of a Gaelic Revival is an overly simplified one. The political decline of the English in Ireland was not matched by parallel changes in the transformation of the socio-economic structure. The decline of feudalism took a different course to events in England where it was a corollary to centralization and the emergence of absolute monarchy. In Ireland, the outcome was a localization and fragmentation of authority, perhaps even more intense than that of the early medieval period. But there was a substantial economic recovery from the crisis of the fourteenth century and the maintenance of trading relationships, urbanization and economic hinterlands over-rode the political fragmentation. As Smyth argues, the later Middle Ages saw

> 'the fusion of a number of relatively powerful port-centred economic regions with the administrative–political superstructures of the great lordships. Beyond these core territories were the rural-based, less stratified and generally (though not invariably) smaller political lordships.'[111]

However, one outcome of that localization was that responses to the demands of the age were themselves localized, which is one reason why it is so difficult to generalize. For example, the models of rural settlement may well be regionally specific. However, the evidence of the tower houses and the friaries, particularly the former, does suggest that there was a certain commonality of ideas across Irish society, irrespective of ethnic division or locality. The investment in these structures indicates too that there was a modest economic recovery from the crisis of the fourteenth century. In answer to the question posed above, the material evidence does suggest that our concern with the political documentation and the ideological issues of this period has exaggerated both the importance of the ethnic divide and the long-term impact of the decline of the fourteenth century.

References

1. See, for example, Terence Reeves-Smyth and Fred Hamond, *Landscape Archaeology in Ireland*, BAR British Series, 116, (Oxford, 1983).
2. B. N. S. Campbell, 'People and land in the Middle Ages, 1066–1500', in R. A. Dodgshon and R. A. Butlin (eds.), *An Historical Geography of England and Wales*, (second edn, London, 1990), pp. 69–122: see p. 93.
3. See, for example, James Lyndon, *The Lordship of Ireland in the Middle Ages*, (Dublin, 1972).

4. Campbell, 'People and land', pp. 100–2; *idem* (ed.), *Before the Black Death: Studies in the 'Crisis' of the Early Fourteenth Century*, (Manchester, 1991).
5. Mary C. Lyons, 'Weather, famine, pestilence and plague in Ireland, 900–1500', in E. M. Crawford (ed.), *Famine: The Irish Experience, 900–1900: Subsistence Crises and Famine in Ireland*, (Edinburgh, 1989), pp. 321–74; see pp. 37 and 44.
6. J. Hatcher, *Plague, Population and the English Economy, 1348–1350*, (London, 1977), pp. 11–20.
7. Mary C. Lyons, 'Manorial administration and the manorial economy in Ireland, *c.* 1200–*c.* 1377', (unpublished PhD thesis, University of Dublin, 1984).
8. G. Twigg, *The Black Death: A Biological Reappraisal*, (London, 1984), pp. 212–13.
9. Campbell, 'People and land', p. 102.
10. For a discussion, see M. Dunford and D. Perrons, *The Arena of Capital*, (London, 1983).
11. J. P. Mallory and T. E. McNeill, *The Archaeology of Ulster: From Colonisation to Plantation*, (Belfast, 1991), p. 285.
12. Art Cosgrove, *Late Medieval Ireland, 1370–1541*, (Dublin, 1981), p. 51.
13. K. W. Nicholls, 'Anglo-French Ireland and after', *Peritia*, **1** (1982), pp. 370–403; see p. 392.
14. Robin Frame, *The Political Development of the British Isles 1100–1400*, (Oxford, 1990), pp. 203–4.
15. Steven G. Ellis, 'Nationalist historiography and the English and Gaelic worlds in the late Middle Ages', *Irish Historical Studies*, **XXV**, no. 97 (May, 1986), pp. 1–18; see pp. 2–3.
16. Brendan Bradshaw, 'Nationalism and historical scholarship in modern Ireland', *Irish Historical Studies*, **XXVI**, no. 104 (Nov. 1989), pp. 329–51.
17. Cosgrove, *Late Medieval Ireland*, p. 79: James Lydon, 'The middle nation', in James Lydon (ed.), *The English in Medieval Ireland*, (Dublin, 1984), pp. 1–26.
18. Art Cosgrove, 'The emergence of the Pale, 1399–1447', in *idem* (ed.), *A New History of Ireland: II: Medieval Ireland, 1169–1534*, (Oxford, 1987), pp. 533–56; see p. 537.
19. Cosgrove, *Late Medieval Ireland*, p. 81.
20. D. B. Quinn, 'Aristocratic autonomy, 1460–94', in Cosgrove (ed.), *New History of Ireland: II*, pp. 591–618; see p. 619.
21. T. E. McNeill, 'Lordships and invasion: Ulster, 1177–1500', in Ciaran Brady, Mary O'Dowd and Brian Walker (eds.), *Ulster: An Illustrated History*, (London, 1989), pp. 44–76; see p. 69.
22. Lyons, 'Weather, famine, pestilence', *passim.*
23. McNeill, 'Lordships and invasion', p. 63.
24. Cosgrove, *Late Medieval Ireland*, p. 90.
25. C. A. Empey, 'The Butler Lordship in Ireland, 1185–1515', (unpublished PhD thesis, University of Dublin, 1970).
26. Frame, *Political Development of the British Isles*, p. 204.
27. Cosgrove, *Late Medieval Ireland*, p. 86.
28. McNeill, 'Lordships and invasion', p. 64.
29. Cosgrove, *Late Medieval Ireland*, p. 55.
30. Campbell, 'People and land', p. 102.
31. Ellis, 'Nationalist historiography', p. 13.
32. Cosgrove, *Late Medieval Ireland*, p. 45.
33. N. Canny, *From Reformation to Restoration: Ireland, 1534–1660*, (Dublin, 1987), p. 8.
34. Cosgrove, *Late Medieval Ireland*, p. 69.
35. Rolf Loeber, *The Geography and Practice of English Colonisation in Ireland from 1534 to 1609*, (Athlone, 1991), p. 9.
36. C. Manning, 'Excavations at Kilteel church, County Kildare', *Journal of the Kildare Archaeological Society*, **16** (1981–2), pp. 173–229.
37. Tadhg O'Keeffe, 'Medieval frontiers and fortifications: the Pale and its evolution', in F. H. A. Aalen and Kevin Whelan (eds.), *Dublin City and County: From Prehistory to Present: Studies in Honour of J. H. Andrews*, (Dublin, 1992), pp. 57–77.
38. Loeber, *Geography of English Colonisation*, pp. 8–9.

39. O'Keeffe, 'Medieval frontiers and fortifications', pp. 70–2.
40. C. T. Cairns, *Irish Tower Houses: A County Tipperary Case Study*, (Athlone, 1987) p. 3; Mallory and McNeill, *Ulster*, p. 289: M. McCauliffe, 'The tower houses of County Kerry', (unpublished PhD thesis, University of Dublin, 1991).
41. H. G. Leask, *Irish Castles and Castellated Houses*, (Dundalk, 1970), pp. 76–7.
42. C. Manning, 'Excavations at Kilteel', pp. 173–2.
43. Information from Mr Sweetman of the Archaeological Survey of Ireland.
44. See, for example, T. O'Keeffe, 'Rathnageeragh and Ballyloo: a study of stone castles of probable 14th to early 15th century date in County Carlow', *Journal of the Royal Society of Antiquaries of Ireland* **117** (1987), pp. 36–7.
45. Mallory and McNeill, *Ulster*, p. 288.
46. Leask, *Irish Castles*, p. 75.
47. *Ibid.*, p. 123; Edwin C. Rae, 'Architecture and sculpture, 1169–1603', in Cosgrove (ed.), *New History of Ireland: II*, pp. 737–79.
48. Leask, *Irish Castles*, p. 72.
49. Rae, 'Architecture', pp. 769–70.
50. K. O'Conor, 'The later construction and use of motte and bailey castles in Ireland: new evidence from Leinster', *Journal of the Kildare Archaeological Society*, **17** (1991), p. 25.
51. P. Dixon, 'Towerhouses, pelehouses and border society', *The Archaeological Journal*, **136** (1979), pp. 240–52.
52. Caoimhin Ó Danachair, 'Irish tower houses and their regional distribution', *Béaloideas*, **45–7** (1977–9), pp. 158–63.
53. Mallory and McNeill, *Ulster*, p. 290.
54. T. Jones Hughes, 'Town and *baile* in Irish place-names', in Nicholas Stephens and Robin E. Glasscock (eds.), *Irish Geographical Studies in Honour of E. Estyn Evans*, (Belfast, 1970), pp. 244–58.
55. A poor distribution map can be found in Ó Danachair, 'Irish tower houses'.
56. Cairns, *Irish Tower Houses, passim.*
57. Ó Danachair, 'Irish tower houses', p. 152.
58. Margaret MacCurtain, 'A lost landscape; the Geraldine castles and tower houses of the Shannon estuary', in John Bradley (ed.), *Settlement and Society in Medieval Ireland*, (Kilkenny, 1988), pp. 429–44; see p. 439.
59. Mary O'Dowd, 'Gaelic economy and society', in Ciaran Brady and Raymond Gillespie (eds.), *Natives and Newcomers*, (Dublin, 1986), pp. 120–47; see pp. 127–8.
60. A. J. Jordan, 'The tower houses of County Wexford', (unpublished PhD thesis, University of Dublin, 1991).
61. *Ibid.*, pp. 190–1.
62. O'Dowd, 'Gaelic economy', pp. 127–8.
63. Ó Danachair, 'Irish tower houses', p. 161.
64. P. O'Connor, *Exploring Limerick's Past*, (Limerick, 1987), pp. 31–3; William J. Smyth, 'Property, patronage and population: reconstructing the human geography of mid-seventeenth century County Tipperary', in William Nolan (ed.), *Tipperary: History and Society*, (Dublin, 1985), pp. 125–6.
65. O'Dowd, 'Gaelic economy', p. 128.
66. Information from Paul Gosling, University College, Galway.
67. M. L. Simpson and A. Dickson, 'Excavations in Carrickfergus, County Antrim, 1972–79', *Medieval Archaeology*, **XXV** (1981), p. 84.
68. Cairns, *Irish Tower Houses*; Jordan, 'Tower houses of Wexford', pp. 207–8.
69. Cosgrove, 'Beyond the Pale', p. 584.
70. Rae, 'Architecture', pp. 750–1.
71. Roger Stalley, *The Cistercian Monasteries of Ireland*, (New Haven, 1987), chapter 5.
72. Mallory and McNeill, *Ulster*, p. 294.
73. John Watt, *The Church in Medieval Ireland*, (Dublin, 1972), pp. 193–4.
74. C. A. Empey, 'The sacred and the secular: the Augustinian priory of Kells in Ossory', *Irish Historical Studies*, **XXIV**, no. 94 (Nov. 1984), pp. 131–51.
75. B. de Breffny and G. Mott, *The Churches and Abbeys of Ireland*, (London, 1970), p. 99.

76. Mallory and McNeill, *Ulster*, pp. 292–7.
77. T. B. Barry, *The Archaeology of Medieval Ireland*, (London, 1987), p. 195.
78. P. Clark and P. Slack (eds.), *Crisis and Order in English Towns*, (London, 1972).
79. P. T. H. Unwin, 'Towns and trade, 1066–1500', in Dodgshon and Butlin (eds.), *Historical Geography of England and Wales*, pp. 123–50.
80. S. G. Ellis, *Tudor Ireland*, (London, 1985), pp. 37–8.
81. Gearoid MacNiocaill, 'Socio-economic problems of the late medieval town', in David Harkness and M. O'Dowd (eds.), *The Town in Ireland*, (Belfast, 1981), pp. 7–22; see pp. 18–19.
82. J. F. Lydon, 'The Medieval City', in Art Cosgrove (ed.), *Dublin Through the Ages*, (Dublin, 1988), pp. 25–45; see pp. 31–2.
83. MacNiocaill, 'Socio-economic problems', p. 20.
84. J. Bradley, 'Ardee: an archaeological study', *County Louth Archaeological and Historical Journal*, **20**, no. 4 (1984) p. 6.
85. W. G. Neely, *Kilkenny: An Urban History, 1391–1843*, (Belfast, 1989), p. 53.
86. *Calendar of Patent Rolls*, 1429–36, p. 68.
87. J. F. Lydon, 'The city of Waterford in the later Middle Ages', *Decies*, no. 12 (Sept. 1979), pp. 5–15; Ellis, *Tudor Ireland*, *passim*.
88. A. F. O'Brien, 'The royal boroughs: the seaport towns and royal revenue in medieval Ireland', *Journal of the Royal Society of Antiquaries of Ireland*, **118** (1988), pp. 13–26.
89. MacNiocaill, 'Socio-economic problems', *passim*.
90. Cosgrove, *Late Medieval Ireland*, p. 95.
91. R. A. Butlin, 'Irish towns in the sixteenth and seventeenth centuries', in R. A. Butlin (ed.), *The Development of the Irish Town*, (London, 1977), pp. 61–100; see p. 74.
92. Killanin and M. Duignan, *The Shell Guide to Ireland*, (London, 1967), p. 159.
93. Barry, *Archaeology of Medieval Ireland*, pp. 159–60.
94. K. W. Nicholls, *Gaelic and Gaelicised Ireland in the Middle Ages*, (Dublin, 1972), p. 122.
95. H. Walton, 'The English in Connacht, 1171–1333', unpublished PhD thesis, University of Dublin (1980), p. 504; B. J. Graham, 'The medieval settlement of County Roscommon', *Proceedings of the Royal Irish Academy*, **88c** (1988), pp. 19–38.
96. MacNiocaill, 'Socio-economic problems', p. 21.
97. See, for example, C. McNeill and A. J. Otway-Ruthven (eds.), *Dowdall Deeds*, (Dublin 1960), nos. 639, 658; Nicholls, 'Anglo-French Ireland', p. 398.
98. Barry, *Archaeology of Medieval Ireland*, p. 179.
99. Lyons, 'Manorial administration', pp. 53–95.
100. Timothy O'Neill, *Merchants and Mariners in Medieval Ireland*, (Dublin, 1987), p. 65.
101. Mallory and McNeill, Ulster, p. 286.
102. Jack Burtchaell, 'The south Kilkenny farm villages', in William J. Smyth and Kevin Whelan (eds.), *Common Ground*, (Cork, 1988), pp. 110–23.
103. *Ibid.*, p. 121.
104. B. J. Graham, 'Anglo-Norman settlement in County Meath', *Proceedings of the Royal Irish Academy*, **75c** (1975), pp. 223–48.
105. T. B. Barry, 'The people of the country ... dwelt scattered': the pattern of rural settlement in Ireland in the later Middle Ages', in Bradley (ed.) *Settlement and Society*, pp. 345–360; see p. 354.
106. O'Dowd, 'Gaelic economy'.
107. William J. Smyth, 'Society and settlement in seventeenth-century Ireland: the evidence of the 1659 Census', in Smyth and Whelan (eds.), *Common Ground*, pp. 55–83; see p. 62; *idem*, 'Property, patronage and population'.
108. Barry, *Archaeology of Medieval Ireland*, p. 54.
109. K. W. Nicholls, 'Land, law and society in sixteenth-century Ireland', O'Donnell Lecture (Cork, 1976), p. 9; *idem*, 'Gaelic society and economy in the high Middle Ages', in Cosgrove (ed.), *New History of Ireland: II*, pp. 397–438.
110. Katherine Simms, 'Nomadry in medieval Ireland', *Peritia*, **5** (1986), pp. 379–91.
111. Smyth, 'Society and settlement', p. 62.

4

Explorers, Exploiters and Entrepreneurs: Early Modern Ireland and its Context, 1500–1700

Raymond Gillespie

The Rhetoric of Empire

British historians have detected a profound change from the beginning of the sixteenth century in the rules and organizing principles of society in the British Isles. One historian has recently characterized the period as 'the making of the British empire'.[1] Legislative changes such as the 1536 Act of Union with Wales, which aimed to eliminate the 'distinction and diversity' then existing between the king's subjects of England and those of Wales, and the 1542 Act of the Irish Parliament, which stated that the king of England was no longer lord of Ireland but its king, created a new constitutional framework. Cruder attempts were made to integrate Scotland into this new entity with the invasions of 1544 and 1545, which became known to later historians as the 'rough wooing'.[2] The process of constructing the 'empire' was part of the creation of modern states in which the old obligations which held groups of people together, such as the ties of lordship which bound Ireland to England, were transformed into a different set of social, economic and political arrangements. The expansive ambitions which lay behind these changes were set out in the preamble to the English Parliament's 1533 Act in Restraint of Appeals to Rome which proclaimed 'where by divers old authentic histories and chronicles it is manifestly declared that this realm of England is an empire and so hath been accepted in the world'. A wider dimension to this claim was provided much later than in other European countries, such as Spain and Portugal, by Henry VII's entry into the scramble for territories in the newly discovered areas of North America through his funding of John Cabot's voyages of discovery in the late 1490s. The gradual emergence of a framework for a 'British Empire' involved changes in the social, economic and cultural geography, not only of the outlying regions being colonized, but of England herself. In particular London had to take an interest in the peripheral regions both within the political bounds of England and far outside them.

In some ways there was nothing new about an English rhetoric of empire and attempts to implement it. Medieval kings had made similar claims and Edward I had gone a long way towards achieving them. However, the claims of the early sixteenth century were different from those made earlier. The ties which held Edward I's imperial concept together were those which also held England itself together: ties of lordship. Royal policy under the Tudors was moving away from reliance on powerful subjects to control the different regions within the kingdom. Instead, royal officials, such as sheriffs, began to play a greater part in controlling the localities. In outlying regions new institutions, such as the Council of the North and the Council of the March of Wales, were set up to wield royal power in the provinces. In this way a 'rediscovery' of the outlying areas of England itself became necessary as well as information about the object of the imperial claims, such as Ireland, Scotland or America. The urge to be better informed about all regions was prompted by new ideas about learning and religion. Historians and topographers followed the claim of the Act in Restraint of Appeals to Rome with a precise description of what was being laid claim to. Topographers, such as John Leland, began to describe the physical appearance and evolution of countryside of England. Renaissance standards of historiography with their concern for textual analysis and the preservation of sources provided the guiding principle for these men.

Within a generation the scope of study had moved to a smaller scale. Men such as Thomas Carew, William Lambarde and John Stow began to describe individual counties and even cities. It was such activity which formed the basis of the strong seventeenth-century tradition of local history in England. Detailed topographical descriptions were paralleled by map-making of smaller areas such as Christopher Saxton's county survey of the 1570s and John Norden's *Speculum Britanniae* of 1592. The rise of the estate map in the late sixteenth century shows concern for yet smaller areas, although more for economic reasons than geographical ones.[3] These exercises in exploration were not simply theoretical but had a considerable practical effect on the way early modern society was organized. One such practical application of the discoveries of the topographers came in the field of religion. The discovery of 'dark corners of the land' was not simply a cartographic exercise, it also revealed groups of people who had not been confronted with the religious changes of the sixteenth century. Puritan clergy immediately saw the need for evangelization in these areas and an accompanying reformation of manners to create the ideal kingdom, uniformly governed, learned and godly.[4] Similarly most of the scholars who set out on the discovery of England were not merely topographers. Leland was an accomplished linguist, historian and collector of manuscripts, concerned primarily not with topography but with recording antiquities. Such men wanted to describe what they saw and in particular how what they saw related to the past and the evolution of society. In that sense they were early anthropologists.[5]

Over the early modern period, perceptions of territories both at home and abroad changed. The idea of the state and the types of bonds which held groups of people together changed radically and this had different effects on both the Old World and the New. The involvement of European states in the New World helped broaden their perspective on the world while the inflow of precious metals from the newly discovered lands had a considerable economic impact at home.[6] The economic and social paths taken by peripheral regions, under the pressures of population change, commercialization and settlement, differed widely. Patterns of acculturation also varied over the British Isles and colonial America. Some Scots, for example, absorbed the culture of the London court while the 'New English' settlers in seventeenth-century Ireland created and developed their own culture in response to the circumstances they found in their adopted country. This chapter does not attempt to describe economic, social or political developments in either the Old World or the New, as that has been done elsewhere.[7] Rather it examines how one region, Ireland, came to terms with some of the pressures placed on it by an expanding 'British Empire'. In particular it will examine how the solutions to the problems of economic and social change which were adopted in Ireland by British settlers compared with those which evolved in the regions of the Old World from which they came, and also with developments in contemporary colonial environments of English and Scots settlers in the New World. In essence it is an attempt to place the development of early modern Ireland in a wider regional context.

Finding out About New Worlds

Ireland and the New World soon came to the forefront of the English process of gathering and sorting information about the outlying regions. The New World was *terra incognita* and information had to be assembled piecemeal from the accounts of explorers and map-makers.[8] These were often sparse given that English interest in North America was slow to gain momentum. Only the coastal regions were explored in any detail and most settlers knew little of the country when they arrived there, depending heavily on the assistance of the local Indians to survive their first few seasons. Tracts commissioned and produced by those intent on creating settlements formed the basis of the information available to the first settlers. The picture presented was unduly optimistic but it was soon tempered by the correspondence of the first settlers with friends and relations in England which provided a more sobering picture of life. By contrast Ireland, particularly the east coast, was a country well known to sixteenth-century English and Scots men. This knowledge partly derived from strong and growing trading connections with England and Scotland. Contemporary maps of Ireland show that by the beginning of the sixteenth century the coastline of Ireland and its main trading ports were well known to English and European traders. Less familiar were the inland regions.[9] One of the main concerns of map-makers in sixteenth-century Ireland was the filling in of the detail of such areas. Elizabeth's principal secretary of state, William Cecil, was a passionate map collector and as English royal authority advanced into Ireland, he commissioned new maps of specific areas which could be shown to the queen. Thus after the defeat of Shane O'Neill in 1567, Robert Lythe was dispatched to Ireland to make maps of Ireland. By 1571 Lythe had surveyed most of the country south of a line from the Lecale in County Down to Killary Harbour, Co. Galway.[10] More local map-making endeavours were undertaken as required, most notably the groups of maps prepared as background for the plantation of Munster in the 1580s.[11] The demands of war in the later part of the century considerably speeded up the process of regional map-making so that by the early years of the seventeenth century, the overall topography of Ireland was well documented. Much of the detail would be filled in during the seventeenth century as repeated inquisitions were held to record the geographical divisions of the country as part of the process of making land grants in plantation schemes.[12] No equivalent process was ever undertaken in colonial America.

Maps alone were often of limited use to those trying to understand Ireland because of the complex and fluctuating nature of its political geography in the early sixteenth century (Fig. 4.1).[13] Part of the reason why the Pale, in the east of the country, was well documented was that it was easy to describe in English terms. It was composed of formally established counties and the landholding system was similar to that of England. In Counties Dublin and Meath, there were a large number of small landowners while outside the formally defined Pale, a larger area was dominated by the larger, more feudal lordships of the Anglo-Irish Earls of Kildare and Ormond. A manorial type of economy with an inheritance system based on primogeniture was characteristic of the Pale region. Most of Ireland's principal towns were concentrated along the east and south coasts. Outside the formal Pale, in the areas of Gaelic-Irish influence, the pattern was different. It consisted of small, more or less independent lordships, many of which were in a continual state of fragmentation and reconstruction. Here political and economic power fluctuated in accordance with military might and political boundaries could change with considerable rapidity. Land was not held from a landlord on lease but by freeholders who owed bonds of service and paid duties to an overlord. In these circumstances, genealogies, which Sir William Cecil also collected and annotated, could be of more importance than maps of territories in understanding Irish political realities. By contrast with the eastern part of the country, towns were few and coinage little used. Between these two apparently well-defined areas there was a cultural frontier zone which had contacts with both regions. Thus in the sixteenth century areas such as Longford and Cavan show features of both types of social and political organization.

Trading contacts and maps were not the only sources of knowledge English and Scots men had about Ireland in the sixteenth century. Ireland was a relatively poor economy beside a rich one and the normal migration flow was from Ireland to England. The English Vagrancy Act of 1572 mentioned the Irish migrants, presumably Gaelic-Irish, in England as a special problem. Arrests for vagrancy in England in the late sixteenth century included significant numbers of men originating from Ireland. In London 3 per cent of arrests for vagrancy in 1574–9 were Irish, increasing to 8 per cent in 1604–10 and the proportion was even greater on the west coast of England. Irish names also occur amongst apprentices in sixteenth-century London, demonstrating the existence of a more stable Irish community there.[14] Moreover, throughout the sixteenth century there was also a steady movement of Gaelic-Irish gentry either to the London court or, as with Hugh O'Neill, later Earl of Tyrone, to be educated in the households of English magnates.

Personal knowledge about Irish life and manners was supplemented by a meagre collection of written accounts. Most important of these was Giraldus Cambrensis's *Topographia Hibernicae* written between 1186 and 1189. Edmund Campion noted in his 1571 history of Ireland that Giraldus was 'the only author that ministreth some indifferent furniture to his chronicle and with what search I have been driven to piece the rest by help of foreign writers (incidently touching this realm) by a number of brief extracts of rolls, records and scattered papers'.[15] For those

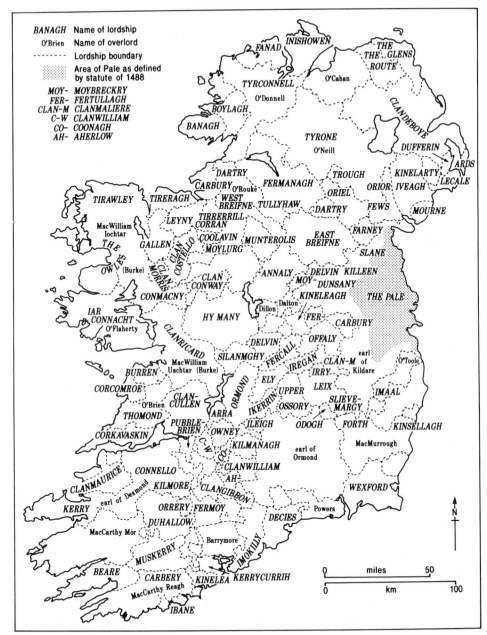

Fig. 4.1. The lordships of Ireland. *c.* 1534. After K. W. Nicholls in T. W. Woody, F. X. Martin and F. J. Byrne (eds.), *A New History of Ireland: III*, (Oxford, 1976), pp. 2–3.

who had no first hand contact with Ireland, the work of Giraldus was the text to which they most often turned for information. The number of manuscript copies made of it in the sixteenth century mushroomed. It was cited in law cases and in the 1569 attainder of Shane O'Neill. In 1609 when Sir John Davies, the Irish attorney general, wanted to present Lord Salisbury with a book on Ireland it was the *Topographia* which he sent.[16] The influence exercised by Giraldus is clear from the number of attacks on him during the late sixteenth and seventeenth centuries. Stephen White, Geoffrey Keating, Richard Stanyhurst, Philip O'Sullivan Beare, Peter Lombard and, most comprehensively, John Lynch all wrote tracts to refute the image which Giraldus had created of the barbarity of the Gaelic-Irish. Conversely his picture was drawn on by hostile seventeenth-century commentators, many of whom had never visited Ireland.

The work of Giraldus was considerably suppplemented in the course of the sixteenth century as other material about Ireland became available. First there were the various analyses sent to the London government by interested parties in Ireland during the sixteenth century. These could take the form of proposals by various lords deputy for the final reconquest of Ireland in the form of a tightly costed programme. The Anglo-Irish of the Pale were also concerned that they should have their views on the government of Ireland heard at the London court. Both groups had a similar aim: to persuade Elizabeth that it was worth asserting English authority over Ireland. One of the main arguments for this was an economic one and the gains to the exchequer were usually spelt out providing details, sometimes more fictitious than factual, about the economic geography of Ireland.[17] Secondly antiquarians in England became increasingly interested in Ireland. The Anglo-Saxon scholar Lawrence Nowell, for instance, was compiling a description of Ireland in 1565 based on materials given to him by Sir William Cecil.[18] By the end of the sixteenth century, it was not possible to produce any sort of respectable work on Britain without at least a description of Ireland. William Camden's *Britannia*, for example, published in 1586 contained a long Irish section. Even if one did not feel competent to write the Irish section of a work, there were always Irish scholars to oblige. The Dubliner Richard Stanyhurst contributed the account of Ireland to Holinshed's Chronicle, and for the 1607 revision of his *Britannia*, Camden used the work of the Jesuit Fr. William Good who had spent time in Limerick during the 1580s.[19]

By 1600 Ireland was a country almost as well known to Europeans as any other in the Old World. America, by contrast was unknown. Thus whereas it was necessary to issue colonizing literature to attract settlers to the emerging American colonies, almost no comparable literature was produced for the settlements in Ireland.[20] Only two tracts could be described as colonizing literature in an Irish context: Barnaby Rich's *New Description of Ireland* (1610) published at the time of the Ulster plantation and Robert Payne's *Description of Ireland* (1589) published after the Munster settlement had been under way for some years. Yet neither of these are colonizing tracts in the way that the examples issued by those promoting the settlement of the Americas were. This highlights a fundamental difference between Ireland and America at the outset of the colonial enterprises. Ireland was an old established society about which a good deal had been known for many years and contacts between Irish men and future settlers were common. America was an unknown quantity. The arrival of John Rolfe's Indian wife at London in 1616 was greeted with great interest by the curious whereas the arrival of an Irishman on the west coast of England in the same year was more likely to have been met with demands for deportation.

Settlement Strategies

These differences between Ireland and the English settlements in the New World had a profound impact on how government viewed the two regions and the solutions they proposed for their development. Ireland was an existing polity which had to be reformed, although men disagreed as to the methods which were required for that reformation. They viewed sixteenth-century Irish society as unstable and they attempted to stabilize and improve it, creating what English social theorists termed a commonwealth. Sir Thomas Smith, the settler of the Ards, Co. Down, in the 1570s, described a commonwealth as 'a society or common doing of a multitude of free men collected together and unto by a common conservation of themselves as well in peace as in war'.[21] The essence of such an institution was order: one king, one law, one religion, one language and an interdependence of master and man so that no one could become what sixteenth-century government most feared; the overmighty subject. According to one early-seventeenth-century commentator, the aim of the English settlement of Ireland was that the Gaelic-Irish would 'grow into a body commoned and into a commonwealth whereas before they wholly consisted of poor proud gentry'.[22] This was to be achieved by the introduction of English law, religion, commercial organization and patterns of landholding. It was expected that cultural barriers, such as language and dress, would disappear as a result of increased interaction between native and newcomer at venues such as markets and schools.

Initial attempts to achieve this improvement by settlement in sixteenth-century Ireland had involved the granting of large areas of territory to individuals, such as Sir Thomas Smith in the Ards and the Earl of Essex in County Antrim. In theory such individuals would lead the way in promoting English civility but the quality of the settlers, as in Virginia, left much to be desired and these settlements had little long-term impact.[23] From the 1580s the approach changed and the government took a direct interest in the formulation of plantation schemes and the allocation of land. Elaborate codes were constructed for the plantations of Munster and Ulster and for the seventeenth-century settlements in the midlands (Figs. 4.2 and 4.3). The social structure of the settlements was set out in the requirements for specific numbers of freeholders and leaseholders and the relationships between the settlers were to be determined by law and set out in leases. The plans for plantation included conditions relating to the creation of towns, including markets, and requirements for a building programme of castles to be carried out by the settlers. The settlers were also expected to follow English agricultural practices. While such schemes were easy to prepare they were much more difficult to implement. The population of any estate in the plantation of Ulster was determined not so much by the demands of government as by the distance of that estate from a port, the landlord's leasing policy and the opportunity for profit.

Similarly, while it was easy to instruct settlers to pursue English-style agricultural practices and to grow grain, such activities could prove totally unsuited to the Ulster or Munster environment and were quickly abandoned in favour of cattle raising. Plantation schemes as such were of less importance than other social and economic factors in shaping the landscapes and society of formally planted regions. Thus, for instance, the most successfully developed part of early-seven-

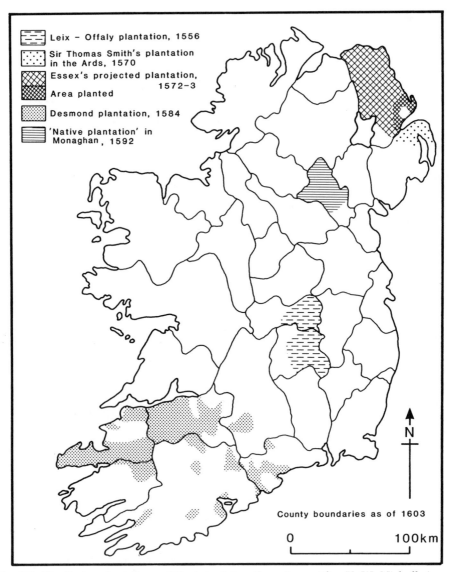

Fig. 4.2. The Tudor plantations of the late sixteenth century. After K. W. Nicholls in Moody, Martin and Byrne (eds.), *A New History of Ireland: III*, p. 77.

teenth-century Ulster was not the formally planted areas but the two eastern counties of Antrim and Down which lay nearest to Scotland and hence were most accessible for settlers.[24]

The London government showed no such direct interest in the shaping of settler society in the American colonies. The charters of Virginia, for instance, assigned the functions of government to the Virginia Company. Virginia codified its own laws and there emerged significant differences from the common law of England. In effect each of the colonies established its own form of government, and each met with varying degrees of success.[25] In colonial New England, the religious ethos of

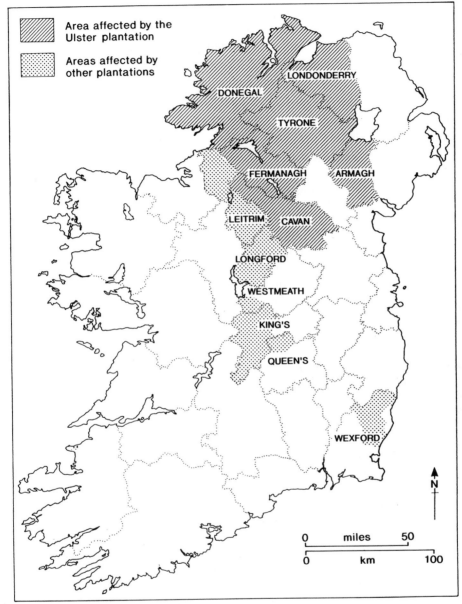

Fig. 4.3. Plantations between 1609 and 1625. After Aidan Clarke in Moody, Martin and Byrne (eds.), *A New History of Ireland: III*, p. 220.

that settlement produced a novel set of legal documents, notably the town charters, which in their content and terms had no Irish parallel. In the case of Lord Baltimore's grant of Maryland and, to a lesser extent, the grant of Pennsylvania to William Penn, near absolute powers were granted to the landlord. Royal policy meant that no settler in Ireland could ever aspire to similar grants. Not until Bacon's rebellion drew attention to the dangers of this position in the mid-1670s was any attempt made to modify the situation.[26] These contrasts illustrate the divergent approach of the London government to the problems of settling the two regions. The social structures of Gaelic Ireland, regarded by the London government as inherently unstable, were to be stabilized and modified under the direct control of the London administration from the late sixteenth century. British America, by contrast, was to be dealt with at arm's length until the late seventeenth century.

Colonial Economic Enterprise

In the context of improved information about Ireland and colonial America, inhabitants of the Old World began to perceive the advantages of settlement in both regions. The picture which had been presented by Giraldus in the *Topographia* of an Ireland where 'the land is fruitful and rich in its fertile soil and plentiful harvests' had been more than confirmed by the sixteenth-century descriptions of the island.[27] There was now added evidence of mineral and fishing wealth, both of which were being exploited by foreigners. The late sixteenth century had seen an expansion of trade between Ireland and England which further confirmed the existence of natural resources in Ireland which could be profitably exploited. The trade in Irish yarn to Liverpool, for instance, grew from 356 packs in 1565–6 to 1555 packs in 1593–4 and wool exports to Liverpool over the same period increased by almost 140 per cent.[28] The timber trade, destined to be an important source of wealth at a time when woodland was becoming scarce in England, also expanded dramatically from the 1550s. In addition to these well known resources there were also rumours of others: for example gold, silver and other minerals were supposed to be abundant in Ireland.

What made these resources seem even more attractive was that the indigenous populations of both Ireland and the New World seemed uninterested in their exploitation. Population levels were low in relation to the available resources in both regions. In Ireland there were some areas of high population density, notably parts of the Pale, where in the late sixteenth century the competition was for land rather than tenants, but this was the exception rather than the rule. The south and west of the country seem to have been reasonably well populated to judge from the returns of composition rent in Connacht in the early 1590s and the 1586 survey for the Munster plantation. However, English contemporaries regarded these areas as underpopulated even by their standards. Population was lowest in Ulster and there was a movement of tenants from the Pale to settle waste areas in south Ulster in the 1580s. While population was probably rising over the sixteenth century as a whole, specific crises such as the Desmond rebellion (1579–83) and the Nine Years War (1594–1603) undoubtedly had a deleterious effect on population, not only from war deaths but also from an increase in migration from Munster to continental Europe and southern Britain.[29]

Secondly, the Gaelic-Irish population in Ireland and the Indian population of the New World seemed uninterested in commercial exploitation of resources because their social structures did not encourage such activities. The concept of the market was poorly developed. The income of a Gaelic-Irish lord was usually received not in money rents but in the form of entertainment or food and the main social bond was not that of landlord and tenant but of warlord and follower. Society was organized around consumption rather than capital investment. One consequence of this was a skill shortage in sixteenth-century Ireland since producers were regarded as of a low social status. The pardons issued to the 990 followers of O'Connor Sligo at the end of the Nine Years War (1594–1603) included only 26 craftsmen but recorded 311 soldiers of various types and 335 agricultural workers, most of the rest having no designation.[30] Gaelic Ireland was a society articulated by warfare and feuding and those who did not take part were marginalized. The shortage of manufacturing skills is also demonstrated by the fact that wool and linen yarn were among the main exports of Dublin in 1611 while woollen and linen cloth were among the main imports. The Irish economy did not have the necessary skill to process its own raw materials. There were attempts to improve this situation. The Irish Parliament of 1569–71 did develop a strategy for improving Irish manufactures by increasing customs duties on exports of raw materials in the hope that it would encourage domestic manufactures and employ 'idle men'. This seems to have had some short-term effect but in the longer term it was not significant.[31] There still remained considerable economic opportunities in Ireland and in colonial America for those prepared to take the risk of settling there.

Migrants' Motives

As evidence increased from both Ireland and the New World of the opportunities available there, so those in the Old World became more restricted. By the late sixteenth century, for example, the Elizabethan religious settlement was proving not to be the universal compromise some had hoped for. Those who came to believe that the Godly nation could not be created in an English context looked elsewhere for another. Religion was to prove a key factor in promoting migration to New England and Pennsylvania. Ireland offered considerably less opportunity for the creation of a Godly commonwealth although some English Catholics migrated to Munster to escape the eye of the London government.[32] In general those who left England or Scotland for America did so to escape an oppressive environment, seeking freedom to build a new society based on their own religious, economic and social beliefs while those who came to Ireland had no such desire as they entered into a society similar to that which they had left. The trans-Atlantic journey needed considerably more commitment than crossing the Irish Sea.[33]

The rather peculiar nature of the New England settlement is reflected in the geography of its recruitment. The New England migrants were drawn mainly from south-east England: Norfolk, Suffolk, Kent and Essex. There was a smaller centre for migrants in Somerset, Dorset and Wiltshire. Conversely, these areas played a relatively small part in the settlement of Ireland with only a small group of men from Norfolk moving to Fermanagh. Rather, it was the area from which New England drew the fewest number of settlers which was to be more important for the settlement of Ireland and the remainder of British North America. Virginia, for example, drew most of its settlers from south-west England as did the Munster settlement. Ulster also attracted men from the south-west. Northern

England, especially Lancashire, Cheshire, Yorkshire, together with Nottingham-shire, provided the bulk of the settlers for the Delaware valley and especially Pennsylvania. Ulster also attracted many settlers from these regions of England, especially in the later seventeenth century. The main source for the Ulster settlers throughout the century was south-west Scotland, and it was migrants from there who also established themselves in the middle colonies of North America. In the 1680s the first Scottish colony in America was established in east and central New Jersey, later to be absorbed in the royal colony of New Jersey in 1702.[34] Colonial America also tended to draw its settlers from a wider geographical region of the Old World than Ireland did. The settlers in Ireland during the seventeenth cen-tury tended to be mainly English, Scottish or Welsh although there were some Dutch, and later in the century, Huguenots, but these were a minority. In Amer-ica, outside New England, which tended to remain English in ethos and settler origin, there was, for example a body of German, Dutch, French, Walloons and a few Swedes, to say nothing of the African slave population, interspersed with the English settlers.[35]

The factors which caused men to settle in Ireland or colonial America tended to vary from region to region. In some cases, religion was important, but more commonly the motivation for migration was economic. Settlers were drawn from a wide social range in both Ireland and America. However, the push factors from Britain and the pull of rapid social mobility in Ireland or America did produce a socially selective process. It was generally not the wealthiest of each social group who moved but those anxious for advancement or those concerned to reverse declining fortunes. As Sir Arthur Chichester, the lord deputy, commented on those Ulster planters who arrived in 1610, 'those from England are for the most part plain country gentlemen ... if they have any money they keep it close for hitherto they have disbursed little ... The Scottish come with greater part and better accompanied, but it may be with less money in their purses'.[36] Most of these settlers had little in the way of the surplus capital necessary to set up new settle-ments to the standard which the London government or the Companies envis-aged. While the Irish settlers, with the exception of the London Companies in County Londonderry, had to rely on their own wealth, the Virginia and New England Companies could, like the Londonderry settlement, count on wider sources of funding through the moneys raised by the Companies from speculative investors. There were links between the investors in both regions in that some of those subscribing to the American companies were also Irish settlers. Their specu-lation in the New World was motivated by the same hope of profit which brought them to Ireland.[37]

Migration was the main dynamic of the population growth in both Ireland and colonial America throughout the seventeenth century although its importance declined towards the end of the century in some regions. All estimates of popu-lation, especially in rapidly growing colonial situations, must be very tentative but while numbers remain elusive the trend is clear. Between 1600 and 1641, the Irish population increased from about 1.4 million to about 2.1 million or about 1 per cent per annum. The growth rates varied regionally. Munster's settler population grew faster than that of Ulster, growing from about 5000 in 1611 to almost 22,000 by 1641, while in Ulster there were about 15,000 settlers in the 1630s when the population

was at its pre-rebellion peak.[38] Much of this early settlement was landlord sponsored. Landlords tried to attract suitable tenants to stock their newly acquired
estates. From the 1660s the influence of landlords in directing the settlement
declined and in Ulster at any rate, the pattern of settlement seems to have been
dictated more by economic opportunity and communications. This meant that it
was the areas in the immediate hinterlands of the main ports of entry to Ulster that
were most heavily settled and lands which were more difficult of access tended to
be settled later and much more thinly.[39]

The fact that the migrants to both Ireland and the New World were drawn from
fairly well-defined regions of the British Isles to fairly well-defined settlements
meant that local traditions could be translated to the country of settlement. In
many cases traditions were modified in the migration process and adapted to the
new environment. In Ireland, for example, the settlers quickly adopted many
Gaelic-Irish agricultural practices such as ploughing by attaching the plough to the
horse's tail. Similarly, for environmental and other reasons, the agricultural tradition of Ulster was more akin to that of Scotland than the arable, wheat-growing
tradition of lowland England which developed in Munster. This does not mean
that the Ulster economy was in any way inferior to that of Munster, although such
a case was argued by contemporaries. In fact the economic indicators such as the
burden of taxation and the scale of trade suggest that the Ulster and Munster
economies may have been on a par by the late seventeenth century.[40]

Changing Patterns of Landownership

It was not only regional characteristics which the settlers brought to their respective new worlds. They also brought a revolutionary attitude to land ownership and
its use. In the sixteenth century, the economies of Ulster, most of Connacht, parts
of the midlands and most of the south-west of Ireland, and the social arrangements
on which they rested, could be described as 'redistributive' in character. This
meant that land was not held by landlords for rent but was carved up among
numerous freeholders who owed bonds of allegiance and tributes to greater lords.
Allegiances were often changed. Surpluses generated by freeholders were not sold
through markets but given to lords who recirculated them in the form of guesting
and feasting. Thus Gaelic-Irish society, like that of the American Indians, was held
together by ties of obligation with few market structures and a man's place in
society was determined by his genealogy and the number of his followers, rather
than by the contracts he entered into. Of course the economy of the lordship was
not totally self-contained. Gaelic-Irish lords did trade to obtain goods such as salt
and wine which were were not produced within Ireland. This trade was not
necessarily conducted by a network of merchants through the main port towns but
often directly through local creeks and havens. Individual lords and Gaelic Irishmen did know about coinage and its relative values. Nor was the strength of these
social ideas uniform throughout the sixteenth century. Gaelic society was changing
rapidly during the sixteenth century independently from the processes of plantation and colonization with results similar to those produced by settlement.[41]

By contrast the economic system operated by the early modern British settlers in

Ireland and the Anglo-Irish of the Pale depended on the market for the redistribution of surpluses at a price governed by supply and demand. One cohesive force in
this society was wholesale trade mediated through a series of local markets and
possibly extending through a hierarchy of towns into the world of international
commerce. Land was held from the king in large blocks by landlords who gave it to
tenants under certain conditions for a fixed period of time in return for a price—the
rent. This system of property rights was underpinned by a legal code, the common
law, which regulated land ownership, customs duties and market rights, for
instance. However, as with the Gaelic system, this framework of land ownership
and economic life did not operate in a pure form. Bonds of neighbourliness,
controls by the church and the guilds, and the shortage of suitable tenants all
prevented the full rigour of the market from operating.

The late sixteenth and early seventeenth centuries saw a marked shift in the
balance between these two economic systems in Ireland with the market becoming
dominant. The local trading rights of Gaelic lords and the trading prerogatives of
the towns, derived from their charters, were broken down, leaving merchants free
to trade over the whole island. In terms of economic structures, the division
between Gaelic and Old English areas of influence became less clear cut. The
emergence of an estate system encouraged the growth of an active land market and
the Old English of the Pale, together with urban merchants, took full advantage of
this to acquire extensive estates for themselves especially in the midlands and
west. At least some Gaelic-Irish landholders who failed to come to terms with the
new system either sold land or mortgaged it with little hope of redeeming the
mortgages. It was this process, almost as much as plantation, which caused a
dramatic fall in Catholic landownership in seventeenth-century Ireland. It was not
that the Gaelic and Gaelicized Irish were incapable of adapting to changed economic structures. Hugh O'Neill, Earl of Tyrone, was already modernizing his lands
at the end of the sixteenth century as were the Earls of Clanricard and Thomond in
Connacht.[42] Rather it was the pace of change which led to problems for most of the
elite from the old order who could not transform their followers into tenants. It is
clear that the rate of spread of these new ideas was very uneven. Some areas, such
as Mayo, were slow to adopt the new standards of wealth measurement and so
from being a relatively wealthy area under one set of perceptions, became poor
under a different economic system.[43]

A New Landscape

The replacement of a Gaelic lordship economy by an English-style market economy
had a significant impact on both the landscape and ecology.[44] Land was managed
in new commercially profitable ways, often by stripping significant amounts of
woodland. Land was valued as an asset, the limits of which had to be defined and
managed carefully. Boundaries, hitherto fluid, had to be more carefully delineated,
especially when population was growing fast and land being leased in large units.
The early seventeenth century saw a considerable increase in the body of Irish law
governing land ownership, and the beginnings of the rise of accurate surveying
techniques and the making of the estate maps. Landlords used existing property

terminology, such as the townland, gneeve or treen, in leases to smooth the transition from one system of landholding to another, but these had to be more clearly defined by detailed written descriptions or by estate maps. Estate maps, such as those made by Thomas Raven for the Clandeboy estate in County Down and the Essex estate in Monaghan, became an essential part of estate management.[45] One other consequence of the rise of a market economy was urbanization. Although this is difficult to measure, its most obvious manifestation was the development of the port towns. Belfast and Derry were new creations of the settlement process, eclipsing the older north-eastern port of Carrickfergus. In the south, Cork more than doubled in size between 1600 and 1641 and its main outports, Kinsale and Youghal, grew even more dramatically. It was Dublin which saw the fastest growth during the seventeenth century as a whole and it attracted a growing proportion of the trade of the island over the century. It is much less easy to show how the many smaller towns which developed in the seventeenth century were established and grew. One very crude measure is the authorizations granted to hold markets and fairs. Between 1600 and 1649 over 500 grants were made in Ireland authorizing the holding of markets and another 130 were made between 1660 and 1690. In addition there were 503 fairs operating in Ireland in 1684. Many of these grants in the areas of Anglo-Irish settlement were regrants of medieval grants to hold markets or fairs. Not all of these grants resulted in the establishment of markets and even when established, markets did not necessarily mean towns. Nevertheless, numerous sites of these grants were centres of population density in the 1660 poll tax (see Fig. 12.6).

Over the seventeenth century as a whole there was a tendency towards centralization of specialist economic activity in Dublin. The growth of banking and insurance services there in the early eighteenth century points to the beginnings of a national economy. By 1700, over 80 per cent of the fine Ulster linen trade was being carried on through Dublin since the city had the specialist skills to support such a luxury trade. Other important regional centres, especially Cork, also emerged but these were not able to provide the range of services offered in Dublin. There are further indications of the evolution of a national economic network in Ireland. These include the development of a nationally accepted system of weights and measures and the growth of interregional trade.[46]

Changing Trade Patterns

Changing ideas about property and other rights led to an increased role for the market in the redistribution of resources within both Ireland and colonial America. One immediate result of this was a trade boom in both countries. In Ireland it is possible to measure this by analysing the quantity of Irish goods imported at English ports such as Chester, one of the main destination ports for Irish exports to England. In the late 1580s, somewhere between 25 and 60 dickers of hides (a parcel of 10 hides) were landed at Chester from Ireland each year. By 1639 this had grown to 1289 dickers. Sixteenth-century Irish tallow exports to Chester had peaked in 1592–3 at 50 hundredweight but in 1639, 619 hundredweight was being landed there. More spectacular was the growth in wool exports from between 100 and 200 stone in the late 1580s to 6666 stone in 1639. However, the success story of the seventeenth-century Irish export trade was the export of live cattle, which rose from almost no shipments in the sixteenth century to 15,000 beasts a year in the late 1630s. This was not a phenomenon evident at Chester alone. In 1640, 45,000 live cattle from Ireland were landed in England and somewhere between 1.5 and 2 million sheep, in various forms, were sent from Ireland to England.[47] Colonial American exports to England expanded from a base of zero in the middle of the sixteenth century to an annual value of almost a million pounds by the middle of the eighteenth century.[48]

The changes in the volume of trade were rather more significant than the changes in its structure, or indeed the structure of the economy as a whole. About half of the total Irish export trade in 1615–16 comprised cattle and cattle products. Grain exports stood at 6 per cent. While grain and cattle had not featured prominently in the records of sixteenth-century trade, they had been staples of the sixteenth-century domestic economy. Penal customs duties on grain had discouraged its export but cattle hides had been an important element in sixteenth-century trade.[49] Fishing, especially pilchards from Munster, continued to be of considerable importance. Pilchard exports trebled between 1616 and 1625 but fell off in the late 1630s. The timber trade, growing from the 1550s, expanded especially rapidly in the early seventeenth century but this was a short-lived growth. By the late 1630s, the best timber, that used for pipestaves, was almost exhausted. Areas such as the Bann valley in Ulster, the Slaney valley in south Leinster and the Blackwater and Bandon valleys in Munster were rapidly denuded of timber. Wool and woollen products which had also featured prominently in the sixteenth-century economy were one of the staples of the early-seventeenth-century economy. Wool exports, especially from Munster, rose dramatically in the early seventeenth century to supply the English clothiers. The amount of raw wool leaving Youghal, for example, rose from 4378 stones in 1616 to 15,716 by 1625. New items in recorded seventeenth-century trade included iron, which was exported in modest quantities throughout the early seventeenth century. This was not to be a lasting development. The rapid clearance of timber from the Irish countryside deprived the iron furnaces of their source of fuel and the local Irish iron ore was of poor quality resulting in a mediocre product which was difficult to market. Profits from iron working were small in comparison to those which could be made in agriculture or landholding. Richard Boyle, the first Earl of Cork, expended £70,000 on his iron works between 1607 and 1643 but received only £95,000 in return. Attempts to set up a clothing trade in Munster also failed because of shortages of capital and because technical problems, such as the supply of fuller's earth for finishing, could not be overcome.

Colonial Trade

In some ways the American trade was similar to that of Ireland since it also specialized in the export of raw unprocessed goods.[50] New England had little to offer in the way of agricultural potential. Initially furs were important but by the middle of the seventeenth century, this trade was on the wane and it had begun to move north to Canada. Fish, from the Newfoundland Banks, remained a staple in the New England economy throughout the century. Sugar from the Caribbean islands formed another key element in the Atlantic trade. However, by far the most important element in the colonial trade was tobacco from the Chesapeake colonies of Maryland and Virginia. In 1620 119,000 pounds of tobacco were exported but by 1700 some 36 million pounds were being exported annually.[51] There were some domestic manufactures. Pennsylvania, for example, had small-scale iron working but none of this was exported. Textiles for local use were produced throughout the colonies but were not traded to any great extent, most demand being met by imports.

The reasons for this similarity in the structure of the Irish and American econ-omies were almost identical: a shortage of capital and skilled labour. The easy availability of land in both regions and the demand for settlers discouraged the growth of urban craft industries since there were larger profits to be made on the land. Indeed it was almost impossible to establish towns in areas such as the Chesapeake since any settlement broke up almost immediately as settlers moved into the countryside to engage in the profitable tobacco trade.[52] The socially selec-tive processes of migration to both regions encouraged those with little capital to move to the newly opened up areas but this lack of capital restricted their scope for improving and developing any holdings they acquired. The possibilities for bor-rowing were also limited by the crude nature of the financial systems which evolved in both areas during the early years of settlement. Since land was cheap in both British America and Ireland, the main sources of loans in pre-industrial societies, merchants, lawyers and clergy, were more prepared to invest in land themselves than make loans for others to do so. As a result, demand for money was high and supply low. Consequently, penal interest rates, up to 30 or 40 per cent per annum, were not uncommon.[53] This situation was exacerbated by the monetary arrangements in both regions. Neither Ireland nor British America, for example, had a mint and therefore had no local control over their money supply. An adequate supply of coin was dependent on a favourable balance of trade. Given the rapid expansion in trade, an equally rapid expansion in the money supply was necessary to fund this. To meet this problem colonial America, especially New England, developed a complex network of book credits in order to ensure that trade ran smoothly.[54]

Conversely there were differences between the economic organization of Ireland and British America which were to be important for the future. The development of a merchant marine and the accompanying merchant community is a case in point. In the main, Irish trade was carried on by foreign merchants in foreign ships. By 1698, for example, two-thirds of the tonnage of ships engaged in the Irish trade with England was English. This had also been the case in the late sixteenth century when one commentator noted 'there be many merchants of staple in the country whereof the most were buyers and the smallest number shippers'. Those who operated as merchants in Ireland were, in the main, little more than shopkeepers or men who shipped one or two small cargoes a year. Contemporaries were scathing in their comments about Irish merchants. One writer in 1683 observed 'the merchants generally throughout the kingdom drive a peddling trade upon credit, having not stock of their own'.[55] This apparent poverty of the Irish merchants was in part the result of the easy availability of Irish land at low rates in which merchants were keen to invest. Thus the wealthy merchant did not remain in trade for long but joined the ranks of the landowners. It was only in the latter part of the seventeenth century when land values increased significantly that many merchants were prompted to remain in towns, thus allowing resident mercantile communities to develop. The implications of this for the pattern of trade were considerable. Since Ireland had almost no independent merchant marine, it became part of a wider European trading network. Dutch and Spanish ships, for example, added Ireland as another port of call on voyages which could visit four or five ports, buying and selling goods on the way. Dutch shipmasters could buy salt in France which would then be sold in Ireland for pipestaves which could then be sold elsewhere. In the late seventeenth century at least some of the Irish exports to England were re-exported to continental destinations. This European network for Irish trade is in sharp contrast to the American experience. America did not fit neatly into pre-existing patterns of Old World trade. Initially the colonies had to establish their own shipping fleets and merchant communities. New England, for instance, had developed a substantial merchant marine and there was a large merchant community in Boston in particular. By 1700 the merchant fleet of New England, excluding fishing vessels, exceeded 2000 ships. In Philadelphia by the end of the seventeenth century, the Quaker community had become legendary for its wealth and its success in trading, especially in the Caribbean trade which had been exploited to generate considerable wealth for the Philadelphia merchants generally.[56]

Perhaps the most dramatic difference between Ireland, America and Great Britain was the experience of the 1640s and 1650s. In demographic terms the Irish war of the 1640s and the uncertainty of the 1650s was disastrous. The outbreak of plague in the early 1650s was significant regionally, especially in towns such as Dublin. Sir William Petty estimated that at the height of the outbreak 1300 people (perhaps 3 per cent of the city's population) were dying in Dublin each week. In Ulster a comparison of the surnames on the 1630 muster roll with the names on the hearth money rolls of the 1660s suggests a turnover of population of more than 50 per cent and in some areas as much as 80 per cent.[57] The disruption of war in both England and Ireland caused a dramatic reduction in Irish trade with England which had severe dislocating effects throughout the economy. The trade of Dublin, in particular, which accounted for about one-third of Irish customs revenue in the 1630s, ground to a halt before the seizure of the port by the Cromwellians in 1647. The principal effect of the war in England on the New England economy was in the fall in demand for colonial exports. This was compensated for by an expanding Caribbean trade which formed an increasingly important part of the colonial trade in the late seventeeth century and provided a source of silver coin from Jamaica.[58]

The economic and social structure of Ireland had to be rebuilt in the 1650s whereas that of colonial America experienced little in the way of disruption. The distance separating the Old World and the New and the different basis of the relationships between native and newcomer isolated the political priorities of the New World from those of the Old. One consequence of that isolation was that colonial America was not as rapidly exposed to the new ideas which emerged in

England and Ireland in the 1650s on the organization of the economy and society. Men such as William Petty, Myles Symner and the Boate brothers all brought to Ireland new ways of developing the economy. These were prompted by the new scientific ideas emerging in England in the mid-seventeenth century but such influential figures had few contemporary American counterparts.[59]

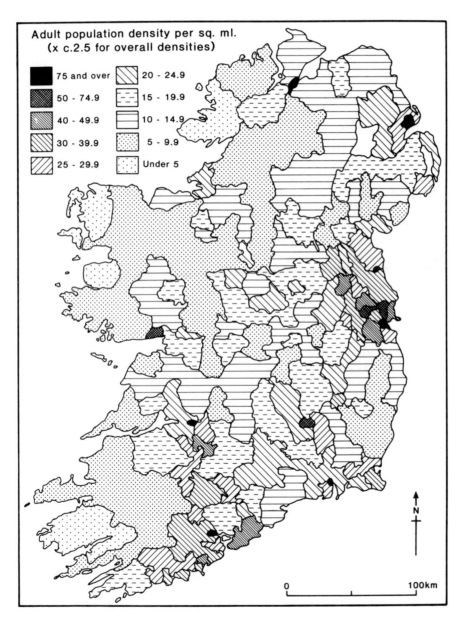

Fig. 4.4. Adult population distribution in 1660. After Smyth, 'Settlement and Society', in Smyth and Whelan (eds.), *Common Ground*, p. 57.

Population Trends in the Later Seventeenth Century

In the later part of the seventeenth century there is evidence for a significant shift in the balance between population and resources within Ireland. The population in late-seventeenth-century Ireland grew faster than it had done earlier in the century (Fig. 4.4). Estimates must remain tentative but population probably increased from about 1.7 million in 1672 to about 2.8 million by 1712, an annual growth rate of 1.26 per cent per annum.[60] This places Ireland midway between the demographic experiences of colonial America and the demographic regime of Europe. In Virginia, for instance, migration into the Chesapeake was running at between 120,000 to 130,000 people over the whole of the later seventeenth century although this is not reflected in the overall population growth rates because of the high death rates arising from unfavourable climatic conditions. In west New Jersey, Pennsylvania and the Delaware valley, the annual growth rate was 10.7 per cent per annum between 1670 and 1710, largely because of the low population base in 1670. Less dramatic was the growth rate of the population of the older settlement of New England but even there population managed to grow by about 2.7 per cent per annum.[61] Such rates of increase were incredible in a European context, where the late-seventeenth-century demographic regime was distinctly unfavourable. The rapid population growth of the late sixteenth and early seventeenth centuries had slowed to almost zero and in some regions population had begun to fall. The Mediterranean regions of Spain and Italy were worst affected but the main sources for Irish migrants, England and Scotland, also experienced a slowdown in population growth. The English population, for instance, remained almost stable, showing only a 2 per cent fall between 1660 and 1700. Estimates for Scotland are somewhat more problematical but a population estimate of one million in 1700 is not significantly different from the probable population in the late sixteenth century.[62]

Given the equation between population size and power made by most political economists in the seventeenth century, it is not surprising that emigration came to be viewed unfavourably. It was actively discouraged by the London government in the later seventeenth century. As one English commentator, Carew Reynolds, observed in 1674,

> 'The country complains of small vend of commodities which proceeds essentially from want of people, for people were consumed mightly in these late years ... two hundred thousand more have been wasted in repeopling Ireland'.[63]

While Reynolds' estimates are too high, it is clear that despite official discouragement there was significant immigration into Ireland in the late seventeenth century. The effect of that immigration varied regionally. Where large-scale immigration occurred it seems to have been the main engine of population change with natural increase, though significant, lagging behind. Population growth in Ulster was much more marked than in Munster since it was Ulster which experienced most of the late-seventeenth-century immigration. The lack of enthusiasm for emigration in England, the main source of Munster's settlers, had curbed population growth there. Meanwhile in Scotland, the Covenanter disturbances and the severe harvest failures of the 1690s ensured erratic bursts of migration to Ulster despite disapproval from the administration in Edinburgh.[64]

Although migration continued to be significant in some regions in Ireland as a whole before 1700, the dynamic of population growth was moving away from immigration towards natural increase. While little demographic evidence, such as parish registers, has survived for the late seventeenth century, the Quakers in Ireland did keep good registers of births, marriages and burials which can go some way to remedying this deficiency. The Quaker records suggest that between 1650 and 1699 Irish Quaker women married earlier than their English counterparts, providing a longer childbearing period with resulting higher fertility rates. Quaker infant mortality seems to have been lower in Ireland than in England and life expectancy was about two years longer in Ireland than in England.[65] This impression is supported by other evidence on age at marriage from non-Quaker women.[66] There is also confirmation of this picture from one of the few surviving parish registers, that for Blaris, Co. Antrim, where the number of baptisms each year in the late seventeenth century was three times the number of burials.[67] Low death rates may be explained in terms of an improved diet in the seventeenth century combined with the relatively few instances of plague during the century.[68]

Natural increase in colonial America remained of lesser importance than immigration throughout the late seventeenth century. While American women, like their Irish counterparts, tended to marry younger than in contemporary Europe and although the incidence of marriage was also higher, the American population was unlike Ireland in that it had a male surplus. This arose from the selective nature of the migration. While migration to Ireland was more akin to internal migration in England with only short distances involved, and with families often travelling together, the move to America was a considerably greater undertaking with the migrants being predominantly young males. Death rates among migrants were considerably higher in some regions of America. While the Irish environment was similar to that of Britain and perhaps healthier in some respects since plague could be kept out by its maritime location, many areas in colonial America, such as the Chesapeake, were environmentally different to England. Fatal diseases in these regions were endemic until immunity had been built up but such a process only took place over several generations.[69] Thus high death rates in these areas served to check natural growth rates and immigration remained the main dynamic of population growth.

Reactions to Population Change

In demographic terms late-seventeenth-century Ireland lay somewhere between the Old World and the New. Population rose faster than in the Old World but considerably slower than in colonial America where immigration continued at a high level. Reactions to demographic change were therefore different in each of these regions. Contemporary theorists in England, for instance, were concerned with the impact of falling population on the labour supply for agriculture, and they turned to the more efficient use of the available resources to maintain output levels. In particular, enclosures were used more extensively to increase the efficiency of agriculture. Products with a high added value were encouraged and this promoted the spread of manufactures. Such intensive measures were not necessary in colonial America. There the ratio of labour to land was so low that it was possible to continue to settle new areas. One English commentator in 1674 stressed this almost limitless supply of land as the main attraction of colonial America. 'What makes New England, Jamaica and the plantations abroad increase so fast', he observed 'but because they have employment and estates for all people and no poor among them which encourages people to come from abroad and their own people to marry and get children'.[70] The Virginian problem was not an oversupply of labour but a dramatic undersupply. To resolve this they turned to indentured servants and later to the importation of slaves. In New England, where the settlement was older and the settlement pattern better developed, the solution to the problem of a rapidly growing population was different. The first two generations accommodated themselves by subdivision of land but by the later seventeenth century this had become impractical, and the colony began to expand territorially down the Connecticut river valley and southward to the New York boundary.[71]

The solutions adopted in colonial America to accommodate an expanding population were not practicable in Ireland. The early seventeenth century had seen the whole of Ireland carved up into great estates. Leases, often of large areas for long terms, were granted to settlers. There was, for tenurial reasons, little unallocated land to expand into by the 1660s. The only option was subdivision. Also, unlike America, the natural resources of Ireland, such as timber and iron, had been worked to the point of exhaustion by the later seventeenth century. The profitable use of natural resources had also been curtailed in other ways. The export of live cattle, for instance, had been prohibited under the Cattle Acts of 1663 and 1667. Emigration provided one short-term solution to the problem of accommodating an increasing population on limited resources. In particular, the expanding economy of the Caribbean provided an outlet for those in Ireland who saw their opportunities restricted at home. By 1660, for example, 20 per cent of the population of the Barbados was Irish in origin. Ulster-based Presbyterians began to show an interest in the New World by the 1680s and a substantial movement took place between Munster and America. The scale and chronology of the emigration from Ireland is impossible to determine but the Quaker records, while providing only a small sample, are suggestive. These show 39 Quakers leaving Ireland for Pennsylvania in the 1680s of whom 16 were from Ulster and five from Munster. The movement slowed down in the 1690s with only three Quakers leaving Ireland but in the first decade of the eighteenth century, 26 Quakers left Ireland for Pennsylvania.[72]

While emigration was a short-term expedient it was clearly not a solution to the problems created by a changing balance between population and resources in Ireland. Throughout the late seventeenth century, contemporaries became increasingly worried about the problem of poverty and attempts were made to draft a suitable Irish poor law.[73] The problem was caused, in part, by the ever increasing population which the island was required to support but there were other factors also. The taxation demands of central government grew significantly in the later part of the century. In the earlier part of the century taxation had been levied sporadically but from the 1660s regular taxes such as the hearth tax, which required regular payments from Irish householders, were introduced. Such taxation demands did not come at a propitious time for Irish economic development.[74] Prices for agricultural produce as a whole were falling during the late seventeenth century. While a decline in food prices certainly gave wage earners greater discretionary expenditure, it meant that primary producers had to rely on increasing volumes of output to ensure that income remained the same. In part this was self-defeating since increasing volumes of output drove prices down further. In 1686 and 1687, for instance, two exceptionally good harvests drove prices down to unrealistic levels which resulted in the economic collapse which underlay the political crisis of 1688–89.

From the later part of the seventeenth century, landlords began to consider ways of diversifying the economy of their estates to ensure that tenants would be able to pay their rent, which was the principal source of landlord income. The income of tenants in the early seventeenth century had been derived from sales of agricultural produce. With falling agricultural prices in the late seventeenth century the income of agricultural producers looked increasingly uncertain. In addition rent levels in the most heavily settled areas were rising as a result of increased demand for land, and in an effort to maximize incomes, landlords increasingly subdivided their estates. Faced with the prospects of higher rent and falling incomes the possibility of default on rent payments was a real one. The main way in which landlords tried to counter this problem was to encourage with renewed vigour the growth of craft industry and the diversification of production on their holdings. The encouragement of fishing on Sir William Petty's estates in Kerry was done 'forasmuch it will be an employment to the people who otherwise would be trouble to pay the rent'.[75] The types of ventures which were promoted varied widely throughout the country. Some landlords tried to promote maufactures on their estates, most importantly linen. Arthur Brownlow at Lurgan, Co. Armagh, encouraged the manufacture of fine linens by promising to buy up all the linens brought to the market, thus providing a guaranteed sale until the trade became established. In the 1690s the Earl of Abercorn promoted spinning and weaving competitions on his estate to boost the linen trade at Strabane.[76] These developments were not confined to Ulster. The Duke of Ormond attempted to establish a linen manufactory at Chapelizod near Dublin by bringing in skilled Dutch weavers. At Carrick-on-Suir, Co. Tipperary, and Callan, Co. Kilkenny, he tried to establish woollen cloth production centres in the same way. One of the most sophisticated of these projects was that of the Earl of Orrery at Charleville, Co. Cork. He encouraged Dutch and French weavers to the town, provided capital to set up a linen industry and tried to set up a joint stock company, the Merchant Adventurers of Munster, to market the goods.[77]

Landlord activities were not confined to manufactures. They also encouraged tenants to diversify their output to fill the vacuum created by the ending of the live cattle trade. These efforts by landlords were complemented by Irish price movements.[78] Late-seventeenth-century price movements favoured butter and wool over cattle and beef which certainly prompted increased production of these items, although there had been a trend in this direction even before the passage of the Cattle Acts. One development which was promoted by these changes in the structure of the Irish economy was the growth of regional specialization. The live cattle trade which had dominated the early-seventeenth-century economy was unspecialized. The rise of the butter and provisions trade, based on barrelled beef, meant greater regional specialization was required to ensure that the most appropriate land was used for each activity. East Connacht and the midlands soon developed as fattening regions with breeding being done on poorer lands. The marginal quality lands of Westmeath, Limerick, Clare and Roscommon emerged as the centre of the wool producing region. Commercial dairying became established in the hinterlands of the major Ulster ports and in south-east Ireland.[79]

Most fundamentally these new developments were dependent on the development of an adequate internal marketing system and the identification of new foreign markets into which these goods could be sold. Contemporaries were well aware of this and as Sir John Perceval commented of Kanturk, Co. Cork, in 1681, 'the place is capeable of a woollen manufacture. But be pleased to mind the fairs first'.[80] The early part of the seventeenth century had seen the rapid rise of the port towns as a result of the export boom but it was the inland towns which were to benefit from the late-seventeenth-century developments (Fig. 4.5). Part of the explanation for the dramatic rise in Dublin's share of the Irish trade, from about 21 per cent of the customs yield in 1616–17 to almost 50 per cent by the beginning of the eighteenth century, was the rise of an inland market system which directed goods to Dublin rather than to the local ports. Dublin could offer access to specialized overseas markets and this capacity helped the capital to dominate overseas trade. Only the Cork region managed to resist the extension of the influence of Dublin to any degree, since it could rely on the colonial trade as a staple for which Dublin was less conveniently sited.

The development of a marketing system was not only a domestic development. Changes in the organization of Irish agriculture promoted efficiency gains and increased output of specialized goods which could not be consumed in Ireland. New markets had to be sought. In 1665 about 74 per cent of Irish exports were destined for England. By 1683 that had fallen to 30 per cent although by 1700 the English share of Irish exports had risen again to 42 per cent.[81] This changing pattern was the result of the development of new markets for Irish exports. Continental Europe took up a greater proportion of Irish trade than hitherto with almost one-fifth of butter exports going to France by the 1680s.[82] The second developing market was the colonial American trade which absorbed increasing amounts of beef and butter from Ireland.[83] This had initially developed in the Galway area in the 1650s but was concentrated in the Cork region by the 1660s. This trade took advantage of the high prices of colonially produced goods, a result of labour shortages, to sell cheaper Irish goods in the American market. However, in the late seventeenth century the balance of trade favoured the colonies. The proceeds of the Irish trade were used to purchase luxury goods of colonial origin. Most dramatic was the rise of tobacco imports into Ireland, which almost doubled between 1665 and 1700. This is only one indication that the strategy adopted to deflect the impact of rising population on limited resources had considerable success. The rise in tobacco imports is paralleled by a rise in wine imports and other luxuries, indicating increased prosperity in late-seventeenth-century Ireland.

Thus while the problems presented by the interaction of demographic change and resources in Ireland were similar to those experienced in colonial America, the solutions found in America were not feasible in Ireland. Paradoxically the solutions which were adopted to the problem of rising population in Ireland were those of the Old World responding to falling population. Changes in organization produced greater efficiencies permitting an increase in the standard of living.

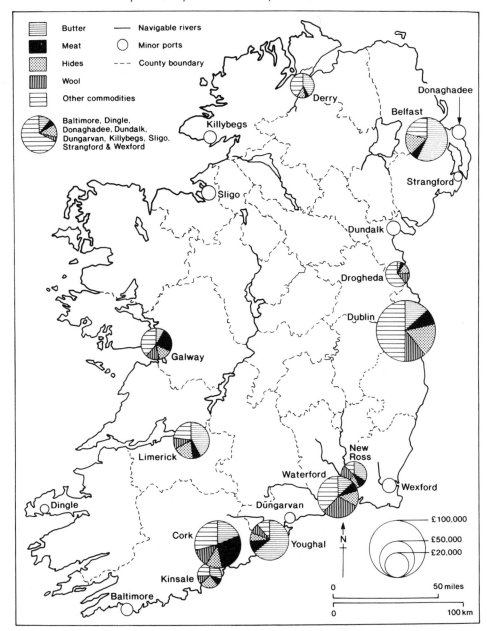

Fig. 4.5. Major navigable waterways and Irish exports, *c.* 1683. After J. H. Andrews in Moody, Martin and Byrne (eds.), *A New History of Ireland: III*, p. 460.

Ireland in the English Colonial System

The experience of economic and social development during the sixteenth and seventeenth centuries suggests that conceptually as well as geographically, Ireland lay somewhere between the Old World and the New. This context is of

considerable importance in understanding Ireland's place in the political geography of the early modern world. Increasingly during the sixteenth and seventeenth
centuries, the idea of the state was ceasing to be that of an entity, often with ill-
defined geographical boundaries, held together by personal alliances and marriages. States began to be seen as internally coherent geographical entities with
their boundaries defined by treaties. The relationship between England and Scotland is a case in point. In 1603 the two kingdoms were united by a union of their
crowns while each continued to exist as a separate political entity which could be
at war with each other, as in 1640. By the end of the seventeenth century this had
become an unacceptable arrangement and a relationship more in keeping with the
new idea of the state was established by the 1707 Act of Union. In this situation a
hierarchy of political entities developed and the contrast between the kingdom,
ruled by a monarch, and the dependent, geographically separate colony became
more sharply defined with the passage of legislation such as the 1679 Navigation
Act.[84]

Ireland's position within this new geopolitical scheme needed to be redefined.
The political organization of medieval Ireland had been characterized by ties of
lordship between the inhabitants of at least part of the island and its lord, the king
of England. Ireland, therefore had the structures of a separate political entity: a
Parliament, a Privy Council, a legal system and a local government structure
modelled on that of England with sheriffs and justices of the peace. It was
governed by the king's representative, the lord deputy or lord lieutenant. These
men were not merely agents. Their powers were considerable; for instance, they
could make peace and war, authorize expenditure and grant pardons which no
English magnate had the power to do. Initially this arrangement had been confined
to the areas controlled by the Anglo-Irish lords but from the middle of the sixteenth
century, military action and one-off agreements with local lords combined to
extend the scheme and new geographical arrangements were put in place. The
creation of new counties, such as Antrim, Down, Longford, Sligo, Mayo, Galway,
Clare and Roscommon in the 1570s, Leitrim, Donegal and Monaghan in the 1580s
and Tyrone in the 1590s, was not simply the creation of geographical units but also
of structures for local government whose head lay in Dublin. In most cases the
administration used the old Gaelic-Irish lordships as they stood at the time of the
creation of the county in order to smooth the transition from one system of government to another.[85]

Thus at the end of the Nine Years War in 1603, the country was completely
shired and had all the appearance of a kingdom similar to England. A proclamation
of 1605 seemed to confirm this declaring all the inhabitants of Ireland to be the
immediate subjects of the king. The 1613 Parliament repealed much of the cultural
legislation against the native Irish. Indeed when a number of MPs tried to raise
problems relating to Ireland in the 1623 Parliament in England, they incurred the
king's wrath since they were impinging on his role as the king of Ireland.[86] Indeed
some features of seventeenth-century Ireland can be seen as the product of the
emergence of an integrated kingdom. The expansion of Dublin, for example, was
part of the more general growth of metropolitan cities in early modern Europe
which was associated with the rise of a centrally organized state. Paris and Madrid,
for instance, had little in the way of an economic rationale for their rapid develop-

ment, which seems to have been largely due to political factors. Despite this evidence that Ireland was regarded as a kingdom there were other conflicting indicators that this was not the case. The address of the lord keeper to the Irish lord chancellor in 1617 commented that the 'civilization' of Ireland 'is not yet conducted to perfection but is in far advance . . . it is likely to become a garden and a younger sister to Great Britain'.[87]

The seventeenth century saw an intensification of the problem of the existence of multiple kingdoms in the British Isles and attempts were made to regularize that situation. In 1640, for example, the English Parliament was seen as increasingly asserting authority over that in Dublin, to the great concern of the Old English. The Cromwellians attempted to solve the problem by a projected union of the three kingdoms but this was not in place before the Restoration. Indeed the experience by the settler community in Ireland of such integration as had taken place during the 1650s suggested that parliamentary separation under the crown of England, which the Old English argued for in the 1640s, was indeed a good idea. Perhaps most decisively, from the point of view of the London administration, the 1641 rebellion had proved how volatile Ireland was, and how necessary it was that increased control should be exercised over it as it was to be over the American colonies after 1676. Thus the late-seventeenth-century lord keeper, Lord Guildford, unlike his early-seventeenth-century predecessor, left no room for doubt in his pronouncement that 'Ireland is a kingdom subject to England in so absolute a manner that the king in his parliament of England may make laws which shall be binding in Ireland,' and that 'it follows that in Ireland they [the judges] are not to be trusted to judge or declare law'.[88] These views were matched by a movement of financial control from Dublin to the London Treasury from the 1670s. By 1677 the English lord treasurer was countersigning all Irish expenditure. Further demonstration that Ireland's status was regarded as similar to the subservient colonies of North America was provided by the extension of the Irish Parliamentary arrangement known as Poynings' law to Virginia and Jamaica. As the Earl of Essex noted in 1674 'Ireland is a plantation (for in reality it is little other)'.[89]

In some ways this late seventeenth-century perception reflected the economic realities of the Irish situation. Ireland had been colonized by both people and capital from England and Scotland during the seventeenth century as part of formal plantation schemes or more informal settlement. Land passed from one ethnic group to another and that passage was validated by Act of Parliament or decision of the London government. In particular the Acts of Settlement and Explanation underpinned and guaranteed the existing social order and were, as one contemporary put it, 'the knot and ligature of all'.[90] Thus the rationale of Irish society and its economic foundation was based on a series of arrangements which can only be described as colonial. As one observer explained in 1698, 'though Ireland be a very contemptible place yet I find some great men and wise men of that kingdom [England] are reconcilable to our land and to our money'.[91] This scramble for land and money, observed by many visitors to Ireland, was characteristic of the colonial society. Sir Thomas Phillips argued in 1685 that Irish society had become corrupted by it 'for there is not the true affection that subjects ought to bear to one another, besides the business of most people here is nothing but getting of money without the least regard to their prince's service'.[92] Such comments apply as readily to the activities of the Earl of Cork in the early seventeenth century as to those observed by Phillips. The colonial element in Irish society was also emphasized by the presence of a majority of Gaelic-Irish among the population who, especially after the rebellion of 1641, were seen as a continual threat to the settlers. Thus James Bonnell, secretary to the commissioners for forfeiture, noted in 1692 that the Irish Protestants were like the colonists in New England 'among the natives of whom they are always in danger'.[93]

Yet for all the apparently conclusive evidence of Ireland's status as a colony many refused to acknowledge this. In the early part of the seventeenth century the Old English refused to accept the rulings of the king's representative in Ireland, the lord deputy, and his Parliament and appealed their case direct to the king in London as many of their sixteenth-century predecessors had done. Increasingly the newcomers came to share this view and by the end of the seventeenth century it was the New English who were arguing the case propounded earlier by the Old English. The most strident statement of this position was that by William Molyneux in his *The Case of Ireland Being Bound by Act of Parliament in England Stated*, published in Dublin and London in 1698. Molyneux objected strongly to the description of Ireland as a colony to be classified with America:

> Does it not manifestly appear by the constitution of Ireland that it is a complete kingdom within itself? Do not the kings of England bear the style of Ireland among the rest of their kingdoms? Is this agreeable to the nature of a colony? Do they use the title of kings of Virginia, New England or Maryland?[94]

A statement of such directness did not command the total support from Molyneux's contemporaries but views similar to it had been circulating for some time. During the passage of the Cattle Acts in the English Parliament, the Earl of Orrery divorced the person of the king of England from that of Ireland and assumed that Charles would refuse royal assent to the Act since it was against Irish interests. He wrote 'Our usage in England amazes me . . . But they [the parliament] have done what they can against us. I doubt not that his Majesty will do what he can for us . . . I will never so much doubt that the king's care for his own prerogative as to fancy an act in England shall be admitted to bind Ireland.'[95] Other New English settlers began to adopt the sixteenth-century tactics of the Old English. They began to bypass the colonial government in Dublin and appeal cases direct to the king. So common did this become that in 1693 an order had to be issued to the Irish lords justice that no complaints would be examined in England until they were first investigated in Ireland.[96] These political actions were paralleled by other developments. In the economic sphere there was increased concern to use Irish manufactures to reduce imports. The Earl of Orrery demanded that the Irish army should be outfitted in Irish cloth and the Cromwellian settler Richard Lawrence railed against the import of foreign luxuries and the money drained out of the country by absentee landlords. The establishment of the Dublin Philosophical Society also reflected an increasing concern with Irish problems within Ireland and over a quarter of the papers read to it between 1682 and 1701 related to Irish problems. In part this stemmed from the effect of the wars of the 1640s which had forced settlers to decide which of the three kingdoms of the British Isles they belonged to, and by the later seventeenth century a generation of settler families had grown up who knew no other home than Ireland. In Ulster, family histories, the best known being the text known as *The Montgomery Manuscripts*, began to appear, making clear the distinctions between Irish and English branches of a family. This process was not confined to the settlers. Old English families, such as the Plunketts of Dunsoghly, Co. Dublin, continued to show an interest in the development of the country's trade and agriculture and to argue for a federal solution of the problem of multiple kingdoms, as the 1541 Act had envisaged.[97]

From the perspective of England or Scotland, Ireland seemed to be developing a distinct identity. According to one writer in the late 1690s, Ireland 'seemed remote to them [the English], independent of them and a people setting up for ourselves'. This change was also reflected in a change in terminology. In the early part of the seventeenth century the registers of the University of Glasgow had noted as the nationality of the sons of Irish settlers coming there 'Scotus' or 'Anglicus' but from the 1660s they began to record them as 'Scoto-hibernicus' or 'Anglo-hibernicus'.[98]

The geopolitical situation of Ireland was a paradox and most settlers living within it simultaneously held contradictory ideas about the constitutional status of the country. Ireland was neither a kingdom on the model of the Old World nor did it wish to be seen as a colony like the New World. This paradox was well expressed in the status of Dublin. At one level it was a largely Protestant English-style city which had no parallel in Ireland. It drew its wealth in part from the colonial economy of the country and thus it acted as a centre for the colony. At another level it was a genuine capital city with its own vice-regal court, which by the late seventeenth century was regarded as not inferior to Whitehall, its own courts of law, its university and its cathedral. It was because of this confusion of function that Dublin—both court and commercial centre—developed an extraordinarily wide range of functions for a pre-industrial city.

The paradox of Ireland's status was also clear from the settlers whose existence and wealth depended on Ireland being regarded as a colony yet proclaimed them-selves to be living in a distinct kingdom. When that became a reality in 1689 with the landing of James II as king of Ireland, they drew back from the full implications of that proclamation. Various formulations were drawn up to express this paradox. One solution was to maintain a federal solution to the problem of multiple king-doms, each entity being held together by its allegiance to the king in the medieval tradition. This approach ignored the role of Parliament and the newer ideas of state building. As one English courtier put it, Ireland was conquered by the king but not by Parliament. A similar view was set out by the English attorney general, Sir Henage Finch, who maintained the sovereignty of both kingdoms, arguing that an Act of the English Parliament could bind Ireland but could be repealed by an Irish Parliament, which was a recipe for legal and administrative confusion. Such formu-lations were a solution to a medieval anachronism in an age of new ideas about the state. A solution could only come about by radical means, an Act of Union as passed for Scotland in 1707. William Molyneux and Sir William Petty both argued for such an approach to Ireland but it found no favour in London.[99] An Act of Union could only be between equal partners with Irish MPs sitting in the House of Commons on an equal basis with their English counterparts. Yet that was not possible because of the London administration's view that Ireland was fundamen-tally a colony to be classified with America. Thus in political, as in social and economic matters, Ireland occupied a mid-Atlantic position neither part of the Old World nor the New. It was a geopolitical problem not to be resolved until the Act of Union in 1801.

A Mid-Atlantic Polity

One way of regarding early modern Ireland is as a mid-Atlantic polity having some features of both the Old World and the New. If colonial America is considered to be the periphery of Atlantic society rather than a frontier then that periphery began with Wales and northern England and extended through Ireland to the edge of the Delaware with degrees of remoteness from the core being the distinguishing features of the regions.[100] Yet all those regions had their own problems. The nature of the interactions between settler communities and indigenous inhabitants was one of the greatest points of contrast between the British Isles and British North America. The approaches used towards Ulster's indigenous population in the seventeenth century resembled the treatment of the inhabitants of the highlands and islands of Scotland and those of the borders of Scotland and England rather than the techniques used towards the native American populations.[101] Unlike the contacts with these people, association with the Gaelic-Irish was no innovation and accommodations between the different ethnic groups in Ireland and with the London government had been in train for centuries. As a result the inhabitants of Gaelic Scotland and Ireland were politically more sophisticated than some older historians have given them credit for. While many of the main families died out or left Ireland, cadet branches emerged to take their place and make accommodations with the new order. The favourable treatment meted out to Hugh O'Neill, Earl of Tyrone, in the 1603 Treaty of Mellifont or to the Duke of Argyll in Scotland would have no New World parallels. As a result many of the features of Scottish and Irish Gaeldom found an enduring place in the new order. This was not confined to place-names or landholding units but individual families themselves who survived through intermarriage. The ethnic patterns of settlement established in the seventeenth century persisted for generations. By contrast the Indian legacy was to prove to be much less enduring. The native American communities had significantly less input in the long-term development of the British settlements in the New World.

One fundamental difference in dealing with the native communities was in the area of religion. Reviewing the course of the seventeenth-century developments in Ireland and America, in 1681 the Earl of Anglesea, himself born in Ireland, observed that the North American Indians had become Christian and peaceable and that only the native Irish remained uncivilized enough to continue massacres. This he attributed to 'the want of policy and good government' in Ireland.[102] Thus the difference between the reactions of the two groups to religious change was not solely a spiritual one. The problem which faced the New World settlers was the religious one of converting the heathen to Protestantism. The religious problem in Ireland was a different one. There the Protestant 'missionaries' found that they were in competition with another mission, that of the Counter-Reformation, which was making considerable strides among the Old English and Gaelic-Irish populations of Ireland. The brand of Catholicism was not that of Baroque Europe, which made it difficult for some European visitors to recognize it as the religion of the Council of Trent, but it carried the same political overtones with threats to the role of the monarch as head of the church. Thus Anglesea's comparison was of a religious problem in North America with a political one in Ireland.

The realization that the Irish experience was not that of other colonies had dawned on administrators from an early date. Francis Bacon, for instance, considered the settlement of Virginia as 'an enterprise in my opinion differing as much from this [the settlement of Ireland] as *Amadis de Gaul* differs from Caesar's *Commentaries*'.[103] There were fundamental differences between the structures created for the settlement of the New World and those which were already in place in sixteenth-century Ireland. Yet in their turn, the latter were different from the new concepts of the state which were emerging in the Old World. There were no universal panaceas for those who settled in Ireland, the various different colonies of British North America or who opted to remain in the Old World. All had to find their own political, economic, religious and cultural salvation in a world of rapid change. The solutions they found to the problems which presented themselves differed from country to country and even between regions within each country. It was in Ireland, a volatile mix of native and newcomer, kingdom and colony and exploiters and entrepreneurs, that the problems were most difficult to solve for contemporaries and remain most complex for the historian to unravel.

References

1. Hugh Kearney, *The British Isles*, (Cambridge, 1989), pp. 106–11.
2. Glamor Williams, *Recovery, Reorientation and Reformation, Wales 1415–1642*, (Oxford, 1987), pp. 263–78; Brendan Bradshaw, *The Irish Constitutional Revolution of the Sixteenth Century*, (Cambridge, 1979), pp. 231–57; William Ferguson, *Scotland's Relations with England: a survey to 1707*, (Edinburgh, 1977), pp. 51–62.
3. For this process V. Morgan, 'The cartographic image of "the county" in early modern England', *Transactions of the Royal Historical Society*, 5th ser., **XXVI** (1979), pp. 129–54; Sarah Tyack and John Huddy, *Christopher Saxton and Tudor Map Making*, (London, 1980).
4. C. Hill, 'Puritans and the dark corners of the land', *Transactions of the Royal Historical Society*, 5th ser., **XIII** (1963), pp. 77–102; Patrick Collinson, *The Birthpangs of Protestant England*, (London, 1988), pp. 1–27.
5. For the interest in anthropology, see Margaret Hodgen, *Early Anthropology in the Sixteenth and Seventeenth Centuries*, (Philadelphia, 1964).
6. J. H. Elliott, *The Old World and the New, 1492–1650*, (Cambridge, 1972); William Brandon, *New Worlds for Old*, (Athens, Ohio, 1986); H. Pohl (ed.), *The European Discovery of the World and its Economic Effects on Pre-Industrial Society, 1500–1800*, (Stuttgart, 1990).
7. For colonial America, see E. J. Perkins, *The Economy of Colonial America*, (2nd edn, Columbia, 1988) and for Ireland, Raymond Gillespie, *The Transformation of the Irish Economy, 1550–1700*, (Studies in Irish Economic and Social History 6, Dundalk, 1991).
8. For New England information flows, David Cressy, *Coming Over*, (Cambridge, 1987), pp. 1–36, 231–34.
9. For a list of the available sources, see R. Dunlop, 'Sixteenth century maps of Ireland', *English Historical Review*, **XX** (1905), pp. 309–37.
10. J. H. Andrews, 'The Irish surveys of Robert Lythe', *Imago Mundi*, **xix** (1965), pp. 22–31.
11. J. H. Andrews, 'Geography and government in Elizabethan Ireland', in Nicholas

Stephens and Robin Glasscock (eds.), *Irish Geographical Studies in Honour of E. E. Evans*, (Belfast, 1970), pp. 178–91.

12. For developments in one region, see Raymond Gillespie, *Colonial Ulster*, (Cork, 1985), pp. 10–21.
13. For an overview, see D. B. Quinn and K. W. Nicholls, 'Ireland in 1534', in T. W. Moody, F. X. Martin and F. J. Byrne (eds), *A New History of Ireland III: Early Modern Ireland, 1534–1691*, (Oxford, 1976).
14. A. L. Beier, *Masterless Men*, (London, 1985), pp. 208–14.
15. Edmund Campion, *Two Bokes of the Histories of Ireland*, ed. A. F. Vossen (Assen, 1963), p. 2. For a modern edition of Gerald of Wales, see *The History and Topography of Ireland*, ed. J. J. O'Meara, (Harmondsworth, 1982).
16. *Calendar of Carew Manuscripts, 1603–24*, pp. 351–5, 374; *Calendar of State Papers Ireland, 1615–25*, p. 215.
17. For an example of these, see Nicholas Canny (ed.), 'Rowland White's discours touching Ireland *c.* 1569', *Irish Historical Studies*, (1977), pp. 439–63.
18. Robin Flower, 'Laurence Nowell and the discovery of England in Tudor times', *Proceedings of the British Academy*, **XXI** (1935), pp. 47–73.
19. D. B. Quinn, *The Elizabethans and the Irish*, (Ithaca, 1966), pp 27–30.
20. Colonizing literature is dealt with in Cressy, *Coming Over*, pp. 1–36. Some examples are printed in L. B. Wright (ed.), *The Elizabethans' America*, (London, 1965).
21. Thomas Smith, *De Republica Anglorum*, ed. L. Alston, (Cambridge, 1906), p. 20.
22. British Library, Harley Ms 3292, f. 30.
23. Hiram Morgan, 'The colonial adventure of Sir Thomas Smith in Ulster, 1571–5', *Historical Journal*, **XXVIII** (1985), pp. 261–78; Nicholas Canny, 'The permissive frontier: social control in English settlements in Ireland and Virginia', in K. R. Andrews, N. P. Canny and P. E. H. Hair (eds.), *The Westward Enterprise*, (Liverpool, 1978), pp. 17–44.
24. See, for example, the scheme for Ulster described in Philip Robinson, *The Plantation of Ulster*, (Dublin, 1984), pp. 55–65.
25. W. M. Billings, 'The transfer of English law to Virginia, 1606–50', in Andrews, Canny and Hair (eds.), *Westward Enterprise*, pp. 215–44. For the evolution of government, see K. A. Lockridge, *Settlement and Unsettlement in Early America*, (Cambridge, 1981).
26. S. S. Webb, *1676: the End of American Independence*, (Harvard, 1985).
27. Gerald of Wales, *History and Topography*, pp. 34–5.
28. The evidence for this trade is in Norman Lowe, *The Lancashire Textile Industry in the Sixteenth Century*, (Manchester, 1972), esp. pp. 10–19.
29. Gillespie, *Transformation*, pp. 13–14.
30. G. Mac Niocaill, *Irish Population Before Petty*, (Dublin, 1981), p. 4.
31. *Calendar of Carew Mss., 1603–24*, pp. 174–6; Victor Treadwell, 'The Irish Parliament of 1569–71', *Proceedings of the Royal Irish Academy*, **65 C** (1966–7), pp. 55–89.
32. Michael MacCarthy Morrogh, *The Munster Plantation*, (Oxford, 1986), pp. 190–7.
33. Cressy, *Coming Over*, pp. 144–77.
34. D. H. Fischer, *Albion's Seed*, (Oxford, 1989), pp. 31–8, 236–40, 438–45; N. C. Landsman, *Scotland and its First American Colony*, (Princeton, 1985), pp. 99–194.
35. Fischer, *Albion's Seed*, pp.429–34, 618.
36. *Calendar of State Papers, Ireland, 1608–10*, pp. 525–6. Cressy, *Coming Over*, pp. 74–106. For the argument that economics was at least as important as religion in New England, see Stephen Innes, *Labour in a New Land*, (Princeton, 1983). Gillespie, *Colonial Ulster*, pp. 29–46; MacCarthy Morrogh, *Munster Plantation*, pp. 177–222.
37. T. K. Rabb, *Enterprise and Empire*, (Harvard, 1967). For an interesting group of Irish adventurers, see Joyce Lorrimer (ed.), *English and Irish Settlement on the Amazon, 1550–1646*, (London, 1989), and for some Irish settlers such as Sir George Calvert and Lord Falkland investing in Newfoundland, see G. T. Cell (ed.), *Newfoundland Discovered*, (London, 1982).
38. The best estimates for Irish population are in L. M. Cullen, 'Population trends in seventeenth-century Ireland', *Economic and Social Review*, **VI** (1974–5), pp. 149–65.
39. Robinson, *Plantation of Ulster*, pp. 123–8.

40. T. H. Breen, *Puritans and Adventurers*, (Oxford, 1980), esp. pp. 3–23; Nicholas Canny, 'Migration and opportunity', *Irish Economic and Social History*, **XII** (1985), pp. 7–32; Raymond Gillespie, 'Migration and opportunity: a comment', *Irish Economic and Social History*, **XIII** (1986), pp. 90–95.
41. Gillespie, *Transformation*, pp. 20–3.
42. For the changing pattern of landownership, see J. G. Simms, 'Land owned by Catholics in 1688', *Irish Historical Studies*, **VII** (1951), pp. 189–90; N. P. Canny, 'Hugh O'Neill and the changing face of Gaelic Ulster', *Studia Hibernica*, **X** (1971), pp. 7–35; Bernadette Cunningham, 'Political and social change in the lordships of Clanricard and Thomond', (unpublished MA, University College, Galway, 1979).
43. For Mayo, see Raymond Gillespie, 'Lords and commons in seventeenth-century Mayo', in Raymond Gillespie and Gerard Moran (eds.), *'A Various Country': Essays in Mayo History, 1500–1900*, (Westport, 1987), pp. 44–66.
44. William Cronon, *Changes in the Land: Indians, Colonists and the Ecology of New England*, (New York, 1983). Ecological changes as a result of the settlement of Ireland, apart from the clearance of woodland, have not been studied at all.
45. J. H. Andrews, *Plantation Acres*, (Belfast, 1989), esp. chs. 1–5.
46. Gillespie, *Transformation*, pp. 27–29.
47. These estimates are taken from data in D. Woodward, *The Trade of Elizabethan Chester*, (Hull, 1970), D. Woodward, 'The overseas trade of Chester, 1600–1650', *Transactions of the Historic Society of Lancashire and Cheshire*, **CXXII** (1970), pp. 25–42, and D. Woodward, 'Irish Sea trade and shipping from the later middle ages to 1660', in M. McCaughan and J. Appleby (eds.), *The Irish Sea: Aspects of Maritime History*, (Belfast, 1989), pp. 35–44.
48. G. M. Walton and J. F. Shepherd, *The Economic Rise of Early America*, (Cambridge, 1979), p. 98.
49. Gillespie, *Transformation*, pp. 31–37.
50. For trade patterns, see Jacob M. Price,'The transatlantic economy', in J. P. Greene and J. R. Pole (eds.), *Colonial British America*, (Baltimore, 1984), pp. 18–42.
51. Walton and Shepherd, *Economic Rise*, p. 43.
52. For a comparative view, see Raymond Gillespie, 'The origins and growth of an Ulster urban network', *Irish Historical Studies*, **XXIV** (1984), pp. 26–8.
53. Michael MacCarthy Morrogh, 'Credit and remittance: monetary problems in seventeenth century Munster', *Irish Economic and Social History*, **XIV** (1987), pp. 5–29; Raymond Gillespie (ed.), 'Peter French's petition for an Irish mint', *Irish Historical Studies*, **XXV** (1987), pp. 413–20.
54. R. B. Sheridan, 'The domestic economy', in Greene and Pole (eds.), *Colonial British America*, pp. 72–73.
55. A. F. O'D Alexander (ed.), 'The O'Kane papers', *Analecta Hibernica*, **12** (1943), p. 76; Historical Manuscripts Commission, *Report on the Manuscripts of the Marquess of Ormond*, n.s **VII** (London, 1920), p. 136.
56. Walton and Shepherd, *Economic Rise*, pp. 90–94; Bernard Bailyn, *The New England Merchants in the Seventeenth Century*, (Harvard, 1955); F. B. Tolles, *Meeting House and Counting House*, (Chapel Hill, 1948).
57. V. Morgan and W. A. Macafee, 'Population in Ulster, 1660–1760', in Peter Roebuck (ed.), *Plantation to Partition*, (Belfast, 1981), p. 47.
58. R. W. Weiss, 'The colonial money standard of Massachusetts', *Economic History Review*, 2nd ser., **XXVII** (1974), pp. 579, 585.
59. Gillespie, *Transformation*, pp. 41–2.
60. Cullen 'Population trends'; David Dickson, Cormac Ó Gráda and Stuart Daultry, 'Hearth tax, household size and Irish population change, 1672–1821', *Proceedings of the Royal Irish Academy*, **82C** (1982), pp. 125–81. For the geography of population at mid-century, see W. J. Smyth, 'Society and settlement in seventeenth century Ireland: the evidence of the "1659 Census"', in W. J. Smyth and Kevin Whelan (eds.), *Common Ground: Essays on the Historical Geography of Ireland*, (Cork, 1988), pp. 55–83.
61. Fischer, *Albion's Seed*, pp. 226–7, 421.

62. Jan de Vries, *The Economy of Europe in an Age of Crisis*, (Cambridge, 1976), p. 5; E. A. Wrigley and R. S. Schofield, *The Population History of England*, (Cambridge, 1981), pp. 531–3.
63. Joan Thirsk and J. P. Cooper (eds.), *Seventeenth Century Economic Documents*, (Oxford, 1972), pp. 758–9.
64. Raymond Gillespie (ed.), *Settlement and Survival on an Ulster Estate: the Brownlow Leasebook, 1667–1712*, (Belfast, 1988), pp. xvii–xix; Gillespie, *Transformation*, pp. 18–19.
65. D. E. C. Eversley, 'The demography of the Irish Quakers, 1650–1850', in J. M. Goldstrom and L. A. Clarkson (eds.), *Irish Population, Economy and Society*, (Oxford, 1981), pp. 57–88.
66. David Dickson, 'No Scythians here: women and marriage in seventeenth century Ireland', in Margaret MacCurtain and Mary O'Dowd (eds), *Women in Early Modern Ireland*, (Edinburgh, 1991), pp. 223–35.
67. Valerie Morgan, 'A case study of population change over two centuries: Blaris, Lisburn', *Irish Economic and Social History*, **III** (1976), pp. 6–12.
68. L. M. Cullen, 'Population growth and diet, 1600–1800', in Goldstrom and Clarkson (eds.), *Irish Population*, pp. 89–112.
69. For a summary see J. Potter, 'Demographic development and family structure', in Greene and Pole (eds.), *Colonial British America*, pp. 148–50. For the problem of the Chesapeake, see C. V. Earle, 'Environment, disease and mortality in early Virginia', in T. W. Tate and D. L. Ammerman (eds.), *The Chesapeake in the Seventeenth Century*, (New York, 1979), pp. 96–125.
70. Thirsk and Cooper (eds.), *Seventeenth Century Economic Documents*, p. 760.
71. For the question of slavery and indentured servants see, E. S. Morgan, *American Slavery, American Freedom*, (New York, 1975); A. E. Smith, *Colonists in Bondage*, (Chapel Hill, 1947); Bernard Bailyn, *The Peopling of British North America*, (New York, 1986), pp. 92–97.
72. Audrey Lockhart, *Emigration from Ireland to the North American Colonies 1660–1775*, (New York, 1976), pp. 1–15; Hilary McD. Beckles, 'A "riotous and unruly lot": Irish indentured servants and freemen in the English West Indies, 1644–1713', *William and Mary Quarterly*, **XLVII** (1990), pp. 503–24; A. C. Myres, *Immigration of Irish Quakers into Pennsylvania*, (New York, 1902).
73. David Dickson, 'In search of the old Irish poor law', in R. Mitchison and P. Roebuck (eds.), *Economy and Society in Scotland and Ireland 1500–1939*, (Edinburgh, 1988), pp. 149–51.
74. Gillespie, *Transformation*, pp. 41–3, 48.
75. Quoted in T. C. Barnard, 'Fishing in seventeenth century Kerry: the experience of Sir William Petty', *Journal of the Kerry Historical and Archaeological Society*, **XIV** (1981), p. 24.
76. Gillespie, *Settlement and survival*, pp. xxxv–xxxix.
77. Liam Irwin, 'The role of the presidency in the economic development of Munster, 1660–72', *Journal of the Cork Historical and Archaeological Society*, **LXXX** (1977), pp. 102–114.
78. L. M. Cullen, *Anglo-Irish Trade*, (Manchester, 1968), pp. 41–42.
79. The regions are discussed in J. H. Andrews, 'Land and people, 1685', in Moody, Martin and Byrne (eds.) *New History of Ireland: III*, pp. 458–62.
80. Historical Manuscripts Commission, *Report on the Manuscripts of the Earl of Egmont*, II (London, 1909), p. 85; Raymond Gillespie, 'The small towns of Ulster', *Ulster Folklife*, **XXXVI** (1990), pp. 23–31.
81. Cullen, *Anglo-Irish Trade*, pp. 31, 36, 40, 42.
82. British Library, Additional Ms. 4759.
83. Thomas Truxes, *Irish American Trade, 1660–1783*, (Cambridge, 1988), chapter 1.
84. For the new ideas of the state, see Mark Greengrass (ed.), *Conquest and Coalescence: the Shaping of the State in Early Modern Europe*, (London, 1991), esp. pp. 1–25; Brian Levack, *The Formation of the British State*, (Oxford, 1987).
85. For the geography of shiring, see T. W. Moody, F. X. Martin and F. J. Byrne (eds.), *A New History of Ireland*, *VII*, I (Oxford, 1984), p. 43.

86. Conrad Russell, *Parliaments and English Politics, 1621–9*, (Oxford, 1979), pp. 128–9.
87. *Calendar of State Papers, Ireland, 1615–25*, p. 167.
88. Library, Additional Ms. 32519, f. 105.
89. Osmund Airy (ed.), *Essex Papers*, I, (London, 1940), p. 201; S. S. Webb, *The Governors General*, (Chapel Hill, 1979), pp. 118, 279, 321–2, 378–80.
90. Historical Manuscripts Commission, *Egmont Ms*, II, pp. 115, 168.
91. Patrick Melvin (ed.), 'Letters of Lord Longford and others on Irish affairs', *Analecta Hibernica*, **32** (1985), p. 109.
92. Historical Manuscripts Commission, *Report on the Dartmouth Manuscripts*, I (London, 1887), p. 132.
93. Trinity College Dublin, Ms. 1430, ff. 189–90.
94. William Molyneux, *The Case of Ireland. . . . Stated*, ed. J.G. Simms (Dublin, 1977), p. 115.
95. Thomas Morrice, *A Collection of the State Letters of the . . . First Earl of Orrery*, II (Dublin, 1743), pp. 93–4, 145–6, 150.
96. *Calendar of State Papers, Domestic, 1693*, pp. 194–6.
97. For example, Raymond Gillespie, 'Continuity and change: Ulster in the seventeenth century', in Ciaran Brady *et al.*, (eds.), *Ulster: an Illustrated History*, (London, 1989), pp. 129–32; Patrick Kelly, 'A light to the blind: the voice of the dispossessed elite in the generation after the defeat at Limerick', *Irish Historical Studies*, **XXIV** (1985), pp. 455–6.
98. Cosmo Innes (ed.), *Munimenta alma universitatis Glasguensis*, **iii**, (Glasgow, 1854), pp. 75, 82, 93, 116, 121, 133; Public Record Office of Ireland, Wynche Mss. 2/143.
99. Thomas Carte, *Life of the Duke of Ormond*, v, (Oxford, 1851), pp. 123; James Kelly, 'The origins of the act of union: an examination of unionist opinion in Britain and Ireland, 1650–1800', *Irish Historical Studies*, **XXV** (1987), pp. 236–43.
100. Bailyn, *Peopling of British North America*, pp. 112–31, and developed in B. Bailyn and P.D. Morgan (eds.), *Strangers Within the Realm*, (Chapel Hill, 1991).
101. The 1609 Statutes of Iona and the attempted plantation of Lewis in 1602 both foreshadowed aspects of the London government's policy towards the native Irish, J. Wormald, *Court, Kirk and Community: Scotland 1470–1625*, (London, 1981), pp. 164–5.
102. British Library, Additional Ms. 4816 f. 30v.
103. J. Spedding (ed.), *The Life and Letters of Francis Bacon*, IV, (London, 1872), p. 123.

5

Birth, Death and Exile: Irish Population History, 1700–1921

Liám Kennedy and Leslie A. Clarkson

Introduction

Population change lies at the heart of modern Irish history. During the seventeenth century successive waves of outsiders sowed the human seeds for an ethnic and a cultural diversity that proved, by times, enriching and divisive. Between 1700 and 1845 population expanded at a rate that was remarkable by European standards: double that of France, and at least equal to the rate of 0.8 per cent per annum achieved by the world's first industrial nation.[1] Many of Malthus' contemporaries, though seemingly not Malthus himself, saw in the squalor of pre-Famine Ireland the sequel to reproductive excess and the prelude to disaster.[2] The Great Famine at mid-century might, with justice, be labelled the last great subsistence crisis of the Western world. In its shadow emerged a new Ireland, notorious for its sexual conservatism, yet nonchalantly sending between a half and a quarter of each generation of its children into alien societies.[3] Emigration itself was of seminal significance for virtually every aspect of Irish society, from marriage and inheritance practices to the forging of revolutionary and constitutional nationalisms.

The structure of the chapter is as follows. First the trends in population levels and population growth rates are charted. The bulk of the chapter is devoted, however, to exploring the demographic mechanisms—changes in fertility, migration and death rates—which determined the course of events both regionally and nationally. These changes have themselves to be explained: hence the need to relate demographic variables to the larger social and economic context of the times. In the conclusion we highlight some of the key issues and draw out their wider implications.

Population Totals and Population Growth

For more than half the period under review most of what we know about population is based on guesses of various degrees of plausibility. There was no census before 1821, apart from an uncompleted attempt in 1813. Neither was there a national system of vital registration before 1864, with the exception of Protestant marriages whose registration commenced in 1844. Demographers of other western European societies faced with similar shortages of data have devised ingenious strategies for filling the gaps. For England Wrigley and Schofield have reconstructed population totals, growth rates, birth, death, and marriage totals and rates, and many other things besides, for the period 1541–1871, from parish registers.[4] Although some registers exist in Ireland for the Church of Ireland community from the late seventeenth century and for the Catholic community from the late eighteenth century, their quality and coverage are poor. Presbyterian and Quaker records are better, but fragmentary. Therefore other approaches are necessary.

From the time of Sir William Petty onwards, demographers of Ireland have used the numbers of hearths (i.e. houses) counted for the collection of the hearth tax. This tax was introduced in 1662 and survived until the end of the eighteenth century. The counts were used, for example, by the census commissioners in 1821 who wanted some idea of population trends over the previous century and a half, by George O'Brien when writing his influential economic history between 1918 and 1921, and most notably by K. H. Connell in his seminal work on population published in 1950.[5]

Two major difficulties attach to the hearth money returns. The more important concerns their completeness. Hearths were under-recorded throughout the history of the tax because of legitimate exemptions, evasion, and corruption. Connell inflated the surviving totals for the 1790s by 20 per cent, those for 1788 by 25 per cent, all earlier eighteenth-century totals by 50 per cent, and those for 1672, 1676 and 1687 by 66 per cent. The effect was to increase the population estimates for the seventeenth and the first half of the eighteenth century, generated by earlier demographers, by a greater degree than for calculations for the late eighteenth century. However, recent work by David Dickson and his colleagues suggests that Connell's revisions before 1753 were too radical. Between 1753 and 1788 errors, corruption and carelessness increased as the rate of population growth accelerated; but the mistakes had been less serious earlier in the century, and major reforms were introduced after 1788, resulting in more efficient collection.[6]

The second difficulty concerns the multipliers required to convert hearths into persons. Connell used national multipliers, based on contemporary estimates, ranging from 5.2 persons per house to six. The size of the multiplier fell slightly during the early eighteenth century but rose steadily from the 1730s, reflecting Connell's belief—and that of contemporaries—that households became larger as population increased. Dickson *et al.* employ multipliers that vary both over time and place; they are generally higher in Leinster and Munster than in Connacht and Ulster, although the relationship changes during the course of the eighteenth century.[7]

The alternative ways of handling the house counts and multipliers produce different estimates of population before the census of 1821. These are presented in Table 5.1, together with Professor Lee's upward revisions of the census totals for 1821 and 1841.[8] More significant than the differences in the totals are the differences implied in the growth rates. Over the period 1687–1821 Connell's estimates produce an annual growth rate of 0.9 per cent, Dickson's 1.0, and Clarkson's 1.1 (Table 5.2). A period of fairly rapid increase in the late seventeenth and early

Table 5.1: Irish population estimates (millions).[9]

Date	Connell	Dickson et al.	Clarkson	Census	Lee
1687	2.2	2.0	1.7		
1712	2.8	2.0–2.3			
1725	3.0	2.2–2.6	2.2		
1753	3.2	2.2–2.6	2.3		
1791	4.8	4.4	4.2–4.6		
1821				6.8	7.2
1841				8.2	8.4
1901				4.5	
1911				4.4	
1926				4.2	

Table 5.2: Annual population growth.

Period	Connell	Dickson et al.	Clarkson	Census[11]
1687–1725	0.8	0.5	0.7	
1725–1753	0.2	0.0	0.02	
1753–1791	1.1	1.6	1.7	
1791–1821	1.4	1.7	1.7	
1821–1841				0.8
1841–1901				−1.0
1901–1926				−0.3

eighteenth centuries was followed by stagnation in the second quarter of the eighteenth century. Then came seventy years of uninterrupted growth between 1753 and 1821. According to Connell the rate of population growth in Ireland was comparable to that in England; but later estimates show it to be higher than anywhere else in western Europe.[10] In the two decades before the Famine, by contrast, population growth was slowing down; and from the Great Famine until the 1920s—and beyond—the population of Ireland fell in a manner unparalleled in Europe.

The national figures conceal regional variations in the pace of population change (see Tables 5.3 and 5.4).[11] At the beginning of the eighteenth century Leinster and Munster each contained around 30 per cent of the Irish population, Ulster a little over a quarter, and Connacht about 14 per cent. Over the next century the most significant gains were made, first in Ulster and then in Connacht; in the former between 1753 and 1791, and in the latter between 1791 and 1821, growth rates exceeded 2 per cent per annum. In the post-Famine years Ulster's share of Ireland's diminishing population increased substantially, largely because of the growth of Belfast. Connacht, at the other extreme, lost population more dramatically than the other provinces.

There was one further significant regional difference. In the mid eighteenth century, Dublin, with a population of 125,000, was the eleventh largest city in Europe, and Cork was the fourth largest city in the British Isles.[13] Even so, only 7 per cent of Ireland's population lived in towns bigger than 10,000. The degree of urbanization in Ireland in the mid eighteenth century was substantially lower than in England although not significantly different from that in Scotland or continental

Table 5.3: Provincial population totals (millions).[12]

Year	Leinster	Munster	Ulster	Connacht
1712	0.64	0.63	0.59	0.30
1725	0.73	0.72	0.61	0.32
1753	0.77	0.64	0.67	0.32
1791	1.18	1.20	1.43	0.61
1821	1.76	1.94	2.00	1.11
1841	2.00	2.40	2.40	1.14
1901	1.15	1.08	1.58	0.65
1926	1.15	0.97	1.56	0.55

Table 5.4: Provincial growth rates.

Year	Leinster	Munster	Ulster	Connacht
1712–25	1.01	1.03	0.26	0.50
1725–53	0.19	−0.42	0.34	0.00
1753–91	1.30	1.67	2.02	1.71
1791–1821	1.34	1.61	1.12	2.02
1821–41	0.64	1.07	0.92	0.13
1841–1901	−0.92	−1.32	−0.69	−0.93
1901–26	0.00	−0.43	−0.05	−0.67

Europe. After 1750 England and Scotland both urbanized rapidly; but the urban percentage in Ireland remained practically unchanged until the Famine (see Table 5.5). Between 1750 and 1845 Ireland experienced rapid population growth without urban growth, a phenomenon characteristic of an economy increasing its output of food without increasing labour productivity. After the Famine, the urban proportion rose sharply as the rural population flowed into the industrializing towns of east Ulster and—to a lesser extent—into Dublin, as well as into the urban centres of North America and Britain.[14] In 1821 just over 2 per cent of Ulster's population lived in towns larger than 10,000. In 1901 the figure was 28 per cent and in 1926 36 per cent. Only Leinster had a slightly higher urban fraction, almost entirely confined to the Dublin conurbation.

Table 5.5: Numbers and proportions living in towns of 10,000 or more in Ireland, England and Wales, and Scotland.[15]

	Ireland		England & Wales		Scotland	
Year	000s	per cent	000s	per cent	000s	per cent
1750	161	7.0	1021	16.7	119	9.2
1800	369	7.4	1870	20.3	276	17.3
1821	517	7.6	—	—	—	—
1841	640	7.8	7906	44.1[16]	—	—
1901	1045	23.4	22489	69.1	—	—
1926	1211	28.6	—	—	—	—

The Determinants of Population Change

Pre-Famine Fertility Trends

The contours of Irish population growth thus display features peculiar by European standards: between 1750 and 1845 there was rapid growth without urbanization; after 1845 there was rapid population decline accompanied by rapid urbanization. Eighteenth-century observers of Ireland were well aware of the fact of population growth and stressed what Arthur Young described as 'the generality of marriage' made possible by cheap shelter and food.[17] This emphasis on fertility remained an important theme in Irish population history until it became overshadowed, in the 1920s and 1930s, by developments in historical demography in England, stressing the importance of declining mortality in explaining English population growth during the Industrial Revolution. However, Connell's *Population of Ireland* (1950), and, even more emphatically, his essay in *Irish Historical Studies* the following year, shifted the attention of demographers, both in England and Ireland, back to fertility.[18] The publication of Wrigley and Schofield's population history of England, firmly re-established the role of high fertility in accounting for English population growth and raises again the question of its importance in the Irish story.

A study of fertility requires a consideration of nuptiality, fecundity, and fecundability.[19] The conventional assumption of Irish demographers is that throughout the century and a half before the Famine marriage became the universal condition for adults. The evidence is more impressionistic than statistical and much of the discussion focuses on the age at marriage rather than its frequency.[20] Nevertheless, there seems to be a clear distinction between the experiences of Ireland and England during the eighteenth century. In the latter country, about 15 per cent of women remained unmarried in 1700; by 1800 the proportion had fallen to about 7 per cent. This decline was an important reason for the increase of population in England.[21] No parallel increase in nuptiality seem to have occurred in Ireland; it started high at the beginning of the eighteenth century and remained high throughout.

All discussions of European marriage stress the importance of economic conditions—access to land or jobs—in determining decisions to marry. In England inheritance and leasing systems restricted access to land, but industrialization opened up other economic niches and so stimulated nuptiality. In Ireland land was available to rent on favourable terms throughout the eighteenth century. As the decades passed, subdivision, the spread of the linen and woollen industries in some parts of the countryside, and cheap potatoes almost everywhere, provided ample economic bases for young and universal marriage. Connell's characterization of Ireland between 1780 and 1845 as a country of 'haphazard, happy-go-lucky marriage'[22] is a touch fanciful but it is not violently at odds with contemporary observations.

The most vigorous debate in pre-Famine demography concerns age at first marriage. According to Connell the peasantry married young, and from the 1780s teenage marriage became almost commonplace. More recent work indicates that on the eve of the Famine, marriage ages in Ireland were little different from those in

England and western Europe.[23] Nevertheless, we should be cautious in rejecting the prevalence of young marriage. In 1841, and probably for several decades before, marital fertility was substantially higher in Ireland than in England and western Europe. This could be interpreted as evidence of a generally low age at first marriage. In Dublin, for example, the age at marriage among poor females was 21.5 in 1810 and 23 on the eve of the Famine.[24]

Age at first marriage is important because of its influence on the alternative three 'Fs' in Irish history: fertility, fecundity and fecundability. Marital fertility is a function of fecundity (the physiological capacity to produce a live birth), fecundability (the probability of conception during the menstrual cycle among women who do not practise contraception), and also post-partum non-susceptibility (the period immediately following a birth or abortion during which a woman does not ovulate or is not sexually active).[25] Fecundity is inversely correlated to age. In pre-industrial England, for example, a decline of one year in the female marriage age resulted in a 7 per cent increase in completed fertility.[26] However, there were almost certainly additional reasons for high marital fertility in pre-Famine Ireland. For one thing, in the early nineteenth century, marital fertility varied between town and countryside without any apparent difference in age at marriage.[27] More significantly, Eversley has shown that fertility among Irish Quakers was higher than among their English counterparts, not only because they married younger, but because they also had short birth intervals. These, he suggested, were features they shared with their Catholic and Protestant neighbours.[28]

The major determinant of fecundability is the frequency of intercourse. Demographers of pre-industrial England, where good parish registers exist, are able to throw some light on this arcane topic;[29] but so far historians have been unable to penetrate the mysteries of Irish coital behaviour. There is, however, a more accessible influence—nutrition—and here we are on firmer ground. Nutrition affects fecundability in various ways. Malnutrition dulls sexual appetites. A poorly nourished woman may be less likely to carry a pregnancy to full term than her well-nourished sister, or she may become prey to infection that reduces coital activity or prevents her conceiving. Chronic malnutrition postpones the age of menarche in females and the onset of sexual maturity in males. However, only extreme hunger, verging on starvation, is likely to result in infertility.[30] During the Great Famine Irish women—and their men—did indeed starve. But during the preceding century, as potatoes captured the diet of the bottom third of the population and made substantial inroads further up the social scale, the Irish population generally was abundantly fed, and indeed well-fed. Pre-Famine diets were 'excellent, not merely when measured by the "recommended daily intake" of the nutritionist, but also when set against the historical reality of the later nineteenth century.'[31] Except for short periods of dearth, fecundability in pre-Famine Ireland was subject to none of the constraints that a chronically inadequate diet might impose.

The potato diet may also have determined the duration of the period of post-partum non-susceptibility and hence birth intervals. Apart from Eversley's work on Quakers we have no direct evidence on this question. However, studies of populations in contemporary Third World countries and biological evidence both indicate that extended lactation postpones ovulation.[32] Breast-feeding practices among human populations vary greatly, depending on economic, social and cultural conditions, but the abundant potato and buttermilk diet of pre-Famine Ireland made early weaning possible. The practice of taking children early from the breast could explain both high marital fertility and also the high level of infant mortality which—as we shall see below—was apparent in pre-Famine Ireland.

Before 1845, therefore, Ireland was a society where marrying and multiplying were almost universal practices. However, during the three decades between the end of the Napoleonic Wars and the Great Famine marriage ages moved gradually upwards and there was a growing aversion to marriage at any age. Consequently there was a decline in both general and marital fertility. These changes were scarcely perceptible in the west of Ireland but they were more pronounced further east.[33] They were related to the attempts by landlords in the eastern counties to restrict subdivision, to the slow shift away from labour-intensive tillage, to the collapse of the woollen industry in the south-east of the country, and to the contraction of the linen industry in the north-east. How such changes in behaviour might have worked out in the absence of the Famine is a matter for conjecture, but that 'tragic ecological accident' is one of the great discontinuities of Irish history. Its effects on population were profound.

Marriage After the Famine

The most striking feature of demographic change between the Famine and the First World War was the halving of the Irish population. Unlike previous famines in Ireland, such as the comparable crisis of 1740–41, and also unlike most famines elsewhere, the Great Famine set in motion a process of continuous decline. The absolute fall in numbers (see Table 5.1) was mainly a rural phenomenon. The proximate causes of this decline were emigration—discussed more fully below—and changing marriage patterns. A slight fall in marital fertility towards the end of the period also has a role to play. These changes, in turn, can only be explained by reference to economic, social and cultural forces—emanating primarily from Ireland's English-speaking neighbours, Britain and North America. These external influences, interacting with conditions within Irish society, determined Ireland's curious demographic pathway.

It is convenient, if seemingly perverse, to begin the exploration of post-Famine marriage patterns by looking at non-marriage. While marriage seems to have been virtually universal in most Asian and African societies, post-Famine Ireland conformed to the distinctive west European pattern in which a significant proportion of the adult population never married. At mid-century, the Irish levels of permanent celibacy (defined here as those in the age range of 45–54 years and still single) were still much the same as in England and Scotland. Roughly one in ten in this age group, both men and women, had not married, and the presumption is that most of these would never do so.

Permanent celibacy made spectacular advances in Ireland over the following century (see Table 5.6). By 1911, celibacy levels for women had doubled; among men, they had more than doubled. So, on the eve of the First World War, about a quarter of the adult Irish population (and almost a third of males in Leinster) were avoiding marriage, and its attendant joys and responsibilities. Why?

We can hardly look for an easy pan-European explanation: Ireland pulled away

Table 5.6: Permanent celibacy in Ireland, 1841–1911: the proportion (per cent) of males still single in the age group 45–54 years.[34]

	1841	1851	1881	1911
Leinster	13	15	22	31
Munster	9	10	14	26
Ulster	10	13	19	26
Connacht	7	7	11	25
Ireland	10	12	17	17

from the experience of neighbouring societies, where celibacy levels showed no such radical changes over the period. This divergence is sharply illustrated by a comparison with England: in 1851 levels of male celibacy were identical; by 1891 the Irish boasted a level which was double that of England. Rome-watchers might have pointed to the swollen ranks of professional celibates—priests, nuns and monks—at the end of the century, but this was an irrelevance. The brides and brothers of Christ were relatively few, if not in influence, then certainly in numbers. Neither is a process of immiseration relevant. On the contrary, absolute living standards rose markedly between 1841 and 1921.[35] Moreover, viewed relatively, the gap in income per capita between Ireland and other west European countries narrowed in these years. A similarly unsatisfactory explanation is that a process of consolidation of farms—reversing the results of previous generations of subletting and subdivision of holdings—was making access to marriage more difficult. In an emigration-prone society, the main effect would have been to reduce the numbers rather than the rate of marriage. In any case, once the Famine clearances had taken their toll, the extent of subsequent consolidation of farms was limited. More plausibly, one might link the decline of subdivision, and the associated shift to impartible inheritance and stem family households, to delayed and less frequent marriage in the countryside.

Perhaps, as argued by Lee, there were important changes in the social structure: as the rungs in the social ladder widened, it became increasingly difficult to locate a spouse of broadly similar socio-economic status.[36] Quite apart from the absence of evidence on such structural changes, the argument is implausible in another direction. In company with other authors, Lee also stresses the importance of dowry payments in post-Famine society. As one function of the dowry was to iron out differences in economic status, its more widespread adoption should have helped lubricate the marriage market. But did the need to accumulate a dowry not act as a barrier to marriage? It almost certainly delayed marriage but it does not seem to have postponed it indefinitely.[37] The evidence for the early twentieth century, at any rate, is that farmers, who along with the aristocracy were the groups most engaged in the business of nuptiality, enjoyed above average rates of marriage.[38]

Earlier writers saw the shock of the Great Famine as forcing a decisive change in attitudes. The dangers of profligate marriage had been laid bare for all to see. Revisionist historians, however, have tended to rob the Famine of causal significance in the demographic as well as in the economic spheres. Arguably, the revisionist impulse has been too easily indulged. Any Famine impact on celibacy levels would have operated with a time lag. Thus, it is quite conceivable that the shift to a higher celibacy plane during the 1860s was related to the mid-century crisis. But clearly, given the sustained upward trend in non-marriage, there were more systematic forces at work.

The standard economic interpretation is that advanced by Robert Kennedy.[39] He sees postponed marriage and non-marriage as attempts to maintain or realize a 'desired' standard of living. Notions of acceptable living standards changed through time, being driven by comparisons between conditions in Ireland and those in the increasingly familiar worlds of America and Britain. These expectations varied in space as well as over time. In many parts of the west of Ireland, despite miserable housing and poor incomes, higher marriage rates prevailed than in the more affluent regions elsewhere. But, by the late nineteenth century, the west was not only awake, but assimilating notions of social decency established at least a generation earlier in the eastern counties. This was not simply a process of geographical diffusion from east to west. Tens of thousands of households along the western seaboard now had their own windows on America. Bypassing Dublin and Belfast, the emigrant's letter linked the old crofting world of the Connacht peasant with the new world of urban, industrial society.[40]

This neo-Malthusian framework has been challenged recently by Guinane.[41] His counter-suggestion is that high levels of celibacy are explicable in terms of increasing economic security at the end of the century, and the availability of marriage-substitutes, such as siblings, nephews and nieces. Thus, for some, the economic burdens of marriage and children, or the vagaries of life as an emigrant, outweighed the comforts of life in an Irish household, albeit under conditions of strict celibacy. This would go some way towards explaining one of the most puzzling features of rural society: a significant incidence of celibacy among large farmers, where economic barriers would seem to be least relevant. It is much less helpful, however, in explaining the surge in celibacy among western smallholders around the turn of this century. Between 1891 and 1911, the levels of male and female celibacy in Connacht almost doubled. This seems more plausibly linked to the traumatic impact of the subsistence crises of the late 1870s, the 'modernization' of mentalities implied by the Land War, and the diverse influences opening up the west. The last ranged from the activities of the Congested Districts' Board to closer contact with the British and American labour markets.

Perhaps the declining absolute size of the major status and class groups in post-Famine society also influenced the marriage rate. This has been demonstrated for the farming population for 1926, when Breen finds that the most important determinant of non-marriage was simply the numbers of farmers within a given farm-size category (the size of the relevant marriage market). In Leinster, for example, the absolute size of the pool of farmers in each of the standard farm-size categories was much smaller than in Connacht. As a consequence, Leinster had much lower marriage rates than Connacht.[42] Whether this delightfully simple explanation can be exported back into the nineteenth century is not known. If so, it also suggests that the influence of a factor we have not considered so far—emigration—was more complex than is usually allowed. The argument might be that the thinning out of the population, and particularly the farming population, through emigration, tended to raise celibacy levels. Quite simply, by reducing the number of players in local marriage markets, emigration may have reduced opportunities for appropriate matches, and hence marriage. However, the more obvious impact of emigration—that of draining away large numbers of young people who, had they remained in Ireland, would have been unable to afford marriage and would, in due course, have multiplied the ranks of the permanently celibate—must have swamped this effect. The regional patterns to emigration and celibacy rates would suggest that the two were *inversely* related.[43]

Finally, there is the possibility of cultural explanations for the avoidance of marriage. Potential candidates are not lacking in the Irish case, be it the puritanical exertions of a celibate Catholic clergy or claims of an ascetic strain in Gaelic culture. Despite much evidence on the nocturnal adventures of priests rooting out courting couples, or stamping on cross-roads dancing and related forms of social inter-course, the conclusion usually drawn is that clerical controls made little, if any, impression on marriage behaviour. To buttress this argument the roughly similar behaviour of Irish Catholics and non-Catholics is frequently invoked.[44] But this may mean simply that Protestants and non-Protestants were both subject to purita-nical clerical regimes. There may well be a case for reinstating some elements of a cultural explanation, particularly as this relates to the growing power of the Irish churches in the later nineteenth century.[45]

Most people, of course, did marry in post-Famine Ireland. But they did so at increasingly later ages. Bridegrooms in 1841 were accustomed to marrying about the age of 28 years. By 1911 Irishmen postponed the marriage date by some five years as compared to their pre-Famine counterparts, entering wedlock in their 33rd year, on average. The maturing of the Irish bride, from 24–25 years to 28 years over the same period, was only marginally less pronounced.[46] The big lurch towards postponed marriage came during the Famine years. Naturally enough, this was due to a change in marriage behaviour on the part of a traumatized population. It was also, and less obviously, a product of the changing balance of social classes in Irish society during the 1840s. Those who survived the holocaust were dispropor-tionately farmers and other property owners, amongst whom cautious attitudes were already deeply ingrained in the generation before the Famine. This more calculating outlook found expression in such practices as dowry payments, impart-ible inheritance and a comparatively late age at marriage.[47]

During the later nineteenth and early twentieth centuries, the drift towards later marriage intensified, to the wonderment of visitors.[48] Interestingly, this prolonged adolescence did not give rise to illicit sexuality, on any scale. The incidence of illegitimate births and pre-nuptial pregnancies remained remarkably low through-out the century. While the north-east of Ireland, particularly those districts which had experienced substantial Scottish immigration during the seventeenth century, showed above-average levels of bastardy, the significant point is that national rates remained well below those of the neighbouring societies of England and Scot-land.[49] Viewed regionally, deferred marriage was most evident in the Leinster counties on the eve of the Famine, and least so in the west. The Famine decade quickly brought Connacht close to national norms. By 1911 late marriage was more pronounced in the west than in the east, this being a remarkable inversion of Connacht's pre-Famine position (Table 5.7).

The transition from an early to a late marrying people has never been explained adequately. The Famine, as noted above, did matter. There is also the slow pace of

Table 5.7: Postponed marriage in Ireland, 1841–1911: the proportion (per cent) of males still single in the age group, 25–34 years.[50]

	1841	1851	1881	1911
Leinster	49	60	63	69
Munster	43	62	61	76
Ulster	40	54	57	62
Connacht	36	57	60	81

urbanization: marriages in the countryside tended to be later than in the towns.[51] Shifting power relationships within the rural family may also be relevant. Thus it could be argued that deeper immersion in production for the market, and the enhanced economic status of landholders in the later nineteenth century, made for the greater subordination of the inheriting son.[52] Farm inheritance, or its promise, was a prerequisite to marriage. The owner of an attractive set of assets could enforce a long, frustrating wait. Still, as against this bargaining-power model of family and inheritance, one attempt to establish a statistical relationship between farm size and age at marriage has proved less than successful.[53] More importantly perhaps, the price of marriage—in the sense of subjective notions of acceptable housing and living standards—rose in post-Famine Ireland, thus leading to the deferral of marriage transactions. Finally, the elusive issue of a causal role for cultural explanations remains unclear. Certainly some contemporaries complained of the 'unnatural' segregation of the sexes in Irish society and an almost obsessive concern with controlling sexuality.[54]

So, by 1911, access to marriage had been severely rationed, giving Ireland an almost freak status among European societies. The mechanisms were lifelong celibacy for some and delayed marriage for many. In relation to the latter, however, Ireland was only the extreme case in a cluster of late-marrying societies which included Switzerland, Sweden and the Netherlands. The country's freak status resided mainly in the fact that a large proportion of the population never married. A principal motive for rationing marriage was, of course, the desire to increase or maintain living standards.[55] Just as pre-Famine Ireland could be described as illustrating aspects of Malthusian population dynamics, so pre-Independence Ireland can be seen as a case study in neo-Malthusian logic.

Post-Famine Fertility

During the second half of the nineteenth century, western Europe moved from a regime of high birth and high death rates to a lower-pressure demographic system in which births and deaths (per thousand of the population) fell steeply. Life expectancy improved; fertility declined, due to deliberate family limitation. This is the European demographic transition.[56] It was a momentous development, not only in the history of population, but also in the evolution of modern society. Ireland participated in the general decline in death rates. But did it share in the fertility transition before 1914?

It has been conventional to assume that Irish couples adhered to a natural fertility regime prior to 1914. However, the observation that fertility among Protestant families in Ulster was diverging from that of Catholic families around the turn of the century might have brought this assumption into question.[57] Recently, Ó Gráda has established that Ireland was a mild participant in the European fertility decline. Change in one of the standard measures of fertility, for example, indicates a 10 per cent fall between 1881 and 1911.[58] Admittedly, this shows a less than striking commitment to reducing family size, particularly as Irish fertility in the later nineteenth century was already high by European standards. Completed family size was still a remarkable 6.8 children in 1911, thereby maintaining Ireland's position as one of the highest fertility zones in Europe.[59]

Fertility varied between the different parts of Ireland. The regions of highest fertility in 1881 were in the west. The midland counties occupied an intermediate position, while the lowest fertility was to be found in the more urbanized eastern counties. This regional picture, which broadly mirrors the pattern of emigration in post-Famine society, provides an important insight into family strategies. Easy access to employment abroad allowed Irish couples to avoid the adverse economic consequences of a deluge of children. Boats and ships were the nation's favourite and most effective contraceptive devices.

By contrast with Ireland's extreme position among western societies in relation to marriage and fertility, its birth-rate story in the century after 1850 seems almost uneventful. The crude birth rate fell from an estimated 38–40 births per thousand of the population in 1841 to 23 in 1911. The latter was below the Scottish rate of 26 but virtually the same as in England and Wales in 1911.[60] For once, in matters demographic, Ireland was cruising in the mainstream. This normality, it should be remembered, was the product of two extreme but conflicting forces: an exceptionally low marriage rate and an exceptionally high fertility within marriage. Unlike the cases of Britain or France, for example, Ireland's pathway to a falling birth rate was achieved by rationing marriage rather than by restricting the numbers of children produced within marriage.

The Demographic Mechanisms: Mortality

In 1950 Professor Connell, after struggling with the ambiguities of the data in the 1841 census of Ireland, concluded that there was only flimsy evidence for any fall in mortality in the century before the Famine. Even the potato diet did more, he thought, to boost fertility than to reduce deaths.[61] In the two decades immediately before the Famine, the crude death rate was about 24 per 1000, with little inter-provincial variation. It was thus a point or two higher than the rate prevailing in England but, given the evidential difficulties, the difference was not significant. Life expectancies in the two countries were broadly similar: 38 years in Ireland and 40 years in England.[62] England was a richer country than Ireland and we might expect that it should enjoy substantially lower mortality. On the other hand, Ireland was less urbanized and a large proportion of its citizens avoided the hazards of insanitary city life. The Irish, too, enjoyed the benefits of the nutritionally superior though economically inferior potato diet.

What had been the trends in mortality before the 1820s? England had enjoyed a modest fall during the 'long eighteenth century' although this did no more than restore mortality to levels prevailing in the Elizabethan period.[63] In Ireland the widespread advance of the potato during the eighteenth century provided the population with a substantial diet. Such a diet was healthy and nutritious. Recent work on heights shows that Irishmen were consistently taller than Englishmen: testimony to the health-promoting qualities of potatoes. Since a well-nourished person is better able to resist infection than a malnourished one, we may surmise that the Irish population was at least as healthy in the eighteenth century as it seems to have been in the 1820s and 1830s.[64]

It is even conceivable that the death rate in Ireland had been lower during the eighteenth century and that it rose during the immediate pre-Famine decades. After 1815 agricultural prices fell and much of industry collapsed. Consequently the 'bottom half or so of the population ... almost certainly grew poorer'.[65] Added to this, the poor were becoming dangerously dependent on potatoes. By the 1830s, the dependence was almost total among the cottier class.[66] There was one final problem. Although the proportion of the population living in large towns rose little, the absolute numbers quadrupled between 1750 and 1841 (see Table 5.5). Irish towns, even small ones, were desperately unhealthy. In 1799, for example, the death rate in Carrick-on-Suir, Co. Tipperary, a decaying cloth town of 11,000 people, was over 40 per 1000 and life expectancy under 30 years.[67]

The trend in infant mortality is particularly intriguing. The uncertain testimony of parish records is that infant mortality declined during the eighteenth century for reasons that are unclear.[68] By the 1820s and 1830s mortality among male infants has been estimated at 173 per 1000 and, among females, 135. Infant mortality was probably higher than in England, partly—we have suggested above—because of the early weaning of babies.[69] Mokyr has calculated infant mortality rates (males and females) in 1841 as 224 per 1000, but this figure sits uncomfortably beside other estimates and is the result of an error. When the arithmetic is corrected the estimate falls to 193. This is still high, but there are other problems with Mokyr's procedures that account for the high figure.[70]

During the Great Famine the angel of death gathered a bountiful harvest. As a result of *Phythophthora infestans*, the poor lost a quarter of their calorie supply; over a million men, women and children perished; death rates more than doubled and life expectancies halved.[71] All this is well known. What is less well known is the kind of mortality regime that was restored when the crisis passed.

Table 5.8 summarizes the course of the death rate between 1820 and 1920 and compares it with that in England and Wales. We do not know what happened immediately after the Famine. The experience of earlier famines in Europe suggests that the death rate might have fallen to below normal levels immediately after the crisis, because disease had culled the weaker members of society. On the other hand, persistent emigration removed the young and healthy from Ireland. What is certain is that the death rate in the 1870s did not fall to a level 15 per cent less than that in England; the population of Ireland was not healthier, merely less efficiently registered.[73]

The most significant feature of Table 5.8 is the stability of death rates in Ireland after 1880. Whereas in England and Wales the death rate fell by 25 per cent between 1881–91 and 1911–20, in Ireland it declined by only 4 per cent. Part of the explanation was simply that registration in Ireland had become more efficient.

Table 5.8: Crude death rate, Ireland and England and Wales.[72]

Period	Ireland	England and Wales
1821–41	23.8	22.8*
1846–51	52.7	23.3
1851–61	?	22.3
1861–71	?	22.3
1871–81	18.2	21.4
1881–91	17.4	19.2
1891–1901	18.2	18.2
1901–11	17.3	15.4
1911–20	16.7	14.4

* England only.

Another was that emigration had left behind an ageing population. But in two important ways, the living conditions of the poor deteriorated after the Famine, notwithstanding a rise in incomes. A larger proportion of them became town dwellers and thus prey to the hazards of unhealthy cities. Perhaps even more important, their diets deteriorated. With more money in their pockets they looked to grocers' shops rather than to cottier gardens for their food and consumed more tea, sugar, bread, jam and bacon but fewer potatoes. The nutritional quality of diets fell, and the poor became prone to diseases that had once passed them by. The most dramatic illustration of this was the increase in the incidence of tuberculosis in the late nineteenth century at a time when the disease was declining in every other part of the United Kingdom.[74]

Trends in infant mortality tell the same story even more graphically (Fig. 5.1).[75] Recorded infant mortality in Ireland is suspiciously low during the 1870s and 1880s. Registration improved in the early 1890s, partly, it was alleged, because parents insured infant lives and then gave nature a helping hand.[76] More importantly, infant mortality failed to decline significantly after 1900 in the way that it did in other parts of the United Kingdom. The explanation was clear to contemporaries. In 1915 infant mortality in 27 town districts in Ireland was 134.4 per 1000 births compared with an average of 69.9 for the rest of the country. In Dublin the figure was 160.3.[77] Irish infants paid a heavy price for the late rush of their parents into urban society.

Taking the long view, mortality was generally low between the mid eighteenth and mid nineteenth centuries. It possibly drifted slowly upward so that on the eve of the Famine the death rate in Ireland was similar to that found in its more heavily industrialized and urbanized neighbour. During the Famine the death rate more than doubled. It may have dipped below 'normal' levels immediately after the Famine; but in the late nineteenth and early twentieth centuries it declined only sluggishly. In the century before the Famine, therefore, there is no evidence that the death rate played more than a minor part in explaining the rapid growth of population. Soaring levels were crucial in reducing the population by more than two million between 1841 and 1851. In the late nineteenth and early twentieth centuries, the relative failure of the death rate to fall contributed to a small degree to the decline of population, but the more dynamic roles were played by persistent emigration and falling fertility.

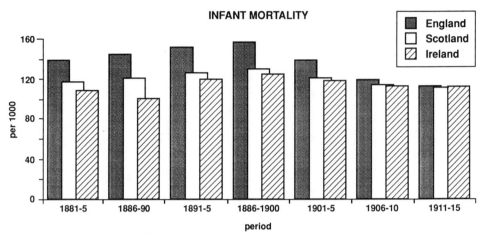

Fig. 5.1. Trends in infant mortality in England, Scotland and Ireland, 1881–1915.

Migration Before and After the Famine

The third component of population change was emigration. While Erin and exile seem inextricably linked, Ireland was not always a land of emigration. During the seventeenth century it had been a net receiver of people from other regions of the British Isles. Thinly populated it was an alternative frontier zone to that of the New World for colonial projects and peoples. But Ireland never again appeared so attractive to settlers from abroad or, increasingly, to some of its own inhabitants. Over the succeeding three centuries the trickle of incomers was swamped by an outward tide of migration. Like other peripheral societies, Ireland's demographic destiny lay in forming and forwarding muscle power to the dynamic centres of economic growth, which in her case, were found principally in Britain, North America and Australasia. The effect of this Irish emigration on its destinations overseas is discussed in Chapters 10 and 11; here, we consider its social and demographic consequences within Ireland.

The volume of emigration ebbed and flowed through time. So also did its regional sources. It is no coincidence that Ulster, which experienced the most extensive immigration at the end of the seventeenth century, should a generation or two later supply many of the pioneering emigrants for the American colonies.[78] It may well be, as is cogently argued by Miller, that the mentalities of the settlers from Scotland and England were different from those of the indigenous Irish.[79] But the shallowness of the newcomers' roots in Ulster landscape and culture must also have facilitated the physical and psychic uprooting that emigration entailed. Crossing the Atlantic was the analogue of earlier migratory moves, particularly for those who had come to define themselves as the Scots-Irish (see Chapter 10).

Typically, emigrants to colonial America were of Presbyterian and Scots-Irish background, though the non-Presbyterian and non-Ulster component expanded through time. Many financed the long passage to the colonies by mortgaging their labour power and becoming indentured servants. Fluctuations in earnings from farming and the domestic textile industry influenced the extent of the outflow. The first major migration, which permanently opened America to the northerners, was in the years 1718–20. The catalyst was a succession of bad harvests and acute agricultural distress in Ulster. Subsequent crises in 1725–29, 1740–41, and in the mid-1750s were reflected in further peaks in overseas migration.[80] Significantly, the abnormal outpouring of people in the early 1770s was precipitated, not only by food scarcity, but also by crises in linen manufacturing. This testifies to structural change in the northern economy over the preceding half century, in particular the widespread diffusion of and dependence on domestic industry.[81] Still, while this emigration was of significant economic, and of even more significant political import for colonial America, its demographic implications for Ireland should not be exaggerated. In most years, no more than 2000 people left for the New World. There was some quickening in the pace of emigration in the three decades after American independence in 1783. Perhaps around 100,000 left.[82] While this is a large cumulative total, it implies an annual flow of just over 3000 per year.

The other major emigrant destination during the eighteenth century was the neighbouring island of Britain (see Chapter 11). In the main, cross-channel migration drew its sustenance from the eastern counties of Ireland, those regions closest culturally as well as geographically to England and Scotland. Essentially it was a movement of the able-bodied poor, tramping through Britain in search of work. The size of this migration is difficult to ascertain, in part because of its fluid character. Some settled permanently; others returned after an interval of years; others still scurried backwards and forwards across the Irish Sea, exploiting the peak seasonal demands for labour in British agriculture during the summer months.[83] Fitzpatrick surmises that more emigrated to Britain than America, which seems plausible in view of the relative costs involved, the larger geographical base of emigration to Britain,and the finality in most instances of a move to the New World.[84] Even if emigration to Britain was double the American level over the eighteenth century, the quantitative dimensions of the combined emigrant streams remain small when set against the background of a rapidly expanding population.

Following the ending of British–Irish hostilities with Napoleonic France in 1815, a new era in the history of Irish emigration opened. Between 1815 and 1845 something like a million Irish men and women disappeared into the New World.[85] Perhaps half that number went to Britain. Thus, when in 1844 Engels came to write his celebrated account of the 'uncivilized' and 'brutish' Irish of Manchester, there were 'Little Irelands' in many of the manufacturing towns of northern England and lowland Scotland. The overseas and cross-channel emigration indicates an *annual* outflow of 45,000 persons. This truly remarkable exodus dwarfs the levels characteristic of the previous century, and was unique also in the context of the Europe of the day. In terms of population change, emigration was the major demographic mechanism restraining 'runaway' population growth in the decades before the Famine.[86]

Large-scale emigration would have been difficult to sustain without an expansion of the phenomenon from its core regions in Ulster and Leinster to the island as a whole. There was, nonetheless, a regional pattern to the process.[87] (Fig. 5.2) Six of the 12 most emigration-prone counties were in Ulster, reflecting not only a heritage of earlier emigration but also the crisis in the rural textile industry during the 1820s and 1830s.[88] The west midland counties of Leinster were also severely affected. These subregions contained pockets of vulnerable industry. More import-

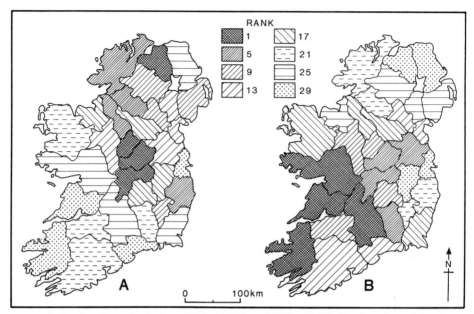

Fig. 5.2. Ireland: cohort depletion, 1821–41 (A) and 1851–61 (B). Rank order relates to percentage depletion over an intercensal decade of the cohort initially aged 15–24 years (6–15 years in the case of depletion over the two decades 1821–41). Each rank group contains four counties. The percentages for each rank group in each map are:

Rank	A 1821–41	B 1851–61
1	51.62	48.40
5	42.06	40.99
9	40.60	40.24
13	40.06	38.98
17	37.24	37.70
21	34.41	35.81
25	29.99	32.77
29	26.29	28.42

(After D. Fitzpatrick, in Vaughan (ed.), *Ireland Under the Union*, (Oxford, 1989), p. 620.)

antly, the advance of commercialized agriculture—with its logic of strict estate management, monetized transactions, impartible inheritance, and less labour-intensive production—was enhancing the prospects of market-oriented farmers. This was at the expense of surplus farming sons and daughters as well as the rural poor. The western seaboard counties were sheltered from these modernizing impulses, in part by distance but also by the cultural barrier to attitudinal change posed by the Gaelic language and its rich storehouse of alternative values and meanings. Clare and Kerry, for example, which, on the basis of socio-economic indicators ranging from population density to income levels, should have been prime recruiting territories for the emigration agent, were among the least affected by the drain of population.[89] These regional variations should not be allowed, however, to obscure the national picture. The central reality remained the fact of massive emigration, with substantial migration from all, including the most 'backward' counties.

The panic-stricken exodus of the Famine years was an altogether different experience. Inhibitions regarding emigration withered, like the potato stalks on a ruined landscape. In the years 1845–55 over two million people escaped the wreckage of the pre-Famine economy, with most of these finding their way to the United States. A less than providential Mother Ireland lost more of her sons and daughters in this decade than in the previous two and a half centuries.[90] Viewed on an annual basis, those fleeing Ireland during the crisis period 1846–50 numbered at least 200,000. The year 1851 was the *annus mirabilis* of Irish emigration history. A staggering one-quarter of a million people left for overseas destinations, the largest number ever, either before or since.[91] Even when the shock waves of the Great Hunger had subsided, the exodus continued, averaging an eighth of a million annually during the 1850s and 1860s.[92] The rate as well as the volume of emigration slackened in the 1870s, picked up again in the 1880s under the impact of agricultural depression, and gradually tapered off during the quarter century of rising living standards prior to the First World War.

The Famine inaugurated, not only a century of population decline, but also a changing regional pattern of emigration. The conventional view was that the most overpopulated western counties had somehow maintained pre-Famine demographic characteristics, without recourse to large-scale emigration.[93] This interpretation has turned out to be a statistical illusion, derived from the under-recording of emigrants from the west.[94] In fact the western peasant, often Gaelic speaking, was disproportionately represented among post-Famine emigrants, something which contrasts sharply with earlier times. The Famine not only accelerated existing demographic trends; it created new ones.

The religious as well as the regional composition of emigration changed through time. The preponderance of Protestants among emigrants to colonial America reduced significantly the potential weight of Ulster Protestants within Irish society, possibly with major long-term political and cultural consequences. In the century before the Famine, the most striking disparity between Protestant and Catholic population growth rates occurred in many of the southern counties. Among the many reasons which might account for the erosion of these minority communities, voluntary (sometimes forced) emigration seems the most likely explanation. While more detailed studies are needed, it is possible that the pattern shown for County Longford approximates the long run fate of many southern Protestant communities (Fig. 5.3).[95]

Differential emigration, aided by internal migration, may also help to explain a profound and largely undocumented set of changes in the spatial distribution of Irish Protestants. In 1731 the six Ulster counties which now comprise Northern Ireland contained slightly less than half of Ireland's Protestant population; by 1861 they contained 64 per cent, or two out of every three. This focus on the north-east continued, intensifying during the revolutionary decade, 1911–21.

Although somewhat neglected, the importance of Protestants to Irish emigration is shown in the strength of Orange politics in nineteenth-century Scotland, in parts of the north of England, New York State, and most of all in Canada.[96] Akenson's startling suggestion that most present-day Irish-Americans are of Protestant rather than Catholic stock, while heavily dependent on the definitions employed, helps restore Protestants to a central role in the drama of Irish emigration.[97] Still, there is

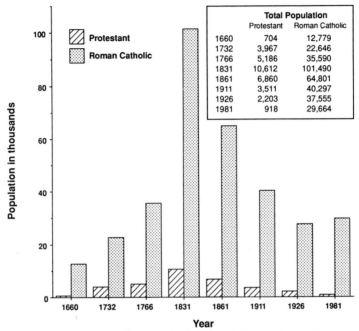

Fig. 5.3. Religious demography of County Longford. (After L. Kennedy *et al.*, in Gillespie and Moran (eds.), *Longford. Essays in County History*, (Dublin, 1991), p. 32.)

no doubt that during the Great Famine, and subsequently, the great bulk of emigrants came from Catholic backgrounds. This numerical concentration in later historical time contributed to the easy, if misleading, equation of emigrant status with Catholicism.

Post-Famine emigrant streams were dominated by single, young people, mainly the surplus sons and daughters of farmers and labourers, although in Ulster the collapse of handloom weaving during the 1850s added a distinct industrial coloration. By contrast with emigration from other European societies, this was not a male-dominated exodus. In most years there was a rough equality of the sexes, though in the later nineteenth century women emigrants came to outnumber the men.[98] This youthful and largely gender-neutral process, as well as the orderly and self-perpetuating nature of Irish emigration, suggest that, while the role of emigrant was filled by the *individual*, the traffic overseas was governed by group decisions originating with the *family* and its various kin extensions. Before the Famine the majority of overseas passengers seem to have travelled in some form of kinship group, and during the Famine itself the removal of whole families was common.[99] The dominance of single emigrants in the later period reflected the greater resources and flexibility of families on both sides of the Atlantic. Thus, the transnational character of many Irish families permitted a controlled sequence of transactions across space and time: as sons and daughters reached adulthood, they were shuttled along kinship networks from the Old to the New World. Emigrants' remittances flowed in the reverse direction.

The magnitude of emigration varied enormously over the course of the eighteenth and nineteenth centuries. Table 5.9 summarizes, in approximate fashion, the scale of these variations.[100] It is worth noting also that, contrary to popular assumption, the pattern revealed bears no simple relationship to overall population change in these centuries.

Table 5.9: Estimates and guess-estimates of the annual volume of Irish emigration in selected time periods between 1700 and 1900 (in thousands).

1715–83	1783–1815	1815–45	1845–50	1850–60	1900–14
c. 5	*c.* 6	*c.* 45	*c.* 200	*c.* 125	*c.* 34

Why did so many Irish emigrate during the two centuries after 1700? Some were driven out, by the state, by the landlords, by communal intimidation. But the overwhelming majority left because *they* had decided to leave, in response to unfavourable conditions at home and the expectation of superior conditions abroad. Between the accession of George I in 1714 and the end of the Great Famine, push factors in the form of industrial, farming and subsistence crises were the predominant forces making for movement. Conceivably, this was more true of Catholic than of Protestant emigrants. The collapse of the cottier economy, centring on potato cultivation and subsistence living, was the single most powerful blow, leading to the destruction of hundreds of thousands of economic niches. During the second half of the nineteenth century, livelihoods continued to disappear: in handloom weaving and other forms of handicraft industry under the pressure of technological change; in agriculture as capital-intensive farming displaced labour.[101] In some backward districts potato failure still carried baleful consequences. Viewed spatially, each of these causes had an uneven incidence, thus making for a regional pattern to emigration. But the dominant set of forces was of the pull rather than the push variety.

There is no doubt that material well-being improved in post-Famine Ireland and that the country could have sustained a larger population.[102] But this would have been at the cost of *per capita* living standards. The Irish were advantaged—self-indulgent notions of exile notwithstanding—by ready access to the two great labour markets of the industrializing world: North America and Britain.[103] The prospect of employment abroad, and higher earning power, persuaded many people of the benefits of mobility. Those who remained were also convinced, as uneconomic household members departed and emigrants' remittances took their place. In this deliberate and orderly efflux, the encouraging hands of earlier emigrants, stretching metaphorically across the seas to Ireland, gave tangible expression to the notion of pull factors.

Migration within Ireland is a minor variation on the larger theme of emigration flows. The census takers of 1841 estimated that about 5 per cent of the Irish population were living in counties in which they were not born.[104] A majority of these were to be found in neighbouring counties; some were visitors rather than migrants. The absence of expanding industrial centres, outside the north-east in the nineteenth century, is probably the chief reason for limited internal migration. In 1911 only Belfast and Dublin had substantial minorities recruited from other counties and countries. Belfast in particular had grown spectacularly during the

nineteenth century on the basis of in-migration. But this flawed New Jerusalem—
importing the sectarian animosities of the Ulster countryside within its palisades—
was the exception. The lack of comparable magnetic poles on the island explains
why emigration, rather than migration, as in the case of Britain, France or Germany, was the dominant pattern.[105]

Internal migration could also take the form of temporary or seasonal flows of
labour. From at least the later eighteenth century, migratory workers (*spailpini*)
moved in droves from the poor or mountainous districts to the lowland and
commercialized farming areas to work on the hay and tillage harvests. Changes in
post-Famine agriculture, in particular the shift to livestock husbandry and the
switch from hand to horse technology, progressively reduced the demand for
labour generally in the rural economy, and for migratory labour in particular.
These temporary movements were replicated also on a larger geographical canvas:
Irish men and, to a much lesser extent, women travelled backwards and forwards
to England and Scotland in search of seasonal work. This traffic, which was directed mainly to harvest work, probably peaked at a level of 100,000 migrants
during the 1860s and subsequently went into steep decline.[106] In the later part of
the century these migrants came disproportionately from the west and the north-
west, where underemployment on smallholdings was most severe and where also
cultural barriers to emigration may have been stronger.[107] Temporary movement
offered a half-way house between life in Ireland and permanent emigration. It was
also a compromise which allowed archaic patterns of landholding and living to
survive for an additional generation or two after the cataclysm of the Famine. Like
land reform, like light railways, like other panaceas for the alleviation of rural
overpopulation, it offered no permanent solution. Ironically, these various adaptations probably smoothed the way to bidding final farewells to the west.

Perspectives on Mortality: Malthus and Ireland

In matters demographic Ireland gravitated towards the extreme of the west European experience. It had the fastest growing population in the century before the
Famine; in the century after, it had the slowest. As in England, population increase
during the period 1700–1845 was driven by changes in fertility rather than mortality. In England an increase in the birth rate is held to account for three-quarters
of the increment to population which occurred during the 'long' eighteenth century. An argument-by analogy, bearing in mind the well-nourished and rural
character of Irish existence, might lead one to the conclusion that the increasing
birth rate accounted for even more of the growth in Irish population.

Post-Famine population change was dominated by two demographic mechanisms, a falling birth rate (due to later and less frequent marriage) and, more
importantly, a huge exodus of people. Once again, changes in mortality seem to be
relatively unimportant. Can we, therefore, take death out of Irish history, in the
demographic sphere at any rate? Possibly so, for the hundred years before 1845,
but certainly not for the following century. It needs to be emphasized: while it is
convenient to treat separately the triad of demographic mechanisms—fertility,
mortality and migration—in practice some interaction between these is likely.
Thus, an analysis of regional patterns in post-Famine society would suggest that

high levels of emigration permitted and sustained high marital fertility and also (relatively) high marriage rates. In time, these two fuelled further emigration. Whether or not there is a relationship between fertility and mortality in this period is less clear. The simple model of the European demographic transition postulates that the birth rate adjusts downwards, after a time lag, in response to a falling death rate. In particular, the greater likelihood of children surviving into adulthood was conducive to a reduction in desired family size. The Irish case seems a heterodox one. Birth and death rates fell after 1850. There was a small reduction in marital fertility towards the end of the century. Curiously, this coincided with a period of stationary rather than falling death rates. Possibly the fertility decline was related to earlier falls in the death rate, though this is a subject which requires further exploration.

There is no doubting, however, a connection between mass mortality, emigration and marriage patterns. The Great Famine was 'no ordinary subsistence crisis': its searing impact affected society in the longer as well as the short term.[108] A terrible, if temporary, surge in the death rate moved emigration onto a higher plane; contributed to a weakening of the propensity to marry; and initiated a secular decline in total population.

Does this suggest that Ireland was overpopulated on the eve of the Famine? Were Malthusian notions of a link between population pressure, low living standards and vulnerability to famine well founded? The most authoritative work on pre-Famine poverty, that by Joel Mokyr, suggests that overpopulation (relative to existing land resources) was not the problem. However, more recent research, using Mokyr's methodology but exploring the question in a local and regional context, concludes that overpopulation was indeed a problem in west Munster, in the west midlands, and in parts of Connacht. In the more industrialized north-east, not surprisingly, this proved not to be the case. A tentative conclusion might be that Malthusian notions have validity in relation to some, though not all, regions of pre-Famine Ireland.

Cultural influences tend to be ignored or downgraded in the international literature on demographic change. We have suggested a broadly Malthusian interpretation of pre-Famine population history. For the post-Famine period we have favoured a neo-Malthusian emphasis in explaining marriage and migration patterns. But we have been conscious also of the need, such is the extreme character of some of the Irish demographic responses, to incorporate cultural elements into the explanatory sketch. The quest for total history is an elusive one, but a deeper understanding of the dynamics of Irish population would seem to require an approach which integrates the economic, the social and the cultural.

References

1. Cormac Ó Gráda, *The Great Irish Famine*, (London, 1989), p. 13.
2. *Ibid.*, 34; D. B. Grigg, *Population Growth and Agrarian Change: An Historical Perspective*, (London, 1980), pp. 138–9.
3. David Fitzpatrick, 'Irish emigration in the later nineteenth century', *Irish Historical Studies*, **22** (1980), p. 126; *idem*, 'Emigration to America', in W. E. Vaughan (ed.), *A New History of Ireland: Ireland under the Union, I, 1801–70*, 5 (Oxford, 1989), p. 608.
4. E. A. Wrigley and R. S. Schofield, *The Population History of England 1541–1871: A*

Reconstruction, (London, 1981). The most recent and succinct summary is R. A. Houston, *The Population History of Britain and Ireland 1500–1750*, (London, 1992).

5. K. H. Connell, *The Population of Ireland 1750–1845*, (Oxford, 1950), pp. 255–61; L. A. Clarkson, 'Irish population revisited, 1687–1821', in J. M. Goldstrom and L. A. Clarkson (eds.), *Irish Population, Economy, and Society: Essays in Honour of the late K. H. Connell*, (Oxford, 1981), pp. 14–18.

6. Clarkson, 'Irish population revisited', 14–18; D. Dickson, C. Ó Gráda, S. Daultrey, 'Hearth tax, household size and Irish population change 1672–1821', *Proceedings of the Royal Irish Academy*, **82C**, no. 6 (1982), pp. 125–50.

7. Connell, *The Population of Ireland*, pp. 14–24; Clarkson, 'Irish population revisited', pp. 18–25; Dickson, Ó Gráda, Daultrey, 'Hearth tax, household size and Irish population', pp. 50–55.

8. J. J. Lee, 'On the accuracy of pre-famine Irish censuses', in Goldstrom and Clarkson (eds.), *Irish Population, Economy, and Society*, pp. 37–56.

9. Joel Mokyr and Cormac Ó Gráda, 'New developments in Irish population history, 1700–1850', *Economic History Review*, 2nd ser., **XXIV** (1984), p. 475; W. E. Vaughan and A. J. Fitzpatrick, *Irish Historical Statistics: Population, 1821–1971*, (Dublin, Royal Irish Academy, 1978), p. 3.

10. Mokyr and Ó Gráda, 'New developments', p. 476

11. The census figures used for 1821 and 1841 are Professor Lee's revisions.

12. Based on Dickson, Ó Gráda, Daultrey, 'Hearth tax, household size and Irish population', p. 155 (averages of the upper and lower-bound totals); and Vaughan and Fitzpatrick, *Irish Historical Statistics*, pp. 15–6, 24, 25–6.

13. P. M. Hohenberg and L. H. Lees, *The Making of Urban Europe*, 1000–1950, (Cambridge, Mass., 1985), p. 227.

14. L. A. Clarkson, 'Population change and urbanization 1821–1911', in L. Kennedy and P. Ollerenshaw (eds.), *An Economic History of Ulster*, 1820–1940, (Manchester, 1985), pp. 137–41.

15. Houston, *Population History*, p. 32; Vaughan and Fitzpatrick, *Irish Historical Statistics*, pp. 28–48; P. J. Waller, *Town, City, and Nation: England 1850–1914*, (Oxford, 1983), pp. 7–8.

16. 1851.

17. Arthur Young, *Tour in Ireland, 1776–9*, (ed. A. W. Hutton, London, 1892), II, pp. 119–20.

18. Connell, *The Population of Ireland; idem*, 'Some unsettled problems in English and Irish population history', *Irish Historical Studies*, **vii** (1951).

19. Strictly, we should also consider legitimacy and illegitimacy, but all studies of pre-Famine Ireland suggest that the latter was at such a low level that it can be ignored.

20. Mokyr and Ó Gráda, 'New developments', pp. 477–9.

21. E. A. Wrigley, 'The growth of population in eighteenth-century England: a conundrum resolved', *Past and Present*, no. 98, 1983, p. 131.

22. K. H. Connell, 'Catholicism and marriage in the century after the famine', in K. H. Connell, *Irish Peasant Society: Four Historical Essays*, (Oxford, 1968), p. 114.

23. Joel Mokyr, *Why Ireland Starved: A Quantitative and Analytical History of the Irish Economy, 1800–1850*, (London, 1983), p. 36

24. Mokyr and Ó Gráda, 'New developments', pp. 477–8. Cormac Ó Gráda, 'Dublin's demography in the early nineteenth century: evidence from the Rotunda', *Population Studies*, **45** (1991), p. 52.

25. It is also influenced by foetal mortality, which cannot be measured historically. However, most studies suggest that its influence has been limited. See Chris Wilson, 'The proximate determinants of marital fetility in England, 1600–1799', in Lloyd Bonfield, R. M. Smith and Keith Wrightson (eds.), *The World We Have Gained: Histories of Population and Social Structure*, (Oxford, 1986), p. 209.

26. Houston, *Population History*, p. 36.

27. L. A. Clarkson, 'The demography of Carrick-on-Suir, 1799', *Proceedings of the Royal Irish Academy*, **87C**, no. 2 (1987), pp. 24–7.

28. D. E. C. Eversley, 'The demography of the Irish Quakers, 1650–1850', in Goldstrom and Clarkson, *Irish Population, Economy and Society*, pp. 86–7.

29. Wilson, 'The proximate determinants of marital fertility', pp. 212–19.

30. John Bongaarts, 'Does malnutrition affect fecundity? A summary of the evidence', *Science*, 208 (1980), pp. 564–9.

31. L. A. Clarkson and E. M. Crawford, 'Dietary directions: a topographical survey of Irish diet, 1836', in Rosalind Mitchison and Peter Roebuck (eds.), *Economy and Society in Scotland and Ireland, 1500–1939*, (Edinburgh, 1988), p. 191; Ó Gráda, *The Great Irish Famine*, pp. 19–27.

32. Bongaarts, 'Does malnutrion affect fecundity?', pp. 566–7; Wilson, 'The proximate determinants of marital fertility', pp. 219–26. For a dissenting view see Thomas McKeown, 'Food, infection, and population', in R. I. Rotberg and T. K. Rabb (eds.), *Hunger and History: the Impact of Changing Food Production and Consumption Patterns on Society*, (Cambridge, 1983), pp. 35–6.

33. S. H. Cousens, 'The restriction of population growth in pre-Famine Ireland', *Proceedings of the Royal Irish Academy*, **64C**, no. 4 (1966), pp. 85–99.

34. Calculated from Vaughan and Fitzpatrick, *Irish Population Statistics*, pp. 87–90. (For 1841 the age group is 46–55 years.)

35. L. M. Cullen, *An Economic History of Ireland since 1660*, (London, 1972), pp. 167–70.

36. J. J. Lee, *The Modernization of Irish Society, 1848–1918*, (Dublin, 1973), p. 4.

37. K. H. Connell, 'Peasant marriage in Ireland: its structure and development since the Famine', *Economic History Review*, 2nd ser., **XIV** (1962), pp. 502–523; C. Arensberg, *The Irish Countryman*, (Gloucester, Mass.,1959), pp. 71–79.

38. Census of Population of Ireland for 1926.

39. R. E. Kennedy, *The Irish*, pp. 153–72.

40. K. A. Miller, *Emigrants and Exiles: Ireland and the Irish Exodus to North America*, (New York, 1985), pp. 357–8.

41. T. Guinane, 'Migration, marriage, and household formation: the Irish at the turn of the century' (abstract of PhD thesis), *Irish Economic and Social History*, **25** (1988), pp. 105–6.

42. R. Breen, 'Farm size and marital status: county and provincial differences in Arensberg and Kimball's Ireland', *Economic and Social Review*, **13** (1982), pp. 89–100.

43. Guinane, 'Migration', pp. 105–6.

44. Kennedy, *The Irish*, pp. 145–8.

45. J. C. Messenger, *Inis Beag: Isle of Ireland*, (New York, 1969); S. O Faolain, *The Irish*, (London, 1947); J. Whyte, *Church and State in Modern Ireland, 1923–1979*, (Dublin, 1980).

46. Based on calculations of the singulate mean age of marriage.

47. Lee, *Modernisation*, p. 3.

48. J. A. O'Brien (ed), *The Vanishing Irish*, (London, 1954).

49. W. P. Gray, 'Patterns of illegitimacy in twentieth-century Northern Ireland' (unpublished MSSc dissertation, The Queen's University of Belfast, 1989), pp. 133–48.

50. Source: calculated from Vaughan & Fitzpatrick, *Irish Historical Statistics*, pp. 104–159. (For 1841 the age group is 26–35 years.)

51. Commission on Emigration and other Population Problems, 1948–54, (Dublin, 1954), pp. 69–70.

52. L. Kennedy, 'Farm succession in modern Ireland: elements of a theory of inheritance', *Economic History Review*, **XLIV** (1991), pp. 477–481.

53. Ibid., p. 491.

54. H. Plunkett, *Ireland in the New Century*, (London, 1904), pp. 115–16; P. Blanchard, *The Irish and Catholic Power*, (London, 1954).

55. Commission on Emigration, pp. 79–80.

56. A. J. Coale and S. C. Watkins (eds.), *The Fertility Decline in Europe*, (Princeton, 1987).

57. Cormac Ó Gráda, 'Did Ulster Catholics always have larger families?', *Irish Economic and Social History*, 12 (1985), pp. 79–88.

58. C. Ó Gráda, 'New evidence on the fertility transition in Ireland, 1880–1911', (Centre for Economic Policy Research, Discussion Paper Series, London, 1991).

59. Commission on Emigration, p. 94.

60. B. R. Mitchell and P. Deane, *Abstract of British Historical Statistics*, (Cambridge, 1971), pp. 30–33.

61. Connell, *Population of Ireland*, p. 240.

62. Mokyr, *Why Ireland Starved*, p. 35; P. P. Boyle and Cormac Ó Gráda, 'Fertility trends, excess mortality, and the Great Irish Famine', *Demography*, **23**, no. 4 (1986), p. 561.

63. Wrigley, 'Population growth in eighteenth-century England', pp. 129, 143

64. Ó Gráda, *Ireland Before and After the Famine*, pp. 16–17; Joel Mokyr and C. Ó Gráda, 'The height of Irishmen and Englishmen in the 1770s: some evidence from the East India Company records', *Eighteenth-Century Ireland*, **4** (1989), pp. 83–92; E. Margaret Crawford, 'Subsistence crises and famines in Ireland: a nutritionist's view' in E. Margaret Crawford (ed.), *Famine: The Irish Experience 900–1900*, (Edinburgh, 1989), pp. 198–219.

65. Joel Mokyr and Cormac Ó Gráda, 'Poor and getting poorer? Living standards in Ireland before the Famine', *Economic History Review*, 2nd ser., **XLI** (1988), p. 211.

66. Clarkson and Crawford, 'Irish diet, 1836', pp. 171–91; Ó Gráda, *The Great Irish Famine*, pp. 19–22; Peter Solar, 'The Great Famine was no ordinary subsistence crisis' in Crawford (ed.), *Famine: The Irish Experience*, pp. 114–18.

67. Clarkson, 'The demography of Carrick-on-Suir', p. 31.

68. Valerie Morgan, 'A case study of population change over two centuries: Blaris, Lisburn 1661–1848', *Irish Economic and Social History*, **3** (1976), p. 16; L. A. Clarkson, 'Armagh 1770: portrait of an urban community', in David Harkness and Mary O Dowd (eds.), *The Town in Ireland*, (Belfast, 1981), p. 92.

69. Boyle and Ó Gráda, 'Fertility trends', p. 561; Wrigley and Schofield, *Population History*, p. 249; Houston, *Population History*, pp. 50–1; Clarkson, 'The demography of Carrick-on-Suir', p. 31.

70. Mokyr, *Why Ireland Starved*, pp. 37, 64–7, 72–5. To measure infant mortality one first has to calculate the number of live births. Mokyr does this for 1840–41 by taking the number of children recorded in the 1841 census aged one month and multiplying by 12. However to the recorded numbers of live infants must be added an estimate of the numbers who died in the first month of life. Mokyr adds this estimate after the multiplication; it should have been added before. The consequence is to underestimate the number of live births against which to set the estimated numbers of infant deaths. The corrected estimate of births also produces a crude birth rate of 44.4 against Mokyr's figure of 40.

71. Mokyr, *Why Ireland Starved*, pp. 265–8; Boyle and Ó Gráda, 'Fertility trends', pp. 561–2; Solar, 'The great famine', p. 125; Crawford, 'Subsistence crises', pp. 198–219.

72. Mokyr, *Why Ireland Starved*, pp. 35, 266; Registrar General of Ireland, *Annual Reports*, 1870–1921, (British Parliamentary Papers); Wrigley and Schofield, *Population History*, pp. 534–5; Neil Tranter, *Population since the Industrial Revolution: the Case of England and Wales*, (London, 1973), p. 53.

73. See, *First and Second Reports from the Select Committee on Death Certification*, (British Parliamentary Papers, 1893–4 [374, 402], vol. XL), pp. 291–303.

74. E. Margaret Crawford, 'Aspects of Irish diet, 1839–1904' (unpublished PhD thesis, University of London, 1985), pp. 342–7; *41st Annual Report of the Registrar General of Ireland, 1904*, (British Parliamentary Papers, 1904 [cd 2673]), p. xvii.

75. Registrar General of Ireland, *Annual Reports*, 1864–1920; R. I. Woods, P. A. Watterson and J. H. Woodward, 'The causes of rapid infant mortality decline in England and Wales, 1861–1921, part 1', *Population Studies*, **42** (1988), p. 349.

76. *First and Second Reports from the Select Committee on Death Certification*, p. 302.

77. The Carnegie United Kingdom Trust, *Report on the Physical Welfare of Mothers and Children*, Volume IV, Ireland (Dublin, 1917), pp. 4–10; Woods, Watterson, and Woodward, 'The causes of rapid infant mortality decline in England and Wales', pp. 353–66.

78. J. G. Leyburn, *The Scotch-Irish: A Social History*, (Chapel Hill, North Carolina, 1978); R. J. Dickson, *Ulster Emigration to Colonial America, 1718–1775*, (London, 1966); Houston, *Population History*, pp. 62–63.

79. K. A. Miller, with B. Boling and D. N. Doyle, 'Emigrants and exiles: Irish cultures and

Irish emigration, 1790–1922', *Irish Historical Studies*, **29**, (1980), pp. 97–125; K. A. Miller, *Emigrants and Exiles: Ireland and the Irish Exodus to North America*, (New York, 1985), pp. 102–135.

80. Leyburn, *Scotch-Irish*, pp. 169–175; Dickson, *Ulster Emigration*, pp. 21–31.
81. *Ibid.*, pp. 78–80; W. H. Crawford, 'The evolution of the linen trade in Ulster before industrialization', *Irish Economic & Social History*, **15**, (1988), pp. 32–53.
82. Miller, *Emigrants and Exiles*, p. 169; although he believes that the numbers could be as high as 150,000.
83. E. J. T. Collins, 'Labour supply and demand in European agriculture, 1800–1880', in E. L. Jones and S. J. Woolf (eds.), *Agrarian Change and Economic Development*, (London, 1969), pp. 76–8
84. Fitzpatrick, 'Emigration' in Vaughan (ed.), *Ireland under the Union*, p. 565.
85. W. F. Adams, *Ireland and Irish Emigration to the New World from 1815 to the Famine*, (New Haven, 1932).
86. C. Ó Gráda, 'Population change', in Vaughan (ed.), *Ireland under the Union* p. 119. G. O Tuathaigh, *Ireland before the Famine, 1798–1848*, (Dublin,1972), p. 141.
87. Fitzpatrick, 'Emigration', in Vaughan (ed.), *Ireland Under the Union*, p.620.
88. L. Kennedy, 'The rural economy', in Kennedy and Ollerenshaw (eds.), *Economic History of Ulster*, pp. 4–6.
89. For detailed local perspectives on the pre-Famine economy see Poor Inquiry (Ireland): Appendix D, (British Parliamentary Papers, 31 ,1836).
90. Miller, *Emigrants and Exiles*, p. 291.
91. Commission on Emigration, pp. 314–16; Vaughan and Fitzpatrick, *Irish Historical Statistics*, p. 260.
92. Fitzpatrick, 'Emigration', in Vaughan (ed.), *Ireland under the Union*, p. 566.
93. S. H. Cousens, 'Emigration and demographic change in Ireland, 1851–1861', *Economic History Review*, 2nd ser., **XIV** (1961), pp. 275–88.
94. C. Ó Gráda, 'Some aspects of nineteenth-century Irish emigration', in L. M. Cullen and T. C. Smout (eds.), *Comparative Aspects of Scottish and Irish Economic and Social History, 1600–1900*, (Edinburgh, 1977), p.70.
95. L. Kennedy, K. A. Miller, with M. Graham, 'The long retreat: protestants, economy and society, 1660–1926' in R. Gillespie and G. Moran (eds.), *Longford: Essays in County History*, (Dublin, 1991), pp. 31–61.
96. D. H. Akenson, *Small Differences: Irish Catholics and Irish Protestants, 1815–1922: An International Perspective*, (Kingston and Montreal, 1988); B. Elliott, *Irish Migrants in the Canadas: A New Approach*, (Kingston and Montreal, 1988).
97. D. H. Akenson, 'The Irish in North America: Catholic or Protestant?', *Irish Review*, **11** (1992), pp. 17–22.
98. R. E. Kennedy, The Irish, pp. 76–78.
99. Adams, *Ireland and Irish Emigration*; C. Ó Gráda, 'Across the briny ocean: some thoughts on Irish emigration to America, 1800–1850', in T. M. Devine and D. Dickson, *Ireland and Scotland, 1600–1850*, (Edinburgh, 1983), pp. 119–20.
100. The pre-Famine estimates are derived from the works of Leyburn, Dickson, Adams and Miller, with a wholly arbitrary allowance being made for emigration to Britain. Even if the latter is wide of the mark, the obvious contrast in emigration before and after 1815 holds good.
101. Liam Kennedy, 'Rural economy', pp. 10–11.
102. K. A. Kennedy, T. Giblin and D. McHugh, *The Economic Development of Ireland in the Twentieth Century*, (London, 1988).
103. L. Kennedy, 'The economic thought of the nation's lost leader: Charles Stewart Parnell', in D. G. Boyce and A. O'Day (eds.), *Parnell in Perspective*, (London and New York, 1991), pp. 182–3.
104. Report of the commissioners appointed to take the census of Ireland for the year 1841, (British Parliamentary Papers, 24, 1843), p. 552.
105. A. S. Milward and S. B. Saul, *The Development of the Economies of Continental Europe, 1850–1914*, (London,1977), pp. 44–6, 104–5, 147; J. Lawton, 'Urbanization and popu-

lation change in nineteenth century England', in J. Patten (ed.), *The Expanding City*, (London, 1983).

106. C. Ó Gráda, 'Seasonal adjustment and post-Famine adjustment in the west of Ireland', *Studia Hibernica*, **13** (1973), pp. 48–76.

107. For data on numbers and their geographical distribution see The Agricultural Statistics of Ireland for the year 1881, (British Parliamentary Papers, 74, 1882).

108. Solar, 'The Great Famine', in Crawford (ed.), *Famine: The Irish Experience 900–1900*, pp. 112–33; Mokyr, *Why Ireland Starved*, pp. 62–4; L. Kennedy, 'Malthusian models and Irish history: a view from the localities', (unpublished paper, Belfast, 1990).

6

Regionalism and Localism: Religious Change and Social Protest, *c.* 1700 to *c.* 1900

L. J. Proudfoot

Introduction

One of the most significant developments in Irish historical writing in recent years has been the growing recognition of the diversity of the social structures and economic experience which characterized Irish life during the post-plantation period. Recent work by both geographers and economic historians has departed radically from the conventional certainties of colonial oppression which imbued the work of earlier historians, writing within the framework of traditional Gaelic nationalism.[1] In place of explanations for social and spatial change which were frequently couched in terms of the subjugation of a (seldom-defined) 'Irish' majority by an intrusive alien 'English' minority, modern studies have emphasized the varied social composition and political and economic motivations of groups such as landlords or tenants, once regarded as relatively homogeneous. Similarly, modern explanations of long-term trends in the Irish economy no longer favour simple monocausal models to account for these. Thus, the performance of the Irish economy in the eighteenth century is no longer explained solely in terms of the effects of restrictive English trade legislation. Rather, it is now held to reflect the varying competitiveness of Irish exports within the changing terms of trade in the European economy at large.[2]

These new perspectives are welcome. Nevertheless, it must be remembered that by the end of the seventeenth century, Ireland had undergone a series of radical and externally-imposed social, political and economic transformations. While these did not succeed in wholly obliterating earlier social and economic structures, they nevertheless fundamentally altered the nature of the country's leadership and landownership, and the social distribution of its wealth. These changes are discussed in more detail in Chapter 7. It is sufficient to note here that they created a structural context for individual and collective action which was characterized by pronounced cultural, social, economic and political inequalities which did not always reinforce each other in a mutual fashion. For example, although the shift in the ethnic composition of landownership following the plantations was never as complete as early writers suggested, by the early eighteenth century, the bulk of Irish land was still nevertheless in the hands of the descendants of the plantations' 'New English' and Scots beneficiaries. However, the religious divisions which were also created by these processes did not invariably conform to the new patterns of landownership. The majority of the population continued to adhere to one or other of the Gaelic or Old English varieties of Catholicism which had coexisted in pre-plantation Ireland. For the most part, however, for much of the eighteenth century the elite groups among them were effectively excluded from landownership by disabling legislation. Most land throughout the country was held by the Anglican minority—many of whom were the descendants of the 'New English' planters. In Ulster, the colonization process created a large Presbyterian minority, but these too were constrained from widespread landownership by the effects of the Penal Legislation.

Thus, in interpreting geographical changes in Ireland in the period after c. 1700, we must take into account the very uneven social, economic and political structures created by the sixteenth and seventeenth-century land reallocations. Clearly, these structures were themselves increasingly modified as time went by. Indeed, the heterogeneous nature and divergent behaviour of different groups in eighteenth- and nineteenth-century Ireland was very much part of this process of change. It reflected the continuous interaction between general processes of change affecting these determinant structures and local processes grounded in the particularities of place. For example, the relative location and varying resource endowment of different geographical localities ensured that they were perceived and developed in different ways by groups of varying social provenance, technological ability and economic resource.

This chapter discusses the characteristics of this geographical localism in the context of religious change and agrarian social protest. Both of these themes necessarily involve some consideration of the changing political structures in eighteenth and nineteenth-century Ireland, but the chapter is not presented primarily as a political analysis. Moreover, even within its chosen themes, some attempt at selectivity has been necessary. Accordingly, by way of introduction, the chapter commences by outlining some of the major characteristics of regional economic change between c. 1700 and c. 1900, before going on to discuss the major dimensions of religious change which paralleled these but did not always conform to them. For clarity's sake, the major dimensions of religious change are presented chronologically in narrative form. They include the economic effects of the eighteenth-century Penal Legislation, the political consequences of nineteenth-century Catholic emancipation, and the spatial evolution of the organizational structures of the Catholic Church. The chapter concludes with an examination of the growth and nature of agrarian redresser movements in the eighteenth century, and the debate over their putative politicization in the post-Famine period. These movements are so called, because their main purpose was usually the 'redressing' or eradication of perceived economic inequalities. Throughout, the discussion emphasizes the structural contexts within which these essentially localized phenomena occurred.

The Course of Regional Divergence

In 1700, Ireland was still relatively underpopulated and, arguably, underdeveloped. Its population of around two million was overwhelmingly rural and was supported by an economy which was almost entirely dependent for growth on the exports generated by its agricultural sector.[3] Given Ireland's constitutionally subordinate status to England, these exports were inherently vulnerable to the disruptive effects of English commercial legislation such as that embodied in the later seventeenth-century Cattle Acts and Navigation Acts. More fundamentally, they, and thus the whole Irish economy, were also vulnerable to periodic fluctuations in the overseas market demand for Irish produce.[4] Despite these fluctuations, however, and the widespread destruction which attended the Cromwellian and Williamite Wars in Ireland, growth *had* taken place. Total exports rose to a peak value of over £996,000 in 1698, when they represented the culmination of a variable but ultimately sustained trend which Cullen claims as evidence that the Irish economy had already begun a process of modernization.[5]

One hundred and fifty years later, on the eve of the potato Famine in 1845–49, Ireland's regional geography had altered radically but the underlying structural weakness of its economy—the dependence on external markets—remained. Despite short-term fluctuations and a varying pace of growth, however, the economy had expanded. Exports had grown slowly in the first 40 years of the eighteenth century to reach over £1.25 million in 1740, but thereafter had risen dramatically. Cullen cites figures of £3.0 million in 1770, £4.8 million in 1790 and over £7.0 million in the year to January 1816.[6] Much of this later rise was accounted for by the increase in the value of Irish agricultural exports to England during the boom years of the Napoleonic Wars. The price collapse which followed the cessation of hostilities ushered in the agricultural depression of 1816–20 with its attendant escalation in misery for a significant section of the agricultural population. The earlier growth had been sustained both by the success of Irish agriculture in responding to the opportunities created by the provisions trade in the period after 1730, and by the significant increase at about the same time in the volume of linen exports. These had risen from a total of 300,000 yards (328,000 metres) in 1700 to over 4.1 million yards (4.5 million metres) in 1730, but thereafter had risen even more rapidly to reach 20.5 million yards (22.4 million metres) in 1770 and over 35.6 million yards (38.94 million metres) in 1800.[7] The increasing concentration of linen production in Ulster from the late eighteenth century onwards was one of the major causes of the growing regional diversification within the Irish economy at that time. Prior to that, however, linen production had been much more widely distributed in Connacht, Leinster and parts of Munster as smallholders sought additional sources of income and landlords tried to diversify their estates' economy and enhance their income.

The other textile industries displayed their own spatial characteristics which added to the regional diversification. Wool combing and spinning provided an important supplementary source of income for the poorer sections of the rural population in many districts in Limerick, Clare, Cork and Kerry between the 1730s and 1780s, but weaving of both the Old Draperies and, to a lesser extent, the lighter and cheaper New Draperies remained a predominantly urban occupation. The production of Old Draperies—thick, heavy woollens such as broadcloths, kerseys or friezes—remained concentrated in and around Dublin, until a progressive decline in the supply of the requisite short-staple wool from the 1780s led to its gradual demise. New Drapery or worsted production was concentrated in the ancient towns of the Suir valley in County Tipperary and, more widely, in towns and villages in County Cork.[8] But in these regions, the higher urban-labour production costs ultimately helped to lessen its competitiveness in the face of growing English competition in the closing decades of the eighteenth century. Cotton production experienced a similar spatial cycle to linen manufacture. The industry had been widely introduced by landlords and other entrepreneurs into areas with an existing textile skill base in the 1770s on a speculative but nevertheless capital-intensive factory basis.[9] However, long before the recession-induced crises of 1819–20 and 1825–6 decimated the industry even in its Belfast heartland, cotton production had begun to pull back from the wilder shores of its original distribution, such as Mayo. The Irish cotton industry's most enduring legacy was the transfer of significant portions of its capital and steam-powered spinning technology into linen in east Ulster in the 1820s, a move which revitalized that industry.[10]

Interacting with this economic restructuring was Ireland's accelerating population growth, particularly after the 1750s. Modest growth in the first quarter of the eighteenth century was cut back by the excess mortality caused by the widespread famines of 1740–41, when between 250,000 and 400,000 may have died.[11] One estimate puts Ireland's total population in 1753 at a little over 2.25 million, only marginally higher than its figure 50 years before. Thereafter, and for reasons which are still disputed, the population growth rate accelerated sharply carrying the total figure to between 4.2 and 4.6 million in the early 1790s, and, more slowly, to perhaps 6.8 million in 1821. This slackening off in the growth rate became more pronounced after 1821 as regionally, emigration rates increased and, as a possible 'preventive check' age at marriage rose. Nevertheless, by 1845 Ireland's population was probably in excess of 8.5 million, more than treble what it had been one hundred years before.[12]

The causes of this extraordinary growth in Ireland's population are discussed in detail in Chapter 5. Current explanations stress the importance of food supply and dietary quality in limiting the impact of subsistence crises and in promoting early marriage and high marital fertility. As Ó Gráda notes, however, so great were the regional variations in the demographic behaviour which lay behind this growth, that any single explanation is probably misleading. What is clear is that this 'heaping up' of population was distributed very unevenly throughout Ireland, in a pattern which, ultimately, did not always conform with the changing capacity of the regional economies to support it. Freeman's map of the distribution of population density recorded in the census of 1841 shows two levels of spatial differentiation (Fig. 6.1). At a macro level, a broad division existed between much of Leinster in the east and south-east, where rural densities were generally below 200 people per square mile, and the remainder of the country where, save for the most barren moors and mountains of west Ulster, Connacht and south-west Munster, rural population densities were generally well in excess of this figure. Within these zones, however, complex local variations existed. As Cullen has implied, these are

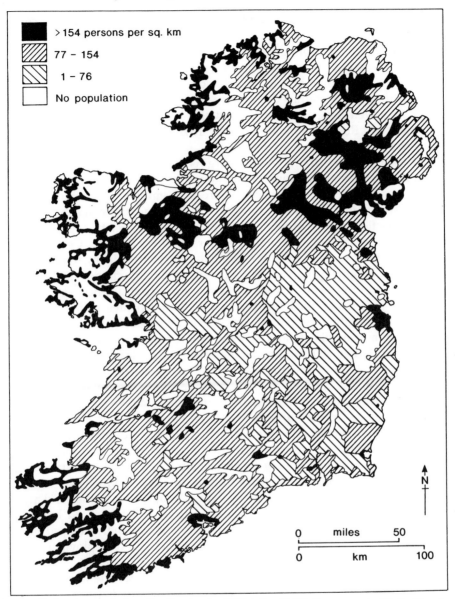

Fig. 6.1. Ireland: population distribution in 1841 (after T. W. Freeman, in W. E. Vaughan (ed.), *Ireland under the Union I, 1801–1870*, (Oxford, 1989)).

only likely to be understood in terms of an explanation which takes into account the relationship between demographic behaviour, social structure and the scale and nature of the local productive economy.[13] Thus the highest rural population densities of over 400 people per square mile (259 ha) which were widely distributed throughout the north and west of Ireland are unlikely to have everywhere resulted from the same mix of economic opportunity and demographic behaviour. In mid and south Ulster, where these densities were recorded in the Bann and Lagan valleys, and in Monaghan, Cavan and south Armagh, they were almost certainly originally a function of the structural characteristics displayed by the rural-based domestic linen industry. From the mid eighteenth century onwards, linen weavers and others engaged in the industry in these districts had shown a willingness— and ability—to pay a premium for smallholdings located close to linen markets, and in turn this had encouraged excessive farm subdivision.[14] Similar industrial processes may well have initiated the equally high densities on the borders of Leitrim, Sligo and Roscommon, although by 1841 the rural linen industry in these areas was very much in a state of decline.

Further west, on the extreme coastal margins of Donegal, Sligo, Mayo, Galway, Cork and Kerry, the similarly high population densities in 1841 had long ceased to reflect the availability of textile-based sources of employment which had been locally widespread in the 1770s. By the eve of the Famine, these may better be seen as a true reflection of the growing inequality of Irish society expressed in the deepening immiseration of its poorest members. In these districts, Connell's classic explanation of the causes of Ireland's population growth is likely to remain valid. Marginal areas became grossly overpopulated, as dietary change and early marriage forced communities ever closer to the margins of subsistence.[15]

To the east, in Leinster, the lower rural population densities in 1841 reflected the very different evolutionary path taken there by society and economy alike. Endowed with a drier climate and generally more fertile soils than in the west of Ireland, farmers in Leinster had proved themselves capable of a more intensive and flexible response to the changing pattern of overseas demand for Irish farm produce. Accordingly, farming in the region very quickly developed social and economic structures which were geared towards commercial production, and which were inimical to the support of a large surplus labour force of marginal productivity. Landowners attempted to maintain the economic viability of the farms on their estates by resisting tenant pressure for subdivision, while the tenants themselves proved willing to participate in a market for farm tenancies which became increasingly competitive during the expansionist years of the later eighteenth century. With a comparatively limited supply of marginal land available for colonization, and with rural tenurial structures still dominated by leases of considerable length, members of the farming class increasingly delayed marriage until a tenancy became available. The rural poor either found employment as wage labourers on the land or migrated to the towns.[16]

The growing social and regional inequalities in the countryside were mirrored by those in the towns. The predominant element in the pattern of urban change in the pre-Famine period was the disproportionate growth of Dublin during much of the eighteenth century. From a population that might have been as low as 5000 in 1600, Dublin had grown—largely in the Restoration period—by more than ten-fold to reach *c.* 60,000 by 1685.[17] By 1800, the city's population had risen to around 200,000. Newly connected via the Grand and Royal canals to an extensive hinterland in the Irish midlands, Dublin had become a significant component in its own right in the evolving pattern of regional demand in the country's domestic economy. Dublin's primacy at this time extended through virtually every aspect of Irish life. Its disproportionately large size reflected the fact that it performed a variety of national political, administrative, social and economic roles which no other Irish town could emulate. The city's monopoly of the apparatus of state attracted a variety of professional groups such as lawyers and bankers, while the presence of the vice-regal court attracted the country's social and political elite. In turn, these groups generated a demand for numerous other high status goods and services, which was supplied in part by artisans living within the city itself, and fuelled the city's further growth.[18]

Within Dublin, these elites created and 'consumed' urban space in characteristic ways. In common with other pre-industrial European cities, the pattern and sequence of Dublin's expansion was largely determined by the existing pre-urban cadastre of landownership.[19] In the immediate post-Restoration period, the main expansion appears to have been to the south of the old medieval city core, where the Earl of Longford's estate was rapidly developed from the 1660s onwards.[20] Thereafter, for much of the eighteenth century, most high status residential growth occurred on the northern bank of the Liffey, and in particular on the extensive Gardiner estate. This property had been amassed by Luke Gardiner, a property speculator and major figure in the city's government, from the 1720s onwards. Gardiner assiduously promoted the development of this estate as an aristocratic residential district throughout the first half of the century. Its social centre was Sackville Street, now O'Connell Street, which functioned as an exclusive *promenade* or mall. In 1795, however, the newly-extended street was linked via the Carlisle bridge to the south of the city, and the Sackville Street district became more closely integrated with the commercial districts to the south of the Liffey. The area subsequently lost its exclusive residential status and became increasingly commercial in tone. Encouraged both by this development and by the increasingly obvious inadequacy of the sewage systems and other amenities on the Gardiner estate, the city's aristocratic elite sought quieter residences in the newly-developed Fitzwilliam and Molesworth estates to the south-east of the city-centre.[21]

This process of incremental estate-based growth did not encourage the coherent organization of the city's spatial structures and traffic flows. Increasingly, this was undertaken by Corporation edict through the Wide Streets Commissioners.[22] Nevertheless, the building controls exercised *within* individual estates encouraged the uniformity of architectural style which remains today such a characteristic feature of the 'Georgian' districts around Merrion Square and St Stephen's Green. When newly built, these streets and squares, assembly rooms and churches were intended to provide the stage on which their elite and fashionable residents could parade their wealth and thus assert their social status before their peers.[23]

In many respects, therefore, eighteenth-century Dublin was typical of the 'consumerist' cities of pre-industrial Europe. As such, its potential for growth was not unlimited, but was constrained by the ceiling imposed by the agrarian economy on the size of the population at large. Dickson makes this point when he notes that Dublin's fastest growth was over by the middle of the eighteenth century. In percentage terms, Dublin's share of Ireland's total population rose from 2.5 per cent in the 1680s to over 5 per cent in the 1750s, but fell away to less than 3.5 per cent by 1800. Arguably, this reduction in the relative rate of growth reflected the fundamental inelasticity in demand for the goods and services Dublin produced. As in all pre-industrial agrarian economies, the need to feed the Irish population from the same agrarian resource-base used for industry ensured that this last sector

could never form the basis for the open-ended growth of population and, therefore, demand for urban manufactures and services.

Clarkson's analysis of the Hearth Money returns of 1798–1800 demonstrates
that, beyond Dublin, the Irish urban hierarchy at this time was broadly based, with
a large number of small inland market towns little differentiated from each other
either in terms of their size or functional complexity. Of the larger towns, Cork,
with a population of about 80,000, performed some of Dublin's functions on a
regional scale within Munster. The major regional ports, Belfast, Drogheda, Limerick and Waterford, had a population of between 12,000 and 15,000.[24] Many towns
and villages of all sizes showed evidence—in however debased a fashion—of
formal replanning and/or rebuilding on neo-classical principles. Sometimes this
was carried out by the town's proprietor, frequently acting in cooperation with his
major tenants, in order to improve local marketing facilities and—occasionally—
for reasons which were tantamount to social or political 'engineering' The motivations and methods involved in this urban and village improvement are discussed
in more detail in Chapter 7, but it is worth noting here that throughout Ireland,
over 750 towns and villages had been at least partly replanned in this way by 1840,
giving rise to the visual uniformity which still characterizes provincial Irish urbanism today.

Current research has suggested that such urban and village improvement was
not an exclusively pre-Famine phenomenon. Occasional instances of later urban
foundation or substantial transformation are known, for example at Charlestown,
Co. Mayo, and at Cahirciveen, Co. Kerry. The latter was rebuilt as a market centre
for the Trinity College Iveagh Estate in the 1870s.[25] Nevertheless, we may question
whether, given the massive reduction in Ireland's population during and after the
Famine and the radical changes in the relations of production which accompanied
this, the country's urban network required significant further transformative extension in the post-Famine period. Although the urban *proportion* of Ireland's declining post-Famine population rose from 17 per cent of the total of just over 6.5 million
in 1851 to 31 per cent of the 4.5 million recorded in 1901, much of this was
accounted for by the growth of Dublin and—more spectacularly—Belfast. Between
them, these cities accounted for 31 per cent (345,431) of the urban total in 1851 but
47 per cent (639,818) in 1901. If they are removed from the calculation, the total
provincial urban population in towns of more than 2000 people actually *fell* slightly
from just over 770,000 in 1851 to approximately 745,000 in 1901.[26] This suggests
that, generally, after the Famine the existing provincial urban network proved
adequate to meet the demands emanating from the diminishing population at large
for marketing and other services. Consequently, although the rapid expansion in
the railway network after the mid-1840s may be argued to have led to increasing
functional differentiation between towns and—in some cases—increased economic vitality within the context of a general shift from industry to retailing, these
developments show no evidence of requiring a significant extension to the inherited pre-Famine urban stock.

Thus, with the exception of the passage through many towns in Munster and
Connacht of significant numbers of impoverished rural migrants between 1841 and
1861, the Famine appears to have had little long-term effect on the Irish urban
network.[27] Its impact on rural society on the other hand, while regionally and

socially selective, was more immediate and lasting. Although we must now recognize that many of the demographic trends and structural economic weaknesses which were once thought to be a consequence of the Famine were evident before it, it remains the case that the scale and spatial unevenness of the population loss between 1845 and 1849 set up regional dissonances which recombined these earlier trends in new and more potent ways. For example, the Famine's impact on the pattern of landownership depended on the extent to which landowners had permitted subdivision and let directly to a numerous class of smallholders as sitting tenants. This had been common practice on many estates in western counties such as Clare and Mayo, and in these instances the potential loss of rents could be severe and the prospects of bankruptcy for the landowner brought ominously close. On the other hand, on those estates which were still dominated by middlemen, the landowners were relatively well protected. In these cases it was the middlemen who had to bear the loss of rents from defaulting tenants, but who nevertheless still had to find the money to pay the head rents due to the landlord.[28] Indeed, Donnelly has argued that one of the chief effects of the Famine on the upper reaches of Irish agrarian society was its extinction of the middleman class: they either paid up or got out.[29]

The landowning class did not escape entirely unscathed, however. Hoppen estimates that approximately a quarter of all land changed hands under the aegis of the Encumbered Estates Court, set up by the government in 1849 to facilitate the sale of bankrupt estates, and its successor, the Landed Estates Court. Contrary to the government's expectations, however, most of this land was bought by other landowners who had successfully survived the Famine and who took advantage of the depressed land prices caused by the glut of properties coming onto the market in such a short period. Relatively few estates were bought either by Irish or English urban capitalists.[30]

It is unclear whether this consolidation by the landowning minority of their grasp on agricultural land in the mid-nineteenth century initiated a more general period of landlord prosperity. The revisionist stance, based on somewhat speculative calculations of the overall changes in agricultural output, rents and labour costs between 1850 and 1876, would have it that the relative position of landowners deteriorated, as they failed to maintain rent increases in line with the increasing value of agricultural output.[31] The argument is extended to account for the growing politicization of tenant farmers in the 1870s and after, and the increasingly antagonistic relations between them and the landowners. By failing to raise rents adequately in line with the value of agricultural production, landowners, it is alleged, denied themselves the opportunity of investing adequately in their estates and thus helping their tenants weather the agricultural crisis of the 1870s and 1880s. In consequence, the latter sought a political solution to their situation at the expense of their landlords rather than an economic one with their aid.

This revisionist argument has not gone unchallenged. Hoppen and, in the present volume, Turner (Chapter 9) offer a recalculation of output, labour, rent and gross farming profits which suggests that while rents and labour costs increased by about 20 per cent between 1850 and 1876, gross farming profits remained virtually unchanged. Despite the caveats—the difficulty of estimating labour costs given the decline in the number of agricultural labourers, the existence among them of many 'assisting relatives', the uncertainties introduced into the calculation of agricultural output by the variation in overseas demand for Irish farm produce and so on—it may be that by 1876 tenant farmers had no more than regained the position they had held in 1850. If this was so, then not only did the landowning class emerge from the Famine in a hitherto unrecognized stronger position, but the extent of their eclipse under the impact of successive interventionist state legislation in the 1870s and after was thus made all the greater.[32]

Religious Change and Political Aspiration

Paralleling this growing economic diversity were the religious divisions created by the sixteenth and seventeenth-century plantations and land confiscations. Between them, these demarcated communities which were of very uneven numerical size and, in the case of the Presbyterians and Anglicans, geographical distribution. Despite the sustained high levels of Presbyterian immigration from lowland Scotland into Ulster in the later seventeenth century, and the more limited French Huguenot and German Palatine migration, the main beneficiary of Ireland's accelerating population growth from the 1750s onwards had been the Catholic community.[33] In the absence of reliable population figures before the first nineteenth-century censuses, precise estimates are impossible. Nevertheless, McCartney suggests that in the later eighteenth century, Catholics comprised over three-quarters of the total population.[34] By 1834, the Commissioners of Public Instruction estimated that 80.9 per cent of the population were Catholic; 10.7 per cent Anglican and 8.1 per cent Presbyterian. If anything, the Catholic proportion is likely to have grown still further by the eve of the Famine, since the bulk of the continued pre-Famine population growth occurred in those regions and among those social classes who most completely shared this particular religious affiliation.[35]

By the same token, however, it was the Catholic community who suffered the greatest proportionate loss as a result of the Famine. Between 1834 and 1861, when the first true religious census was taken, their numbers fell by nearly 30 per cent from just under 6.5 million to just over 4.5 million, or just under 78 per cent of the total population. By comparison, the numbers of Anglicans and Presbyterians fell by less than one-fifth in the same period. Nor did the Catholic decline stop there. By 1901, the Catholic proportion of the population had fallen to 74.2 per cent, while the proportion of Anglicans and Presbyterians had risen to 13 per cent and 9.9 per cent respectively.[36]

These adjustments in the relative numerical strength of the three main denominations were clearly a function of the changing size of the population at large. Despite the eighteenth-century Penal Legislation, and the efforts of Protestant missionary societies in the 1830s and 1840s during the so-called 'Second Reformation', and the widespread revivalism in all the main denominations in the immediate post-Famine period, there is no evidence of long-term mass-transfers of allegiance from one denomination to another. For example, no more than 4000 Catholics registered their formal conversion to the Established Church between 1704 and 1771. Similarly, the much publicized 'souperism' of the Famine years, in which Protestant missionaries in the west of Ireland attempted to induce Catholic conversions by means of food aid, was as limited in effect as it was local in extent.[37] Consequently, the regional differences in denominational support in the 1861 census may be argued to reflect patterns which had been relatively stable over the preceding century and a half. The concentration of Presbyterians in east Ulster has already been alluded to, and has remained a continuing characteristic of the regional identity of this part of Ireland until the present day. In 1861, over 96 per cent of all Irish Presbyterians lived in Ulster, where they formed the largest single denomination in Antrim, Down, Belfast and Carrickfergus. Anglican support was equally localized. Over 56 per cent of Irish Anglicans lived in Ulster, where they showed a more central and westerly distribution than the Presbyterians. The most significant numbers lived in Counties Armagh and Londonderry, and were supplemented by smaller communities in Counties Fermanagh and Tyrone and elsewhere. Beyond Ulster, the greatest concentration of Anglicans lay in Dublin and its hinterland. Generally, Leinster contained about one-quarter of the total Anglican Communion in Ireland in 1861, while Munster and Connacht recorded 12 and 6 per cent respectively.

The distribution of Catholic denominational support was broadly the reverse of the combined Anglican and Presbyterian patterns. In 1861, despite their relatively greater loss of membership during the Famine years and after, Roman Catholics continued to form the majority of the population in all save four of the 32 Irish counties. Only in Antrim, Armagh, Down and Londonderry were they in an absolute minority. In Fermanagh and Tyrone they constituted a relatively small majority. Elsewhere, the Catholic majority remained massive. They constituted over 86 per cent of the population in Leinster and over 90 per cent in both Connacht and Munster.[38]

Disability and Adjustment, *c.* 1694–1760

The recitation of denominational population figures of the sort given here indicates little about the changing social and economic complexion of that support, and nothing about the changing organizational character of the Churches themselves. Both of these aspects are crucial to any appraisal of the role played by denominational allegiance in determining the local variations in the pattern of human experience in eighteenth- and nineteenth-century Ireland. Recent studies of eighteenth-century Irish Catholicism have recognized this particularism, especially in their re-examination of the effects of the Penal Legislation directed against Catholics and Dissenters in the late seventeenth and eighteenth centuries.

The origins of this Penal Legislation lay in the defensive mentality of Protestants in England and Ireland in the wake of the Jacobite War of 1688–91. Although that war had resulted in a crushing military defeat for the Irish Jacobite forces, the dispersal of the Catholic leadership and the further erosion by confiscation of the Catholic economic base in landownership, Irish Protestants in particular were still anxious lest these benefits be wrested from them. James III, the Stuart Pretender to the English throne, was still recognized as the rightful king by both the Vatican and the French king, Louis XIV; while more ominously, Irish Protestants remained a small minority in their own country. Perhaps not surprisingly, when called on by an English House of Commons Committee in 1694 to pass 'such laws as shall be necessary for the security of Protestants', the lord deputy, and the overwhelmingly Protestant Irish Parliament willingly complied.[39]

On paper, the provisions of the anti-Catholic legislation passed by successive Irish Parliaments between 1694 and 1728 were severe. They were directed both specifically against the Catholic clergy and against the property rights of Catholics at large. Earlier legislation predating the 1690s already existed to prevent Catholics from exercising effective political power. The major anti-clerical provisions were contained in the Banishment Act of 1697, the Registration Act of 1704 and the Act of 1709. The Banishment Act provided for the expulsion from Ireland of those priests who exercised 'jurisdiction', that is members of the Catholic diocesan hierarchy together with monks and nuns in regular orders. Within 18 months, over 440 priests had been expelled together with 383 members of religious orders.[40]

The Registration Act required Catholic diocesan clergy to register with the County Sessions and to provide securities for their own 'good behaviour', but also promised legal recognition of the right of those who did so to continue functioning as priests. Whether, as Wall has suggested, the ultimate intention of the Registration Bill was to create a situation in which the existing Catholic clergy would simply wither away through the effects of old age and mortality, is not certain. What is clear is that in the short term it had the opposite effect of removing some of the disabling pressure on the parish clergy, and—in the spirit of the Treaty of Limerick signed at the end of the Williamite Wars in 1691—enabled them to continue the business of parochial reconstruction. This interlude was short-lived, however. In 1709, in the wake of renewed alarms at the apparent prospect of an imminent Jacobite invasion of England in 1708, an amending Act was passed. This closed various loopholes in the 1704 legislation, and required all Catholic priests to take the same oath of abjuration which office holders in Ireland had been required to take in 1703. By this, priests would confirm their loyalty to the reigning monarch, Queen Anne, and forswear allegiance to the Stuart Pretender. In practice, less than 100 of the 1089 Catholic priests who registered under the Act of 1704 took the oath, and their widespread non-compliance rendered this part of the Act unenforceable.[41]

The most important disabling provisions against Catholic property rights were contained in the 'Popery Act' of 1704 and its amendments in the Act of 1709. An earlier Act in 1695 had already attempted to limit both the opportunities for Catholic education in Ireland, and some of the social manifestations of the Catholic gentry's status.[42] The Popery Act went further and sought to strike at the property basis of Irish Catholicism in general. Under its provisions, Catholics were prevented from purchasing land or taking out leases of more than 31 years' duration or from paying a rent of less than two-thirds the property's annual value. Existing Catholic landowners—who after the Williamite confiscations still owned some 14 per cent of the country's land—were obliged to abandon primogeniture and divide their estates equally among their male heirs under a system of gavelkind. If, on the other hand, the eldest son conformed to the Established Church, the entire reversionary interest in the estate would descend to him, effectively reducing his father to the status of a tenant for life. Further provisions required Catholic freeholders to take an oath of abjuration before Parliamentary elections, and required Protestant

Dissenters to take a sacramental test before they could become MPs, receive a commission, or sit in a municipal corporation.[43]

Subsequent anti-property legislation between 1714 and 1728 was essentially reactive in character, and designed to remedy any deficiencies in earlier Acts.[44] Significantly, however, the 1728 Act also formally excluded Catholics from the franchise. The rapid passage through the Irish Parliament of the 1704 and 1709 Acts thus marked the high point of discriminatory legislation against Catholic property ownership in Ireland. However, whatever the formal provisions contained in this legislation, it is highly debateable whether it had a major crippling effect on the economic performance of the Catholic community. In the most recent reassessment, Bartlett suggests that for the most part, the Penal Legislation was already a 'dead letter' by the 1730s. Long before then it had become quite clear that the Penal Laws were 'neither going to eliminate Catholicism, nor bring about the mass conversion of Catholics, nor [keep them] poor'. In general, most Irish Protestants were content to leave the laws on the statute books, where they could be reactivated in times of national threat, such as the Jacobite rebellion in 1744–45. For most Irish Catholics, they remained a source of petty oppression rather than serious discrimination.[45]

Moreover, as Osborough has shown, both the provisions against Catholic landownership and Catholic tenancies could be—and were—evaded. Catholic younger sons might be pressurized into giving up their claim to a share of the estate under the gavelling (equal-division) clause, while Protestant landlords and Catholic tenants might collude in the fabrication of misleadingly onerous leases or in forestalling the activities of Protestant 'discoverers'. Under the provisions of the 1709 Act, if a Protestant could establish at law the existence of a 'discoverable interest', that is a property granted illegally to a Catholic under the terms of the Act, he could then obtain possession of that property for the duration of the original lease. If a landlord suspected that the 31 year lease he had granted to his Catholic tenant was too generous under the terms of the 1709 Act and therefore constituted a 'discoverable interest', he might agree with the tenant to bring an early ejectment against him, thereafter replacing the first lease with a second, more secure agreement. Osborough's general conclusion is that though the provisions of the Penal Legislation were severe in the letter of the law, in practice the various forms of evasion and the general unwillingness of Irish lawyers to act illegally in their pursuit, greatly ameliorated them.[46]

Despite such amelioration, it is nevertheless true that Catholic landownership in fee continued to decline throughout the eighteenth century, reaching about 5 per cent of the total at the century's close. Moreover, as Cullen has emphasized, those Catholic landowners who did survive were among the poorest of their class, many having incomes of less than £500 a year. Very few figured among the great landowners of the realm, the Earl of Kenmare being one exception. Instead, in a conclusion which accords with Wall's earlier work, Cullen depicts the eighteenth century as a period when Catholic *leasehold* wealth rather than wealth in fee grew— and grew remarkably. Despite the prohibition which prevented Catholics from taking leases for lives or for more than 31 years prior to the Relief Act of 1778, the number of substantial Catholic tenant farmers grew in concert with the expansion in the agrarian economy after the 1740s. Thus, whatever disabilities this Catholic tenant group suffered from their limited leaseholds, these seem to have been more than outweighed by their success in renegotiating leases. Consequently, instances of deliberate discrimination against prospective Catholic tenants, such as those practised in the 1770s and 1780s by the Duke of Devonshire's Irish agent, William Conner, seem to have been outweighed by the straightforward commercial competitiveness of many Catholic tenants.[47]

But just as the scale and nature of this agrarian expansion varied, so too did the extent of the Catholic participation in it. The most prosperous Catholic tenant communities were to be found in the rich farming lands of south Leinster and east Munster, and also in the grazing lands of east Clare. Catholic participation divided too on social grounds: the less substantial yeoman farmers being clearly distinguishable from the quasi-gentry groups. Occasionally of true gentry origin, the latter were frequently middlemen, and indulged in more conspicuous 'gentry' life styles.[48]

Catholic participation in the eighteenth century urban economy is as yet imperfectly understood. Conventional interpretations have stressed, almost as an article of faith, the proposition that Catholic merchants dominated the economies of most towns other than Dublin and those in Ulster from well before the 1780s, despite their exclusion from municipal authority. The argument has been most persuasively expressed by Wall. She postulated a massive growth in the capital resources of Catholic townsfolk which was used to fund their participation in trade. This concentration of wealth in urban hands resulted from the Catholics' inability to purchase land or lend money on mortgages, as well as from their politically-desirable inconspicuous patterns of consumption. Thus, trade not only represented the most respectable means of obtaining a living which remained open to Catholics, but also constituted the only effective way of using Catholic savings. A new Catholic urban middle class was thereby recruited, drawn mainly from the ranks of Catholic landowners or ex-landowners.[49]

Although subsequent studies of the mercantile communities in various eighteenth-century Irish towns have stressed the importance of Catholic merchants, Dickson has challenged the basic assumption that Catholic urban wealth was in fact growing in *relative* terms during this period. He argues that since urban wealth in general grew in the later eighteenth century as the Irish economy expanded, evidence of increasing numbers of Catholic traders does not constitute evidence for an increase in the Catholic share of urban wealth. Moreover, given the relatively low capital entry requirements for retail traders and craftsmen, increasing numbers of Catholics among the latter would not necessarily indicate an increased Catholic share of urban wealth either. And in the case of Catholic entry into the wholesale merchant elite, whose capital requirements were much higher, Dickson argues that this continued to be limited by the landownership disabilities suffered by the Catholic community. Their consequently narrow rural property base prevented them from recirculating landed capital into urban commerce, in the way which enabled their Protestant competitors to refinance their trading operations.[50]

Relief and Reaction, *c.* 1761–1800

During the last forty years of the eighteenth century, the legal position of Catholics in Ireland was transformed. A variety of factors, including the growing military requirements of Empire, the decline in anti-Catholicism among the English elite, and their concern at the continued legislative discrimination against Irish Catholics, prompted the British government to press for the dismantling of the Penal Laws. This was mirrored by a growing body of opinion among the Anglican gentry who were convinced, not so much of the desirability of religious toleration (although this did exist), but of the general benefits to the economy which would flow from a relaxation of the tight inheritance and property laws. Accordingly, beginning in 1761 with the so-called 'Bogland Act', which permitted Catholics to take 61-year reclaiming leases, successive Relief Acts in 1778, 1782 and 1793 allowed Catholics to take 999-year leases, purchase and inherit land on the same terms as Protestants (save in Parliamentary boroughs); and finally, vote—subject to property qualifications. The extent of this sea-change was signalled in 1795, when the Irish Parliament voted £8000 towards the establishment of a Catholic seminary at Maynooth.[51]

If the revisionist interpretation of the true extent of the economic disabilities suffered by the Catholic community in the earlier eighteenth century is correct, these Relief Acts did little more than rectify formal penalties against Catholic property which had been as frequently honoured in their breach as their observance. Nevertheless, their removal must have accelerated Catholic participation in the late-eighteenth-century expansion of the agrarian economy. Even so, the most important of the Relief Acts, as far as the long-term constitutional and political situation of the Catholic community was concerned, was arguably that of 1793, which gave a significant section of the Catholic population a vote for the first time in over 60 years.

To be precise, this Act extended the existing 40 shillings freeholder franchise to Catholics. The concept of a vote acquired by virtue of possession of freehold property was of considerable antiquity in Ireland, and had been available to Protestants throughout the eighteenth century. The diagnostic characteristic of freehold property was that it was owned outright or else was leased for an indeterminate period of years. A lease for one life was a freehold, a lease for 999 years was not. During the eighteenth century, the commonest form of property qualification for freehold votes was 40 shillings. That is, the would-be voter had to prove that his property was worth at least that amount to him each year over and above the rent he paid. This was a minimum and not an absolute value, and prior to 1793, many freeholders registering under this qualification held tenancies worth a great deal more than 40 shillings. By extending this franchise to the much more numerous and relatively impoverished Catholic tenantry, the Act effectively transformed what had been a nominal 40 shillings freehold electorate into a near 40 shillings electorate. In Malcomson's phrase, 'the Roman Catholic rabble' which was thereby enfranchised was objected to by many Protestant gentry not because it was Roman Catholic, but because it was a rabble.[52]

Their concern mirrored one salient feature of this extension to the franchise. It created an opportunity whereby politically active landowners might seek deliberately to increase the number of 40 shillings freehold tenancies on their estates. By letting these for leases of one decayed life, they could hope to marshall a theoretically politically obedient army of tenant voters who would support their candidate at parliamentary elections. The potential scope for this sort of electoral manipulation was most extensive in the county constituencies, where there was a large reservoir of enfranchisable Catholic tenants. In the boroughs, on the other hand, the franchise was much more restricted. It was based either on a higher property requirement, such as the £5 qualification in Downpatrick, Dungarvan, Lisburn and Newry, or else on membership of the Corporation, as at Athlone, Bandon, Dungannon or Sligo. In the latter case, the franchise remained exclusively in the hands of the Protestant community, as Catholics continued to be excluded by a variety of legal or technical considerations. These narrow urban electorates were themselves frequently under the political patronage and control of some local grandee, who was perhaps also their ground landlord. A notable example of such a patron was Richard Boyle, 2nd Earl of Shannon (1728–1807). For much of the late eighteenth century following his father's death in 1764, he controlled the parliamentary representation of the County Cork towns of Castlemartyr, Charleville, Clonakilty and Youghal, and influenced the representation at Bandon, Doneraile, Dungarvan, Midleton and Tallow.[53]

By thus enhancing the importance of the Catholic-dominated county constituencies, the 1793 Act had the potential to alter the political map of Ireland. However, this could not be fully realized until Catholics were also permitted to become MPs. As it was, the 1793 Act had been passed by an Irish Parliament which had enjoyed considerable legislative independence since 1782, and which was, and remained, the embodiment of an *exclusive* Protestant elitist nationalism. This legislative independence had been granted by the newly-installed Whig government under Lord Rockingham, which had replaced Lord North's Tory administration following British defeats in the American War of Independence. Prior to 1782, successive Whig administrations had capitalized on Irish discontent over the constitutionally subordinate status of their Parliament. Thus Rockingham's government was poorly placed to resist the demands for Irish constitutional reform being made by the increasingly radical and predominantly-Protestant Volunteer Movement and Irish 'Patriot' MPs.[54]

The prompting for the 1793 Act had nevertheless still come from the British government, alarmed at the increasing revolutionary fervour on the continent, and at the influence this and events in America had on radical Catholic and Dissenter political opinion in Ireland. For these radicals, the pace of constitutional change moved too slowly, and in any case showed little likelihood of accommodating their demands for complete religious emancipation and political reform. Constitutional radicalism had first appeared in 1784 but had been revived in 1791, with the establishment of United Irishmen's Societies in Dublin and Belfast. By 1795, a radical and mainly Presbyterian conspiracy centred in east Ulster was actively considering an offer of French help to instigate an Irish revolution. A year later, this group had established links with the more overtly sectarian Catholic Defenders. The Defenders had originated in County Armagh in 1784, in clashes with Protestant Peep O' Day Boys. These clashes had arisen out of the economic tensions generated within the local weaver–farmer community by the growing prosperity of Catholic tenants. Defenderism had subsequently spread widely through Leinster and east Munster as an anti-Protestant, pro-French and proto-Nationalist secret society. By late 1796, it had been subsumed by the newly-revitalized Dublin-based United Irishmen's Society, as part of a wider revolutionary structure in the southern counties.[55]

This combination of radical Ulster Presbyterians and southern Catholics was inherently unstable. When armed insurrection finally broke out in May–June 1798, following an abortive French attempt at invasion in December 1796 and subsquent government repression, the disparate nature of the conspirators quickly became apparent. The early enthusiasm of the Ulster Presbyterian activists quickly evaporated following military reverses at Antrim and Ballynahinch, and as news of the sectarian massacres of Protestants in County Wexford by their fellow United Irishmen filtered north. Indeed, Connolly argues that it was the Presbyterians' regional strength in Ulster, which, by protecting them from the sectarian realities of life and encouraging their politically parochial outlook, had prompted their participation in the rebellion in the first place.[56] Despite the tardy arrival of a small French expedition under Humbert at Killalla, Co. Mayo, in August 1798, and a later, unsuccessful French attempt at invasion in Donegal in October of the same year, the government had little difficulty in suppressing the rebellion. The most tenacious rebel opposition occurred in County Wexford, where a relatively wide social spectrum from among the local Catholics took part, including members of the professional and commercial classes, as well as the rural poor and the sons of minor gentry.[57]

The significance of the United Irishmen's rebellion lay in what it signalled about the nature of the divisions within Irish society. In the first place, it forced a reassessment by Ulster Presbyterians of their aspirations for political independence. In the new century, this led them slowly but inexorably towards Unionism, and a closer alignment with the Anglican community than either party would have previously thought either possible or desirable. Secondly, the rebellion signalled quite clearly the potential for revolutionary change in Ireland, as long as the existing political structures conformed to minority rather than majority aspirations. The progressive formal economic rehabilitation of Catholics had not been paralleled by anything approaching complete political emancipation. Catholic freeholders might vote, but only for Protestant MPs. Political authority was still monopolized by the Anglican minority. Indeed, after 1782 this had been enhanced. Accordingly, when the major constitutional sea-change of Union with Britain was enacted in 1801, it followed a political debate in Ireland which had been led by the Anglican elite and dominated by their perspectives. Chief among these, alongside the prospective benefits to be gained from closer constitutional links with the foremost economic world power at the time, was the apparent security offered by the Union against further Catholic challenges to Anglican supremacy.[58]

Assertion and Consolidation, 1801–1870

The Act of Union became law on 1 January 1801, after considerable political management by the British government in the face of strong opposition from an unlikely alliance of ultra-Tories and Reformers. The Tories feared that Union would soon be followed by Catholic Emancipation. The Reformers had hoped that the constitutional changes in 1782 would eventually open the Irish Parliament to representation by the Catholic propertied classes. The British government had sought the Union as a counter to the continued danger of insurgency within Ireland and the threat posed by French hostility abroad. In order to secure the Roman Catholic hierarchy's compliance in the measure, the British Prime Minister, Pitt the Younger, had promised full emancipation for their co-religionists in post-Union Ireland. Under the Act's provisions, the Dublin Parliament was abolished, and the Irish seats—reduced from 300 to 100—were transferred to the Imperial Parliament at Westminster.

Pitt's failure to secure emancipation—not the least as the result of George III's inexorable opposition to it—had lasting consequences for the course and nature of political change in Ireland. It ensured that the 'Catholic Question' remained a constant feature in the wider arena of British politics. Successive Emancipation Bills in 1808, 1813, 1819, 1821 and 1825 were defeated by a combination of royal opposition and government equivocation. As Hoppen notes, these contained offers of emancipation which were grudgingly made, and attached to numerous conditions. These would have reduced the Catholic franchise and, by establishing a government veto over the appointment of Catholic bishops, aligned the Catholic Church closely with the interests of the state.[59] The failure of these Bills, combined with the government's procrastination, engendered an increasingly militant attitude among Catholics. The conservative and aristocratic leadership of the Catholic Committee—established in the eighteenth century to represent Catholic interests—was replaced by radical middle class urbanites led by Daniel O'Connell, who were prepared to espouse both constitutional politics and extra-parliamentary activity in order to obtain emancipation.

The turning point in the campaign for emancipation came in 1824, when associate membership of O'Connell's Catholic Association was made available for a penny a month, rather than for the annual guinea subscription which the 46 founding members had paid the previous year. In McCartney's phrase, this 'transformed the Association from a middle-class political club into a mass-movement which politicised the countryside'.[60] By paying this so-called 'Catholic Rent', a significant proportion of the relatively impoverished Catholic peasantry were able to participate, or at least made to feel they participated, in the electoral process. As such, they constituted an impressively large and well-disciplined political body. In exercising their democratic power through the 40 shillings freeholder franchise in the elections for Counties Waterford, Louth, Westmeath and Monaghan in 1826 and for County Clare in 1828 (where O'Connell himself was elected), members of the Association demonstrated their commitment to electoral politics. At the same time, they signalled the potential for civil disruption which existed if their demands for emancipation were not met. Recognizing the reality of Catholic freeholder electoral power and its ability to displace traditional landed patronal influence, and conscious too of the possibility of at best, a Radical Irish party being returned to Westminster which could paralyse Parliament, and at worst, civil war, Peel surrendered and introduced the Catholic Relief Bill in March 1829. The Bill was passed, and Catholics were able for the first time in over 130 years to enter Parliament, to sit in any corporation and to hold the higher civil and military offices of State. The *quid pro quo* was an increase in the property qualification for the predominantly Catholic county franchise from 40 shillings to £10.[61]

O'Connell's tactics in pursuing emancipation were influenced by the localism which was to pervade Irish politics for much of the nineteenth century. The reduction in the number of Irish seats by the Act of Union, and their transfer to Westminster, led to a major reappraisal of their political worth. Arguably, the proprietorial attitude displayed by many landowners towards the political representation of the towns and rural communities on their estates before the Union, and their willingness to trade this for personal political or financial advantage, was the consequence of the 'closed' nature of Irish politics at the time. Political aspirations and rivalries were essentially internalized within a ruling elite. Although this elite was conscious of the potential challenge from the only recently and partly enfranchised majority, it still retained its traditional monopoly of power. Thus, political influence could be traded on a relatively casual and pragmatic basis, since this was unlikely—in the short term at least—to lead to a major external challenge to the elite's political dominance.

The Union altered matters fundamentally. Although retaining their political dominance in the short term, the Protestant Ascendancy now operated within a wider political arena. In this, the imperatives determining government action were no longer necessarily consonant with their own continued defence of their minority elitist position in Ireland. Moreover, the growing demands for emancipation, and the skill with which O'Connell orchestrated these in the predominantly Catholic county constituencies, meant that the potential for political change which had existed since 1793, finally looked like being realized. This would undoubtedly lead to a realignment of political representation along lines which would further the aspirations of the majority. Accordingly, in looking to the defence of their increasingly precarious political position, the Ascendancy survivors of the Union had to rely increasingly on the 33 borough seats which had been retained under that Act. Even here, however, the tide of events was moving against them. In the 1820s, the Protestant electors in some of the unreformed Corporations showed increasing signs of political independence. Paradoxically, this usually took place if they felt that their political representatives were too quiescent in the face of what they conceived of as the challenge of sectarian Catholicism. At Bandon and Youghal, Co. Cork, for example, the Whiggish Devonshire interest was challenged by local ultra-Protestants because it was perceived to be too supportive of Catholic rights in general. At Youghal, which the 6th Duke of Devonshire had succeeded in wresting from the Tory Shannon interest in 1822, the Duke's attempt to introduce Catholic freemen-at-trade into the Corporation in 1829, and thereby shore-up local electoral support for his preferred candidate, barely succeeded in the face of strong Protestant Conservative opposition. At Bandon, where the parliamentary representation was shared between the Duke and the Conservative Lord Bandon, a revolt by Protestant voters in 1831 prevented the election of the Duke's nominee, Captain A. W. Clifford. Clifford was eventually elected, but a subsequent revolt by the Protestant electorate two years later finally persuaded Lord Bandon to resign his interest in the borough, as he could no longer fulfil his electoral obligations to the Duke.[62]

Events such as these bore witness to the declining political authority of the

Ascendancy in the post-Union period. Their continued management even of the Protestant-dominated boroughs was only tolerated as long it remained compatible with the electorate's own aspirations. The irony, of course, was that prior to the Irish Reform Act of 1832, these Protestant urban electorates were themselves still structured in an elitist fashion, and were perceived to be so by both government and Catholic majority alike. The Reform Act was passed by Lord Grey's Whig government against substantial Tory opposition, and was intended to make the urban franchise more representative of the changing social and economic dimensions within Irish society at large. As with the parallel Act in England, it was designed to defuse the potential for radical assault on the increasingly non-representative structures of social authority. As Stewart notes, it was thus not a deliberate step towards 'democracy', but rather a pragmatic attempt to secure the stability of the state.[63] Irish Whigs regarded it as the logical culmination of the various processes of reform which had been going on since the Union. Irish Tories regarded it as a further threat to the Protestant Ascendancy, the established position of the Church of Ireland and the legislative Union itself. O'Connell's radicals welcomed it for precisely these reasons, but quickly became disillusioned when the much more limited nature of the real reforms became apparent.[64] Under the Act, the borough franchise was extended to include all householders who either occupied premises worth at least £10 or who paid at least £10 a year in rent. At the same time, provision was made to retain for life the voting rights of the existing £5 and 40 shillings freeholders who happened to live within the newly revised and generally reduced borough boundaries.[65] Unlike the 40 shillings county freeholders, this group had not been disenfranchised as part of O'Connell's deal with the government to secure the passage of the 1829 Catholic Emancipation Act.

The Reform Act thus effectively destroyed the closed Protestant Corporations, and with them, the last reasonably assured bastion of Ascendancy political privilege in pre-Famine Ireland. It did not, however, make the electoral process in the urban constituencies any more democratic. Although widened in membership and broadened in sectarian composition, the urban electorates remained a very small proportion of the expanding urban populations of the time. At Bandon, for example, the electorate increased from 13—the provost and 12 free burgesses— under the unreformed Corporation, to a total of 240 with the inclusion of the £10 householders. Nevertheless, these still only represented 2.4 per cent of the town's 1831 population.[66] Consequently, the same potential for political intimidation and violence existed at elections in the 'reformed' boroughs as had occurred previously. Indeed, the renewed impetus given by Reform to the assertion of Catholic political demands, now increasingly centred around the cause of Repeal, ensured that in the 1830s and 1840s, levels of political violence if anything increased.[67]

The issue of Repeal represented the end of the early-nineteenth-century phase of active Catholic clerical involvement in Irish politics. The Catholic clergy had formed the organizational backbone of O'Connell's Catholic Association in the 1820s. Their willingness to add the moral authority of the Church to the political urging of the secular leadership had done much to strengthen the resolve of the Catholic freeholders in the face of landlord hostility. Despite the refusal of some Catholic bishops to join O'Connell's Repeal Association when it was founded in 1840, the mass of the Catholic clergy enthusiastically supported it and added the same 'confessional air' to its proceedings as they had done to the Catholic Association. Despite their support, however, by 1843—designated by O'Connell as 'Repeal year'—it was manifestly clear that the movement had failed. Indeed, the very formation of the Association and its resort to mass demonstrations was in some ways itself an admission of the failure of the previous ten years of parliamentary agitation in the same cause. The main reason for its failure was the British government's firm resistance to the idea of Repeal, backed by the hostility of moderate Catholic and Protestant middle class opinion on both sides of the Irish Sea. But O'Connell's timing and tactics were also misjudged. The growth of the tithes issue in the 1830s had distracted the attention of the rural communities who might otherwise have supported the movement. While in Parliament, O'Connell had consistently failed to marshall Radical Irish MPs as an effective lobby, possibly because of the slow but steady on-going programme of Government-sponsored reform.[68]

O'Connell's death in 1847 deprived the Catholic clergy of sustained and coherent political leadership. As a result, the Catholic clergy's political role entered a phase in which it was essentially localist in character. This lasted until the revival of agrarian reform as a national issue in the 1870s, particularly with the foundation of the Land League in County Mayo in 1879, and, following its proscription two years later, the National League in 1882. The localism of Catholic political involvement during the intervening period mirrored the structure of Irish politics at large. Political issues were generally local, immediate and pragmatic, and priests thus responded as one interest-group among many to local rather than national agendas. This localism was matched by the Catholic hierarchy's suspicion of those putatively national political movements which emerged during the same period From its perspective, these were either tainted by cultural radicalism, like the Catholic Defence Association of the 1850s, or else were overtly revolutionary, like the Fenian Irish Republican Brotherhood, established more successfully at much the same period.[69]

Significantly, the attempt by the Church to establish its own national platform for reform, and thereby detach its members from the appeal of radical republicanism, failed. The National Association set up by Archbishop Cullen in 1864 to promote the dis-establishment of the Anglican Church of Ireland, as well as educational and (mild) agrarian reform, was unable to win widespread support even from among the Catholic clergy themselves. Its failure bore witness to the changed post-Famine relationship between the Catholic Church and Irish politics. Before the Famine, the politicization of the largely-illiterate rural peasantry was greatly aided, and was perhaps only possible, through the agency of an institution like the Catholic Church, which could use its organizational structures and moral authority to promote this. In the wake of the Famine, this was no longer necessary. The Famine had destroyed precisely those labouring and cottier groups which had formed such a significant part of O'Connell's Emancipation constituency. At the same time, it had radically strengthened the economic position of tenant farmers, who in consequence had acquired a new assertiveness independent of the moral authority of the Church. Accordingly, as the events of the Land War demonstrated, they operated their own political agenda, driven by economic imperatives, and in this the Catholic Church had much less of a role to play.

The Structures of Irish Religious Observance

The changing legal status of the Catholic Church in eighteenth- and nineteenth-century Ireland was paralleled by equally far-reaching changes in its spatial organization and ethos. The main concern of the eighteenth-century Church was its need to adjust to the spatial disinheritance it had suffered as a result of the seventeenth-century plantations and confiscations. Many of the earlier, medieval, parish centres, had been 'fossilized' by the processes of seventeenth-century land reallocation. Frequently, they had been reused as the cores of the new estates which were carved out of the existing structures of landownership, by their New English and Scots owners. In such cases, frequently all that remained of their earlier ecclesiastical functions were the semi-ruined churches or graveyards incorporated into the demesnes of the new owners (Fig. 6.2).

For the Catholic Church, therefore, the urgent need was to recreate a parish network together with its associated places of worship. However, the pace and scale of this adjustment was hindered by the relative weakness of the Church's organization following the loss of its diocesan clergy under the Act of Banishment in 1697, and by its impoverished state and lack of adequate parochial clergy. As conditions ameliorated during the later eighteenth century, these deficiencies were gradually rectified, but the fact remains that for much of this period, the Catholic Church was engaged on a process of reconstruction. One consequence of this, however, was the close congruity between the new Catholic parishes and the realities of social and economic life. Each parish had to be economically self-sustaining, and accordingly, their size and distribution closely reflected the variations in the relative distribution of Catholic wealth. The wealthiest and most numerous parishes were created in the south-east, in Leinster and east Munster, where in 1800 virtually all the parishes valued at over £150 were located.[70] As already noted, a significant sub-stratum of relatively wealthy Catholic farming tenants had survived the effects of the Penal Legislation in these districts, and were complemented by Catholic urban merchant communities who maintained significant trading links with France and Spain. This combination of urban and rural Catholic wealth provided a firm basis for the early reconstruction and modernization of the organizational structures of Catholicism in this part of Ireland by the end of the eighteenth century. In west Ulster and Connacht, on the other hand, the relative poverty of the Catholic population delayed this process until the mid nineteenth century.[71]

During the nineteenth century, the removal of the remaining impediments against Catholic observance and the final incorporation of its adherents into the mainstream of political as well as commercial life, created a climate of expansionism. This found expression not simply in the 'Devotional Revolution' encouraged by the reforms of Archbishop Cullen and his immediate predecessors, but also in the extensive replacement and extension of the existing stock of chapels.[72] The relatively simple, barn-like chapels of the Penal Era, were replaced by larger and more ornate buildings, frequently constructed in one or other of the 'Gothic Revival' styles. As Jones Hughes and Whelan have both noted, this widespread reconstruction frequently involved various types of settlement adjustment. Jones Hughes has argued that by the mid nineteenth century, the location of various institutional buildings in many towns and villages reflected both the dominance of

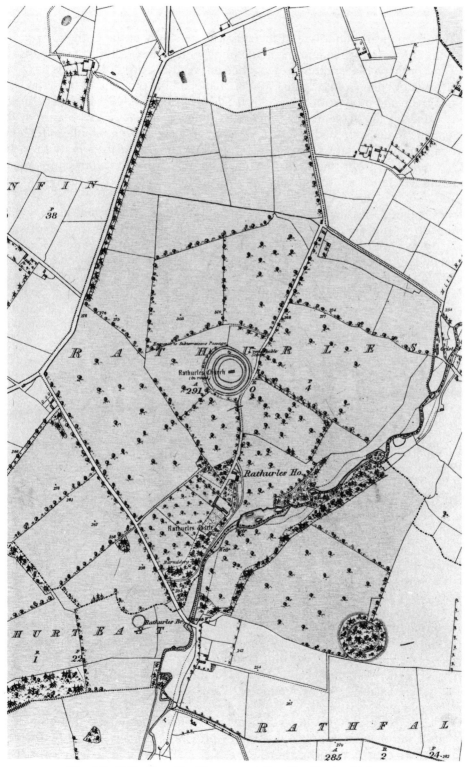

Fig. 6.2. Rathurles, Co. Tipperary: a 'fossilized' parochial core.

the ruling Anglican minority and the subordinate status of the Catholic majority. Thus the Anglican church and the market house, together with the court house (if any) and perhaps the landlord's own mansion, might occupy prominent positions in the town or village centre. The Catholic chapel on the other hand, together with the fair green and other socially-specific facilities like ball parks, would be peripherally located on the settlement's fringe. He argues that where this occurred, the settlements in question had almost invariably previously been rebuilt under landlord patronage as 'estate' towns. Thus the social and sectarian polarity they displayed reflected, in his view, the 'colonial' nature of the social structures which underpinned much of the urban and village refurbishment in early modern Ireland.[73]

Jones Hughes' ideas have a pleasing symmetry, but as O'Flanagan has shown, in some Irish 'estate' towns at least, this sort of crude urban sectarian polarity had broken down well before the mid nineteenth century. Using a variety of estate, valuation and parochial sources, he has demonstrated, for example, that between the 1770s and 1850s, the traditional central Protestant 'cores' of Bandon and Youghal, Co. Cork, were thoroughly infiltrated by Catholic tenants, who established themselves in these central zones on a highly segregated basis. At Dungarvan and Tallow, Co. Waterford, the Catholic preponderance which was already displayed by the 1770s was further enhanced by 1851. At Lismore, Co. Waterford, the relatively mixed community of the 1770s was replaced by an almost exclusively Catholic one by 1851. All of these towns were dominated politically, financially and socially by a limited number of patronal families or Corporate institutions. Of them all, only Lismore corresponded in any way to the morphological model proposed by Jones Hughes. Ironically, Lismore was owned by the Duke of Devonshire, an absentee English landlord, known for his liberal treatment of his Irish tenants, and his sympathy towards parliamentary reform and Catholic Emancipation.[74]

Whelan's analysis of the settlement changes which accompanied the chapel building campaigns emphasizes two scales of adjustment: those which were internal to existing settlements, and those which created entirely new settlements. Internal adjustments involved the relocation of existing chapels to more central and socially prominent locations. Invariably, this only occurred where the local landlord was Catholic or else sympathetic to Catholic aspirations. Thus in 1815 at Dungarvan, Co. Waterford, the 6th Duke of Devonshire provided a prominent site for the new Catholic chapel together with substantial grant aid.[75] In the same county, Lord Stuart de Decies built a chapel at Toor 'for the accommodation of his mountain tenantry'. Elsewhere, De Vere Hunt planned and built the new chapel at New Birmingham, Co. Tipperary, in the early nineteenth century as part of his proposed new town. In County Wexford, where nineteenth-century Catholic landowners were both relatively wealthy and numerous, their patronage resulted in the construction of a variety of centrally-located chapels, including those at Tomhaggard—where one of the few remaining 'Penal Chapels' also survives—Kiltealy, Piercestown and Murntown.[76]

Whelan's second class of settlement adjustment postulates the growth of hamlets around the new functional nodes provided in many places by the construction of a chapel, parochial house and National School. He envisages these as being characteristically irregular in plan and appearance, and the consequence of

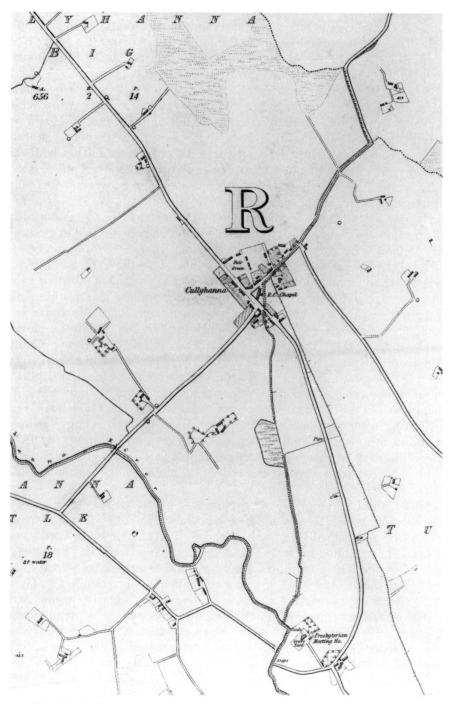

Fig. 6.3. Cullyhanna, Co. Armagh: a nineteenth-century 'chapel-village'.

the episodic accretion of additional retail and other services which were attracted to the chapel complex by its increasingly predominant centrality within the life of the parish. This centrality was reflected in the characteristic location of many of these 'chapel-villages' at important nodes in the local road network (Fig. 6.3). Whelan estimates that over 400 chapel-villages existed in Ireland by the early twentieth century, before the growth of new forms of communication broke down the localism of rural life. They were mainly located in the south-eastern heartland of modern Catholicism in Leinster and east Munster, as well as in the drumlin belt of the north Midlands. Whelan thus conceives of the chapel-villages as a late settlement form, inserted into the interstices of the existing settlement pattern. He argues, consequently, that many existed in a dialectical relationship with earlier settlement types created by other social forces unsympathetic to Catholicism. For example, a strong polarity can be shown to have existed between chapel-villages and estate villages, as at Valleymount and Blessington, Co. Wicklow, Caltra and Castleblayney, Co. Galway, and Newtown and Kilmacthomas, Co. Waterford.[77]

If the territorial and structural adjustments of the Catholic Church in nineteenth-century Ireland were consistently expansionist in character, those of the established Anglican Church were less emphatically so. Like the Catholic Church, the Church of Ireland entered the nineteenth century in urgent need of reform. Bishops were appointed by government, usually for political reasons. Many failed to reside in their dioceses, some even failed to visit them at all. Consequently, the local Anglican parish clergy were also characterized by non-residence, plural livings and—in the spirit of the times—a general lack of religious fervour. Churches were frequently in poor repair, and 10 per cent of all parishes had no church at all. Between 1800 and 1830, however, a general improvement in Church discipline and organization occurred, as individual reforming bishops sought, with tacit government approval, to raise standards of observance and behaviour. The Board of First Fruits, set up in the eighteenth century to finance church building, was reorganized and its income supplemented by generous government grants. By 1832 the number of churches had increased by 30 per cent, and the number of parishes by 25 per cent, as large parishes were subdivided and plural livings and non-residence discouraged.[78]

Thereafter, the Church of Ireland experienced a gradual but sustained loss of privilege, which culminated in its dis-establishment in 1869. It had started the century as the Established Church. Its bishops sat in the House of Lords, and its members still constituted Ireland's ruling political elite. Gradually, however, this status was eroded. The growth in Catholic political assertiveness helped to foster the concept of the 'neutral state', in which the government recognized that it could only rule effectively if it was not associated with any one sectarian group. Accordingly, successive governments sought to adjust the pattern of denominational privilege in ways which would reflect in more sensitive fashion the sectarian realities of Irish life. In 1831, the government established the ostensibly non-denominational National School system, in a move which was widely seen to erode one of the traditional areas of Anglican social authority. Ironically, the new schools were quickly absorbed and transformed by the Catholic Church into an overtly sectarian educational system, funded entirely at state expense. In 1833, the Church Temporalities Act reformed and reduced the Anglican hierarchy, and set up a body of Church Commissioners who were responsible for administering most of its income. At the same time, the contentious issue of the tithes payable to the Church of Ireland by all sections of the community was temporarily diffused by converting these into a reduced payment subsumed in the tenants' rent. Nevertheless, the underlying issue of the established status of the Church of Ireland remained unresolved. When renewed demands for reform were made in both Britain and Ireland by Catholics and Nonconformists alike in the 1850s and 1860s, they could no longer be resisted. In 1869, the Irish Church Act was passed, which abolished all state endowments of religion, including the *regius donum* to the Presbyterian clergy and the annual grant to the Catholic seminary at Maynooth. Although compensated by substantial endowments, the Church of Ireland was thereby reduced in status to an independent institution, serving an increasingly marginalized and politically-discredited minority.[79] The forlorn Anglican steeples of the west of Ireland, beacons of a small and politically-beleaguered community, foundering in a rising tide of sectarian nationalism, provided an eloquent metaphor for the change.

Agrarian Society and Social Protest

The third component in the *troika* of social, religious and political protest which occurred in Ireland during the eighteenth and nineteenth centuries was comprised of various agrarian movements. The earliest of these occurred in Connacht and south-west Ulster in 1711–12, but they were most widespread between the 1760s and the 1840s. Their varied and colourful nomenclature hid a common purpose: namely, the defence of their members' position within the agrarian 'moral economy', in the face of threats to their livelihood from other socio-economic groups. Lee argues that prior to the Famine, most of the antagonism occurred between farmers and their labourers, rather than between farmers and landlords. For this reason, he argues that there was little direct connection between these pre-Famine redresser movements, and the Land and National Leagues of the 1870s and 1880s. These were comprised of tenant farmers who pursued direct confrontation with their landlords, in a confrontation which itself reflected the fundamental reordering of the agrarian social structures of the post-Famine period. Before the Famine, an inflated and increasingly impoverished smallholder and labouring community saw the basis of their existence eroded by the progressive extension of commercial tenant farming. In the 1870s, a relatively well-capitalized tenant community, faced with the consequences of agrarian depression, sought a solution to their problems at the expense of the landlords via a redistribution of the rewards of agriculture.[80]

Lee's argument has found general acceptance, although Donnelly has suggested that the social composition of the groups involved in pre-Famine agrarian agitation depended on the immediate economic circumstances. In times of agricultural prosperity, only the poorest sectors of rural society were likely to feel marginalized and thus likely therefore to be involved in protest. In periods of depression, on the other hand, a wider social spectrum was likely to become involved, as increasing numbers of farmers found themselves faced with falling incomes but inelastic fixed costs such as tithes or rents.[81] In either case, however, we may conclude that although the precise nature of the perceived threats varied according to the state and nature of the local agrarian economy, these movements shared a similar structural origin in the profound inequalities in the social distribution of agrarian wealth in general.

By the late nineteenth century, of course, such inequalities were also the stuff of political protest. Consequently, one of the major debates over the earlier redresser movements has concerned whether, and when, they became politicized. Conventional opinion suggests that the earliest redresser movements in the eighteenth century were economic in purpose and were neither sectarian nor political in intent. For example, the Houghers, who were active in maiming and slaughtering cattle in Counties Clare, Galway, Fermanagh and Sligo between 1711 and 1712, were arable smallholders concerned at the spread of highly-capitalized extensive pastoralism in these districts.[82] Similarly, the more extensive Whiteboy agitation which broke out in southern County Tipperary during the early 1760s, and spread through parts of Counties Cork and Waterford by 1765, also had its origins in the local smallholders' perception of the threat posed by the expansion of commercial pastoralism. While it is true that the package of grievances presented by the Whiteboys was gradually extended, most notably to include the payment of tithes to the Church of Ireland, the movement remained resolutely non-sectarian. The tithes issue was resented by both Catholic and Protestant farmers alike. Contemporary imprecations by the local Protestant gentry that it was a 'popish plot' reflected their antagonism towards the growing economic success of Catholic tenant farmers. In much the same way, in Ulster, the Oakboys were most concerned about the size of the county cess being raised for road building. When this was abolished, the movement faded away.[83]

The politicization issue becomes more pertinent in the case of the later-eighteenth and early-nineteenth-century agrarian movements. It has already been shown that in the 1780s in County Armagh, both the Catholic Defenders and Protestant Peep O'Day Boys operated in an emphatically sectarian manner, as they sought to resolve economic rivalries which were internalized within what was, essentially, a group of equal socio-economic status. However, the subsequent alignment of the Defenders with the United Irishmen and the Peep O'Day Boys with Orangeism, demonstrated the potential for political activism which agrarian redresser movements might possess in the uncertain political conditions of the time.

Nevertheless, it seems that these Ulster movements represented a particular variant in the pattern of pre-Famine social protest. For it is reasonably clear that few of the later agrarian societies which flourished in the immediate pre-Famine period were primarily political in intent. For example, the Threshers, Carders, Caravats, Shanavests and Rockites were also all driven by the desire to rectify economic inequalities. The first four of these groups operated widely but episodically in north Connacht, central and south Leinster and Munster between 1806 and 1816.[84] The Rockites operated in an even more widespread fashion in Counties Cork, Kerry, Limerick and Tipperary between 1821 and 1824, and at times seemed close to fomenting a social revolution in the countryside. While maintaining links with the contemporary urban-based Ribbon movement, the Rockites' objectives were similar to those of the previous groups and were emphatically agrarian. They included the abolition of tithes and priests' dues, rent reductions and an end to 'land-grabbing'—the competitive outbidding of one tenant by another for a vacant farm.

Thus of all the early-nineteenth-century movements with agrarian origins or linkages, only the Ribbon Societies were avowedly political and sectarian in purpose. They originated on the Ulster–Leinster border prior to 1820, and spread rapidly through much of Connacht and north Leinster on a predominantly urban basis during the 1830s. In the post-Famine period, Ribbonism became increasingly localized in the Westmeath area, where the final outbreak occurred in the late 1860s. The longevity of the movement, its urban basis but widespread links with rural societies such as the Rockites, and the varied and contradictory nature of the contemporary descriptions of it, make an overall assessment of the movement difficult. McCartney probably comes closest to the truth when he stresses its origins in Defenderism, its sectarian antagonism to Orangeism and Protestant proselytization, but above all, its willingness to exploit local variations in the causes of sectarian tension and potential political disaffection. He notes, however, that although there were organizational and recruiting similarities between the Ribbon Societies and the Fenians of the 1860s, there is no evidence to indicate a direct link between them.[85] Beames and Garvin, on the other hand, have argued for precisely such a link.[86] They suggest that the Ribbon Societies provided a platform for the coherent articulation of working class nationalism in pre-Famine Ireland. As such, they argue that the Ribbon Societies constituted an important intermediate stage in the evolution of widespread nationalist consciousness, which linked the pre-Famine redresser movements with overtly nationalist post-Famine movements such as Fenianism, the Land League and the National League. However, this interpretation has been challenged by Murray, who has argued that the last outbreak of Ribbonism, in County Westmeath in 1869, showed no evidence of self-conscious nationalism, but was instead typical of the earlier economic redresser movements.[87]

Thus a link between the pre-Famine Ribbon Societies and the nationalist land agitation of the late 1870s and after, remains to be established. Consequently, interpretations which would see an early and widespread politicization of the Irish countryside in terms of a coherent sense of exclusive nationalism must find their evidence elsewhere. Moreover, to reiterate Lee's original argument, the differences in the structure of the pre-Famine and post-Famine land agitation indicate significant differences in their social complexion and motivation. These really demand explanation in terms of the particularities of place and time, rather than by means of some over-arching construct which links them together by means of some spurious uniformity. The antagonisms between the tenant farmers and the smallholders and cottiers who dominated the pre-Famine societies represented a form of social confrontation which had vanished from rural Ireland by the 1870s. The farmers who supported the Land League and Parnell during the Land War of 1879–82, sought a major redistribution of the rewards of agriculture at the expense of an entirely different sector of rural society.

The origins of the Land War were economic, although its solution was political. It was triggered by an unusually severe agricultural depression in 1876–79, which ended more than 20 years of rising prosperity for Irish tenant farmers, and faced them with the prospect of the loss of all their previous economic gains. Moreover, the depression coincided with a world-wide trade depression, which effectively cut off the safety-valve of emigration to America. The consequences of this were particularly severely felt in Connacht, where the post-Famine tradition of emigration had been especially widespread, and it was here that the Land League was first established in the autumn of 1879.

From the outset, the League attracted wide-ranging support from every spectrum of Irish rural society. This, however, was to prove divisive. The smallholders in the western districts wanted above all the redistribution of land—something which could only be done at the expense of local cattle ranchers. The more substantial tenant farmers wanted rent relief. The tactics employed by the Land League and, after its proscription in 1881, its successor, the more centrally-organized National League, varied in different places according to the nature of the agricultural economy and the structure of landownership. They included widespread rent-strikes, as well as more picturesque forms of protest aimed at disrupting gentry pastimes such as fox-hunting. They also included violence and intimidation. The government's response was at first equivocal, but latterly resolved upon the suppression of the various acts of violence coupled with an accelerated programme of land reform. Gladstone's Land Act of 1881 provided the means for the judicial reduction in rents via the Land Courts. So generous were the reductions that few tenants were initially enthusiastic about taking advantage of the opportunity to purchase their holdings provided by the Ashbourne Act of 1885 and its successors. By the end of the century barely 60,000 tenants had purchased their own farms. It was not until the Wyndham Act of 1903 made available state loans at significantly lower rates of repayment than the already reduced rents that the major transfer of landownership began. Except in Ulster, Irish landlords were generally glad to oblige. Faced with falling rents, a collapsing land market, and fixed costs and incumbrances which did not decline in line with their income, they had little option to do otherwise.[88]

Conclusion

This chapter has attempted to demonstrate the complexity of the religious and political changes which occurred during the eighteenth and nineteenth centuries in Ireland, and their consequences for the structures of everyday life. Two major themes have been identified: first, the inadequacy of earlier accounts which interpret these changes in terms of alienation and marginalization; and second, the complex local spatial and social textures to which these changes gave rise. If a single dominant characteristic for the period could be identified, it might be that of 'protest'. However, as the discussion has sought to show, the discourse of protest did not depend solely on a colonial dialectic, although this of course formed part of it. Rather, it reflected more fundamental inequalities in the structures of society and in its economic base, which had been reinforced, but not caused, by the seventeenth-century colonial transformations. Indeed, the evidence reviewed in this chapter suggests that the time has come to abandon the old stereotypes of repression and triumphalism, no matter how comforting they might be. Instead, due recognition should be given to the manifestly complex nature of society in eighteenth- and nineteenth-century Ireland, and to the complex nature of the spatial structures which were fundamental to it.

References

1. E. R. Hooker, *Readjustments of Agricultural Tenure in Ireland*, (Chapel Hill, North Carolina, 1938); N. D. Palmer, *The Irish Land League Crisis*, (New Haven, 1940); J. E. Pomfret, *The Struggle for Land in Ireland, 1800–1923*, (Princeton, 1930).
2. L. M. Cullen, *An Economic History of Ireland Since 1660*, (2nd edn, London, 1987), pp. 37–8.
3. L. A. Clarkson, 'Irish population revisited, 1687–1821', in J. M. Goldstrom and L. A. Clarkson (eds.), *Irish Population, Economy, and Society*, (Oxford, 1981), pp. 13–35; L. M. Cullen and T. C. Smout, 'Economic growth in Scotland and Ireland', in L. M. Cullen and T. C. Smout (eds.), *Comparative Aspects of Scottish and Irish Economic and Social History 1600–1900*, (Edinburgh, 1977), p. 6.
4. Cullen, *Economic History*, pp. 36–42.
5. *Ibid.*, p. 39; *idem, The Emergence of Modern Ireland 1600–1900*, (Dublin, 1983), pp. 25–30.
6. Cullen, *Economic History*, p. 54.
7. *Idem, Anglo-Irish Trade 1600–1800*, (Manchester, 1968), p. 60.
8. *Idem, Economic History*, p. 60.
9. D. Dickson, 'An economic history of the Cork region in the Eighteenth Century', (unpublished PhD thesis, University of Dublin, 1977), pp. 594–600.
10. E. Boyle, 'Linenopolis: the rise of the textile industry', in J. C. Beckett *et al.* (eds.), *Belfast. The Making of the City 1800–1914*, (Belfast, 1983), pp. 41–56; P. Ollerenshaw, 'Industry, 1820–1914', in L. Kennedy and P. Ollerenshaw (eds.), *An Economic History of Ulster 1820–1939*, (Manchester, 1985), pp. 66–9.
11. D. Dickson, 'The gap in famines: A useful myth?', in E. M. Crawford (ed.), *Famine: The Irish Experience 900–1900*, (Edinburgh, 1989), p. 97.
12. Clarkson, 'Irish population', p. 27; C. Ó Gráda, 'Poverty, population, and agriculture, 1801–1845', in W. E. Vaughan (ed.), *A New History of Ireland V, Ireland Under the Union, I, 1801–70*, (Oxford, 1989), pp. 118–22.
13. Cullen, *Emergence*, pp. 96–7.
14. W. H. Crawford, 'Ulster landowners and the linen industry', in J. T. Ward and R. G. Wilson (eds.), *Land and Industry. The Landed Estate and the Industrial Revolution*, (Newton Abbot, 1971), pp. 136–7.
15. K. H. Connell, *The Population of Ireland 1750–1845*, (Oxford, 1950), *passim*; Cullen, *Economic History*, pp. 110–19.
16. L. J. Proudfoot, 'Urban patronage and estate management on the Duke of Devonshire's Irish estates (1764–1891): A study in landlord–tenant relationships', (unpublished PhD thesis, Queen's University, Belfast, 1989), pp. 388–95.
17. J. H. Andrews, 'Land and people, *c.* 1685', in T. W. Moody, F. X. Martin and F. J. Byrne (eds.), *A New History of Ireland III, Early Modern Ireland 1534–1691*, (Oxford, 1976), p. 474; A. Sheehan, 'Irish towns in a period of change, 1558–1625', in C. Brady and R. Gillespie (eds.), *Natives and Newcomers*, (Dublin, 1986), p. 97.
18. H. Carter, *An Introduction to Urban Historical Geography*, (London, 1983), p. 112; D. Dickson, 'The place of Dublin in the eighteenth-century Irish economy', in T. M. Devine and D. Dickson (eds.), *Ireland and Scotland 1600–1850*, (Edinburgh, 1983), pp. 177–92.
19. The classic study of this phenomenon in England is D. Cannadine, *Lords and Landlords. The Aristocracy and the Towns 1774–1967*, (Leicester, 1980). See also Carter, *Urban Historical Geography*, pp. 130–42.
20. N. T. Burke, 'An early modern Dublin suburb: the estate of Francis Augnier, Earl of Longford', *Irish Geography*, 4 (1972), pp. 365–83.
21. E. Walsh, 'Sackville Mall: the first one hundred years', in D. Dickson (ed.), *The Gorgeous Mask. Dublin 1700–1850*, (Dublin, 1987), pp. 30–50.

22. E. McParland, 'The Wide Streets Commissioners: their importance for Dublin architecture in the late eighteenth and early nineteenth century', *Quarterly Bulletin of the Irish Georgian Society*, **XV** (1972), pp. 1–27.

23. T. Mooney and F. White, 'The gentry's winter season', in Dickson (ed.), *Mask*, pp. 1–16.

24. P. Butel and L. M. Cullen (eds.), *Cities and Merchants: French and Irish Perspectives on Urban Development, 1500–1900*, (Dublin, 1986), Section III, 'Merchant Communities and Politics', *passim*; L. A. Clarkson, 'An anatomy of an Irish town: the economy of Armagh, 1770', *Irish Economic and Social History*, **V** (1978), pp. 27–8.

25. R. B. McCarthy, 'The estates of Trinity College, Dublin, in the nineteenth century', (unpublished PhD thesis, University of Dublin, 1982), pp. 293–325.

26. W. E. Vaughan and A. J. Fitzpatrick, *Irish Historical Statistics. Population 1821–1971*, (Dublin, 1978), pp. 27–40.

27. Cullen, *Economic History*, pp. 142–3.

28. J. S. Donnelly, 'Landlords and tenants', in Vaughan (ed.), *Ireland Under the Union*, pp. 332–49.

29. *Ibid.*

30. *Ibid.*, pp. 347–8; K. Theodore Hoppen, *Ireland Since 1800. Conflict and Conformity*, (London, 1989), pp. 87–8.

31. Summarized in W. E. Vaughan, *Landlords and Tenants in Ireland 1848–1904*, (Studies in Irish Economic and Social History 2, 1984), *passim*.

32. Hoppen, *Ireland*, pp. 90–4.

33. Cullen, *Economic History*, pp. 28–9; P. Robinson, *The Plantation of Ulster*, (Dublin, 1984), pp. 91–128.

34. D. McCartney, *The Dawning of Democracy: Ireland 1800–1870*, (Dublin, 1987), p. 3.

35. S. Connolly, *Religion and Society in Nineteenth-Century Ireland*, (Studies in Irish Economic and Social History 3, 1985), p. 3.

36. *Ibid.*, p. 3; McCartney, *Dawning*, pp. 36–7.

37. Connolly, *Religion and Society*, p. 26; D. Dickson, *New Foundations: Ireland 1660–1800*, (Dublin, 1984), p. 74.

38. Connolly, *Religion and Society*, pp. 3–4.

39. T. Bartlett, 'The origins and progress of the Catholic Question in Ireland, 1690–1800', in T. P. Power and K. Whelan (eds.), *Endurance and Emergence*, (Dublin, 1990), pp. 1–2; *idem*, *The Fall and Rise of the Irish Nation, The Catholic Question 1690–1830*, (Dublin, 1992), pp. 17–29, 82–170. Dickson, *New Foundations*, p. 42.

40. M. Wall, 'The Penal Laws, 1691–1760', in G. O'Brien (ed), *Catholic Ireland in the Eighteenth Century*, (Dublin, 1989), p. 10.

41. *Ibid.*, pp. 17–18.

42. Dickson, *New Foundations*, p. 43; J. G. Simms, 'The establishment of Protestant Ascendancy, 1691–1714', in T. W. Moody and W. E. Vaughan (eds.), *A New History of Ireland IV, Eighteenth-Century Ireland 1691–1800*, (Oxford, 1986), pp. 16–20.

43. Dickson, *New Foundations*, p. 44; Simms, 'Establishment', pp. 16–20.

44. Dickson, *New Foundations*, p. 73.

45. Bartlett, 'Origins and progress', pp. 1–3.

46. W. N. Osborough, 'Catholics, Land and the Popery Acts of Anne', in Power and Whelan (eds.), *Endurance*, pp. 21–56.

47. L. M. Cullen 'Catholic social classes under the Penal Laws', in Power and Whelan (eds.), *Endurance*, pp. 58–9; Wall, 'Penal Laws', *passim*.

48. Cullen, 'Catholic social classes', pp. 57–84; K. Whelan, 'The regional impact of Irish Catholicism 1700–1850', in W. J. Smyth and K. Whelan (eds.), *Common Ground. Essays on the Historical Geography of Ireland*, (Cork, 1988), pp. 253–77.

49. Dickson, *New Foundations*, p. 173; M. Wall, 'The rise of a Catholic middle class in eighteenth century Ireland', in O'Brien (ed.), *Catholic Ireland*, pp. 73–84; *idem*, 'Catholics in Economic Life', *Ibid.*, pp. 85–92.

50. Butel and Cullen (eds.), *Cities and Merchants*, Section III, *passim*; D. Dickson, 'Catholics and trade in eighteenth-century Ireland: an old debate revisited', in Power and Whelan (eds.), *Endurance*, pp. 85–100.

51. Bartlett, 'Origins and progress', p. 9; Dickson, *New Foundations*, pp. 152–5; R. B. McDowell, 'Ireland in 1800', in Moody and Vaughan (eds.), *Eighteenth-Century Ireland*, pp. 688–9.
52. A. P. W. Malcomson, *John Foster. The Politics of the Anglo-Irish Ascendancy*, (Oxford, 1978), pp. 297–303.
53. E. Hewitt (ed.), *Lord Shannon's Letters to His Son*, (P.R.O.N.I., 1982), pp. 223–36; P. Jupp, 'Urban politics in Ireland, 1801–31', in D. Harkness and M. O'Dowd (eds.), *The Town in Ireland*, (Belfast, 1981), pp. 103–24.
54. Dickson, *New Foundations*, pp. 152–5, 164–5; J. McGuire, 'The Act of Union', in L. de Paor (ed.), *Milestones in Irish History*, (Cork, 1991), p. 75.
55. Dickson, *New Foundations*, pp. 173–4, 187.
56. Connolly, *Religion and Society*, pp. 32–3.
57. L. M. Cullen, 'The 1798 Rebellion in Wexford: United Irishman organization, membership, leadership', in K. Whelan (ed.), *Wexford History and Society*, (Dublin, 1987), pp. 248–95; K. Whelan, 'The role of the Catholic priest in the 1798 rebellion in county Wexford', *Ibid.*, pp. 296–315.
58. McGuire, 'Act of Union', p. 75.
59. Hoppen, *Ireland*, pp. 22–3.
60. McCartney, *Dawning*, p. 110.
61. *Ibid.*, p.118.
62. I. d'Alton, *Protestant Society and Politics in Cork 1812–1844*, (Cork, 1980), pp. 102–3; Devonshire Papers, Lismore Castle Estate Office, Ms C/1/20 Bundle: 'Bandon Election correspondence 14 Jan. 1830–26 Aug. 1831', *passim*.
63. R. Stewart, *Party and Politics 1830–1852*, (London, 1989), pp. 19–20.
64. J. C. Beckett, *The Making of Modern Ireland*, (London, 1981), pp. 308–17; N. Gash, *Politics in the Age of Peel*, (London, 1977), pp. 50–64.
65. K. Theodore Hoppen, *Elections, Politics, and Society in Ireland 1832–1885*, (Oxford, 1984), pp. 1–33.
66. 'Instructions given by the Chief Secretary for Ireland with reference to the Cities and Boroughs of Ireland, sending representatives to Parliament', *Parliamentary Sessional Papers, Reports and Plans*, **6** (1831–2), pp. 65–7, 145–50.
67. K. Theodore Hoppen, *Elections, Politics, and Society in Ireland, 1832–1885*, (Oxford, 1984), *passim*.
68. Hoppen, *Ireland*, pp. 26–31.
69. *Ibid.*, pp. 158–9.
70. Whelan, 'Regional impact', p. 261.
71. *Ibid.*
72. Connolly, *Religion and Society*, pp. 12–15; K. Whelan, 'The Catholic Parish, the Catholic chapel, and village development in Ireland', *Irish Geography*, **16** (1983), pp. 1–15.
73. T. Jones Hughes, 'Village and town in mid-nineteenth century Ireland', *Irish Geography*, **14** (1981), pp. 99–106.
74. P. O'Flanagan, 'Urban minorities and majorities: Catholics and Protestants in Munster towns, c. 1659–1850', in Smyth and Whelan (eds.), *Common Ground*, pp. 124–148.
75. W. Fraher, 'The reconstruction of Dungarvan, 1807–c. 1830: A political ploy', *Decies*, **XXV** (1984), p. 19.
76. S. Lewis, *A Topographical Dictionary of Ireland*, Vol. 2 (London, 1837), p. 208; Whelan, 'The Catholic Parish', pp. 1–15.
77. *Ibid.*
78. Connolly, *Religion and Society*, pp. 7–10.
79. *Ibid.*, pp. 18–30; McCartney, *Dawning*, pp. 26–31.
80. J. Lee, 'Patterns of rural unrest in nineteenth-century Ireland: a preliminary survey', in L. M. Cullen and F. Furet (eds.), *Ireland and France 17th–20th centuries*, (Paris, 1980), pp. 223–37.
81. J. S. Donnelly, 'The social composition of agrarian rebellions in early nineteenth century Ireland: the case of the Carders and Caravats 1813–16', in P. J. Corish (ed.), *Radicals, Rebels and Establishments*, (Belfast, 1985), pp. 151–70.

82. S. J. Connolly, 'Law, order and popular protest in early eighteenth-century Ireland: the case of the Houghers', *Ibid.*, pp. 51–68.
83. Dickson, *New Foundations*, pp. 132–6.
84. McCartney, *Dawning*, pp. 62–82.
85. *Ibid.*, pp. 82–9.
86. Cited in Donnelly, 'Social composition'. See also A. C. Murray, 'Agrarian violence and nationalism in nineteenth-century Ireland: The myth of Ribbonism', *Irish Economic and Social History*, **XIII** (1986), pp. 56–73.
87. *Ibid.*
88. Hoppen, *Ireland*, pp. 94–8.

7

Spatial Transformation and Social Agency: Property, Society and Improvement, *c.* 1700 to *c.* 1900

L. J. Proudfoot

Introduction

Calendar dates rarely provide a convenient framework for the analysis of processes of historical and geographical change, and Ireland in the eighteenth and nineteenth centuries provides no exception. Nevertheless, the two hundred years which followed the final assertion of English political authority over the country in the 1690s may be identified as a period of significant social, economic and demographic change which in combination radically transformed but, ultimately, failed to strengthen Ireland's regional economy. Some of these changes, for example those in the composition of landownership, had their origins in the colonial transformations brought about by the sixteenth- and seventeenth-century plantations and land confiscations. Many of the 'colonial' patterns of settlement and social organization established at that time were themselves subsequently modified by later social and political change. Other transformations were more characteristic of the latter part of the period. For example, the growing concentration of industry in the north-east of the island was essentially a nineteenth-century phenomenon, while the complex adjustments in demographic behaviour which were associated with the rapid growth in population before the Famine only really became apparent after *c.* 1750. All such changes, however, were profoundly uneven in their regional and social impact, and consequently had far-reaching and sometimes contradictory implications for the way in which all levels of Irish society perceived and used space.

Although there is reasonable agreement among historians concerning the periodicity of these changes, there is less consensus about their causation. For example, considerable debate has surrounded the role played by different social groups as agents promoting or hindering Ireland's economic development, with particular attention being paid to the landowning minority. Conventionally, geographers and historians have identified landowners as *the* main arbiters of socio-economic change in pre-Famine Ireland, but recent discussion has suggested that this view requires modification. Early analyses of the landowners' socio-economic role presented this in an almost uniformly unfavourable light. These studies were frequently framed by an overtly nationalist ideology which emphasized the colonial origins of these landowners—which was itself unusual in a European context. They depicted landowners as an economically parasitic and culturally alien group, intent on expropriating the maximum rent value from their tenants and willing to indulge in a wide variety of social coercion to achieve this. Moreover, by accepting contemporary eighteenth-century tracts such as Thomas Prior's, *List of the absentees of Ireland*, published in 1729, at face value, nationalist historians added the sin of absenteeism to the general obloquy attached to landowners. The view was promulgated that much of the rents exacted under coercion from the tenantry were then exported in the form of remittances for landlord use in England or elsewhere.[1]

Early geographical contributions to the debate reinforced the emphasis on the allegedly extensive and interventionist nature of the landowners' authority, by arguing that this was frequently used to create 'estate landscapes'. Characterized by relatively formal settlement and land-use patterns, these were held to embody both the landowners' own social codes and values and their ability to impose these on other social groups. Most recently this argument has been promulgated in an urban context by O'Connor,[2] but its classic exposition was by Jones Hughes, who wrote that

> the impact of the estate system is so overwhelming in places that it is difficult to decipher the type of landscape that immediately preceded it.

He concluded that

> in those parts of Ireland most intimately affected by landlordism little of the framework of the existing landscape, whether this is thought of in terms of the arrangements of settlement and associated patterns of enclosure, or the communications pattern, or even the details of the lie of the boundaries of the smallest administrative units, may be said to have evolved slowly and spasmodically over lengthy periods of time.[3]

Thus in this view, the landowner was the supreme arbiter of local life, and was able to adjust the conditions of existence of those around him to suit his own purposes. If necessary, he could even recreate the geography of Ireland in order to do so.

Recent attempts to re-evaluate the Irish landowners' socio-economic role have eschewed the nationalist commitment of earlier writers. These studies have challenged both the concept of a 'predatory landlordism' and its capacity for untrammelled unilateral action. In so doing they have recognized implicitly that some of the evidence which in the past has been taken to denote such unilateralism may be better interpreted as arising from the constraints imposed on that action by the property rights which the landowner had previously delegated to his tenants.[4] Thus in their studies of the construction of demesne landscapes in Tipperary and Kildare, Smyth[5] and Horner[6] both emphasize the important influence exerted by existing tenurial structures in determining when and how these improvements were completed. More generally, Malcomson[7] has demonstrated that eighteenth-century landlord absenteeism was less pernicious than contemporary observers supposed, while Vaughan has argued plausibly that landowners were as often the victims of circumstance as the perpetrators of malign social injustice. In post-Famine Ireland, he argues, evictions were less frequent, rent increases lower and insecurity of tenure less pervasive than earlier writers supposed. Indeed, in his view, if landowners conspicuously failed in anything in the long term, it was in their failure to raise rents sufficiently in line with price movements to permit them to invest adequately on their estates.[8]

Arguably, however, this revisionist argument may well have *overemphasized* the limits to the discretionary powers available to Irish landowners—at least to those who had not been beggared by falling rents in the wake of the post-Napoleonic agricultural crisis or the Famine. Prior to the land legislation of the 1880s, the fundamental division in Irish society lay between a minority class of property-*owners* and the majority who enjoyed only delegated rights of property *use*. The distinction between them arose on the basis of their relationship to the production process—the ways in which wealth was created.[9] In what was still, outside Ulster, an agrarian economy, the property-owning minority was comprised predominantly of landowners, who thus monopolized the ownership of land as the basic source of production. Within eastern Ulster—the only industrializing region in the island—this minority also included growing numbers of industrial capitalists. These owned the means of industrial production and thus also stood in a relationship of exploitation with the groups in society who were using these to produce wealth—the industrial workforce. The majority of the population who did not own property in their own right thus included not simply the tenant farmers and their own dependent wage labourers and cottiers in the countryside, but also the burgeoning array of industrial and service workers, who became increasingly urban-based as the nineteenth century progressed.

This majority stood in an entirely different relationship to the production process when compared to the property-owners. Whether directly or indirectly, all its members relied on negotiation with that minority for access to the means of production—land or industry—on which their livelihood depended. However frequently or extensively the minority delegated some or all of their property rights to these other socio-economic groups, whether by means of agricultural leaseholds or by industrial wage-bargaining, the fact remained that these rights would ultimately revert to the property-owners at a time and in a manner determined by them. Similarly, no matter how extensive and generous the delegated property rights received by the property user—be he tenant farmer or industrial worker—it was equally certain that these had to be bought at the cost either of rent or labour and would one day have to be relinquished to the property-owner. Significantly, there is considerable evidence from the 1770s onwards of landowners deliberately trying to minimize the property rights delegated to their tenants by reducing the length and security of their tenurial contracts.[10] Arguably, therefore, while it is true that as Ireland's economy diversified, social access to wealth widened, as the rise and growing independence of the Ulster Linen Drapers testifies,[11] these developments did not distort the underlying and grossly uneven social pattern of property *ownership*. Until the Ashbourne and Wyndham Acts of 1885 and 1903,[12] this remained dominated by a minority who, although broadened in social composition and in the types of property they owned, succeeded in preserving their monopoly of the means of production until largely divested of these by state intervention. Thus the tenurial and other constraints on the landowners' actions, and their inability always to maximize their share of the rewards from agriculture, was evidence of continuing adjustments to the process of property-delegation, and not evidence of the loss of those rights altogether.

This chapter attempts to further understanding of the social origins of the geographical transformations which characterized eighteenth- and nineteenth-century Ireland. It offers a general assessment of the role of landowners in promoting these changes, prior to the state intervention which led to their progressive eclipse as a class after *c.* 1870. This focus of attention on the landowners is warranted by their continuing importance within the property-owning minority throughout the greater part of the nineteenth century. As in eastern Prussia and southern Spain, two of the other main regions of 'great estates' in Europe,[13] the landowning elite in Ireland managed to survive the nineteenth century with most of their estates intact, at least until the 1880s. Even the massive land sales which followed the Famine tended to redistribute the land among existing landowners rather than lead to an extension in the social composition of landownership.[14] Thus the four million or so people who earned their living in the Irish countryside in 1871 did so through negotiation with a landowning class comprised of perhaps 20,000 families,[15] some of whom, moreover, also possessed extensive urban and industrial interests. The discussion begins with an analysis of the origins and social composition of landownership in eighteenth- and nineteenth-century Ireland, which pays particular attention to its diverse and fluid nature. This is followed by an examination of the motivations for landowner involvement in those spatial transformations which can loosely be termed 'improvement', and relates these to the major modernizing trends in Ireland's regional economy between 1700 and 1900.

The Origins and Character of Landownership in Ireland, 1700–1870

Origins

In large measure, the origins of the eighteenth- and nineteenth-century landowning class can be traced to the arrival in Ireland of New English and Scots settlers in the sixteenth and seventeenth centuries. These incomers were the beneficiaries of the land reallocations which were part and parcel of the successive plantation schemes implemented in Munster, the Irish midlands and Ulster between 1550 and 1640, and the more widespread Cromwellian and Williamite land confiscations of the 1650s and 1690s. Despite the English government's willingness to subsidize the capital costs incurred by individual planters, the initial plantations struggled in the face of poor planning, lack of interest in England and continuing native hostility in Ireland, to establish and maintain their financial and demographic viability.[16] Consequently, save in Ulster, the major transfer of landownership from the hands of the existing Catholic Gaelic and Old English social elites occurred not during the plantations as such, but as a result of the Cromwellian and Restoration land confiscations which followed the 1641 rebellion and those carried out after the Williamite Wars of the 1690s. In 1641, Catholics owned most of the profitable land in Ireland. The only exceptions were Ulster, where they owned between 4 and 49 per cent, and Counties Carlow, Leitrim and Wicklow, where they owned between a quarter and a half. By 1703 only 14 per cent of the country's profitable land remained in Catholic hands, and in every county Catholic landowners were in a minority.[17] Significantly, however, the majority of the Catholic landowners dispossessed in this way remained on their erstwhile estates as head tenants, where their presence could act as a substantial curb to the depth and stability of subsequent incoming Protestant settlement. Relatively few were reassigned estates in Connacht under the Cromwellian scheme.[18]

Among the English government's purposes in promoting the plantations was the desire to reinvigorate the exploitation of Ireland's resources, and this was reflected in the terms and conditions of the land grants and leasehold tenures made available to the new settlers. An ethos was thereby created which encouraged the commercial exploitation of the newly created or recreated estates by their new owners.[19] Accordingly, the new landowners and their tenants have been credited with importing new commercial ideas of land management and economic exploitation which were at variance with existing Gaelic and Gaelicized economic systems. These are thought to have organized economic exchange on a social basis, which recognized a complex web of status-based mutual obligation between family and clan members.[20] In time, the new commercial ideas are thought to have imposed more formal spatial signatures on the agrarian landscape. In parts of Tipperary and Kilkenny, for example, Smyth argues that they gave rise to geometric 'commercial' landscapes which had virtually replaced the earlier and more irregular medieval settlement patterns by the 1670s.[21] In some parts of Ireland too, notably Ulster, Laois and Offaly, the plantations involved a significant extension to the existing urban network.[22]

Smyth's argument is persuasive but probably requires modification. In the first instance, it is quite clear that the plantations also involved processes which were socially and spatially adaptive rather than obliterative, which in turn suggests a significant degree of continuity with earlier patterns of economic exploitation. Thus in the Ulster Plantation of 1610, for example, the land reallocation utilized existing Gaelic *ballybetaghs* and *ballyboes* as the basic units of measurement to accommodate both the incoming 'planter' settlers and the surviving original Gaelic-Irish and Old English tenants. These latter groups remained on the escheated territories in much larger numbers than had originally been anticipated, largely because of the scheme's failure to attract sufficient numbers of New English and Scots settlers onto lands whose size had in any case been grossly underestimated.[23] The successful incorporation of these existing occupiers within the plantations suggests a degree of familiarity on their part with the concept of a cash-based rent economy which lay at the scheme's heart. Moreover, it also suggests that the existing Gaelic-Irish and Old English concepts of ordered economic space retained some residual utility in the new arrangements. In short, the plantations did not necessarily involve the 'clear felling' of all the component structures in the existing cultural landscape. Rather, wherever existing features such as settlement nodes or units of landownership displayed some continuing usefulness, they were retained, but were recombined as part of a new property matrix to form new patterns of administration and landownership which were not, however, necessarily completely divergent from what had gone before.

It is also clear, moreover, that the Irish space-economy was not as devoid of significant commercial enterprise by the mid sixteenth century as the advocates of the plantations as a 'new beginning' would have us believe. Market economies, for example, had continued to function in various parts of Ireland both within and beyond the area of rapidly fragmenting centralized English authority prior to the first plantations of the mid sixteenth century. The most successful of these were centred either on towns such as Kilkenny, which enjoyed the protection of a powerful patron, in this case the Duke of Ormond, or on well-circumstanced ports such as Galway, Waterford or Youghal. Galway in particular flourished for much of the immediate pre-plantation period on the basis of its extensive trade with France and Spain. Significantly, as in Waterford, this trade involved many of the county's leading Catholic gentry. The continued existence of these urban markets and their regional hinterlands provides further evidence of the commercial potential within the pre-plantation Irish economy, and adds weight to Cullen's contention that it would have modernized irrespective of the land settlements. In his view, the presence of New English or Scots was not a necessary precondition for the growth of a commercial economy in seventeenth-century Ireland; the presence of an adequately capitalized gentry, whether English, Scots or Irish, was.[24]

If the degree of continuity between some of the existing economic structures and those created by the seventeenth-century land settlements was greater in parts of Ireland than has previously been realized, it is nevertheless still true that this process of dispossession created significant social divisions which had a lasting effect on Irish society. In reconstructing the pattern of landownership, the land settlements reinforced the existing differences in wealth between the landowning minority and the landless majority, with newly-emphasized differences in language, religion, cultural mores and perceived ethnicity. Arguably, however, the most important characteristic of this recreated landowning elite was its continuing near-monopoly of agricultural land, which remained the basic source of production throughout the period. By the 1770s, over 95 per cent of all land is estimated to have been held by no more than 5000 'landed' families, less than one per cent of the total population.[25] By the early 1840s, when Ireland's population had more than doubled, roughly the same proportion of land was in the hands of roughly the same proportion of the population, some 10,000 families.[26] Thirty years later, the total had doubled again to reach *c.* 20,000 but this time in the context of an overall population which had fallen from just under 8.2 million in 1841 to approximately 5.4 million in 1871.[27] Hoppen estimates their gross annual rental at this time to have exceeded £10 million.[28]

The size distribution of the estates owned by these families was strongly pyramidal in character. By 1870, the first rank comprised the 300 or so families who owned estates of over 10,000 acres (4048 hectares), but even among these a small coterie of magnate landowners stood out, including the Marquis of Lansdowne with 120,000 acres (48,582 ha) in Dublin, Kerry, Leix, Limerick, Meath and Offaly; the Earl of FitzWilliam with over 90,000 acres (36,437 ha) in Kildare, Wexford and Wicklow; and the Duke of Devonshire with 60,000 acres (24,291 ha) in Cork and Waterford. The second rank was over 10 times as numerous, and comprised 3400 estates of between 1000 and 10,000 acres (405–4048 ha). Finally, beneath these again, a group of some 15,000 families owned less than 1000 acres (405 ha), many of them much less, as this category also included a locally numerous class of squatters who had colonized common land and acquired freeholders' rights over their smallholdings.[29]

The hierarchical and therefore inevitably unequal nature of this landownership pattern has sometimes been taken as further evidence of the allegedly 'predatory' basis of the landlord system in Ireland. In reality, it was a pattern which was well within the range of nineteenth-century European experience. In the 1850s in Prussia, for example, the 15,000 *Junkers* who owned estates of more than 375 acres (152 ha) between them accounted for over 40 per cent of the land area of a country twice the size of England.[30] In England itself the disparities were even more pronounced. In 1874 over 55 per cent of all land was held by landowners with estates of over 1000 acres (405 ha), with the proportion rising to 65 per cent if a 300 acre (121 ha) threshold size for estate status is adopted. Even this does not tell the full story, since over 25 per cent of all land was in the hands of 363 landowners with estates of more than 10,000 acres (4048 ha).[31] In Spain, the plurality of landed elites and the absence of reliable nineteenth-century statistics makes comparison diffcult, but even here it seems that despite the enforced sale of previously entailed ecclesiastical, municipal and crown lands between 1798 and 1855, the lay aristocracy succeeded in retaining most of their land until the present century. In the 1930s, over 52 per cent of all Spanish land was contained in the 50,000 estates of more than 250 acres (101 ha).[32] Even in France, long characterized—perhaps misleadingly—as a country of 'peasant proprietorship' after the Revolution of 1798, the landed elite held on to about 20 per cent of all land in the early nineteenth century.[33] Thus what was remarkable about the pattern of landownership in Ireland was not the relative size or number of the estates; rather, it was that they were owned in the main by families of relatively recent origin in the country, whose rights of possession were acquired at the expense of an earlier, largely displaced, landed elite.

The Changing Character of Irish Landownership

Nevertheless, it is too simple to conceptualize the landowning class as a homogeneous entity, uniformly separated by a seamless array of cultural attributes from the mass of Ireland's rapidly growing population. This was never completely true even in the heyday of the 'Protestant Ascendancy', as correctly and narrowly defined in a political sense during the last quarter of the eighteenth century,[34] and became progressively less so during the nineteenth century. Whatever the cultural differences which may have separated many landowning families from the majority of their fellow countrymen, these were not truly diagnostic of their separate status, since similar divisions existed among the landowners themselves. Politically, landowners reflected every shade of opinion from the High Toryism espoused by Lord Bandon and the Marquis of Waterford, to the Whiggish Liberalism of the Villiers-Stuarts and the Radicalism of Daniel O'Connell, himself a minor Kerry landlord. Their sectarian affiliations and ethnic origins were equally varied. The majority of landowners were Anglicans of English descent, many of whom by the 1790s regarded themselves as the embodiment of a patriotic Protestant Irish nationalism—the quintessential Protestant Ascendancy.[35] In addition, a regionally varied minority of estates remained in Catholic Old English or Gaelic-Irish owner-ship or in the hands of Scots Episcopalians. Some of the Catholic minority con-formed to the Anglican faith during the Penal Era, but others adopted a variety of other strategies to retain effective control of their land.[36] Indeed, Whelan suggests that over 5 per cent of land remained in Catholic hands during the eighteenth century, despite the operation of the Penal Legislation which prior to 1778 attempted to discriminate against Catholic landownership.[37]

These divisions within the landowning class left a persistent imprint on the cultural landscape. In the 1830s, for example, it was still possible to identify a cluster of landowners of Scots origin in northern part of County Down. This was precisely the locality where informal Scots colonization in the late sixteenth and early seventeenth centuries had been densest in an area of otherwise generally strong English settlement.[38] By contrast, in County Waterford, which was an area which had not experienced widespread seventeenth-century resettlement but which had been densely settled by Anglo-Norman colonists in the Middle Ages, over 58 per cent of all landowning families in 1851 were of Gaelic-Irish or Old English origin. Interestingly, however, they were significantly under-represented in terms of the aggregate and average value of their estates. In aggregate, their estates accounted for only 46 per cent of the total Poor Law valuation for the county's landed property at large, compared to the 54 per cent of the valuation provided by the minority of estates in New English ownership (42 per cent). Similarly, whereas the average valuation of the estates owned by families of Gaelic and Old English origin was, respectively, £1409 and £1752, the average figure for the New English estates was £2614.[39] Clearly, although the most valuable property in the county had been acquired by seventeenth-century settlers or their descend-ants, including, notably, the Marquis of Waterford, the existing landowning com-munity were sufficiently well entrenched to resist complete displacement and to retain a significant proportion of the county's land in their hands.

The landowning class was thus far from seamless. It was also, in aggregate, socially highly mobile. This mobility involved both advancement, as successful merchants, industrialists and tenant farmers sought to enhance their social status through land purchase,[40] and decline, as indebtedness periodically forced the owners of estates of all sizes to shed land and, sometimes, status. The latter process reached its apotheosis in the enforced post-Famine sales of bankrupt landed property in the Encumbered Estates Court and Landed Estates Court referred to in Chapter 6. Prior to this, however, the doubling in the overall number of the landowning families between the 1770s and 1840s suggests that the net effect of this social mobility had been to favour admission to, rather then demotion from, the ranks of landownership. This was despite the fact that, as Large has demon-strated, the potential for landowner indebtedness long predated the agricultural crisis of 1815 which was once considered to be its prime cause.[41] Recent regional studies have tended to validate this view. In his analysis of agrarian society in eighteenth-century Tipperary, Power concludes that analogous processes of social mobility led to an overall doubling in the size of the county's landed community from c. 100 families in 1700 to 200 a century later. One major cause of this growth was the opportunistic purchase of lands shed by the owners of some of the mag-nate estates in the first half of the century in an attempt to solve their chronic indebtedness. Notable among these in Tipperary were the Dunboyne, Everard and Ormond estates, but these were simply local examples of a more widespread eighteenth-century phenomenon, identified in County Cork by Dickson and in County Waterford by O'Flanagan.[42]

Thus the one truly diagnostic characteristic of landowner status in Ireland was not perceived ethnicity, cultural origins or wealth, nor yet the antiquity or recency of the acquisition of such status. Rather, it was that, whether as fee-simple owners or tenants in chief holding in perpetuity or for terms of hundreds of years, the families in question held a sufficiently secure title to most or all of their property to allow them, in theory at least, extensive discretionary control over it. In reality of course, this theoretically limitless authority was heavily circumscribed. Indeed, the nature of these constraints goes some way to explaining why and how landowners reacted as they did to such economic opportunities as presented themselves during the eighteenth and nineteenth centuries. In towns and countryside alike, existing leases might limit the landowner's opportunity to intervene in the management of his property, while inherited jointures and other financial obligations might limit the income available to him for discretionary spending.[43] Increasingly too, the collective action taken by agrarian groups such as the Oakboys and Steelboys in Ulster or the Whiteboys in Munster to defend what they saw as their position within the 'moral economy' provided a further powerful constraint on landowners' managerial independence in the later eighteenth and nineteenth centuries.[44]

Landowners and Improvement, *c.* 1700–1900

The concept of 'improvement' as understood by eighteenth- and early nineteenth-century landowners in England has recently been defined as the progressive 're-structuring [of] the landscape for social and economic, as well as aesthetic ends and, by extension, restructuring the conduct of those who lived in, worked in and looked upon it'.[45] Quite how far these notions would have been understood by contemporary landowners in Spain or France or Germany is debateable. By 1800 the 'new agriculture' which formed the economic basis for much of this improvement had made very little headway beyond Belgium and Holland and very restricted parts of Germany and France.[46] Consequently, the eighteenth-century French *châteaux* and German *schloss* were evidence not so much of the benefits of this very 'English' concept of improvement, but of patterns of conspicuous consumption supported by relations of production which in many parts of Europe were still essentially feudal.[47]

In Ireland, the landowners' apparent willingness to engage in extensive transformations of the landscape has been traditionally ascribed to a rather narrower range of motivations. Despite the involvement of some landowners in institutions such as the Royal Dublin Society, founded in 1731 to improve 'Husbandry, Manufactures and other Useful Arts',[48] this interpretation of the landowners' role has minimized their importance as economic 'improvers'. Instead, it has stressed their capacity for far-reaching but seemingly unproductive landscape transformations carried out for aesthetic and social or familial reasons, for example in the construction of demesnes and country houses.[49] Thus even as an 'improver', the Irish landowner is held to have been a consumer rather than a producer of resources, a view which reinforces the stereotype of the landowner as an essentially parasitic figure. Moreover, recent research has also revived the notion of a 'political econ-omy' of improvement, in which members of the property-owning minority sought to reinforce their control of the political representation of different constituencies by the discriminatory delegation of property-rights to sections of the electorate.[50]

Clearly, these motivations were not mutually exclusive. Urban improvements, for example, could be carried by landowners anxious not only to improve the aesthetics of their 'estate-core' settlements but also as a means of reinforcing their tenants' political fidelity.[51] Similarly, the construction of demesne parks might serve the double purpose of encoding in the landscape—for peer group assess-ment—the landowner's cultural values, as well as providing local employment.[52] All such conspicuous improvement, however, depended crucially for its periodi-city and extent on the levels of disposable income available to the landowner. Accordingly, it is misleading to assess the motivations behind these improvements without reference to the financial contexts within which they were carried out. When all was said and done, the landowner's success either in raising his income or reducing his existing expenditure determined his opportunity to indulge his finer aesthetic sensibilities in country house or landscape park design, or his taste for 'politicking' or social 'engineering'.

Improvement and Production

Agriculture

Despite the continuing interest among historians in the structures and functions of Irish agrarian society, the patchy survival of data relating to landowners—particu-larly in the eighteenth century—and the idiosyncratic role played by many of them, makes any assessment of their importance as agricultural improvers a very tentative one. At present, we may reasonably conclude that current research has yet to show that Irish landowners were significantly more active as agricultural improvers than historians have traditionally supposed. While analyses of individ-ual regions or estates such as Donnelly's study of nineteenth-century Cork, Maguire's study of the Downshire estates and Proudfoot's study of the Devonshire estates[53] have demonstrated that *some* landowners were actively involved in improving drainage, rebuilding tenant farmhouses and rationalizing existing field systems, other more general studies have concluded that on the whole, Irish landowners did *not* invest significant amounts of capital in this way. In his study of eighteenth-century Tipperary, for example, Power concludes that though there were some exceptions, most 'landlords spent little of their income on estate im-provements, [with] little evidence of regular reinvestment in agriculture'.[54] Mokyr has argued for a general failure of direct landowner investment throughout the pre-Famine period. He sees this as resulting from continuing high levels of land-lord absenteeism, which he perceives as crucial 'because it made a co-operative effort between landlord and tenant, so vital for progressive and efficient agricultural production, impossible'.[55] Ó Gráda's earlier research suggests that this general lack of landowner investment continued into the post-Famine period, even though, as subsequent work has shown, their share of the rising levels of gross agricultural output may have increased. He estimates that agricultural reinvestment by Irish landowners averaged no more than 3 per cent of gross rents between 1850 and 1876.[56] This compares to Beckett's more recent calculation of a rising trend of investment on many nineteenth-century English estates which in some cases consumed more than a quarter of all rent income.[57]

Donnelly has argued that these relatively low levels of agricultural investment reflected both the Irish landowners' general lack of external capital and the nature of Irish farming. Unlike their counterparts in England, few landowners in Ireland had access to significant sources of urban or industrial capital with which to finance farm modernization, while the pastoral emphasis in Irish agriculture precluded significant investment anyway.[58] A more immediate reason for these low levels of investment may have been the survival of considerable numbers of lengthy leases on many Irish estates. A growing body of evidence indicates that as agricultural prices rose from the 1740s onwards, many Irish landowners increasingly sought to shorten leases and raise rents. In so doing, they not only effectively regained control of their property, but also ensured for themselves a greater share of the enhanced rewards from agriculture.[59] It may well be that, as Donnelly has argued for County Cork in the 1850s, the propensity among landowners to invest directly in agriculture was conditioned by their previous success in regaining such control by letting directly to occupying tenants as the earlier, 'middleman' leases fell in.[60] In this situation it was the landowner rather than his head tenants who stood to gain from any increase in agricultural values created by direct investment in drainage, enclosure or new buildings. Where landowners were still faced with lengthy leases inherited from the earlier eighteenth century, both their incentive and their opportunity to expend capital in this way was more limited. Thus the relative lack of landlord investment in agricultural improvement in Ireland may well have had as much to do with the sectoral and tenurial constraints on their opportunities to improve, as with any general disinclination on their part to do so.

On this interpretation, therefore, the key to understanding the apparently limited nature of direct landowner involvement in agricultural improvement for much of the eighteenth and early nineteenth centuries, in particular, lies in the character of the tenurial bargains being struck between landowner and tenant at this time. The variety of tenures available in eighteenth-century Ireland was considerable, and was conditioned by both political and economic factors. Under the so-called 'Popery Act' of 1704 and its subsequent amendment in 1709, Catholics were prevented from buying land or leasing it for more than 31 years and from paying a rent that was less than two-thirds of its annual value.[61]

Doubt has been expressed about the real severity of these laws,[62] however, and by the early 1770s the process of amelioration had begun. The 'Bogland' Act of 1772 permitted Catholics to take 61-year reclaiming leases of marginal lands, while the Catholic Relief Act of 1778 enabled them to take leases of 999 years and to inherit land on the same terms as members of other denominations.[63] Nevertheless, for much of the eighteenth century, the opportunity for Catholic tenants to participate in the tenurial process was formally limited by purely political legislation in a way which would have limited their incentive to engage in productive agricultural improvement.

Even for those sections of the community unaffected by the Penal Laws, the types of leases commonly offered by landowners changed radically during the course of the eighteenth century as the latter's perception of prevailing economic conditions altered. Every lease represented a compromise between the interests of the landowner and those of his tenant. On the one hand, most landowners presumably wished either to maximize or, on a longer view, optimize the net income they derived from their estates given the current state of the economy. The tenant, on the other hand, would wish to balance considerations such as security and length of tenure against the level of rent, the type of contractual obligations demanded and the amount of income the property could generate. In short, each bargain had to provide for the interests of both parties, and it was by no means certain whether subsequent economic trends would favour one party more than the other.

For much of the eighteenth century, the system seems to have favoured the tenant rather than the landowner. The troubled conditions of the 1690s led to low rents being set for relatively long leases which, when they expired in the 1720s, were reset at higher rents more in line with the rising agricultural prices and land values of the time. These increases were relatively substantial and initially caused some distress to the tenant community.[64] As the century progressed, however, the steady rise in agricultural prices made these rents progressively more affordable. Most of the agricultural leases set in the 1720s were for 21 or 31 years or for three lives, and did not fall in until the 1750s or 1760s. Accordingly, most of the added value which accrued to Irish agriculture during the boom years of the 1740s and after was appropriated by the head tenants or 'middlemen' rather than their landlords. The tendency to grant long leases during the early and middle years of the century had been encouraged by the desire for 'good' solvent tenants, and by the general perception that such leases were intrinsically beneficial, insofar as they were thought to encourage farm improvement by the tenants.[65] This belief may explain why, as late as the 1760s, at a time when land values generally were rising, many landowners still responded by 'tying up' their interest in their estates for relatively long periods, an apparently perverse reaction which was ultimately to prove harmful to their financial interests. By the last quarter of the eighteenth century, however, the increasing general awareness among landowners of the deleterious effects of this practice led to a sustained swing towards shorter leases and direct letting to occupying tenants rather than middlemen.[66]

The trend towards shorter leases let to occupying tenants continued throughout the early nineteenth century. So great was the inherited stock of lengthy leases for lives, however, that as noted earlier, the final demise of the middlemen did not occur until the Famine years. Even then, as the sale particulars in the records of the Encumbered Estates Court make clear, on many estates in the 1850s, there was still a considerable residue of occupying tenants holding for lengthy periods of years or lives.[67] If nothing else, their continued presence prevented the more innovative landowners from taking their farms in hand and operating them as demesne holdings.

Tenurial constraints thus acted in many cases to limit the landowners' opportunity for direct agricultural investment, particularly in the eighteenth and early nineteenth centuries. In addition, the nature of agricultural production may also have tended to limit the need for such investment. Prior to the expansion in tillage in the 1780s, stock-rearing figured largely in many regional agrarian economies in Ireland, particularly in the west and south. Although capital intensive in terms of the cost of stock, pastoral agriculture required less in the form of fixed capital investment than arable agriculture. Moreover, in counties such as Cork, Kerry and Waterford, it was the middlemen who provided much of the capital for stock purchase. By acting as brokers between their own occupying sub-tenants and cattle merchants, the middlemen effectively financed the former's stock raising activity and did much to hasten the spread of the cattle trade there during the 1720s and 1730s. By the 1770s, however, the growing commercialization of the Irish rural economy, coupled with the increasing solvency of many small farmers and the progressive reassertion of tenurial control by many landowners over their properties, rendered the middlemen increasingly anachronistic.[68]

Given these limitations to the opportunities for landowner investment in agriculture, it is not surprising to find that the pace of improvement in pre-Famine Irish agriculture was relatively slow compared to England, although probably less so compared to France or Spain.[69] Its most visible effects were seen in the attempts to modernize demesne agriculture and, more generally, in enclosure. The attempts by some improving landowners to modernize agricultural practice on their demesne farms are well documented. Contemporary sources, such as Arthur Young's *Tour in Ireland*, published in 1780, or the 23 *County Statistical Surveys* published under the aegis of the Royal Dublin Society between 1801 and 1832,[70] record with approval the activities of individual landowners in importing improved breeds of sheep and cattle, adopting integrated systems of livestock/arable management and purchasing improved ploughing and other equipment. On properties as diverse as the French demesne, Co. Roscommon, the Baltiboys estate, Co. Wicklow, and the Farnham estate, Co. Cavan, for example, drill-sown turnips formed one course in a rotation system which was geared towards winter stall-feeding of stock.[71] By contrast, despite attempts by some landlords to encourage the growth of Farming Societies,[72] the attitude of most tenants remained ambivalent to the advantages of the new technologies and practices. Conventionally this caution has been ascribed to the allegedly inherent conservatism of the Irish peasantry. More recently, however, Bell and Watson have argued that it indicated instead the tenants' awareness of the advantages of traditional labour-intensive methods of husbandry, particularly in marginal environments.[73]

Enclosure probably constituted the most lasting of the improving landowners' attempts to modernize Irish agriculture. Although the chronology of post-medieval enclosure in Ireland has yet to be fully established, previous research suggests that a broad regional distinction may be drawn between the so-called 'commercial' farming districts of south and east Ireland, where enclosure occurred relatively early, and the agriculturally more marginal maritime environments of the west and north where it occurred rather later.[74] In both regions enclosure was an essentially private process, involving the landowner and his tenants alone. Only in the case of the enclosure of common land were Acts of Parliament required. The difference with contemporary practice in England is marked. Arguably, the absence in Ireland of the legal apparatus which so characterized the English enclosure movement[75] reflected the relatively greater discretionary powers of action enjoyed by Irish landowners—once they had regained tenurial control over their estates.

In the 'commercial' farming districts of Leinster, south-east Ulster and east Munster, the twin processes of engrossing and enclosure were widespread throughout the seventeenth and eighteenth centuries. Engrossing consolidated existing small strips into larger land units; enclosure parcelled out existing common fields into fields held in severalty. Both processes transformed what had been an open 'champion' landscape—itself the probable relict of complex late medieval and Tudor agrarian systems—into one approximating to today's fragmented field-scape.[76] We should be careful to note that much of this was probably the result of indirect landowner influence rather than direct landowner investment, and was due to tenants fulfilling the covenants in their newly acquired leases. On numerous estates, including, for example, the Cork and Orrery Caledon estate, Co. Tyrone, the Downshire estates in Counties Down, Offaly and Wicklow, and the Midleton and Bernard estates in County Cork,[77] incoming tenants were required to hedge and ditch their farms as part of their tenurial obligations. In each case, the motive seems to have been the same: the creation of more efficient farm units which would in turn encourage greater efficiencies in livestock production before the 1780s and in cereal production thereafter.[78]

The later enclosure of more marginal areas in western and northern districts was closely associated with attempts by landowners to resolve the problems caused on their estates by the Famine and the unprecedented population growth which preceded it. Arguably, therefore, it had as much to do with rural social adjustment as with the maintenance of proprietorial incomes. The rapid growth in population densities in these areas from the 1780s onwards was accompanied by massive and frequently unauthorized subletting and subdivision of the existing tenants' holdings. The microscopically fragmented smallholdings that resulted bore eloquent testimony to the growing imbalance between land and labour. They also effectively precluded any reordering by the landowners of the structures of agricultural production, unless this was accompanied by some means of displacing the surplus population from the land. Where this was done, usually by resettling the surplus tenantry onto marginal land elsewhere, or else by encouraging them to migrate to the nearest town or emigrate, landowners might hope to accommodate their by-now reduced tenant communities with larger holdings of a more viable size and disposition. The so-called 'ladder' farms, found extensively in marginal areas in the north and west, are one result of these attempts by landowners to regulate subletting in the face of the pre-Famine population growth. Rectangular in shape, they formed part of an imposed geometrical agrarian landscape which was laid out so as to ensure that, theoretically, no tenant was disadvantaged by the size and location of his plot.[79]

The Famine of 1845–9 accelerated this process of consolidation, particularly in the worst affected smallholder districts of the west and south-west. Faced with catastrophically reduced rent rolls and rising demands for payment of the Poor Relief for which they were responsible on behalf of their poorest tenants, many landlords calculated that their only chance of financial survival lay in clearing their estates of these tenants who were by now a complete drain on their resources.[80]

Evictions followed, with or without tenant consent. Consequently, one major result of the Famine was to offer landowners in the west of Ireland further opportunities to dismantle the existing patterns of economically sub-marginal smallholdings, and thereby engage in new relations of production with a numerically reduced tenant community. Not every landowner was able to to do so. Hoppen's estimate that up to a quarter of all land changed hands under the aegis of the Encumbered and Landed Estates Courts in the aftermath of the Famine masks the regional dimension to these sales.[81] Most occurred in districts such as those in the south-west, where the pre-Famine landowners had let land directly to smallholders, and where they accordingly had borne the full brunt of their tenants' inability to pay their rents. In these districts, the Famine altered relations of production by restructuring the composition of the landlord and tenant communities alike.

Industry

The rural basis of much industrial production in Ireland prior to the 1820s, coupled with the predominant position of landowners within the property-owning minority, combined to ensure that landowners played an early and important role in the promotion of the textile, food-processing and mining industries in eighteenth-century Ireland. Cullen has emphasized the importance to this of the rise in landowner incomes resulting from the general resetting of leases in the 1720s and 1730s,[82] and recent research has demonstrated the breadth of the landowners' industrial interests in the ensuing decades. Mineral deposits were widely exploited by landowners as an additional, if sometimes erratic, source of income. In County Tipperary, for example, copper, lead or coal deposits were variously mined in the late eighteenth century on the Langley estate at Coalbrook, the Prittie estate at Silvermines, the Stanley property at Gortdrum and the De Vere Hunt estate at Glengoole.[83] Mining operations further to the east on the Wandesworth estate on the Castlecomer plateau, Co. Kilkenny, appear to have been on an altogether larger scale. Begun on a commercial basis in the late seventeenth century, by 1716–17 these coal and iron ore mines cost over £1000 a year to run. Sixty years later, they were estimated to be generating £10,000 a year profit for their Wandesworth proprietors.[84] In County Cork, landowners were involved in various phases of industrial exploitation during the eighteenth century. These were marked, in Dickson's phrase, more by 'the insuppressible optimism of the landowners' and the absence of external investment by urban capitalists, than by any substantial degree of success. Charcoal-based iron production continued in the Blackwater valley and in the extreme south-west of the county largely under the direction of the Petty and White families until the 1750s, when a combination of dwindling supplies of local timber and erratic price fluctuations for pig-iron forced its demise. Elsewhere in the county, coal was mined from the 1760s on the Philpott/Leander estate and in the upper Blackwater valley, largely to meet the demands of local food-processing industries. The short-lived copper mines which were worked on the Herbert estate near Killarney between the 1750s and 1770s were reported to have produced ore worth £25,000 during that time. Copper mining continued intermittently on the nearby Kenmare estate from the 1750s until 1811, when despite the investment of

£50,000 by the leasing company, continuing problems with flooding forced their closure.[85]

Elsewhere in Ireland, coal deposits were worked at Coalisland, Co. Tyrone, and on the Boyd estate at Ballycastle, Co. Antrim, while copper continued to be mined in County Wicklow. Andrews' conclusion that, given the prevailing ignorance of the true state of Ireland's mineral resources, the prospects for further exploitation still seemed promising as late as the 1780s, seems warranted.[86] In practice, increasing geological difficulties combined with relatively high costs of extraction and transport in the face of growing British competition, led to the decline of much of this extractive industry by the mid nineteenth century.

Landowner involvement in the textile industries was generally more successful in the short term, and was carried out for much the same motive—the enhancement of proprietorial incomes. The foremost example was of course the part played by Ulster landowners in promoting the growth of the domestic linen industry in that province during the eighteenth century. But it should be remembered that this was but one example of a more widespread phenomenon. Thus the activities of Mr Justice Coote, of Cootehill, Co. Cavan, or Edward Lucas of Castleshane, Co. Monaghan, or Arthur Brownlow at Lurgan, Co. Armagh, in establishing brown linen markets and setting favourable leases to encourage weavers to take up smallholdings, were paralleled elsewhere in Ireland.[87] For example, in Munster textile towns such as Bandon, Co. Cork, or Thurles, Co. Tipperary, landowners such as the Duke of Devonshire and George Mathews played an important role in either attempting to establish textile production or in encouraging its survival during the difficult years after the 1780s by providing favourable urban leaseholds for manufacturers.[88] For other landowners, membership of the Linen Board, established by Act of the Irish Parliament in 1711, provided the means by which to promote that industry on their own estates as on others throughout Ireland.[89] On the Lloyd estate in County Roscommon, the weaving of friezes and druggets was widespread prior to the collapse of the rural textile industry in this area in 1819.[90] The ultimate failure of the Linen Board's attempts to regulate linen production and its disbandment in 1828 was not simply the result of its bureaucratic inefficiency,[91] but reflected a more fundamental shift in the balance of power within the industry away from the landowning and government interests which had originally promoted it, in favour of the (Ulster) drapers and bleachers who by then effectively capitalized it. This shift marked a significant stage in the transition from proto-industrial production to factory-based production. In the first, landowners—as the most heavily capitalized members of society—played a significant role in industrial promotion. Under the second, an entirely new set of production relationships was created, in which agrarian sources of capital became progressively less important.

Improvement and Marketing

Urban and Village Transformation

A characteristic feature of the provincial urban and village network in eighteenth- and nineteenth-century Ireland was the widespread transformation of plan and morphology carried out in individual settlements. Estimates of the total number of towns and villages affected by these improvements between *c*. 1700 and 1900 vary. Lockhart identified 188 'planned villages' but on unspecified criteria.[92] These appear to have been both new foundations of the eighteenth and nineteenth centuries as well as remodelled earlier settlements. Cullen refers to around 500 'estate villages' apparently defined again on essentially morphological criteria but notes that if informal criteria are used, the total could easily double.[93] The most recent estimate, based on an analysis of the First Edition of the Ordnance Survey Six Inch Maps, indicates that by the 1840s, over 750 provincial towns and villages of all sizes throughout Ireland displayed some evidence for cohesive planning or partial reconstruction.[94]

Conventionally, these settlement transformations have been ascribed to proprietorial intervention, although the nature and overall extent of their collective involvement remains to be established in detail.[95] Nevertheless, previous writers have interpreted the regional variation in the distribution of these 'improved' settlements in terms of the variation in the size and distribution of the landed estates owned by their owners and improvers. Thus Jones Hughes argues that 'barren estate cores'—those without improved towns or villages—were most likely to occur in regions where 'landlordism' was relatively weak and unstable such as Sligo, Limerick and Tipperary. Conversely, in his view, they flourished most in Ulster.[96] Smyth concludes that most of the formally planned 'estate villages', newly founded in the eighteenth and nineteenth centuries, were located beyond the heavily feudalized heartlands of east Munster and Leinster. Here, earlier medieval settlement nodes survived into the nineteenth-century landscape, and while some acquired the appurtenances of estate management, others, for example the 'farm villages' of south Kilkenny, remained functionally and morphologically entirely outside the estate system.[97]

The nature and extent of the individual morphological transformations involved in this process of settlement modernization varied considerably. One of the few attempts to classify them has been by Cullen, who uses a variety of chronological and morphological criteria to distinguish between 'settlement villages, functionally-planned villages and re-developed villages'.[98] Settlement villages were those established during the seventeenth-century colonizations and were frequently consolidated for defence around triangular greens or open spaces. Functionally-planned villages are defined by Cullen as those deliberately endowed with church and market place. Frequently located in close proximity to the landlord's own residence, they generally display a high degree of formal planning. Redeveloped villages, on other hand, were later, dating from the late eighteenth and early nineteenth centuries and represented a reworking or modernization of earlier settlements.

Cullen's classification has the merit of comprehensiveness but suffers from the ambiguity of its definitional terms. The distinction between functionally-planned and redeveloped villages is particularly debateable: some settlements, for example Cookstown and Hillsborough, were both. A simpler and more informal classification might be based on the extent of the morphological transformations involved in the process of modernization, and the nature of the social agencies involved. At one end of the spectrum of change were the towns and villages which had been either newly constructed on 'greenfield' sites or else had been totally reconstructed on or near their earlier sites. Notable examples of completely new towns include Castlewellan, Co. Down, laid out by the Annesley family before 1764, Westport, Co. Mayo, built by the Brownes in the 1770s and Mitchelstown, Co. Cork, begun by the King family a decade later.[99] Cookstown, Co. Tyrone, and Maynooth, Co. Kildare, on other hand, were both laid out in the 1750s by their respective land-lords, Colonel Stewart and the Duke of Leinster, to replace earlier decayed or destroyed settlements.[100]

Whether new or rebuilt, these settlements were characterized by coherent planning which utilized a variety of formal elements, including orthogonal or linear street plans, squares, crescents, architecturally important buildings treated as visual foci and processional axial vistas. The latter are a particularly widespread feature of this kind of comprehensive replanning. At Strokestown, Co. Roscommon, for example, this linearity is especially pronounced. It is emphasized by the length and width of the main street, which focuses on the Anglican church at its west end, and much more emphatically, on the early-nineteenth-century castellated entrance to Strokestown demesne at the other. At Cookstown, Co. Tyrone, and Kingscourt, Co. Cavan, the linear emphasis also derives from the formally planned and widened main street, but at Cookstown the plan is developed a stage further as a simple orthogonal grid (Fig. 7.1). Similarly emphatic linear planning is to be seen on a smaller scale at Summerhill, Co. Meath, and at Dunlavin and Stratford upon Slaney, Co. Wicklow.

These attempts at formalism, on however small and reduced a scale, mirrored the much more ornate and grandiose use of the same plan forms in the numerous planned extensions or reconstructions which were carried out in European cities during the seventeenth and eighteenth centuries. Whatever their scale, they shared a common origin in the Renaissance—literally the 'rebirth' of interest in the art and architecture of classical Greece and Rome which first occurred in fifteenth-century Italy, and spread to France and England by the early seventeenth century.[101] The most immediate exemplars for the small Irish towns, however, are likely to have been the formally planned eighteenth-century extensions to Dublin and Limerick.[102] Here, these neo-classical plan forms were utilized on a scale which was more immediately comparable to important French examples such as Charleville, Philippeville or Versailles,[103] or those German *Residenzstadte* which were rebuilt in the wake of the Thirty Years' War (1618–1648). These were towns which emerged as the capitals of the 200 or so petty German states which existed during the late seventeenth century, and many were remodelled under the patronage of their princely rulers.[104]

In Ireland, the towns and villages at the other end of the transformation spectrum were more numerous. These are places where the improved plan and morphology are less formally regular and may be inferred to have resulted from a process of modernization which was incremental in character. Perhaps as the fortunes of the local economy permitted, a market house or court house or a new market place might be built, to be followed by the gradual replacement of the existing housing stock by buildings which were more in tune with the fashion for vernacular 'Georgian' architecture. Examples where the existence of formally planned public buildings or public space combined with irregular housing suggest

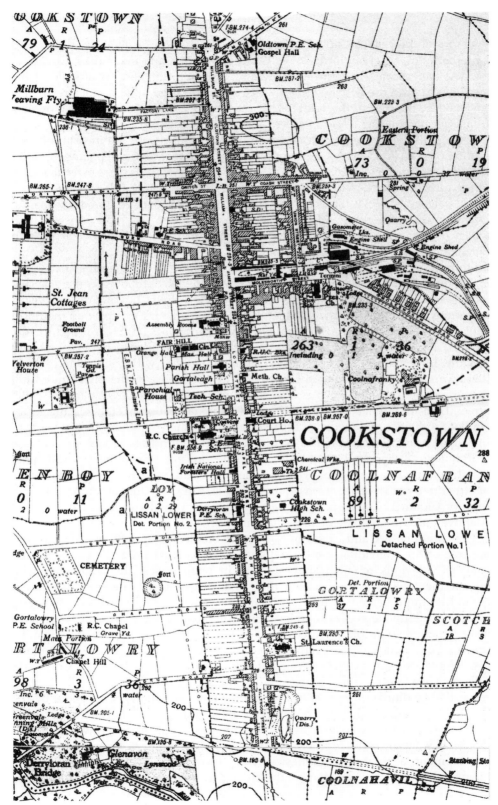

Fig. 7.1. Cookstown, Co. Tyrone: a regularly-planned 'estate town' (*By permission of the Ordnance Survey*).

this sort of process include Hacketstown, Co. Carlow, Edgeworthstown and Lanesborough, Co. Longford, Boyle, Co. Roscommon, and Baltinglass, Co. Wicklow. At Lanesborough the irregularity and disproportionately small scale of the buildings around the widened main street may reflect the influence of a restrictive covenant in the title to the estate. This prevented its nineteenth-century owners from offering building leases of more than 21 years' duration.[105]

Between these two extremes and merging with both were the most numerous group of towns and villages. Although not formally planned or replanned in their entirety, they display an element of ordered formality which is more extensive than in the category just described. At Bailieborough, Co. Cavan, this stems from the visual balance between the small rectangular market square and adjacent market house which define one end of the main axis, and the Anglican parish church which defines the other, although the housing in between is irregular in both height and plot size. At Cootehill, Co. Cavan, on the other hand, it is precisely the uniformity in the size and architectural style of many of the buildings lining the main street—itself leading towards the Anglican parish church as its major visual focus—which provides the visual coherence. At Athy, Co. Kildare, the visual uniformity is provided by the eighteenth-century marketing complex on the north bank of the River Barrow. The most striking components in this are the formally planned Emily Square, named after an eighteenth-century Duchess of Leinster, and the adjacent neo-Classical market house. Together with the bridge of 1763, these were built by the Duke of Leinster, whose influence as the then landlord of this originally medieval town is also commemorated in the street names—Duke Street, Leinster Street and William Street. This juxtaposition of eighteenth-century landlord influence and medieval urban origins is a timely reminder that in many of the larger provincial towns in eastern and south-eastern Ireland in particular, the morphological changes brought about by the process of eighteenth- and nineteenth-century modernization were themselves conditioned by an inherited legacy of structured urban space. Consequently, as at Athy, or Dungarvan, Co. Waterford, or Clonmel, Co. Tipperary, these processes of modernization tended to be adaptive rather than obliterative in their impact.

The varied nature and extent of these settlement transformations suggests that the role of the individuals and groups involved in their promotion was equally complex. Previous research suggests that in many cases, the landowner who owned the town was the major—though not necessarily the only—promoter behind its improvement. Cullen, for example, cites a wide range of towns and villages of all functions, sizes and locations where landowners are thought to have been largely responsible for their modernization. His examples include Sixmilebridge, Co. Clare, created by the Levers in 1733 as a textile centre; Ballymote, Co. Sligo, Dromana, Co. Waterford, Dunmanway and Inishannon, Co. Cork, Killarney, Co. Kerry, and Monivea, Co. Galway, all planned or rebuilt by their respective landlords in the 1740s; and Edenderry, Co. Offaly, refurbished by the Downshires as a market centre between 1809 and 1829.[106] Byrne's analysis of Tullamore, Co. Offaly, demonstrates the importance to urban growth of a proprietorial willingness to compromise their property interests in order to further development, a point also emphasized in a study of the five 'Devonshire' estate towns in Munster.[107] Thus many of these extensively replanned towns and villages also received landowner investment in the construction of public buildings such as court houses or market houses, as well as, more occasionally, in the provision of housing. More usually, the practice was for the landowner to spread the investment risk by offering building leases on suitably favourable terms to encourage tenants or speculative builders to share the capital costs involved. This device was used, for example, by the Bury family to promote the extensive reconstruction of Tullamore in the period after 1786, by the Annesleys at Castlewellan and by the Downshires at Edenderry at much the same period.[108]

Research is currently being directed towards establishing the true extent of the landowners' collective role in urban and village modernization, but in the meantime the concept of proprietor-led improvement seems to be a reasonable proposition. With their effective monopoly of the means of production, landowners were, in theory, the group best able to provide the resources necessary to fund these improvements and the one likely to reap the greatest benefit from them in the long-term. Individual instances of extensive replanning, such as those at Dungarvan and Lismore between 1806 and 1830, can be shown to be the result of the landowner's willingness to exert the full range of his economic and social authority, in order to effect the desired improvement.[109] In other cases, however, either through the landowner's lack of interest, or because the survival of property rights they had previously delegated to tenants constrained their freedom of action, the landowner's role was more limited, perhaps to the provision of public buildings in the manner described above. Thus where towns and villages display evidence of extensive cohesive replanning, the implication is that some individual or group— probably including the landowner—were able to ensure that *their* values were encoded in the structure of the urban space being recreated. In contrast, where the morphological outcomes were more irregular, the encoded values were by implication more varied and to this extent imply an absence of any singular unity of purpose. This would seem to be the situation Sir Charles Coote found at Mount Mellick in 1801. Describing the town's irregular appearance, he concluded that 'it has hitherto laboured under the great disadvantage of disputed claims between proprietors, by which means no encouragement of leases could be given'.[110]

The landowners' motivations for their involvement in agrarian improvement were generally economic, though there are well-attested examples of social motivations such as the 'moral agency' practised on Lord Farnham's estates in County Cavan.[111] Similarly, it is probable that the landowners' primary objective in facilitating urban and village improvement was the improvement of marketing and thus the enhancement of their own incomes.[112] That this was so is suggested by the results of a Spearman Rank correlation test, which indicated a statistically significant positive relationship between the number of improved towns and villages recorded by the First Edition Ordnance Survey Six Inch Map, and the total *cultivated* area in each county (+0.775; significant at the 99% probability level). The implication is that by the 1840s, a functional balance had been achieved between the size of the agrarian economy in each region, the number of local market centres which were perceived to be capable of improvement, and the ability of local communities to effect this. Figure 7.2 indicates that this relationship was spatially complex, and did not conform to any simple east–west bipolar model of economic activity, nor, completely, to Smyth's 'feudal' or Jones Hughes' 'landlordism'-based regional appraisals. It reminds us that each instance of settlement improvement was the unique outcome of the interaction between the trends in Irish society and economy which encouraged this sort of improvement, and the local opportunities for such change to occur.

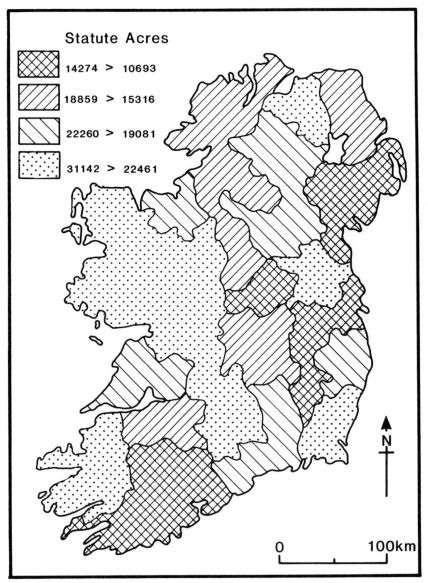

Fig. 7.2. Ratio of improved towns and villages to cultivated area by county, *c.* 1840. The value for each category represents the ratio of the extent of the cultivated area (in statute acres) to each improved settlement.

Previous research suggests that, on occasion, the interactions which gave rise to urban and village transformations were distinctly non-economic in character. In short, as well as seeking to maximize income, landowners also engaged in settlement improvement in pursuit of a variety of other, less tangible goals. For example, on the Duke of Devonshire's urban estate in Counties Cork and Waterford, the urban improvements carried out between *c.* 1760 and 1890 were geared towards achieving aesthetic, social and political goals, as well as increasing the size and reliability of the rent-roll. Thus the improvements begun at Lismore between 1792 and 1798 were intended to develop the town as a major regional marketing centre; those carried out at Dungarvan between 1801 and 1830 were designed first to recapture and then retain representation of the parliamentary borough by the Duke; while the renewed work at Lismore after 1820 was intended to enhance the town's visual appearance as an estate-core and provide local employment.[113]

How far lesser landowners who did not enjoy the Devonshires' magnate status could afford to indulge in such non-economic motivations is as yet unclear, but individual studies indicate the importance attached to such considerations by some landowners. Thus at Hillsborough, the completion of the market square after 1810 was perceived by the 3rd Marquis of Downshire to have the added advantage of replacing an existing cabin suburb with 'polite' housing, thus improving the view from his mansion.[114] More generally, the use of functionally superfluous architectural ornament either in set-pieces, such as market houses or court houses, or more widely, in 'estate housing', indicated a willingness to invest in encoding aesthetic values in the townscape to a point beyond that justified by mere economic considerations. Thus the cruciform market house built at Dunlavin by the Tynte family in 1743, or the market house at Hillsborough started 20 years later,[115] both utilize an architectural repertoire far in excess of that applied to many contemporary but plainer market houses. Similarly, the use of the early-nineteenth-century 'cottage ornee' style for estate housing, as at Adare, Co. Limerick, Castlebellingham, Co. Louth, Dromahair, Co. Leitrim, or Virginia, Co. Cavan, arguably indicates precisely the same primacy of aesthetics over economics.

The politically-oriented provision of public buildings and new housing on the massive scale carried out at Dungarvan is likely to have represented one extreme of the spectrum of politically-motivated urban improvement. Over £71,000 was spent by the 5th and 6th Dukes of Devonshire on the construction of wharfs, streets, markets, a square, a bridge and upwards of 350 cabins there between 1801 and 1830.[116] Much more typical was the relatively small-scale incidental expenditure indulged in by most politically active landowners as a matter of course in an attempt to bribe or otherwise coerce the electorate during elections.[117] Nevertheless, the timing of the Devonshire expenditure at Dungarvan—and indeed at Youghal, where over £28,000 was spent for similarly political reasons—is noteworthy. It reinforces Jupp's argument that borough representation only became particularly sought after by landowners *after* the Act of Union had reduced the number of borough seats by two-thirds to 33. Concurrent changes in the county electorate had created a large Catholic freeholder electorate, which was potentially politically hostile to the landowners' perceived interests in a way which the limited Protestant electorates in the remaining boroughs were not. Accordingly, the importance of the remaining boroughs to the 'Ascendancy' political interest rose, precisely because that interest was coming under increased pressure from the growth of sectarian nationalism in the county constituencies where it had once also held sway.[118]

Communications

As a further means of improving local economic exchange, landowners were also involved in promoting improvements to inland road, canal and, latterly, rail communications. Just as they sought the sanction of the state for their urban improvements, by petitioning for the grant of market or fair patents,[119] so too landowners utilized the structures of local administration—particularly the County Grand Jury system—to further their attempts to improve communications at least partly for their own benefit.[120] Latterly, however, as Ireland's economy expanded and diversified, their role in this regard came to be augmented by urban-based mercantile and industrial capitalists and by direct state investment.

Arguably, the landowners' collective importance as a social agency promoting communications improvement lay in their domination of the system of County Grand Juries. These were set up under an Act of 1765 to finance and oversee the improvement and extension of Ireland's road and bridge network. Prior to this, local road improvements had been carried out on a parish basis under an Act of 1613, which had laid a statutory obligation on each parish to raise sufficient direct labour each year to maintain the roads within it.[121] The parishes' responsibility did not extend to the construction of new roads, and between the 1730s and 1750s, most new arterial routes were constructed by turnpike trusts, set up as self-financing commercial ventures. However, the deficiencies of the turnpike system soon became apparent. Income was rarely sufficient to cover the maintenance and capital costs of the roads which had been constructed, and there was little incentive for turnpikes to be established in marginal areas offering few prospects of adequate traffic.

The 1765 Act was intended to encourage road building by no longer making it conditional on its likely prospect of success in attracting minimum levels of traffic. Under the new system, each proposal or *presentment* for a new road was submitted to the County Grand Jury, and if accepted, was funded by an acreable cess or tax imposed by the Jury on the baronies through which the road was to pass. Arthur Young estimated the average cess at between 3d and 6d per acre although it rose to as high as one shilling in County Meath.[122] As the Grand Juries were themselves composed of local landowners newly appointed for each county court session by the county sheriff,[123] the opportunities for maladministration were perceived by contemporary opinion to be immense. As an unelected taxing body, the Grand Juries came under frequent criticism, and from 1817 they were only permitted to consider presentments once they had been first assessed by local Justices of the Peace.[124] Nevertheless, landowner participation in these County Grand Juries represented a tradition of unpaid public service, and long before their disbandment in 1898, the Juries had provided Ireland with a road network which, if anything, was more than adequate for the needs of its economy.[125]

Canal and railway construction was much more capital intensive than road building, and in Ireland seems to have suffered from long-term problems of capital availability. The extent of landowner investment in canals and railways is difficult to determine. Cullen has argued for significant 'passive' landowner investment in canal stock in periods of rising income in the eighteenth century such as the 1740s and 1770s.[126] As well as this, there is occasional evidence for more direct landowner involvement. Between 1792 and 1796, for example, the 5th Duke of Devonshire spent over £2300 on constructing the Lismore Canal, while in the same period the Marquis of Abercorn part-financed the Strabane Canal, built at a reputed cost of £12,000.[127]

In addition to this private funding, which between 1801 and 1845 may have amounted to over £1 million, the government also invested a similar sum of public money in promoting Irish waterways.[128] Even with this investment, however, Ireland's inland navigations never achieved the level of success of their English counterparts. For example, the country's two most successful canals, the Grand and Royal, carried no more than 350,000 tons of goods between them in their peak years immediately before the Famine, and consequently both remained vulnerable to competition from cheaper or more efficient forms of transport. The Grand Canal was begun in 1756 and the Royal thirty years later in 1789, but canal construction had first begun in Ireland in 1734 with work on the Newry Canal, undertaken under the aegis of the Commissioners for Inland Navigation, set up by Act of the Dublin Parliament in 1729.[129] By the mid 1790s, major integrated canal and river navigations had been established along the Barrow, Lagan, Shannon and Suir rivers, as well as minor ones on the Blackwater, Boyne and Slaney. Together with the Newry, Grand and Royal Canals, navigable waterways extended for over 600 miles (965 km) and represented, in theory at least, a major advance in the integration of Ireland's regional economies (Fig. 7.3).

In practice, the potential advantages offered by the canal system were undermined by the nature of the Irish economy. Canals were most suited to the uninterrupted transport of heavy or bulky goods over long distances, provided that this trade was regular. Consequently, the highly seasonal trade in agricultural commodities—which formed the bulk of economic exchange in Ireland—was by itself unlikely to make any Irish canal particularly profitable. As Cullen notes, the only Irish canals with any prospect of profitability either served an increasingly industrialized region, as did the Lagan Navigation, or else, like the Grand Canal, served a population centre of sufficient size to generate an assured and extensive aggregate trade. In reality, the relatively high costs of canal transport, together with the slow and incremental nature of their regionally limited construction, ensured that they never effectively challenged the rapidly improving and more flexible system of road transport which was already in place. Thus, arguably, government and landowner investment in Irish canals was equally misplaced.[130]

Although ambitious proposals for Irish railways had first been made in 1825 and again in 1835–36 after the opening of the Dublin–Kingston line a year earlier, Ireland's 'railway age' really only began in the flurry of speculative investment which followed the standardization of the Irish gauge in 1846. By 1850, some 400 miles (640 km) of line had been opened including the main line between Dublin and Cork.[131] Four years later, the total network had increased to 865 miles (1400 km), including the link between Belfast and Dublin which had been completed with the construction of the Boyne viaduct at Drogheda in 1853. By 1866, the

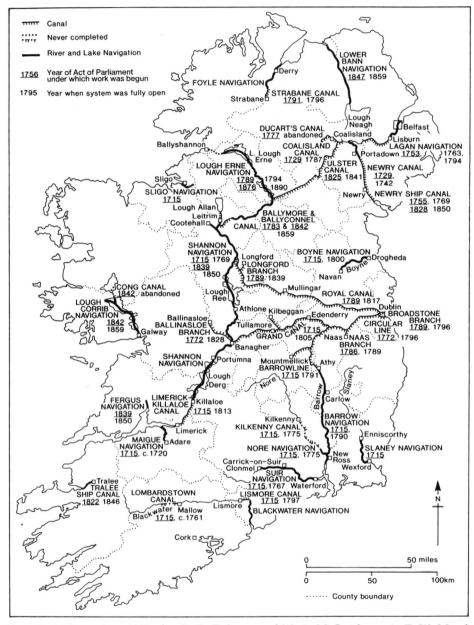

Fig. 7.3. Irish canals, *c.* 1890 after D. R. Delaney and W. A. McCutcheon, in T. W. Moody, F. X. Martin and F. J. Byrne (eds.), *A New History of Ireland, IX. Maps, Genealogies, Lists* (Oxford, 1984).

network had more than doubled to over over 1900 miles (3057 km), but as this by now included all of the potentially most profitable routes, the rate of investment slowed down, and only a further 461 miles (742 km) were added by 1880 (Fig. 7.4).[132]

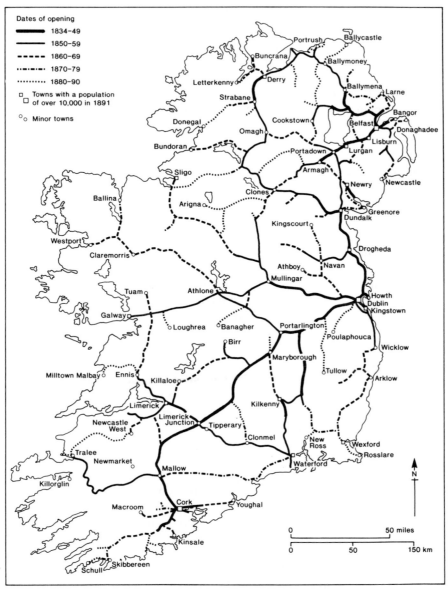

Fig. 7.4. Irish Railways 1834–1890 After K. M. Davies, in T. W. Moody, F. X. Martin and F. J. Byrne (eds.), *A New History of Ireland, IX, Maps, Genealogies, Lists* (Oxford, 1984).

Although individual landowners can again be shown to have made extensive direct investments in certain projects, Lee argues that the bulk of the capital required for Irish railways came initially from English sources, only latterly from Ireland, and generally from speculative, business and government sources in that order.[133] McCutcheon's regional analysis of Ulster railways points to much the same conclusion.[134] Consequently, when a landed magnate like the 7th Duke of Devonshire came to invest over £200,000 of externally-derived capital in regional railways in Cork and Waterford between 1858 and 1878, the likelihood is that this was relatively unusual in an Irish context. Indeed, in this case, the explanation for the 7th Duke's investment is largely external to Ireland. He had already invested heavily in urban, industrial and transport undertakings in England, and this Irish investment simply represented another attempt to develop a non-agrarian source of income which would restore the family's ailing finances. Like the concurrent English investments it failed, and indeed contributed largely to the £2 million debt which faced the 8th Duke of Devonshire on his accession in 1891.[135]

Improvement and Ornamentation

In addition to their involvement in the improvement of production and marketing structures in Ireland, landowners also engaged in *ornamental* improvement in the construction of country houses and their associated landscaped parks. These parks formed part of the estate owner's *demesne*, that portion of his land reserved for his exclusive use and which might include agricultural as well as recreational land. Bence-Jones estimates that at least 2000 major country houses were built in Ireland between 1660 and 1900.[136] By contrast, the First Edition of the Ordnance Survey Six Inch Maps identifies some 10,188 individual country houses by name. However, many of these lacked demesnes or any other appurtenances of estate-core status and were probably no more than substantial farm houses or rectories.[137] Bearing more immediate comparison with Bence-Jones' estimate, are the 2596 houses identified by these maps as standing in demesnes of 50 acres (20 ha) or more.

Figure 7.5 depicts the complex regional variation in the density of these larger demesnes *c.* 1840. Broadly speaking, they were least frequent in mid and west Ulster, west Connacht and Kerry, and most numerous in an eastern midland belt running from Longford and Westmeath in the north through Laois and Offaly to Tipperary in the south. Previous research has indicated a strong positive relationship between the size of the demesne and the parent estate.[138] Thus in this midland zone and, to a lesser extent, in the counties immediately adjacent to it to the east and south-east, we may tentatively conclude that the structures of land ownership which had evolved prior to the 1840s were characterized by the survival of significant numbers of relatively large estates. The relative absence of similar large estates from mid and west Ulster may be a distant echo of the seventeenth-century plantations. In these, most undertakers and servitors were restricted—in theory at least—to holdings of 3000 acres (1214 ha) or less.[139] The absence of many truly 'great estates' from the region in the 1840s suggests that subsequent land transactions had not tended to consolidate many of these plantation estates into larger units. These regional differences remind us once again that the nature of landownership was very uneven, and that these variations were significant in affecting the extent to which individual landowners were able to invest in urban and rural modernization.

Conventionally, landowner investment in country house construction and in laying out landscaped parks has been regarded as an exercise in conspicuous consumption, which, though it might have had an important role in affirming the landowner's social status, added nothing in the long term to the growth of the

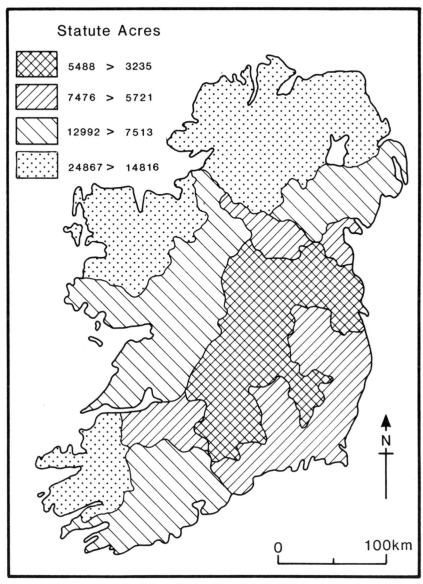

Statute Acres

5488 > 3235
7476 > 5721
12992 > 7513
24867 > 14816

Fig. 7.5. Density distribution of demesnes of more than 50 acres in size by county, *c.* 1840. The value for each category represents the ratio of the extent of the total area (in statute acres) to each demesne of over 50 acres.

productive economy.[140] Recent research on the distribution of early nineteenth-century demesnes in County Down, however, has suggested that their resource implications may have been less negative than was previously supposed. Between them, the 134 demesnes in the county in 1834 accounted for only 14,820 acres (6000 ha), or less than 2.5 per cent of the county's total agricultural land. Moreover, many of the largest demesnes were located in marginal areas on land of relatively limited agricultural potential, for example around the flanks of the Mourne Mountains. Finally, the admittedly relatively limited documentary evidence available suggests not only that comparatively small amounts of capital were invested in their construction, but that on some demesnes, the ornamental land also supported ancillary pastoral and forestry enterprises and thus provided local employment. For example, construction of the Marquis of Downshire's park at Hillsborough, between 1742 and 1800, cost at most £4800, or rather less than 1 per cent of the total income generated by the estate during this period. At Castlewellan and Tollymore, on the other hand, the demesne woods provided a significant part of the overall estate income. On the Annesley's Castlewellan estate, sales of timber from the park averaged £320 during the 1790s, at a time when the overall rental was between £5000 and £6000. At Tollymore, the Earl of Clanbrassil's sustained treeplanting in the 1770s and 1780s was estimated in 1792 to have created a resource worth over £2500.[141]

Thus although a highly visual reminder in the contemporary Irish landscape of the landowning class's previous ability to negotiate transformations in rural space, demesnes may have had fewer resource implications than the stereotype of the landowner as 'parasite' would suggest. This is not to deny, however, that both demesnes and country houses had an important symbolic role to play in reinforcing the status differential between the landowning minority and the remainder of society. It was for this reason that many successful urban merchants and industrialists sought to enhance their perceived social status by purchasing country estates.[142] The basis of this emblematic social-distancing lay in the susceptibility of country house and park design to changes in architectural and landscaping fashion. By reconstructing his house or park in line with these changes, the landowner reaffirmed his social standing by signalling his adherence to his peers' aesthetic norms. These in their turn transcended the social milieu of landownership in Ireland, and were in fact of essentially European provenance.

As in the case of urban planning, these norms were initially of Renaissance origin. Just as classical Greek and Roman principles of architecture and planning were used to transform urban space in early modern Europe, so too they were applied to country house and landscape design. Initially in fifteenth-century Italy and subsequently in France, England and Holland, country houses were built or redesigned using various interpretations of the classical idiom, while gardens were laid out in an intricately formal geometrical manner which emphasized axial vistas and linearity. By the mid seventeenth century, the leading exponent of this type of formal design was a Frenchman, André Le Nôtre, who laid out the royal park at Versailles for Louis XIV around 1660.[143] Le Nôtre's work was initially influential elsewhere in Europe, but by the early eighteenth century, reaction had set in to his extreme formalism. First in England and subsequently in France, this style gave way to the so-called 'picturesque' school of landscape design. This found its inspiration in the contemporary French and Italian 'Romantic' schools of landscape painting, and especially in the work of Salvator Rosa, Claude le Lorrain and Poussin. The 'picturesque' school sought to create seemingly natural but in reality man-made landscapes, which by the careful arrangement of their component parts—woodland, water, grassland and so on—emphasized 'nature's sweet disorder'.[144] Leading practitioners of the 'picturesque' in England included William Kent, Capability Brown and Humphrey Repton, and although each made their individual contribution to the idiom, its fundamental characteristic—naturalism—continued to dominate English landscape park design throughout the eighteenth century.

In Ireland too, the architectural formalism of the Versailles school gave way in the 1730s to increasingly naturalistic landscape designs. Consequently, very few examples of the early formal style of park design survive. The most complete is at Kilruddery, Co. Wicklow, where the use of rectangular canals, radial walks and focal statuary combine to create a sense of 'architectural' space. Similarly formal canals survive in the grounds of the now demolished Antrim Castle, while in the 1840s examples of this and other types of axial planning still survived in part at Mount Uniacke, Co. Cork, Castle Coole, Co. Fermanagh, Grange House, Co. Kilkenny, and Golden Grove, Co. Offaly.

The completeness with which these early formal designs were lost beneath the welter of mid- and late-eighteenth-century naturalism bears witness to the appeal of this new style. Nevertheless, despite utilizing the relatively great variety of natural features in the Irish landscape, these later landscaped parks were still effectively man-made. In the spirit of the age, the carefully contrived woodlands and vistas were embellished with Romantic shell houses, grottoes or Classical statues. The contrast between these and their 'natural' surroundings was intended to emphasize the 'wildness' of Nature, and provoke in the observer feelings of awe at its grandeur.[145] Figure 7.6 illustrates a typical example, the 812 acre (329 ha) Dromoland demesne in County Clare. The present 'Gothick Revival' castle was built *c.* 1826 on the site of a large early-eighteenth-century house, and post-dates the demesne.[146] The major landscaping elements were contrived to enhance the position of the original house, and included sinuous woodland shelter belts, copse planting and an artificial lake, Dromoland Lough, fed by a leet from the Ardsollus river. Hidden in the trees were follies—a turret and a grotto—while adjacent to the house and farmyard buildings lay the small formal garden. To the south, the woodland planting gave way to the deer park and a more open fieldscape.

By the 1840s most of these design features were replicated in numerous large demesnes throughout Ireland. Previous research in County Waterford suggests that generally speaking, a consistent relationship existed between the size of a demesne and the extent to which its design was dominated by such ornamental features. Larger demesnes in the county tended to be more exclusively ornamental in their design, smaller demesnes were much more likely to contain a significant proportion of agricultural land, indicated on the Ordnance Maps by clearly defined field boundaries. The implication is that only larger estates could afford to devote significant amounts of land to uses which were only partly economic in character, whereas smaller estates required the maximization of the property's agricultural potential. Consequently, the ornamentation on many smaller demesnes was limited to a relatively restricted area immediately adjacent to the house.[147]

The imperatives of fashion which led to the rapid alteration in landscaped park design in eighteenth-century Ireland dictated similar changes in the style of country house architecture. Consequently, despite the proliferation of house building by landowners benefiting from the upward adjustment of rents in the 1720s and 1730s, few of these survive unaltered. Most were modified or extended in the later eighteenth century or replaced altogether in the building boom of the early

Fig. 7.6. Dromoland Demesne, Co. Clare, c. 1840.

nineteenth century.[148] Thus, for example, the Palladianism reputedly introduced into Ireland in the 1720s in the work of Sir Edward Lovett Pearce and his pupil, Richard Castle, only survived into the present century in a few major houses, such as Bellamount Forest, Co. Cavan, Desart Court, Co. Kilkenny, Carton, Co. Kildare, and Russborough, Co. Wicklow. These displayed, variously, typical Palladian features such as giant pilasters or pedimented porticoes often extending to the full height of the house, as well as a ground plan consisting of a central block joined to subordinate wings by straight or curved and sometimes colonnaded links.[149]

This type of plan continued to be used in Ireland into the early nineteenth century—much later than in England—and is a good example of the architectural conservatism which characterized Irish country house building. This was equally true of the other major design tradition in eighteenth-century Irish country houses, that of the tall neo-classical 'box' of perhaps five or seven bays and as high as it was long. While the earliest examples of this genre such as Mount Ievers in County Clare date from the 1730s, the majority date from the later eighteenth and early nineteenth centuries. They represent the widespread building response among all types and conditions of landowner to the agricultural boom years between c. 1770 and 1820. Neo-classical houses were distinguished from earlier Palladian examples by their simpler ground plans and their more restrained detailing. Like the Palladian houses—and the various 'Gothick' and 'Tudor' or 'Elisabethan Revival' houses built in increasing numbers from the 1820s onwards—they represented individual landowners' attempts to signal both their ability and willingness to affiliate to the changing norms of their peers.

Conclusion

As members of the property-owning minority, Irish landowners enjoyed a dominant status within the county's economy throughout the eighteenth and for much of the nineteenth century. There was nothing extraordinary about this by the standards of contemporary Europe; similar landed elites existed in Britain, Prussia, parts of Spain and to a lesser extent, France. What was unusual about the landed elite in Ireland was the circumstances of their origin. For the most part, they were the descendants of an 'inserted' sixteenth- and seventeenth-century colonial minority, whose arrival necessarily partly displaced the existing earlier elite, itself of partly colonial origin. Although this process of displacement was never as complete as traditional nationalist historiography has alleged, it nevertheless set up significant new cultural, ethnic and political tensions within Ireland, which were ultimately resolved in the later nineteenth and early twentieth centuries at the expense of the landowning minority.

Because of these nationalist connotations, the issue of landownership in Ireland has frequently been treated in political terms. As this chapter has sought to demonstrate, however, it is important to realize that such analyses misconstrue the fundamental characteristics of landownership in Ireland, which were essentially economic. Thus the present discussion of the landowners' economic performance as 'improvers' has shown that, in many respects, this was entirely normative by the standards of their peers elsewhere in Europe. If Irish landowners on the whole invested less in agricultural improvement than, say, their English counterparts, there is a strong argument to suggest that this was because of the constraints imposed by the existing system of extensive agrarian leaseholds, not to mention the varying capital requirements of the very different enterprise mix in British and Irish agriculture. Even with these constraints, Irish landowners were a formative influence in furthering—directly or indirectly—the enclosure of the Irish landscape. A similar pattern of direct intervention, coupled with more numerous instances of indirect tenurial encouragement, seems also to have characterized the landowners' promotion of urban improvement. The final assessment of their role in this regard must await the results of current research. Nevertheless, it is already clear that a far greater number of Irish towns and villages display evidence of the cohesive reordering which has been shown to be the hallmark of landlord intervention than was once thought. Some landowners, too, were active promoters of early industrial investment and communications improvement, although in the latter instance their role was increasingly taken over by industrial and government capital as the nineteenth century progressed. The most visible, if not the most deeply-rooted, contribution by Irish landowners to the evolution of Ireland's cultural landscape probably lay in their assiduous promotion of country-house building and emparking. In their variety and easy familiarity with an essentially European cultural idiom, these parks and houses provide an eloquent metaphor for the landowning class itself.

References

1. E. R. Hooker, *Readjustments of Agricultural Tenure in Ireland*, (Chapel Hill, North Carolina, 1938); N. D. Palmer, *The Irish Land League Crisis*, (New Haven, 1940); J. E. Pomfret, *The Struggle for Land in Ireland, 1800–1923*, (Princeton, 1930).
2. P. J. O'Connor, *Exploring Limerick's Past*, (Newcastle West, 1987), pp. 81–6.
3. T. Jones Hughes, 'Society and settlement in nineteenth-century Ireland', *Irish Geography*, **5** (1965), pp. 79–96.
4. A. A. Horner, 'The scope and limitations of the landlord contribution to changing the Irish landscape, 1700–1850', *Collected Papers Presented at the Permanent European Conference for the Study of the Rural Landscape, Denmark Session, 1979*, (Copenhagen, 1981), pp. 71–8.
5. W. J. Smyth, 'Estate records and the making of the Irish Landscape: An example from County Tipperary', *Irish Geography*, **9** (1976), pp. 29–49.
6. A. A. Horner, 'Carton, Co. Kildare. A case study of the making of an Irish demesne', *Quarterly Bulletin of the Irish Georgian Society*, **XVIII** (1975), pp. 45–103.
7. A. P. W. Malcomson, 'Absenteeism in eighteenth-century Ireland', *Irish Economic and Social History*, **I** (1974), pp. 15–35.
8. Usefully summarized in W. E. Vaughan, *Landlords and Tenants in Ireland 1848–1904*, (Studies in Irish Economic and Social History, 2, 1974), pp. 21–6.
9. M. Dobbs, *Studies in the Development of Capitalism*, (Rev. Ed., London, 1978), pp. 13–15.
10. L. J. Proudfoot, 'Urban patronage and estate management on the Duke of Devonshire's Irish Estates (1764–1891): A study in landlord-tenant relationships', (unpublished PhD thesis, Queen's University, Belfast, 1989), pp. 121–30.
11. W. H. Crawford, 'Ulster landowners and the linen industry', in J. T. Ward and R. G. Wilson (eds.), *Land and Industry. The Landed Estate and the Industrial Revolution*, (Newton Abbot, 1971), pp. 117–144; *idem*, 'Drapers and bleachers in the early Ulster linen industry', in L. M. Cullen and P. Butel (eds.), *Négoce et Industrie en France et en Irelande aux XVIIIᵉ et XIXᵉ Siècles*, (Paris, 1980), pp. 113–20.

12. P. Travers, *Settlements and Divisions. Ireland 1870–1922*, (Dublin, 1988), pp. 24–9.
13. N. J. G. Pounds, *An Historical Geography of Europe*, (Cambridge, 1990), pp. 274–6.
14. K. Theodore Hoppen, *Ireland Since 1800: Conflict and Conformity*, (London, 1989), p. 87.
15. Travers, *Settlements and Divisions*, p. 15; W. E. Vaughan and A. J. Fitzpatrick, *Irish Historical Statistics. Population 1821–1971*, (Dublin, 1978), pp. 3, 5–26.
16. M. MacCarthy-Morrogh, *The Munster Plantation*, (Oxford, 1986), pp. 30–8, 119–30; P. Robinson, *The Plantation of Ulster*, (Dublin, 1984), pp. 91–128.
17. F. H. A. Aalen, *Man and the Landscape in Ireland*, (London, 1978), p. 148; A. R. Orme, *Ireland*, (London, 1970), p. 130.
18. L.M. Cullen, *The Emergence of Modern Ireland 1600–1900*, (Dublin, 1981), pp. 33–7; T. P. Power, 'Land, politics and society in eighteenth century Tipperary', (unpublished PhD thesis, Trinity College, Dublin, (1987), p. 13.
19. N. Canny, *Kingdom and Colony. Ireland in the Atlantic World, 1560–1800*, (Baltimore, 1988), pp. 69–98; MacCarthy-Morrogh, *Munster Plantation*, pp. 30–45; Robinson, *Ulster*, pp. 66–90.
20. Aalen, *Man and the Landscape*, pp. 137–40; R. Mitchison, 'Ireland and Scotland: the seventeenth-century legacies compared', in T. M. Devine and D. Dickson (eds.), *Ireland and Scotland 1600–1850*, (Edinburgh, 1983), pp. 2–11; Orme, *Ireland*, pp. 112–17.
21. W. J. Smyth, 'Property, patronage and population—reconstructing the human geography of mid-seventeenth century County Tipperary', in W. Nolan and T.G. McGrath (eds.), *Tipperary History and Society*, (Dublin, 1985), pp. 104–38; idem, 'Territorial, social and settlement hierarchies in seventeenth-century Kilkenny', in W. Nolan and K. Whelan (eds.), *Kilkenny History and Society*, (Dublin, 1990), pp. 127–60.
22. R. Gillespie, *Colonial Ulster*, (Cork, 1985), pp. 167–94; Robinson, *Ulster*, pp. 150–71; A. Sheehan, 'Irish towns in a period of change, 1558–1625', in C. Brady and R. Gillespie (eds.), *Natives and Newcomers*, (Dublin, 1986), pp. 93–119.
23. Robinson, *Ulster*, pp. 66–90.
24. Cullen, *Emergence*, p. 32.
25. J. H. Andrews, 'Land and People, *c.* 1780', in T. W. Moody and W. E. Vaughan (eds.), *A New History of Ireland IV, Eighteenth-Century Ireland 1691–1800*, (Oxford, 1986), p. 237; L. A. Clarkson, 'Irish Population Revisited, 1687–1821', in J. M. Goldstrom and L. A. Clarkson (eds.), *Irish Population, Economy and Society*, (Oxford, 1981), p. 27.
26. C. Ó Gráda, 'Poverty, population, and agriculture, 1801–45', in W. E. Vaughan (ed.), *A New History of Ireland V, Ireland Under the Union I, 1801–70*, (Oxford, 1989), p. 118.
27. Vaughan and Fitzpatrick, *Irish Historical Statistics*, pp. 3, 5–26.
28. Hoppen, *Ireland*, p. 87.
29. J. H. Andrews, 'The struggle for Ireland's public commons', in P. O'Flanagan, P. Ferguson and K. Whelan (eds.), *Rural Ireland. Modernisation and Change 1600–1900*, (Cork, 1987), pp. 1–23; Hoppen, *Ireland*, p. 87; Travers, *Settlements and Divisions*, p. 15.
30. D. Spring, 'Landed elites compared', in D. Spring (ed.), *European Landed Elites in the Nineteenth Century*, (Baltimore, n.d.), p. 4.
31. *Ibid.*, pp. 4–5.
32. R. Herr, 'Spain', *ibid.*, p. 104.
33. *Ibid.*, p. 5.
34. J. C. Beckett, *The Anglo-Irish Tradition*, (London, 1976), pp. 28–43; J. Hill, 'The meaning and significance of "Protestant Ascendancy"', in British Academy, *Ireland After the Union*, (Oxford, 1989), pp. 1–22.
35. J. C. Beckett, *A Short History of Ireland*, (5th edn., London, 1977), pp. 119–29; idem, *Anglo-Irish Tradition*, pp. 44–62.
36. Malcomson 'Absenteeism', pp. 15–35; Power, 'Land, politics and society', p. 67.
37. A slightly lower estimate for the end of the eighteenth century is given in L. M. Cullen, 'Catholic social classes under the Penal Laws', in T. P. Power and K. Whelan (eds.), *Endurance and Emergence*, (Dublin, 1990), p. 57. See also L. J. Proudfoot, 'The estate system in mid-nineteenth century Waterford', in W. Nolan and T. P. Power (eds.), *Waterford History and Society*, (Dublin, 1992), p. 523.
38. Gillespie, *Colonial Ulster*, pp. 57–63; L. J. Proudfoot, 'Landscaped parks in pre-Famine

Ireland: a regional case-study', in A. Verhoeve and J. A. J. Vervloet (eds.), *The Transformation of the European Rural Landscape: Methodological Issues and Agrarian Change, 1770–1914*, (Brussels, 1992), pp. 230–7.

39. Proudfoot, 'Estate system', pp. 532–4.
40. D. Dickson, 'An economic history of the Cork region in the eighteenth century', (Unpublished PhD thesis, University of Dublin, 1977), pp. 88–98; Power, 'Land, politics and society', p. 38.
41. D. Large, 'The wealth of the greater Irish landowners, 1750–1815', *Irish Historical Studies*, **15** (1966–7), pp. 21–45.
42. Dickson, 'Economic history', pp. 67–73, 81–6; P. O'Flanagan, 'Rural change south of the River Bride in Counties Cork and Waterford: The surveyors' evidence 1716–1851', *Irish Geography*, **15** (1982), pp. 51–69; Power, 'Land, politics and society', pp. 33–44.
43. Large, 'Wealth', pp. 37–42; Proudfoot, 'Urban patronage', pp. 239–40, 259–60.
44. J. S. Donnelly, 'The social composition of agrarian rebellions in early nineteenth-century Ireland: the case of the Carders and Caravats, 1813–16', in P. J. Corish (ed.), *Radicals, Rebels and Establishments*, (Belfast, 1985), pp. 151–70; D. McCartney, *The Dawning of Democracy: Ireland 1800–1870*, (Dublin, 1987), pp. 63–109.
45. S. Daniels and S. Seymour, 'Landscape design and the idea of improvement 1730–1914', in R. A. Dodgshon and R. A. Butlin (eds.), *An Historical Geography of England and Wales*, (2nd edn, London, 1990), p. 487; S. Wilmot, *'The Business of Improvement': Agriculture and Scientific Culture in Britain, c. 1700–1870*, (London, 1990), pp. 39–46.
46. Pounds, *Historical Geography*, pp. 285–6.
47. *Ibid.*, p. 276.
48. J. Meenan and D. Clarke (eds.), *RDS. The Royal Dublin Society 1731–1981*, (Dublin, 1981), p. 1.
49. Jones Hughes, 'Society and settlement', pp. 70–80; *idem*, 'The estate system of landholding in nineteenth century Ireland', in W. Nolan (ed.), *The Shaping of Ireland*, (Dublin, 1986), pp. 145–50; O'Connor, *Limerick's Past*, pp. 77–83.
50. Proudfoot, 'Urban patronage', pp. 253–300.
51. J. Gardner, 'Landlord motivation for improvement in an Ulster estate Town: the case study of Hillsborough, 1780–1820', (unpublished BA dissertation, Queen's University, Belfast, 1991), *passim*; Jones Hughes, 'Estate system', pp. 138–42; Proudfoot, 'Urban patronage', pp. 253–300.
52. Proudfoot, 'Landscaped parks', pp. 235–6.
53. J. S. Donnelly, *The Land and The People of Nineteenth-Century Cork*, (London, 1975); W. A. Maguire, *The Downshire Estates in Ireland, 1801–1845*, (Oxford, 1972); L. J. Proudfoot, 'The management of a great estate: patronage, income and expenditure on the Duke of Devonshire's Irish property, c. 1816–1891', *Irish Economic and Social History*, **XIII** (1986), pp. 32–55.
54. Power, 'Land, politics and society', p. 54.
55. J. Mokyr, *Why Ireland Starved*, (London, 1983), pp. 203–13.
56. C. Ó Gráda, 'Agricultural rents, pre-Famine and post Famine', *Economic and Social Review*, **7** (1974), pp. 385–92; idem, 'The investment behaviour of Irish landlords 1850–1875: some preliminary findings', *Agricultural History Review*, **XXIII** (1975), pp. 139–55.
57. J.V. Beckett, *The Aristocracy in England 1660–1914*, (Oxford, 1986), pp. 178–9.
58. Donnelly, *Land and People*, p. 169.
59. Cullen, *Economic History*, pp. 77–82; Dickson, 'Economic history', pp. 271–90.
60. Donnelly, *Land and People*, pp. 165–9.
61. J. G. Simms, 'The establishment of Protestant Ascendancy, 1691–1714', in Moody and Vaughan (eds.), *Eighteenth-Century Ireland*, pp. 16–20.
62. Cullen, *Economic History*, p. 167.
63. J. E. Doherty and D. J. Hickey, *A Chronology of Irish History since 1500*, (Dublin, 1989), p. 84.
64. Cullen, *Economic History*, pp. 78–86.
65. Dickson, 'Economic history', p. 145 ff.
66. J. Barry (ed.), 'Henry Bowman. Reports on the Duke of Devonshire's Irish estates,

1794–1797', *Analecta Hibernica*, **XXII** (1960), pp. 275–6; C. Maxwell (ed.), *Arthur Young, A Tour in Ireland*, (Rev. edn, Belfast, 1983), pp. 174–8.

67. W. Nolan, *Tracing the Past*, (Dublin, 1982), pp. 109–10.
68. Cullen, *Economic History*, pp. 78–80, 114–5.
69. F. Braudel, *The Identity of France. 2, People and Production*, (London, 1990), pp. 237–285, 400–414; A. Schubert, *A Social History of Modern Spain*, (London, 1990), pp. 57–104.
70. Maxwell, *Arthur Young, passim*; Meehan and Clarke, *RDS*, p. 22.
71. P. J. Carty, 'The historical geography of County Roscommon', (unpublished MA thesis, National University of Ireland, 1970), pp. 109–15, 139; E. McCourt. 'A study of the management of the Farnham estates in County Cavan during the nineteenth century', (unpublished MA thesis, University of Dublin, 1973), pp. 25–56; A. M. Tod, 'The Smiths of Baltiboys. A County Wicklow family and their estate in the 1840s', (unpublished PhD, University of Edinburgh, 1978), pp. 153–8, 177.
72. J. Bell and M. Watson, *Irish Farming 1750–1900*, (Edinburgh, 1986), pp. 1–14.
73. *Ibid.*, pp. 229–39.
74. F. H. A. Aalen, 'The origin of enclosures in Eastern Ireland', in N. Stephens and R. E. Glasscock (eds.), *Irish Geographical Studies*, (Belfast, 1970), pp. 209–23.
75. See, for example, J. A. Yelling, *Commonfield and Enclosure in England 1450–1850*, (London, 1977), *passim*.
76. Aalen, 'Origin of enclosures', pp. 209–23; R. H. Buchanan, 'Field systems of Ireland', in A. R. H. Baker and R. A. Butlin (eds.), *Studies of Field Systems in the British Isles*, (Cambridge, 1973), pp. 584–607.
77. Dickson, 'Economic history', pp. 153–68; Harvard University Library, Ms Eng. 218, Cork and Orrery papers, vol. 3, Lease Book and Account of the Caledon Estate, *c.* 1714–1745; Maguire, *Downshire Estates*, pp. 110–6, 259–61.
78. F. Mitchell, *Shell Guide to Reading the Irish Landscape*, (Dublin, 1986), pp. 189–90; Orme, *Ireland*, pp. 132–3.
79. Aalen, *Man and the Landscape*, pp. 169–92.
80. J. S. Donnelly, 'Landlords and tenants', in Vaughan (ed.), *Ireland Under the Union*, pp. 332–341.
81. Hoppen, *Ireland*, p. 87.
82. Cullen, *Economic History*, pp. 45–6.
83. Power, 'Land, politics and society', pp. 50–1
84. W. Nolan, *Fassadinin. Land, Settlement and Society in South-East Ireland 1600–1850*, (Dublin, 1979), pp. 92–7.
85. Dickson, 'Economic history', pp. 542–5.
86. J. H. Andrews, 'Land and people', p.259.
87. Crawford, 'Ulster landowners', pp. 117–44.
88. Proudfoot, 'Urban patronage', pp. 121–39; Power, 'Land, politics and society', pp. 237–8.
89. Public Record Office of Northern Ireland, Clanbrassil–Hamilton Correspondence, 1744–1780, M.I.C. 147, Reel 9, Vol. 17.
90. Carty, 'Roscommon', p. 124.
91. H. D. Gribbon, 'The Irish Linen Board, 1711–1828', in L. M. Cullen and T. C. Smout (eds.), *Comparative Aspects of Scottish and Irish Economic and Social History 1600–1900*, (Edinburgh, 1977), pp. 77–87.
92. D. G. Lockhart, 'Planned village development in Scotland and Ireland, 1700–1850', in Devine and Dickson, (eds.), *Ireland and Scotland*, pp. 132–45.
93. Cullen, *Emergence*, pp. 61–82.
94. This estimate is based on the preliminary results of a research project on Irish Estate Towns which is jointly directed by the editors. They wish to acknowledge the generous funding provided by the Leverhulme Trust which has made this work possible.
95. Jones Hughes, 'Estate system', pp. 138–43; O'Connor, *Limerick's Past*, pp. 77–83.
96. T. Jones Hughes, 'Village and town in mid-nineteenth century Ireland', *Irish Geography*, **14** (1981), pp. 100–1; *idem*, 'Estate System', pp. 137–150.
97. J. Burtchaell, 'The south Kilkenny farm villages', in W. J. Smyth and K. Whelan (eds.),

Common Ground. Essays on the Historical Geography of Ireland, (Cork, 1988), pp. 110–23; Smyth, 'Territorial, social and settlement hierarchies', pp. 140–60.

98. Cullen, *Emergence*, pp. 61–82.
99. *Ibid.*, p. 74; Ulster Architectural Heritage Society, *Historic Buildings . . . in the Mourne Area of South Down*, (Belfast, 1975), p. 24.
100. Aalen, *Man and the Landscape*, pp. 281–2; Ulster Architectural Heritage Society, *Historic Buildings . . . in and near Dungannon and Cookstown*, (Belfast, 1971), pp. 22–3.
101. A. E. J. Morris, *History of Urban Form Before the Industrial Revolution*, (London, 1979), pp. 121–54.
102. Aalen, *Man and the Landscape*, pp. 292–7; D. Dickson, 'Large-scale developers and the growth of eighteenth century Irish cities', in P. Butel and L. M. Cullen (eds.), *Cities and Merchants: French and Irish Perspectives on Urban Development, 1500–1900*, (Dublin, 1986), pp. 109–24.
103. Morris, *Urban Form*, pp. 155–84.
104. A. Sutcliffe, *Towards the Planned City, Germany, Britain, the United States and France, 1780–1914*, (Oxford, 1981), pp. 10–13.
105. West Yorkshire Archives, Leeds, Lane-Fox Papers, L. F. LXXXXVI.11, Dromahair Estate Rent Roll, n.d. but after *c.* 1780; L. F. CXIV.21, 'Report on the Dromahair Estate by Joshua Kell, 1843'.
106. Cullen, *Emergence*, pp. 61–83.
107. M. Byrne, 'The development of Tullamore, 1700–1921', (unpublished MLitt thesis, National Union of Ireland, 1980), pp. 123–5; Proudfoot, 'Urban patronage', pp. 121–46, 255–81.
108. Byrne, 'Tullamore', pp. 123–5, 129–38.
109. Proudfoot, 'Urban patronage', pp. 253–311.
110. Sir Charles Coote, *Statistical Survey of Queen's County*, (Dublin, 1801), p. 146.
111. McCourt, 'Farnham estates', pp. 27–40.
112. W. H. Crawford, 'The significance of landed estates in Ulster, 1600–1820', *Irish Economic and Social History*, **XVII** (1990), pp. 44–61; P. O' Flanagan, 'Settlement development and trading in Ireland, 1600–1900', in Devine and Dickson (eds.), *Ireland and Scotland*, pp. 146–50; B. J. Graham and L. J. Proudfoot, 'Landlords, Planning and Urban Growth in Eighteenth- and Early Nineteenth-Century Ireland', *Journal of Urban History* **18(3)** (1992), pp. 308–329.
113. Proudfoot, 'Urban patronage', pp. 253–311.
114. Gardiner, 'Landlord motivation', pp. 50–3.
115. Ulster Architectural Heritage Society, *Historic Buildings . . . in the Towns and Villages of Mid Down*, (Belfast, 1974), p. 14.
116. Proudfoot, 'Urban patronage', p. 323 ff.
117. K. Theodore Hoppen, *Elections, Politics, and Society in Ireland 1832–1885*, (Oxford, 1984), *passim*.
118. P. Jupp, 'Urban politics in Ireland, 1801–31', in D. Harkness and M. O'Dowd, *The Town in Ireland*, (Belfast, 1981), pp. 103–24.
119. Crawford, 'Significance', pp. 57–60.
120. W. A. McCutcheon, *The Industrial Archaeology of Northern Ireland*, (HMSO, London, 1980), pp. 4–5.
121. *Ibid.*, pp. 2–6.
122. Arthur Young, *A Tour in Ireland . . . Made in the Years 1776, 1777, 1778 and . . . 1779*, Vol. 2, Part 2, (Dublin, 1780), pp. 56–7.
123. J. C. Beckett, 'Eighteenth-century Ireland', in Moody and Vaughan (eds.), *Eighteenth-Century Ireland*, p. XLVIII; J. L. McCracken, 'The social structure and social life, 1714–1760', *ibid.*, p. 67.
124. R. B. McDowell, 'Ireland in 1800', *ibid.*, p. 704.
125. C. Ó Gráda, 'Industry and communications, 1801–1845', in Vaughan (ed.), *Ireland Under the Union*, p. 150.
126. L. M. Cullen, 'Economic Development, 1750–1800', in Moody and Vaughan (eds.), *Eighteenth-Century Ireland*, p. 179.

127. S. Lewis, *A Topographical Dictionary of Ireland*, Vol. 2, (London, 1837), p. 576; Proudfoot, 'Urban patronage', pp. 246–50.
128. Ó Gráda, 'Industry and communications', pp. 148–9.
129. *Ibid.*; McCutcheon, *Industrial Archaeology*, p. 53.
130. Cullen, *Economic History*, pp. 88–9; Ó Gráda, 'Industry and communications', pp. 148–9.
131. *Ibid.*, p. 150; R, V, Comerford, 'Ireland 1850–70: Post-Famine and Mid-Victorian', in Vaughan (ed.), *Ireland Under the Union*, pp. 374–5.
132. Cullen, *Economic History*, pp. 143–4.
133. J. Lee, 'The provision of capital for early Irish railways, 1830–53', *Irish Historical Studies*, **16** (1968–9), pp. 33–63.
134. W. A. McCutcheon, 'Transport, 1820–1914', in L. Kennedy and P. Ollerenshaw (eds.), *An Economic History of Ulster, 1820–1939*, (Manchester, 1985), pp. 109–36; *idem, Industrial Archaeology*, pp. 95–222.
135. D. Cannadine, 'The landowner as millionaire: The finances of the Dukes of Devonshire, *c.* 1800–*c.* 1826', *Agricultural History Review*, **25** (1977), pp. 77–97.
136. M. Bence-Jones, *A Guide to Irish Country Houses*, (London, 1988), p. xi.
137. W. Nolan, 'Patterns of living in Tipperary, 1750–1850', in Nolan and McGrath (eds.), *Tipperary*, pp. 288–324.
138. Proudfoot, 'Landscaped parks', p. 231; *idem*, 'Estate system', pp. 535–6.
139. Robinson, *Ulster*, pp. 72, 77.
140. Orme, *Ireland*, pp. 136–8.
141. Proudfoot, 'Landscaped parks', pp. 235–6.
142. Power, 'Land, politics and society', p. 38; Proudfoot, 'Estate system', pp. 528, 536–7.
143. Morris, *Urban Form*, pp. 176–7.
144. E. Hyams, *Capability Brown and Humphrey Repton*, (London, 1971), pp. 1–10.
145. E. Malins and the Knight of Glin, *Lost Demesnes. Irish Landscape Gardening, 1660–1845*, (London, 1976), pp. 73–188.
146. Bence-Jones, *Guide*, pp. 109–10.
147. Proudfoot, 'Estate system', pp. 536–7.
148. Cullen, *Emergence*, pp. 43–4; B. de Breffny and R. ffolliott, *The Houses of Ireland*, (London, 1975), p. 84.
149. Bence-Jones, *Guide*, pp. xi–xxiv.

8

Industrialization, Urbanization and Urban Society in Post-Famine Ireland, *c.* 1850–1921

Stephen A. Royle

Introduction

Figure 8.1 is a simple representation of Ireland's urban network as revealed by the first full and reasonably accurate count of the island's population, the census of 1821. Most of the towns it depicts were market towns or had marketing and central place activity as part of their functions. Such towns were to be found across Ireland, but their maximum density was in the fertile agricultural districts of the east and south. By contrast, the more barren western districts contained few settlements of any size, while County Leitrim could not boast of a town at all. The few larger towns tended to be regional central places, and were often ports. These larger towns and some of the others, too, might also have had some industry, usually food processing or textiles. Dublin served as the commercial, financial and administrative centre for the entire country. It dominated the urban hierarchy, and was almost twice the size of Cork, the next largest town. This urban system of 1821 has resonances of both central place theory and the rank-size rule. Such resonances faded away as the network became transformed over the following century, and different explanations for Ireland's changing urban character must be sought. The task of research on Ireland's urban development in the nineteenth and early twentieth centuries is to demonstrate and explain these changes. The issues that have to be addressed include the causes of urban growth, where this occurred, and conversely, the explanation for the decline in the urbanization of large parts of Ireland. The growth of industry is an important factor here. The different types of town that existed or that emerged need to be identified; the urban structure in both functional and socio-spatial terms has to be considered and the operation of the urban society discussed. This chapter will attempt to deal with these issues.

Urbanization and Industrialization in Ireland

Weber's pioneering book on the growth of cities in the nineteenth century refers only briefly to Ireland (pp. 64–7), and notes that, apart from the growth of Belfast

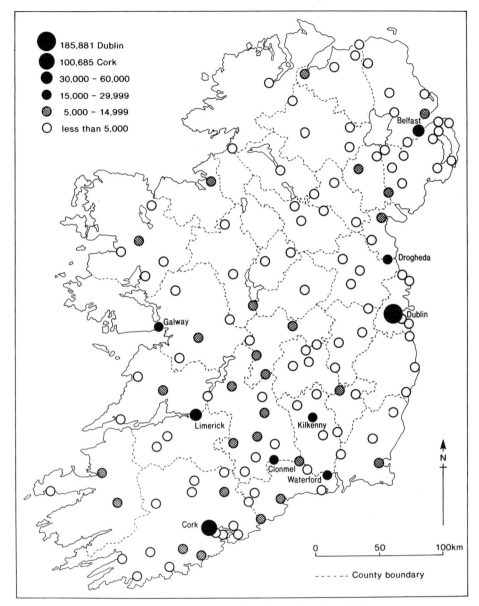

Fig. 8.1. The urban network in Ireland in 1821.

and Dublin, Ireland's 19 cities of more than 10,000 people actually lost aggregate population between 1841 and 1891.[1] Thus, there was not a general urbanization of the island during this period. Kemp's much later survey of the parallel and associated phenomenon of industrialization in Europe makes no mention of Ireland.[2] This may be partly due to the country's small size and peripheral location, for isolated places are often neglected in works dealing with an entire continent. Thus, in Stearns' survey of European social history after 1750, references to Ireland are confined to three brief entries in the index under 'Ireland, hunger in', nothing else happening there seemingly being worthy of note in a continental context.[3] However, there is another, more significant, reason for Ireland's exclusion from Kemp. Ireland, to use the terminology of the mythical 'trenchant businessman' employed by Weber as a pedagogic device to sum up the 'basic cause of nineteenth-century European industrialization in a single word', did not develop 'steam'.[4] So Ireland as a whole neither urbanized nor industrialized.

Urbanization can take place without industrialization. This is happening in the contemporary world in many of the less developed countries where high rates of rural–urban migration are not being matched by the growth of employment opportunities in urban manufacturing (or other sectors) to soak up this surplus labour. Difficult social, economic and infrastructural problems are the result. In nineteenth-century Europe, however, the two processes were usually matched, and employment was provided for those either pulled to the city by these perceived opportunities or pushed from the land anyway. In Ireland, however, some urban growth was associated with causes other than industrialization. Dublin grew from 232,726 in 1841 to 304,802 by 1911, but as a commercial rather than as an industrial city. It is noteworthy that this rate of growth, 131 per cent over 60 years, was actually fractionally below the mean for Irish urban growth as a whole. Weber's engine of urban growth, the steam engine, was to be found operating in only a small corner of the island, the north-east. Here, in Belfast, Ireland's only major Victorian industrial city, population grew 514 per cent from 75,308 in 1841 to 386,947 by 1911, when its population exceeded that of Dublin.

In the pre-Famine period, Ireland's failure to industrialize, save in the north-east, could not have been foreseen. The returns to the 1841 census show that over 27 per cent of the Irish labour force was in manufacturing. Contemporary observers hardly expected either the demographic and economic shock of the Famine itself, or a decline in Irish manufacture. Kane, for example, argued that a population of 35 million might be supported by agriculture and, additionally, that industrialization could develop in Ireland despite its lack of major coalfields.[5] Noting that in Leeds the cotton industry spent less than 2 per cent of its total manufacturing costs on fuel, he argued:

> That the cost of fuel to generate steam power bears so small a proportion to the value of the products of mechanical industry as to be totally unimportant in comparison with money wages and raw material, regarding which this country [Ireland] labours certainly under no natural disadvantage.[6]

Recent work seems to support Kane's contention. Mokyr, using data for the Mulholland flax mill in Belfast in the mid 1830s, noted that despite coal in Belfast being about four times its price in Leeds, the cost still represented only 3.8 per cent of the total value of output, compared to 0.4 per cent in Leeds (note that Mokyr is considering output values; Kane looked at input costs).[7] To compensate Mulholland, and presumably other Irish manufacturers, wages in Belfast were much lower than those paid in Leeds. Kane concluded that Ireland could become industrialized, and only 'indolent ignorance' led her to retreat behind complaints about a shortage of fuel and its high cost.[8] Rather, he argued, the factors holding Ireland back were poor communications,[9] a lack of common industrial raw materials,[10] a lack of education[11] and a want of capital.[12] These problems overcome, he foresaw an industrial future for Ireland, which if not so vibrant as that of England, might avoid some of the latter's problems. In particular 'the evils of vast unhealthy manufacturing cities need not be feared' because Ireland's power sources of coal, turf (peat) and water were distributed fairly uniformly.[13] Hence he felt that Ireland would be able to develop a dispersed pattern of industry.

Table 8.1: Irish occupational regions in 1841: summary of cluster analysis.

Dendrogram of final seven steps in cluster analysis	Final seven clusters and counties included	Characteristics of seven clusters
	1. Carlow, Wexford, Wicklow, King's (Offaly), Cork, Tipperary, Clare, Kerry	High incidence of shopkeepers, pigjobbers, labourers and farmers. Low incidence of spinning and weaving trades; average incidence of all other occupations.
	2. Longford, Sligo, Louth	Large numbers of flax spinners, flax dressers.
	3. Kildare, Meath, W. Meath, Limerick, Kilkenny, Queen's (Laois), Waterford, Roscommon	Highest incidence of cattle dealers and labourers; many ploughmen, carpenters and other tradesmen.
	4. Galway, Mayo	Large numbers of carders, wool spinners, wool weavers; low incidence of tradesmen, service occupations.
	5. Dublin	Many tradesmen of all sorts: bakers, papermakers, writing clerks; high incidence of ploughmen, land agents and domestic servants.
	6. Antrim, Down, Armagh, Londonderry, Tyrone	Extreme incidence of linen weavers, unspecified weavers, and other domestic industry occupations.
	7. Cavan, Monaghan, Donegal, Fermanagh, Leitrim	Many unspecified spinners, flax spinners, flax dressers; highest incidence of farmers.

Based on a hierarchical cluster analysis using a conventional Euclidean distance measure of points (counties) in multivariate space. The vertical bars show the last seven steps of the combination of points into relatively homogeneous clusters, or groups of counties. The final cluster consists of all Irish counties. The SAS algorithm CLUSTER was used.
Source: Almquist, 1980.

Almquist has argued that pre-Famine Ireland did indeed display industrial potential in that by 1830, both spinners and labourers represented potential sources of workers for urbanized industry.[14] However, he was able to show that even before the Famine a regionally-concentrated pattern of industry was developing. Almquist considered the occupational data from the 1841 census which he subjected to a cluster analysis. His results (reproduced as Table 8.1) demonstrate that the most significant spatial division in Irish occupations was between the nine counties of Ulster (plus Leitrim), which had a heavy concentration of flax weavers and spinners, and the rest of the island, where such jobs were less common. A later step in the analysis then separated the western Ulster counties (plus Leitrim) where most of the flax workers were spinners, from the eastern counties where more weavers were to be found. Most of these textile workers were not yet urban or factory-based and Almquist concludes his paper by noting the subsequent destruction of the economic structure of pre-Famine, pre-industrial Ireland, by a combination of factory mechanization and hunger. However, some of the spatial and economic distinctions between the regions of Ireland which he identified did continue into the post-Famine period.

In their different ways, Almquist, Kane and Mokyr present a picture of a pre-industrial economy that could have industrialized. That it would not was clear within a generation of Kane's optimistic predictions. Table 8.2 demonstrates that the rural counties tended to lose what industry they had, the decline in industrial employment being particularly striking in Connacht.[15] Here, in the west, there was also considerable decline in agricultural opportunities with what Fitzpatrick identifies as the virtual disappearance of the agricultural labourer.[16] The western counties became trapped into a downward spiral for they were

> those counties most reliant upon foreign markets to absorb their labour surplus [and] were least successful in developing alternative sources of employment at home.[17]

Thus, there was no fairly even distribution of industry lacking vast manufacturing cities as Kane had hoped, but only a partial industrialization of one corner of the landmass with the development of a classic industrial city in Belfast.

Table 8.3, which is based on data supplied by the late-Victorian statistician, Charles Booth, compares the occupational structure of Ireland as a whole with that of the rest of the British Isles during the nineteenth century.[18] It shows that the gradual decline in population engaged in agriculture in Ireland was accompanied by a parallel fall in the proportion in manufacturing, with agriculture remaining overwhelmingly predominant. This relationship between the two occupational groups was the converse of that in England and Wales (considered together in Booth's analysis) and Scotland (Fig. 8.2). Booth's comparisons of Ireland to Great Britain are instructive. He pointed out that in 1881 the land in England and Scotland supported nearly as many in absolute terms as it did in 1841, with the increased population supported by industry. In nineteenth-century Ireland on the other hand, only half the rural workforce remained on the land and other productive industries did not take up the slack. He concluded that 'if a reduced population finds less work to do per man it is hard to obtain any encouragement from the figures'.[19] Occupations which did increase in importance in Ireland in the nineteenth century included transport and public and professional services. These are certainly sectors necessary to develop and modernize the economy, but the greatest increase was in people employed in domestic or 'industrial' service, the latter being largely general labourers. Booth noted that general labourers could

Table 8.2: Percentage of the labour force in industry, 1821–81.

	1821	1841	1881
Ulster			
Antrim	57.2	48.7	43.2
Carrick	54.7	43.7	—
Belfast	n.a.	57.0	68.2
Armagh	60.7	48.7	43.2
Cavan	45.8	37.4	15.3
Derry	60.1	47.3	34.2
Donegal	52.5	41.8	22.6
Down	57.0	51.2	45.3
Fermanagh	45.1	41.1	19.5
Monaghan	56.1	40.0	17.8
Tyrone	56.2	47.8	26.3
Total	55.3	45.9	37.1
Leinster			
Carlow	21.2	19.8	22.1
Dublin (city)	54.6	39.8	55.1
Dublin (county)	32.7	19.5	29.0
Kildare	23.4	18.5	22.2
Kilkenny (city)	60.3	37.7	—
Kilkenny (county)	17.4	8.2	22.6
King's (Offaly)	26.8	19.8	21.2
Longford	42.5	29.4	18.0
Louth	46.8	28.3	31.5
Drogheda	63.1	48.9	—
Meath	32.7	22.4	20.9
Queen's (Laois)	23.1	19.2	20.4
Westmeath	32.6	24.6	19.9
Wexford	22.9	24.2	22.5
Wicklow	48.7	20.0	22.0
Total	33.6	24.1	29.9
Munster			
Clare	24.2	23.5	19.1
Cork (city)	40.9	38.2	48.3
Cork (county)	19.4	19.0	22.2
Kerry	26.8	22.4	19.7
Limerick (city)	38.3	27.1	43.9
Limerick (county)	28.0	21.9	20.9
Tipperary	17.8	16.8	22.0
Waterford (city)	45.7	34.2	50.8
Waterford (county)	14.9	14.4	20.6
Total	23.7	20.8	24.3
Connacht			
Galway (county)	33.9	26.4	16.3
Galway (town)	30.6	35.0	—
Leitrim	47.0	37.2	13.5
Mayo	48.8	28.2	13.3
Roscommon	40.4	23.9	15.2
Sligo	46.5	30.7	17.8
Total	42.9	28.4	15.2

Source: Ó Gráda (1988).

Table 8.3: Occupations of the people of the UK 1841–91.

	1841		1851			1861			1871			1881		1891
	Ireland	England & Wales	Scotland	Ireland	England & Wales	Scotland	Ireland	England & Wales	Scotland	Ireland	England & Wales	Scotland	Ireland	Ireland
Agriculture	50.9	20.9	22.7	48.4	18.0	20.1	42.9	14.2	17.3	40.7	11.5	14.2	41.1	43.7
Fishing	0.2	0.2	1.5	0.4	0.2	1.7	0.3	0.2	1.8	0.4	0.3	1.9	0.5	0.5
Mining	0.2	4.0	4.0	0.4	4.5	4.5	0.4	4.5	5.1	0.3	4.8	5.0	0.4	0.2
Building	2.0	5.5	5.2	2.0	5.8	5.9	2.4	6.3	6.3	2.2	6.8	6.7	2.4	2.6
Manufacture	27.3	32.7	36.5	22.8	33.0	35.0	20.7	31.6	34.7	19.5	30.7	33.8	16.0	17.8
Transport	0.5	4.1	3.6	1.4	4.6	4.1	1.8	4.9	4.9	2.1	5.6	5.2	2.2	2.6
Dealing	2.6	6.5	5.6	3.6	7.1	6.5	4.1	7.8	7.1	4.6	7.8	7.5	4.8	5.4
Industrial service	1.2	4.5	3.8	2.3	4.0	3.9	7.5	6.0	4.5	7.5	6.7	6.2	6.7	6.6
Public/Professional service	1.6	4.6	3.5	2.2	5.3	3.9	3.7	5.5	3.8	4.3	5.6	4.2	5.0	5.8
Domestic service	9.4	13.3	10.5	9.4	14.6	12.0	13.3	15.8	10.7	15.2	15.7	11.1	18.0	12.2
Others	4.1	3.7	3.1	7.1	2.9	2.4	2.9	3.2	3.8	3.2	4.4	4.2	2.9	2.6

Source: 1841–81, Booth, 1886; 1891. Booth, 1901.

hardly be counted as being involved in productive industry, as they stemmed from the destitute groups which sprung 'into existence not from any need of their services, but as the outcome of agriculture and industrial distress and charitable doles on an enormous scale'.[20]

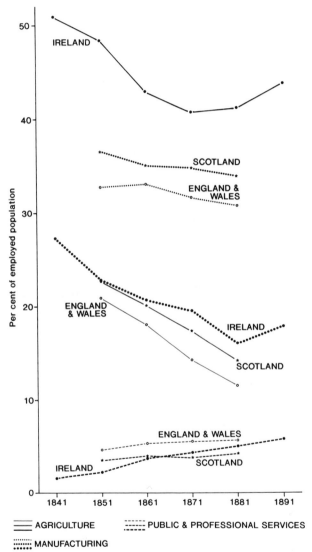

Fig. 8.2. Occupational breakdown for the British Isles, 1841–1891. *Source:* Booth 1886, 1901.

Within the continental context, Mokyr points out that Irish industrialization was so slow and in so few areas that the island was probably regressing in its relative position compared to the rest of Europe.[21] His explanation for this touches upon core–periphery concepts, with the core area of Great Britain holding back the Irish periphery as part and parcel of the British political and economic domination and exploitation of the smaller island. He introduces, too, the idea of risk aversion, with Irish entrepreneurs seemingly less willing than those in other countries to take the chances that might have led to industrial success. However, the principal reason for Ireland's backwardness, he avers, was the mobility of its labour force. Ireland's cheap labour became part of a labour market which extended far beyond the island. Instead of building up its own industrial sector, Ireland provided workers for economies elsewhere which, using this cheap labour supply, could produce higher profits and foster capital formation. Thus

> Ireland industrialised but unfortunately, for the Irish, its industrialisation took place outside its borders in north west England, the Scottish lowlands and New England ... The unusually large dimension of Irish emigration is one reason why Ireland, unlike Belgium ... was unable to take advantage of a cheap labour force.[22]

Ireland's nineteenth-century urbanization can also be set into a wider context, using the statistics gathered by Weber (Table 8.4).[23] These data enable comparisons

Table 8.4: Nineteenth-century European urban growth.

	Early century		Mid century			Late century		
	Year	%[a]	Year	%[a]	% change p.a. early-mid[b]	Year	%[a]	% change p.a. mid-late[b]
England & Wales	1801	21.3	1851	39.5	0.36	1891	61.8	0.56
Scotland	1801	17.0	1851	32.2	0.30	1891	49.9	0.44
Belgium	1810	13.5	1846	20.8	0.18	1890	34.8	0.32
Saxony	1815	8.9	1849	13.6	0.14	1890	34.7	0.52
Netherlands	1795	29.5	1849	29.0	−0.01	1889	33.5	0.11
Prussia	1816	7.3	1849	10.6	0.10	1890	30.0	0.47
France	1801	9.5	1851	14.4	0.10	1891	25.9	0.29
Denmark	1801	10.9	1840	9.6	−0.03	1891	23.6	0.28
Spain	1820	14.0	1857	16.2	0.06	1887	29.6	0.45
Ireland	1800	7.8	1851	10.1	0.05	1891	18.0	0.20
Norway	1801	3.3	1848	5.3	0.05	1890	16.7	0.25
Switzerland	1822	4.3	1850	7.3	0.11	1888	16.5	0.24
Austria	1800	4.4	1843	5.8	0.03	1890	15.8	0.21
Hungary	1800	5.6	1850	9.1	0.08	1890	17.6	0.21
Sweden	1805	3.9	1850	4.7	0.24	1890	13.7	0.23
Portugal	1801	12.7	1857	12.9	0.004	1890	12.7	−0.005
Russia	1820	3.7	1856	5.3	0.04	1855	9.3	0.14

[a] % of population in towns above 10,000.
[b] Average annual urban growth.

Source: Adapted from Weber, 1899.[23]

to be made between the urban proportions of 17 European countries for the early, mid and late century. In each case Ireland lay in tenth position, consistently ahead of rural countries such as Norway, Portugal and Sweden, but lagging far behind the urban and industrial leaders such as England, Belgium and Saxony. With regard to rates of urban growth, Ireland lay eleventh comparing early to mid century, whilst the mid to late century period saw Ireland's urban growth rate exceed only that of Russia, the Netherlands and Portugal. Russia was yet to experience its late, quick spurt of industrial and urban growth; the Netherlands possessed a largely commercial economy which had been heavily urbanized by the late eighteenth century; while Portugal, which by then was still very much a developing country, had a single primate city in Lisbon.

Much of Ireland's distinctive industrial and urban experience in the nineteenth century can be traced to her demographic history. The Famine and its associated and long-continued massive population decline were hardly incentives to industrialists to base themselves in Ireland. As Mokyr, Almquist and others have shown, the Irish who became industrial workers usually found their jobs outside the island. In 1851, 734,000 people of Irish birth were resident in Great Britain, mostly in the growing industrial cities, growth which was paralleled in many other urban settlements across the globe.[24] Table 8.5, based on data collected by Doyle, shows the Irish migration data for Canada, the USA and Australia. It indicates that over 6 million Irish people migrated to just these three countries between 1815 and 1921.[25] The Famine might also be seen as the key to the continued, indeed growing, divergence in urban and industrial terms between Ulster and the rest of Ireland. The slower rate of population loss from that province[26] has been explained in terms of Ulster's development of industry.[27]

Table 8.5: Irish emigration to Australasia, Canada and the United States (totals in thousands; percentages relate to aggregate emigration for each period).

Years	Australasia		Canada		United States	
1815–1845	c. 60.0[a]	(6.2%)	570.0	(54.0%)	420.0	(39.8%)
1846–1855	69.7	(3.8%)	336.3	(18.2%)	1443.7	(78.0%)
1856–1870	130.6	(11.6%)	53.6	(4.8%)	940.5	(83.6%)
1871–1880	61.9	(11.5%)	25.7	(4.8%)	449.5	(83.7%)
1881–1900	66.9	(5.7%)	55.1	(4.7%)	1053.9	(89.6%)
1901–1921	29.5	(4.1%)	74.5	(10.4%)	610.7	(85.5%)

[a] Between 1815 and 1845, records were incomplete; a minimum of 50,000 and a maximum of 65,000 seem the most convincing figures.

Source: Doyle, 1989.[25]

In sum, it can be said that as a whole, and despite some industrial and urban potential, nineteenth-century Ireland failed to capitalize upon its opportunities. It is thus now appropriate to move beyond this general picture and consider in more detail the growing regional differentiation in the industrialization and urbanization which did take place.

Ulster: Ireland's Industrial Province

Pre-Famine Industry

Even by the late eighteenth century, parts of Ulster already stood out from the rest of Ireland because of the extent of manufacturing. At this period industry was mostly still based in the rural areas with the involvement of the local towns as marketing centres. Crawford notes that in 1816, around 14,500 weavers attended local linen markets and traded more than 24,000 pieces of cloth in the nine Ulster counties.[28] These markets were in towns such as Lisburn, Armagh, Dungannon and Belfast, the last beginning to take over Dublin's earlier dominance of the final marketing of linen. Early in the eighteenth century, Ulster drapers had taken their bleached linen webs to Dublin, for sale in a Linen Hall erected there for them in 1728. The linen was then exported to London. In 1782, in a reaction by the Ulster drapers against the regulation of their trade by the Dublin merchants, they sought to market the final product from Ulster. A Brown Linen Hall had already been erected in Belfast in the 1740s; in 1784 Belfast's White Linen Hall started operation and the city became not only a principal trading place for bleached linen but also its port of export.[29] It was typical of early industrialization of this type that the product should have both a national and international market.[30]

Clarkson and Collins have set this early industrial picture into its theoretical framework. Discussing proto-industrialization, otherwise 'industries in the countryside', they note that

> the labour for proto-industry was provided by peasant farmers on a part-time basis. They turned to industry to supplement with cash the inadequate living their farming provided them.[31]

Such part-time manual work could be fitted both into the domestic arrangements of the farmer and into the seasonal nature of farm work. Clarkson and Collins suggest that proto-industrialization had two possible outcomes, either the development of factory-based industrialization, presumably in towns or industrial villages, or a fading away to de-industrialization. A third possibility also existed—the straightforward continuation of these part-time 'industries in the countryside'. The home working of knitting in places like Donegal is one example or, outside Ireland, the part-time domestic weaving of the Harris Tweed industry of the Western Isles.

Although Clarkson and Collins' study was based on an analysis of data for Lisburn in 1821, most Ulster proto-industrialization was rural. Kennedy shows how it was organized and on what scale.[32] In 1750, 11 million yards (10.1 million metres) of linen cloth, most of it Ulster produce, were exported from Ireland; by 1815 the figure was 43 million yards (39.4 million metres).[33] Typically, the flax was grown on the farm, spun, usually by the women of the household on a wheel, and woven by the men on a handloom. Even young children had to help, and were often used to wind on the spun yarn. Farms which were large and/or more remote from the market towns, particularly in the west of Ulster, were less involved. In the nineteenth century, the putting-out system (whereby a weaver contracted his output to a single draper rather than selling it in the open market) became more widespread and the independence of the individual farmer/weaver households was undermined. Now the greatest opportunities to acquire wealth were in the hands of the bleachers who processed the brown linen and organized the putting-out.

The organization of cotton spinning on a factory basis started in the 1770s, and led to what Geary has called Belfast's 'brief flirtation with cotton'.[34] This peaked in 1826, when the town had 21 mills and about 3600 operators, and involved the transference of many linen weavers to cotton to keep pace with the output from the spinning factories. The demand for cotton led to its weavers being much better rewarded than those remaining in linen, although the growing demand for weaving skills in general led to higher wages for all. Periodically, however, the economic downturns in the cotton industry, such as that from 1817 to 1819 after the end of the Napoleonic Wars, and again from 1826 to 1829, led to considerable hardship. Wages fell and Ulster manufacturers had little incentive to invest in new machinery to cut labour costs, even though the Belfast factories were not undercapitalized compared to their English counterparts. However, when in 1824 the United Kingdom government removed all duties on goods passing between Ireland and Great Britain, Irish cotton proved to be uncompetitive against the Lancashire goods of higher and more consistent quality which were now being woven as well as spun by steam power.[35] Presumably, the local industrialists could have invested to compete with Lancashire cotton, but instead, many of them transferred their capital as well as their factory-based technological expertise to linen.

Flax spinning, particularly of fine yarns, remained a hand industry until 1825, when James Kay of Preston discovered that soaking flax in cold water enabled it to be machine-spun, and the factory production of even fine-yarned flax thread became possible. When Thomas Mulholland's Belfast cotton mill burnt down in 1828, he decided not to try and compete once again with English and Scottish cotton manufacturers, but to take up instead the new wet-spinning process for linen. Mulholland's venture was successful and the new technique was widely adopted. The diffusion of factory linen spinning to Ulster within a short time brought both the cotton industry and, over a longer period, the domestic linen spinning industry to a virtual close. The latter disappeared from the more remote areas first, but survived a little longer closer to the towns, especially if the farmers could grow their own flax and maintain a couple of hand looms on their premises. Flax acreage peaked at 278,000 acres (112,500 hectares) in 1864. Indeed, the widespread introduction of factory-woven linen was somewhat delayed in Ireland because of the large numbers of handloom weavers prepared to work at cheap rates. However, post-Famine migration reduced the rural labour supply and hastened the factory-based industrialization of all aspects of textile production, which increasingly was concentrated in either towns or industrial villages. Kennedy places the major collapse in handloom weaving between 1851 and 1861, although a few domestic weavers would still be found until the turn of the century.[36]

For some decades factory and domestic production had advanced together with different processes being carried on by each, but eventually all production became factory-based. In some parts of Ulster this led to de-industrialization and a reversion to agriculture. This was particularly evident in those areas where the coarser cloth was produced and which were hit by competition from factory-produced cotton. Thus there was not a steady shift everywhere from one mode of production to another, nor from proto-industrialization to industrialization. Kennedy emphasizes the importance of the economic nerve centres of proto-industry, the points in a region where it was concentrated.[37] Here, the major possibilities for capital formation existed and the large-scale entrepreneur could flourish. It was these poles of accumulation, rather than the vast hinterlands of lowly paid labour over which they held sway, that were of primary importance for further industrial development and its associated urbanization. Crawford notes that 'only in few

places outside the linen triangle (Belfast–Dungannon–Newry) would linen spinning mills be erected'.[38]

Belfast

One such early 'economic nerve centre' was Belfast. Though heavily involved in
the trading of linen in the late eighteenth century, Belfast's major thrust into urban
industrialization came from cotton. Cotton spinning was initially introduced as a
means of providing employment within the Poor House by the Belfast Charitable
Society. This was so successful that the trade spread and a factory system developed, linked financially with English and Scottish textile towns. Initially the west
bank tributaries of the Lagan were used for power but steam had become more
important than stream by the late 1820s.[39] After the adoption of wet flax spinning,
linen took over, either taking advantage of a decline in cotton or causing this
decline.[40] By the early 1850s there were 28 flax mills but only four cotton mills.[41]
Belfast's linen industry was supported by vertical economic linkages in a manner
that did not develop in many Irish settlements. This was of considerable benefit to
Belfast as further employment was provided by the circulation of trade and capital
within the town. For example, in the suburb of Ballymacarrett on the east or Down
side of the Lagan where many of the ancillary industries were situated, two tile
factories, a timber pond, a glass works, an iron foundry and a flax spinning mill
were built between 1846 and 1849. In 1849 this area also contained chemical, glass,
iron, rope and timber works.[42]

Another major Belfast industry that could look back to pre-industrial and pre-
Famine roots was shipbuilding. There had been shipbuilding in Belfast since at
least the eighteenth century, initially on the west or Antrim bank of Belfast Lough,
although its major development came later after a fresh beginning in a new location
from the second half of the nineteenth century. Access to the harbour at Belfast
was impeded by the constricted bends in the River Lagan, and in 1785 the Corporation for Preserving and Improving the Port of Belfast, the Ballast Board in general
parlance, was empowered to provide a deep water channel. This had been
achieved by 1795 but access to the city by ship still remained tortuous. In the 1840s,
further dredging work of what became the Victoria Channel was authorized under
the newly constituted Harbour Commissioners.[43] The spoil from this was dumped
on to the slob lands at the sides of the cut to make a training bank to modify the
river's flow. This land was named Dargan's Island after the supervising engineer,
but was later renamed Queen's Island. Initially it was used as a pleasure park but
when the Harbour Commissioners concentrated trade activities on the Antrim
bank, shipyards such as Thompson and Kirwan moved across to Queen's Island.
In 1853 Robert Hickson also opened a shipyard there, largely to consume plate
from his iron foundry which he was having trouble selling in the British market.
His manager, Edward Harland, bought him out in 1858 and brought in Gustav
Wolff as partner. Wolff was the nephew of Gustav Schwabe, a Liverpool ship-
owner. Schwabe's orders, together with the Harland and Wolff directors' links
with shipping companies, helped to establish the firm. Harland and Wolff
absorbed Thompson and Kirwan in 1859 and by 1870 employed 2400 workers,
when they began their long association with the White Star Line as a major world

shipbuilder. Around the turn of the century Harland and Wolff employed 9000 workers and three times launched the world's then largest ship: Oceanic II (17,274 tons gross) in 1899; Olympic (45,324 tons) in 1911: and the Titanic (46,328 tons) in 1912. Across the Lagan on the west bank stood the 'wee yard', Workman and Clark, established as a subsidiary company for British owners in 1879 who wished to take advantage of the local availability of skilled, experienced labour.[44] From 1878 to 1913 Belfast shipbuilding output grew by 7.8 per cent per annum, compared to a United Kingdom average of only 2.5 per cent.[45] By the start of the First World War the two Belfast yards had become responsible each year for about 8 per cent of the world's shipping construction.

Other Belfast industries fed off orders from the linen and shipbuilding industries as well as from the port. The vertical linkages that first developed in the early linen industry remained characteristic of Belfast's industrial scene. The city (as Belfast became in 1888) had rope works, engineering factories, chemicals works and, early on, foundries. By 1907 Cullen estimates that about one-third of Irish net industrial output and two-thirds of total industrial exports originated in or around Belfast.[46] Table 8.6 presents data drawn from the official census statistics on employment in Belfast from 1871 to 1921.[47] These data tend to obscure rather than reveal the precise nature of Belfast's industrial activity, but can be used to confirm the importance of various industrial activities within the city. Thus, although linen is buried amongst 'other textiles', it in fact dominated this category and its significance to Belfast can hardly be overstated. Belfast was a 'Linenopolis', and this had considerable effects on its culture,[48] society and even its health.[49] Shipbuilding also is not properly identified by the official statistics. Many of those recorded as being employed in 'other engineering' or 'other manufacturing' between 1871 and 1911 actually worked in the shipyards, but, again, their importance and scale is still apparent.

Belfast thus became a Victorian industrial city, recognizably British in type. It bore comparison to places like Leeds, Bradford or Newcastle and, as Ollerenshaw confirms, it also cooperated 'far more closely with industrial regions in Britain . . . than it did with other parts of Ireland'.[50] Like the mainland British cities, by the 1900s Belfast had about 75 per cent of its workforce in industry, 5 per cent in professions and 8 per cent in domestic service.[51] This contrasts with Dublin where only 54 per cent of the working population was in industry and of this a much higher proportion than in Belfast lacked skills. For example, more than 80 per cent of the workforce at the Guinness Brewery, Dublin's largest industrial employer, was unskilled.[52]

Belfast achieved this notable industrial pre-eminence

> even though it is practically devoid of native sources of minerals and power and is separate from the principal domestic markets by the Irish Sea and for most goods supplies only a very small market of its own.[53]

Further, with regard to shipbuilding, Geary and Johnson stress that the yards appear to have had a particularly unsuitable location on a narrow river.[54] However, although the Irish Sea cut Belfast off from Britain, its position on it, relatively close to Liverpool and Glasgow with which it developed links, allowed easy delivery of raw materials, whilst its peripheral but coastal location was one preferred by

Table 8.6: Employment patterns for specified occupations[a], Belfast County Borough[b, c] 1871–1926.

	1871		1881		1891		1901		1911		1926[d]	
Shipbuilding[e]	821	(0.9)	1,308	(1.2)	2,890	(2.2)	5,138	(3.1)	6,935	(4.0)	19,286	(9.5)
Other engineering[f]	1,242	(1.4)	1,361	(1.3)	2,842	(2.2)	3,985	(2.4)	5,967	(3.4)	7,328	(3.6)
Rope[g]	206	(0.2)	300	(0.3)	584	(0.4)	1,168	(0.7)	1,166	(0.7)		
Other textiles	14,673	(16.2)	26,297	(23.9)	34,625	(26.4)	34,642	(21.1)	35,731	(20.4)	50,969	(25.1)
Tobacco	144	(0.2)	303	(0.3)	479	(0.4)	813	(0.5)	1,144	(0.7)	2,271	(1.1)
Other manufacturing	20,778	(23.0)	21,301	(19.4)	29,899	(22.8)	36,268	(22.1)	37,696	(21.5)	28,571	(14.1)
Domestic service[h]	9,543	(10.6)	16,669	(15.2)	9,969	(7.6)	12,354	(7.5)	11,075	(6.3)	7,824	(3.6)
Transport and communication	5,848	(6.5)	6,256	(5.7)	8,008	(6.1)	10,401	(6.3)	11,704	(6.7)	10,847	(5.3)
Distributive trades[i]											22,105	(10.9)
Public administration, defence	1,819	(2.0)	2,679	(2.4)	3,784	(2.9)	4,105	(2.5)	4,142	(2.4)	12,686	(6.3)
Total employed	90,356		109,886		131,076		164,314		175,494		202,904	

[a] Statistics refer to population classified by occupation 1871–1911, population classified by industry 1926.
[b] Statistics refer to population of County Borough (boundary change 1896).
[c] Statistics refer to population according to place of residence.
[d] Statistics for 1926 include those out of work.
[e] Shipbuilding consists of manufacture of hull, masts, rigging 1871–1911 (an unknown proportion of 'Other engineering' or 'Other manufacturing' would have worked at the shipyards), shipbuilding, ship repairing and marine engineering 1926.
[f] Other engineering includes vehicles 1926.
[g] Rope manufacture not separately categorized 1926.
[h] Domestic service excludes charwomen.
[i] Distributive trades not separately categorized 1871–1911; partly included in other categories.

Source: Boal and Royle, 1986.[47]

shipbuilders.[55] Contemporaries wondering about the reasons for Belfast's industrial success saw it as a product of the qualities of its people, many of whom were
descended from seventeenth-century migrants from Britain. In 1834 at an early
period in Belfast's industrialization Inglis remarked that he

> thought it impossible that Cork, Limerick or Waterford could ever become cities like
> Belfast for the people in the southern cities are addicted to pleasure which in Belfast was a
> very secondary consideration.[56]

Inglis went on to say that Belfast was bound to flourish because so many of its
inhabitants were of Scottish origin but then, as Freeman wryly notes, Inglis was
himself Scottish.[57] Today such ethnic explanations do not find favour and there is
more merit in the points which Freeman himself made to explain Belfast's industrial growth. These included the considerable and growing maritime trade in agricultural produce and linen which necessitated so much port activity, the ready
availability of level, reclaimed land by the deep waters of Belfast Lough which
could be easily worked to provide suitable accommodation for shipyards and other
industries, and the vertical linkages between so many Belfast industries which
enabled an efficient, prompt delivery of the ultimate final product of many of them,
the ships. With regard to the workers, Geary and Johnson's recent verdict is that
the main attraction of the workforce to employers was not their ethnic origin but
their abundance and low wage cost.[58] The links with Britain led to the possibility of
bringing in specialists from outside Ulster whenever necessary. Further, as Moss
and Hume's magisterial history of Harland and Wolff has made clear,[59] Belfast was
fortunate in having in Harland a brilliant engineer and in Wolff, despite his self-
effacing claim that 'as for me, I smoke the cigars for the firm', a man of financial
acumen and the useful family ties which eased the shipyard's entry in to Liverpool
shipping circles.[60]

Figure 8.3 sums up the development of industrial Belfast up to the turn of the
century. It shows that the industrial development was superimposed onto a townscape long divided into separate residential areas for its competing ethnic groups:
Inglis's Scots who with others originally from Great Britain were largely Protestant,
and the Catholic Irish. Hepburn and Collins confirm the relevance of a map of this
date to the contemporary geography of Belfast, writing of the 'stable population
pattern and segregation level of the twentieth century [having been] established by
1901'.[61] In fact, the basic lineaments of the segregation evident by this time can be
traced back to the seventeenth century, when the location of the future core of the
Catholic area in west Belfast was determined by a 'decree that the native people
should live outside the wall'.[62] Jones points to the 'tradition' of this western Catholic sector which had spread along the Falls Road and its containment by industrial
Protestant working class areas along the Shankill and Crumlin Roads and the older
Sandy Row.[63] The eastern side of the city was largely Protestant, the population
having mainly been drawn from Protestant areas of County Down.

Hepburn and Collins provide a detailed study of Belfast in 1901 based on the
manuscript census returns of that year. Much of their analysis concerns the differentiation between Protestant and Catholic groups. They demonstrate that the latter
were disadvantaged in a number of ways, including low levels of literacy (12 per
cent of Catholics were illiterate compared to 5 per cent Protestant), poorer housing

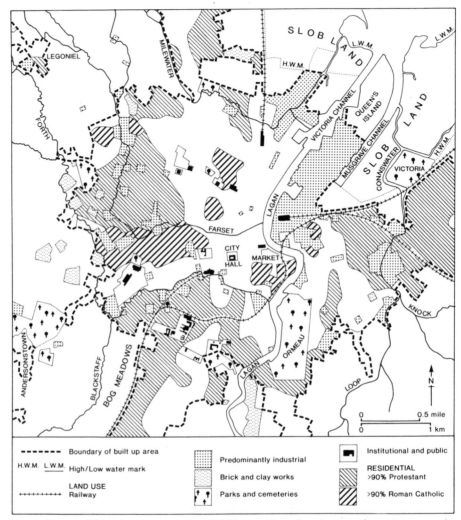

Fig. 8.3. The suburban growth of Belfast during the nineteenth century.

(Catholic-headed households lived in property of a mean value of £6 6s 0d compared to the Protestant-headed mean of £9 19s 0d), and industrial employment. Finally, their data on social class (Table 8.7) demonstrate that Catholics were more predominant in the lower status groups. These inequalities thus added a sectarian dimension to a socio-spatial pattern which was otherwise essentially similar to those Lawton and Pooley have identified in contemporary industrial cities of similar size in Britain.[64]

These sectarian inequalities, combined with the more normative patterns of residential segregation, might help to explain the periodic bouts of sectarian rioting which afflicted Belfast, this 'seat of mischief'.[65] Another source of sectarian rivalry was the two groups' mutual intolerance of each other's political aspirations—Home Rule was a sensitive issue in this divided city. Riots occurred in 1852, 1864, 1872, 1880, 1884, 1886, 1889, 1901 and from 1920 to 1922 over the issue of Partition.

Table 8.7: Social class by religion, Belfast 1901: male household heads (%).

	Catholic	Other denominations	Great Britain 1911
Classes I and II	13	13	15
Class III (non-manual)	8	12	7
Class III (manual)	31	35	33
Classes IV and V (semi-, unskilled)	44	36	45
Not classified	4	4	—
N =	897	3153	—

Source: Hepburn and Collins, 1981.[61]

However, on rare occasions the working class would unite in common cause as in the 1907 dock strike. The strike's leader, James Larkin, 'looked first to Belfast and then to Dublin to organise Ireland's more poorly-paid workers'.[66]

Throughout the second half of the nineteenth century, Belfast's municipal government was firmly in the hands of the Conservative and thus Unionist, and to some extent, Anglican and industrial interests. Notable industrialists who served as Mayor were Andrew Mulholland and Sir Edward Harland. O'Leary notes that after the Irish Reform Act of 1832, Belfast's two MPs were always Conservative apart from a brief spell in the 1830s and 1868 when a Liberal was elected.[67] The first municipal election after the Irish Municipal Corporation Act of 1840 saw all 40 seats in Conservative hands. However, O'Leary notes that the corporation tended to be as reform minded as equivalent Liberal administrations in British cities. Thus, although the completion of a satisfactory water supply was long delayed and Belfast's public health record was not comparable to English cities such as Birmingham, the city's housing record, thanks to the by-laws of 1848 and 1878, was good. Indeed, partly due to a considerable period of speculative building in the 1880s and 1890s, most Belfast families were able to live in their own (rented) house. The houses were mainly terraced but, even so, accommodation was far superior to that available for equivalent social groups in Dublin or Glasgow. Belfast even ended the century in a burst of civic pride. In a manner reminiscent of English industrial towns, an extravagant 'Civic Temple' in the form of the City Hall was laid out in 1906 on the site of the White Linen Hall.

In addition to taking on civic political duties, many industrialists also served as Harbour Commissioners. This was another reformist body and the help it gave to the continued development of Belfast's port was very important. Having a major port on the doorstep was of considerable benefit to Belfast industrialists, and gave an impetus to their economic activity which has sometimes been overlooked.[68]

Nor should the role of landownership in Belfast's development be disregarded. As Carter and Lewis note, landowners could exert considerable influence over the process of urban development by releasing or retaining land, or by inserting restrictive covenants into their building leases.[69] In the early nineteenth century Belfast was the property of the Marquis of Donegall. Ballymacarrett belonged to Lord Templemore, a cousin of the Donegalls and also a member of the Chichester family to whom the land of Belfast had been granted in the early seventeenth century. When the 5th Earl of Donegall (later the 1st Marquis) inherited Belfast in 1757 it was in poor condition, but he was a caring landowner and made many much needed improvements to the town. By granting leases requiring the erection of high quality buildings, he also improved its appearance. His eldest son, who inherited Belfast as the 2nd Marquis, exerted less control. As a young man he had accumulated a massive personal debt of at least £200,000. Consequently from 1822 onwards, he began to sell the leases of plots in and around Belfast at fixed rents and in perpetuity, thus sacrificing future income for ready money. After the death of the 2nd Marquis in 1844, it was discovered that most of the money raised by the sale of Belfast had been spent on his house and estate at Ormeau in the east of the city, and the 3rd Marquis was consequently obliged to raise more cash to clear the debts. This was achieved by the sale of almost all the remainder of the Belfast holdings, mainly through the mechanism of the Encumbered Estates Court. Purchasers of the leases could build what and how they liked, guided only by the local by-laws, and thus Victorian Belfast took on its rather crowded, unplanned and incoherent built form. In Ballymacarrett, Lord Templemore began building his planned industrial suburb in the late 1840s. However, after the eponymous Templemore Avenue was built, this plan was abandoned probably because of the cost involved and east Belfast, too, was allowed to develop with few constraints.[70]

The transformation of Belfast's socio-spatial structure was more typical of that of other north European towns during the nineteenth century. Thus, a gradual change in status distribution occurred as the urban wealthy moved out of their original central locations[71] to peripheral high-status wedges to the north or south of the city or on its eastern edge.[72] The inner east and the west of the city became working class with great wedges of industrial housing along the (Protestant) Shankill and (Catholic) Falls, which even by 1901 stretched away towards the city's natural western limits at the foot of the Antrim plateau (Fig. 8.3).

Other Ulster Towns

Industry developed in other Ulster towns, especially Londonderry where the local production of 'Coleraines'—half bleached cloths ⅞ yard wide and suitable for good quality shirtmaking—was associated with the rise of that industry. In the 1870s, some 4000–5000 workers were employed in 12 shirtmaking factories in the city, together with an additional 15,000 rural outworkers who made up the garments.[73] By 1902 Londonderry had 38 factories and 80,000 employees.[74] In his classification of Ulster towns, Clarkson lists Lurgan, Gilford, Ballyclare and Ballymena as additional manufacturing centres.[75] Such towns needed good access to raw materials and markets to enable their industry to flourish. Consequently, the development of transport facilities went hand in hand with Ulster's industrialization, and Ballymoney, Cookstown, Omagh and Portadown developed as railway centres. The coming of the railway was of considerable importance, too, in the development of the late Victorian or Edwardian seaside resorts such as Bangor, Bundoran, Newcastle and Portrush. The growth of Belfast and Londonderry was also influenced by railway development, and, as at Coleraine and Larne, by their port facilities. However, two towns were left behind by these improvements in transport technology. Newry's pre-eminence in the canal age which had given the town the vitality that so impressed W. M. Thackeray in 1843, was not maintained into the railway era.[76] By contrast, Donaghadee was a failed ferry port, its service to Portpatrick which had started in 1825 being withdrawn in 1849, to be revived only briefly in the 1860s. To this day the town retains the impressive harbour built by the Rennies, father and son, from 1821 to 1837, although it is overlarge for present needs.[77] Finally, Clarkson's categorization also includes dormitory settlements, one example being Holywood, which served Belfast.

Industrial Villages and Paternalism

In Ulster, industrialization also gave rise to a number of functionally-specialized industrial villages. In some cases, these were planned and built on greenfield sites by entrepreneurs; others developed from pre-existing settlements. Macneice notes that most Ulster industrial villages were founded between 1830 and 1870. Prior to this, the Coulsons of Lisburn had built houses for their damask weavers and as early as 1784, John Barbour of Paisley had established the 'Plantation' at Hilden near Lisburn, which became the centre of production for Barbour's Threads.[78] Villages established in the mid nineteenth century included Annsborough near Castlewellan, built by the Murlands, Dunbarton near Gilford built by Dunbar McMaster and Company, and the Martins' village of Shrigley near Downpatrick, all in County Down. Sion Mills, Co. Tyrone, was built by the Herdmans from 1835, while Bessbrook, Co. Armagh, was a larger-scale model village and textile factory begun by the Richardsons in 1847. It attracted wide attention and might be seen as a forerunner of George Cadbury's model industrial village at Bourneville near Birmingham.

No single motivation can be identified for the building of so many places over a couple of generations. Macneice suggests that entrepreneurs were often stimulated by genuine religious or social motives, and wished to improve the lot of their workers in spiritual and moral as well as economic terms. Many provided schools, churches, reading rooms and recreational facilities within their developments. Macneice and Ollerenshaw both speak of the sense of community imbued in these villages.[79] The latter quotes Clarke's (1882) comment that Bessbrook 'has neither pawn shop, nor public house nor police office and seems to get on excellently well without any of these customary resources of civilization'.[80] However, it cannot be doubted that economic factors were of the first importance. These Ulster industrialists were usually making a sound investment, and Macneice implies that they received a return from capital invested in excess of the 4 per cent gained by Titus Salt from the building of Saltaire, his industrial suburb outside Bradford.

The successful development of an industrial village required a suitable labour supply, and this was true even of the proto-industrial period. Lockhart's work on the advertising of early industrial villages stresses this:

> the residence of weavers in a community stimulated demand for the services of tradesmen ... provided employment for spinners and created a sales outlet for ... agricultural produce.[81]

Lockhart reproduces newspaper advertisements from across Ireland seeking weavers to come and live in potential manufacturing centres. To attract such workers to these new industrial villages, particularly in the nineteenth century, when there were often many opportunities for skilled labour, the employer had to provide good housing. However, this also gave him an opportunity to exert a paternalistic influence over the behaviour of his labour force, perhaps for economic motives. Given good, employer-owned, housing, 'workers would be grateful and employers would reap the benefits of a sober and industrious work force with little desire to strike'.[82] In fact, this paternalism was essentially coercive, since it invariably limited the freedom of action of those exposed to it. Thus, in his discussion of the labour movement in Ulster, Patterson cites the example of Ligoniel in north-west Belfast, where the Ewart family had provided housing for their linen workers, but at a price:

> the negative aspects of paternalism were ... clear when an employee came into conflict with the firm, for to lose one's employment would also mean the loss of one's home.[83]

The Ewarts' paternalism extended into politics. Their workforce was encouraged to be loyal to the Conservative interests favoured by their employers. Other paternalists cited by Patterson included the Barbours of Hilden, near Lisburn, who built 350 houses for their workers, together with a primary school and a hall to provide rooms for lectures, reading and recreation. The Barbours were also amongst those employers who tried to manipulate their workforce for their own political aims, in their case to gain political power for themselves at Lisburn. Prior to the 1850s, the borough had been a 'typical' example of a safe Tory constituency, dominated by its local landlord, but in that decade, candidates from manufacturing families had taken the seat.[84] In the by-election of 1863, there was a renewed struggle between the old guard and these new men. As the local newspaper put it:

> The ... conservative candidate [E. W. Verner] belonged to an old-fashioned political family of the sort that had held seats in Protestant Ulster earlier in the century ... the Liberal candidate [J. D. Barbour of the Hilden family] was a radical Presbyterian textile manufacturer seeking ... to establish the despotism of the mill.[85]

The contest was bitter, dishonest and rumbustious although there were no deaths. Property was damaged and there were well-founded allegations of bribery, intimidation and assault on both sides. The Liberal interests kidnapped voters to Hilden; the Tories, to Belfast. The election itself had to be overseen by 362 police officers and 340 soldiers. Barbour, representing paternalistic capitalism and the Liberal party, probably in that order, won by 140 votes to 134 (the electorate was only 313). However, a parliamentary enquiry into the election campaign unseated him and a fresh election was ordered. This time another mill owner stood for the Liberals, while Verner again represented the Conservative landed interest. Verner won by 151 votes to 90 in a less disruptive contest. Nevertheless, the defeated Liberals petitioned Parliament anyway to try to have the result overturned. In the end it stood.[86]

Consideration of the literally bloody strife in Lisburn in 1863 is instructive, not just because of its portrayal of the unsophisticated state of urban industrial society in mid-century Ulster, but also as an example of the struggle for social and political control between the old order and the new men, the capitalists who were bringing change in so many ways to north-east Ireland.

Nineteenth Century Urbanism in the Rest of Ireland

Market Towns

Outside the north-east, most of nineteenth-century Ireland remained what it had long been, a rural area studded by a network of small agricultural service towns. The nature and role of these towns is becoming clearer as several have been scrutinized by the Royal Irish Academy's Irish Historic Towns Atlas project. The first fascicle, issued in 1986, was on Kildare, Co. Kildare, by John Andrews.[87] Others dealing with small market towns have included Bandon, Co. Cork,[88] and Kells, Co. Meath.[89] Connell's detailed work on nineteenth-century Navan, Co. Meath, is another source of information.[90] Commonalities in the experiences of these towns, which are spread widely across Ireland, can be identified and, by implication, can be applied to other market towns.

Table 8.8: Occupational structure Navan, Co. Meath, 1821 and 1901.

Occupation	1821		1901	
	1821	%	1901	%
Professional	42	3.9	187	10.7
Domestic services	157	14.5	290	16.6
Commercial	136[b]	12.5	126	7.2
Agriculture	56	4.8	167	9.5
Industry[a]	463	42.6	629	36.0
Unspecified (mostly labourers)	235	21.7	347	19.9
Total	1085		1746	

[a] 1821 189 Domestic boot/shoe, clothing;
     164 Domestic flax spinning, linen weaving.
   1901 More than 500 in manufacture; furniture and textiles.
[b] 1821 101 retailing; 35 hawkers.

Source: Adapted from Connell, 1978.[90]

Industry was never significant in Kildare, and in the other towns it tended to decline. Lace making lasted in Kells only from 1825 to 1851. Bandon's cotton mills had declined from their earlier importance in the late eighteenth century, and one founded in 1805 had turned to the manufacture of whiskey by 1825. Early in the century Bandon and its environs contained 2000 weavers, but by 1850 this number had fallen to less than 30, the industry being unable to compete against larger centres of production. The changes in Navan's occupational structure between 1821 and 1901 provides further evidence of industrial decline in many small towns (Table 8.8). Data for 1901 comes from the manuscript census returns of that year. This information is available for every town in Ireland but only in the case of Navan can the 1821 Census Enumerators' Books be used in comparison. These records have not survived for any other urban area.[91] The 1821 statistics conceal much underemployment, especially with regard to servants and industry, but it is clear that over the 80 year period, there was both a relative decline in industry and a rise in numbers of professionals, a growing proportion of whom were clergymen.

Surprisingly, perhaps, despite a growth in the number of specialist shops and a 50 per cent increase in shop numbers since 1821, the proportion of the town's work-force employed in commerce actually fell by 1901.

The built form of many small towns also changed during the nineteenth century, usually as the result of infilling and infrastructural improvements rather than outright expansion. The socio-spatial structure of many Irish market towns tended not only to be like one another, but also tended not to change very much during the century. Thus, the 1841 map of Kildare (Fig. 8.4), which records the highest valued buildings in the centre around the market place, bears considerable resemblance to the later town depicted by Andrews' analysis of the 1901 census housing returns. This identified houses in the central streets as having, on average, more rooms, less overcrowding and more out-offices than those further from the market place, although by 1901 there was also some good quality housing in the 'outer suburbs'. This pattern aptly describes the socio-spatial structure of Navan at that date.

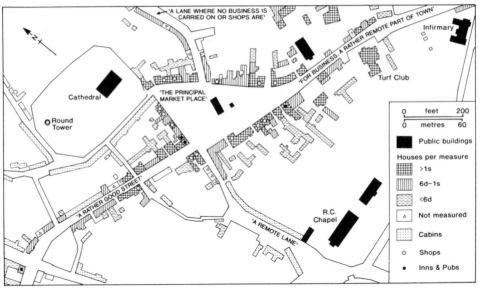

Fig. 8.4. Kildare in 1841 (After J. H. Andrews, 'Kildare', *Irish Historic Towns Atlas*, (Dublin, 1986) p. 5).

Finally, with regard to social control, we tend to find not the paternal capitalist control or attempted control of industrial towns like Lisburn, but increasingly power wielded by local government and the Roman Catholic Church. Socially, the growing role of the Catholic Church was notable in the small towns as many of them experienced an influx of Catholic residents during the nineteenth century. As the discussion in Chapter 6 demonstrates, however, this did not always involve a significant change in the sectarian composition of the urban community, although in towns such as Bandon, Co. Cork, which had remained under the active control of Protestant-dominated Corporations into the early nineteenth century, this did happen. Frequently, legislation had been passed in the seventeenth century deliberately excluding Catholics from living in central areas. In other towns, such as Dungarvan or Tallow, Co. Waterford, where the Corporation's authority had decayed at a much earlier date, nineteenth-century Catholic migration simply reinforced their already-existing numerical dominance.

Commercial Cities

In addition to the network of market towns, and situated at a higher level in the urban hierarchy, were a few large commercial towns and cities including Cork, Galway, Limerick and Waterford, which in addition to a marketing role, often possessed administrative and port functions. At the top of the Irish urban hierarchy, and leaving aside the north-east of the island which was dancing to a different, British, tune, was the capital, Dublin. Cork will be taken as an example of the commercial city and port, whilst Dublin will be considered in its own section.

Cork

In 1800, Cork's merchants and manufacturers expected the forthcoming Act of Union with Britain to bring increased prosperity to the city's commerce and manufacture.[92]

The optimism did not last long. Much of Cork's industrial and commercial activity was connected with the supply of provisions—butter, alcoholic beverages and other foodstuffs. With the ending of the Napoleonic Wars, there was a slump generally throughout the British Isles, exacerbated in Cork's case by the loss of naval provisioning contracts. In peacetime, the British navy did not need to be so large and, therefore, required less food. In addition, the city's textile manufacturing industry began to be hit by competition from the increasingly mechanized textile production of some other parts of the British Isles. Only Cork's role as the regional central place of the south, with retail, administrative, professional, legal, financial and educational services, helped to cushion the economic decline of this 'pork and butter salting provincial town'.[93]

Murphy quantifies this industrial decline and sets it against an increase in services, including transport, between 1841 and 1901 (Table 8.9).[94] The growing differences between Cork and Belfast are clear (Table 8.6). Cork was not and did not become an industrial city. In fact there was not just the relative decline of industrial jobs shown in Table 8.9. There was also an absolute decline, male jobs in industry falling from about 8000 to 4000 between 1841 and 1901, while female numbers declined from 3500 to 3200.[95] Some of the city's food processing industries kept up reasonably well, particularly distilling and brewing, but there was a quick turnover of small manufacturers in trades such as tailoring, whilst the textile industry fell away. This industrial specialism in the processing of locally-produced foodstuffs added to Cork's role as a regional central place. The nature and volume of the goods shipped through its port, and also through the outport at Queenstown, later Cobh, confirms that this was a commercial rather than an industrial city.

The growing numbers of middle class people engaged in this commerce had an effect upon the city's socio-spatial structure. Fahy notes that such people tended to

Table 8.9: Proportion of males and females employed in each occupational sector in Cork City (1841–1901) as a percentage of the total occupied male and total occupied female population.

	1841	1851	1861	1871	1881	1891	1901
Males							
Agriculture	9.99	7.94	3.64	3.78	3.98	3.15	2.86
Mining	0.07	0.37	0.03	0.10	0.12	0.10	0.18
Building	7.95	6.81	6.73	7.10	7.79	8.53	9.17
Manufacture	40.88	27.23	22.88	23.67	19.14	19.57	19.15
Transport	1.60	8.37	—	10.77	10.76	14.33	15.29
Dealing	10.29	10.51	9.31	10.75	11.22	11.95	11.47
Industrial service	18.50	27.56	31.32	25.81	25.59	18.51	23.22
Public service and professions	3.63	3.86	13.72	10.15	14.15	14.48	15.69
Domestic service	4.16	3.81	2.63	2.03	2.59	3.06	2.30
Indefinite	3.36	3.14	1.51	5.77	4.76	6.70	0.66
Females							
Agriculture	0.42	1.63	0.22	0.39	0.11	0.21	0.26
Manufacture	30.89	41.10	26.54	21.08	21.93	24.94	28.09
Transport	—	—	—	—	0.07	0.16	0.10
Dealing	13.68	16.23	17.75	14.85	11.85	14.14	19.01
Industrial service	0.99	1.60	1.92	1.49	0.77	1.02	0.25
Public service and professions	2.39	3.10	3.08	2.49	2.83	5.29	7.76
Domestic service	49.19	48.14	43.62	39.86	57.27	40.00	41.87

Source: Murphy, 1986.[94]

settle in the suburbs and commute by tram into the city centre.[96] The once elegant houses of the western city gradually filtered down to poorer people and were converted to multiple dwellings. By 1863, 'Cork had taken on much of the morphological character which it presents today'.[97]

There was little paternal industrial capitalism in Cork since the structure of the city's economy did not encourage this. Nor did the old landed interests dictate. Instead, Cork was dominated by its merchant class. Murphy notes that there was a growing acceptance that Cork's representation in national politics could be in the hands of men from outside the city, but in local politics, the merchant community remained dominant through its control of the Town Council (Table 8.10).[98] While this merchant domination remained a feature of the city's politics for most of the nineteenth century, its sectarian complexion changed. After the Famine, Catholic merchants began increasingly to dominate local political life at the expense of the Protestant oligarchy which had ruled during earlier years.[99] Only in the mid 1880s did the first signs of trade union dissatisfaction with the local council emerge, and it was not until 1898 that organized labour stood for local government. Even then they did not present any coherent political platform and won only seven out of 56 seats.[100]

Thus, change came to Cork in the nineteenth and early twentieth centuries, as it did to many places in Ireland. However, these developments did not alter the city's economy and appearance almost beyond recognition, as was the case with Belfast, once a functionally not-dissimilar regional market town and port. For, unlike Belfast, Cork did not industrialize, and in consequence its nineteenth-century development modified rather than obliterated its existing commercial role.

Table 8.10: Composition of the Cork Town Council, 1841–99.

	1841	1853	1863	1871	1883	1898	1899
Merchants	23	23	23	27	23	29	24
Retailers	10	5	3	3	3	4	5
Vintners	1	1	2	1	2	3	2
Master tradesmen	4	2	3	2	3	4	4
Legal and professional men	6	13	14	13	6	7	6
Gentlemen	4	4	6	8	7	4	5
Manufacturers	16	8	5	4	5	—	—
Journeymen	—	—	—	—	—	—	7
Others	—	—	—	2	7	5	3

Source: Murphy, 1979.[98]

Dublin

Like Cork, Dublin entered the nineteenth century in a well-placed position. Its population had trebled in the eighteenth century to reach around 180,000 by 1800, when it was the second city of the British Isles and one of the great cities of Europe. As Daly notes, Dublin had achieved the rare combination of being both a parliamentary and administrative centre, as well as an important industrial, commercial and banking centre and a major port.[101] In that respect it was comparable only to London within the British Isles, and was unlike all other Irish places. By the end of the nineteenth century, Dublin was by contrast not even the largest city in Ireland, having experienced a rate of urbanization from 1841 to 1911 which was below the Irish average, itself slow in European terms (Table 8.4).

The Act of Union of 1801 saw Dublin lose its Parliament to Westminster and was a prime cause of the city's relative decline. Many of the gentry who used to attend the Dublin Parliament migrated, taking with them their expenditure and the social activities which had been an important source of employment for other sectors in the city's population. In some cases, the housing they vacated ended up in the hands of religious orders or institutions. To the north of the Liffey in particular, it frequently degenerated into multiply-occupied tenements. The city did retain many administrative and central-place functions, but lost its financial pre-eminence in face of competition from the north of Ireland and England. In Ulster, the Belfast Bank, the Northern Bank and the Ulster Bank took on much of the local industrial business. The administrative integration of Ireland with Britain saw Dublin lose other financial activities to London. For example, the London Stock Exchange took over much Irish business. Two of the largest nineteenth-century Dublin industrial issues—Guinness (brewery) and Jacobs (biscuits)—were floated in London and not on the local Dublin exchange.[102] Further, many of the top jobs in the civil service, commerce and railways were taken by immigrants from Britain, even as Irish migrants were pouring out of the island.

Another early-nineteenth-century factor in the city's decline was the loss of its role in shipping Ulster linen exports. It ceased to be the financial and organizational centre for that industry when Belfast and the other Ulster towns and ports took on more responsibility for all aspects of the trade. However, some compensation came from the city's role as the hub of Irish railways. This, combined with the local processing of food and drink for export, led to a steady growth in the port's traffic until the mid-1870s. However, by the end of the century this had lost ground to Belfast as that city's major industrial growth spurt sent its port's tonnage figures up.

Unlike Belfast, Dublin did not experience much industrialization during the nineteenth century. The absolute number of skilled workers in manufacturing actually fell from 1851 to 1891. The increase in their numbers by 1911 was more a reflection of the city's boundary extension, which inflated the Dublin's total by including artisans living in the suburbs. In relative terms, the proportion of skilled workers fell from 35 per cent of the total workforce in 1851 to only 22 per cent in 1911. This decline reflected the existence of alternative employment opportunities elsewhere, in North America, Great Britain and locally, in Ulster. Consequently, it is likely that Dublin entrepreneurs would have faced problems in recruiting suitable labour even if they had tried to industrialize on the British model. It is significant that the industrial sectors of the economy that did thrive in the nineteenth century were all connected with food processing, and relied on local sources for many raw materials and a ready market in, rather than competition from, the much larger British economy. Firms such as Guinness, Jacobs, and Jameson's and other distillers were capital rather than labour intensive. They did not provide many jobs despite the value of their output. Guinness had a capital value of £7 millon in the early twentieth century but employed only 2500 manual workers who, with the exception of the coopers, were mostly unskilled.[103] Jacobs employed mainly female labour. Nor did distilling or brewing produce much ancillary work. Their requirements were limited except for items such as bottles and some engineering needs. Thus unlike Belfast's linen and shipbuilding staples, in Dublin vertical industrial linkages were not set up. Where integration and free trade with Britain led to competition rather than complementarity, as with Dublin's tanning or textile industries, the smaller economy of the Irish city inevitably suffered.

Table 8.11: Mortality rates from contagious diseases, 1851 census of population, Dublin.

	Deaths per thousand people		
Census ranking of streets	Cholera	Fever	Consumption
1st class private: south	0.9	3.4	12.3
1st class private: north	1.3	2.0	11.8
2nd class private: south	4.5	7.0	21.1
2nd class private: north	4.1	7.6	18.8
1st class shop: south	3.3	4.8	12.8
1st class shop: north	3.3	2.8	17.8
2nd class shop: south	9.5	9.5	28.5
2nd class shop: north	6.3	7.7	28.5
3rd class shop: south	8.8	11.8	31.5
3rd class shop: north	8.1	12.2	33.3
Mixed streets: south	6.1	8.6	23.8
Mixed streets: north	6.4	7.4	23.7

Private: residential streets.
Shop: commercial and tradesmen's streets.
Mixed: 'small shops and the private residence of the middle classes'.
Source: Martin, 1988.[107]

Table 8.12: Death rates per 1000: Dublin and selected English cities.

	a 1864–80	b 1895–1904	% decline a–b
Dublin City	31.6	28.2	10.75
Dublin City and suburbs	29.6	25.3	14.5
London	23.4	18.2	28.6
Liverpool	29.3	23.2	20.8

Source: Tabulated from Daly, 1979,[109] and Lampard, 1973.[108]

Table 8.13: Dublin City accommodation quality 1841–1911.

	First class[a]		Second class[b]		Third class[c]		Fourth class[d]		
	Numbers	%	Numbers	%	Numbers	%	Numbers	%	Total
1841	5605	11.3	8412	17.0	12,297	24.8	23,197	46.8	49,511
1851	5604	9.7	9345	16.3	14,330	25.0	28,039	48.9	57,318
1861	5158	8.8	9815	16.8	16,163	27.7	27,290	46.7	58,426
1871	5033	8.6	10,523	18.0	16,819	28.8	25,952	44.5	58,327
1881	4692	8.4	11,013	19.8	16,660	29.9	23,360	14.9	55,725
1891	4694	9.1	13,279	25.6	14,536	28.0	19,342	37.3	51,851
1901[e]	4635	7.8			33,199	56.0	21,429	36.2	59,263
1911	4599	7.4			37,202	59.7	20,564	33.0	62,365

[a] First class accommodation was one family in a first class house. A first class house had 10 or more rooms.
[b] Second class accommodation was one family in a second class house (5–9 rooms with windows), or 2–3 families in a first class house.
[c] Third class accommodation was one family in a third class house (2–4 rooms with windows), 2–3 families in a second class house; or 4–5 families in a first class house.
[d] Fourth class was one or more families in a fourth class house (one room with window); 2 or more in a third class house; 4 or more in a second class house; more than 6 in a first class house.
[e] Second and third class houses were combined.

Source: Adapted from Daly, 1979.[108]

Thus like Cork but unlike Belfast, Dublin was a commercial city in the nineteenth and early twentieth centuries. In 1911 only three of the 26 members of its Chamber of Commerce were manufacturers, and its Corporation was dominated by tradesmen such as grocers and publicans.[104] The migration of the wealthy to the southern suburbs outside Dublin city proper, and their consequent withdrawal from city politics, also had an effect on the composition of the council. Their movement had left the city predominantly working class, Roman Catholic and nationalist, in contrast to suburbs such as Rathmines and Pembroke which were wealthier, more Protestant and more conservative. As a result the Corporation had to manage what became a very poor population and had few resources with which to do so. Dublin's income, largely from rates, was 'remarkably modest' compared to British cities.[105] Financial problems were exacerbated by the fact that by its very poverty, the city and its ratepayers had to support many workhouse inmates. This was a burden which the rich suburbs were spared, to the benefit of their already wealthier ratepayers. In 1872 the total rate in north Dublin city was 9s 3d in the pound, compared to only 4s 0d in Rathmines. Daly comments that the late-nine-

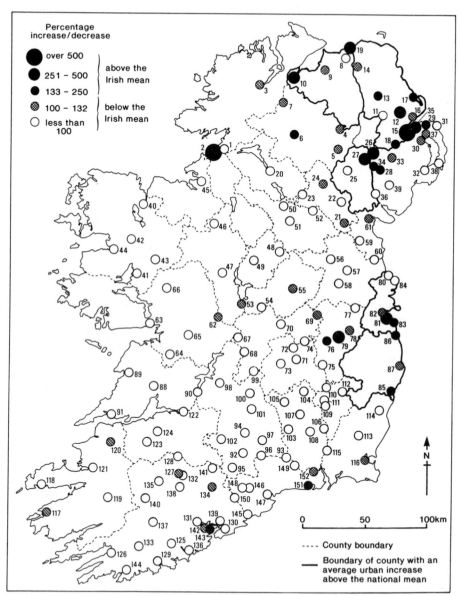

Fig. 8.5. The population of Irish towns in 1911 expressed as a percentage of their 1841 population.

Co. Donegal: 1, Ballyshannon; 2, Bundoran; 3, Letterkenny.

Co. Tyrone: 4, Cookstown; 5, Dungannon; 6, Omagh; 7, Strabane.

Co. Londonderry: 8, Coleraine; 9, Limavady; 10, Londonderry.

Co. Antrim: 11, Antrim; 12, Ballyclare; 13, Ballymena; 14, Ballymoney; 15, Belfast; 16, Carrickfergus; 17, Larne; 18, Lisburn; 19, Portrush.

Co. Fermanagh: 20, Enniskillen.

Co. Monaghan: 21, Carrickmacross; 22, Castleblaney; 23, Clones; 24, Monaghan.

Co. Armagh: 25, Armagh; 26, Lurgan; 27, Portadown.

Co. Down: 28, Banbridge; 29, Bangor; 30, Comber; 31, Donaghadee; 32, Downpatrick; 33, Dromore; 34, Gilford; 35, Holywood; 36, Newry; 37, Newtownards; 38, Portaferry; 39, Rathfriland.

Co. Mayo: 40, Ballina; 41, Ballinrobe; 42, Castlebar; 43, Claremorris; 44, Westport.

Co. Sligo: 45, Sligo.

Co. Roscommon: 46, Boyle; 47, Roscommon.

Co. Longford: 48, Granard; 49, Longford.

Co. Cavan: 50, Belturbet; 51, Cavan; 52, Cootehill.

Co. Westmeath: 53, Athlone; 54, Moate; 55, Mullingar.

Co. Meath: 56, Kells; 57, Navan; 58, Trim.

Co. Louth: 59, Ardee; 60, Drogheda; 61, Dundalk.

Co. Galway: 62, Ballinasloe; 63, Galway; 64, Gort; 65, Loughrea; 66, Tuam.

King's Co./Offaly: 67, Banagher; 68, Birr; 69, Edenderry; 70, Tullamore.

Queen's Co./Laois: 71, Maryborough/Portlaoise; 72, Mountmellick; 73, Mountrath; 74, Portarlington.

Co. Kildare: 75, Athy; 76, Kildare; 77, Maynooth; 78, Naas; 79, Newbridge.

Co. Dublin: 80, Balbriggan; 81, Blackrock; 82, Dublin; 83, Kingstown/Dun Laoghaire; 84, Skerries.

Co. Wicklow: 85, Arcklow; 86, Bray; 87, Wicklow.

Co. Clare: 88, Ennis; 89, Ennistymon; 90, Killaloe; 91, Kilrush.

Co. Tipperary: 92, Cahir; 93, Carrick-on-Suir; 94, Cashel; 95, Clogheen; 96, Clonmel; 97, Fethard; 98, Nenagh; 99, Roscrea; 100, Templemore; 101, Thurles; 102, Tipperary.

Co. Kilkenny: 103, Callan; 104, Castlecomer; 105, Freshford; 106, Graiguenamanagh; 107, Kilkenny; 108, Thomastown.

Co. Carlow: 109, Bagenalstown/Muine Bheag; 110, Carlow; 111, Leighlinbridge; 112, Tullow.

Co. Wexford: 113, Enniscorthy; 114, Gorey; 115, New Ross; 116, Wexford.

Co. Kerry: 117, Cahirciveen; 118, Dingle; 119, Killarney; 120, Listowel; 121, Tralee.

Co. Limerick: 122, Limerick; 123, Newcastle; 124, Rathkeal.

Co. Cork: 125, Bandon; 126, Bantry; 127, Buttevant; 128, Charleville/Rath Luirc; 129, Clonakilty; 130, Cloyne; 131, Cork; 132, Doneraile; 133, Dunmanway; 134, Fermoy; 135, Kanturk; 136, Kinsale; 137, Macroom; 138, Mallow; 139, Midleton; 140, Millstreet; 141, Michelstown; 142, Passage West; 143, Queenstown/Cobh; 144, Skibbereen; 145, Youghal.

Co. Waterford: 146, Cappoquin; 147, Dungarvan; 148, Lismore; 149, Portlaw; 150, Tallow; 151, Tramore; 152, Waterford.

teenth-century campaign to widen the municipal boundaries was not just a competitive desire to become bigger than Belfast again, but was also a financial necessity.[106]

Two interlinked social problems, themselves associated with the city's poverty, were housing and health. In each case the districts to the north of the Liffey and the Liberties suffered particular difficulties. Martin neatly links these two issues by comparing the mortality figures from certain contagious diseases, collected by Sir William Wilde's special report to the 1851 census, with a social ranking of Dublin streets also made at that census (Table 8.11).[107] While the generally wealthier south of the city did not stand out as being particularly healthier, the comparison between the classes of street is clear with death rates increasing as status decreased. This analysis looks within Dublin; others have compared the city's health record with that of different cities (Table 8.12).[108] The gap between Dublin mortality levels and those of major English cities actually widened between the mid and late nineteenth century, despite the fact that it should have been easier to reduce Dublin's figures given their higher initial levels. Dublin's health and sanitary legislation was the equivalent of English measures at this period.

Table 8.13 reworks Daly's figures for Dublin housing in the period between 1841 and 1911.[109] The dreadfully overcrowded conditions in which huge numbers of Dublin families lived is clearly revealed. The poorest conditions and most overcrowding occurred in the tenemented Georgian houses of the north bank of the Liffey. Despite the activities of bodies such as the Dublin Artisans Dwelling Company, who provided 3300 dwellings for 16,000 tenants of their chosen artisan class from 1870 to 1908, and the substantial activities of the Guinness/Iveagh Trust, the improvement in housing conditions was very slow. Just before the turn of the century, the Corporation had to join in to provide subsidized housing. By 1914 in multi-storey blocks as large as and next to those of the Iveagh Trust near the cathedrals, and elsewhere, the Corporation had housed around 7500 people, 2.5 per cent of the total population, and a proportion higher than that housed by the local authorities in London or Glasgow. Combining the corporation and philanthropic housing schemes, 18.7 per cent of the total city housing stock was subsidized by 1914, but the extent of the housing problem which remained at that time is evident from Table 8.13.[110]

Conclusions

The summation of Ireland's urban experience from 1841 to 1911 is presented in Fig. 8.5, which shows the 1911 urban populations expressed in terms of their 1841 equivalents. The majority of Irish towns not only failed to match the ponderous rate of mean Irish urbanization, which by 1911 saw a town grow to 133 per cent of its 1841 size, a mean annual growth of 0.47 per cent, but failed to grow at all and were smaller in 1911 than at the pre-Famine census of 1841. In most cases, as the population of the rural hinterland emptied, so the population of their agricultural service towns fell too. Only 12 of the 32 counties had any towns with a growth rate above the mean. The two towns with above average growth rates in the southern counties of Cork and Waterford were coastal, and the business that enabled Queenstown to grow was the export of Irish people to urbanize other countries.

Otherwise, apart from the late spectacular growth of Bundoran, Co. Donegal, as a resort for Ulster trippers, all the towns growing at above the mean, and all five counties which urbanized generally at above average rates, were in the east of Ireland. They fell into two clusters. Around Dublin, towns such as Bray, another seaside resort, and the ferry port at Kingstown, later Dun Laoghaire, grew. The city itself, like other commercial centres such as Cork, Limerick and Galway, failed to grow at the average rate. The second and more substantial cluster was in Ulster, reflecting with precision the only area of Ireland to industrialize. The most rapidly growing town, except for Bundoran, was Belfast. This city's surrounding industrial, transport and resort towns also stand out. The Ulster towns that did not develop included old market towns and central places that failed to acquire much industry, such as Downpatrick, Armagh and the Fermanagh and Monaghan towns. Thus, Fig. 8.5 encapsulates much of nineteenth- and early-twentieth-century Irish settlement geography, with its depiction of a declining rural economy associated with the loss of population at and after the Famine, contrasted with extensive urbanization based around the commerce of Dublin, and more particularly, the industrialization of Belfast and eastern Ulster.

References

1. A. F. Weber, *The Growth of Cities in the Nineteenth Century*, (New York, 1899).
2. T. Kemp, *Industrialisation in Nineteenth Century Europe*, (2nd Edn, London, 1985).
3. P. N. Stearns, *European Society in Upheaval: Social History Since 1750*, (New York, 1975).
4. Weber, *The Growth of Cities*, p. 158.
5. R. Kane, *The Industrial Resources of Ireland*, (Dublin, 1845).
6. *Ibid.*, p. 59.
7. J. M. Mokyr, 'Industry and poverty in Ireland and the Netherlands', *Journal of Interdisciplinary History*, **X** (1980), pp. 429–58.
8. Kane, *Industrial Resources*, p. 69.
9. *Ibid.*, p. 387.
10. *Ibid.*, Chapter 10.
11. *Ibid.*, p. 402; p. 423.
12. *Ibid.*, p. 408
13. *Ibid.*, p. 426.
14. E. L. Almquist, 'Labour specialisation and the Irish economy in 1841 an aggregate occupational analysis', *Economic History Review*, **XXXVI** (1983), pp. 506–17.
15. C. Ó'Gráda, *Ireland Before and After the Famine: Explorations in Economic History 1860–1925*, (Manchester, 1988).
16. D. Fitzpatrick, 'The disappearance of the Irish agricultural labourer 1841–1912', *Irish Economic and Social History*, **VII** (1980), pp. 66–92.
17. *Ibid.*, p. 74.
18. C. Booth, 'Occupations of the people of the United Kingdom 1801–1881', *Journal of the Royal Statistical Society*, **XLIX** (1886), pp. 314–444; C. Booth, 'The economic distribution of population', in Department of Agriculture and Technical Instruction for Ireland, *Ireland, Industrial and Agricultural*, (Dublin, 1901), pp. 54–62
19. *Ibid.*, p. 56.
20. *Ibid.*, p. 58.
21. Mokyr, 'Industry and poverty in Ireland'.
22. *Ibid.*, pp. 449–450.
23. Weber, *The Growth of Cities*.

24. Mokyr, 'Industry and poverty in Ireland', p. 450.
25. D. N. Doyle, 'The Irish in Australia and the US: some comparisons 1800–1939', *Irish Economic and Social History*, **XVI** (1989), pp. 73–94.
26. L. A. Clarkson, 'Population change and urbanisation 1821–1911', in L. Kennedy and P. Ollerenshaw (eds.), *An Economic History of Ulster 1820–1939*, (Manchester, 1985), pp. 137–58.
27. P. Ollerenshaw, 'Industry 1820–1914', *Ibid.*, pp. 62–108.
28. W. H. Crawford, 'The evolution of the linen trade in Ulster before industrialisation', *Irish Economic and Social History*, **XV** (1988), pp. 32–51.
29. J. Bardon, *Belfast: an Illustrated History*, (Belfast, 1982).
30. L.A. Clarkson and B. Collins, 'Proto-industrialisation in an Irish town: Lisburn, 1820–21', in *VIIIe Congrès International D'Histoire Economique, Section A2: La protoindustrialisation: théorie et réalitié*, (Budapest, 1982).
31. *Ibid.*, pp. 1–2.
32. L. Kennedy, 'The rural economy 1820–1914', in Kennedy and Ollerenshaw (eds.), *An Economic History of Ulster*, pp. 1–61.
33. Crawford, 'The evolution of the linen trade in Ulster'.
34. F. Geary, 'The Belfast cotton industry revisited', *Irish Historical Studies*, **XXVI** (1989), p. 250.
35. Bardon, *Belfast*.
36. Kennedy, 'The rural economy 1820–1914'.
37. *Ibid.*
38. Crawford, 'The evolution of the linen trade in Ulster', p. 51.
39. F. Geary, 'The rise and fall of the Belfast cotton industry: some problems', *Irish Economic and Social History*, **VIII** (1981), pp. 30–49; J. Butt, 'Belfast and Glasgow: connections and comparisons, 1790–1850', in T. M. Devine and D. Dickson (eds.), *Ireland and Scotland 1600–1850; Parallels and Contrasts in Economic and Social Development*, (Edinburgh, 1983), pp. 193–203.
40. Geary, 'The Belfast cotton industry revisited', p. 266.
41. Bardon, *Belfast*.
42. S. A. Royle, M. E. Pringle and F. W. Boal, 'New information on the development of Ballymacarrett: Lord Templemore's plan of 1853', *Ulster Journal of Archaeology*, **46** (1983), pp. 137–42.
43. R. Sweetnam and C. Nimmons, *Port of Belfast 1785–1985*, (Belfast, 1985).
44. M. D. Thomas, 'Manufacturing industry in Belfast, Northern Ireland', *Annals of the Association of American Geographers*, **XLVI** (1956), pp. 177–96; R. Sweetnam, 'The development of the port', in J. C. Beckett *et al.* (eds.), *Belfast: the Making of the City*, (Belfast, 1983), pp. 57–70; M. Moss and J. R. Hume, *Shipbuilders to the World: 125 Years of Harland and Wolff 1861–1986*, (Belfast, 1986); F. W. Boal and S. A. Royle, 'Belfast: boom, blitz and bureaucracy', in G. Gordon (ed.), *Regional Cities in the United Kingdom 1890–1980*, (London, 1986), pp. 191–215.
45. F. Geary and W. Johnson, 'Shipbuilding in Belfast 1861–1986', *Irish Economic and Social History*, **XVI** (1989), pp. 42–64.
46. L. M. Cullen, *An Economic History of Ireland Since 1660*, (2nd Edn, London, 1987).
47. Boal and Royle, 'Belfast: boom, blitz and bureaucracy'.
48. B. Messenger, *Picking Up the Linen Threads: A Study in Industrial Folklore*, (Belfast, 1978).
49. H. Patterson, 'Industrial labour and the labour movement 1820–1914', in Kennedy and Ollerenshaw (eds.), *An Economic History of Ulster*, pp. 158–183.
50. Ollerenshaw, 'Industry 1820–1914', p. 62.
51. W. Black, 'Industrial change in the twentieth century', in J. C. Beckett and R. E. Glasscock (eds.), *Belfast: the Origins and Growth of an Industrial City*, (London, 1967), pp. 157–168.
52. A. C. Hepburn, *The Conflict of Nationality in Modern Ireland*, (London, 1980).
53. K. S. Isles and N. Cuthbert, 'Industries', in British Association, *Belfast in its Regional Setting*, (Belfast, 1952), p. 149.
54. Geary and Johnson, 'Shipbuilding in Belfast 1861–1986'.

55. Thomas, 'Manufacturing industry in Belfast'.
56. Cited in T. W. Freeman, 'Irish towns in the Eighteenth and Nineteenth Centuries', in R. A. Butlin (ed.), *The Development of the Irish Town*, (London, 1978), p. 124.
57. *Ibid.*
58. Geary and Johnson, 'Shipbuilding in Belfast 1861–1986'.
59. Moss and Hume, *Shipbuilders to the World*.
60. Bardon, *Belfast*, p. 128.
61. A. C. Hepburn and B. Collins, 'Industrial society: the structure of Belfast 1901', in P. Roebuck (ed.), *Plantation to Partition*, (Belfast, 1981), p. 208.
62. E. Jones, 'Belfast: a survey of the city', in British Association, *Belfast*, p. 203.
63. E. Jones, 'The distribution and segregation of Roman Catholics in Belfast', *Sociological Review*, New Series, **IV** (1956), pp. 167–89.
64. Hepburn and Collins, 'Industrial society'; R. Lawton and C. Pooley, *Britain 1740–1950. An Historical Geography*, (London, 1992), pp. 187–192, 205–209.
65. A 1796 comment cited in S. Gribbon, 'An Irish city: Belfast 1911', in D. Harkness and M. O'Dowd (eds.), *The Town in Ireland: Historical Studies*, **XIII** (Belfast, 1981), p. 217.
66. *Ibid.*, p. 208.
67. C. O'Leary, 'Belfast urban government in an age of reform', in Harkness and O'Dowd (eds.), *The Town in Ireland*, pp. 187–202.
68. Gribbon, 'An Irish city: Belfast 1911'.
69. H. Carter and C. R. Lewis, *An Urban Geography of England and Wales in the Nineteenth Century*, (London, 1990). pp. 151–2.
70. W. A. Maguire, 'The 1822 settlement of the Donegall estates', *Irish Economic and Social History*, **III** (1976), pp. 16–32; W. A. Maguire, 'Lord Donegall and the sale of Belfast: a case history from the Encumbered Estates Court', *Economic History Review*, **XXIX** (1976), pp. 570–584; W. A. Maguire, 'Lords and landlords: the Donegall family', in Beckett *et al.* (eds.), *Belfast*, pp. 27–40; Royle, Pringle and Boal, 'Ballymacarrett'.
71. S. A. Royle, 'The socio-spatial structure of Belfast in 1837: evidence from the First Valuation', *Irish Geography*, **24** (1991), pp. 1–9.
72. E. Jones, *A Social Geography of Belfast*, (Oxford, 1960).
73. Ollerenshaw, 'Industry 1820–1914'.
74. See also Crawford, 'The evolution of the linen trade in Ulster'.
75. Clarkson, 'Population change and urbanization 1821–1911'.
76. W. M. Thackeray, *The Irish Sketch Book* (London, 1843).
77. W. A. McCutcheon, *The Industrial Archaeology of Northern Ireland*, (Belfast, 1980).
78. D. S. Macneice, 'Industrial villages of Ulster 1800–1900', in Roebuck (ed.), *Plantation to Partition*, pp. 172–90.
79. Ollerenshaw, 'Industry 1820–1914'.
80. *Ibid.*, p. 72.
81. D. G. Lockhart, 'The linen industry and the advertising of towns and villages in Ireland 1700–50', *Textile History*, **VIII** (1977), pp. 168–76.
82. Macneice, 'Industrial villages', p. 174.
83. Patterson, 'Industrial labour', pp. 175–6.
84. K. T. Hoppen, *Elections, Politics and Society in Ireland 1832–85*, (Oxford, 1984), p. 288.
85. *Belfast Telegraph*, 6 June 1863.
86. S. A. Royle, 'The Lisburn by-elections of 1863', *Irish Historical Studies*, **XXV** (1987), pp. 277–91.
87. J. H. Andrews, *Kildare*, Fascicle Number 1, Irish Historic Towns Atlas, Royal Irish Academy (Dublin, 1986).
88. P. O'Flanagan, *Bandon*, Fascicle Number 3, Irish Historic Towns Atlas, Royal Irish Academy (Dublin, 1988).
89. A. Simms and K. Simms, *Kells*, Fascicle Number 4, Irish Historic Towns Atlas, Royal Irish Academy (Dublin, 1990).
90. P. Connell, *Changing Forces Shaping a Nineteenth Century Irish Town: a Case Study of Navan*, Occasional Paper Number 1, Geography Department, St Patrick's College, (Maynooth, 1978).

91. S. A. Royle, 'Irish manuscript census records: a neglected source of information', *Irish Geography*, **11** (1978), pp. 110–26.

92. M. Murphy, 'Cork commercial society 1850–1899', in P. Butel and L. M. Cullen (eds.), *Cities and Merchants: French and Irish Perspectives on Urban Development, 1500–1900*, (Dublin, 1986), pp. 233–247.

93. J. Johnson, *A Tour in Ireland with Meditations and Reflections*, (London, 1844), p. 140 (cited in Murphy, 'Cork commercial society', p. 233). See also A. M. Fahy, 'Residence, workplace and patterns of change, Cork 1787–1863', in Butel and Cullen (eds.), *Cities and Merchants*, pp. 41–52.

94. Murphy, 'Cork commercial society', p. 233.

95. M. Murphy, 'The economic and social structure of nineteenth century Cork', in Harkness and O'Dowd (eds.), *The Town in Ireland*, pp. 125–55.

96. A. M. Fahy, 'The spatial differentiation of commercial and residential functions in Cork City 1787–1863', *Irish Geography*, **17** (1984), pp. 14–27; Fahy, 'Residence'.

97. *Ibid.*, p. 51.

98. Murphy, 'Nineteenth century Cork'.

99. J. B. O'Brien, 'Merchants in Cork before the Famine', in Harkness and O'Dowd (eds.), *The Town in Ireland*, pp. 221–32.

100. Murphy, 'Nineteenth century Cork'.

101. M. E. Daly, 'Dublin in the 19th century Irish economy', in Butel and Cullen (eds.), *Cities and Merchants*, pp. 53–65.

102. Daly, 'Dublin in the 19th century Irish economy'.

103. M. E. Daly, 'Late nineteenth and early twentieth century Dublin', in Harkness and O'Dowd (eds.), *The Town in Ireland*, pp. 221–56.

104. *Ibid.*

105. *Ibid.*, p. 235.

106. *Ibid.*

107. J. H. Martin, 'The social geography of mid 19th century Dublin city', in W. J. Smyth and K. Whelan (eds.) *Common Ground* (Cork, 1988), pp. 173–88.

108. Eric Lampard, 'The urbanising world', in H. J. Dyos and Michael Wolff (eds.), *The Victorian City: Image and Reality* (2 vols, London, 1973), I, pp. 13–41; see p. 21.

109. Daly, 'Late nineteenth and early twentieth century Dublin'.

110. *Ibid.*; F. H. Aalen, 'Approaches to the working class housing problem in late Victorian Dublin: the Dublin Artisans Dwelling Company and the Guinness (later Iveagh) Trust', pp. 161–184 in R. J. Bender (ed.) *Neuere Forschungen zur Sozialgeographie von Irland Mannheimer Geographische Arbeiten 17* (Mannheim, 1984), pp. 161–184; R. J. Bender, 'Sozialer Wohnungsbau und Stadtenwicklung in Dublin 1886–1986', *Mannheimer Geographische Arbeiten 31*, (Mannheim, 1991).

9

Rural Economies in Post-Famine Ireland, *c.* 1850–1914

Michael Turner

Introduction

This chapter examines the changes in Ireland's agricultural economy from the Famine of the 1840s until the onset of the First World War. However, some reference will be made to the pre-Famine inheritance and especially to the idea that many post-Famine features continued trends which already existed before the Famine. The agricultural economy of the later nineteenth century is discussed under three main headings: firstly, the working of the land, in which land use and livestock adjustments, the role of agricultural exports, and regional changes are explored; secondly, the occupation of the land, which looks at landholding and occupancy patterns and changes; and finally the product from the land, in which the performance of agriculture, measured by the gross value of output, is examined under a number of sub-headings. In each instance, previous statistical estimates are critically examined and new calculations offered. The chapter relates agricultural performance to ongoing debates about productivity, both within Ireland and in contrast to Great Britain. Finally, its conclusions concerning the distribution of income from agriculture to tenant farmers and their landlords support the argument which suggests that the political moves after 1880 towards greater Irish independence originated, in part, from the maldistribution of rewards from agriculture. Thus—combining its revised estimates of agricultural statistics and contrasting Ireland with Great Britain—the chapter questions the stance of revisionist historians who argue that tenant farmers achieved a relatively favourable position in late-nineteenth-century Irish agriculture.

   Three watersheds in Irish rural history are defined: the Famine; the depression of 1859–64; and the Land War period which followed the agricultural depression of 1879–82. The Famine is a thread which runs through the entire story. It was a traumatic event, but the recovery from it in terms of agricultural production and organization was remarkably rapid. The depression of the early 1860s was severe and, in terms of its permanent impression on the landscape, it marked the final turning point in the eclipse of the arable sector by livestock. But it was the depression of the early 1880s which had perhaps the most profound effect. As a result of it, by 1914 possibly one-half of Irish land was both farmed and owned by the Irish themselves and substantial economic independence from British and Anglo-Irish dominance had been gained.

Working the Land

Land Use

Ó Gráda's observation that by the end of the nineteenth century, 'the humble farmyard hen and duck were adding more to agricultural output than wheat, oats and potatoes combined, crops which in the early 1840s accounted for more than half of output', tells much of the story of post-Famine agricultural change.[1] The arable sector shrank, the animal sector expanded. The increase in ducks, hens and poultry does not measure this but highlights it. The more important changes involved the rise of cattle and milk. The country became greener, and while hay (meadow and clover) might be included under rotational crops and hence under tillage, ultimately most of the hay was intended for animal use. A doubling of the hay acreage, from 1.2 million acres in 1850 to over 2.4 million in 1910, readily expresses both the overall land-use changes and the movement towards animal husbandry and away from crops, especially away from cash crops. The acreage of hay and pasture increased from 9.995 million acres in 1851 to 12.08 million in 1881 and 12.42 million by the First World War. By contrast, the arable declined from 4.6 million acres in 1851 to 3.2 million in 1881 and 2.3 million by 1911.

Table 9.1 summarizes land use for each population census year from 1841 to 1911. Data for 1841 are included, but the criticism of these by Bourke must be noted.[2] The apparent increase of 10 per cent in cultivated land from *c.* 1841 to 1851 is not necessarily large, but the distribution of that change at the county level is so uneven as to be suspicious. Six counties (Dublin, Louth, Meath, Westmeath, Kilkenny and Roscommon) apparently experienced a fall in cultivated acres. These were by no means *all* remote counties or those which were at the sharp end of the Famine crisis. In 10 counties, apparently, the increase in the cultivated acreage was greater than the national average. In Donegal, Kerry and Mayo this amounted to 76, 49 and 30 per cent respectively, statistics hard to believe given the trauma of the 1840s and its known regional impact.[3] Such problems with the 1841 data have been attributed to anomalies in conducting the census, and to changes in the classification of marginal grazing land. It was in the counties where this type of land was most abundant that the differences were greatest.[4] When Bourke revised the 1841 estimates he added just 100,000 acres to the cultivated area from 1841 to 1851, as compared with the officially designated increase of 1.3 million acres.[5] On the revised basis there was no substantial overall change in the extent of the cultivated area during the Famine decade.

During the first 20 years or so after the Famine the total cultivated acreage rose. This was not merely a redistribution of existing agricultural land uses, but also involved the addition of previously uncultivated land. Subsequently there was a downturn which continued into the twentieth century. Given the backcloth of a severe decline in population from 6.552 million in 1851 to 4.39 million by 1911, and

Table 9.1: Ireland; the division of the land, 1841–1911.

Date	Crops	Hay	Grass	Woods and plantations	Grazed and barren mountain	Bog and marsh	Waste
In millions of acres							
1841	←	13.464	→	0.375	←	6.49	→
1851	4.613	1.246	8.749	0.305	←	5.416	→
1861	4.344	1.546	9.534	0.317	←	4.588	→
1871	3.792	1.829	10.071	0.352	←	4.311	→
1881	3.194	2.001	10.075	0.329	2.118	1.72	0.892
1891	2.759	2.06	10.299	0.312	2.211	1.744	0.949
1901	2.452	2.179	10.577	0.31	2.223	1.574	1.018
1911	2.349	2.512	9.847	0.3	3.084	1.198	1.061
Percentage distribution							
1841	←	66.2	→	1.8	←	31.9	→
1851	22.7	6.1	43.0	1.5	←	26.6	→
1861	21.4	7.6	46.9	1.6	←	22.6	→
1871	18.7	9.0	49.5	1.6	←	21.2	→
1881	15.7	9.8	49.6	1.6	10.4	8.5	4.4
1891	13.6	10.1	50.6	1.5	10.9	8.6	4.7
1901	12.1	10.7	52.0	1.5	10.9	7.7	5.0
1911	11.5	12.3	48.4	1.5	15.1	5.9	5.2

Subject to rounding errors.

Note: The 1911 figures are misleading when compared with other years because from 1906 there was a change in definitions. In 1911 there were 2.584 million acres of grazed mountain land much of which would formerly have been counted as grass.

Source: Agricultural Statistics of Ireland, 1911, British Parliamentary Papers, cd. 6377, (Dublin, 1912), pp. 2–3.

ignoring the fall directly associated with the Famine itself, the initial rise in the cultivated area may seem surprising.[6] However, it is readily explained. Even with a reduced population, pastoral farming was more land extensive than arable culti-vation. Although tillage production fell in the 50 or 60 years after the Famine, it did not fall as much for some crops as for others. The enhanced value of the root and green crops as animal feedstuffs, related to the growing emphasis on livestock production, kept tillage acreage high.[7]

Figure 9.1 summarizes the long-run trend in land use. Tillage includes hay since this was employed as a rotational crop. Exports of wheat, barley and oats to Britain had been at a peak in the 1830s and wheat at least continued to be an important export item up to and including 1845.[8] On the eve of the Famine wheat accounted for 11.5 per cent of Irish agricultural output by value, barley and oats contributed 4 and 19 per cent respectively, and wheat and flour exports constituted about 40 per cent of the net output of these products.[9] Bourke estimated that nearly 80 per cent of the domestic production of oats before the Famine was retained in Ireland. Therefore, although the export trade was important it did not overwhelm the home use of those crops. This has a bearing on any discussions about British economic imperialism, since the food deficiency at the time of the Famine, which was essentially the loss of the potato crop, could not have been met simply by prohibiting the export of grain. Clearly, the potato loss had been too great.[10]

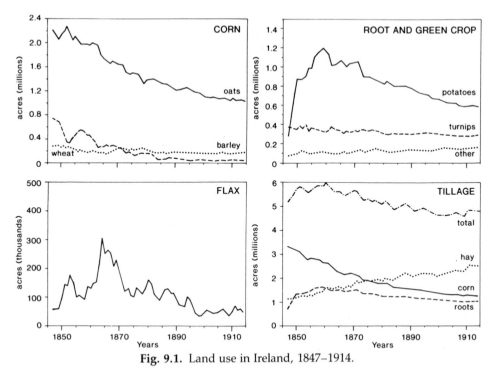

Fig. 9.1. Land use in Ireland, 1847–1914.

Perhaps 27 per cent of agricultural output was exported on the eve of the Famine.[11]

From around 1847 and into the 1850s, there was a clear move to increase the amount of arable land. Thereafter, the long-lasting impact of the Famine began to be realized. Wheat declined dramatically from half a million acres in 1851 to 150,000 by 1881, and settled at a modest 45,000 acres by 1911. At its lowest extent in 1904 it was just under 31,000 acres. The largest absolute decline of 157,000 acres took place in the 1860s. There was also a large decline in the acreage under oats.

The flax acreage rose from 58,000 acres in 1847 to 175,000 in 1853. This represented the recovery of an important cash crop to a once important cash industry. But from 1853 there was a decline until the 1860s, at which point the American Civil War seriously impeded cotton supplies to Britain, and the Irish flax/linen industry received a large, if short-lived, boost. The acreage rose to 302,000 acres in 1864, but thereafter dwindled, with some minor recoveries, to a low of 35,000 acres at the turn of the century and 50,000 by the First World War. However, the national importance of flax should not be exaggerated. It was rarely as large as 1 per cent of the total area of Ireland nor as much as 3 per cent of the cultivated area, and it was always heavily concentrated in Ulster. In 1851 all 32 counties had some flax, but by 1911 this had shrunk to 12. Of the 66,618 acres of flax in Ireland in 1911 there were just 49 in Leinster, 327 in Munster and 99 in Connacht, leaving 66,143 in Ulster.

Of the arable crops only mangels and cabbage increased in acreage, signalling the extended use of green crops for animal consumption. 'It is an old saying that without green crops there can be no cattle; and without cattle, no manure; and without manure, no corn.'[12] The final link in this circle of production became increasingly diluted over time. Before the Famine turnips had been a neglected crop. They were grown in quantity in 1847 as an emergency human food, and remained in cultivation afterwards at high levels, but as a fodder for livestock. They stood at nearly 400,000 acres in 1850 but declined steadily to about 270,000 in 1914.[13] Potatoes rose from 869,000 acres in 1851 to 1.134 million in 1861 before declining to 590,000 in 1911. The acreage had risen from 284,000 in 1847 to 719,000 in 1849, and again this had been a bid to return to some kind of pre-Famine norm before the long-term changes took effect. The bid finally failed, but by then the dependent population had declined considerably.

The importance of the potato in Irish history cannot be overstressed. Bourke in particular has written widely about it. His reconstruction of the pre-Famine potato acreage was derived from official returns produced as a reaction to the Famine crisis. These revealed potato acreages of 2.378 million acres in 1844, 2.516 million in 1845 and 1.999 million in 1846. Such acreages were never attained again in Ireland. These years represented just about the peak of potato cultivation with a probable actual peak in the early 1830s.[14] Because the potato is a key issue in debate in Irish history, various historians have questioned the precise extent of the crop. Crotty, for example, has challenged Bourke's estimates and suggested an alternative pre-Famine acreage of only 1.4 million acres.[15] Bourke stressed the likely confusion to the authorities as a result of the possible use of three different sizes of acre—the Statute, Irish and Cunningham.[16] The Irish and the Cunningham acres were equivalent to 1.62 and 1.29 Statute acres respectively. Bourke suggested that the Irish or plantation acre was the one in use for around 80 per cent of the time. Crotty's alternative assumption that Statute acres were in use inevitably means that his estimates were lower than Bourke's. Mokyr too has questioned Bourke's methods of reconstruction, and his assumptions and statistical procedures, and has settled for a pre-Famine potato acreage of 2.187 million acres.[17] It is sufficient to note here that the potato acreage never attained the pre-Famine levels after the famine had passed. But it did remain high, in spite of the large fall in human population, and this was because of the extension of animal husbandry and the use of potatoes as a feedstuff, especially for pigs.

The general decline in arable farming was partly due to the decline in population. This meant a decline in demand for arable products and consequently a decline in aggregate arable consumption. But in addition there was a general rise in the demand for meat and dairy products in western Europe, especially after the 1870s and particularly in England. This last factor was linked to the increase in the quantity of North American grain reaching western Europe at progressively lower prices from the 1870s, with the effect of improving working class real incomes. In England this led to the final demise of corn growing, but in Ireland the economy had already adjusted output, concentrating more on cash products other than wheat *before* the 1870s. This is partly because the decline in population had meant a decline in the supply of labour available for arable production at a time when that sector was still labour intensive. To some extent, therefore, the move into animal husbandry responded to this constraint.

Market and agricultural adjustments can be identified by an inspection of price relativities. Figure 9.2 compares crop and livestock prices, by dividing a livestock price by an index of crop prices. The resulting price relativity can be viewed as a terms of trade index. In the case illustrated in Fig. 9.2 the rising long-term trend meant that livestock prices advanced at a greater pace than crop prices (or declined less fast than crop prices). In short, the terms of trade moved pretty well in favour of the livestock sector, and it therefore made economic sense for farmers to adjust their output to livestock products.[18]

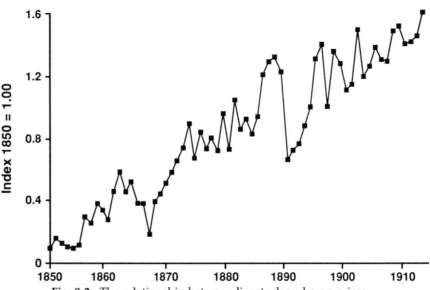

Fig. 9.2. The relationship between livestock and crop prices.

Crop Yields

A catalogue of acreage trends over time is only part of the story and should not lead us to suppose that there were parallel adjustments in output. Farmers are environmentalists. If they switch crops they are mindful of the suitability of the soil for those crops. The desertion from wheat and other grains in favour of other land uses tended to increase the long-term yields per acre, because land less suited to cereal cultivation was converted early, and therefore average yields of wheat, barley and oats naturally increased.[19] As the author of *The Agricultural Output of Northern Ireland* put it in 1925, 'the increase obtained in the average yield per acre had, in the case of a number of the crops, had the effect of neutralizing the decline in acreage' and this was 'particularly noticeable with oats, potatoes and turnips' (see Fig. 9.3).[20]

Post-Famine changes point to even higher pre-Famine yields brought about by spade labour with a large manual labour force, constantly weeding and hoeing, combined with prodigious applications of manure. Large potato acreages serviced a rising pig and bacon trade leading, in turn, to more manure and spade labour, and all the while weeds were kept in check. This was a crude, but effective and

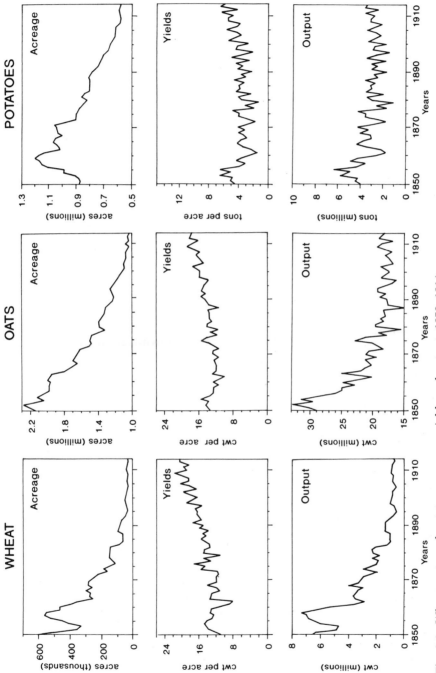

Fig. 9.3. Wheat, oats and potatoes: acreage, yields and output, 1850–1914.

expanding circle of pre-Famine land and labour productivity, which, however, could not be maintained in the post-Famine period. Less intensive agricultural practices took over, the plough replacing the spade while there was a decline in intensive manuring.[21] The result was that from about 1870 onwards, potato output reached its lowest point, perhaps for more than a century. If Bourke's estimates of potato acreages and yields at the time of the Famine are followed, much enhanced by spade cultivation and heavy manuring, we derive an estimated 14.8 million tons of potatoes from the 1844 crop, 10 million tons in 1845 but only 2.999 million tons in 1846. Yields recovered to 6.3 million tons in 1855, but the decennial average between the 1850s and the end of the century varied between only 2.6 and 4.7 million tons.[22]

Depression

The depression of 1859–64 was the first crisis to hit the Irish rural economy after the Famine. It began with a severe drought in the critical months of July to September 1859, when rainfall was 30–40 per cent below average. This was followed by unusually heavy rain between 1860 and 1862, years which became 'almost certainly the wettest three consecutive years of the entire nineteenth century in Ireland, with the significant exception of 1846–8.'[23] The year 1861 was especially bad because of the concentration of rain from July to September. Then in 1863 there was an unusually dry spring, and a drought which continued into the summer. When this broke in September the grain harvest had hardly begun. Finally, although the spring of 1864 brought luxuriant pastures, the following summer saw an intense drought in which the grasslands shrivelled and food for livestock was in severely short supply.

Thus for six seasons either grassland suffered with drought, or conversely the arable/fodder sector suffered from drought or, more particularly, heavy rain. Crop yields fell dramatically and the trend of declining corn acreages accelerated. Green and root crops and hay acreages were either stabilized or actually increased, accelerating the trend into livestock. Cash crop prices did not rise as might be expected during this supply shortfall because grain prices were influenced more by the larger British or even European market than by conditions in Ireland itself.[24] After an astronomical rise in 1859, the price of hay fell almost as dramatically in 1860. It settled down in the early 1860s at much the same level characteristic of the four years before the depression, although with a higher acreage. This stabilization of hay prices was beneficial for the livestock economy, as was the dramatic fall in potato prices in 1862–5. They had been at high levels in the previous two years precisely because of rain damage, which promoted the blight. Potato yields were reduced to between 42 and 61 per cent of the average yield of 1856–8 in each of the three years between 1860 and 1862.[25] Without potatoes, the pig population could not be sustained and their numbers fell from 1.1 million aged less than one year in 1858, to 858,000 in each of 1863 and 1864, but with an as yet incalculable mortality loss before maturity.[26]

The depression was deepened by other factors. The wet conditions had a bad effect on turf, which could not dry out. A severe fuel shortage ensued.[27] Coincidentally, the cotton famine resulting from the United States Civil War encouraged an increase in flax production.[28] If for this reason alone, the depression hit Ulster less severely than elsewhere. Nationally there was a downturn in bank deposits and the imposition of credit restrictions. At a time when they needed it most, farmers found credit was most expensive.[29] This first depression lasted from 1859 to 1864 and twenty years later, it was to be followed by the severe downturn in agricultural fortunes which led to the Land War of the early 1880s (see below). In addition, in the 1890s a more localized depression was to afflict the 'Congested' counties of the west.[30]

Regional Land-use Change

The ratio of pasture (hay and grass combined) to tillage rose from just over 2 in 1851 to over 5.5 in 1911 (Fig. 9.4). Connacht and Munster were the provinces with least arable in 1851, but this did not necessarily mean that they were the most grassed. While the broad rule of least arable/most grassed did apply to Ulster, Connacht was paradoxically the least arable but also one of the least grassed provinces. Through-out the period, 35 per cent or more of Connacht was bog, waste or water. In comparison, Leinster was one of the most arable *and* most grassed provinces and throughout the period had the smallest proportion under bog or waste (only 15–16 per cent) for the whole period compared with a national average of 21–26 per cent.

Despite these variations, however, the trends in national land use were roughly replicated at the provincial level. Everywhere corn declined from being the leading 'crop' to second or even—in Connacht—third-placed ploughed land use. In con-trast, hay became the most prominent cultivated crop by 1871 or 1881 and grass cultivation rose steadily up to *c.* 1901. In Connacht, Leinster and Munster over half of all land was under permanent grass. The move towards pastoralism was slower in Ulster than elsewhere, due to a combination of physical and socio-economic factors. These included soil endowment and topography, and the prevalence of small farms which emphasized farm-family labour with an historic local product emphasis on flax. Mixed farming came to characterize Ulster in the second half of the nineteenth century.[31] Thus the relatively complicated agricultural geography observable in 1851 was much simplified by 1911. These land use adjustments generally proceeded without bringing woods, bogs and wastes into cultivation. An exception was the reclamation for cultivation of over half a million acres of bog and waste during the first decade after the Famine, although some had reverted by the end of the century.

The national increase of 7 per cent in cultivated land from 1851 to 1871 disguised provincial variations. The increase was as high as 17 per cent in Connacht and 10 per cent in Munster, but only 3 per cent in each of Leinster and Ulster. In 1851, north of a line from Dublin to Galway (but excluding Mayo and parts of the east coast), wheat and barley rarely exceeded 10 per cent of the cropped area whereas to the south of this line these crops generally occupied over 10 per cent, reaching 30 per cent in parts of the most southerly and south-easterly counties.[32] Connacht was the province with the least arable but it was also one of the least grassed. Here, the ratio of pasture to tillage was the highest in 1851 and remained so throughout the period. In Munster and Leinster this ratio replicated the national average, while at

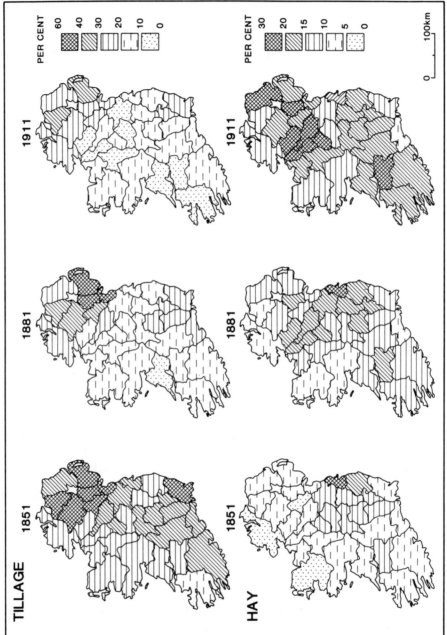

Fig. 9.4. Tillage and hay cultivation as a percentage of the total cultivated area, 1851, 1881 and 1911.

the opposite extreme, Ulster remained more determinedly a tillage province. Yet the change from tillage to pasture was largest in the already dominant pasture areas of Connacht and Munster. Arguably, therefore, regional specialization was already present, and post-Famine changes may have merely reflected pre-Famine developments already underway. Thus, the *degree of change* was heightened by the mid-century crisis, but was not necessarily caused by it.

In 1851 there was a crude east to west split in the distribution of cultivated land. Connacht and Munster stand out for the proportion of land *not* cultivated. In Ulster too, there were significant areas of uncultivated land, especially concentrated in Donegal, Fermanagh and Londonderry. Here, as elsewhere, the ability to bring extra land into cultivation was often limited by environmental factors.

In all but 11 counties the maximum amount of cultivated land was recorded in 1871, and of these exceptions five had their maxima within the adjacent decade. Conversely, in 21 counties the minimum point of cultivation was 1851, and of the 11 exceptions, seven (six of which were in Ulster, with Dublin the seventh) had a low point in 1911. Although the difference between maximum and minimum extent of cultivation was often insignificant, in the cases of Antrim, Fermanagh and Donegal the decline in the cultivated area from 1901 to 1911 was large.[33] The post-Famine recovery *might* be well illustrated in Clare, Galway, Kerry, Roscommon, Londonderry and Sligo where there were large increases in the proportion of cultivated land between 1851 and 1861, but without a reliable pre-Famine datum we cannot be sure if this was a recovery to former levels.

There was not much movement in the density of cultivation in individual counties over the period. In each of Donegal, Galway, Mayo and Kerry less than 60 per cent of the area was cultivated in 1851, and this remained so by 1911. There are perhaps two reasons for this. Environmentally these counties had a disproportionately large distribution of unusable land, and second, they suffered the greatest impact of the Famine. In 1851, Mayo (at 48.1 per cent) was the least intensively cultivated of all counties, remaining so in five out of the seven census years (1851, 1861, 1871, 1891 and 1901; in 1881 and 1911 it was second only to Donegal). These statistics imply that while there were great national changes in the agricultural face of the country, the relative geography of agriculture hardly varied at all.[34]

However, if the *relative* position of the counties with respect to *total cultivation* did not change a great deal over time, this is not to deny the dramatic flight from arable cultivation which covered 22 per cent of Ireland in 1851 but just 11 per cent in 1911 (based on five year averages and excluding flax and hay). In 1851 the country was in two halves divided by an axis running roughly from the south-west to the north-north-east. East of that line every county except Wicklow had at least 20 per cent of its area under arable crops, rising to over 30 per cent in Wexford and in the Ulster counties of Cavan and Monaghan, and over 40 per cent in other parts of Ulster and on the Ulster/Leinster border. Ulster was still the arable centre in 1881. Only 12 of the 32 counties experienced an increase in arable cultivation between any of the seven census years between 1851 and 1911. In all cases these were marginal increases, mostly between the censuses immediately after the Famine, and all in the west and north.

Land-use changes were only minimally regionally specific. The country moved more or less as one, but wherever arable was replaced by animal production, the clearest land-use indication of this was through the extension of hay production. This was a truly national movement. Only one county—Waterford with less than under 10 per cent of its cultivated area under hay—refused to 'move'. The pattern in 1851 is of a concentration of hay production in Dublin and the immediate counties. The requirement for bedding and feeding materials for the urban horse population in a large city dominated by horse transport helps to explain this relative concentration.

However, by 1881 widespread hay cultivation extended well beyond Dublin, especially in the counties to the north-west. The national change from arable to livestock was all but complete by 1911 and this was reflected in hay cultivation. Some of the counties producing least amounts of hay in 1851 had become some of those producing the most by 1911. Yet the apparently uncomplicated substitution of hay for arable identified at the national level hides different regional rates of change. Factors such as labour supply and proximity to the urban areas will have influenced whether hay or grass replaced arable. Hay was relatively labour intensive and it had a derived demand which was partly related to non-agricultural usage (urban horses). By grass we generally refer to permanent grass, non-mown and directly grazed by livestock.[35] The greenest county in 1851 was Kerry (74.2 per cent of the cultivated area under grass), followed by Galway and Mayo. The least green was Louth (30.3 per cent) followed by Armagh (34.8 per cent). By 1911 the greenest county was Westmeath (78.5 per cent) with Meath and Waterford close behind, and then the counties of the south and south-west. The least green county was Armagh (49.6 per cent) with Down (54.8 per cent) close behind. In this context too, Ulster, in general, was not green!

Table 9.2: Irish animal numbers, 1841–1914 (to the nearest thousand).

Year	Cattle	Sheep	Pigs	Horses	Goats	Poultry	Mules and asses
1841	1863[a]	2106	1413	576	[b]	8459	93
1847	2591	2186	622	558	164	5691	126
1849	2771	1777	795	526	183	6328	140
1850	2918	1876	928	527	201	6945	145
1851	2967	2122	1085	522	235	7471	159
1852	3095	2614	1073	525	278	8176	165
1853	3383	3143	1145	540	296	8661	170
1854	3498	3722	1343	546	311	8630	169
1855	3564	3602	1178	556	284	8367	172
Ave 1850s	3412	3131	1161	563	257	8646	171
Ave 1860s	3557	3959	1164	564	185	10373	190
Ave 1870s	4039	4212	1310	542	254	12536	203
Ave 1880s	4084	3399	1275	551	271	13910	223
Ave 1890s	4430	4320	1328	606	315	16590	254
Ave 1900–1914	4739	3949	1261	600	270	22013	273

[a] According to Bourke's re-estimates the true number could easily be 2220–2330 thousand.
[b] Goats were not included in 1841.

Sources: Derived from Annual Agricultural Statistics.

Livestock and Land-use Change

The 1841 population census includes an animal census. Bourke doubts its accuracy especially with regard to cattle numbers and also the reported size of the pre-Famine pig population. If the survival of pigs was at all related to the potato harvest then the enumerated pig population in 1841 was certainly an underesti-mate of the normal pre-Famine population. There was a potato scarcity in the spring of 1841 prior to the June census, a scarcity related to successive crop failures in 1838 and 1839 and the below normal year in 1840. Bourke has re-estimated the likely size of the pre-Famine animal population as follows.[36]

Cattle	2,250,000	Poultry	8,458,517
Pigs	1,412,813	Horses and mules	576,115
Sheep	2,106,189	Asses	92,365

Table 9.2 compares 1841 with the annual agricultural returns for the years 1847, 1849–55 and the 1860s. A closer definition of animal ages is not possible for 1841, and so post-Famine numbers have been standardized on 1841 definitions. The repercussions of the Famine hardly touched the horse population and did not apparently affect cattle at all (based on Bourke's re-estimates). The largest casual-ties were pigs and poultry, which, like humans, were dependent on potatoes.[37] Moreover, these livestock formed a stopgap in human diets when the potato crop failed, and this further reduced their numbers. But pig and poultry populations made fast recoveries after crises because of multiple births. Additionally they did not constitute as large a proportion of farm capital as the larger animals. Thus, sheep and poultry numbers recovered by the early 1850s, but if the 1841 census did capture an abnormally low year in pig numbers, then it is doubtful whether pig numbers ever did fully recover to pre-Famine levels. The peak year for the pig population was 1871 with 1.621 million animals.

By the 1850s the *immediate* effects of the Famine on livestock numbers had passed. These included abnormal circumstances such as the pilfering of growing crops, and more importantly the stealing or killing of cattle, sheep and poultry. In Cork this was organized by gangs of cattle stealers.[38] The greater greenness of Ireland was reflected in rising animal numbers, especially of beef rather than dairy cattle. From a high point in 1859 when milch cows constituted over 40 per cent of all cattle, there was a general downturn in their numbers to 1883 (33 per cent). We have here the *relatively* declining fortunes of the milk and butter trades giving way to the rise in the fat and store cattle trades round about 1880.[39]

The seriousness of the depression of 1859–64 is seen in the length of time it took animal numbers to recover. On the export side the worst years were at the end of the depression in 1864 and 1865. The stock of young cattle aged two years or less was built up until they matured as beasts of at least two years of age in 1867. This was the year when the least number of these cattle disappeared from the enumer-ation—disappeared in the sense of being slaughtered, sold or exported. We have, therefore, what John O'Donovan referred to as a paradox. There was a decrease in the number of milch cows, and therefore a likely decrease in the number of calves born, *but* an increase in the number of cattle of all ages. This is partly explained by a decrease in the trade for veal. Calves were living longer and had a greater chance of surviving for subsequent inclusion in the annual enumeration.[40]

Three choices faced the farmer with his newly born calves. He could rear them, or conversely, dispose of them and concentrate on the milk/butter trade, or he could do both. The evidence suggests a switch in emphasis as time proceeded. In 1854 there were 45 cattle of less than one year of age to every 100 milch cows, but by 1861 there were only 34. This suggests the second alternative, an emphasis on milk and butter. Thereafter, the ratio of young to old cattle rose dramatically, until in about 1865 there were 74, and numbers remained on or about 70 thereafter. Thus, the store cattle trade was coming into its own as the second half of the century proceeded. Additionally, the decrease in the veal trade meant that cattle born between censuses had a greater chance of being enumerated.[41] With the decline of the veal trade, calves were of little value, and in terms of feed they were high cost consumers, but once there was an increase in the demand for mature cattle, then the ratio of calves to milch cows increased. Figure 9.5 shows the density of cattle in Ireland in 1851, 1881 and 1911 per 100 acres of hay and pasture. In 1851 and again in 1881, the greatest density of cattle was in the northern counties; by 1911 the counties of the south-west had become substantial cattle producers.

The trend in sheep numbers was more variable. The short gestation period of a ewe in lamb allows for crises to be short-lived and the incidence of multiple births is more common with sheep than with cattle. Stocks were more easily reduced, but they also recovered more easily, as for example after the depression in 1868. Between then and the First World War, the number of yearling or older sheep generally fell, whereas the trend for sheep aged less than one year was flatter, or even slightly rising. The sharp rise from 1864 to 1868 was a ripple effect arising from disruptions in cotton supplies at the time of the Indian Mutiny of 1857–8, but more particularly from the United States Civil War and the associated cotton famine. These disruptions gave a fillip to both the flax (linen) and wool industries. The index of wool prices increased by over 100 per cent between the mid 1850s and 1864, or in general terms by 40–60 per cent during the Civil War compared with the mid 1850s. A decline in sheep numbers to around 1880 coincided with a near continuous downturn in wool prices from 1871 to 1881, but while sheep numbers recovered from 1881 to 1883, wool prices continued to decline into the twentieth century.

The main source of food for pigs was the potato. It was widely believed that their numbers fluctuated in response to the size of the potato harvest. For example, O'Donovan claimed that variations in the size of the pig population in the nineteenth century could be traced through variations in potato yields.[42] Thus, in '1881 there was an excellent potato harvest in Ireland, and the number of pigs kept in the year 1881–2 was as a result much greater than the number of pigs in 1880–1 and the preceding years'.[43] Table 9.3 suggests that this relationship between pigs and potato yields was more complicated. Arguably, it was the acreage as well as the yield of potatoes which was important. And it was the product of both which determined the availability of food. The relationship also depended on the slaughter and disposal of animals in the face of a glut or shortage of food available for them. Although pigs have large litters and are able to recover quickly from mortality crises, in particularly bad potato years some of the breeding stock may

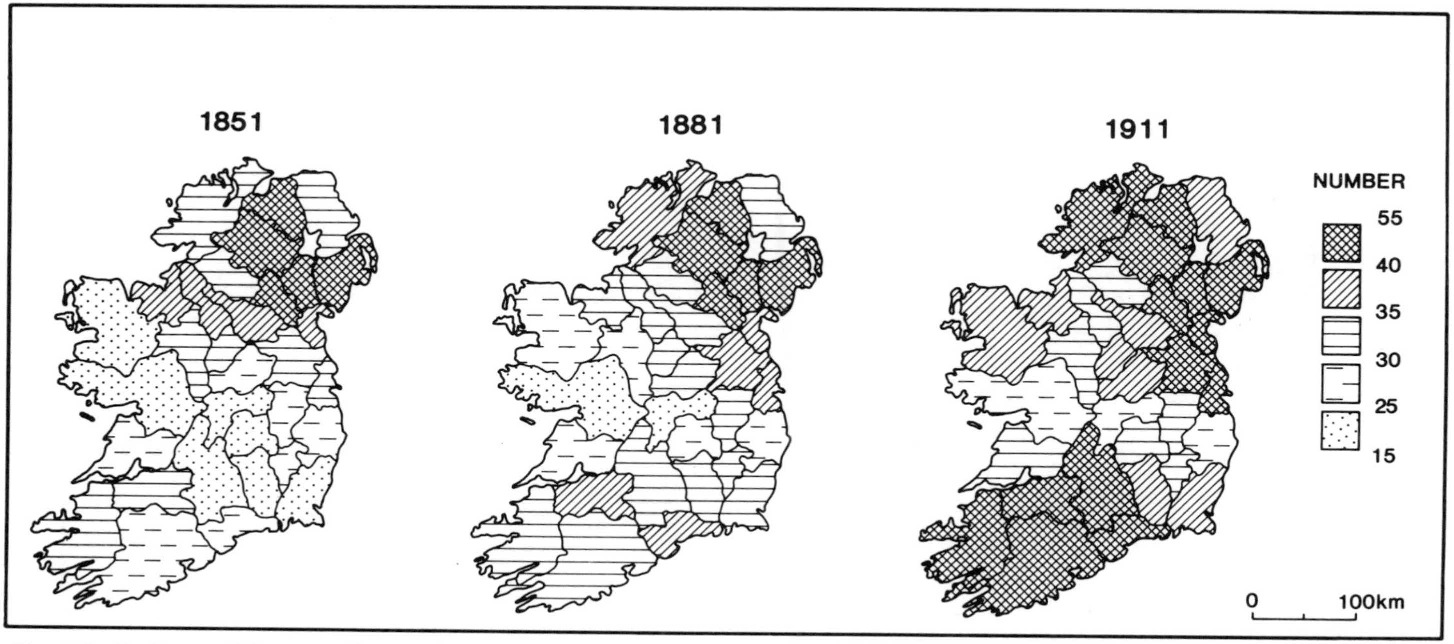

Fig. 9.5. Cattle per 100 acres of hay and pasture, 1851, 1881 and 1911.

have been slaughtered as well. In 1877 there was a lower potato output than in 1878, and significantly, by 1878 the pig population was reduced. But the good potato year of 1878 was also followed by a reduction in the pig population by 1879. Thus, the size of the pig population was not so obviously correlated to variations in the availability of food. A better model might include the provision of milk for pigs. For example, in Cork in 1884, after a long summer drought and reduced milk yields, there was a sharp downturn in pig numbers, as farmers were obliged to curtail breeding.[44] But in general, pigs weather crises better than sheep or cattle and therefore, for instance, although the depression of 1859–64 did affect pig numbers, in the long term it was not important.

Table 9.3: Pigs and potatoes, 1877–83.

Date	No. of pigs (millions)	Average potato yield (tons per acre)	Potato acreage (000s acres)	Potato output (000s tons)
1877	1.469	2.0	0.873	1.746
1878	1.269	3.0	0.847	2.541
1879	1.072	1.3	0.843	1.096
1880	0.850	3.6	0.821	2.956
1881	1.096	4.0	0.855	3.42
1882	1.430	2.4	0.838	2.011
1883	1.348	4.3	0.806	3.466

Sources: Derived from Annual Agricultural Statistics.

Livestock Exports

By 1900, the policy of British free trade, instituted in the mid nineteenth century, had combined with later improvements in international transport and the opening up of previously virgin land in North and South America and the Dominions to produce cheap supplies of grain which were flooding the British market. Although the free trade policy extended to livestock products, livestock production was afforded partial protection by the contagious diseases legislation of the 1860s which required the slaughter of animals before they entered British waters. This enabled Britain to take advantage of its island location and thus preserve the general health of its livestock from external infection. However, the legislation did not apply to trade across the Irish Sea, and consequently, the British market for livestock products partly drove agricultural change in Ireland. Coupled with these factors was a general improvement in British living standards towards the end of the century which instituted changes in demand.

Table 9.4 shows the livestock exports to Britain from 1854 to 1914.[45] In the 1850s 35–40 per cent of the cattle which 'disappeared' each year from the annual enumeration were exported to Great Britain, rising to 50 per cent by the mid 1860s, over 60 per cent by the early 1870s, and finally to 70 per cent by the end of the century. From 1850 to 1875 between 30 and 50 per cent of Irish sheep were exported, over 30 per cent of Irish pigs were exported as live pigs, and a further untold proportion in the form of bacon.[46] By 1908 no less than 58 per cent of the net value of Irish livestock output was derived from exports.

Table 9.4: Livestock exports from Ireland to Britain, 1854–1914.

Date	Cattle	Sheep	Pigs
Annual averages (thousands)			
1854–56	242	483	241
1865–69	407	584	350
1870–74	558	635	421
1875–79	656	710	493
1880–84	670	569	435
1885–89	687	633	464
1890–94	676	771	563
1901–04	790	887	592
1905–09	808	703	415
1910–14	790	691	269
As a proportion of the annual enumeration			
1854–56	6.8	13.1	21.1
1865–69	10.7	13.1	26.9
1870–74	13.8	14.6	31.9
1875–79	16.2	17.4	36.7
1880–84	16.7	17.3	36.5
1885–89	16.5	18.0	34.4
1890–94	15.4	20.9	40.4
1901–04	16.7	21.4	47.4
1905–09	17.2	18.0	34.0
1910–14	16.7	18.2	22.4

Sources: Annual Agricultural Statistics for the years 1891, 1901, 1911 and 1916. See also, R. Perren, *The Meat Trade in Britain, 1840–1914*, (London, 1978), p. 96.

The cattle trade first appeared to take off in the decade preceding the Famine. There was an annual average export of 47,000 between 1821 and 1825 rising to 98,000 in 1835 and over 200,000 annually between 1846 and 1849.[47] The growth of this trade was encouraged by the development of an efficient cross-Irish Sea steam navigation before the Famine, perhaps complemented by railway development in Ireland soon after.[48] However, the overall impact of the latter is doubted by some. For example, Kennedy suggests that post-Famine trends in livestock exports had roots 'firmly established' in the early nineteenth century, in other words before the development of railways.[49] His doubts contribute to the wider debate over the pre-Famine origins of post-Famine agricultural trends. In essence, it is argued that to a considerable extent, the rise in the animal trades and the *relative* decline in the grain trade (although that trade peaked in the 1830s and was still high up to 1845), predated the less ambiguous trends of the post-Famine years. Thus Crotty has argued for a dramatic shift out of tillage and into livestock from 1820, though this has been challenged by Ó Gráda, whose analysis of agricultural output leads him to conclude that there was little scope for a large-scale switch to pasture before the Famine. Indeed Ó Gráda's estimate suggests that tillage output, even after deducting for intermediate use as fodder, still constituted over 60 per cent of total output immediately prior to the Famine.[50]

Although live cattle exports did rise between 1815 and 1845, it is doubtful that a realignment of general agricultural production prior to the Famine can so easily explain the trend in exports. Perhaps the most that can be said, unambiguously, is that post-Famine developments were accelerated by the crisis of the 1840s, even if they had an earlier origin.[51] Another problem is that trends which rely on animal numbers alone underestimate the true increase in Irish meat reaching the English market because animal carcass weights improved over the century. On the other hand, this increase was probably less than it might otherwise have been, because of the debilitating effect of disease among the Irish livestock entering the British market. The contagious diseases legislation of the 1860s did not apply to Irish animals which therefore entered Britain on the hoof. This led to much contemporary criticism and suspicion over the health of Irish animals whenever there were outbreaks of disease.[52]

The Occupation of the Land

Short-term Crisis

The 1841 population census is also a partial census of landholding structure, although concerns over the accuracy of that census material apply particularly to the landholding data.[53] As noted earlier, it is unclear as to which acre was in use at the time. Was the Statute acre used throughout the country, or were there regional variations in the employment of Irish or Cunningham acres? Furthermore, while a holding included a combination of arable and pasture, there is doubt if bogs and wastes were included too. Although marginal, such lands were useful contributors to the overall income of a landholder. For example, in 1912 the value of turf was about £3 million, or 7 per cent of gross agricultural output.[54]

The contemporary (1845) Land Commission Office used Poor Law Commissioners' Returns to assess pre-Famine farm size distribution. Their findings suggested that 54 per cent were under 10 acres, 20 per cent 10–20 acres, 15 per cent 20–50 acres and 7.5 per cent over 50 acres with a residue of about 3.5 per cent unclassified.[55] These are unhelpful divisions with respect to the subsequent annual returns, but they do give some idea of the pressure on land at the bottom end of the socio-economic hierarchy. Table 9.5 combines Mokyr's revision of the pre-Famine base with Bourke's revision of the immediate post-Famine situation.[56] The former is based on the percentage distribution of farms in size groups while the latter is derived from an estimate of the number of holdings in each size group. Mokyr calculated that 40 per cent of all pre-Famine holdings were between one and 10 acres, which compares reasonably with Bourke's revision of the 1841 estimates which shows 45 per cent of all holdings at between two and 10 acres. Either way, the small farms or holdings which dominated Ireland on the eve of the Famine, were radically restructured immediately thereafter. In contrast the long-term changes from about 1851 were gradual rather than cataclysmic.

If these modern revisions are correct then the reduction in the numbers of the smallest farms or holdings abstracted from the 1841 census is easily explained in the aftermath of the Famine. It resulted from death and emigration, and from the financial hardship facing the survivors. Those who ate potatoes but grew cash

Table 9.5: Distribution of holdings and farm sizes, *c.* 1845–51.

(a) *Distribution of holdings 1845–51*

Size categories (in acres)	1845	1847	1851	% Change 1845–47	% Change 1847–51
<1	135,314	73,016	37,728	−46.0	−48.3
>1– 5	181,950	139,041	88,083	−23.6	−36.6
>5–15	311,133	269,534	191,854	−13.3	−28.8
>15	276,618	321,434	290,401	+16.2	−9.7
Total	905,015	803,025	608,066	−11.3	−24.3

(b) *Farm sizes in pre-Famine Ireland (after Mokyr)*

No. of farms	915,513
Mean farm size (acres)	14.69
% of farms <1 acre	14.8
% of farms 1–5 acres	19.7
% of farms 5–10 acres	20.5
% of farms <10 acres	55.0
% of farms 10–20 acres	20.2
% of farms <20 acres	75.2

Sources: P. M. A. Bourke, 'The agricultural statistics of the 1841 Census of Ireland: A critical review', *Economic History Review*, 2nd ser. **XVIII** (1965), p. 380; J. Mokyr, *Why Ireland Starved: A Quantitative and Analytical History of the Irish Economy, 1800–1850*, (London, 1985 edn), p. 19.

crops to earn their rents were forced to eat those grains and default on their rents. Smallholder farming, never viable without supplementary employment, became impossible for many. The crisis left the small man in particular short of the barest capital, even for seed. Thus, there were reports of desertion, as well as eviction.[57] Daly's conclusion is inescapable: 'The decline in the number of small farms is therefore not surprising, even ignoring the active role of the landlord in evicting farmers.' Generally the gap between the rich and poor in Ireland widened.[58] In Cork the opportunity was taken to oust 'bankrupt middlemen' and weed out 'struggling or broken tenants, and (of) enlarging the farms of those who remained'. This was one of the worst hit counties for mortality and therefore a substantial amount of slack was created in the land market. Nevertheless, landlords too were hit by cash-flow problems arising from the Famine, which worsened existing patterns of indebtedness. Many insolvent landlords disposed of their property through the Encumbered Estates Court set up under the Encumbered Estates Act of 1849. Some of these landlords had been absentees, living outside Ireland. Accordingly, a proportion of the rents which had previously accrued to these now-bankrupt estates had in the past been 'exported' out of the country. The new, incoming landowners were very often Irish-domiciled, and therefore these landownership adjustments at least set in motion the move towards Irish land which was now Irish owned.[59]

It might be thought that such a traumatic event as the Famine would have dealt a blow to traditional forms of settlement and field or farming systems, in particular the 'rundale' system of agriculture once thought to be widely practised in Ireland.[60] It is difficult to comment effectively on this issue because so little recent research has been carried out on the system or its supposedly cognate settlement form, the clachan, within the context of the re-evaluations of the Famine period being discussed here. It is possible that field systems were rather more diverse than traditional models suggest and again, the clachan is very much an enigma. It is now clear that what was once thought to be a settlement form ubiquitously characteristic of much of Ireland, was polygenetic in origin and function. Many of the nucleated rural settlements identified in the nineteenth century were of Anglo-Norman origin, although conversely, a number represent expansion onto marginal land during the eighteenth century, especially in the south and east of the island. Further, it is probably best to abandon the idea and terminology of the clachan as the traditional nucleated settlement form of the west of Ireland. The volatility of clusters there was in direct contrast with the relative stability apparent in the settlement pattern in the south and east of the island.[61]

Table 9.5 points to a decrease in the number of the smallest holdings of less than one acre during the Famine years. These fell by perhaps 46 per cent between 1845 and 1847 with a further fall of 48 per cent by 1851. In the next two size groups there were decreases of 24 and 13 per cent, but then a rise of 16 per cent in the number of holdings of over 15 acres. However, there were wide regional differences. In Wexford, holdings of less than one acre increased by as much as 67 per cent from 1844 to 1847, while the total number of holdings in each of the size groups 1–5, 5–15, and over 15 acres all declined (by 27, 15 and 13 per cent respectively). Many small farmers in the county were forced to give up their holdings. They became day labourers, exchanging their farms for small plots or vegetable gardens of less than one acre.[62] In contrast, in Cork, there was a decrease in the number of holdings under one acre. These different experiences have been attributed to the success of the local relief schemes in Wexford which created employment and allowed labourers to survive on the land, albeit at much reduced farming levels.[63]

But the fund of land which became available has also been attributed to a policy of deliberate—and perhaps necessary—government intervention which led to what Hoppen describes as 'social engineering'. He concludes that the creation of a network of soup kitchens, and the authorization of outdoor relief by the Poor Law Amendment Act of 1847 in breach of a central principle of the Irish poor law, which allowed for indoor relief only, was the fulfilment of a British political ambition. Hoppen calls this the 'sovereign remedy for Irish rural discontent, namely the reduction of cottiers and smallholders to the status of wage labourers'. This policy was assisted by the Gregory clause in the Irish poor law which, '(denied) relief to all those occupying more than a quarter of an acre of land, (and) represented a decisive step towards the achievement of such a policy.'[64]

Long-term Trends

In the longer term, holdings under one acre constituted 6 or 7 per cent of all holdings in all but two years of the 1850s, when there were between 35,000 and 38,000 holdings of this size. By 1890, these had risen to 50,000, reaching 70,000 by 1900 and 100,000 by the First World War. The depression of 1859–64 seemed not to influence this general upward trend in numbers except perhaps to accelerate it. In the decade or so before 1914 the trend was further emphasized by the move to greater owner-occupancy. This began with legislation in the 1880s and 1890s, and continued into the Edwardian period, whereby tenants were encouraged to purchase their land by borrowing the funds from the state. In 1870 only 3 per cent of Irish holdings were owner-occupied, but by 1908 this had reached 46 per cent and was rising rapidly. By 1910, 58 per cent had become owner-farmed and by the First World War it was over 60 per cent.[65]

While the number of smallest holdings therefore rose, the converse was true of those between one and five acres, which declined from over 80,000 in the 1850s to 70,000 by the mid 1870s, and further to just over 60,000 from the late 1870s onwards. A similar pattern of change took place for holdings of between five and 15 acres, and a less pronounced one for those of 15–30 acres. For holdings of 30–50 acres, 50–100 acres and 100–200 acres, the general trend was in the other direction and their numbers increased. The message is emphatically clear, however. Apart from the immediate Famine years, the changes were small, and more or less evenly distributed over time (Fig. 9.6).

As noted above, the definition of a landholding adopted in the Irish Agricultural Statistics is somewhat ambiguous.[66] Most of the time a landholding defines the autonomous integrity of, literally, a holding on the ground. The national figures abstracted from the census enumerators' reports were constructed by aggregating county totals. However, holdings which were divided by a county boundary may have been counted twice. Additionally, one landholder could have had more than one holding, wherever it was located. Thus, to obtain a complete picture of land distribution in 1861, the enumerators collected the number of occupiers in various size groups, regardless of the county in which they were located, and regardless of how many holdings they occupied. In 1861 there were 41,561 holdings of less than one acre (including some double counting) but 39,210 occupiers (now without double counting), and there were 53,933 holdings of 50–100 acres but only 49,654 occupiers. Overall there were 610,045 holdings and only 553,664 occupiers. While there were thus considerable discrepancies between the numbers of holdings and occupiers, the trends over time already described for holdings were the same for occupiers (see Fig. 9.6).

At around one acre it was difficult to distinguish between gardens and agricultural premises (however small). Equally, it was difficult to distinguish between agricultural holdings, gardens, town gardens and allotments.[67] Officially, it was felt that holdings of less than one acre contributed very little to agricultural output, and although they were large in number, they could be safely excluded from contemporary discussions concerning Irish agriculture.[68]

On closer inspection, this apparently straightforward tale of landholding and occupancy adjustments becomes more complicated. The rate of turnover of property is obscure, and the aggregate numbers employed here mask individual cases and identities. Moreover, there is a missing element in that traders gained a wider access to the land. During difficult years (for example, the depression of 1859–64 and the Land War), it may have been in the interest of both the farmers and the traders who serviced them to obtain rent reductions. By the end of the century, however, many traders were rivals for land, and the shopkeeper–grazier emerged as an important force in the countryside.[69] Ill-feeling between farmers and traders was worsened when the farmers embraced the cooperative system.[70] The

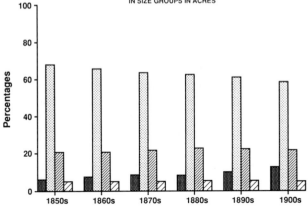

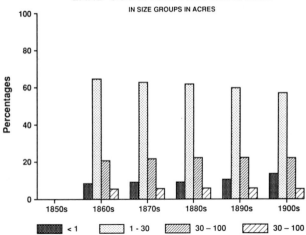

Fig. 9.6. Landholding and occupancy by size groups.

situation is further confused because there was also a move by farmers towards off-farm occupations, such as trading. As farming became less labour intensive so farmers responded accordingly.[71] In addition, as the country became 'greener' and the rural economy driven more by the production of dry cattle and sheep, the grazier–rancher emerged. They farmed large areas, often over 300 acres, and normally their land was held in scattered multiple holdings. To a degree they were absentees. When they acquired small holdings formerly occupied by tenants close to or below the subsistence level, there was an inevitable erosion of traditional rural society and reduced employment opportunities. Thus, conflict could emerge between peasants and ranchers as in the grazing regions of Connacht, north Munster and north Leinster.[72] Cattle driving, or the illegal removal of cattle from graziers' lands, was rampant from 1906 to 1909. Ranching was characterized by low output per acre, but ranchers' costs were also small. In this lay the seeds of the conflict;

'narrow profit margins impelled territorial expansion', but the opportunities to accomplish this, such as during times of heavy evictions, were limited in time and localized in space.[73]

A further complication was the system by which landlords let their untenanted pastures on 11 month lettings. This had two effects. Graziers tended to outbid other would-be holders of that land, but they could not claim formal tenancy or interest in it. The landlord remained occupier in law and his 'tenant' (not really the desired term), was a temporary occupant. There is uncertainty whether this system was fully registered in the annual returns. So again the record of occupiers may be in doubt. In 1906 2.6 million acres was devoted to this system, or nearly 13 per cent of the whole country, and nearly 18 per cent of the cultivated area (crops and grass). The trend in the late nineteenth century was for landlords to increase the amount of 'untenanted' land in their possession, and to extend the 11 month system. For instance, in 1901 between 30 and 50 per cent of commercial pasture and ranch land in Kells Barony, Co. Meath, was untenanted in this fashion. This feature became more marked as the terms of trade moved in favour of livestock production, and the graziers' appetite for more pasture increased. Increasingly, the peasantry were deprived of access to land. This resulted in overcrowding, particularly in the congested counties of the west coast. The fresh supply of untenanted lands was achieved by drastic measures such as eviction, and a traditional rural way of life was permanently changed.[74]

Average Size of Holding

Table 9.6 shows the average size of holdings by size groups. While there was remarkable continuity over time (at its largest the average size was 36.13 acres, in 1888), this should not obscure the significant adjustments in land use. Of every 100 acres cultivated on holdings of less than one acre in 1851, 33.4 per cent was under cereals, 63.2 per cent under root and green crops, and less than 3 per cent under meadow. But of every 100 acres on holdings of over 500 acres, 35.2 per cent was under cereals, but only 18.4 per cent under root and green crops, and 45.6 per cent under meadow. Potato cultivation dominated holdings of under one acre, but on holdings up to 200 acres 47–57 per cent of the land was under cereals, the percentage under root and green crops fluctuating widely between 19 and 36 per cent. The extent of meadow increased from 9 per cent on holdings of one to five acres to 33 per cent on holdings of 100–200 acres. In 1861 small farms were comparatively arable-intensive while larger holdings were dominated by grass. The division between the two, with an approximately equal cultivation of crops and grass, took place around the 15 acre level. Some of these features are captured in Table 9.7 a summary of land use by holding size groups for 1853, 1861, 1871.[75]

The relative importance in a farm economy of cattle, sheep and pigs cannot be assessed simply by looking at their numbers, because the resource-requirements of these animals are so very different. First, they must be reduced to a common unit for study. The conventional method is based on the relative amounts of feed which animals of different shapes and sizes require, using the cow as the standard against which to make the comparison. Using such livestock unit equivalents for the years 1854, 1861 and 1871 (Table 9.8), it can be seen that there were more livestock units

Table 9.6: Long-term trends in landholding, distribution and average size of holding, 1853, 1861, 1871, 1902.

Size groups (acres)	Holdings as a % of all holdings	Average size of holdings	Holdings as a % of all holdings	Average size of holdings
	1853	*1853*	*1861*	*1861*
<1	6.1	0.7	6.8	0.6
1–5	13.6	3.5	14.0	3.5
5–15	30.5	10.2	30.1	10.4
15–30	23.7	22.2	23.1	22.3
30–50	12.0	40.5	11.9	40.3
50–100	8.8	74.5	8.9	73.3
100–200	3.5	154.1	3.5	149.8
200–500	1.4	357.7	1.4	340.4
>500	0.3	1344.5	0.3	1244.7
Total	100.0	34.5	100.0	33.1
	1871	*1871*	*1902*	*1902*
<1	8.2	0.5	12.6	0.5
1–5	12.6	3.6	10.6	3.0
5–15	28.9	10.5	26.2	10.0
15–30	23.4	22.3	22.7	22.5
30–50	12.3	40.4	12.6	40.0
50–100	9.3	73.5	9.7	75.0
100–200	3.6	150.2	3.9	150.0
200–500	1.4	342.0	1.4	350.0
>500	0.3	1320.2	0.3	1295.9
Total	100.0	34.3	100.0	34.5

Sources: Derived from Annual Agricultural Statistics.

on the larger holdings than on the small. In terms of stock density, however, there was a nearly perfect gradation from high stocking levels on small holdings to low levels on large holdings.[76] While these findings are not surprising, there were two interesting patterns at work which are hidden in the data. First, *it appears* that cattle were bred on holdings of less than 50 or 100 acres and passed on to larger holdings for fattening and final disposal. Second, important regional variations in the age distribution of cattle suggests the operation of a regional filter from the west to the east of Ireland.

To take the discussion further, it has to be admitted that farm-size groups are not always a useful basis for classification because all acres are treated as equal. Obviously, land quality varies enormously. Thus, an intensively arable farm in a fertile area might be small in size but large in output, while conversely, a hill farm might be extensive in size but small in output.[77] A solution to this problem is to reduce all crops and animals into a standard form. In order to combine arable and livestock agriculture a measurement can be employed which is based on the amount of labour each acre of crop and each animal requires through the year. This is expressed in terms of standard man days (Table 9.9).[78] This is the closest we can come to looking at Irish agriculture and all of its *major* elements together, land use, the relative importance of tillage and grass, farm sizes and labour.

One man with his own labour and with up to 365 days available, *theoretically*, could have farmed a holding of around 15 to 30 acres. At certain times of the year,

Table 9.7: Land use by holding size groups, 1853, 1861 and 1871.

Size groups	Total average size (acres)			Average extent of crops and fallow (acres)		
	1853	1861	1871	1853	1861	1871
<1	0.7	0.6	0.5	0.6	0.5	0.5
1–5	3.5	3.5	3.6	2.3	2.3	2.3
5–15	10.2	10.4	10.5	5.1	5.1	5.0
15–30	22.2	22.3	22.3	9.4	9.4	9.1
30–50	40.5	40.3	40.4	14.9	14.9	14.3
50–100	74.5	43.4	73.5	22.3	22.3	21.3
100–200	154.1	150.0	150.2	34.1	33.3	32.2
200–500	357.7	341.2	342.0	47.6	45.4	43.8
>500	1344.5	1249.9	1324.5	55.1	48.7	42.3
Total	34.5	33.3	34.3	9.9	9.7	9.5

	Average extent of grass (acres)			Average extent of other land (acres)		
	1853	1861	1871	1853	1861	1871
<1	0.04	0.04	0.03	0.04	0.05	0.05
1–5	1.0	0.9	1.0	0.2	0.3	0.3
5–15	4.4	4.3	4.5	0.7	1.0	1.0
15–30	10.4	10.2	10.7	2.4	2.8	2.5
30–50	19.9	19.5	20.6	5.7	5.9	5.5
50–100	38.1	37.3	40.3	14.1	13.8	11.9
100–200	80.9	79.4	85.9	39.1	37.4	32.2
200–500	170.3	170.9	179.5	139.8	124.9	118.7
>500	384.5	424.9	438.7	904.9	776.1	840.5
Total	16.0	15.6	17.0	8.6	8.0	7.7

Sources: Derived from Annual Agricultural Statistics.

Table 9.8: Livestock densities by holding size groups (livestock unit equivalents).

Size groups (acres)	Per holding 1854	Per 100 acres 1854	Per holding 1861	Per 100 acres 1861	Per holding 1871	Per 100 acres 1871
1–5	1.0	28.8	0.9	26.4	1.1	31.6
5–15	2.6	25.1	2.4	23.3	2.9	27.8
15–30	5.0	22.7	4.8	21.4	5.6	25.1
30–50	8.5	20.9	8.1	20.1	9.3	23.0
50–100	14.2	19.1	13.9	18.9	15.5	21.0
100–200	27.0	17.5	26.7	17.8	28.8	19.2
200–500	49.6	13.9	49.7	14.6	51.9	15.2
>500	79.2	5.9	82.7	6.6	85.5	6.5
Total	6.7	18.1	6.4	18.0	7.5	20.1

Sources: Derived from Annual Agricultural Statistics.

farming activities compete with one another for labour time, but if 15 to 30 acres defines a 'peasant' or self-sufficient family holding, then it also points to the precarious position of holders of less than say 15 acres who, doubtless, had to supplement their incomes by working for others. This can be viewed another way. The bigger holdings with their larger animal populations and relatively smaller

Table 9.9: Labour requirements by holding size group (in standard man days).

Size groups (acres)	Per holding (1854)	Per 100 acres (1854)	Per holding (1861)	Per 100 acres (1861)	Per holding (1871)	Per 100 acres (1871)
1–5	79.2	2263.7	79.0	2257.3	81.8	2272.7
5–15	170.8	1674.9	172.8	1661.3	177.6	1691.2
15–30	305.5	1376.3	306.2	1373.1	306.5	1374.5
30–50	470.6	1162.1	472.0	1171.2	468.5	1159.7
50–100	694.7	932.5	700.2	955.2	690.8	939.9
100–200	1055.3	684.8	1052.2	702.4	1034.7	688.9
200–500	1516.6	424.0	1505.2	442.2	1459.4	426.7
>500	2024.5	150.6	2058.3	165.4	1989.7	150.7
Total	338.4	919.6	338.1	947.1	346.8	929.8

Sources: Derived from Annual Agricultural Statistics.

emphasis on tillage could get away with quite low labour densities per acre (last column of Table 9.9).

In summary some important conclusions can be drawn from this section on landholding changes. First, over the period between 1851 and 1911, the number of all landholders stayed remarkably stable, fluctuating narrowly between 563,000 and 610,000.[79] Second, although the immediate post-Famine years were clearly a time of turmoil, especially for smaller landholders, once that trauma had passed the long-term changes were gradual. Third, even during the two depressions those changes might have been accelerated, but not dramatically so.

Table 9.10 summarizes the landholding changes from the 1840s to 1911. A further important conclusion emerges. Even lacking confidence in the 1841 base and interposing the pre-Famine estimates for 1844–45 from Bourke and Mokyr, it looks as though the Famine was a watershed in terms of landholding distributions. There was a large redistribution of holdings immediately after the Famine, especially of those between one and five acres. Some smaller farmers were able to join the ranks of those with holdings greater than 30 acres. This change was rapid but short-lived. By the early to middle 1850s, the repercussions arising from the Famine, and the major reorganization of agriculture which followed, had been mainly worked out.[80]

The national patterns in landholding by size groups were not necessarily replicated at the provincial and county level (for example, see Fig. 9.7). In particular, the relationship between size of farm and land use is by no means clear. The 'relative' abundance of small intensively farmed arable units in Ulster contrasts with the larger extensive farms, whether arable or pasture, of Leinster and Munster. But by the twentieth century, Connacht was characterized by relatively small holdings although it was also dominantly pastoral compared with other parts of Ireland. In Ulster, at least to begin with, the presence of much rural industry and the generally reduced impact of the Famine were factors which helped to slow down the trend towards larger average farm sizes.[81] Over time there was an increase in the average size of holding, especially in the south and south-east of the country in Munster and Leinster. Here, larger than average holdings emerged in the counties surrounding Dublin and in Cork. This pattern and the trend which

Table 9.10: Percentage distribution of landholding by size groups, 1841–1911.

(i) *Short term*

Size groups	1841	Pre-Famine (a)	(b)	1847	1849	1850	1851
1–5 acres	44.9	23.1	23.6	19.0	15.8	15.5	15.5
5–10 acres		24.1					
5–15 acres	36.6		40.4	36.9	34.5	34.2	33.6
10–20 acres		23.7					
>20 acres		29.1					
15–30 acres	11.5		35.9 }	22.5	24.2	24.5	24.8
>30 acres	7.0			21.5	25.3	25.7	26.1
Number >1 acre (in 000s)	691	780	770	730	619	593	570

(ii) *Long term*

Size groups	1861	1871	1881	1891	1901	1911
1–5 acres	15.0	13.7	12.7	12.3	12.2	12.0
5–15 acres	32.4	31.5	31.1	30.3	29.9	29.6
15–30 acres	24.8	25.5	25.8	25.9	26.0	26.3
>30 acres	27.8	29.3	30.4	31.5	31.9	32.1
Number >1 acre (in 000s)	568	544	527	517	516	521

(a) After Mokyr, recalculating percentages and eliminating holdings (farms) of less than one acre.
(b) After Bourke.

Sources: Annual Agricultural Statistics; Mokyr, *Why Ireland Starved*, p. 19; Bourke, 'The agricultural statistics of the 1841 Census', p. 380.

underpinned it was virtually complete by 1881. Along the Leinster–Munster border, King's County (Offaly), Queen's County (Laois) and Kilkenny emerged as the nucleus of a large group, amounting to just over half the country, in which the average size of holding by 1881 was greater than 30 acres. The exceptions were Longford and Louth which from 1851 to 1911 continuously recorded average sizes of 20–30 acres.

These patterns exclude holdings of less than one acre. If these are included, counties in Leinster and Munster emerge in 1911 with not only a predominance of large holdings, but also with a very large proportion of holdings of less than one acre. By 1911 the counties in Connacht and Ulster were dominated by holdings in the one to 30 acres groups, uniformly so in Connacht, where by 1911 over 70 per cent of all holdings were less than 30 acres. Not surprisingly, Connacht is the region to which the Congested Districts legislation of the 1890s was directed. While the average size of holdings was not necessarily much smaller than elsewhere, the concentration of smaller holdings, which on their own offered an insecure economic living, was larger than average.[82]

Ireland was not a closed economy, but if it had been, the changes described here may have looked quite different. As it was, emigration acted as a safety valve which could operate at times when the pressure on the land was greatest. The rate of emigration usually increased in times of agricultural distress, or even at times of moderate potato shortage, and this created a fund of land for subsequent redistribution. In Cork at least, there were times when the flow of remittance funds from family members, from America in particular, propped up otherwise evictable

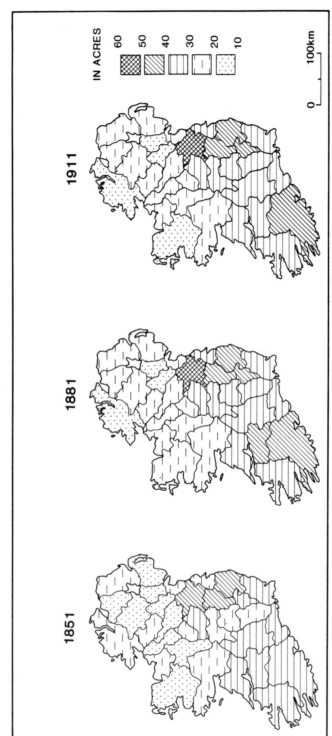

Fig. 9.7. Average size of holdings, 1851, 1881 and 1911 (excluding holdings less than 1 acre).

holders of land or potential emigrants. 'American money', as distinct from 'passage money', made it possible for others in the west (of County Cork) 'to maintain an otherwise hopeless position on uneconomic holdings and to persist in an irrational, if understandable, resistance to emigration'. A margin for redistribution, change and consolidation was thereby held in check in this, the premier county for emigration.[83]

The Performance of Irish Agriculture

Output in Nominal Terms

If, 'statistics of agricultural production' constitute 'an index of national prosperity', then without doubt the wealth of such material for Ireland provides a better opportunity to construct that index than is normal in most nineteenth-century studies.[84] Output, in the sense used here, is that part of total production which was marketed. It is calculated by first estimating total production and then deducting for seed retained, for the recycling of products within agriculture such as fodder crops or milk which was fed to calves or pigs, and for estimated animal mortality. It included an assessment of that part of production which represented farmers' own consumption. Table 9.11 is a half-decade summary of the latest estimates available. Figure 9.8 provides a graphical illustration of the full estimates.

Tillage output fell from £21 million per annum in 1850 to £7 or £8 million by 1900, before rising to £10 million by the start of the First World War. This long-term trend was disrupted early on, when output rose to between £33 and £34 million in both 1854 and 1855. In western Europe in general there were grain supply problems emanating from the Crimean War with a knock-on effect for grain prices. In contrast, the equivalent steep rise in livestock production through the 1850s, unlike the rise in tillage output, can be viewed as part of a long-term trend and not a short-term aberration.

Livestock output rose from £10 million in 1850 to about £32 million in the mid 1870s, falling to £24 million in the middle of the following decade. It recovered to about £40 million by the outbreak of the First World War. The agricultural depression of 1859–64 shows up in the livestock trend, but not particularly dramatically. Livestock output has almost certainly been overestimated for the depression period. There was an incalculable loss of pigs through a likely rise in mortality, and both milk yields and prices were probably down on the contemporary average. Current estimates do not, or cannot, properly capture all of these and other effects.[85]

In total output terms there were three main phases: a general rise to the mid 1870s; a fall to the mid 1890s; and finally an upturn to the First World War. Overall, off-farm crop output fell by nearly 60 per cent, animal output increased by 192 per cent , and total output increased by nearly 30 per cent. Tillage represented over 60 per cent of total output until the mid 1850s, but slumped more or less progressively thereafter to a level of 21 per cent by 1900. Conversely, the livestock share rose from about 35 per cent in the early 1850s to nearly 80 per cent by the close of the century. The single most important contribution became the combined milk and

Table 9.11: Annual averaged marketed agricultural output, 1850–54 to 1910–14.

Period	Crops	Animals	Total
In £s million			
1850–54	24.8	13.2	38.0
1855–59	22.1	20.8	42.8
1860–64	15.1	21.9	37.0
1865–69	17.5	23.7	41.1
1870–74	14.3	29.7	44.0
1875–79	13.2	30.5	43.8
1880–84	11.6	28.3	39.9
1885–89	9.0	25.6	34.7
1890–94	9.8	27.1	36.9
1895–99	8.2	27.2	35.3
1900–04	8.7	30.8	39.4
1905–09	9.2	33.7	42.9
1910–14	10.2	38.6	48.8
Percentage changes			
1850–54 to 1870–74	−42.3	125.0	15.8
1870–74 to 1890–94	−31.7	−8.6	−16.1
1890–94 to 1910–14	4.4	42.3	32.2
1850–54 to 1910–14	−58.9	192.7	28.4
1855–59 to 1910–14	−53.8	86.1	14.0

Source: Michael Turner, 'Agricultural output and productivity in Post-Famine Ireland', pp. 410–38, in B. M. S. Campbell and M. Overton (eds.), *Land, Labour and Livestock: Historical Studies in European Agricultural Productivity*, (Manchester, 1991), p. 419.

cattle output. From over 30 per cent of total output in 1860 rising to 40 per cent and more from the early 1870s, this peaked at 50 per cent in 1903.

Output in Real Terms

To some extent, the broad outlines of the trends in nominal output should be familiar from the preceding discussion. The international prices peak of the early 1870s is more or less mirrored in animal and total output terms, followed by the prices depression down to the mid-1890s, before the progressive recovery of prices thereafter. But for a more detailed explanation, output needs to be viewed in 'real terms'. Figure 9.8 shows output at constant prices in two ways. The deflators are an index of wholesale prices and an agricultural prices index.[86]

If output is deflated by a wholesale prices index, an unmistakably upwards trend becomes apparent *in the long term*. The early depression, however, was a major blemish upon the industry, and agriculture held its head above water continuously, so to speak, only from about 1873. Such a calculation of the 'real income' effect of agriculture before the 1870s runs counter to the view expressed by Lee, for example, of a long boom or tide of prosperity, in the rural economy in the three decades after the Famine.[87]

When the value of output is compared with the price trend of agricultural products alone, using an agricultural prices index as the deflator, a measure of the

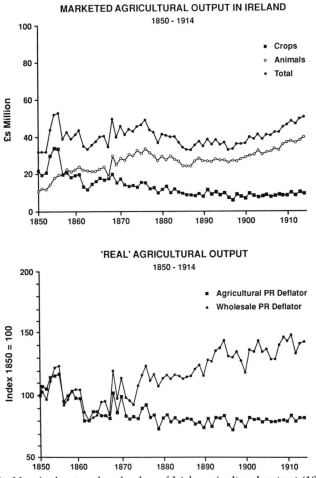

Fig. 9.8. Nominal net and real value of Irish agricultural output (1850–1914).

'real volume' of agricultural output can be produced. Farmers' real incomes may have improved (wholesale prices deflator), but this was achieved through favourable price changes. For the industry as a whole, the real volume of output certainly did not improve over the full course of the period. Give or take short-term fluctuations there seems to have been a decline in real volume down to the early 1860s, a rise to about 1870, and a decline to about 1880. The downturn of real output in 1879 reached the lowest point thus far in the chronology. The coincidence here with Donnelly's theory of 'rising expectations' is appealing (see below), although those rising expectations from the mid 1860s look rather flat in trend terms with one or two outstanding years at odd intervals. Nevertheless, 1879 was an outstandingly poor year in volume terms.

Irish Agricultural Productivity

Thus, an assessment of the value of output compared with its volume leaves us questioning the general performance of Irish agriculture. But Ireland at the time was part of the wider United Kingdom economy. In comparison with the output of agriculture in Britain, there are some reasons to adopt a more optimistic view of the Irish performance.[88] The share of United Kingdom tillage output coming from Ireland rose from 15 per cent in 1870 to nearly 19 per cent by 1913. This may seem impressive, but since Irish tillage acreage was in absolute decline, these estimates more properly expose the very poor performance of mainly English tillage output from about 1870 to 1913. The contribution of Irish livestock rose from about 20 per cent in 1870 to 23 per cent by the First World War. This was a modest increase in monetary terms but again an indication of the depressed performance of British agriculture at the time. Overall, therefore, Irish agriculture contributed about one-sixth or one-fifth of United Kingdom agricultural output in the 1860s rising to between one-fifth and one-quarter on the eve of the First World War.

The implied productivity difference between Ireland and the rest of Britain is reinforced when we look at crude income/labour productivity estimates. Irish agricultural output per capita improved over the period while British output declined. Irish output increased from about £6 or £7 per head in the 1850s to £8 in the 1870s and nearly £10 per head by 1910, while in Britain the £7 or £8 per head achieved in the 1870s fell to £4 per head by about 1910. Although the nominal level of output per head of the agricultural labour force was higher in Britain than in Ireland, by 180 per cent early on and still by over 100 per cent on the eve of the First World War, there was in fact a decline in that output from about £110 per head in the 1870s to £100 in the late 1890s, before recovering to about £112 per head in 1910.

Since the value of Irish output per head of the agricultural workforce was just over one-third of the size of its British counterpart in the early 1870s, but just under one-half by the First World War, we can say with some justification that Irish agriculture was performing well. In real terms, Irish output, whether per capita or per head of the agricultural labour force, nearly doubled from the mid 1860s to the First World War. In Britain, it fell dramatically in per capita terms over the whole period, while per head of the agricultural labour force it improved only during the Agricultural Depression of the 1890s, and then fell in Edwardian times.[89] In real volume terms the productivity trend in Ireland was less encouraging, but still generally positive.[90]

Since the amount of land in Ireland under cultivation did not change very much, land productivity followed the course of output. Output per acre rose modestly from *c.* 1850 to the mid 1870s, from about £2.2 per acre to a little under £3, then fell back to £2.4 towards the end of the century before rising steeply to £3.5 per acre by the First World War. Output per occupier rose from about £60 to £90 between 1860 and 1876, before declining to a little over £60 by 1887. Thereafter, it rose modestly to over £70 before falling back to just over £60 (between 1887 and 1897) before finally expanding almost continuously to over £90 by 1914. This last period of expansion coincided in part with changes in tenure and land law, and with the general move towards greater owner-occupancy and Irish peasant independence.

Rising Expectations and the Depression of 1879–82

During the 1870s, the nominal value of total output peaked in 1876 at £49 million, rather less than in 1868, although that was an exceptional year. The year 1876 can be viewed as the opposite pole of prosperity (measured solely by value of output) from the low of 1862.[91] This conforms neatly with Donnelly's 'rising expectations' argument in which the relative fortunes of landlords and farmers are held to have acted as a precursor to the Land War of the 1880s. The argument portrays discontent among the tenantry, who were faced with relatively fixed costs in the form of rents which nevertheless rose in real terms in comparison with the squeezed tenant incomes after 1876. Thus, Donnelly does not suggest that there was a rent problem prior to that. Rather he argues that tenants received the main benefits from price and production increases from the early 1850s through to the mid 1870s. His point is that the events of 1877–9 effectively reversed the flow of benefits from the tenants' point of view.[92] The coincidence with the period of Land War and land reform which followed is appealing.

However, it is the depression of 1859–64 which has been prominent in the discussion so far, and this points to an important question. If there was a Land War in the 1880s, why did a similar economic downturn not produce one in the 1860s? By Donnelly's estimation, 'the value of the seven major crops was depressed by an average of twenty per cent for *three* years' in 1877–9 compared with 1876, 'whereas in the earlier depression their value was reduced by an average of twenty-one per cent for five years', compared with 1859.[93] His calculations are based on total output, not marketed output, and therefore they cannot be compared directly with the new estimates. In addition crop production was much more subservient to livestock by about 1880. But as an alternative we can say that total marketed output in each of the years between 1860 and 1864 compared with 1859 differed by +6.0, −15.5, −18.7 , −13.5 and −9.2 per cent, whereas the differences in 1877–79 compared with 1876 were −10.8, −13.4 and −24.6 per cent. This comparison does not answer the question conclusively one way or the other. It exposes 1879 as the deepest depression year, but the depression in the early 1860s was more protracted. Even though the depth of the 1859–64 depression has probably been underestimated, it should be noted that 1876 was an exceptionally good year, the best since 1868, while 1879 was exceptionally bad, the worst year since 1863. Therefore, the choice of dates is important because it dictates the analysis. Donnelly would have found a worse crisis earlier if he had used 1858 as his base, but 1876 is the best possible year he could have chosen to highlight the later depression.

What did rising or falling expectations look like from the farmer's *initial* point of view? He might observe his standing crops or harvested crops. Donnelly also did this when he looked at crop yields. Yet he may have misrepresented the case. He compared crop yields for 1859–64 as a percentage of the average of 1856–8. He then compared 1877–9 as a percentage of the average of 1870–6. In other words, in value terms he played up the good year of 1876, but in yield terms he played it down by diluting it with six other years. If his deviation of yields from the average for 1877–9 is reworked using 1874–6 for comparison, 1879 emerges as a year of particularly deep depression, deeper than Donnelly demonstrated (Table 9.12). This was especially the case for the fodder crops in an economy which since the early 1860s had moved further and further towards the pastoral side.

Thus 1879 saw a sharp dip in the value of output: it was a year of exceptionally bad weather with low tillage yields everywhere, and probably an even sharper fall

Table 9.12: Crop yields, 1877–9, (a) Donnelly, percentages of the mean of 1870–76; (b) *revised* percentages of the mean of 1874–6.

	Oats		Wheat		Barley		Flax		Potatoes		Turnips		Hay	
	(a)	(b)	(a)	(b)	(a)	(b)	(a)	(b)	(a)	(b)	(a)	(b)	(a)	(b)
1877	91	84	101	87	94	85	113	91	59	48	82	76	121	117
1878	102	94	111	96	98	88	125	100	88	71	109	104	121	117
1879	88	81	84	73	78	70	93	75	38	31	50	46	100	97

Sources: Derived from Annual Agricultural Statistics.

in livestock output than has been calculated, given the fixed weights for carcass sizes and milk yields employed, and the probability of inferior fodder. There was some compensation for falling physical output in an augmented price for some products, but a rise in potato and hay prices meant a corresponding increase in fodder prices. Besides, prices were increasingly determined internationally, or else in Britain, the main market for Irish produce. To this extent 1879 was indeed a deep trough in the recent better fortunes of Irish agriculture, but the depressed incomes in that year must be viewed against the background of the relatively fixed cost of renting land. Even so, the depression resulted in the withholding of 25 per cent of the rents which were due in 1879–82; the opening shots in the Land War of the early 1880s had been fired.[94]

There is other evidence of changing prosperity. If bank deposits can be used as a barometer for agricultural incomes and prosperity then in the 1870s there was an extension of bank branches and a transfer of funds from, for example, the mattress to the bank. This was followed by a large decline in bank deposits in the late 1870s to early 1880s. Credit restrictions were introduced, and applied both to farmers and, of wider rural importance, to the service sector on which many of those farmers relied, especially the shopkeepers.[95]

The Land War was obviously a major watershed in the political moves towards greater Irish self-determination, and consequently, contemporary Irish political rhetoric interprets it less pragmatically than the agricultural historian. Solow characterizes the period in terms of agricultural failure, prefacing the relevant chapter of her book with Healy's interpretation that: 'The Land League was not begotten by oratory, but by economics'.[96] Eventually what emerged was a decline in the economic power of the landed elite, and correspondingly, its acquisition by other groups within agrarian society in Ireland.[97] There was a rent strike and therefore the loss of income to proprietors. In addition, there was the more general inability—which was not always an unwillingness—of farmers to discharge their other debts and accounts to the service sector of shopkeepers and suppliers.[98] Thus it was in the interests of both farmers and tradesmen alike to obtain rent reductions, and this brought town and country together in what Kennedy refers to as their mutual 'coincidence of interests'.[99] But the connections between landlords and tenants were also important, and 'anything likely to cause hardship among the tenantry was bound, sooner of later, to affect the economic position of the landlords.'[100] Rental arrears filtered up to the landlords and down to the shopkeepers. For landlords it resulted in mortgages.[101] Not all outstanding debts, however, derived from the immediate depression of the late 1870s. For example, many landlords were already encumbered by debt. In the aftermath of the legislation which followed the depression they were faced with reduced revenues from rents, and the link between reduced economic power and reduced political power could be made.[102]

The two depressions in the second half of the nineteenth century were important to the course of post-Famine Irish agricultural history. The first may have finally moved the economy towards pastoralism, though this clearly had pre-Famine origins, but the second heralded the arrival of the Land War and the final drive to Irish independence. To this extent, it was the more important of the two as a landmark in Irish history. The repercussions of tenant unrest began with the granting of the 'three Fs' under the 1881 Land Act—fair rent, freedom of sale of tenancy, and the fixity of tenure. This focused attention on the land question and the distribution of returns from agriculture.[103] Occupiers had managed to improve the gross value of their output during the first half of the period (1850 to the mid 1870s), and then again from the mid 1890s, but they also took part in a move to greater independence from 1880. By 1914 there were 349,000 owners (now substantially if not mainly owner-occupiers) and 217,000 tenants. The idea that productivity change was linked to this move towards tenurial independence is seductive for the period after about 1890. Seductive it might be but the improvements in both farmers' real incomes and the real volume of output are less than certain.

Table 9.13: Land, labour and gross farming profits, 1852–4 to 1905–10.

Date	Output	Rent	Labour	Gross farming profits
In £s million				
1852–54	42.3	10.0	9.3	23.0
1872–74	44.4	12.0	10.6	21.8
1882–84	39.0	11.5	11.0	16.5
1905–10	43.6	8.0	10.6	25.0
In real terms, 1852–54 = 100				
1852–54	100.0	100.0	100.0	100.0
1872–74	89.9	102.7	97.6	81.2
1882–84	104.7	130.6	134.4	81.5
1905–10	125.1	97.1	138.4	131.9

Source: Turner, 'Agricultural output', p. 430.

Land Reform, the Distribution of Profits and the Land War

Before the discussion can be taken further, it must be admitted that it lacks an appreciation of the scale of the costs or factor inputs which faced the Irish farmer. Table 9.13 combines Hoppen's summary of factor inputs with the latest estimates of output.[104] While output was fairly stable and the fluctuations in gross rents and the labour bill quite small, the combination of outputs and inputs still produced a narrowing of profit margins down to the early 1880s, especially when compared to the early 1870s. Farmers' profits eventually recovered, but mainly as a result of the decrease in the rent bill in the aftermath of the successive land legislation which began with the Land Act of 1881, and included the Ashbourne Act of 1885, the

Land Purchase Acts of 1891 and 1896, and Wyndham's Land Act of 1903 and its successor of 1909. The tenurial adjustments towards owner-farming stretched into Edwardian times. The variation in rent and output in real terms suggests a similar conclusion. The decrease in real output down to the early 1870s was not compensated by comparable decreases in farming costs, and 'real' rent actually rose modestly. 'Real' farming profits therefore slumped, and remained depressed until the early 1880s. Thereafter, they rose significantly. This expansion in 'real' profits came about through a combination of improved 'real' incomes, and the emergence of occupiers who were now increasingly independent and therefore faced a much reduced national rent bill. In 1870 only 3 per cent of Irish holdings were owner-occupied, but the corresponding figure for 1908 was no less than 46 per cent.[105]

The Land War was central to the rural economy in so far as it highlighted the issue of the distribution of rewards from Irish land and Irish labour. The significance of output estimates in relation to the cost of inputs relates to the distribution of farm income between landlords, tenants and labourers, but particularly between landlords and tenants. An appraisal of the distribution of rewards relative to the factors of production opens up the whole debate about the economic circumstances of the early 1880s. The previous paragraph suggests a happy link between increased independence and improved agricultural output, but the calculation of output is problematic, and estimates of rent and wages even more so.

The definition of labour is not straightforward. Farmers' relatives often assisted in an unpaid capacity and occupiers also acted as labourers. Payment was often largely in kind and labour service was highly seasonal. This leads to an uncertain estimate of the labour force and, since the equation which gives the wages bill is based on the size of the labour force, the estimate of a national wages bill is surely no better than a guess.[106] The trend in rents is also by no means certain. There are many choices for the rent profile,[107] but if we adopt modest, middle-of-the-road estimates of £12–13 million in 1852–54, rising to £15–16 million in the 1870s and early 1880s, the broad conclusions reached here are not upset. 'Real' rent would have risen more steeply and gross farming profits would have been squeezed even more, to two-thirds their level in the early 1880s compared with the early 1850s.

Clearly the cost of the factor inputs in relation to the output can lead to different assessments of the rewards to tenants and owners. Vaughan has suggested that there was a 20 per cent increase in rent between the Famine and the late 1870s, claiming that if the course of rents had followed the course of agricultural output, as he had estimated it, then rents should have risen by another 13 per cent.[108] Thus for him the returns to farmers (profits) were greater than to the landlords (rents). This is a view pretty well followed by Donnelly in his study of Cork.[109] This is what we might call the orthodox revisionist view of the distribution of farming incomes. The latest output estimates summarized in this chapter indicate a different course of events. In showing that output rose from £38–42 million (1850–4, 1855–9) to £43–44 million (1870–4, 1875–9), or at most by 16 per cent, they suggest that the increase in the returns to farmers was less than the accepted increase in the return to landlords. This is important to an understanding of the economic background to the Land War, and its central issues of tenure and rents. The revised estimates encourage the view that there was a relative switch in incomes to landlords rather than to tenants. So whereas Vaughan talks of the 'remarkable prosperity' of Irish agriculture in one study and concludes in another that, 'on the whole tenants were in a relatively privileged position, holding their land at what were in real terms falling rents', the new estimates presented here suggest quite a different background.[110] If these newly revised figures are secure, then the tenants' victory arising from the Land War was preceded by a real deterioration in their incomes.[111] And if we adopt Ó Gráda's estimate for rent of £8.5 million in about 1852, then his view that the landlords' share of output had increased from the early 1850s to the 1870s falls easily into place.[112] The time-series analyses used here depend crucially on their choice of base-year, but if the interpretation offered here is correct then it follows an old traditional line.[113] The consequences are equally important. The economic and perhaps social background of tenants in agriculture in the years from the Famine to the Land War needs to be reassessed, as should the impact of the Land War on changing the political as well as the economic map of Ireland.

Land Reform and Peasant Independence

The enaction of Irish land reform heralded the tenurial independence of the Irish peasant. From 22 August 1881 to 31 March 1900, 328,220 tenants had a fair rent set under the provisions of the 1881 Land Act. They farmed 9,859,970 acres. Thus 60 per cent or so of all occupiers farming 65 per cent of the cultivated land area had fair rents set for a first time or term. There was a marginal bias to the larger occupiers. At the end of 15 years 52,396 of them with 1,432,515 acres had obtained a fair rent set for a second time or term. On average rent was reduced by 21 per cent in the first term rising to 22 per cent in the second.[114] Annual average output fell by 19 per cent from the half decade prior to the 1881 Act to the last half decade of the century. The adjustment to a fair rent, therefore, pretty well matched the decline in the nominal value of output.

Under the provisions of the Ashbourne Acts of 1885 and 1888, and their successors the Balfour Acts of 1891 and 1896, tenants were encouraged to purchase their land by way of a 100 per cent advance from the state as cash or stock. But that tenant was liable to an annuity of 4 per cent for a period of 49 years. In practice, the effect was to transfer what was a rent to an interest charge, which by any other name, for 49 years at least, was a form of rent. However, it was terminable and not perpetual and in its operation seemed to imply a decrease in 'rent' at inception, although without any allowance for future price changes (that is in contemporary terms, no allowance for deflation).[115] There is one problem with this history, however, which relates to the distribution of the rewards of agriculture. Have the interest charges under this and other schemes been included in estimates of the national rent bill? Undoubtedly they should be included in any calculation which seeks to clarify the level of farming profits.

The end result of the buy-out scheme was certainly to reduce the cost of the land input.[116] By March 1911 £66.5 million had been advanced for land purchases for something close to six million acres, with agreements to purchase a further 4.5 million acres pending at a price of £46.5 million. By mid 1913, purchases fulfilled or pending under Wyndham's Act of 1903 and its successor the Birrell Act of 1909, totalled £96 million, plus £4 million for labourers' cottages, and £24 million for purchases of land prior to 1903. Thus, £125 million had been expended with an estimated £60 million still needed to complete the transfer from occupancy to owner-occupancy.[117] The movement was strongest in Ulster. By 1913, 69 per cent of its farmers owned their holdings.[118]

Conclusion

The Famine's traumatic impact on Irish history is beyond doubt, and while it was a watershed it is evident, nevertheless, that the rural economy adjusted rapidly to changed circumstances. The first post-Famine decade determined the shape of things to come to a large degree, although some of the agricultural adjustments identified here were already in motion before the Famine. After the 1850s the changes in land use and land occupancy were gradual—attritional—rather than dramatic. The land became greener as the arable acreage shrank and livestock output increased, in particular following the rise of the cattle and milk trades. Despite doubts about quality of the data available for the Famine period, it seems clear that there was a rapid restructuring of land occupancy. The overwhelming dominance of very small farms or holdings was dealt a severe blow by the Famine, and then for a half century or more two dominant features were characteristic. Very small holdings, those below one acre, remained numerically important and actually increased in numbers, but so also did holdings of over 30 acres as a less subsistence-orientated, more commercial agricultural economy evolved. The holdings in between acted as the 'slush fund' of adjustment. It must be emphasized, however, that apart from the Famine decade itself, the changes were relatively small most of the time, and the trends were more or less evenly distributed over time.

The post-Famine changes had profound influences on the landscape itself and on the methods of production. Partly this arose as a result of the increasingly constrained labour supply and the necessary decrease in labour intensive spade cultivation. The national trends had subtle regional expressions, and they were accelerated modestly by the depression of 1859–64. The sum total of changes meant that when the international arable prices depression hit Britain and western Europe after the 1870s, Irish agriculture had already adjusted to cash products other than grain. To this extent, in comparison with the rest of the United Kingdom, Irish agriculture performed well.

The depression of 1879–82 and the Land War which ensued were major landmarks in their own right. They heralded the most long-lasting change of them all— the move towards greater Irish independence. The acquisition of land by the Irish peasantry threw into reverse the opposite, centuries-old process of the English acquiring Irish land, but the really clever trick of this last move to economic independence was that it was British or even English capital which paid for the buy-out. By 1914 Ireland had certainly gained a large share of its economic independence and in the end achieved it rapidly. The power of the people (as distinct from the power of the politicians) in securing this independence in the aftermath of the depression of 1879–82 hinges largely on interpretations of the performance of Irish agriculture. At times and by certain analyses that performance looks good, especially when compared with Britain, but we are left with an unresolved debate on the prosperity of, and more particularly, the distribution of rewards from agriculture, both before and after the depression of the early 1880s.

Acknowledgements

While this chapter is a synthesis and overview of its topic, it does rely on ongoing research into Irish agricultural structure, output and performance between 1850 and 1914. I thank The Nuffield Foundation for their financial support.

References

1. C. Ó Gráda, 'Irish agricultural output before and after the Famine', *Journal of European Economic History*, **13** (1984), p. 154.
2. P. M. A. Bourke, 'The agricultural statistics of the 1841 Census of Ireland. A critical review', *Economic History Review*, 2nd ser., **XVIII** (1965), pp. 383–4. This chapter draws heavily on the annual agricultural statistical returns. The 1841 details were repeated without qualification in those annual agricultural statistics.
3. Bourke, 'The agricultural statistics', pp. 386–7.
4. J. Mokyr, 'Reply to Peter Solar', *Irish Economic and Social History*, **XI** (1984), p. 119. See also P. Solar, 'Why Ireland starved: A critical review of the econometric results', *Irish Economic and Social History*, **XI** (1984), p. 113.
5. Bourke, 'The agricultural statistics', p. 391.
6. Population figures here and elsewhere taken from J. P. Huttman, 'Institutional factors in the development of Irish agriculture, 1850–1915' (unpublished PhD thesis, University of London, 1970), p. 414.
7. In the absence of fertilizers or other artificial additives, an acre of root or green crops yields more in nutritional terms than an acre of hay, meadow or rough pasture. See Huttman, 'Institutional factors', pp. 366–7. See also J. T. Coppock, *An Agricultural Geography of Great Britain*, (London, 1971), pp. 135–6.
8. M. Daly, *The Famine in Ireland*, (Dublin, 1986), p. 22, based on J. M. Goldstrom, 'Irish agriculture and the Great Famine', in J. M. Goldstrom and L. A. Clarkson (eds.), *Irish Population, Economy, and Society: Essays in Honour of the late K. H. Connell*, (Oxford, 1981), p. 160.
9. C. Ó Gráda, *Ireland Before and After the Famine: Explorations in Economic History, 1800–1925*, (Manchester, 1988), p. 48. See also P. Solar, 'Agricultural productivity and economic development in Ireland and Scotland in the early nineteenth century', in T. M. Devine and D. Dickson (eds.), *Ireland and Scotland 1600–1850. Parallels and Contrasts in Economic and Social Development*, (Edinburgh, 1983), p. 87 n. 32; J. S. Donnelly, *The Land and the People of Nineteenth-Century Cork: The Rural Economy and the Land Question*, (London, 1975), p. 82.
10. P. M. A. Bourke, 'The Irish grain trade, 1839–48', *Irish Historical Studies*, **XX** (1976), 165.
11. Ó Gráda, *Ireland Before and After the Famine*, p. 51.
12. R. O. Pringle, 'A review of Irish agriculture, chiefly with reference to the production of live stock', *Journal of the Royal Agricultural Society of England*, 2nd Series, 8 (1872), p. 32.
13. See P. M. A. Bourke, 'The extent of the potato crop in Ireland at the time of the Famine', *Journal of the Statistical and Social Inquiry Society of Ireland*, **XX**, part III (1959–60), p. 13.
14. Bourke, 'The extent of the potato crop', p. 11.
15. R. D. Crotty, *Irish Agricultural Production: Its Volume and Structure*, (Cork, 1966), p. 315.
16. See Bourke, 'The agricultural statistics', p. 379. On this general issue of standard and

non-standard units of measurement, see P. M. A. Bourke, 'Notes on some agricultural units of measurement in use in pre-Famine Ireland', *Irish Historical Studies*, **XIV** (1965), pp. 236–45.

17. J. Mokyr, 'Irish history with the potato', *Irish Economic and Social History*, **VIII** (1981), p. 20.

18. See also T. Barrington, 'A review of Irish agricultural prices', *Journal of the Statistical and Social Inquiry Society of Ireland*, **XV** (1927), pp. 249–80; Mokyr, *Why Ireland Starved*, 1985 edn, pp. 147–9.

19. See also T. Barrington, 'The yields of Irish tillage crops since the year 1847', *Journal of the Department of Agriculture*, **XXI** (1921), pp. 212–13, and 289–305.

20. *The Agricultural Output of Northern Ireland, 1925*, Cmd. 87 (Belfast, 1928), p. 11. L. Kennedy, 'The rural economy, 1820–1914' in L. Kennedy and P. Ollerenshaw (eds.), *An Economic History of Ulster, 1820–1939*, (Manchester, 1985), p. 23; P. M. A. Bourke, 'The average yields of food crops in Ireland on the eve of the Great Famine', *Journal of the Department of Agriculture*, **LXVI** (1969), especially pp. 27–30; Barrington 'The yields of Irish crops'; B. Solow, *The Land Question and the Irish Economy, 1870–1903*, (Harvard 1971), pp. 112–13.

21. See Daly, *The Famine*, pp. 23, 55; P. Solar, 'Harvest fluctuations in pre-Famine Ireland: Evidence from Belfast and Waterford Newspapers', *Agricultural History Review*, **37**, Part II (1989), pp. 157–65.

22. Bourke, 'The extent of the potato crop', pp. 11–14, and derived from the annual agricultural statistics.

23. This paragraph based on J. S. Donnelly, 'The Irish agricultural depression of 1859–64', *Irish Economic and Social History*, **3** (1976), especially pp. 34–7.

24. See Crotty, *Irish Agricultural Production*, p. 69 on supply price determination.

25. Donnelly, 'Irish agricultural depression', p. 37. See also Barrington, 'Review of prices', p. 251.

26. Donnelly, 'Irish agricultural depression', pp. 38–9.

27. *Ibid.*, p. 47.

28. See also Kennedy, 'The rural economy', pp. 30–1.

29. P. Ollerenshaw, *Banking in Nineteenth-Century Ireland: The Belfast Banks, 1825–1914*, (Manchester, 1987), pp. 102–5.

30. T. P. O'Neill, 'The Food Crisis of the 1890s', in E. M. Crawford (ed.), *Famine: The Irish Experience 900–1900*, (Edinburgh, 1989), pp. 176–97.

31. Kennedy, 'The rural economy', pp. 18–20.

32. T. J. Hughes, 'Society and settlement in nineteenth-century Ireland', *Irish Geography*, **5**, no. 2 (1965), p. 88.

33. This could easily be the result of changed definitions in 1906 when mountain land was differentiated as either barren or grazed. Before 1906 much of this land was probably returned as pasture.

34. If we rank the 32 counties for 7 census years in order from most to least cultivated, we can derive Spearman rank correlations coefficients of between 0.92 and 0.99.

35. If we rank pasture by county as a percentage of cultivated area, we can derive rank correlation coefficients which vary from 0.68 to 0.98, with a gradual deterioration over time.

36. Bourke, 'The agricultural statistics', pp. 381–2. *Census of Ireland for the Year 1841*, B[ritish] P[arliamentary] P[apers], Vol. 24 for 1843, pp. 454–7.

37. P. M. A. Bourke, 'The use of the potato crop in pre-Famine Ireland', *Journal of the Statistical and Social Inquiry Society of Ireland*, **21** (1967–8), pp. 84, 86. For local studies see M. E. Turner, 'Livestock in the agrarian economy of counties Down and Antrim from 1803 to the Famine', *Irish Economic and Social History*, **XI** (1984), pp. 19–43; Donnelly, *The Land and the People of Cork*, pp. 76–9.

38. Donnelly, *The Land and the People of Cork*, pp. 87–8.

39. For a local study see Donnelly, *ibid.*, pp. 135–58 and *idem*, 'Cork Market: Its role in the nineteenth-century Irish butter trade', *Studia Hibernica*, **11** (1971), pp. 130–63.

40. J. O'Donovan, *The Economic History of Livestock in Ireland*, (Cork, 1939), p. 207.

41. See Pringle, 'A review of Irish agriculture', pp. 32–3. See also Crotty, *Irish Agricultural Production*, p. 85.

42. O'Donovan, *Livestock in Ireland*, p. 256; see also, H. Staehle, 'Statistical notes on the economic history of Irish agriculture, 1847–1913', *Journal of the Statistical and Social Inquiry Society of Ireland*, **18** (1950–51), pp. 444–71.

43. O'Donovan, *Livestock in Ireland*, p. 266 based on an inspection of the data in Saorstat Eireann, *Agricultural Statistics 1847–1926: Reports and Tables*, Department of Industry and Commerce (Dublin, 1930), p. 16.

44. Donnelly, *The Land and the People of Cork*, p. 293.

45. R. Perren, *The Meat Trade in Britain 1840–1914*, (London, 1978), pp. 96–7; *Agricultural Statistics of Ireland . . . 1891*, BPP, Cd. 6777 (Dublin, 1892), p. 23; *Agricultural Statistics of Ireland . . . 1901*, BPP, Cd. 1170 (Dublin, 1902), p. xvii; *Agricultural Statistics of Ireland . . . 1911*, BPP, Cd. 6377 (London, 1912), p. xxi; *Agricultural Statistics of Ireland . . . 1916*, BPP, Cmd. 112 (Dublin, 1919), p. xiv; *Report from the Committee. . . . Transit of Animals by Sea and Land*, BPP, Cd. 116 (London, 1870), Appendix XXV, p. 110; *Minutes of Evidence. . . . Upon the Inland Transit of Cattle*, BPP, Cd. 8929 (London, 1898), Appendix III; *Agricultural Statistics, 1907 . . . Acreage and Livestock Returns of Great Britain*, BPP, Cd. 3870 (London, 1908), where pp. 272–5 is 'Trade in Livestock with Ireland'.

46. *The Agricultural Output of Ireland 1908*, (Department of Agriculture and Technical Instruction for Ireland, Dublin, 1912), p. 6. See also Huttman, 'Institutional factors', pp. 538–40 for 1850–1915.

47. O'Donovan, *Livestock in Ireland*, pp. 212–13. Though see P. Solar, 'The agricultural trade statistics in the Irish Railway Commissioners' Report', *Irish Economic and Social History*, **VI** (1979), pp. 24–40, especially 30–2, for criticism of the original data.

48. O'Donovan, *Livestock in Ireland*, pp. 213–14. See also Donnelly, *The Land and the People of Cork*, pp. 137–8.

49. L. Kennedy, 'Regional specialization, railway development, and Irish agriculture in the nineteenth century' in Goldstrom and Clarkson (eds.), *Irish Population, Economy, and Society*, pp. 173–93, especially 187, 191.

50. Crotty, *Irish Agricultural Production*, chapter 2: Ó Gráda, *Ireland Before and After the Famine*, p. 50 and *idem*, 'Poverty, population and agriculture, 1801–45', in W. E. Vaughan (ed.), *A New History of Ireland V: Ireland Under the Union, I 1801–70*, (Oxford, 1989), pp. 122, 130, and the trade statistics outlined on pp 132 and 136.

51. J. M. Goldstrom, 'Irish agriculture and the Great Famine', in Goldstrom and Clarkson (eds.), *Irish Population, Economy and Society*, pp. 155–71, especially 162–3, 170–1.

52. O'Donovan, *Livestock in Ireland*, p. 215; *Report of Mr Chambers and Professor Ferguson on Pleuro-Pneumonia among Cattles imported from Ireland into Norfolk*, BPP, LX (1875).

53. See Bourke, 'The agricultural statistics', p. 378; Mokyr, *Why Ireland Starved*, pp. 17–19. For criticism of Bourke's original doubts over the 1841 statistics see the discussion by T. P. O'Neill, K. B. Nowlan and R. Dudley Edwards appended to Bourke, 'The extent of the potato crop', pp. 26–35, where 20–35 is an appendix on the 'Uncertainties in the statistics of farm size in Ireland, 1841–51'; see also Bourke, 'Notes on some agricultural units', pp. 236–45; Donnelly, *The Land and the People of Cork*, esp. pp. 119–22; D. Fitzpatrick, 'The disappearance of the Irish agricultural labourer, 1841–1912', *Irish Economic and Social History*, **VII** (1980), esp. p. 72.

54. R. O'Connor and C. Guiomard, 'Agricultural output in the Irish Free State area before and after Independence', *Irish Economic and Social History*, **XII** (1985), p. 93.

55. Bourke, 'The agricultural statistics', p. 380; see also Bourke, 'The extent of the potato crop . . . Uncertainties in the statistics', pp. 20–6.

56. Bourke, 'The agricultural statistics'; and Mokyr, *Why Ireland Starved*, pp. 18–19. Based on *Appendix to the Minutes of Evidence taken before Her Majesty's Commissioners of Inquiry into the State of the Law and Practice in respect to the Occupation of Land in Ireland*, BPP, XXII (1845), 280–3 and 288–9, known more popularly as *The Devon Commission*. See Solar, 'Agricultural productivity', p. 77.

57. Daly, *The Famine*, pp. 65–6. See also Donnelly, *The Land and the People of Cork*, pp. 100–3.

58. Daly, *The Famine*, pp. 65–6, also 94–7; J. S. Donnelly, 'Production, prices, and exports, 1846–51', in Vaughan (ed.), *A New History of Ireland V*, p. 292.
59. Donnelly, *The Land and the People of Cork*, p. 100, also 114–20. More generally see J. S. Donnelly, 'Landlords and tenants' in Vaughan (ed.), *A New History of Ireland V*, pp. 332–49.
60. R. H. Buchanan, 'Field systems of Ireland', in A. R. H. Baker and R. A. Butlin (eds.), *Studies of Field Systems in the British Isles*, (Cambridge, 1973), pp. 590–8, especially p. 596.
61. M. E. Cawley, 'Aspects of continuity and change in nineteenth-century rural settlement patterns: findings from County Roscommon', *Studia Hibernica*, (1982–3), pp. 106–27; B. J. Graham, 'Clachan continuity and distribution in medieval Ireland', in P. Flatrès (ed.), *Paysages Ruraux Europeens*, (Rennes, 1979), pp. 147–58; K. Whelan, 'The Catholic parish, the Catholic chapel and village development in Ireland', *Irish Geography*, **16** (1983), pp. 1–16; see also W. Nolan, *Fassadinin: Land, Settlement and Society in South-east Ireland, 1600–1850*, (Dublin, 1979). Kevin Whelan, 'Settlement and society in eighteenth century Ireland', in Gerald Dawe and John Wilson Foster (eds), *The Poet's Place: Ulster Literature and Society: Essays in Honour of John Hewitt, 1907–87*, (Belfast, 1991), pp. 45–62.
62. M. Gwinnell, 'The Famine years in county Wexford', *Journal of the Wexford Historical Society*, **9** (1983), p. 47 citing the *Devon Commission* as evidence.
63. Gwinnell, 'The Famine years', p. 47; and the Cork evidence based on Donnelly, *Land and the People of Cork*, p. 119.
64. K. T. Hoppen, *Ireland Since 1800: Conflict and Conformity*, (London, 1989), p. 54. See also *idem, Elections, Politics, and Society in Ireland 1832–1885*, (Oxford, 1984), p. 96.
65. Solow, *The Land Question*, p. 193. See also M. J. Bonn, 'The psychological aspect of land reform in Ireland', *Economic Journal*, **19** (1909), pp. 374–94, especially, 376–8 and 384n; see also E. Barker, *Ireland in the Last Fifty Years (1866–1916)*, (London, 1916), pp. 53–4, 98–116.
66. The figures for holdings and occupiers before and after 1909 are not directly comparable as the enumeration went through some subtle changes. See *Agricultural Statistics of Ireland ... 1916*, p. xvi and *Agricultural Statistics of Ireland ... 1914*, BPP, Cd. 8266 (Dublin, 1916), p. xvii.
67. *Agricultural Statistics of Ireland ... 1911*, pp. xxiv, 12.
68. *Agricultural Statistics ... 1916*, p. xvi.
69. L. Kennedy, 'Farmers, traders, and agricultural politics in pre-Independence Ireland', in S. Clark and J. S. Donnelly (eds.), *Irish Peasants. Violence and Political Unrest 1780–1914*, (Manchester, 1983), pp. 346–7; D. S. Jones, 'The cleavage between graziers and peasants in the land struggle, 1890–1910', in *idem, Irish Peasants*, pp. 394, 401, 412–13.
70. Kennedy, 'Farmers, traders, and agricultural politics', pp. 347–9, 356.
71. L. Kennedy, 'Traders in the Irish rural economy, 1880–1914', *Economic History Review*, 2nd ser., **XXXII** (1979), pp. 201–10, especially 209.
72. In general see Jones, 'The cleavage'.
73. Jones, 'The cleavage', pp. 392, 394.
74. Much of this section on 11 month lettings derives from Jones, 'The cleavage', especially pp. 396–404.
75. 1853 was the first year when data was presented in this form, 1874 was the last year, but in 1902 the enumerators gave an estimate of average holding size in each size group. See *Agricultural Statistics of Ireland ... 1861*, BPP, LXIX (Dublin, 1863). p. xv; *Agricultural Statistics of Ireland ... 1902*, BPP, Cd. 1614 (Dublin, 1903), p. xxvi. See also *The Census of Ireland for the year 1851. Part II. Returns of Agricultural Produce in 1851*, BPP, XCIII (Dublin, 1852–3), p. vii, for more detail and comment. See also Pringle, 'A review of Irish agriculture', p. 21 for a breakdown for 1869, and Solow, *The Land Question*, p. 108 for a breakdown for 1871.
76. In this table we use the year 1854 as the first year of study, whereas in an earlier table we began with 1853. Milch cows were not separately enumerated until 1854. Livestock unit equivalents as in Coppock, *An Agricultural Geography*, p. 150.

77. See J. T. Coppock, *An Agricultural Atlas of Scotland*, (Edinburgh, 1976), p. 42.
78. There is a large literature on this subject. A good starting point might be Coppock, *An Agricultural Geography*, p. 150.
79. Though this choice of date hides the dramatic fall from 1847 to 1853 of 27 per cent (803 to 585 thousand).
80. *Agricultural Output of Northern Ireland*, p. 43.
81. Kennedy, 'The rural economy', p. 20.
82. Barker, *Ireland in the Last Fifty Years*, pp. 116–20.
83. This paragraph is heavily dependent on Donnelly, *The Land and the People of Cork*, pp. 227–32. By premier we mean emigrants as a proportion of county population 1851–91.
84. Bonn, 'The psychological aspect', p. 377. For the latest revisions and reviews see M. E. Turner, 'Output and productivity in Irish agriculture from the Famine to the Great War', *Irish Economic and Social History*, **XVII** (1990), pp. 62–78; *idem*, 'Agricultural output and productivity in post-Famine Ireland', in B. M. S. Campbell and Mark Overton (eds.), *Land, Labour and Livestock: Historical Studies in European Agricultural Productivity*, (Manchester, 1991), pp. 410–38. See W. E. Vaughan, 'Potatoes and agricultural output', *Irish Economic and Social History*, **XVII** (1990), pp. 79–92 for criticisms of the estimating procedures.
85. C. Ó Gráda, *The Great Irish Famine*, (London, 1989), p. 68; Donnelly, 'Irish agricultural depression', pp. 42–4; *idem*, 'Cork market', pp. 154–7; *idem*, *The Land and the People of Cork*, pp. 150–3.
86. For the methods of construction see Turner, 'Agricultural output', pp. 419–21.
87. See the bald statement of this in J. J. Lee, 'Patterns of rural unrest in nineteenth-century Ireland: a preliminary survey', in Cullen and Furet (eds.), *Ireland and France*, p. 230.
88. For a greatly expanded analysis on comparisons between Ireland and Britain see Turner, 'Agricultural output', pp. 422–8.
89. Official sources tend to confirm this impression of the real improvement in Irish agricultural performance, *Agricultural Statistics, Ireland, 1915, Return of Prices of Crops, Livestock, and other Irish Agricultural Products*, BPP, Cd. 8452 (1917), pp. 5–8.
90. Turner, 'Agricultural output', p. 428.
91. See also Solow, *The Land Question*, pp. 121–2; and more generally for the agricultural distress of the late 1870s, see S. Clark, *Social Origins of the Land War*, (Princeton, 1979), pp. 225–45.
92. Donnelly, *The Land and the People of Cork*, pp. 184–200. See also Hoppen, *Ireland Since 1800*, Chapter 4, pp. 83–109, especially pp. 94–5 and the antithesis to the Donnelly view, 'The background to the Land War of 1879–82 was not, therefore, "a revolution of rising expectations" . . . but a state of deep anxiety that the economic roller-coaster was once again heading in a downward direction.' For different arguments against the rising expectations theory see W. E. Vaughan, *Landlords and Tenants in Ireland 1848– 1904*, (The Economic and Social History Society of Ireland, Dublin, 1984), especially pp. 31–5.
93. Donnelly, 'The agricultural depression', pp. 52–3, his emphasis.
94. Vaughan, *Landlords and Tenants*, p. 30, who curiously added a loaded value judgement when he said that '*only* about 25 per cent of rents due between 1879 and 1882 were not paid', my emphasis.
95. Ollerenshaw, *Banking in Nineteenth-Century Ireland*, pp. 114–22, 198, though he cautions against using bank deposits as evidence; Donnelly, *The Land and the People of Cork*, p. 377; Clark, *Social Origins*, p. 231.
96. Solow, *The Land Question*, p. 117 *et seq*.
97. See in this context S. Clark, 'The social composition of the Land League', *Irish Historical Studies*, **XVII** (1971), p. 450.
98. Briefly touched upon by P. Bew and F. Wright, 'The agrarian opposition in Ulster Politics, 1848–87', in Clark and Donnelly (eds.), *Irish Peasants*, p. 209. See also S. Clark and J. S. Donnelly, 'Introduction' to part III of Clark and Donnelly, *idem*, pp. 279–80; Donnelly, *The Land and the People of Cork*, p. 254; Ollerenshaw, *Banking in Nineteenth- Century Ireland*, pp. 121–2; Clark, *Social Origins*, pp. 231–5; Kennedy, 'Farmers, traders,

and agricultural politics', especially pp. 342–3; L. Kennedy, 'Retail markets in rural Ireland at the end of the nineteenth century', *Irish Economic and Social History*, **V** (1978), pp. 46–61.

99. Kennedy, 'Farmers, traders, and agricultural politics', pp. 343–4, 346. See also Clark, 'The social composition', pp. 450–1; *idem*, *Social Origins*, p. 245 and Chapter 8 in general, pp. 246–304.

100. L. P. Curtis, 'Incumbered wealth: landed indebtedness in post-Famine Ireland', *American Historical Review*, **LXXXV** (1980), pp. 335.

101. Curtis, 'Incumbered wealth', pp. 340–53. See also R. W. Kirkpatrick, 'Origin and development of the Land War in mid-Ulster, 1879–85', in F. S. L. Lyons and R. A. J. Hawkins (eds.), *Ireland under the Union: Varieties of Tension: Essays in Honour of T. W. Moody* (Oxford, 1980), pp. 201–35.

102. Summarized in Clark and Donnelly, 'Introduction', p. 272. See also Curtis, 'Incumbered wealth', 367.

103. See M. J. Winstanley, *Ireland and the Land Question 1800–1922*, (London, 1984); Solow, *The Land Question*; Vaughan, *Landlords and Tenants*.

104. Hoppen, *Ireland Since 1800*, p. 100.

105. Solow, *The Land Question*, pp. 161–7, 174–6, 189–94.

106. Fitzpatrick, 'The disappearance', especially pp. 80–2. See also Hoppen, *Ireland Since 1800*, pp. 91–2, where we note that the use of Vaughan's wage estimates will narrow the bad experience for the farmer in terms of his profits, but not make that bad experience disappear altogether.

107. Solow, *The Land Question*, pp. 62–9, 176, 178–9. J. Lee, 'Irish agriculture', *Agricultural History Review*, **17** (1969), pp. 74–5; Mokyr, *Why Ireland Starved*, p. 28. See also C. Ó Gráda, 'Agricultural head rents, pre-Famine and post-Famine', *Economic and Social Review*, **5** (1973–4), pp. 386–7.

108. Vaughan, *Landlords and Tenants*, pp. 14, 21; *idem*, 'An assessment of the economic performance of Irish landlords, 1851–81', in Lyons and Hawkins (eds.), *Ireland under the Union*, pp. 173–99, especially 177–8.

109. Donnelly, *The Land and the People of Cork*, pp. 189, 194, 199–200.

110. Vaughan, 'An assessment of the economic performance', p. 180; *idem*, *Landlord and Tenant*, p. 23. See also his 'Landlord and tenant relations in Ireland between the Famine and the Land War, 1850–1878' in L. M. Cullen and T. C. Smout (eds.), *Comparative Aspects of Scottish and Irish Economic and Social History 1600–1900*, (Edinburgh, 1977), pp. 216–17; Winstanley, *Ireland and the Land Question*, p. 30; R. F. Foster, *Modern Ireland 1600–1972*, (London, 1988), pp. 375–7; O. Macdonagh, 'Introduction: Ireland and the Union, 1801–70' in Vaughan (ed.), *A New History of Ireland V*, p. lviii.

111. Vaughan, *Landlord and Tenant*, pp. 27–35. See also Hoppen, *Ireland Since 1800*, Chapter 4, 'Agricola Victor'; R. W. Kirkpatrick, 'Origin and development of the Land War in mid-Ulster, 1879–85', in Lyons and Hawkins (eds.), *Ireland under the Union*, pp. 201–35; P. Bew, *Law and the National Question in Ireland 1858–82*, (Dublin, 1978), chapter 1, but especially pp. 25–33.

112. Ó Gráda, 'Agricultural head rents', pp. 389–90, or a 30 per cent increase from the early 1850s to the mid 1870s.

113. J. Johnson, *Irish Agriculture in Transition*, (Dublin and Oxford, 1951), p. 5.

114. Donnelly, *The Land and the People of Cork*, pp. 296–7, for Cork in the early 1880s suggests the size of initial rent reductions was only about 16 per cent. See also C. F. Bastable, 'Some features of the economic movement in Ireland, 1880–1900', *Economic Journal*, **XI** (1901), p. 33. By the time Bonn was writing in 1909, 369,483 holdings had rents fixed for a first term, 131,637 for a second term. In addition, tenants on 143,564 holdings had been converted into owners and on a further 173,343 holdings purchase agreement had been conducted, Bonn, 'The psychological aspect', pp. 376–8. See also Curtis, 'Incumbered wealth', pp. 332–67.

115. Suppose a tenant redeemed a £100 rent at 18 years' purchase. On the £1800 borrowed at 4% over 49 years he would become liable to an annual interest repayment of £72, or £28 less than his *current* rent. This example comes from Johnson, *Irish Agriculture in Tran-*

sition, p. 8, citing Bonn, 'The psychological aspect of land reform'. See also Barker, *Ireland in the Last Fifty Years*, pp. 100–16.

116. J. P. Huttman, 'The impact of land reform on agricultural production in Ireland', *Agricultural History*, **46** (1972), pp. 354–5.

117. Barker, *Ireland in the Last Fifty Years*, pp. 53–4, 98–116. See also Barrington, 'The yields of Irish tillage crops', pp. 290–1, for a summary table of the purchase of land under the various acts from 1870–1920.

118. Kennedy, 'The rural economy', p. 60, note 129.

10

The Irish Diaspora: Emigration to the New World, 1720–1920

C. J. Houston and W. J. Smyth

Introduction

Some five million people inhabit the island of Ireland today but the world wide community of Irish, by descent and by birth, totals more than seventy million. In cities as diverse as London, New York, San Francisco, Toronto, Melbourne, Auckland, and Buenos Aires, Irish communities are present. Likewise, many farming regions and mining towns of former British colonies became their home. This widespread dispersal abroad from such a small European source region, is the product of a series of migrations that extends over two and a half centuries. In the history of international migration the Irish experience is distinctive by virtue of its scale, duration and geographical spread. In recent years the evocative term, diaspora, has been employed, thereby linking in metaphor the dispersal of the Irish with that of the Jews. The concept of the diaspora, with its emphasis upon the displacement of people from their home and its connotations of exile, is a compelling but limited description of the Irish experience. Certainly, poverty, hunger, force and desperation drove hundreds of thousands out of Ireland, but many more exited voluntarily, motivated more by a perception of future loss of social status and drawn by opportunities in colonies abroad. They were caught in the imperial ambitions driving their British neighbour's effort to occupy and colonize new territories. Whether in Australia or New Zealand, or the Americas, or in Britain itself, much of the modern Irish emigration experience was propelled by the demands and consequences of the English imperial quest.

Ireland's location between Britain and the lands and resources of North America gave the island an intimate role in England's overseas expansion. In particular, the island's position astride the main trans-Atlantic shipping lanes has meant that British ships have had to sail either to its south or north, creating in the process a complex interrelationship with adjacent Irish ports. South-east coast ports such as Cork and Waterford and the northern ports of Derry and Belfast, together with a number of smaller centres in both those coastal regions, were integrated into the British Atlantic trade from the start. Originally supplying fresh water and provisions for outbound voyages, these centres evolved into intrinsic components of much of the trans-Atlantic activity. In the eighteenth century the south-eastern ports assumed a position of pre-eminence in the shipping of flour and salted meats to the British colonies of Newfoundland and the Caribbean, and then, as in the following century, it was through these and the northern ports that tens of thousands of emigrants were conveyed annually to the New World. These ports and their hinterlands were also responsible for partially supplying the British navy with crews. Logistically, therefore, Ireland was well integrated into the Atlantic economy and the form of that integration was in large measure dictated by the reciprocal but ever-changing nature of the economic and demographic demands of both sides of the ocean. Given the nature of the Irish economy, however, it was scarcely surprising that agricultural products and emigrants should constitute the bulk of Ireland's outgoing trade.[1]

Irish emigration developed within the dynamic of imperial trade in staple goods drawn from Britain's colonies in the New World. From 1675 and the defeat of the Dutch, the North Atlantic had become increasingly a British sea. By 1740 upwards of 30,000 mariners drawn from Britain and Ireland were employed in the Atlantic traffic, and in a coastal strip running from Newfoundland southwards to the Caribbean, complex and increasingly sophisticated regional societies were emerging.[2] The principal exports from the colonies were primary products—fur, tobacco, fish and seed. In the early nineteenth century, timber and wheat were added. These unprocessed staple products were easily marketed in a contemporary Britain then experiencing the first stages of the urban and industrial revolutions: in return the colonies purchased the finished manufactured goods such as textiles, machinery, iron bars and household goods. Thus, in a classical example of mercantilism at work, the mother country and its colonies established a coherent reciprocal relationship. However, a disequilibrium existed in the volume, if not in the value, of the goods transported. The eastbound primary staples were bulky low-value items and some of them, for example, timber, required wide bottomed boats for carriage. The westward bound goods were, by contrast, of high value but low volume and much spare shipping capacity existed. Extra ballast in the form of rocks frequently supplied the weight necessary to ensure a safe voyage and many breakwaters and quaysides along the eastern shore of North America testify to this bulky but highly unprofitable trade. Merchants, ship captains and owners assiduously sought alternative ballast and, legal and social problems notwithstanding, they increasingly turned to the emigrant trade for a fare-paying westward bound cargo. Such then was the logistical context within which operated the process of emigration, an increasingly preferred economic option in an overcrowded rural Ireland.

Emigration was not always the preferred alternative. At any time, it is a selective process and not all elements of society will be equally prone to abandon their homeland in search of an uncertain future. In Ireland emigration as a concept had to filter through barriers erected by socio-economic class, religion and regionalism. Most popular in eighteenth-century Presbyterian Ulster and in the hinterland of the major port cities, emigration had, by the eve of the Great Famine in 1845, attained a status of ubiquity, indeed inevitability, among all but the very poorest and the very richest classes in every part of the country. Assailed by newspaper reports, the propaganda of emigration agents, land clearances, and fortified by emigrant letters, remittances and pre-paid passages, the rural Irish, and indeed some of their urban counterparts, turned in their tens of thousands towards the lure of the New World. Lack of finance and attachments to place of birth and kin, rather than ignorance of other geographical alternatives, acted as the factors restricting the outflow. The catastrophe of the Famine undermined even those barriers and made emigration, either to neighbouring Britain or to the New World, part of an individual's maturation process, assuming the status of a *rite de passage* whereby adulthood was confirmed.[3] From the 1820s emigration was to be endemic in Irish society to a degree unknown in any other European country.[4]

This represented a dramatic turnaround in behaviour from the situation two centuries earlier. Seventeenth-century Ireland had experienced a net demographic balance in favour of immigration from abroad. The Munster, Ulster, Cromwellian, and Williamite Plantations and their aftermaths had all generated a considerable immigration of English and Scottish settlers. Prior to 1641 over 100,000 had settled in Ireland and by the opening years of the eighteenth century perhaps as many as a quarter of the Irish population was of immigrant stock—proportionately the largest immigration of any contemporary European country.[5] By way of contrast emigration from seventeenth-century Ireland had tended to be episodic; the product of such military and political crises as the Flight of the Earls and the Flight of the Wild Geese, whereby the native Irish leadership and the native armies sought refuge in Europe in 1607 and 1690 respectively. Transportation to the West Indies as punishment for alleged social and political crimes was the lot of hundreds of others, especially during the Cromwellian period. However, overall the net balance was in favour of immigration. It was the last time (apart from a few years in the 1970s) that more people were to migrate into Ireland than were to forsake it.

No other European country has experienced such a sustained demographic haemorrhage. From the 1720s onwards every generation has been affected, and Irish communities overseas have been constantly renewed by the latest arrivals. The Irish abroad have been the product not of any single episode in demographic history; rather, they are but elements in an ongoing continuum. From the seventeenth century through to the eve of the First World War, probably seven million Irish had emigrated to North America, a further third of a million had gone to Australia and New Zealand, while smaller groups settled in Argentina and South Africa. More than a million sought a new life in Britain. Overall, the Irish constituted more than 10 per cent of the 60 odd million Europeans who crossed the Atlantic in this, the era of mass migration, and as such were disproportionately over-represented by at least a factor of ten. Among the European migrants of the period the Irish were among the earliest and, arguably, were the most consequential.

Emigration in the Eighteenth Century

The eighteenth-century migrants were drawn to North America for the most part from Ulster, and were predominantly Presbyterian, although Anglicans and Catholics were present in number. It was for this Protestant group that the appellation Scotch-Irish was devised by nineteenth-century descendants in the United States, anxious to create a heritage that would distinguish them from the Catholic Irish whose communities had grown dramatically from the emigrations of the Famine and subsequent decades. Estimates of the scale of the eighteenth-century exodus vary considerably and more recent writings have tended to revise downwards the overall totals, while simultaneously widening the debate on the social and religious composition of the emigrants.[6] For the period 1700–76, emigration estimates vary from 250,000 to 400,000, and this from a national population which totalled no more that 2.4 million in mid century. Estimates for the period following upon the American Revolution suggest that a further 100,000 may have left Ireland for the newly independent United States of America between 1783 and 1815. Such estimates have been based upon incomplete port data, newspaper advertisements and ambitious inferences based upon tonnage of shipping and would appear to overestimate the extent of the outflow, particularly in the early years of the century. Nonetheless, it is clear from both Irish and American sources that the movement was of major significance in the international context of the time. It is also clear that the majority of the emigrants were drawn from the Presbyterian communities of Ulster. However, increasingly evidence is being offered to support the case that perhaps as many as one-third of the eighteenth-century trans-Atlantic migrants were derived from among the Catholic communities of the major urban centres in the south and east of Ireland. Furthermore it has been argued that by the last quarter of the century, upwards of 5000 per year were going to the Newfoundland fisheries, albeit mostly as seasonal fishermen. Despite these refinements the preponderance of Ulster folk remains unquestioned.[7]

The Ulster link with colonial America had tenuous beginnings in the seventeenth century but its dimensions only crystallized in the post-Williamite period. In 1718 James McGregor, Presbyterian minister at Aghadowey, Co. Londonderry, chartered five boats to sail to Boston and announced to his congregation:

> Brethren, let us depart for God has appointed a new country for us to dwell in. It is called New England. Let us be free of these Pharaohs, these rackers of rent and screwers of tithes and let us go into the land of Canaan.[8]

McGregor's exhortation to his congregation reveals two of the underlying motives for what was to become a sustained emigration of co-religionists. Presbyterians in eighteenth-century Ireland suffered under legal and social impediments which effectively reduced them to the status of second class citizens. A largely Anglican landowning class and an Anglican Church to which all inhabitants had to pay tithes cemented in power an Ascendancy which was jealous of its exclusive power base and less than tolerant of any challengers, be they Presbyterian or Catholic. Religious freedom and an aspiration for social equality therefore provided a powerful rhetoric for those seeking to encourage or justify the emigration. But more prosaic factors were also involved. The initial exodus emerged from the west Ulster communities of east Donegal and western County Londonderry—the Foyle valley and its tributaries. There the Scottish immigrants of the previous century had settled on rich but spatially confined agricultural land and their sons and grandsons were faced with either subdividing the original holdings or moving out. Endowed with less extensive natural resources and facing the consequences of environmental limits, west Ulster was the first part of the region to experience the phenomenon of rural emigration. The prospect of diminishing economic possibilities was further reinforced by the clear realization that the centre of economic power in Ulster was irrevocably shifting from Derry and the Foyle valley eastwards to Belfast, the Lagan valley and the lowlands of north Armagh and Down.[9]

The emigration was encouraged, and indeed moulded, by the flax and linen trade which was developing between Ulster and Pennsylvania. Ulster's linen industry, based upon local cultivation of flax, required the imported seeds for both agricultural reasons and also for the production of linseed oil, and it was not long before enterprising ship-captains and merchants perceived a renumerative reciprocal trade in passengers. By mid century a network of small town merchants servicing the larger import and export merchant interests of Derry, Belfast, Newry and Coleraine had sprung up throughout Ulster. Passages to America could be booked as easily in Enniskillen as Derry; local newspapers, and especially the *Belfast Newsletter*, carried advertisements for ships, giving estimated departure dates and details of the level of comfort offered on board. Passage was offered only on cargo ships, temporarily converted and despite the rhetoric the comforts were meagre and the dangers from shipwreck great.[10]

The Ulster bias in this early migration was to last throughout the century and, apart from young artisans leaving from Dublin, Cork and Limerick, there was relatively little enthusiasm for overseas emigration elsewhere in the country. One notable exception to this was the south-east of Ireland where long established links with continental Europe persisted. Cullen argues that in the first half of the eighteenth century, several hundred young men were recruited annually for French and Spanish armies from Counties Wexford, Waterford, Kilkenny, Tipperary and Cork.[11] After the peace of 1763, the European armies were reduced in size, the recruitment ceased and coincidentally there was, within south-eastern Ireland, a development of interest in Newfoundland. Initially, the link was prompted by trade; ships carrying provisions from Bristol and Poole in Dorset used to stop en route to Newfoundland to take on fresh water and additional provisions at Waterford. Soon young men were being recruited as seasonal fishermen and conventionally they would sign on with a ship for two summers and a winter— overwintering in Newfoundland and fishing the Grand Banks during the summer season. *Talamh An Eisc*, the fishing ground, was the local Irish name applied to Newfoundland and a rich lore grew up in the region concerning the seasonal fisheries migration. Eventually permanent Irish settlements emerged in Newfoundland and between 1770 and 1830 some 30–50,000 settled there, adopting a lifestyle of subsistence farming and cod fishing and retaining the distinctive accents of Wexford, Waterford and Kilkenny.[12]

The motivation and expectations of those leaving for Newfoundland contrasted markedly with those of the emigrants from Ulster. Those who left from Ulster were generally of farming backgrounds and apart from group schemes such as that of McGregor in 1718, they very often emigrated as family units, having sold their interest in the lease of a farm or travelling by means of a dowry or inheritance. A significant number of children among the passengers testify to the family status of the migrants and in personal records, references to older parents and even grandparents making the long trip to the New World indicate the strongest of family motivations. Entire families investing their savings in such voyages, the presence of extended kin groups, and the persistence of emigration over several generations in the same localities, all indicate the deliberate nature of a movement which was neither haphazard nor impulsive. By way of contrast, emigration of artisans and the younger sons of south-eastern farmers had more of an image of adventurous youth. A virtual absence of women, except in the later migrations to Newfoundland, confirmed that image and also implied an inevitable pattern of intermarriage and rapid cultural assimilation in the New World. Thus, many Irish tended to disappear into the mix of the new societies, inadvertently hiding the eighteenth-century contributions of a few Irish regions to the New World. Many of these emigrants (and indeed the same applied to adventurous but impoverished weavers from Ulster) had insufficient funds to pay for their passage and so they sold themselves as indentured servants to willing captains and merchants. Upon arrival they were auctioned off for specified periods as servants and only upon completion of that time were they deemed freemen. This system of indenturing carried with it many risks for those in the shipping industry as there was always a risk that the servant might disappear before being auctioned off. Consequently, as demand for travel from fare paying passengers rose later in the century, the system of indenturing was gradually abandoned.[13]

What the emigration regions of Ulster, the major metropolitan ports, and the south-eastern counties had in common, apart from overseas links, were complex and changing regional economies. Collectively they represented the most advanced sectors of the contemporary Irish economy and their established merchant and shipping links with the British colonies across the Atlantic provided not only the logistics but also the mentality for emigration. The earliest emigrants emerged not from the hopelessness of a backward depressed economy but rather they were opportunists from economic regions affected by structural change and restricted growth. Their leaving was not motivated by abject poverty but rather by a perception of diminished opportunities for themselves and future generations, and the critical perception that emigration offered a solution to their dilemma. Catholic artisan and Presbyterian farmer alike were motivated by such a sense of individualism and the desire for improvement. Other regions, and other members of the community who were less motivated, were to await the greater popularization of emigration in the following century.[14]

Emigration in the Pre-Famine Nineteenth Century

The nineteenth century opened with emigration in the doldrums but by 1820, with the resumption of trans-Atlantic commerce in the aftermath of the Napoleonic Wars and because of agricultural depression in Ireland, emigrants were leaving the country in historic number. Their exodus signalled that the great European era of mass trans-Atlantic migration had commenced what would be its century-long run. The Passenger Act of 1803, which raised the standards of conditions on board ship and as a consequence led to a doubling of the cost of passage, had acted as a damper initially on the emigration trade and with the resumption of war with France and, later, the declaration in 1812 of war between Britain and America, the trans-Atlantic flow of emigrants had virtually ceased. However, with the cessation of hostilities in 1815, emigration resumed, fuelled by the pent-up demand of the previous few years and further stimulated by a looming agricultural recession. In the next thirty years almost one million Irish made their way to the United States and Canada and by virtue of its size and composition this exodus differed markedly from that of the previous century.[15] By 1820 the emigrants totalled 20,000 per year. In the early 1830s, the annual figure exceeded 50,000 and in 1842 alone more that 90,000 embarked for North America—averaging five hundred emigrants per day during the course of the shipping season (Table 10.1). North America was overwhelmingly the destination of note, the colonization potential of Australia not having yet caught the popular imagination. The attraction of destinations thus varied but Ireland's role as a source was set. Clearly, the emigration had become massive in scale and contemporaries frequently referred to it as a mania. Only the very poorest classes were precluded from participation and by the eve of the Famine there was scarcely a single parish in the whole of Ireland which had not contributed to the mass migration.

Table 10.1: Irish emigration to North America, 1825–45.

Year	Canada	USA	Total
1825	8,893	4,826	13,719
1826	13,629	4,821	18,450
1827	11,969	9,772	21,741
1828	8,824	7,861	16,685
1829	10,148	9,995	20,143
1830	25,679	12,765	38,444
1831	54,514	13,598	68,112
1832	50,305	15,092	65,397
1833	23,139	14,177	37,316
1834	32,315	16,928	49,243
1835	10,764	13,307	24,071
1836[a]	22,300	4,400	26,700
1837	26,102	22,089	48,191
1838	2,908	8,149	11,057
1839	10,943	20,790	31,733
1840	28,756	25,957	54,713
1841	30,923	36,428	67,351
1842	42,884	49,920	92,804
1843	14,668	23,597	38,265
1844	17,725	37,569	55,294
1845	26,708	50,578	77,286

[a] The figures for 1836 are probably incomplete.

Source: W. F. Adams, *Ireland and Irish Emigration to the New World, from 1815 to the Famine*, (Yale, 1932), pp. 413–14.

The overall trend indicated in Table 10.1 is extremely uneven but suggests nonetheless long-term incremental growth. Thus, for example, the partial potato failures of 1831 and 1842, and the cholera year of 1832 all prompted greater than average emigration. By contrast, 1838 recorded relatively few emigrants to Canada, where the rebellion of the previous year had temporarily cast a shadow of political instability and the cancellation of ships departing from Derry for Quebec. Overall, however, the pre-Famine movement of emigrants was stimulated primarily by the deepening economic crisis at home and the demand for labour in the settlement districts of Canada and the United States.

Population pressure alone would have implied a growing exodus but the socio-demographic situation was worsened further by evolving structural alterations in the economy. Since the end of the Napoleonic Wars agriculture had reverted in its emphasis to a more pastoral emphasis, rendering the landless labouring class redundant. Furthermore, in the linen textile region of Ulster and adjoining counties of north Connacht and north Leinster, machines were replacing domestic spinners, thereby wrecking the proto-industrial support of a rural population which could be classified as being either agricultural or industrial depending on the seasonal rhythm of work demands. It was this structural alteration of the textiles economy which was most significant in the 1820s and 1830s, creating a distortion in the emigration figures in the form of a very disproportionately high representation of Ulster folk.[16]

When large-scale emigration resumed after the Napoleonic Wars, the continued prominence of Ulster as the source region of the majority of emigrants was reminiscent of patterns in the eighteenth century. With a population of approximately two million in 1821, the northern province was home to almost one-third of the national population and was, in fact, as populous as contemporary Scotland; it was therefore a region of considerable demographic significance. Probably between 50 and 60 per cent of all Irish emigrants emerged from the province in the 1820s and early 1830s, making an Ulster person twice as likely to emigrate as any contemporary elsewhere in Ireland. The Ulster counties and the adjoining counties of Sligo, Leitrim, Longford and Louth were facilitated in the population movement by the traditions and expertise established during the eighteenth century in the ports of Derry, Belfast and Newry together with Sligo. Other smaller ports such as Donegal, Ballyshannon, Larne, Portaferry and Carlingford contributed slightly by means of occasional ships. As the earlier logic of emigration reasserted itself so also did the pattern of dependency upon converted cargo boats for passage. But while flax seed imports continued to offer reciprocal passages, a new trade in timber entered the picture to divert emigration to more northerly destinations. During the Napoleonic blockade of European ports Britain had turned to her remaining colonies in British North America for supplies of timber required for the construction and repair of the navy. When the war ended that trade continued, though now serving the merchant fleets and the construction demands of the rapidly growing British urban centres. The chief supply regions of timber were the Saint John River valley in New Brunswick and the Ottawa valley in central Canada and it was to those regions that the settlers were primarily directed by the logistics of trade. The cheapest trans-Atlantic passage was to be found on a timber boat sailing from Derry to Saint John, and for a time in the 1820s and 1830s Canada exceeded the United States in terms of numbers of Irish arrivals. Once landed, however, many Irish made their way southwards to Maine, Massachusetts, New York State or Ohio.[17] Nonetheless, there was a clear northern dimension to the destinations sought by the early-nineteenth-century emigrants compared with their predecessors in the previous century, who had been more inclined to settle in the middle colonies of Pennsylvania, Delaware, Virginia and the Carolinas.

The Ulster emphasis in the emigrations of the 1820s and early 1830s was characterized also by the prominence of Protestants in the exodus. Anglicans outnumbered Presbyterians, reflecting the regional importance of counties such as Armagh
and Fermanagh, but Catholics were still proportionately under-represented. 'You
can almost tell, from the counties they come from, what persuasion they belong to'
commented A. C. Buchanan, Quebec based emigration agent, in 1826.[18] This
prevalence of emigration among the Protestant community was largely a by-
product of tradition and social class, with the Catholic communities being in
general somewhat poorer and less able to afford passage money. It is also possible
that cultural factors such as individualism versus attachment to place and kin may
have operated to distinguish between the two broad groupings. Beyond Ulster the
importance of religion in predicting emigration was also evident. In the midland
counties of Laois and Offaly, in south Wicklow and Wexford, in Tipperary and
Cork, Protestant communities were among the first to seize the opportunity to
emigrate once peacetime shipping had been resumed. Some of these communities
sought British government support for group migration schemes and once abroad
they often founded distinctive community-based settlements.[19] Accurate religious
data do not exist for this period but recent studies have indicated that Protestants
constituted somewhat more than half of all the emigrants going to Canada, itself
the most popular of all destinations before the mid 1830s. Because of its British
colonial status, Canada may have been more attractive to Irish Protestants than
was the republic of the United States and it is most probable that Catholics predominated in the inflow into the latter county. At that time Protestants numbered
about one-quarter of the Irish population and as such they were over-represented
by a factor of two in the exodus to Canada, and may have been slightly over-
represented also in the American flow (Fig. 10.1). But even within the United
States the city of Philadelphia, for example, appeared to retain its long-standing
popularity with Protestants, in contrast to New York and Boston, which had a
greater attraction for Catholics. The selectivity of this religious geography within
the migration stream is illustrated by the partial data which do exist for County
Londonderry for the years 1833–5 (Table 10.2). For that northern county where
Presbyterians were the largest denomination, both Anglicans and Catholics were
under-represented in the outflow but each of the four main destinations exerted
their own distinctive pull on the composite emigration.[20]

Following the cholera outbreaks and regional famines of the early 1830s, emigration assumed massive proportion and with this development came an expansion of source regions and a widening of the social classes involved. Derry, Belfast,
Dublin and Cork remained the most important ports for embarkation, but Galway
and Limerick grew in importance, although the older established ports of Waterford and Wexford exhibited relative decline. Emigration became a national mania,
gripping virtually every parish, and apart from the obvious intensity of push
factors, the exodus was encouraged by the falling cost of passage as ships competed for the lucrative trade.

The majority of the emigrants from 1834 onwards were Catholic and increasingly
they were coming from the more impoverished, but not the very destitute, classes.
Those at the bottom of the social spectrum, the cottiers and landless labourers,
were in large measure immobilized by their poverty. They might seek some refuge

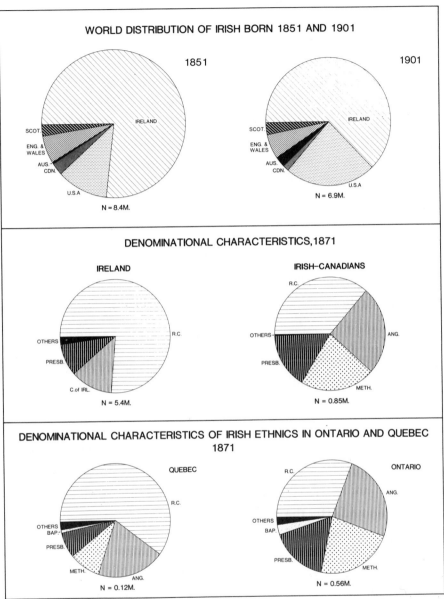

Fig. 10.1. World distribution of Irish born, 1851 and 1901. The nineteenth century witnessed the growing importance of the United States as a destination for the Irish emigrants. The selectivity of the emigrant stream is best illustrated by the data pertaining to Canada, where the under-representation of Irish Catholics is striking. At provincial level the data (derived from a sample analysis of A. G. Darroch and M. D. Ornstein, and presented in C. J. Houston and W. J. Smyth, *Irish Emigration and Canadian Settlement*, (Toronto, 1990), p. 229) are even more revealing: French-speaking Quebec retained a disproportionately high percentage of the Catholic Irish; Protestants disembarking at Quebec City tended to travel further westwards to Ontario.

Table 10.2: Denominational characteristics of County Londonderry emigrants, 1833–35.

Destination	No. of emigrants	% Anglican	% Presbyterian	% Catholic
Quebec	817	13.9	59.9	25.2
Saint John	210	9.5	60.5	30.0
New York	374	9.0	46.9	44.1
Philadelphia	373	4.8	74.6	20.6
Total of emigrants	774	10.5	61.7	28.8
Religious composition of County		15	46	39

in seasonal and permanent migration to Britain but even though emigration was seen increasingly as a solution to Ireland's dilemma, the very poorest remained predominantly confined to their homeland. In the eighteenth century in the face of a predominantly Protestant outflow, the British government had opposed emigration as a drain on resources and a threat to the security of the country, but by the 1820s emigration had full government approval. Shovelling out the paupers was seen as a means of ridding Ireland of a surplus population and simultaneously building up the population of the colonies. Canada, in particular, was the target and for a time in the mid 1820s the government had experimented with subsidizing emigration to the North American colony. Worried by the apparent mounting cost of such an operation, it reverted to a policy of benign encouragement.[21] This enlargement of the social classes contemplating the realistic possibility of emigration was marked also by a steady reduction in the age of emigrants and a corresponding increase in the proportion of single people. The importance of family migration in the eighteenth century has already been noted, and this pattern had extended well into the nineteenth century. Even as late as the 1830s the majority of emigrants probably travelled either as members of family groups, or as individuals on their way to join other members of their family, but by the time of the Famine young, and probably single, emigrants aged 15–24 years composed 45 per cent of the total emigration.[22]

Emigration During and After the Famine

The great blight that descended upon Ireland's potato crop in 1845 and the crop failures in subsequent years magnified emigration's role. What was an established process of adjustment to economic stress and population increase acquired heightened urgency in 1845, and in 1847 became a panic stampede. Emigration offered hope amidst horrific spectacles of starvation, disease, fever and death. It also encouraged such a marked increase in remittance money (so many having gone abroad in such a short period) that the outflow continued at a fast rate well beyond the actual years of crop failure. The decade 1845–55 has been dubbed the 'famine decade' and during that period approximately two million Irish emigrated overseas, representing almost a quarter of the pre-Famine population.[23]

No other modern European country has ever lost through emigration such a large percentage of its population in such a short space of time. In addition, more than one million died of hunger and disease on the roadsides and in the workhouses of Ireland. Even for those fortunate enough to board an emigrant ship, life was not secure, and in 1847 alone, 20,000 Irish died in Canadian quarantine stations at Grosse Isle and Partridge Island, 10,000 died on board ship during the voyage and many thousands of others died within months of arrival.[24]

The scale and nature of the exodus during the Famine confirmed for some the helpless failure of a political economy which, although attached by legislative union to the most advanced nation in the world, could do little by way of containment. The Famine as catharsis has been strongly asserted by MacDonagh.

> The failure was not merely economic, not merely the long prophesied disintegration of an iniquitous, top-heavy system of land tenure, which reduced more than half the entire population to a struggle for mere subsistence. It was a failure of morale as well. The mood prevailing from 1848 onwards seems to differ from the earlier terror and excitement. It is marked by a note of doom, an air of finality, a sense that a chapter in history had come decisively to its close.[25]

An emigration mania, regionally strong but nationally evident, had been slowly gaining momentum before the Famine, but thereafter obstacles to this demographic action of last resort were swept aside. Emigration had become virtually a natural part of the life cycle, a step to adulthood. In the post-Famine period young, unmarried emigrants formed the majority of the movement and the emigrant's marriage would likely take place in the New World. The Famine ensured that future generations of Irish would perceive emigration as inevitable, affecting all regions and every class: condemning, in the eyes of many, the Irish to wander the face of the earth in exile.[26]

At no time in the sixty years after the Famine did the emigration drop below 20,000 a year and, indeed, in more than half these years the number of emigrants was greater than 50,000 and thus exceeded all but the worst years of the pre-Famine period. The latter emigrants were, of course, drawn from a much smaller national total population. The temporal variation was mainly the result of generational pulsations in the Irish outflow and fluctuation in the United States economy. Emigration was endemic, fuelled by the numbers coming of age and drawn overseas by relatives from earlier migrant generations and the possibility of work. The pull of a rapidly industrializing United States on a society in which urbanization was so slow kept the level of emigration consistently high until the American recession of the late 1870s, and as that economy recovered so also did the level of Irish emigration. Only the onset of the First World War, with its opportunities of military service and work in wartime British industries, was capable of temporarily reducing the exodus overseas to a trickle. In contrast to every other set of European emigrants Ireland stood alone. Uniquely, the country had pioneered mass trans-Atlantic emigration and throughout the century every generation produced its own cohort of emigrants. Scottish, English, German and Italian emigrations were all associated with particular decades; none of those countries maintained such a proportionately large emigration over so prolonged a period as Ireland. The implications of such sustained behaviour were great for both Ireland and the recipient countries. In the United States, especially, the urban ghettoes of the north-eastern cities were continually renewed by fresh waves of immigrants. They replaced the earlier generations now departing for the suburbs and guaranteed a vibrant and organic link with the homeland. For Ireland the ongoing haemorrhage left its imprint on a landscape of abandoned houses, a virtually extinct agricultural labouring class, an introspective and defensive value system, and above all an abiding sense of fatalism.

The Emigration Process

The growth in the numbers leaving the country from the early eighteenth century onwards was the result of factors which were neither random nor haphazard. Rather, emigration was in itself a cumulative, causative process in which precedents, once established, became significant directive influences on subsequent movements. Merchants and trading systems built around colonial resources were often the founding links in the eventual chain and, in particular instances, government colonization schemes and the settlement of army pensioners likewise established the nuclei of subsequent settlements. As the settlements developed, letters home, remittance money and pre-paid passages, and the boosterism of pamphleteers, emigration agents, and travelling writers all served to clarify and embellish in the eyes of those remaining at home the geographies of the new lands. In this manner parochial and family links were emphasized especially in the earlier movements and particular geographical relationships emerged between regions in the New World and identifiable localities in Ireland. The intensity and endurance of these links is one of the most striking aspects of the migration.

The best documented of these linkages are those which connected Ulster and the middle colonies of colonial America in the period 1720–76, the equally emphatic but much less populous migration from south-east Ireland to Newfoundland in the second half of the eighteenth century, and the pre-Famine links between Ulster and the Canadian territories now known as Ontario and New Brunswick. Less well documented migrations contain evidence of particular relationships linking Australia with Limerick, Tipperary and Clare, and also between Argentina and Westmeath and Wexford. Central to the explanation of these distinctive geographical relationships is an understanding of the early directive role of trading links whether in the form of Pennsylvanian flax seed boats, the Newfoundland fisheries, the timber trade of the Ottawa valley, or the livestock economy of Argentina. For this reason it is valid to consider just how mercantile trade did operate as a directive influence in the emigration process.

Prior to the 1850s emigrants were forced to entrust themselves to the questionable safety of sailing ships whose primary function was that of cargo vessels. Sailing according to no fixed schedules these ships generally crossed the Atlantic during the April–November season in voyages which could average six weeks, but frequently extended to 10, 12 or even 14 weeks. Storage holds were temporarily converted and furnished with crude bunks upon arrival in an Irish port, passengers would be loaded together with their own provisions for the voyage, and the vessel would depart with the minimum of regulation. Prior to 1803 no legislation governed the conditions under which passengers travelled, and even after that date the comfort and safety of the emigrants was largely dependent upon good fortune, an absence of storms or mid-Atlantic becalming weather, and the skill and social conscience of the captain. At best, conditions on board suffered from a lack of privacy, an absence of sanitary facilities and the boredom and loneliness of long hours spent under deck. At worst, fire and storms destroyed many ships and disease was induced by overcrowding and polluted river water carried for drinking purposes. Deaths on board were not uncommon, and neither were births. For many travellers the voyage must have appeared as a telescoping of all of life's miseries into a chaotic and character-altering experience.[27]

Until the 1850s emigration had a marked localism. In general passengers did not travel more than 40 miles to the emigration port and they would have been advised of the impending arrival and projected departure date of the vessel through local newspapers and especially via the network of merchants and agents who operated in the hinterland. In the eighteenth century the regionalism implied in the migrations meant that the number of ports involved in the trade was surprisingly small. In the period 1750–75, for example, the majority of emigrants from Ulster left from five ports—Belfast (32 per cent), Derry (29 per cent), Newry (19 per cent), Larne (13 per cent) and Portrush (7 per cent).[28] Similarly, the Newfoundland trade was dominated by Waterford, Wexford, New Ross, and Youghal. With the dramatic widening of the emigration field in the second quarter of the nineteenth century, and the concurrent growth in the timber trade, there was also a noticeably increased involvement of smaller ports whose rudimentary quays provided berths for perhaps one or two ships in the year. Nonetheless, as emigration became general there was also a marked commercial restructuring and concentration of the passenger trade in fewer hands. In Derry, for example, the number of companies operating ships was reduced from seven in the mid 1820s to two in the late 1830s. This process was extended further when, after mid century, the trade came to be dominated by purpose-built, steam-powered passenger ships and the era of the converted cargo vessel came to an end. Henceforth, the passenger trade was a lucrative trade in its own right, not merely a convenient, if profitable, form of ballast. Thus with the growth in size of vessels and the development of fixed scheduled sailings, a revolution was wrought. In a marked phase of geographical concentration port hinterlands expanded. Road improvements and railway buildings funnelled emigrants to a handful of dominant ports—Derry, Belfast, Dublin, Cork, Limerick and Galway. By the end of the century two ports at opposite ends of the country, and tangential to the main shipping lanes from Britain, controlled the direct trade—Derry and Cork's outport, Queenstown. From those two centres tenders ferried passengers offshore to the great Cunard and Allen liners whose voyages originated in Glasgow, Liverpool and Southampton. In mid-Ireland emigrants availed themselves of cheap transport by railway and steamship directly to Liverpool and Glasgow, where they boarded trans-Atlantic liners in company with European emigrants who had travelled halfway across the continent to begin the final stage of their travel to the New World. Emigration had become a capital-intensive and highly specialized industry.

Likewise, as the emigration process came to be subsumed into a sophisticated industry the recruitment of emigrants became more organized. The eighteenth-century local advertisements gave way to mass produced pamphlets in the nineteenth century. Initially produced by individuals, entrepreneurs and philanthropists the pamphlets were, by the second half of the nineteenth century, the product of the railway and shipping companies, and also of colonial governments.

They were supplemented by an increasingly sophisticated network of private and governmental emigration agents whose primary task was to generate a constant supply of emigrants. In 1869, for example, after the government of Ontario authorized 10,000 dollars for the publication of a forty-page pamphlet which extolled the virtues of the province, 30,000 copies were distributed in Britain and Ireland. Immediately before the First World War, the Canadian Dominion government spent hundreds of thousands of dollars on emigration promotion in Europe, Ireland included. What was perceived as a demographic problem on one side of the Atlantic was clearly recognized as a good investment when relocated.[29]

The success of such recruitment schemes is difficult to evaluate, but it is probable that their role in such an established emigration region as Ireland was secondary. Personal contacts, letters and remittances were more significant contributors to the emigration process. They were at once symbols and memorials of emigration and causative forces in that process. Despite the somewhat primitive organization of the international postal system, letters appear to have crossed the Atlantic, and later on the Pacific, in considerable numbers. Dozens have survived from the eighteenth century and many hundreds from the nineteenth. Apart from familial greetings the letters contained important information about employment opportunities, the cost of acquiring land, profits to be expected from farming, and countless other issues. Through this correspondence there was created in the minds of the family members remaining at home a distinctive but personalized geography of Canada, America, Australia and the other lesser known destinations. Thus was removed the alien character and mystery of faraway places, and for many potential emigrants, Melbourne and Chicago were more familiar than Dublin.[30]

Not infrequently, the letters also contained remittances in the form of cash or else by way of pre-paid passages. In the 1830s upwards of one-third of those leaving through Derry did so by means of tickets paid for by earlier emigrants and in the period 1843–6 the Canada Company, a land colonization company, sent almost 2000 remittances to Ireland, most of which were no larger that £4. As a shipping agent commented in 1834 '. . . the most enterprising of a family goes first, he sends home for part of his family, and then in some time longer for more of them, until the whole are brought out'.[31] The incidence of remittance payments rose greatly during the closing years of the Famine and by 1850 it was estimated that 75 per cent of the emigrants received their fare from the United States, and it is possible that this percentage remained valid for the rest of the century. While the figures are somewhat incomplete it has, nonetheless, been argued with some credibility that in the period 1847–67 about 120 million dollars were remitted from the United States.[32] Not all of this sum would have been invested in furthering emigration, but the scale of the transactions does give some indication of the financial cost of financing the emigration process.

The Irish Abroad

North America

Extending over more than two centuries, the Irish diaspora was not a homogeneous phenomenon. In its early years, and arguably for the century prior to

1830, the majority of the emigrants were drawn from the Protestant communities of Ulster and identifiable landlord settlements in the southern part of the country. Even in the later period when Catholics predominated in the exodus, sizeable Protestant representation persisted. On the basis of religion, and also social class and regions of origin, the emigrants do not bear easy stereotyping. Likewise, considerable variation is derived from the multiplicity of destinations espoused by the emigrants. From Newfoundland's fisheries, to frontier Pennsylvanian farmers, Ontarian lumbermen and Argentinian sheep ranchers; from domestic servant in Boston to Australian goldminer and American railroad labourer, the Irish spanned an enormous range of economies and occupations. In a sense they were chameleon-like, and in their search for new livelihoods they proved capable of adjusting to the particular demands of period and place. Very often the nature of the place was a function of the time of arrival and so it is important to bear in mind the temporal dimension of the diaspora, as well as its geographical extent.

The eighteenth-century Irish were over-represented in the European emigrations of the day and were among the first to pioneer in many regions of what is now the United States. They were, in sociological terms, not only an ethnic minority but often a charter group, injecting into the cultural foundations of the new societies many of their own societal attitudes and values, thereby helping to establish the cultural norms to which subsequent immigrants would be expected to adjust.[33] In many instances the vitality and durability of the cultural contributions of the Irish were the result of a strongly articulated sense of group identity, and a corresponding reluctance to assimilate rapidly into the host societies. In eighteenth-century Pennsylvania, the Irish Presbyterian settlers may not have been any more able on the frontier than their English or German counterparts but a century after their initial settlement they were still a recognizable cultural group and constituted local majorities in many areas. Doyle argues that 'before and during the American Revolution, Ulster-Americans were the predominant minority, apart from slaves, especially in the nine colonies south of New England, outnumbering other Irish, Scots and Germans'.[34]

This pre-revolutionary group was extended by the subsequent waves of immigrants from by-now traditional core areas in Ireland and by the 1830s they had created a distinctive and extensive settlement geography. Their initial heartland had been created westward from the eastern seaboard of colonial America, in the Appalachian ridge and valley country running southwards from Pennsylvania to as far south as Tennessee (Fig. 10.2). By 1800 they had begun to extend westward through the Cumberland gap into the plains of Ohio, Tennessee, Mississippi, and even across the Mississippi river into Missouri and Arkansas. Simultaneously, the immigrants were settling along the coastal areas of northern New England, where they were grafted onto existing settlements such as Londonderry, New Hampshire and Belfast, Maine. The timber industry drew them into northern Maine where they formed settlements adjacent to the newly formed Ulster-Irish communities of the Saint John valley in New Brunswick. Northwards and westwards they also formed the majority of settlers in the timbered lands of the Great Lakes Basin in Ontario and in the Ottawa valley stretching northwards into the Canadian Shield. In that northerly region of the continent the tone and cultural ethos of the emerging Canadian society was profoundly influenced by the Irish immigrants who

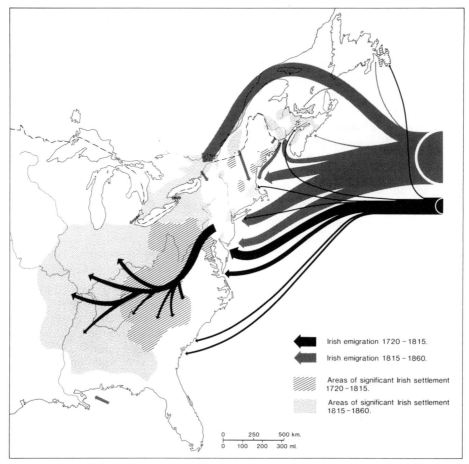

Fig. 10.2. Irish trans-Atlantic migration flows. Striking variances between eighteenth- and nineteenth-century migration flows are evident with respect to the scale of the movement and the destinations. The 1815–60 migrants tended to prefer more northerly destinations and the emergence of the St Lawrence artery is particularly noticeable.

constituted 60 per cent of all immigrants at the time, outnumbering the Scots and English in combination by a margin of two to one.[35]

The Irish settlements in Canada were a logical outcome of a settlement trend which had first become apparent in the third quarter of the eighteenth century, namely the opening up of a northern frontier at the same time as the westward movement through the Cumberland gap was commencing. In Maine, Vermont and along the northern shore of the Bay of Fundy, Irish settlements emerged. The most famous of these was the McNutt settlement of Londonderry, Nova Scotia. In 1760, McNutt, an Ulsterman and sometime resident of Londonderry, New Hampshire, persuaded the British government to grant him more than one hundred thousand acres of Crown land in the colony of Nova Scotia. In 1761 McNutt recruited about three hundred Protestant settlers, mainly from Donegal and Londonderry; earlier Irish emigrants in New Hampshire were also enticed northwards.

However, the British government, alarmed at the exodus 'of such great numbers of His Majesty's subjects' revoked McNutt's land grant except where it was applied to emigrants who had 'been resident either in Nova Scotia or some other of His Majesty's Colonys in America for the space of five years'. Despite this abrupt termination of the colonization scheme, the McNutt settlement survived in isolation until the development of the timber trade in the nineteenth century brought an advancing wave of Ulster settlers into the area via the Saint John River valley of New Brunswick.

The settlers who poured into the river valleys and Great Lakes lowlands of eastern and central Canada, especially in the second quarter of the nineteenth century, confirmed the importance of the northern settlement frontier. By 1850 the Irish were the largest English-speaking group in British North America, straddling the long established French-Canadian colony of Quebec in the lower St Lawrence valley. In 1871, the first census taken after Canadian Confederation revealed that 850,000, a quarter of the population of the new nation, claimed Irish ancestry and only the French Canadians outnumbered them. That census also revealed that there were two great core areas of Irish settlement in Canada, namely Ontario and New Brunswick, in which 35 per cent of the population was Irish, but significant Irish preserves were also evident in Prince Edward Island and Nova Scotia where they represented 20 per cent and 15 per cent of the population respectively. Even Quebec's population contained a 10 per cent component of Irish, living mainly in Montreal, Quebec City, and in agricultural settlements in the Eastern Townships. Offshore, the colony of Newfoundland, which was not to join the Canadian Confederation until 1949, represented the other great enclave of Irish in the northerly region. There, the Irish, derived almost exclusively from the south-eastern counties, had located themselves in fishing settlements that clung to the coves and inlets of the highly indented coastline of the southern shore of the island. In those, often isolated, settlements the Irish alone, without the complicating influence of settlers from other cultures, maintained an element of ethnic cohesiveness unrivalled anywhere else outside of Ireland.

The geographical concentration of the Irish along the eastern seaboard of North America and stretching inland through the Great Lakes Basin to the Mississippi was, in large measure, a function of the time of arrival. These were the major settlement zones of the eighteenth and nineteenth centuries and once Irish communities were established therein, they tended to attract further influxes of fellow countrymen long after the frontier of settlement had pushed further westward. As Fig. 10.3 shows, there is a distinctive temporal pattern associated with the emergence of Irish communities in the period of mass migration during the century following upon 1820. Notwithstanding the fact that many who disembarked in Canada subsequently migrated southwards, it is apparent that Irish emigration to Canada was largely a pre-Famine event. Half of all the Irish emigrants to Canada during the nineteenth century had arrived by 1846, and in the more easterly province of New Brunswick, the median year was *c*. 1834.[36] By 1855 when the last tremors of the Famine exodus had been exhausted, emigration to Canada had coincidentally largely ceased, continuing as a mere trickle for the remainder of the century. The implications of this temporal pattern are significant. The Canadian arrivals came during a period when Protestants were predominant in the exodus,

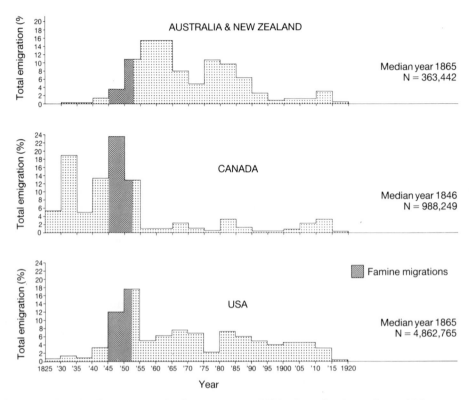

Fig. 10.3. Temporal variance in Irish migration to USA, Canada, Australia and New Zealand, 1825–1920. The data indicate the early, but confined, importance of Canada. Famine migrations were of far greater significance to USA, Australia and New Zealand.

and they arrived in a country whose economy was centred largely on primary activities such as fishing, lumbering and farming. Industry and urbanization were weakly represented. Consequently, the Irish in Canada settled mainly in dispersed rural settlements or else in small villages and towns, and while concentrations were evident in cities such as Quebec, Montreal, Toronto and Hamilton, these urban neighbourhoods contained only a minority of the population. Even as late as 1871, 75 per cent of Irish-Canadians were described as rural dwellers. In that respect they were even more rural than their counterparts back home in Ireland.

The pattern was very different in the United States. As Fig. 10.3 indicates, the bulk of the Irish in that country arrived during and after the Famine, the median year, the year by which half of them had arrived, being 1865. Unlike Canada, where the Famine spelt the end of massive Irish immigration, that traumatic demographic event represented for the United States more of a critical surge in Irish immigration, and the crystallizing of a pattern which was to be sustained for more than half a century. For the American-Irish, therefore, the Famine is an important part of their ethnic heritage and a consciousness of it has coloured Irish-American politics over many decades. Moreover, because this phase coincided with the great upsurge in Catholic emigration a fundamental contrast emerged with Canada, some 80 per cent of the arrivals in the United States being Catholic. The time of arrival and the more advanced state of the American economy produced another major distinction between the United States and Canada. In the former country the majority of the Irish rapidly urbanized. As the Canadian-based Irish politician, D'Arcy McGee, remarked in 1866 of the migration,

> 'Never in the world's history were so purely an agricultural population so suddenly and unpreparedly converted into mere town labourers ... Tens of thousands ... were peasants in Ireland in the spring and town labourers in America the same summer.'[37]

The classic depiction of the urbanization of the Famine Irish is that provided half a century ago by Oscar Handlin when he described the clustering of the immigrants along the docksides of Boston where, immobilized by poverty, they sought a living in casual labouring.[38] The emergence of an urban-industrial 'Paddy Camp' in the textile town of Lowell, Massachusetts, provides another part of the American pattern.[39] But casual labouring and Paddy Camps, while obvious, were just a veneer of transitoriness on a situation of great complexity and flux. The lot of most Irish, caught in America's almost insatiable demand for urban labour, was cast in a livelihood of security and well-being unknown in Ireland. The great cities of the United States were burgeoning and the Irish arrived coincidentally with one of the world's great phases of industrial-urban expansion. The construction of roads, railroads, bridges, mills, factories and tenements on an unprecedented scale demanded energy, skills, and enthusiasm. Given the opportunities, it is not surprising that immigrants got little further than the east coast and that when they travelled inland it was to Chicago or St Louis rather than a rural locality. It should also not be a surprise that a rural people were urbanized so rapidly for there existed in American wage labour a form of security and reward unavailable in Irish rural communities. Rurality had also been the scene of Famine. Although the mass of Irish emigrants had exchanged the lower rungs of one society for the lower rungs of another, the great difference was that the new society offered higher rungs and a sounder ladder to climb. Lace curtains declared that possibility.

Doyle has demonstrated that throughout the second half of the nineteenth century the immigrant Irish urbanized at a rate considerably faster than native-born Americans, but during the decades 1850–70 they did not urbanize faster than the Germans or other European immigrant groups. However, by 1920 the Irish were increasingly concentrated in large cities and with the exception of Russian Jews they were more urbanized than any other immigrant group.[40] The employment niches occupied by the Irish in all the large American cities had a resounding quality of sameness typically providing 'much of the heavy labour and, through the employment of young women in service, many of the household amenities which the growth of these cities required'.[41] Overall a majority of the Irish were urbanized and living in cities of more than 100,000 in 1920. While a small town and rural component did exist, it was a minority of the American-Irish population. Few rural settlements attracted the Famine Irish and their successors, and schemes such as a church-led settlement of Wexford people in Iowa in 1850 are remarkable as exceptions which succeeded in spite of the general trend of the time. In the main, city residential quarters and urban ghetto were the more striking legacy of the new wave of Irish immigrants and for a century after the Famine, new generations of immigrants sustained and renewed those Irish urban strongholds as their own progeny filtered off into the suburbs.[42]

So strong has been the image of the American-Irish that the Irish diaspora is often seen in terms of Irish Famine victims and subsequent urban settlers, people whose chances were limited totally by circumstance. British conditions seem to confirm that view of a group confined within narrow social and economic horizons stuck in working class poverty and beset by the attitudes and discriminatory behaviour of the host society, but the experience of the Irish in British colonies suggests a greater complexity. Canada's case shows that the American model fails badly. The Irish in Canada were rural more than urban, pre-Famine in the main, Protestant more than Catholic, and they occupied a wide range of social and economic niches. They joined in the forming of a new society and not in an effort simply to assimilate to an established mould of someone else's creation. Regional differences were also there, as they were in the United States, although few observers took the time to notice. The Canadian experience signalled a departure from the notions of the American-Irish. In general, in the colonies there is no adequate parallel to the American experience and that lack emphasizes the importance of recognizing the national and regional contexts in which Irish culture was inserted. It also calls attention to the notion that the story of the Irish abroad, although initially an Irish tale, is in fact the story of a new group, no longer simply Irish, in new settings.

Australia, New Zealand and Argentina

In Australia, the Irish community was largely attributable to the post-Famine era with a consequent preponderance of Catholics. A trickle of free migrants made their tedious way before the Famine but not until the 1850s did Irish migrants arrive in number, drawn by previous migrants and the dramatic lure of gold. Getting to Australia demanded a different sort of migrant than that who went to America, one with an immense sense of adventure and confidence, one with backing, one with connections in place. A three month journey to the other side of the world conjured more dread, not to mention costs, than one ocean's stretch to America. Many went in schemes involving passage fares subsidized by landlords, workhouses and official government schemes: a minority were transported felons and men convicted of participation in the 1798 rebellion. Australian legends built around the figures of Ned Kelly and Captain Moonlite of bushranger fame have served to enlarge the aura of rebellion and lawlessness. But of the 300,000 Irish emigrants to Australia in the nineteenth century, perhaps only an eighth were transported and only a minute fraction took to the bush and lives of crime. Most of the transported convicts eschewed rebelliousness, sought the refuge of normal life and accepted absorption within the greater forces and social movements creating colonial Australia. They gave colour and tradition to a mass of rather ordinary emigrants arriving later in search of a better living, and perhaps adventure or gold, in a remote corner of the globe.[43] The Australian experience of the Irish diaspora was similar in timing to that of the American in which again the median year of arrival was 1865, and the experience was largely attributable to the post-Famine era, with a consequent preponderance of Catholics among the settlers. Fitzpatrick argues that a greater percentage of Australian as opposed to American immigrants received aid in the form of passages subsidized by landlords, workhouses and government agencies.[44] Without such enticements, the tyranny of distance would have dissuaded most from travelling literally halfway around the world. Within Australia, Sydney and Melbourne, Perth and Adelaide absorbed many of the Irish as did many smaller resource towns and mining settlements. Ranching attracted some but overall it would appear that notwithstanding the weak urban-industrial character of the country, the settlement pattern of the Irish in Australia was more equivalent to that of the United States than Canada.

The timing of the Irish settlement of New Zealand is roughly coincidental with that of Australia. In 1840 only 2000 European settlers had established themselves in New Zealand but during the next decade that number increased ten-fold. One of the earliest Irish strongholds emerged in the Auckland Isthmus where, between 1847 and 1849, some 2000 discharged Irish soldiers and their families were settled in what became known as the Fencible settlements of Onchunga, Otuhuhu, Panmure and Howick, all of which were located within ten miles of the emerging administrative centre, Auckland.[45] About half of the Fencibles were Catholic and were drawn largely from the vicinity of garrison towns in Ireland. In 1847, for example, the freight ship 'Clifton' sailed from Galway to Auckland with 322 passengers made up of 79 ex-soldiers, 72 women and 171 children and in planned urban settlements such as Panmure, their ethno-religious background was recognized in the creation of St Patrick's Church and glebe land at the heart of the settlement.[46] Elsewhere in New Zealand, a strong rural Irish Catholic community developed on the west coast of the South Island in the vicinity of Greymouth where amid the isolated sheep ranches the immigrant culture was long preserved. Overall, however, it would appear that Protestant Irish emigration to New Zealand, particularly Auckland and the North Island, was more popular than to Australia and in some respects there are grounds for suggesting that in terms of selectivity of migration, New Zealand was closer to the Canadian than to the Australian or American model.

Australia and New Zealand represented the extremities of the Irish diaspora but they did, however, conform to the overall pattern of destinations sought by the emigrants—they were English speaking and closely linked to Britain by economic and political ties. For the most part the Irish diaspora was remarkably conservative in its choice of destinations and rarely expanded beyond the familiar culture zones of the Anglophone world. French Canada was one exception, but there the Irish tended to isolate themselves within urban ghettoes or in self-contained rural settlements. Over time, and facilitated by a commonality of religion, they overcame the linguistic barrier and intermarried with the French-speaking majority population. The other significant Irish settlement in a non-English-speaking world was Argentina, but that Spanish-speaking country was for all practical purposes a quasi-British mercantile colony in the nineteenth century. It would appear that upwards of 30,000 Irish settled in Buenos Aires and in the rural *estanchiaros* of the adjoining River Plate. Enticed out to work in the slaughterhouses and sheep farms of the temperate grassland area, they managed to accumulate sufficient capital to enable them to become independent ranchers in their own right. With their hurling clubs, and regularly published *Southern Cross* newspaper, these Argentine-Irish were able to maintain a distinctive lifestyle until well into the twentieth century when they finally assimilated into the Spanish-speaking population. Despite a commonality of religion, they had successfully resisted assimilation for well over a century, surviving as an exotic but numerically strong strand in the Irish diaspora. Approximately 30,000 Irish also settled in Africa, mostly in South Africa and in the territory then known as Rhodesia, during the nineteenth century but they tended to become rapidly absorbed into mainstream European settlements in the region and soon ceased to exist as a distinctive cultural group.[47]

Legacy of the Irish Abroad

The sheer volume of the Irish diaspora has ensured that cultural transfer did successfully occur. But the range of destinations and settlements and the huge timespan over which emigration was prolonged have complicated the nature of the transfer and have mitigated against any simple stereotyping. In the realm of material cultural transfer, it is fair to argue that this was successful and most evident only when the emigration occurred early on, certainly before the Famine, and where settlement took place either in isolated areas, or in places where the Irish constituted a significant regional majority. Mannion argues very forcefully that Irish emigrants who settled in rural areas in Canada did manage to transfer a surprisingly large amount of material culture ranging from house styles, to farm tools, and kitchen furniture.[48] However, his work also demonstrates that a study of transferred material culture is really a study of rates of attrition rather than a measurement of successful preservation, for only in the remote settlements of Newfoundland was retention beyond the first generation significant. By contrast, in the openly commercial and ethnically mixed society of rural Ontario the prognosis for retention was much less favourable. This theme of transferral of material culture has also been examined by Evans in a seminal article in which he pointed out the obvious architectural links between the Appalachian log cabin and the Ulster farmhouse. However, like Mannion, he based his study on a somewhat isolated rural settlement.[49] By the mid-nineteenth century the vast majority of the emigrants were settling in urban areas, frequently in older inner-city housing stock, and apart from occasional pieces of inherited furniture, and perhaps the arrangement of other purchased pieces, there was little evidence of material cultural transfer. The same was true of Australia and Argentina where different economies and challenging environmental conditions rendered most transfers anachronistic.

In the non-material arena, however, several very significant cultural transfers did take place. Primacy of place in analysis of such must be given to religion, for it was the cultural trait most obviously associated with the emigrant communities. Prior to the mass exodus of the nineteenth-century Irish, the British colonies and former colonies had been almost exclusively Protestant. French Canada was an exception. In 1800 4 per cent of the United States was Catholic; by 1851 this had reached 25 per cent. There, the universal Roman Catholic Church had attained the status of an ethnic church and the Irish dominance of it was not to be successfully challenged until the twentieth century when Italian and Polish immigrants began to assert themselves. Similarly, in Canada, outside of Quebec, the Catholic Church was the prerogative of the Irish and the unfolding network of dioceses, parishes, and other institutional manifestations of the religion were created to serve the demands of the immigrants. In Australia, the Catholic Church was again an Irish creation and in Melbourne, religious and secular politics was dominated for the first half of the twentieth century by the towering figure of Archbishop Daniel Mannix, former president of Maynooth College. As both Quebec and Argentina exemplify, the interlinkage of Irishness and Catholicism was apparent even in destinations where the religion of the majority may have been Catholic but where language differences created the opportunity for Irish enclaves to emerge within the Church.[50]

Not all Irish emigrants were Catholic, but even their Protestant counterparts managed to inject a distinctive tone to church life in their chosen destinations. The Protestant Irish tended to be rapidly assimilated into the denominational pluralism of the majority religions in the New World, and only in isolated communities were they insulated from other Protestant believers. They did not create an ethnic church. However, in places such as Ontario they did inject a particular element of low Anglican theology into the majority religion, and in other instances such as the American middle-colonies and New Brunswick, they displayed a remarkable propensity for conversion to the Baptist Church, and to fundamentalism. For the most part, however, religion offered a means of assimilation for the Protestant Irish; for the Catholics it acted as a conservative defence of their ethnic distinctiveness. But the ideological transfer of Protestant Ireland is clearly to be perceived in politico-religious, rather than in purely religious sociofacts and mentifacts. As an indicator of this one may quote the example of the Orange Order, that distinctive anti-Catholic creation of eighteenth-century Irish sectarianism. The Orange Order was transferred to all the Protestant Irish settlements created after its establishment in 1795. Even in the late twentieth century sizeable Orange halls may be found in Auckland, Melbourne, Sydney, Philadelphia and Toronto, and all of these communities still support annual Orange parades or public ceremonies. But it was in Canada that the Order achieved its greatest success, and nowhere more evidently than in New Brunswick and Ontario. By 1871 there were far more Orange lodges in Canada than in contemporary Ireland, and upwards of one-third of all adult Protestant males were reckoned to be either current or former members of that voluntary organization. Municipal politics, and, to a lesser extent, provincial and national politics, had their Orange pressure groups and for a century and a quarter every mayor of Toronto, the premier city of English Canada, could boast membership of the Order.[51]

The politico-religious distinctiveness of Protestant Irish emigrants had a counterpart in Catholic communities, but to a less obvious extent. In up-state New York and Pennsylvania, the Ancient Order of Hibernians represented a distinctly American-Irish pressure group with close links to the Church, but for the most part the political expressions of Irish Catholicism abroad were rooted more in a perception of ethnicity rather than upon quasi-theological arguments. Frequently too, those political groups fell foul of the authorities of the Catholic Church. Thus the Fenians, the Irish Republican Brotherhood and Clann na Gael all had uneasy relations with the official voices of the Church. These groups were designed in part to remedy political conditions in Ireland, but they were ultimately the creations of a distinctive Irish-American culture which had grown up in the urban ghettoes in the wake of the Famine. Likewise the municipal base of politics in organizations such as New York City's Tamanny Hall were responses to the political realities of the New World rather than simple transfers from the Old. However, it is perhaps fair to argue that ultimately the most durable transfer of political culture lay in the highly politicized outlook of the Irish, who, in the wake of O'Connell's mass agitations, had a finely-tuned sense of power brokerage, and employed it to full advantage in the new settings.[52]

At other levels, and in different contexts the transfers from Ireland are less obvious. Certainly, one of the most significant weaknesses in the process of cultural diffusion is to be found in the realm of language. In 1891 a quarter of all Irish were still using Gaelic as their everyday language in the homeland but apart from incidences in Saint John, New Brunswick, and perhaps among individual families elsewhere, there is very little evidence of language transfer. The Irish abroad adopted English as the means of advancement. Certainly, the Scots would appear to have been much more successful in transferring their Scotch Gaelic than were their fellow Celts. Other badges of Irishness survived with mixed fortunes. The nineteenth-century Ulster accent is reputed to be a strong ingredient in the Ottawa valley accent of today, and certainly the cadence and rhythms of Waterford and Kilkenny are still recognizable in Newfoundland. Folk music in Appalachia owes its origins directly to Ireland and Scotland, and the Australian ballad has a similar Irish genesis. French Canadian music has an Irish sound. Significantly, Irish music was rapidly assimilated into music traditions abroad, but met with a singular lack of success when transferred by emigrants to England. Irish games also survived in particular regions and in Argentina, for example, hurling is still a popular sport, while Australian rules football in an obvious late-nineteenth-century import. For the most part, however, such transfers are limited in extent and are but partial expressions of ethnicity. For many, Irish and non-Irish alike, the most evident cultural transfer remains as the Catholic religion and for the very sizeable minority who cannot be so identified, ethnicity has been recognized in political outlooks— God's Frontiersmen.[53]

References

1. The growth of the provisions trade and consequent emigration in the south-east of Ireland is especially well documented in the writings of John J. Mannion. For example, see 'The maritime trade of Waterford in the eighteenth century', in K. Whelan and W. J. Smyth (eds.), *Common Ground*, (Cork, 1988), pp. 208–34. The functioning of the northern ports in the eighteenth century is best illustrated in R. J. Dickinson, *Ulster Emigration to Colonial America, 1718–1775*, (Belfast, 1966).
2. For a review of recent literature dealing with this Atlantic World see Nicholas Canny, 'The British Atlantic World: working towards a definition', *The Historical Journal*, **33**, 2, (1990), p. 486. See also Donald W. Meinig, *Atlantic America, 1492–1800*, (Oxford, 1985).
3. This interpretation of the significance of emigration was first advanced by John A. Jackson, *The Irish in Britain*, (London, 1960).
4. An extensive body of literature on Irish emigration has now been created. Amongst the

earlier contributors the best work is William F. Adams, *Ireland and Irish Emigration to the New World*, (Yale, 1932). Also of interest is Arnold Schrier, *Ireland and the American Emigration 1850–1900*, (Minneapolis, 1958). Among the more recent works the most important are Kerby A. Miller, *Emigrants and Exiles*, (Oxford, 1985), the chapters by David N. Doyle, David Fitzpatrick and Patrick O'Farrell in W. E. Vaughan (ed.), *A New History of Ireland: V*, (Oxford, 1989).

5. L. M. Cullen, *The Emergence of Modern Ireland 1600–1900*, (London, 1981), pp. 87–8.
6. The best discussions of the variance in emigration figures are to be found in Miller, *Emigrants and Exile*, pp. 131–69 and in David N. Doyle *Ireland, Irishmen and Revolutionary America 1760–1820*, (Dublin, 1981). The presence of Catholics among the emigrants has been discussed by Doyle, *The Irish in North America*, pp. 682–725. For an earlier discussion see Dickinson, *Ulster Emigration*, pp. 229–38.
7. The figure for Newfoundland is derived from Arthur Young, *A Tour in Ireland 1776–1779*, (reprinted Dublin, 1970), p. 406.
8. Quoted by Rory Fitzpatrick, *God's Frontiersmen : The Scots-Irish Epic*, (London, 1989), p. 52.
9. W. Macafee, 'The colonization of the Maghera region of South Derry during the seventeenth and eighteenth centuries', *Ulster Folklife*, **XXIII** (1977), pp. 70–91. Also, G. Kirkham, 'Economic diversification in a marginal economy', in Peter Roebuck (ed.), *Plantation To Partition*, (Belfast 1981), pp. 64–82.
10. Dickinson, *Ulster Emigration*, pp. 98–125.
11. Cullen, *The Emergence*, pp. 115–20. See also L. M. Cullen, 'Merchant communities overseas', in L. M. Cullen and T. C. Smout, (eds.) *Comparative Aspects of Scottish and Irish Economic and Social History, 1600–1900*, (Edinburgh, 1977), p. 173.
12. John J. Mannion, 'Patrick Morris and Newfoundland Irish immigration', in C. J. Byrne and M. Harry (eds.), *Talamh An Eisc*, (Halifax, 1986), pp. 180–203.
13. Doyle, *Ireland and Revolutionary America*, pp. 120–69.
14. This sense of individualism amongst the emigrants is discussed in James T. Lemon, *The Best Poor Man's Country*, (Baltimore, 1972).
15. For an excellent discussion of the numbers see Adams, *Ireland and Emigration*. A partial revision of the data is to be found in Donald H. Akenson, *The Irish in Ontario: A Study in Rural History*, (Toronto, 1984). See also Cormac Ó Gráda 'Across the breny ocean: some thoughts on Irish emigration to America, 1800–1850', in T. M. Devine and David Dickson (eds.), *Ireland and Scotland 1600–1850*, (Edinburgh, 1983), pp. 118–30. And also Cormac Ó Gráda, 'A note on nineteenth-century Irish emigration statistics', *Population Studies*, **29** (1975), pp. 143–9.
16. Cecil J. Houston and William J. Smyth, *Irish Emigration and Canadian Settlement: Patterns, Links and Letters*, (Toronto, 1990), pp. 13–43. For structural changes in the Ulster economy see Liam Kennedy and Philip Ollerenshaw, *An Economic History of Ulster, 1820–1939*, (Manchester, 1985).
17. Houston and Smyth, *Irish Emigration*, pp. 79–121.
18. Minutes of evidence of A. C. Buchanan in *Report from the Select Committee on Emigration from the United Kingdom with Minutes of Evidence, Appendix and Index*, 1826 (404), 1, pp. 170–1.
19. Bruce S. Elliott, *Irish Migrants In The Canadas: A New Approach*, (Montreal, 1988).
20. These emigrant data are obtained from Ordnance Survey of Ireland, *Memoirs, Co. Londonderry*, (Ms. Royal Irish Academy Dublin). For a fuller discussion of them see Houston and Smyth, *Irish Emigration*, pp. 72–3.
21. The Government assisted schemes of emigration in 1823 and 1825 are well documented in Wendy Cameron, 'Selecting Peter Robinson's Irish emigrants', *Histoire Sociale/Social History*, **9** (1976), pp. 20–9.
22. Houston and Smyth, *Irish Emigration*, pp. 66–7.
23. Oliver MacDonagh, 'The Irish Famine emigration to the United States', in *Perspectives in American History*, **10**, (Harvard University, 1976).
24. Donald MacKay, *Flight from Famine: The Coming of the Irish to Canada*, (Toronto, 1990).
25. MacDonagh, 'The Irish Famine', p. 416.

26. This theme is drawn by Miller in *Emigrants and Exiles*, and is also a recurring theme in popular ballad and folk songs. In this image the metaphorical link with the Jewish diaspora is strong.

27. T. Coleman, *Passage to America*, (London, 1972).

28. Dickinson, *Ulster Emigration*, p. 98.

29. Houston and Smyth, *Irish Emigration*, pp. 95–107.

30. E. R. Green, 'Emigrant letters' in *Essays in Scotch Irish History*, (Belfast, 1968); also Miller, *Emigrants and Exiles*.

31. Quoted in MacDonagh, 'The Irish Famine', p. 395.

32. Estimate of the amount of money sent as remittances in MacDonagh, 'The Irish Famine'.

33. The term 'charter group' is analysed by John Porter, *The Vertical Mosaic*, (Toronto, 1968). In North America the British immigrants are widely regarded as establishing the cultural norms which have proved to be so powerful in directing the process of Anglo-conformity followed by subsequent non-British emigrants. It is argued here that the Irish contributed an important sub-set of those 'Anglo' norms.

34. Doyle, *The Irish in North America*, p. 687. See also Lemon, *Best Poor Man's Country*. They arrived early, occupied critical economic niches, and often set the standards and created the models of living which subsequent immigrants would follow.

35. Houston and Smyth, *Irish Emigration*, pp. 188–241. The spread of the Irish in the USA is also discussed by Fitzpatrick, *God's Frontiersmen*, and in a much earlier article by E. E. Evans, 'Cultural relicts of the Ulster-Scots in the Old West of North America', *Ulster Folklife*, **XI** (1965), pp. 33–8.

36. The figure for New Brunswick has been ascertained by the researches of Professor Peter Toner, University of New Brunswick. Personal communication.

37. Quoted in Kenneth Duncan, 'Irish famine immigration and the social structure of Canada West', *Canadian Review of Sociology and Anthropology*, (1965), pp. 19–40.

38. Oscar Handlin, *Boston's Immigrants*, (New York, 1976). See also L. H. Lees and J. Modell, 'The Irish countryman urbanized: A comparable perspective on the Famine migration', *Journal of Urban History*, **3** (1977), pp. 391–408.

39. B. Mitchell, *The Paddy Camps: The Irish of Lowell, 1821–1861* (Urbana, 1988).

40. David N. Doyle, 'The Irish as urban pioneers in the United States, 1850–1870', in Ciaran Brady (ed.), *The American City: Papers presented to the 1988 Conference of the Irish Association for American Studies*, (Dublin, 1989), p. 21.

41. Lees and Modell, 'Irish Countryman Urbanized', p. 406.

42. For a contrary view on the importance of urban centres for the Irish see Donald H. Akenson, *Being Had, Historians, Evidence and the Irish in North America*, (Port Credit, 1985). See also J. King and M. E. Fitzgerald, *The Uncounted Irish in Canada and the United States*, (Toronto, 1990).

43. The best descriptions of the Irish in Australia are to be found in Patrick O'Farrell, *The Irish in Australia*, (New South Wales, 1987). See also O. Mac Donagh and W. F. Mandle (eds.), *Ireland and Irish Australia : Studies in Cultural and Political History*, (London, 1986).

44. David Fitzpatrick, 'The settlers: immigration from Ireland in the nineteenth century', in Colin Kiernan (ed.), *Ireland and Australia*, (Dublin, 1984), pp. 23–34.

45. E. R. Simmons, *In Cruce Salus: A History of the Diocese of Auckland 1848–1980*, (Auckland, 1982), pp. 31–37. The authors are indebted to Sr. Ann Warren, Holy Faith Convent, Auckland for drawing this source to their attention.

46. Nominal roll of the fifth detachment of enrolled pensioners of the New Zealand Force embarked on board the freight ship 'Clifton', Auckland City Archives 165090/1436. For a summary discussion of the Irish in New Zealand, particularly with reference to the importance of Ulster settlers, see D. H. Akenson, *Half the World from Home: Perspectives on the Irish in New Zealand 1860–1950*, (Wellington, 1990).

47. Patrick McKenna, 'Irish migration to Argentina', (MA Thesis, St Patrick's College, Maynooth, 1992).

48. John J. Mannion, *Irish Settlements in Eastern Canada*, (Toronto, 1974). Also P. M. Toner (ed.), *New Ireland Remembered, Historical Essays on The Irish in New Brunswick*, (Fredericton, 1988).

49. E. E. Evans, 'The Scotch-Irish in the New World', *Journal of the Royal Society of Antiquities of Ireland*, **95** (1965), pp. 39–49.
50. Nancy Schmitz, *Irish for a Day*, (Quebec, 1991); M. O'Gallagher, *St. Patrick's Quebec, 1824–1934, the Building of a Church and a Parish*, (Quebec, 1982).
51. Cecil J. Houston and William J. Smyth, *The Sash Canada Wore. A Historical Geography of the Orange Order in Canada*, (Toronto, 1980). Also by the same authors, 'Transferred loyalties, Orangeism in the United States and Ontario', *The American Review of Canadian Studies*, **XIV** (1984), pp. 193–213. See also Sallie A. Marston, 'Public rituals and community power: St. Patrick's Day parades in Lowell, Massachusetts, 1841–1874', *Political Geography Quarterly*, **8** (1989), pp. 255–69.
52. David N. Doyle and Owen Dudley Edwards (eds.), *America and Ireland 1776–1976: The American Identity and the Irish Connection*, (New York, 1980).
53. Fitzpatrick, *God's Frontiersmen*, repeats a very prevalent argument that the Protestant Irish brought a distinctive politico-religious outlook to their new settlement homes. Referring to the Protestant Irish in New Zealand, Akenson has commented that they were distinguished by 'The conviction with which they held their Protestantism and their imperial loyalism, the energy with which they adhered to the "British" way of life, the ability with which they articulated "British" ideas of government, law and politics . . .'; Akenson, *Half the World*, p. 158.

11

The Irish in Britain, 1780–1921

Brenda Collins

Introduction

Over eight million men, women and children emigrated from Ireland between 1800 and 1921. Almost every generation of people born in the island during the nineteenth century contributed, to a greater or lesser degree, to this movement. Growing up in Ireland meant preparing to leave it as emigration became part of the expected cycle of nineteenth- and twentieth-century Irish life.

As discussed in Chapter 10, it is important to understand that this was not a pattern related solely to the Famine years; rather it was a movement established early in the first quarter of the nineteenth century, if not the last quarter of the eighteenth century. Thus by 1841, when the first reliable national census figures of Great Britain became available, there were 415,000 Irish born people living in Great Britain (which was 77 per cent of known Irish-born emigrants world-wide). Between 1851 and 1881 each successive British census recorded around three-quarters of a million Irish-born and, as Table 11.1 indicates, during the 60 years from 1851 to 1921, the number of Irish-born people living in Great Britain was never fewer than about one-quarter of all Irish migrants everywhere in the world.[1] However, while Great Britain as a destination is often considered as one unit, it is essential to remember that there were distinct differences in the settlement patterns between Scotland, England and Wales. In essence, the number of Irish-born in England and Wales dropped steadily after the peak in 1851 down to the First World War, whereas in Scotland the numbers remained stable; in 1901 there were 205,000 Irish-born, a similar figure to the 207,000 of half a century earlier.[2] This meant that a stream of fresh Irish migration to Scotland continued for each generation in the nineteenth century and this had implications for the type of lifestyle and community living which developed in urban working class Scotland.

Although emigration was a phenomenon common to every generation of Irish-born people in the nineteenth century, it drew on certain sections of society more than others. More emigrants came from the adolescent and young adult age groups than from among older people, and much of the emigrant movement consisted of unmarried people rather than those encumbered with families. Certainly, family emigration did exist particularly during the crisis years of the 1840s but, prior to the mid-1830s and after mid-century, the Irish emigrant, more so than any other

European emigrant was more likely to be an unmarried adult. This is not to imply, however, that he or she travelled alone, but to emphasize the extent to which they entered the British or North American labour market at the precise time when their labour could be used effectively without the burden of dependants.

A second general feature of nineteenth-century Irish emigration patterns was the extent of parity of the sexes, a characteristic which distinguished it from other European migratory movements.[3] Certainly, in the general movement to Britain there were migrant harvesters and navvies, close knit male groups often moving from specific regional origins to particular destinations, and in Scotland there was always a slight majority of male Irish immigrants. Nevertheless, women formed a virtually equal proportion of each Irish immigrant generation in Britain as they did elsewhere in the world.

Table 11.1: Permanent residence of Irish-born persons living outside Ireland, 1851–1921 (percentage distribution).

	England and Wales	Scotland	Total GB	USA	Canada	Australia
1851	27	11	38	50	12	N/A
1861	22	7	29	60	11	N/A
1871	20	7	27	65	8	N/A
1881	19	7	26	61	6	7
1891	16	7	23	65	5	8
1901	17	8	25	64	4	7
1911	18	8	26	63	4	7
1921	21	9	30	59	5	6

Source: Commission on Emigration and Other Population Problems: 1948–54, (Dublin, 1954), Table 95.

The Reasons for Emigration to Great Britain

Pioneering demographic studies by Connell, since refined by others, pointed to emigration as a response to the problem of limited food resources in coping with the rising rate of population increase which took place in Ireland after 1780.[4] The complexity of the mechanisms surrounding the population increase hinged round two main themes. First were the changes in land utilization which were evident in the swing from pastoral farming to labour-intensive cereal crops at the beginning of the nineteenth century, and in the subdivision of landholdings and the cultivation of waste land. Second, there was the more generalized dependence on the potato as a staple food in the Irish diet. The swing towards tillage farming was reinforced by the favourable grain price obtainable from Britain during the 30 years of the Napoleonic Wars and took place against a background of lax land leasing which permitted inherited farm holdings to be subdivided by each generation. The availability of the potato as a basic foodstuff permitted this type of farming practice to become extensive because more families were able to live on a given area of land. Potato acreage and dependence expanded right up to the 1840s. This gave rise to an inequitable land structure and reinforced the vulnerability of dependence on a single food crop. The 1841 census recorded that 70 per cent of the rural households in Ireland were headed by landless labourers or cottiers with smallholdings of less than five acres. Many in these groups were dependent on stretching their scanty money wages from intermittent day labour to buy food to supplement their own home grown crops. Their vulnerability lay in precisely this combination, for a bad season led to a poor harvest and high prices. This occurred on at least five occasions in the 1820s and 1830s. Emigration was an obvious response to the intolerability of this situation. When the potato harvest failed extensively in 1845 and sucessive years, it meant not merely a fall in living standards but the prospect of imminent destitution for those who had no other livelihood. The increase in pauper emigration in the 1845–49 period reflected a truly vast increase in abject poverty, as what had previously been a considered action became a reactive flight from destitution and death. The reality of the crisis can be seen in the 20 per cent decline in the Irish population which took place between 1841 and 1851, attributable to a combination of emigration and excess deaths.

After the mid-1850s, the urgency of emigration lessened but the basic contributory factors diminished only slowly. In the western province of Connacht, for example, the continuation of high marriage rates and high marital fertility among communities living on uneconomic smallholdings meant that there continued to be occasional crop failures and long-term deprivation. However, the short-term push out of Ireland in response to crisis was no longer as important as the incorporation of emigration into the family life cycle of events as a means of the growth and placing of each new generation. Emigration came to represent an expected life cycle stage and children were reared with the knowledge of likely emigration, in the same way that in other rural communities they were accustomed to moving to the nearest big cities to seek employment opportunities. But because there was only sluggish urban growth in Ireland (with the exception of Belfast), the Irish sought their 'urban hierarchies' abroad. The prospect of emigration for some children in every family in each generation after 1850 was reinforced by the spread of impartible inheritance patterns whereby only one child could expect to inherit a family property and the others had to migrate in search of marriage and employment. The power of the emigration movement lay in the fact that it represented decisions made in a family context, subjugating individualist aspirations to collective aims. These were underpinned by the growing reliance on 'the American letter'—the acknowledged financial dependence of those at home on the examples of resolution shown by earlier emigrants in their letters home.

As the 'nearest place that wasn't Ireland', Britain provided the easiest and cheapest destination. By the later eighteenth century there were already sizeable Irish communities in London and some Lancashire towns, containing men who had fought in the Napoleonic Wars and settled in England after their discharge. As the volume of emigration increased, the three main routes became those operating from Derry and Belfast to Glasgow, from Cork to Bristol and London, and from Dublin to Liverpool.[5] To some extent, the regional distribution of Irish people in Britain reflected these routes and their catchment areas. Thus Irish settlement in Scotland tended to originate from the northern half of Ireland, while those in southern England tended to have emigrated from Munster and Leinster. Emigrants from the poorest province, Connacht, sailed from Dublin to Liverpool, and thence moved on to the Lancashire and Yorkshire industrial towns. These broad generalizations linking origins to destinations are indicators of trends which remained remarkably persistent into the early twentieth century.

Seasonal and Casual Employment

Seasonal Employment

However, it was in agricultural work rather than in the towns that the Irish were first noted in any numbers. From the mid-eighteenth century there were both seasonal and permanent Irish agricultural workers in Dumfries, Galloway and Ayrshire. Seasonal agricultural work provided an important living for those who could not find employment at home, affording a means of earning sufficient cash to pay the rent on Irish farms and to acquire cash to buy whatever would supplement the marginal existence of their families at home. The frugal lifestyle of the migrant harvesters, living in their employers' barns and sheds with bare cooking and washing facilities, and working all the daylight hours, enabled them to save the bulk of their earnings for the return to Ireland. Their thriftiness and mobility pleased the farmers also, because it released them from the responsibility of providing for a year-round workforce, either in terms of employment and housing or in rateable support.

The vast majority of the nineteenth-century Irish seasonal workers in Britain were adult men, cottiers or small farmers and their kinsmen. The self-selected able-bodied were likely to reap the most rewards; the one general count attempted by census enumerators of harvest migrants leaving Irish ports in the summer of 1841 showed that of the 57,000 tallied, almost all (87 per cent) were male and aged between 16 and 35 years.[6] Most came from the western counties of Connacht where farm sizes were smallest, landless labourers were in the majority and seasonal movement for work was commonplace. Lees and Modell calculated that in County Mayo the equivalent of one person for every six households, and in County Roscommon, one person for every eight households, travelled across the Irish Sea in the summer of 1841.[7] The number of young men who, during their lifetimes, would have gone at least once to work in Britain was thus very large, as was the number of families throughout the century who benefited from such journeys.

The visibility of Irish seasonal harvesters was heightened by their spread through regions and village communities which were otherwise relatively stable. This was particularly the case in the south-west of England and in the Fens and led to isolated physical attacks by local people. These were probably stimulated by drink but there is evidence of connection with the Captain Swing movement against the introduction of threshing machines in the late 1820s.[8] The common factor in the attacks was the perceived threat to local employment and customary work patterns. Even where working patterns were otherwise unchanged by technology, such as in Yorkshire, south Wales and central Scotland, Irish harvesters were viewed as having supplanted the local people in field labour. While the exact nature of this displacement had regional variations, in many instances the substitution was not one of locally born workers but of other migrants. Thus in the 1830s,

Scottish Highland migrants shifted from seasonal work in the Lowland counties of the Lothians, Renfrew and Ayr to more permanent settlement in Glasgow and other Clydeside towns, yet the rate of economic growth in west central Scotland was such that there was no glut of labour in town or country.[9] This local experience supports Williamson's contention that, contrary to received wisdom, agricultural output would have suffered without the Irish.[10]

Seasonal migration was concentrated overwhelmingly in the months of May to September and, as it became more commonplace, its patterns of movement became more routine. Migrants usually travelled as groups, either from their place of origin, or in associations formed during the sea crossing to Liverpool or Glasgow. These gangs moved around the country and followed the successive harvests of early potatoes, corn, turnips, hay and maincrop potatoes in an elliptical movement which traced the agricultural calendar. Their mobility was increased by the development of the railway network in the 1840s and 1850s. This regularization of movement became even more pronounced in the later nineteenth century. By then, the numbers of seasonal harvesters arriving directly from Ireland was much reduced as many turned to permanent urban migration. The consequent diminution in what had been the farmers' most elastic source of labour led some to instigate contractual arrangements at the end of their harvests in order to be sure of workers from one year to the next.

Such arrangements were made not only with migrants directly from Ireland, but also with casual workers, many of Irish origin, from the industrial cities. Thus in Staffordshire, according to Herson, improved agricultural techniques in the 1860s 'High Farming' period increased the demand for farm labour at precisely the same time as industrial opportunities were opening up for native rural workers to leave the land to work in heavy industry elsewhere in the county.[11] In Stafford from the 1860s, a pool of known local Irish residents was given much of the casual farm work, while in Lincolnshire, Irishmen from the Midland towns were known as 'the English Irish'. Throughout the century, Irish farm workers lived in the city of York but worked at outlying villages up to 20 miles distant. For many urban Irishmen, seasonal agricultural work became a means of smoothing over slackness in their winter employment in breweries, gas works and other heavy industries. Migrant Irish labour from the towns was not confined to the male workforce; in the 1880s, market gardens on the fringes of London took on young Irish women who worked in London during the winter as fruit-sellers, in sweet factories and in clothing workshops, while the Cockney Irish families constituted a lasting element in the annual exodus of hop pickers.[12]

Prior to 1870, when officialdom intervened, there is only impressionistic evidence of the numbers of agricultural workers leaving Ireland, but there is agreement that they peaked during the 1840s and 1850s. During the period 1880–1915 the annual numbers of those arriving at British ports fell from 20,000 to 8000 and it is reasonable to infer that there had been a steady decline after mid-century.[13] This decline can be traced to the changes within the Irish land structure which came to favour permanent emigration and to changes in demand for the type of agricultural worker, but also increasingly to intervening urban job opportunities which reduced the attractiveness of long distance travel from the ports. Just as seasonal migration became a localized movement from certain Irish counties (by 1910, 79 per cent of those involved came from Donegal and Mayo), so too it became a move-ment to a shrinking agricultural belt in Britain, and was associated with the higher wage agricultural counties where local labour was scarce. By the last quarter of the nineteenth century harvest earnings represented on average £12 for a season and were recognized by the Department of Agricultural and Technical Instruction in Ireland as essential to the preservation of the rural family system, contributing up to one-third of a typical family's annual earnings in Donegal. These earnings, together with remittances from family members who had left permanently, en-abled the small farm units of north-west Ireland to continue to eke out a meagre existence.[14]

Casual Employment

Halfway between seasonal work and settled employment were the casual workers whose image has provided a popular stereotype of the Irish migrant. The navvies employed on railways and canals were generally on group piecework contracts over a fixed time period. Physical strength and endurance were the prime requi-sites and the only common bond between the men was the work, the pay, and the drinking sessions on pay day. The transient nature of railway construction repli-cated the bursts of work in the farming sector, and most immigrant navvies moved from contract to contract. This confinement within a fairly narrow branch of the labour market meant that navvies tended to remain marginal men, isolated from the mainstream of industrial and social life in Britain, while their impermanence prevented settlement in the communities which they encountered.[15] The autobio-graphical works of Patrick MacGill, a Donegal navvy in central Scotland around the end of the nineteenth century, convey the rootless mercenary existence within the navvy gangs where men were known only by nicknames and violence was com-monplace.[16] According to Treble, this marginality was fostered by some contractors of railway labour, who segregated English and Irish workmen in order to secure Irish labour at a reduced wage, as well as to prevent tensions arising from mutual animosity.[17]

Overall estimates of the Irish proportions of the total navvy workforce are rendered almost impossible by the ephemeral nature of the job. It seems clear, however, that there was a specifically regional pattern of much greater Irish partici-pation in Scotland and the north of England than in the southern counties. During the railway boom of the 1840s, certain railway companies in the south of Scotland may have had a workforce which was at least 50 per cent Irish. In the north of England they were found working on lines in Lancashire, Cheshire, the West and East Ridings of Yorkshire and in Cumberland. In contrast, the navvy gangs in the south of England were drawn mostly from the native population.

Permanent Urban Migration

Urban Settlement Patterns of the Irish in Britain

The majority of Irish emigrants to Britain settled in the areas which offered the greatest job opportunities, the towns and cities of the Industrial Revolution, particularly as several of these (Liverpool, Glasgow and London) were also their main ports of entry. Their preference for urban settlement was part of a much wider pattern of rural to urban migration within a developing Atlantic economy. The pattern was laid down in the early years of the nineteenth century and reinforced by the mass influx of the late 1840s; thus the later-nineteenth-century picture was one of diffusion rather than a fundamental readjustment. At the 1841 census, the Irish-born population was already equivalent to 2.24 per cent of the British population and just under half of the Irish immigrants (48.5 per cent) lived in the four biggest cities, London, Liverpool, Manchester and Glasgow. Table 11.2 indicates

Table 11.2: Percentage distribution of Irish-born population within Great Britain.

	London	Liverpool	Manchester	Glasgow	Elsewhere
1841	17.6	11.9	8.3	10.7	51.5
1851	14.9	11.5	7.2	8.2	58.2
1871	11.7	9.9	5.6	8.8	64.0
1891	10.2	7.2	4.9	10.1	67.6
1911	9.6	6.3	4.5	9.6	70.0

Source: Census data for relevant years.

that this concentration was maintained throughout the nineteenth century, being partly explained by the size of these cities as a whole; as Williamson explains, 'while London absorbed the largest share of Britain's Irish (just under 10 per cent of the Irish-born resident in England and Wales in 1911), it did not have, overall, a very high Irish density'.[18] There was, however, a gradual diffusion of settlement from those larger cities from a situation at mid-century where they accounted for just over 40 per cent of all the Irish-born settlers, to a position on the eve of the First World War when they accounted for barely 30 per cent. The sharpest period of this diffusion occurred between 1841 and 1871 as the Irish drifted to smaller rapidly growing towns. For example, their spread throughout the whole county of Lancashire, away from the largest cities, was in contrast to the overall tendency of increasing urbanization in Britain as a whole.

Table 11.3: Irish-born in Britain and selected British cities, 1851–1911 (percentage of total populations).

	England and Wales	Scotland	London	Liverpool	Manchester	Glasgow
1851	2.9	7.2	4.6	22.3	13.1	18.2
1871	2.5	6.2	2.8	15.6	8.6	14.3
1891	1.6	4.8	1.6	9.1	4.6	10.0
1911	1.0	3.7	1.1	4.6	2.6	6.7

Source: Census data for relevant years.

The densities of Irish population in the same cities is shown in Table 11.3 and this confirms the necessary distinction between high absolute numbers of Irish-born settlers, and the proportions within a given city. Table 11.3 also shows that the urban Irish in Scotland showed less inclination to move beyond their initial places of settlement. This was a reflection, not only of the economic dominance of Glasgow and the more continuous pace of development in the urban west of

Scotland, but also of the recurring waves of Irish immigrants. The number of Irish-born in Scotland remained at over 200,000 throughout the 60 years after 1851 (apart from a small dip in 1891 to 195,000). As Table 11.2 shows, Glasgow's proportion of all the Irish-born in Great Britain thus remained at around 8 to 10 per cent throughout the period. The situation in Edinburgh afforded a neat contrast on all these points. Developing rather sluggishly as a centre of administration and commerce rather than manufacture, it was of similar size to Glasgow in 1851 but only 7 per cent of its population were Irish; by 1911 it was only two-fifths the size of Glasgow and its Irish-born population was less than 2 per cent. The reality of the Irish-Glaswegian dominance was intensified by the fact that the later-nineteenth-century spatial diffusion of the Irish in Scotland took place within the Strathclyde region, where the highest densities of Irish-born in Great Britain were to be found. According to the 1871 census, four of the 'top five Irish' towns in Great Britain were in Strathclyde (Dumbarton, Greenock, Glasgow and Airdrie), and this region came to dominate the Scottish economy.[19] The combination of economic growth, urban expansion and continuing high levels of Irish settlement put a particular character stamp on the region in the years prior to 1914.[20]

Urban Employment of the Irish in Britain

If the main feature of Irish settlement in Britain throughout the nineteenth century was an initial clustering in the areas of arrival, coupled with a slow rate of diffusion to the smaller towns, the actual choice of towns was the outcome of an immigrant response to localized demands for labour. This meant that outside the large urban centres, smaller centres offered small-scale job opportunities, and places as diverse as Newport in south Wales, Gateshead and Newcastle in the north-east, and Stockport in Cheshire, all had about 10 per cent of their population Irish-born. Local labour market factors operated in both general and specific ways. While the large cities and ports of entry provided a wide range of low-skill manual employment in labouring and service jobs, as well as sufficiently buoyant commerce to support casual hawkers and street sellers, there were particular instances where Irish settlement patterns were related to specifically local factors. This can be seen most readily in gender specific occupations. Textile towns, in particular, offered mill and factory work to girls and women. The most telling example of the extent of the Irish response to this was in Dundee where, in 1851, among the young Irish adults aged 20–24 years there were twice as many women as men.[21] Other textile towns which also had high proportions of Irish-born women by the 1870s included Preston, Bradford and Stockport. Indeed the correlation between Irish settlement patterns and work opportunities in textile manufacture was succinctly phrased, as early as 1836, by the reporter from Hull to the Poor Law Commission: 'there are few Irish in Hull because we have no large factories to afford them employment'.[22] On a general scale, a gender analysis of the 1871 distribution of the Irish-born population confirms the earlier pattern. In military or naval towns such as Colchester, Winchester, Portsmouth and Plymouth, there was heavy male dominance among the Irish-born just as there was in those towns as a whole. The distribution of heavy industry was also important. Between 1861 and 1891, for example,

Barrow-in-Furness grew to a population of over 50,000. The Irish formed 8 per cent of its 1891 population and just under two-thirds of the Irish people were men.[23]

Where specifically local opportunities were absent, there was a considerable sameness about the types of jobs which Irish immigrants took up, both in different towns and at different times. As Fitzpatrick has said, 'everywhere, the Irish were over-represented among unskilled and semi-skilled workers, under-represented among skilled and professional people'.[24] This characteristic image can be partly explained by their position as adult migrants. Too old to be apprenticed to a trade and lacking any of the relevant skills except stamina and a desperation for work, they moved into the lowest positions in the job structure. In the major ports, and in London, the construction of docks and harbours and the infrastructure of warehouses and mercantile premises provided ready work which the Irish took up. Jackson describes how Irish navvies, recruited to construct the Liverpool docks in the early 1840s, stayed on in dock employment when the building work was finished, and this seems to be confirmed by Lawton's findings from the 1851 census enumeration books for Liverpool that 76 per cent of all the dock labourers were Irish-born.[25] Where there was a hierarchy of employment such as in the building trade, Irish men were usually found working as bricklayers' labourers rather than bricklayers, as casual workers rather than craftsmen. By far the most common type of job was that of builder's labourer. Table 11.4 suggests the degree to which the prevalence of unskilled work translated into low social status. Research on other towns not listed here, such as Bristol, Leeds and Bradford, also confirms this trend even though the groupings do not correspond directly with the table. Other Irish people became street traders, hawkers or general shopkeepers dealing in basic provisions, clothing or hardware. Street trading was a basic refuge of the casual labourer (Irish or not) when he was thrown out of work by trade depressions, the end of a contract or just bad weather, and in the mid-nineteenth century, many Irish folk in London made their living by hawking fruit, vegetables and fish. Henry Houldsworth, a cotton factory owner in Glasgow, commented in 1836 that jobs such as brokers, old clothes dealers and hawkers of provisions were almost entirely confined to the Irish, and that he considered that the Irish 'had all the elements of the mercantile character, they are very fond of bargain making, of buying and selling and of adventure'.[26] This view continued to hold credibility; in 1909 another Scottish commentator asserted that the Irish 'constituted the great body of unskilled casual labour in Glasgow'.[27]

Yet despite the over-riding impression of a sunken stratum of society, it must be clear, even on the basis of the figures in Table 11.4, that not all the immigrants were clustered in casual or unskilled work. Despite the differing occupational profiles of particular towns, the distribution of the Irish social class structure within those towns tended to follow similar patterns and to differ only in degree from the class structure of the general populace. Therefore, as Table 11.4 shows, in urban centres with long-established Irish settlement (London, York, Paisley), upwards of one-quarter of the Irish migrants were in skilled or trade occupations. Elsewhere in the country, in a middle rank town like Bristol, where the Irish (at fewer than 5000) constituted a relatively small group in 1851, Large found that tailoring was their third most important occupation after labouring and hawking and, more importantly, that they comprised 1 in 10 of all the tailors in Bristol.[28] Similarly, certain

Table 11.4: Socio-economic distribution of the Irish-born population of selected cities and towns in 1851 (percentage of total Irish populations).

Location	SEG 1 and 2	SEG 3 and 4	SEG 5 and 6
London	3	26	71
York	8	24	56
Hull	6	31	63
Cardiff	2	15	83
Dundee[a]	3	14	82
Paisley[a]	9	29	62
Greenock	1	38	61

Note:

SEG 1/2 – Professional and intermediate occupations.
SEG 3/4 – Skilled non-manual and manual occupations.
SEG 5/6 – Semi-skilled and unskilled occupations.

[a] Adult males only.

Sources: Taken from C. Pooley, 'Segregation or integration: the residential experience of the Irish in mid-Victorian Britain', in R. Swift and S. Gilley (eds.), *The Irish in Britain, 1815–1939*, (London, 1989), Table 2.4, p. 71; Brenda Collins, 'Aspects of Irish immigration into two Scottish towns (Dundee and Paisley) during the nineteenth century' (unpublished MPhil thesis, University of Edinburgh, 1978).

one-industry towns with high numbers of Irish-born people employed in those industries tended to retain that pattern throughout the century. Thus, in Greenock, over 60 per cent of the labour force in the sugar refineries was Irish-born, both in 1851 and 1891.[29] St Helen's, too, with its glass-making and chemical industries, attracted and retained many Irish settlers after 1840.

Personal networks played a large part in the formation of such occupational clusters. Lobban discusses the extent of personal recruitment by Greenock sugar refinery foremen of new immigrants introduced by friends and relatives already in employment.[30] In factory work in Manchester, too, the Irish were quick to send home news of openings for fellow countrymen and women. As an employer said, 'I know the Irish constantly invite their friends and relatives in Ireland, and when they come, receive and entertain them in their habitations for a certain period or until they find work.'[31] Not only did the immigrants recruit their fellow countryfolk but employers also sent to Ireland to supplement their workforce when labour was in short supply. Manufacturers and industrial employers likened the 'boundless mines of labour existing for us in Ireland' to the 'boundless coalfields beneath us' as together forming the basis of their prosperity.[32]

This applied particularly to the textile industries, whether cotton in Stalybridge and Stockport, silk in Newton Heath, wool in Bradford or linen and jute in Dundee. In all of these there was a large amount of formal and informal recruitment of Irish people as, apart from fine linen production, much textile manufacture in Ireland declined in the face of British competition and Irish workers moved to maintain their existing job skills. Richardson's work on Bradford suggests that, by mid-century, its woollen and worsted industries occupied about two-thirds of the adult Irish immigrants, many of whom came from counties like Queen's County

(Laois) and from Cork where coarse woollen manufacture was in decline.[33] In the coarse linen and jute industries of Dundee, three-fifths of the hand loom weavers in 1851 were Irish-born, many from north-central Ireland where the domestic linen-producing family units were threatened by mechanization.[34] In the Lancashire cotton industry, there were claims that the Irish and their descendants had taken over the cotton hand loom weaving trade. However, analysis of the spatial distribution of the Irish population throughout Lancashire during the period before mid-century shows its concentration confined to Liverpool, where cotton weaving scarcely existed, and to Manchester, where power looms had superseded hand looms before the mass Irish influx. Again, when the Irish spread into the smaller Lancashire towns in the 1860s, cotton hand loom weaving was already mechanized.

The place of the Irish in the Scottish cotton industry is less ambiguous. Estimated at around one-third of all hand loom weavers in Scotland in 1840, they dominated the sector of plain cotton cloth weaving at precisely the same time as it was being undermined by mechanization. Although contemporaries blamed the immigrants as newcomers flooding the trade, many of the Irish had already been cotton or linen weavers in Ireland. The point was that, in comparison with other trades, hand loom weaving was easy to enter, especially in loom shops where there was no formal apprenticeship and where looms were supplied by the putters-out. The seeming ease of mobility into hand loom weaving, and the relative immobility of the Irish out of the industry during a period of declining wages, led to an identification of that decline with the Irish presence. However, the bulk of the evidence suggests that though the involvement of the Irish prolonged the existence of the industry, their participation was a symptom of its decline rather than a cause.[35]

The fact that many Irishmen were hand loom weavers at a time when mechanization was making such skills redundant is explained by the extent to which Irish women and children participated in other textile work. Irish peasant families were accustomed to the notion that each family member contributed to household maintenance; hence the comments in the 1830s on the extent that 'the Irish come over with their families with a view to obtain labour for their children as well as themselves, so as to prevent starvation'.[36] Each of the towns with hand loom weaving work for men also had a far larger (mainly adolescent) workforce of women and children in spinning mills, bleach and dye works and packing warehouses. Employers in the cotton mills claimed that they would have been 'ruined' without the Irish while in the mid-century mill workforces of both Bradford and Dundee, Irish women were in the majority. At this period of mass immigration, mill and factory regulations permitted children as young as 10 years to be employed half-time and their weekly earnings of half-a-crown (12 pence) or more were higher than could be obtained at that age in any other employment. With two or three adolescents' earnings, the family of an Irish unskilled casual labourer was at least as well off in the short term as that of a skilled tradesman depending on a single income.

Textile manufacturers recognized that the Irish family employment patterns were crucial to their own progress; 'without the Irish there would have been a want of supply of children for the factory employments'.[37] The ability of the Irish to fill this niche was contrasted with the seeming reluctance of the southern English labourer to move north, and the supposed disadvantage in time and cost of travel for a Scottish Highlander to move south to Glasgow. More correctly, it seems that in English towns the Irish immigrants competed for jobs equally with short-distance migrants, but that in Scotland they were disadvantaged in comparison with Scottish (though not necessarily Highland) migrants who tended to monopolize the craft and commercial sectors of many central Scottish towns.[38]

While the expansion of textiles was important for Irish immigrant families, there were other male-dominated clusters of Irish working men, such as in coal and ironstone mining in the west of Scotland, north-east England and, to a lesser extent, south Wales. Campbell's work on the Lanarkshire coalfield outlines perhaps the most extreme picture of an industrial frontier during the 1840s–1870s. The combination of an almost equal ethnic balance between the mineworkers and unskilled metal workers of Coatbridge, and, within the mines, the clustering of the Irish into the most arduous and insalubrious ironstone works, coupled with mutual antagonism which often resulted in violent confrontations, all contributed to a particularly unyielding form of Irish-Scottish working class culture.[39]

Elsewhere in the mining sector, Irish labour was less renowned for providing the basis for rapid expansion than resented as short-term strikebreakers. In the north-east, Cooter outlined the limited extent to which the 'notorious' mine- and land-owner, Lord Londonderry, brought in men from his County Down estates to break a strike organized by his Seaham colliers. Many of the imported Irishmen only remained as miners for a matter of months. It was not until the opening of new inland pits in Durham in the 1860s that the Irish began to penetrate the north-east industry, and then mostly in the lower paid surface jobs.[40] There was much greater Irish movement into the newly expanding Durham iron industry where there was no traditional local pride or competition to bar entry, and also the strength of physique of the Irish newcomers was preferred by the employers. In Wales, too, the Irish immigration of the 1840s coincided with general expansion in both coal and iron ore mining so that their labour was relatively readily absorbed without friction.[41]

The armed services were also traditional employers of Irish men, some of whom were recruited in British towns during slumps in trade. The first recorded army statistics on nationality, published in 1830, showed that over 42 per cent of the non-commissioned ranks had been born in Ireland. Between then and 1870 the number of Irish-born 'other ranks' remained at c. 50,000 although, as the army grew, their proportion dropped to one-quarter. After this date, the classification was made on the basis of religion instead of nationality and the proportion of Roman Catholics in the 1870s was around 30 per cent. Between 1890 and 1913 the actual numbers of enlisted Catholics remained stable at between 20,000 and 30,000 but their proportion of the total decreased to 10 per cent.[42] Increasingly, the measurement of either place of birth or religion became an unrealistic indicator of direct Irish participation as the army recruited large numbers of English- and Scots-born sons of Irish Catholics and non-Catholics. Only Irish officers remained disproportionately numerous in relation to the size of the Church of Ireland membership from which they were drawn. One consequence of the long-term recruitment of the Irish as soldiers, in contrast to the much lower level of Scottish enlistment, was that the Irish were used as a pool for making up regimental numbers. They were therefore much more dispersed than the Scots who were concentrated into certain distinctively Scottish regiments. One exception to this was the formation of the Tyneside Irish Brigade of about 5500 men which was attached to the Northumberland Fusiliers and was to see action at Mons and Ypres.[43]

If the most common Irishman's job was as a labourer, one of the most typical jobs for Irish women was that universal female work, domestic service. Indoor domestic servants and those in personal services, such as laundresses and charwomen, accounted for upwards of one-eighth of the entire female population of England in the second half of the nineteenth century, and a considerably higher proportion of Irish women. The towns with administrative or commercial functions were more likely to support servant-keeping families; at mid-century, almost one-quarter of the Irish working women in York and Liverpool, and over half of those in Bristol, worked in indoor and outdoor service. Lees' research on the Irish in London at the same period has highlighted the extent to which this was an avenue for the single Irish woman and, to a lesser degree, the widow unencumbered with children.[44] There was competition from native country girls and popular prejudice against the rawness of the Irish girls. In Glasgow, Highland girls were preferred to the Irish: 'people do not like employing the Irish in their homes', and so 'they find it less easy to get respectable employment than the Highlander'.[45] By the closing decade of the century, the domestic service sector had contracted, though the more casual aspects of outdoor service persisted into the twentieth century. The Irish girls' position within the service sector probably reflected this trend.

Changes in the Pattern of Employment

How much did this overall picture change? The answer depends, quite simply, on which picture is studied. If the focus is on the cohort of Irish-born people in Great Britain at any one time, such as is provided by the census, there were only minor degrees of difference in the 1890s and early 1900s compared to the mass immigrant profile of the 1840s and 1850s. For each adult Irish-born generation, the preoccupation was with getting a living and maintaining themselves and their dependants. Bringing little in the way of assets and much in the way of liabilities, such as unfamiliarity with urban modes of living (though this attribute was shared with most Scots, Welsh and English country migrants), many Irish adults were glad to secure any foothold in society. Initially also, difficulties in speaking English in an accent intelligible to an unaccustomed ear, and certainly with writing in English (at the 1851 census only half of the Irish population in Ireland was defined as literate in English), must have been effective barriers against moving too far beyond familiar circumstances. Because urban labour markets were local, newly arrived immigrants tended to gravitate to earlier settlers and thus reproduce employment patterns. Job networks perpetuated this through the generations. In 1871 the Irish-born continued to make up 40 per cent of the Liverpool dock labour force, while in 1891 a special sub-group study by the census commissioners showed that nearly half of those Liverpudlians of Irish birth were dock labourers, five times the proportion for the entire local workforce.[46]

However, structural changes like those which created new industrial employment, such as in the north-east in the 1880s, provided a new balance within the

Irish occupational structure. Similarly, Irish female employment patterns probably reflected both the overall shift away from personal services towards the manufacturing sector, and the increasing relegation of women's work to the household sphere where it was redefined as non-economic activity. It was alongside such structural changes that the Irish communities came to consist of British-born descendants of earlier Irish migrants, and this tended to mask occupational mobility. For individual families, it was those in self-employment, especially in the commercial side, who were most likely to improve their circumstances. Thus *Blackwood's Magazine* recorded in 1901 that 'your typical coster is your London Irishman,' and claimed that the retail vegetable trade in London had largely passed into such hands.[47] Fitzpatrick has asserted that by 1911 in Scotland, Irish men were fully represented in such lower middle class jobs as railway clerks and insurance and telegraph workers (notably occupations with bureaucratic rather than informal selection criteria).[48] Only case histories of individual families can document the protracted nature of any inter-generational occupational and social mobility which occurred. Long-established Irish families were themselves often the most concerned to establish a social distance between themselves and those who had just 'come over with the cattle'.[49]

Residential Characteristics of the Irish in Britain

Patterns of Segregation

The networks which so effectively created the occupational profile of many Irish immigrant communities also gave rise to specific residential patterns with identifiable Irish quarters or streets in numerous towns and cities. These have been described by nineteenth-century commentators and defined by twentieth-century analysts. Segregated housing was common in most European towns which experienced distinctive rural–urban migration. In nineteenth-century Britain, the Irish clusters were followed by those of east European Jews, but as the Irish were the forerunners the trait of segregation was popularly identified with them.

Most of the recent work on Irish residential patterns has used evidence from the census enumeration books. This method suffers to the extent that the census, taken in isolation, can only identify Irish immigrants by birthplace and so can take no account of their descendants born in Britain. Attempts to operationalize the phrase 'effectively Irish' have been made for Lancashire, but some researchers have been content to estimate intuitively, or (even less rigorously) to define as 'Irish' all those living with an Irish-born head of household. However, this latter definition becomes increasingly unworkable when applied to the later nineteenth century, so it is perhaps a fortuitous match of method and available data that the census enumeration books which have been used for these studies cover the period of heaviest Irish settlement from the 1840s to the 1870s. Yet the very feasibility of this approach has had the further effect of masking the inevitable changes in the type of people settled in an area or in the ambience and function of the area itself. Moreover, an extension of the labelling logic of identifying 'Irish' people with 'Irish' areas also applies in denying the 'Irishness' of those who lived apart from such areas.

Geographers and sociologists have developed three statistical measures of segregation: the index of dissimilarity, which compares the residential distribution of one group with another; the index of segregation, which compares the residential distribution of one group with that of the total population; and the location quotient, which defines areal differences. In the context of the Irish in Britain, the most explicit demonstration of these techniques has been Pooley's work on Liverpool in 1871, which explored the extent of segregation in the city. His conclusions were that while the Scots and Welsh migrant groups did display distinctive residential segregation, the Irish-born migrants did not differ greatly from the non-migrants in their spatial distribution apart from one small but particularly poor central district composed of unskilled Irish working class families. Overall, such patterns were based on the differing social class structures of each migrant group.[50]

There are problems, however, in the use of these techniques because of the varied scale of analysis at which they are conducted. The most commonly available unit is the census enumeration district which was often an artificial paper unit created with little regard for the topographical or social structural features which may have influenced residential patterns. Consequently, such a unit may provide, quite randomly, a picture which seems at variance with contemporary description; thus the census analysts' view of the Manchester Irish as a spatially dispersed group is hard to reconcile with Engels' famous description of the unsavoury slums of 'Little Ireland'. In Leeds, too, Dillon found that although the Irish were dispersed through all eight wards of the township in 1851, nevertheless 80 per cent lived in only three of them.[51] Clustering and dispersal were therefore hardly mutually exclusive modes of living even within one town, and Pooley has warned against imposing a 'ghetto' model of residential segregation upon the Irish in the absence of other evidence of perceived alienation from fellow town dwellers.

Rather than being employed in aggregate statistical measures, it is at the neighbourhood level, revealing who lived next to whom, that the census material provides the most direct evidence of housing choice and therefore attitudes. In Scotland, because of the prevalence of tenement housing, segregation by social status took place vertically as well as on the ground. In Dundee, 90 per cent of the Irish households in 1851 lived next to another Irish household, either in the same tenement or an adjoining one, while over half the Scottish migrants to the city lived apart from the Irish in terms of this definition. This neighbourhood pattern of small-scale Irish clusters (without the vertical dimension) was evident also in the English towns of Oldham and South Shields. Elsewhere, in Cardiff, Falkirk, Leeds, Huddersfield, Bradford and of course, London, other census-based studies have confirmed that there were urban courts and alleys which were virtually monopolized by the Irish.[52]

Housing Conditions and Housing Choices

The Irish districts within Victorian towns fell into two main types. Firstly, the immigrants gravitated to central areas to live in older, previously grand houses which had been 'made down' (in the descriptive Scottish phrase) to house eight or ten families. Liverpool, York, Glasgow and central London had many examples of this process. The rookeries of St Giles in London comprised former merchants' mansions with additions of small cottages built as infill along their backs and sides, creating a mass of dense housing with no direct street access. Lees referred to such residence patterns as 'dead end locations', literally as well as figuratively. In such neighbourhoods the living quarters were mixed up with stables and cowsheds and the apparatus of small-scale food and animal processing industries. Thus, they were 'crowded with pigs, with fowls and with dogs; they are strewn with oyster shells and fish refuse . . . their drainage lies in pools wherever it may be thrown.'[53] The Walmgate district in York also exhibited this pattern, its Britannia Yard being an extreme example of densely occupied infill cottages, juxtaposed with stables, pigsties and slaughterhouses; in 1851, its 16 two-roomed cottages were occupied by 171 people, 154 of whom were Irish-born.[54] More degrading still were the cellar dwellings used by the Irish in Liverpool. Lawton described these as 'wells of stagnant water' where, in 1851, lived nearly 6000 people.[55] All of these forms of older housing had one feature in common in that they had been constructed for purposes other than that for which they were in use. This frequently meant that they lacked even a hearth, while the provision of a common water tap or a dry privy was totally inadequate for all the inhabitants.

The second pattern of Irish residence was in newer urban housing built not in the town centres but on the outskirts of existing housing and initially often outside civic jurisdiction, to cater for the masses of rural immigrants, Irish and others. In the middle of the century, such housing was quickly erected to minimal standards for fast returns and little regard for the long term. In Leeds East ward, which housed half the Irish in the entire township in 1839, the newly constructed two- and three-roomed houses were built back to back with only one face open to the air. In Cardiff, speculative builders developed the Newtown district with two- and four-roomed cottages which, because of the city's housing shortage, they were able to let at high rents to Irish families who then sublet rooms and bed space within rooms to fellow immigrants in order to afford the rents. In Dundee, the lack of concern over shoddy flats built in the 1840s and immediately occupied by Irish newcomers was justified on the grounds that 'in a town like Dundee, where trade fluctuates so much, we of course have a rush of people into it and of course a number of families go into one house and live in it'.[56]

It was not only the new urban housing lived in by the Irish which was of low standard, but also the settlements constructed round collieries and iron works. In the Durham coalfields, the newly built pit houses of the 1880s were erected on unpaved and undrained land, flanked by dustheaps, dunghills, pigsties and heaps of coal. In 1882 the Irish miners at Ushaw Moor colliery described their housing as 'the most wretched dwellings it is possible to conceive'.[57] In the company towns of Consett and Jarrow, the employers provided the bulk of the housing and therefore its letting reflected the class structure of the workforce. The Irish, if they were provided for at all, were housed at the lower quality end of the terrace rows, but, because they were mainly contracted in labour gangs, they were also not considered to be regular employees and were directed to lodging houses or sheds known as 'paddy houses'.

Residential choices for any nineteenth-century town dweller were constrained ultimately by the level of rents. As a generalization, up to mid-century, the earnings of unskilled labourers did not keep pace with rising rent levels so housing costs took up an increasing share of an Irish household budget. Rents for two- or three-roomed cottages at mid-century were typically four or five shillings out of a typical labourer's earnings of 12 shillings per week. Rooms which were sub-let cost proportionately more for less space while shared beds in lodgings were let out at one shilling per night. The Irish paid dearly for their lowly position. Moreover, when competition for housing was strong, landlords exercised individual power by demanding references or key money and weekly rentals rather than monthly or quarterly payments. Neighbourhood status thus related to the ways of paying as well as to the absolute level of rent and the Irish were often doubly disadvantaged.

Such a volatile situation contributed to the turnover of population which was commonplace in the poorer city districts. Microanalysis between censuses has indicated the extent to which Irish families moved about within small areas, taking advantages of better housing, cheaper rents or just anticipating eviction. At the time of peak Irish movement to London in the 1850s, priests and local officials claimed that the Irish never stayed in an area long enough to strike roots and settle into local life. Booth commented on the same phenomenon two generations later. Yet neighbourhood contacts (not least the shops and credit networks which were vital to everyday living) and support in shared common experiences encouraged people to stay among those with whom they were familiar. Dillon's study of the Leeds Irish population between 1851 and 1861 found that in a typical court of Irish-headed households, nearly two-fifths remained in the court though not at the same address. A similar example has been described by Herson in Stafford where Plant's Square had eight of its nine courthouses occupied by Irish families in 1861; seven of these eight households still lived in the area in 1871, though not all in the Square. Finnegan's work on the Irish in York also confirms that, although there was a high degree of transience among the Irish community, those families who did remain shifted repeatedly from one address to another within the same district.[58]

The reluctance of the Irish to move away from the districts in which they first settled was also connected with the practical need to live sufficiently near places of work to get there on foot in as short a time as possible. Whole streets or districts were identified with particular industries or firms; thus Irish mill workers in Leeds lived within sound of the mill bell or hooter, the Irish in Greenock lived near the sugar refineries, while in Liverpool the Irish dockers lived in the Waterloo Road area where they were close enough to respond to the daily or even hourly availability of casual work. Even skilled tailors or shoemakers in domestic workshops could not afford to live any distance from their warehouses. This was especially the case for the London Irish whose lives were circumscribed by local job opportunities, limited mobility and dependence on the familiar. For them, as Hobsbawm has said, 'all that lay beyond a tiny circle of personal acquaintance or walking distance was darkness'.[59] Perception of distance also varied; where two or three miles would have been a long distance in London, Treble estimated that in Glasgow the greater density of tenement housing narrowed the perspective to under three-quarters of a mile. Hence, specifically local conditions intensified the attachment of Irish families to neighbourhoods where 'they feel almost as if they were coming to an Irish town . . . and though they have little to give, they give what they have'.[60]

Nevertheless, the mid-century Irish residential patterns did not remain unchanged throughout the period, principally because of the influence of national and local legislation. Public health improvements, which were intended to raise living standards, often exacerbated them in the short term. Usually, street widening and slum clearance were undertaken without provision for relocation which meant that many sought refuge among adjacent surroundings and families. In Liverpool, the clearance of Dale Street in 1867 affected 2000–3000 people who crowded into neighbouring districts. Railway construction also wrecked the established pattern of inner-city housing, and affected the Irish huddled in old courts and alleyways of Manchester and in London, where some 56,000 people were said to have been displaced from their homes between 1853 and 1885. The same phenomenon was noted during the construction of the Union Railway in Glasgow in the 1860s.[61] By the turn of the twentieth century, the attempts to create socially mixed housing areas had been largely abandoned by reformists in favour of a distinction between families in primary and secondary poverty. This led to embryonic attempts at local government level to relocate clusters of families into more salubrious housing and deliberately perpetuated the Irish neighbourhoods instead of breaking them up. The enduring pattern of Irish community life in Ship Street, Liverpool, with its emphasis on the strength of household and family ties, which was described by Kerr in the 1950s, was a typical third-generation outcome of this early-twentieth-century policy.[62]

Multiple Occupancy

Perhaps the most lasting image of Irish living conditions was the overcrowded homes which lowered already humble living standards and led to the succinct observation that the homes of the Irish contained more people than furniture. Living in cramped conditions, or in lodgings, minimized the effects of all the external influences simply by reducing the money outlay required for shelter. In addition, giving house room reinforced the ties with other Irish immigrants. The taking-in of lodgers was a common reaction at certain stages of the family life cycle of the urban working class when money was tight. This also helped supplement irregular wages, particularly for elderly widows. Lees, indeed, sees this strategy among the London Irish as consistent with the emphasis placed by the Irish in Ireland on the family as a productive unit.[63] Virtually all the studies of first-generation Irish communities in Britain have found that they were much more likely to have lodgers, and more of them, than other town dwellers, even those in similar socio-economic circumstances. Two or more families sharing accommodation was part of the hurried immigration of the most impoverished Irish of the 1840s. That it was to a degree a product of such conditions is demonstrated by Haslett and Lowe's research on Lancashire towns. This suggests that the sharing of house room which had been common among the Irish in the 1850s had become much less usual by the 1870s. Once newly arrived immigrants had achieved a more settled way of life, they relegated lodger-taking to periods of specific hardship, although of course such times were likely to be relatively frequent for families dependent on low wage casual work.[64] Lodgers were often young and single migrants for whom lodgings were the most useful accommodation. Lodging also seems to have been more than a pecuniary relationship, for there is evidence that the arbitrary category of lodger, defined by census enumerators, under-recorded kin relationships. Detailed analysis of Irish households in Dundee in 1851, almost half of whom contained lodgers, suggested that in nearly 90 per cent of the latter a lodger was probably a relative, most commonly a sibling of the Irish head or his wife.[65]

The Cultural Identity of the Irish in Britain

Cultural Solidarity

If lodger-taking represented an aspect of cultural values and emotional attachments within Irish families and neighbourhoods which extended beyond their material needs, this was also to be seen in other areas of migrant Irish family life. Samuel discusses the extent to which Father Matthew's temperance crusade appealed to those brought up on a reliance on folk medicine and the efficacy of superstition.[66] The Irish language remained for many, especially the wives, a primary cultural resource at times of high emotion, births, burials or other celebrations. Such events were used as a focus to reaffirm communal solidarity. William Luby, born in the 1880s, whose grandfather had been an Irish immigrant, recalled that 'in Ireland they all had a sort of clannishness ... so it made my grandfather try to keep a hold on his children ... funerals were good, the only times we really did get good feeds ... really, funerals, weddings and christenings we children done well' (sic).[67]

Cultural bonds have also been examined, more prosaically, through Irish immigrant marriage patterns, although there is a practical difficulty that, logically, the communities where Irish people were few were least likely to leave any trace of Irish marriages. This was the case in York in 1841 where the Irish comprised fewer than 2 per cent of the population and 31 per cent of all the Irish married at the time of the census had English-born partners. It would seem that York was the exception which proved the rule. Probably the majority of Irish immigrants who were married in Britain by Catholic priests chose other Irish partners; in a little enclave such as St Patrick's, in London's Soho, Lees' analysis of the marriage registers of the 1840s and 1850s revealed that most marriages took place between Irish people who lived within a quarter mile of each other and had come from the same region in Ireland.[68] The extent to which this was a choice based on common religion or common nationality is by no means fully resolved because of the unknown number of Irish-born people in Britain who married outside the Catholic Church. In Scotland, where civil marriage registers of the 1850s have been analysed to this end, it seems that the Protestant Irish of Greenock and Paisley were much more likely to inter-marry with the Scots than were the Catholic Irish. Both Greenock and Paisley had long-established Irish communities with Scottish-born descendants, and the contrasting evidence from Dundee, a centre of recent settlement in the late 1840s, shows that most Irish marriages were between Irish-born spouses regardless of religious differences.[69] This suggests that it was length of residence which was the prime determinant in leading to inter-marriage between the Irish and the English and Scots. Clearly, an additional aspect throughout Britain as the century developed was the extent to which apparently British-born spouses were descendants of earlier Irish immigrants. It is probable that in the last quarter of the century most Catholic marriages in Britain were between people of Irish birth or descent, but it is largely impossible to identify how many non-Catholic ones were.

Irish Catholics in Britain

Membership of the Catholic Church created a badge of identity for many Irish immigrants but, equally important, the Catholic Church in England, Scotland and Wales was profoundly altered by the Irish influx. Between 1800 and 1900 it was transformed both doctrinally and in practical terms. The introduction of ultra-montanism raised the public face of Catholic belief in Britain and, as in the British Empire generally, initiated some popular suspicion of Catholic practitioners as alien to English civil society. In practical terms, the growth in numbers of adherents was begun and sustained by first-generation Irish immigrants and their descendants. Cardinal Manning reminisced in the 1880s that he had 'spent his life working for the Irish occupation of England'.[70] Probably by the early twentieth century, between 50 and 75 per cent of all Catholics in England were Irish by birth or descent. In 1911, 40 per cent of all Roman Catholics in the British Isles lived in Great Britain, three-quarters of them in the urban dioceses of England and Wales.[71] The Catholic Church in Britain was dominated by the Irish immigration to a much greater degree, therefore, than any of the Protestant churches which absorbed Protestant Irish immigrants with little outward show.

However, there was a wide gulf between the estimates of adherents and the numbers actually attending weekly mass or the Easter duties. While the clerical hierarchy attributed this 'leakage' to the failure of priestly pastoral zeal among the urban masses, it seems probable that the mid-century immigrants may have brought little tradition of church-going from a background of relatively lax parish administration in pre-Famine Ireland.[72] Certainly, estimates suggest that at most 30–40 per cent of the baptized Catholic population attended church weekly, whether they were Cockney Irish or in Lancashire. Connolly's recent estimate that fewer than half of all the Irish immigrants before the 1850s attended church regularly confirms the indication that it was not until the second half of the nineteenth century that the extent of Catholic observation and practice among the Irish immigrants came to follow the devout forms subsequently accepted as standard.[73]

If formal adherence was lacking, a much larger number retained a Catholic identity which was increasingly equated, by others, with Irish patriotism; a London Irish street sweeper in the 1860s described himself as 'being a Catholic for I'm not ashamed to own my religion before any man,' and this contrasted with his Cockney workmate whose own religious convictions were lukewarm, church attendance non-existent and who saw the Catholic Church as offering 'an Irish religion [he] wasn't to be expected to understand'.[74] Irish Catholic indifference to religious practice did not imply indifference to belief. Mayhew describes the reception given to the parish priest in ordinary concourse with women curtseying and boys touching their hair in salute. The 'fayther' who commanded respect in the street and was arbiter of family disputes was also the point of reference in all dealings with non-Catholic activity, whether in local authorities, voluntary organizations or even the workplace.

With the restoration of the Catholic hierarchy of bishops in England in 1850 the imbalance between the numbers of serving clergy and the regional distribution of Irish settlers became apparent. In the north-east the ratio of priests to people was 1:1000 in county Durham and even worse in Newcastle. Similar shortfalls existed in Lancashire. On census day 1851, the five masses held at St Anthony's in Liverpool were attended by over 7000 people. Ten Catholic churches were built in Liverpool between 1850 and 1856. Shortage of priests at mid-century was compounded by language and dialect differences. In south Wales, an Italian parish priest compiled a small conversation book in Irish so that he could hear confessions. The pressing problem of church accommodation was tackled by the use of attics and sheds, disused warehouses and factories to house temporary missions. These avoided the high rentals of prime sites and were in the heart of Irish enclaves. Religious orders were assigned specific districts: in London, the Marists went to Spitalfields and the Oratorians to the Strand area.[75] The missions were hard to ignore. The semi-public street life of the rookery encouraged a conformity in communal behaviour of which religion was one expression, especially with the mission emphasis on public repentance, candlelit ceremony and togetherness. The success of these forms of mission has also been attributed to the particular forms of dormant Irish Catholic faith in superstition, comparable in intensity to evangelicalism or Methodism in uncovering belief systems rooted in providence.[76]

In Scotland, organizational structure and the growth in numbers of Catholic adherents paralleled the continuing influx of Irish immigrants. Scottish Catholicism, particularly in the western central belt and the south-west, came to be dominated numerically by Irish-born Catholics as early as 1830. Before mid-century, clerical resources were constantly outstripped by needs. Between 1840 and 1854, the number of Catholic churches in the west rose from five to 49, several of which held over 700 sittings. The shortage of priests meant that many priests served different centres. As in England, the parish missions extended membership: the Passionists' three week mission at Airdrie in 1871, for example, secured some 3500 communicants and 540 confirmations.[77]

In contrast to the mid-century situation in England where Irish-trained priests were rarely welcomed, many priests working in Scotland had been ordained in Ireland. The Scots clergy perceived this as a mixed blessing because of their fear that the Irish element would take over the resources of Scottish Catholicism under a hierarchy of bishops in Ireland. Their response to the vociferous and militantly Irish consciousness of a small group of the younger Irish clergy in Scotland, in the 1860s, was the successful restoration of the hierarchy of Scottish bishops in 1878. The Irish influence continued, however, precisely because of the episcopal void at the time of heaviest mass Irish immigration. One specific instance of this Irish orientation was during the issue of Highland land reform in the 1880s. This united those clergy who combined religion and nationalism, whether in Ireland or Scotland. The bishops and more conservative clergy acted quickly and visibly to condemn public rallies shared by Home Rulers and the Highland Land Law Reform

Association, but the mutual sympathies remained and gained additional credibility from emigrant support in North America.[78]

Anti-Catholicism and Sectarianism

In both England and Scotland, the Irish presence crystallized popular anti-Catholicism which mixed theological and moral objections. The Scots' antagonism had two additional elements, the first of which was the much higher proportion of Irish Protestants in its Irish immigrant population. Taking the nineteenth century as a whole, between one-quarter and one-third of new arrivals from Ireland were Presbyterians, Episcopalians or Methodists, and these immigrants brought a cultural baggage of social distinctions already neatly labelled.[79] Secondly, anti-Catholicism was an ideology which had bound together all urban Lowlanders since the mid-eighteenth century. To these sentiments, the backcloth of the constitutional liberalism of Catholic Emancipation, government sponsorship of the Catholic training college at Maynooth, Co. Kildare, the perception of the restoration of the English hierarchy of bishops as papal aggression, and the declaration of papal infallibility fanned each generation's suspicion of the papist's divided allegiance. Such feelings were fuelled by colourful preachers who travelled throughout Britain using theatrical techniques to agitate and titillate their audiences. Former priests or imposters were often sponsored by Protestant organizations to harangue their listeners on the trappings of Catholic faith and the outcome of such speeches was rioting and looting the homes of Irish Catholics.[80] Apart from the annual ritual sectarian brawls in Liverpool, there were anti-Irish riots in Stockport in 1852, Oldham in 1861 and the more widespread Murphy riots of 1867–71, which took their name from the Protestant Evangelical, William Murphy, whose inflammatory rhetoric stirred up anti-Irish feeling at the time of the Fenian activities.

Anti-Irish expression also surfaced out of underlying job competition when manipulated for local party political ends. The Orange Order in Lancashire recruited members from the British as well as the immigrant Irish Protestant working class when job competition was at its fiercest during the Famine influx. Swift argues, indeed, that the ethnic violence was a reflection of other deeper structural divisions within local communities.[81] By the end of the century, reaction against Irish Catholics was more subtle than physical attack. Residential segregation contributed to the reduction in community tensions, particularly in Glasgow, by reducing contact between the social classes and enabling a social distance to be maintained. The job segregation between Protestant craftsmen and Catholic labourers in the Clydeside shipyards also restrained the level of religious friction. Similar forces plus a buoyant local economy—the north-east was called the poor man's Eldorado—may account for the relative lack of conflict in the Newcastle and Durham area. In contrast, the more open labour market in Liverpool, with its preponderance of casual work, provided an arena in which Catholics challenged non-Catholics on a daily basis. With weak trade unionism until the 1890s, the lack of a strong Co-operative movement or other working class organizations which could have provided meeting points, the tensions in Liverpool's municipal politics in the closing decades of the nineteenth century mirrored those of the Irish question on the centre of the stage.[82]

The Consolidation of Irish Catholic Communities

The response of the Irish to anti-Catholicism was retrenchment and the adoption of a 'pugnaciously defensive' pose. The mid-century missions had sought to capture their flocks by parish-based clubs and associations and to instil feelings of commitment through financial support. All over Britain the weekly pennies and halfpennies provided income for church building to replace sheds and provide school rooms in lieu of basements. From this developed the duplication and reproduction at local parish level of all the non-Catholic and secular social institutions of the Victorian era. By this means, the Church tried consciously to dominate the whole non-working lives of its members and their families, providing clubs for every distinctive group within the parish, in a cradle-to-grave mentality.[83] To belong to a confraternity meant acceptance of the Church's code of social behaviour. In return, membership offered elevated status in church-based rituals and, in general, the chance to mark oneself out from the general run of poor humanity. This social discipline was underpinned with the more practical aspects of friendly societies such as sick and burial schemes and eventually, loans for house purchase. Societies like the Catholic Young Men's Society expanded nationally in the 1860s, developing not only a sense of mutual and parish belonging but also a fellowship of association beyond their immediate locality. Membership of confraternities offered most Irishmen the main opportunity, apart from moving out of their class, to display their distance from the rough counter cultures of drink and petty crime which were considered part of low Irish neighbourhoods.

Where the father was involved at this level, Irish families had Catholic devotion built into their upbringing. Tom Barclay, recalling a Leicester Irish childhood of the 1860s, described how he chalked an altar on the bedroom wall at the age of 12 and regularly attended mass and communion.[84] Even at a less doctrinal level, the Church tried to control its youth by the provision of boys' and girls' clubs, sporting activities and the teaching of social accomplishments such as Irish dancing. In this way, second- and third-generation Catholic children were encouraged to conform to an identity as Irish Catholics. In urban Scotland especially, the emergence of local football clubs in the 1870s and 1880s consolidated working class loyalties and did much to herd fathers and sons along a conformist path.

As far as Irish family life was concerned, the Church's doctrine emphasized the woman's place as wife and mother. An anonymous writer in *Blackwood's Edinburgh Magazine* in 1901 considered that the Catholic Church had an even stronger hold upon Irish wives than it did upon their husbands. As controllers of the family budget, they were perhaps moree aware of the vulnerability of their families' well-being to the chance interventions of unemployment and sickness and hence more open to belief in the effective ends of popular devotion. The doctrine of Holy Poverty was particularly successful among immigrant Irish working class wives and mothers as it justified the endurance of hardship as part of their guarantee of salvation in heaven.[85] Their place in rearing the next generation was vital to the continued growth in Catholic Church membership, particularly in the face of the late-nineteenth-century spread of the practice of family limitation. In England and Wales, Catholic fertility has been estimated at two-thirds higher than non-Catholic fertility in the early twentieth century with baptism into the Church almost universal for the infants of Catholic parents, while in the 1920s, eugenicists and alarmists predicted a repeopling of Scotland, based on a combination of the high birth rate among the Irish Catholics in Scotland and heavy rates of Scottish emigration.[86]

One of the most far-reaching areas of Irish Catholic social discipline was its education which was primarily intended to produce good Catholic citizens. The religious orders staffed many of the schools and the tradition of voluntary subscriptions for their maintenance persisted even after 1847, when Catholic schools in England and Wales were granted eligibility for financial aid in return for inspection of their secular education. Sources of funding were imaginative; in Cardiff subscriptions were sought from ships berthing in the port and also, according to tradition, from the superintendent of police. Even with the state aid, improvements in school accommodation were very gradual. Nor were there sufficient schools to cope with the numbers of children. At the 1851 census, under 30 per cent of the Irish children in London were listed as scholars, although in York and Bristol the proportions were nearer half. Between then and 1871, the number of Catholic school places over the whole of England more than doubled.

However, attendances were irregular and absenteeism continued to be frequent although probably no worse than that among non-Catholic schoolchildren. The outcome was that educational achievment was low with most attaining only minimum standards after repeating years in the lower classes. In the Lancashire factory towns, the high levels of half-time working by Irish immigrant children meant that the Catholic Church relied more on Sunday than on day schools. It was only after elementary education became compulsory in the 1870s in Scotland and the 1880s in England that the numbers attending Catholic day schools improved. Catholic schools were only partly within the school board system in Scotland until 1918, and their relative paucity of funds led to a widening gap in attainment between those pupils fully in the system and those outside it. This was because of the Catholic Church's dual educational role: stretched resources for salaries and books necessitated priority being given to the inculcation of Catholic morality and doctrine at the expense of any studies beyond basic literacy.[87] Defensiveness, moreover, meant that schoolbooks contained little which acknowledged the Irish origins of most of the children. One autobiography describes a Liverpool Irish upbringing of the 1900s where the contrast was stark between the schools where the children were 'patriotised and Britishised' and their homes where they were 'sternly Irishised'.[88] As the political agitation of the last quarter of the nineteenth century moved Irish affairs more to the centre of intellectual as well as popular discussion, Catholic schooling became more self-effacing in its promotion of sobriety and respectability. The relatively slow growth of an Irish Catholic middle class in early-twentieth-century Britain has been attributed to this, and to the difficulty for the individual, clergy or laity, of coming to terms with the fact that social advancement implied a rejection of at least some of the trappings of the formative years of development.

Irish Immigrants and the Maintenance of Social Order

Drink and Criminality

If papishness provided a badge of identity for many Irish immigrants, it was often juxtaposed in the British public mind with other supposed threats to the social order. One of the most notorious of these menaces was Irish drunkenness, to which was attributed both the cause and the effect of poverty. In the nineteenth century, consumption of alcohol was enormous, viewed both in per capita terms and in visible carousing. Its scale implies it was far from confined to the Irish. Whether the Irish brought with them a predilection for spending in the pub what was left after the rent was paid, or conversely this trait was intensified as a result of their experience as poor urban immigrants, is a debatable point. Certainly the British condemnation of the public nature of that consumption, where Irish wives and husbands were seen together in pubs, says as much about their perception of wifely roles as it does about Irish culture.[89] Drink was a traditional part of British working class life as a relief for a harsh existence at work, attractive to those overcrowded at home and part of a weekly round of sociability uniting workplace and neighbourhood. Because of this, temperance campaigns were only partly successful. It was only when alternative ways of spending developed in the last quarter of the nineteenth century such as cheaper mass-produced clothing, day trip excursions and social clubs which were not pub-based, that overall alcohol consumption fell. Even then, the uncertainty of earnings of casual workers, among whom were many of Irish descent, left them with little interest in the long term—'a prosperous week means, too often, a Saturday spent in booze',[90] and this trait saw no distinction between the British and the Irish of the same low social grouping.

Immigrant spokesmen like John Denvir, writing at the end of the century, attributed the charges of high criminality against the Irish to drink rather than to innate evil. Certainly statistics of arrests throughout Great Britain confirm the criminal reputation. Fitzpatrick has calculated that between 1861 and 1911, Irish immigrants were five times as likely to go to prison as the entire English population, and nearly ten times as likely as the Scots. He also suggests, tentatively, through an ingenious analysis of the intake of Barlinnie Prison, Glasgow, in the 1880s, that class rather than mere birthplace was a greater influence on the likelihood of criminal conviction. In contrast, the patterns of listed offences indicated a greater difference between the Irish immigrants and the rest. The Irish-born were much more likely to carry out assaults and breaches of the peace, offences against the person rather than against property.[91] Drunkenness on a Saturday night, combined with noisy and casual violence, invited attention to Irish neighbourhoods and reinforced popular perceptions of the need to contain the disorderly elements. The over-representation of Irish people in statistics relating to assaults on police could thus be seen as a reaction to police interference. Indeed, Swift suggests that the specific targets of the 'new' police forces created during the nineteenth century were precisely these varieties of street crimes.[92] Thus, the police role and mandate brought them into direct contact with the Irish communities who were renowned for the very transgressions which they were directed to combat.

Criminality was also linked to poverty, young offenders and petty theft, and the connection was drawn by middle class observers between the alienating effect of uprooted urban settlement and the difficulty in rising above a hand-to-mouth way of subsistence. The line was indeed finely etched between the London Irish family survival strategies of hawking, odd jobs and casual labour, and arrest for over-stepping the mark. Yet, analysis of that most harsh outcome of such an arrest, transportation, confirms that both the Irish-born migrant convicts and the English convicts came from similar class backgrounds and that, while guilty of larceny, they did not live by crime alone but were workers who stole from need or greed.[93] For the Irish widows and orphaned young people left destitute by bereavement, such crimes were actions of desperation.

The Treatment of the Poor Irish Immigrant

Another British response to evidence of poverty was seen in the variety of policies of poor relief. Whereas in Ireland, paupers were given relief mainly by entering the workhouse, in Britain outdoor relief was more common. Many British observers believed that the Irish poor preferred to exist in Britain on a meagre allowance than to enter a workhouse in Ireland, and they were probably correct. During the Famine years and immediately afterwards, the Irish were greatly over-represented among recipients of relief in Liverpool, and in Leeds they actually made up the majority of poor relief claimants between 1847 and 1853.[94] Elsewhere in Lancashire, Yorkshire and London, the Famine decade saw an immense increase in the number of Irish families making claims for outdoor relief and seeking workhouse accommo-dation. In other areas they were directed towards alternative agencies, generally on the grounds of their being Irish people and Catholics. Thus in Bristol, even at the height of the Famine influx in 1851, only 2 per cent of the workhouse paupers were Irish. This contrasted with the supply of free meals provided by a local Mendicity Society, nearly half of which were taken up by Irish folk.[95] Local attitudes clearly determined the method as well as the degree of help. In Scotland, it was often stated that the Catholics should look after their own. The Scots administrators, who relied on outdoor relief even more than the English, tightened the Scottish laws of settlement in 1845 by increasing the parish residence qualifications from three to five years. The equivalent condition in England was one year. The Scottish qualification remained in force until 1898. Scottish parish authorities also exercised individual autonomy with regard to the Irish poor: during the economic distress in Paisley in 1842, labourers were struck off the relief list regardless of their length of residence.

> 'This affected the Irish congregation; they made applications again and again . . . many who had a feeling of indignation and disgust at being singled out and struck off in this way moved away permanently from Paisley to Canada, the Californian goldfields and to Glasgow.'[96]

The Scots also more frequently invoked what was for many the final test, deport-ation or removal back to Ireland. In the late 1840s this accounted for nearly 6000 Irish people being sent back 'voluntarily' each year from Scotland.[97] The numbers deported through Liverpool peaked at about 15,000 in 1847 but were annually around 9000 in the 1820s and in the early 1850s. By the 1880s, removal from

England had virtually ceased but the Scots continued with the deportation policy, removing the equivalent of one-eighth of the recorded Irish immigrants during the period 1875–1910. While for some migrant agricultural labourers a claim on the parish may have been a means of getting a free passage home, far more of those removed were likely to be the elderly with no means of support. The fear and practice of removal caused many Irish immigrants to turn to their own networks for survival, and discouraged their identification with a wider community and with the rights and duties of citizenship in mid- and late-Victorian Britain.

Irish Immigrants in British Politics

It was in the political arena that the late-nineteenth-century strains between the developing notions of citizenship within British society and the 'apartness' of broadly nationalist Irish aspirations came into collision. This trend was less apparent earlier in the century during the Chartist struggles. Thompson has argued that there was a considerable rank and file Irish presence in the Chartist movement, and that nationalist heroes such as Emmet were openly toasted at radical dinners in the 1840s.[98] This contrasts with Treble's suggestion that the Catholic church was successful in persuading the mass of Irish workers against the movement.[99] The teaching voice of the Church was certainly hostile to secret societies, as was the official voice of O'Connell's Catholic Association, but Thompson argues plausibly that the Irish immigrant workers had much more in common with their northern English co-workers than they had differences. Thus the radical response to potential ethnic conflict was to turn attention to altering political structures rather than to attacking the individuals within them. There was also a strong Irish Chartist influence in England in the Young Ireland movement in 1848 and in the broad anti-establishment ethos and mass organization techniques of the political actions of the Fenians in the 1860s. At the same time, the rise of popular Protestantism and the consequent localized anti-Catholic and anti-Irish disturbances in the 1850s and 1860s, strengthened the image of the Fenians' actions as those of 'subversive aliens'. The combination of these two strands drove a wedge between Irish nationalist and British working class aspirations.

This showed itself in electoral representation at national level following the 1867 Reform Act. In south Lancashire and north Cheshire, the heartland of English cotton manufacture, the Conservative Party virtually swept the board, in part because of working class antipathy towards Irish Catholics. In contrast, T. P. O'Connor was elected for Scotland Ward, Liverpool in 1885, as the only Irish Nationalist MP on the British mainland. At the Liverpool local council level, Orange Toryism had more than two generations of domination, before giving way to the strength of the Liberal-Nationalist block.[100] The scene of large anti-Irish Tory majorities on local councils was replicated all over England. Significantly, perhaps, in view of the relative prosperity of the north-east in the last quarter of the nineteenth century, the first Irishman to sit on a town council in England is said to have been Bernard McAnulty in Newcastle-upon-Tyne, elected as a Home Ruler between 1874 and 1882. In Scotland, where issues of local politics were traditionally deemed separate from party matters, mobilization of the Irish in Glasgow began with organization of the Catholic vote at School Board elections in the 1870s and gained strength in the formation of the Glasgow branch of the Home Government Association (the first outside Ireland). This subsequently became part of the Irish National League which was formed to mobilize Irish opinion and votes behind the Home Rule cause as an auxiliary of the Irish Parliamentary Party led by Parnell.[101] The pivot of the whole relationship of Irish immigrants to British politics changed after the Irish cause gained a decisive measure of respect from Gladstone's conversion to Home Rule in 1886.

Yet the alignment of Irish Home Rule politics with Liberalism did not provide the Irish immigrant communities with the invincibility which might have been considered due reward for participation in the electoral process. Athough the franchise was extended in 1867 and 1884, McCaffrey's analysis of voting patterns in Glasgow suggests that the high rates of mobility among working class ratepayers, including the Irish, mitigated against their registration and their exercise of the vote. His estimate is that at best, one in two of those Irishmen eligible managed to cast a vote.[102] Similarly, O'Day has argued that, in the case of the London Irish, the single member constituencies which were created in 1884 actually undermined the importance of the Irish vote, because the units were too large to require the appeasement of the Irish as a group or for the Irish to have leverage in decision making.[103]

Ironically, the respectability afforded to the Home Rule movement through its association with the Liberals also provided a place for the rise of organized labour. Once the Irish nationalist case was no longer 'out of court,' the Irish immigrant voter and his representatives could openly debate British bread-and-butter issues. This coincided with the rapid extension of trade unionism in the 1880s and 1890s among unskilled and semi-skilled workers, which thus drew disproportionately on the Irish workforce. Irish immigrants or their sons, including Ben Tillett and Will Thorne, became prominent organizers of the gas and dock workers while according to Hunt the intervention of Cardinal Manning in the 1889 London dock strike constituted something of a watershed in consolidating the respectability of the Irish influence in the labour movement.[104] Thus the United Irish League (as the Irish National League had been renamed) supported both Liberal and Labour candidates in the elections of 1906 and 1910, depending on the specific constituency and personal credibility of the candidates. With the Home Rule Act passed in 1914 and in suspension for the duration of the War, the United Irish League became a recruiting agency for the British army. The movement from Nationalism to Labour became a stampede by 1918, and the process was reinforced by the sight of the consequences in Ireland of the rise of Sinn Féin following the treatment of the leaders of the 1916 Easter Rising. The auxiliary organ of Sinn Féin took over some support from 'old activists under new banners' but mostly former United Irish League members turned their aspirations to the British labour movement or to mass apathy. As in Ireland, the Irish-Ireland movement flourished with Gaelic sports, Irish music and literature although the enthusiasm was temporary, and extended beyond those with Irish connections to those with a romantic view of nationhood.[105] Still, the acceptance of the Irish immigrant working man and woman was grudging at best, racialist at worst, and the establishment of the Irish national state did little to reduce the prejudices.

Conclusion

Emigration from Ireland continued after partition from both Northern Ireland and
the Irish Republic. Indeed, due partly to the imposition of a quota system in the
USA, there was a shift of orientation towards Great Britain. Between 1926 and
1936, 40 per cent of Irish emigrants went to Britain compared with 12 per cent in the
period 1876–1921.[106] Emigration has been one of the major factors in the development of modern Irish society. In theoretical economic terms, it removed the surplus population from the poorer districts, thereby reducing underemployment and
raising wage levels of those actually employed. Another theoretical consequence
was the revenue lost because of the costs incurred (in familial and national expenditure terms) in raising to adulthood those who left the country during their most
productive years. This analysis, however, ignores the extent to which children
were viewed as assets, rather than liabilities, through the reality of emigrant remittances which became essential to the survival of rural family life. The number of
emigrants who used their savings to this end is obviously unquantifiable, but
possibly the value of such remittances may have been equivalent to 2 per cent of
Irish gross national income during the nineteenth century. The most important
result of continuing emigration has been to reduce the pace of economic and social
change and (after the immediate post-Famine massive reorganization of land structure), to preserve some archaic features of Irish economic and social life.[107] The
disappearance of the poorest cottier class and the redistribution of the landed
estates consolidated the importance of the middle ranking farmers in the rural class
structure where their authority and conservatism endorsed the influence of the
Church. Post-Famine emigration also provided an option in the sorting out of
denominational rivalries, as can be seen in the decline of the proportion of Catholics in the six counties which became Northern Ireland. This fell from 41 per cent
of the population in 1861 to 34 per cent in 1911, pre-dating partition. Similarly,
from 1911 to 1926, the differential in emigration reduced the Protestant population
of the Irish Free State by almost a third, while the Catholic population fell by only 2
per cent. Above all else, emigration enabled the post-Famine development and
then perpetuation of a demographic structure which related inheritance patterns
(the change to impartibility), high rates of permanent celibacy and large family
sizes. The typical family farm was handed down to one heir who could marry and
raise a family. Less fortunate siblings remained in economic terms as family labour,
and in social terms as dependants, with the whole system buttressed by financial
support from emigrant relatives. The certain knowledge that the possibility of
emigration existed could be considered to have contributed to the continuance of
large families, and if emigrant relatives cut themselves off, they severed their
family rights as well as their obligations. Emigration thus concentrated the aspirations of the Irish upon the standards of living which were obtained in Britain and
America, while reinforcing the gap between those standards and the actuality of
Irish rural life. Finally, the time-warped perception which so many Irish immigrants and their descendants in Britain and elsewhere continued to hold of 'the oul
counthry', frozen in development at the time of their own departure, has contributed, not only to the maintenance of this pattern of Irish society, but also to the
retardation of mature international relationships.

Acknowledgements

Research for this chapter was greatly facilitated by an award from the Twenty Seven Foundation.

References

1. *Commission on Emigration and other Population Problems, 1948–54*, (Dublin, 1954), table 95, p. 126. See also D. H. Akenson, *Small differences*, (Kingston, 1988), Appendix H.
2. Brenda Collins, 'The origins of Irish immigration to Scotland in the nineteenth and twentieth centuries', in T. M. Devine (ed.), *Irish Immigrants and Scottish Society in the Nineteenth and Twentieth Centuries*, (Edinburgh, 1990), pp. 1–18.
3. D. Fitzpatrick, *Irish Emigration 1801–1921*, (Dundalk, 1984), p. 7.
4. A summary of the work by Connell and subsequent scholars is provided by L. A. Clarkson, 'Marriage and fertility in nineteenth-century Ireland', in R. B. Outhwaite (ed.), *Marriage and Society*, (London, 1981), pp. 237–55.
5. See J. A. Jackson, *The Irish in Britain*, (London, 1963), pp. 6–11.
6. *Report of the Commissioners to Take the Census of Ireland for the Year 1841*. Parliamentary Papers (hereafter P.P.) 1843 XIV, pp. 450–1. See also A. O'Dowd, *Spalpeens and Tattie Hokers*, (Dublin, 1991).
7. L. Lees and John Modell, 'The Irish countryman urbanised: a comparative perspective on the Famine migration', *Journal of Urban History*, **III** (1977), p. 13.
8. E. J. T. Collins, 'Migrant labour in British agriculture in the nineteenth century', *Economic History Review*, 2nd ser. **XXXIX** (1976), pp. 38–59.
9. T. M. Devine, 'Urbanisation, in T. M. Devine and R. Mitchison (eds.), *People and Society in Scotland*, **I**, (Edinburgh, 1988), pp. 41–7.
10. J. Williamson, 'The impact of the Irish on British labour markets during the Industrial Revolution', *Journal of Economic History*, **XL** (1986), pp. 693–721.
11. J. Herson, 'Irish migration and settlement in Victorian Britain; a small town perspective', in R. Swift and S. Gilley (eds.), *The Irish in Britain 1815–1939*, (London, 1989), pp. 84–103.
12. R. Samuel, 'Comers and Goers', in H. J. Dyos and M. Wolff (eds.), *The Victorian City: Images and Realities*, **I**, (London, 1973), p. 133.
13. *Reports and Tables Relating to Irish Migratory Agricultural Labourers, 1880–1915*, reproduced in D. Fitzpatrick, 'A curious middle place', in Swift and Gilley (eds.), *Irish in Britain*, pp. 10–59. See pp. 16–17.
14. The seasonal earnings of migrant husbands and sons and the sewing outwork done by wives and daughters propped up these family units. See Brenda Collins, 'The origin of sewing outwork in nineteenth-century Ulster', in M. Berg (ed.), *Markets and Manufactures in Early Industrial Europe*, (London, 1990), pp. 139–56.
15. J. H. Treble 'Irish navvies in the north of England, 1830–50', *Journal of Transport History*, **6** (1973), pp. 227–47.
16. P. MacGill, *Children of the Dead End*, (London, 1914), p. 227.
17. Treble, 'Irish navvies', pp. 238–40.
18. Williamson, 'Impact of the Irish', p. 700.
19. The statistical material in this paragraph is drawn from C. Pooley, 'Segregation or integration? The residential experience of the Irish in mid-Victorian Britain', in Swift and Gilley (eds.), *Irish in Britain*, pp. 60–83.
20. See Devine, *Irish Immigrants and Scottish Society*.
21. Brenda Collins, 'Irish emigration to Dundee and Paisley during the first half of the nineteenth century', in J. M. Goldstrom and L. A. Clarkson (eds.), *Irish Population, Economy and Society*, (Oxford, 1981), pp. 195–212. See p. 201.
22. *Poor Inquiry, Ireland. Appendix G, State of the Irish Poor in Great Britain*, P.P. 1836 XXXIV, p. 161.

23. *Census of Population (England) 1891*, P.P. 1893–4 CVI, p. 388.
24. D. Fitzpatrick, 'A peculiar tramping people—the Irish in Britain, 1801–70', unpublished paper, no date, p. 16.
25. R. Lawton, 'Irish immigration to England and Wales in the mid-nineteenth century', *Irish Geography*, **IV** (1959), pp. 35–54. See p. 50. Jackson, *Irish in Britain, passim*.
26. *Poor Inquiry, I.P.G.B.*, p. 111.
27. J. H. Treble, 'The market for unskilled male labour in Glasgow, 1891–1914', in I. McDougall (ed.), *Essays in Scottish Labour History*, (Edinburgh, 1978), pp. 115–42. See p. 122.
28. D. Large, 'The Irish in Bristol in 1851; a census enumeration', in R. Swift and S. Gilley (eds.), *The Irish in the Victorian City*, (London, 1985), pp. 37–58. See especially pp. 43–4.
29. R. D. Lobban, 'The Irish community in Greenock in the nineteenth century, *Irish Geography*, **XVI** (1971), pp. 270–81. See p. 271.
30. *Ibid.*, p. 274.
31. *Poor Inquiry, I.P.G.B.*, p. 60.
32. *Poor Inquiry, I.P.G.B.*, p. xxxvii.
33. C. Richardson, 'Irish settlement in mid-nineteenth century Bradford', *Yorkshire Bulletin of Economic and Social Research*, **20** (1968), pp. 40–57. See pp. 42–3.
34. Brenda Collins, 'Proto-industrialization and pre-Famine emigration', *Social History*, **7** (1982), p. 145.
35. On this point see N. Murray, *The Scottish Hand Loom Weavers, 1790–1850: a Social History*, (Edinburgh, 1978).
36. *Poor Inquiry, I.P.G.B.*, p. 81.
37. *Poor Inquiry, I.P.G.B.*, p. 65.
38. *Reports on Emigration, Scotland*, P.P. 1841 VI, sections 1224–5.
39. Alan B. Cambell, *The Lanarkshire Miners*, (Edinburgh, 1979), Chapter 7.
40. R. J. Cooter, 'The Irish in County Durham and Newcastle, *c.* 1840–1880', (unpublished MA thesis, University of Durham, 1973), pp. 156–66.
41. The standard work, A. H. John, *The Industrial Development of South Wales, 1750–1850*, (Cardiff, 1950) makes no reference to anti-Irish feeling in the mines and ironworks. However, J. V. Hickey, *Urban Catholics*, (London, 1967), refers to two occasions in mid-century when animosity developed after Irish men were used as strike breakers.
42. H. J. Hanham, 'Religion and nationality in the mid-Victorian army', in M. R. D. Foot (ed.), *War and Society*, (London, 1973), pp. 158–75.
43. Felix Lavery, *Irish Heroes in the Great War*, (London, 1917).
44. Lynn Lees, 'Mid-Victorian migration and the Irish family economy', *Victorian Studies*, **XXI** (1976), pp. 25–43. See pp. 30–1.
45. *Emigration Scotland*, pp. 115–18.
46. Fitzpatrick, 'Middle place', pp. 20–1.
47. 'The London Irish', *Blackwoods Edinburgh Magazine*, **CLXX** (July, 1901), pp. 124–34.
48. Fitzpatrick, 'Middle place', pp. 21–3.
49. R. Roberts, *The Classic Slum*, (London, 1971), p. 110.
50. C. Pooley, 'The residential segregation of migrant communities in mid Victorian Liverpool', *Transactions Institute of British Geographers*, New Series, **2** (1977), pp. 364–82.
51. T. Dillon, 'The Irish in Leeds 1851–1861',*Thoresby Society Publications*, **LIV** (1973), pp. 1–28.
52. B. Collins, 'Aspects of Irish immigration into two Scottish towns (Dundee and Paisley) during the mid-nineteenth century', (unpublished MPhil thesis, University of Edinburgh, 1978). For other towns cited, see M. Hartigan and M. Hickman, *The History of the Irish in Britain, A Bibliography*, (London, 1986).
53. Quoted by Lynn Lees, *Exiles of Erin*, (Manchester, 1979), pp. 71–87.
54. F. Finnegan, *Poverty and Prejudice*, (Cork, 1982) p. 39.
55. Lawton, 'Irish Immigration to England and Wales', p. 50.
56. Dillon, 'Irish in Leeds', p. 12; C. Roy Lewis 'The Irish in Cardiff in the mid-nineteenth century', *Cambria*, **7** (1980), pp. 13–41; *Buildings Regulations, Minutes of Evidence*, P.P. 1842 X, 1190 (Town Clerk, Dundee).

57. Cooter, 'Irish in Durham and Newcastle', p. 30.
58. Dillon, 'Irish in Leeds', pp. 10–11; Herson, 'Irish small town perspective', p. 93; Finnegan, *Poverty and Prejudice*, pp. 157–9.
59. Quoted by Lees, *Exiles of Erin*, p. 91.
60. Treble, 'Market for unskilled labour', p. 131; *Poor Inquiry, I.P.G.B.*, p. 66.
61. G. Best, *Mid-Victorian Britain*, (London, 1979), p. 80.
62. M. Kerr, *The People of Ship Street*, (London, 1958). The framework of explanation used by Kerr, however, lacks any historical conviction.
63. Lees, 'Irish family economy', pp. 29–35.
64. J. Haslett and W. J. Lowe, Household structure and overcrowding among the Lancashire Irish 1951–71'. *Histoire Sociale–Social History*, **10** (1977), pp. 45–58.
65. Collins, 'Aspects of Irish immigration', p. 209.
66. R. Samuel, 'The Roman Catholic Church and the Irish Poor', in Swift and Gilley (eds.), *Victorian City*, pp. 285–7.
67. Extract from *Before my time*, interview by John Berger, Granada T.V. recording (5.6.1963), printed in J. Burnett, *Useful Toil*, (London, 1976), p. 91.
68. Finnegan, *Poverty and Prejudice*, p. 70; Lees, *Exiles of Erin*, p. 154.
69. Lobban 'Irish in Greenock', p. 279; Collins, 'Aspects of Irish immigration', Chapter 5.
70. D. Gwynn, 'The Irish immigration', in G. A. Beck (ed.), *The English Catholics 1850–1950*, (London, 1950), p. 265.
71. Calculated from A. E. C. W. Spencer 'Catholics in Britain and Ireland: regional contrasts', in D. C. Coleman (ed.), *Demography of Immigrants in the United Kingdom*, (London, 1982), pp. 211–44. See pp. 218–19.
72. D. W. Miller, 'Irish Catholicism and the Great Famine', *Journal of Social History*, **9** (1975), pp. 81–98.
73. G. Connolly, 'Irish and Catholic: myth or reality', in Swift and Gilley (eds.), *Victorian City*, pp. 225–54.
74. H. Mayhew, *London Labour and the London Poor*, quoted by Connolly, 'Irish and Catholic', p. 233, and Samuel, 'Irish Poor', p. 279, in Swift and Gilley (eds.), *Victorian City*.
75. K. Inglis, *Churches and the Working Classes in Victorian England* (London, 1965), pp. 122–30.
76. On this point, see H. McCleod, *Class and Religion in the Late Victorian City*, (Oxford, 1981).
77. B. Aspinwall, 'The formation of the Catholic community in the West of Scotland', *Innes Review*, **33** (1982), pp. 44–81.
78. J. Hunter, 'The Gaelic Connection: the Highlands, Ireland and nationalism, 1873–1922', *Scottish Historical Review*, **54** (1975), pp. 184–5.
79. G. Walker, 'The Protestant Irish in Scotland', in Devine (ed.), *Irish Immigrants and Scottish Society*, pp. 44–66. See p. 49.
80. G. Best, 'Popular Protestantism in Victorian Britain', in R. Robson (ed.), *Ideas and Institutions of Victorian Britain*, (London, 1967), pp. 115–42.
81. R. Swift, 'The outcast Irish in the British Victorian City: problems and perspectives, *Irish Historical Studies*, **XXV**, no. 99 (May, 1987), 272–4.
82. T. Gallagher, 'A tale of two cities: communal strife in Glasgow and Liverpool before 1914', in Swift and Gilley (eds.), *Victorian City*, pp. 106–29.
83. Aspinwall, 'Formation of Catholic community', pp. 50–5.
84. Samuel, 'Irish Poor', p. 286.
85. *Blackwood's*, 'London Irish', p. 132; S. Gilley, 'The Catholic faith of the Irish slums: London 1840–70', in Dyos and Wolff (eds.), *Victorian City: Images and Realities*, **II**, pp. 837–53.
86. A. E. C. W. Spencer, 'The demography and sociography of the Roman Catholic community of England and Wales', in L. Bright and S. Clements (eds.), *The Committed Church*, (London, 1966), pp. 74–5. An academic interpretation of the Scottish viewpoint is to be found in J. H. Clapham, 'Irish immigration into Great Britain in the nineteenth century', *Bulletin of the International Committee of Historical Sciences*, **V** (1933), pp. 596–604.

87. T. Gallagher, 'The Catholic Irish in Scotland', in Devine (ed.), *Irish Immigrants and Scottish Society*, pp. 19–43. See pp. 22–3.
88. P. O'Mara, *The Autobiography of a Liverpool Irish Slummy*, (London, 1934), p. 75.
89. *Poor Inquiry, I.P.G.B.*, xiii.
90. *Blackwood's*, 'London Irish', p. 127.
91. Fitzpatrick, 'Middle place', pp. 25–7.
92. R. Swift 'Crime and the Irish in Nineteenth Century Britain', in Swift and Gilley (eds.), *Irish in Britain*, pp. 163–82. See p. 177.
93. S. Nicholas and P. R. Shergold, 'Human capital and the pre-famine Irish emigration to England', *Explorations in Economic History*, **24** (1987). pp. 158–77.
94. Dillon, 'Irish in Leeds', pp. 21–2.
95. Large, 'Irish in Bristol', in Swift and Gilley (eds.), *Victorian City*, pp. 55–6.
96. *Report on Distress, Paisley*, P.P. 1843 VII. Evidence of Rev. John Bremner D.D., 1273–1285. M. Blair, *The Paisley Thread*, (Paisley, 1907), p. 117.
97. M. A. Crowther, 'Poverty, health and welfare' in W. H. Fraser and R. J. Morris (eds.), *People and Society in Scotland*, II, (Edinburgh, 1990), p. 281. This is probably an under-estimate since 1000 Irish people were sent back from Dundee alone in 1842, *Poor Law Inquiry Scotland*, P.P. 1844 XXII, p. 107.
98. D. Thompson, 'Ireland and the Irish in English radicalism before 1850', in J. Epstein and D. Thompson (eds.), *The Chartist Experience: Studies in Working Class Radicalism and Culture 1830–60*, (London, 1982), pp. 120–51.
99. J. Treble, 'The attitude of the Roman Catholic Church towards trade unionism in the north of England, 1833–62, *Northern History*, **V** (1970), pp. 93–113.
100. Gallagher, Tale of two cities, p. 116, refers to Tory Opportunism in Manchester when, on a visit in 1872, Disraeli was inducted into the Orange Order by the Salford Orange Lodges.
101. Ian S. Wood, 'Irish nationalism and radical politics in Scotland 1880–1906', *Scottish Labour History Journal*, (1975), pp. 21–38.
102. J. McCaffrey, 'The Irish vote in Glasgow in the later nineteenth century: a preliminary survey', *Innes Review*, **21** (1970), pp. 30–6.
103. A. O'Day, 'Irish influence on parliamentary elections in London 1885–1914: a simple test', in Swift and Gilley (eds.), *Victorian City*, pp. 98–105.
104. E. H. Hunt, *British Labour History 1815–1914*, (London, 1981), p. 170.
105. See Fitzpatrick, 'Middle place', pp. 41–4.
106. Collins, 'Origins of Irish immigration to Scotland', pp. 12–16.
107. Some of these points are discussed by R. Foster, *Modern Ireland, 1600–1972*, (London, 1988), pp. 369–72, and by Fitzpatrick, *Irish Emigration 1801–1921*, pp. 37–42.

12

The Making of Ireland: Agendas and Perspectives in Cultural Geography

William J. Smyth

Introduction

James Joyce said that truth is a prism, a many-angled gem of brightness and shadow, demanding illumination through a multiplicity of perspectives and lenses.[1] Arriving at an understanding of Ireland requires such a plurality of out-looks in order to unravel and distinguish the many strands that make up the Irish experience. Viewed from the air, the Irish landscape is a tangled series of inscriptions, signs and symbols which reflect the complicated prehistory and history of settlement and culture in this relatively small but diverse island. However, the landscape is only one such multi-layered, eroded and rewritten text. Since *c.* 550 A.D., a whole variety of other interwoven texts and materials have been constructed, reconstructed, reworked and reinterpreted through time, and these must also be interrogated to help reveal the inner realities of Ireland and Irish cultures. And behind all these texts and artefacts are the voices, the stories and the actions of the millions of people who lived, loved, fought and died on this island. The aim of this chapter is to extend the discussion on the meaning of Ireland and Irishness which has permeated every aspect of the preceding analysis. Above all, it seeks to set aside the simplified stereotypes and explore instead, the diversity and plurality of Irish identity.

Even to answer the simple question, 'where is Ireland?', is not at all easy. Ireland is very much a European country in its sensibilities, religious traditions, literature and art. At one scale, it has shared much of the experiences of the other countries and regions of Atlantic Europe from Portugal and Galicia through Atlantic France to highland Britain, the Orkneys and western Norway. All these insular–peninsular worlds, sharing a common 'Ceann Tíre/Land's End' location at the edge of western Europe, are characterized by a wet and relatively mild Atlantic climate and most came to endure minority cultural status within their respective states. For the most part, too, they share disadvantaged positions in relation to the dominant economic cores of mainland Europe.[2] At another scale, Ireland has been profoundly influenced by continental-wide processes, ranging from the expansion of Celtic cultures from a north-central European core and the diffusion of Christianity from the eastern Mediterranean under the protection of the Roman *imperium*, to the genesis and subsequent evolution of urbanization and trade.

But Ireland is also very much part of the wider colonial world created at a global scale in the early modern period. The Anglo-Norman colonization of the high Middle Ages created a sharp cultural and settlement frontier across the island, a 'colonial' pattern deepened and intensified with the Tudor conquest and later plantations. Much of Ireland's colonial experiences, especially since *c.* 1530, were not shared by other western European countries. Like many cultures in South America, Africa and Asia, Ireland saw much of its ancient ways of living—language, law codes, system of territorial and landed organization, settlement and social structures—either replaced or radically reconstructed by a powerful English-speaking state and its agents.

The decolonization process has also been long and complicated. The achievement of political independence by the greater part of the island, following the creation of a national consciousness in the nineteenth century, was accompanied by the incision of a new international boundary across the northern landscape. The period after 1700 also saw Ireland solidly established as a member of the widespread English-speaking world which straddled the Atlantic and the South Pacific. A 'settlement and a spiritual empire' was created through the massive emigration and by Irish church missionaries. More recently, since the 1960s, Ireland's locational axes have again shifted, focusing more strongly on the European mainland, reconnecting with a deeper European heritage which stretches back to prehistory.[3]

Nevertheless, ascribing to Ireland a range of cultural locations remains a simplification. A relatively small island of 32,000 sq. miles (70,000 sq. km) is still large and varied enough to sustain and reveal significant cultural diversities, different regions of the island having long developed their own orientations and experiences. Since prehistory, the north and especially the north-east has had powerful if oscillating links across the narrow straits to Scotland, and beyond to northern England and the Scandinavian world. In contrast the south-west of the country has looked more to France and Spain, a perspective shared with the south-east. But this latter region has also always been intimately connected with Wales and the English West Country, while historically, the 'Pale' region around Dublin had strong linkages along an axis from London to Chester.[4] The far west was more weakly tied into a west European, more Iberian orbit, but since the days of the Newfoundland fisheries in the early sixteenth century, its destiny has increasingly been interlocked with the cities of the eastern seaboard of America, stretching from Boston south to Savannah.[5]

At the same time, the compacting insular qualities of Ireland as place have meant that many different experiences have had to be contained and shared within a narrow, often introverted ground. The ubiquity of the settlements and symbols of the Celtic Christian centuries point to a degree of earlier cultural—if not political—unity. Again, the apparently universal character of the 'Big House' and its culture also speaks of possible uniformities underlying the landlord culture which blossomed in the eighteenth century.[6] And the seemingly eternal quality of the dialectic between the northern and southern halves of the island also reveals the compacting qualities of the island. Whether we look at the distribution of megalithic court tombs, or Iron Age art, or seventeenth-century population patterns or twentieth-century maps of farm size, an old cultural frontier runs across the map, roughly dividing Leath Cuinn (the northern half) from Leath Moga (the south).[7]

Therefore, the answer to the simple question, 'where is Ireland?', cannot be answered in the singular. There have been and there are many Irelands. One of the objectives of this chapter is to explore the origins and nature of these diversities and the processes by which places and societies have reconstructed themselves at different times on this island. This chapter also seeks to grapple with the essential, central features of Irish culture as it evolved and crystallized and transformed itself within its broader European, colonial, Atlantic and global frameworks.

The Location, Diversity and Ecology of Ireland

We can begin by assessing the cultural implications of the sum total of the physical conditions that characterize this island world of Ireland.[8] The first crucial point is that Ireland *is* an *island*, the size, shape and space relations of which have had a profound influence on the cultural history of the Irish peoples. An island's relative location, in terms of its relationship and interconnections with other peoples and places, changes over time, depending on levels of technology, modes of communication and a range of political, economic and cultural developments. Therefore, the presence or absence of an 'insular' mentality is not strictly a product of an island environment *per se*. Islands like countries can tend to be 'closed' and introverted or, conversely, more 'open' and accessible, depending on a range of cultural conditions. In Ireland's history, there have been critical periods when the interchange of external and internal contacts appears to have released great energies and renewed regional vitalities. The era of Celtic Christianity, of the Anglo-Norman medieval settlement, Ireland's incorporation into the Atlantic world in the seventeenth and eighteenth centuries and the more recent European engagement since the 1960s could all be described as phases of opening out.

The view of Ireland's insular position as seen from the heart of continental Europe is of course different. Early maps point to the clear recognition of a bulky island to the west of a much larger island, Britain. For better or worse, Ireland's external relations have been intertwined with those of its larger neighbour. *Physical closeness* but significant *cultural distance* have been two critical if misunderstood features in the often obsessive and confused relations between the peoples of these two islands. Ideas and peoples have moved to Ireland directly from the continent but throughout prehistory and history, Britain has often been a kind of mediator of those influences. European feudalism, the Reformation, democratic and parliamentary procedures and styles of architecture are just four examples of Britain's role in this filtering process. Conversely, Ireland, unlike Britain, was never directly part of the Roman world although its cultural and political life was profoundly influenced by impulses flowing from the edge of that empire.[9] Thus, Ireland experienced a relatively late fully-fledged urban life, allowing the maturation of a complex 'rural, hierarchical and familiar' culture over the space of a thousand years.[10] Likewise, the post-Roman Germanic waves of conquests and settlement did not immediately impinge on Irish society, although there was a substantial Viking influence. Later, only faint echoes of the Renaissance reached these shores, and even in this century, the experiences and destruction of the Second World War, Belfast excepted, were to be rather muffled and distant.

In some ways, Ireland's insular position has thus made it more difficult of access, more remote. Clearly, island life has had a profound influence on the nature of social relations, making for much intimacy but also introversion and bitterness. Smaller nations on the European mainland have, on average, land boundaries with two or three neighbours, resulting in much greater interaction. In Ireland, isolation was compounded by marriage and kinship linkages which reinforced the tightness of the social networks, bringing mutual support but also claustrophobia. Insularity allowed for the slow maturation of distinctive cultural expressions—the artistic and literary achievements of the early medieval church are but one expression of this distinctive kind of cultural synthesis. Yet in its later phases, the same institution became more introverted and conservative, its scholarship, texts and laws hardening and fossilizing in the absence of a constant dialectic with external sources.

As we have seen, part of Ireland's regional diversity springs from the orientations and experiences of different regions of the island. The historic provinces reflect these different regional orientations. In the heart of the country the middle kingdom of Ríocht na Mídhe never became an effective political centre for the whole island until the seventeenth century. But Ireland's diversities also spring from other sources. No other European country has such a fragmented peripheral arrangement of mountain land all along its borders. This has enriched Ireland with a diversified scenic heritage but the complicated distribution of massifs presented severe difficulties to would-be conquerors.[11] Likewise, the topography has meant that the richer lowland regions are scattered and fragmented all over the island, facilitating the evolution of strong regional subcultures. In turn the hills and boglands came to serve as territorial bases for local lordships and, with later phases of conquest and colonization, often became regions of retreat and refuge. Thus, the regional dialectic between peoples of the plains and those of the hills or bogs is a recurring island-wide feature of Ireland's cultural geography, revealing complex and often faulted cultural strata, as complex as the geological base itself.

The temperate Atlantic climate is also a central part of this story. It has been raining in Ireland for close on 12,000 years. This island is wet not just through the amount of precipitation which it receives but also because of the persistence of the water due to the weakness of the forces of evaporation. This mild and wet climate led to the expanses of peatbog. 'Bog'—meaning 'soft/wet/treacherous'—is an Irish word which has wandered into the English language. Thanks to their preservative powers, the bogs, which expanded progressively from the end of the Climatic Optimum right up to the Early Christian period and beyond, contain and cover a rich record of our biological and human history, dating back to the big Neolithic field fences of the earliest cattlemen. The bogs occupy close on one-fifth of the island and for millennia have been a source of fuel, grazing, beauty, poetry and leisure. The boglands also helped conserve and define old cultural regions and often demarcate farms, townlands, parishes, counties and dioceses—even provinces (Fig. 12.1).

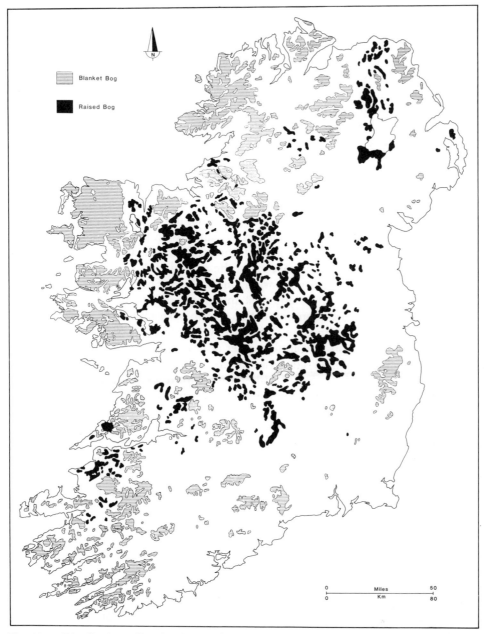

Fig. 12.1. Distribution of boglands in Ireland (after Royal Irish Acadamy, Atlas of Ireland, (Dublin, 1979), pp. 26–7.

The climatic regime also enters profoundly into the creation of Ireland's rich grasslands. Except for brief periods of amelioration, Ireland has lain beyond the climatic limit for the safe sustained production of good corn, especially wheat. Thus, stock-rearing has been a dominant tradition in the Irish countryside for millennia although too much emphasis may have been placed in the literature on its overwhelming importance. Three of the most creative eras in the cultural history of the island, the early medieval period, the high Middle Ages and the brief but dramatic period from *c.* 1770 to *c.* 1840 were all epochs when tillage was a central and, in some regions, a dominant element in shaping economy and society. It should also be remembered that the grasslands of Ireland are cultural creations, reflecting a cumulative assault on the woodlands over thousands of years, culminating in the final clearances of the Tudor conquest after 1600. This left the landscape bare of trees and required the state to legislate in favour of tree-planting as early as 1700, in an age when the commercialization of the pastoral tradition reached its zenith.

The wetness of the land and the mildness of the climate also make for the great fertility in tree and shrub growth.[12] The earliest Mesolithic peoples followed the line of the coast, lake and river fen margins and the earliest 'rancher' farmers spread out across the less densely forested uplands with their lighter more easily worked soils.[13] For the lowland Neolithic farmers, the dense woodlands presented a great challenge. The elm may have been the crucial 'cultural' index to the best land. These were killed off by ring-barking and, like the native North Americans, the farmers planted their crops amongst the stumps.[14] In these clearings, they developed a mixed farming economy with a strong pastoral bias in a kind of long-term system of shifting cultivation. After a few hundred years, when soils were exhausted, they moved on to colonize other adjacent woodlands, their descendants returning again in later centuries to recolonize the secondary woodland growth. Mitchell sees this period of early farming from 5000 B.C. to 300 A.D. as the era when the woodlands were damaged but still remained dominant in the landscape.[15] However, it is clear from the scientific and literary evidence that the great assault on the woodlands and the first great historic 'Age of Clearing' in Ireland began *c.* 300–400 A.D. and continued for at least another 400 years.[16] Underpinning these transformations were three major cultural forces: the introduction of iron as the new technology of warfare, ploughing and farming, the crystallization of a Celtic conquest and culture, expressed in distinctive linguistic, legal and settlement terms and the introduction of an innovative, universalizing script religion—Christianity.

The Crystallization of a 'Celtic' Christian Culture

It is probably valid to see the spread of a Celtic culture in Ireland as a consequence of the invasions of a few waves of iron-welding warrior elites, taking over a long inhabited and already diversified cultural realm and creating a minority ruling caste.[17] Evans is quite correct in noting that we get a very restricted view of the Irish people if we think of them only as 'Celts', overlooking not only the productive mingling of many varieties of *historic* settlers but also, and more critically in Evans' view, ignoring the substantial contributions of pre-Celtic stocks of people.[18] Clearly the Celts in Ireland inherited a great deal from these earlier peoples. A striking feature of the Celtic settlement was the continued use of Neolithic sacred sites such as Tara and Knowth, both in County Meath. Therefore, Evans is critical of historians who tell the story of Ireland as if little or nothing was achieved in Ireland before the coming of the Celts, or the Anglo-Normans or the New English in the seventeenth century. He would see all of these as imperialist kinds of history, which suggest completely new beginnings at certain periods and ignore the complex *unwritten* alterations and adjustments that are very much part of cultural processes.[19] Evans' philosophical position insisted upon patterns of cultural continuity in Ireland which reach deep into the prehistoric past rather than placing too much emphasis on conquest and change. He held that the enduring success of Celtic Christianity spoke of its ability to assimilate old and new features into a powerful new synthesis which expressed itself in art, architecture, literature, mythology and law.

While recognizing the validity of Evans' critique of narrow nationalist interpretations of a 'pure Celtic race' (and also noting his failure to engage the equally circumscribed ideology of Unionism),[20] arguably he did not sufficiently emphasize the impact of the new complex of technologies, crops, elites and institutions that came with the Celtic conquests. Nevertheless, he did note the formidable complex of material and cultural changes from the early Iron Age—the introduction of oats (the great colonizer of wet acidic soils, ripening quickly in the short summer season), rotary querns, harrows, axes, iron ploughs, spades and horse-drawn carts.[21] Evans also pointed to the significance of the *ráth*—or ring-fort—and cashel (see Chapter 1) (Fig. 12.2). Graft on to this, he argued, a long established stock and one has the material essentials of a society which persisted in many areas until the seventeenth century and survivals of which have come down to our own time.

Particularly crucial in the period from *c.* 400 to *c.* 800 A.D. was the establishment of a *permanent sedentary* culture as evidenced by the ring-forts, cashels and *crannógs* and the literal rebaptizing of the whole landscape with an array of family names and place-names. The early medieval Celtic elites and families, using these place-names and the myths and stories associated with the nature and meaning of places—the *Dindsenchas*[22]—invested these now permanently settled and bounded places with enduring symbols of their own identities. The spread of a universalizing Christian religion provided a powerful impetus to the dramatic achievements of this new hybrid culture. The distribution of the place-name element *cluain* or *cloon*—meaning bog or woodland clearing—is but one key to the whole complex story. The overall distribution of this place-name highlights the comprehensive colonization of the wetlands and lakelands of Ireland. These extended all over the central midlands but also embraced the difficult lakeland and drumlin country extending from Clew Bay through Sligo to Carlingford Lough. This pattern of place-names indicates the filling in of the gaps in the settlement pattern between the long occupied uplands and foothills and the completion of population expansion over most of the island, especially in the sixth and seventh centuries.

As yet, we know little about the system of territorial organization.[23] It appears that regionally varied yet coherent systems of territorial organization evolved from the level of the 'proto-townland' or *baile bó* (cowland) at the base of the system, to the later provincial over-kingdoms at the top of the hierarchy. It may be that extended family-owned 'estates' were carved out in such a way as to include the full range of agricultural resources, arable, meadow, bog, woodland and pasture. In the more fertile lowlands these may have comprised segregated parts of a single

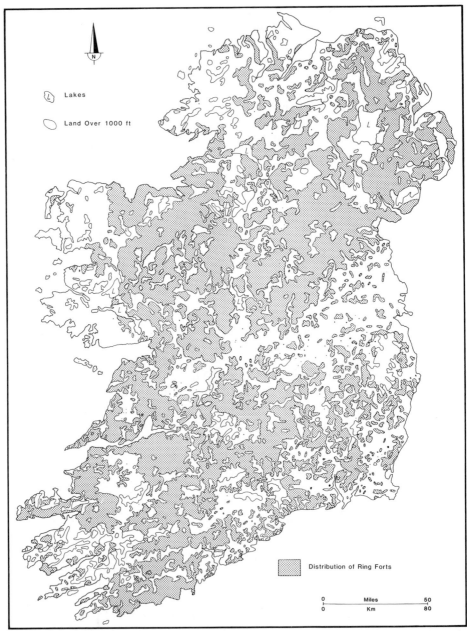

Fig. 12.2. Distribution of ring-forts in Ireland (after D. McCourt, 'The dynamic quality of Irish rural settlement', in R. H. Buchanan, Emrys Jones and D. McCourt (eds.), *Man and his Habitat*, (London, 1971), pp. 158–9).

compact territorial unit. However, in coastal, mountainous, woodland and bog-land regions they clearly involved the kind of land units which combined arable 'infield' lowlands as well as fenced 'outfield' pastures with more distant common grazing lands of forest, upland and bog. These discrete sections were linked by droving lanes (*bóthair*) along estate boundaries. These innovations in agricultural structures and practices significantly augmented the amount of land under arable cultivation.[24] But as in the Neolithic period, beef was the important meat element in the diet, and stock-rearing and dairying in particular the dominant features in the economy. Social rank, taxes, tribute and fines were all reckoned in terms of the number of milch cows or fractions thereof. And most critical for the whole social system, cows rather than land formed the normal fief granted by the lord to his clients.[25]

The changing socio-political geography of early historic Ireland also presents many related difficulties. As yet, we do not possess any satisfactory island-wide maps of the distribution of petty kingdoms, *tuathas*, monastic *paruchiae* or diocesan-type territories for the period 600–1100. Estimates of the number of *tuatha* range from *c.* 100–185 with a tendency for a figure of 150–175 to emerge most often in the debates.[26] Byrne's outstanding analysis of provincial kingdoms and sub-kingdoms remains central to our understanding of these and other levels of pre-Norman systems of territorial organization (Fig. 12.3).[27] In a brilliant synthesis, he illuminates the layers of peoples and territories as they existed across the island *c.* 900, demonstrating that the marginalization of former ruling elites was a major feature of Ireland's cultural and political geography during this time. In Leinster, the former kings of Laigin, the Uí Garrchon and Uí Enechglaiss, ended up on the then remote eastern slopes of the Wicklow mountains. In Munster, the Corco Loígde and related peoples lost their control of the inland core of the province yet still commanded the southern and south-western coastal and peninsular regions. In Ulster, the Ulaid began their retreat east of Lough Neagh and the River Bann *c.* 450, although they were to retain command of the north-eastern corner of Ireland until the Anglo-Norman conquest and settlement of east Ulster.[28]

Byrne also skilfully locates the arrangement of 'vassal' peoples in strategic buffer-lands. The distribution of these peoples, such as the Airgialla in Ulster, the Loígis in Leinster and the Gailenga and Luigní in Connacht, highlights the pivotal position of the key dynasties which dominated all the core regions by *c.* 800. Most of these had come to power with the transformation of political structures during and following the Roman occupation of Britain, which had created new alignments along the Irish Sea and within Ireland.[29] The Uí Néill dynasty was at the heart of these historic transformations, advancing from its Connacht base in the first centuries A.D. to eventually command both the rich lands and symbolic centres including Usnagh and Tara. The ecclesiastical capital of Armagh also emerged as a significant nucleus of ideology in the Uí Néill drive for the high-kingship of the whole island, symbolically centred on Tara. But as Byrne points out, the idea of high-kingship never became institutionalized and ritualized: from the mid-ninth century onwards, high kings conquered and ruled by force. They claimed the elusive title but did not achieve an effective island-wide government or administration.[30] Whatever long-term institutional possibilities the notion of the high-kingship might have had, were rudely shattered by the Anglo-Norman conquest.

West of the Shannon, Connacht was a mosaic of old surviving peoples and newly expanding dynasties. The lowlands of the Moy valley to the north and the rich limestone plains of what is now south Galway came to be dominated by branches of the Uí Fiachrach. But the future control of the province lay with the

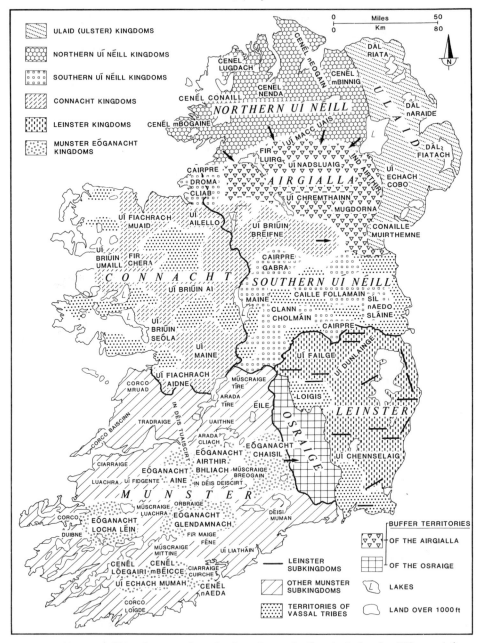

Fig. 12.3. Provincial kingdoms and territories of vassal tribes in Ireland *c.* 900 A.D. (after
F. J. Byrne, *Irish Kings and High-Kings*, (London, 1973), pp. 120–1, 133, 172–3 and 234–5).

branches of the Uí Briúin dynasty, spreading out from their ancient core around
Cruachain in Roscommon to establish a powerful territorial lordship that controlled
secondary cores around Tuam, Lough Corrib and along the Shannon. In Leinster,
the ancient peoples of the Osraige (now County Kilkenny) came to occupy a

strategic buffer zone with Munster. Their rulers grew in authority and autonomy at the time of the Viking invasions as a result of their control of the key river access to the new town of Waterford. Leinster had a north–south political structure with the prehistoric axis of the kingdom pivoting around the ancient hillfort lands of the mid-Barrow valley. The Uí Dúnlainge came to control the Liffey plains and Kildare, while the Uí Chennselaig, protected by the bulky frame of the Blackstairs mountains, dominated the lowland south-eastern core of the island centred on Ferns, Co. Wexford.[31] To the north-west, the old kingdom of Uí Fáilge had contracted under constant Uí Néill pressure while, along the ambiguous wetland boundaries with north Munster, reputedly ancient Laigin peoples such as the Éile, the Arada Cliaich and the Arada Tíre were ultimately integrated within the flexible overlordship of the Eóganacht over-kingdom of Munster.

Munster appears in the historical record as the least disrupted, most stable and culturally and politically the most durable of all the early medieval provinces.[32] The Eóganacht dynasty and its various branches controlled its richer river valleys and plains from *c.* 600. The most powerful dynasties were to be found in the Tipperary plains, in the rich plains of east Limerick and along the Blackwater, Awbeg and Bandon river valleys. In the far west, the Eóganacht Locha Léin dominated the Kerry lowlands north of Killarney. In Munster, therefore, the mainly east–west topographic structure was complemented by a loose Eóganacht hegemony along the valleys which in turn was matched by strategic criss-cross alignment of related and powerful vassal peoples. The Déisi (the name literally means 'vassal') occupied the lands between Waterford and the Shannon estuary, while the Múscraige were settled from north Tipperary to west Cork. In the southern and western coastal regions, a number of ancient but still powerful seafaring tribes seem to have formed a kind of west Munster federation.[33] They provided the old Munster corridor in the midlands with the founders of monasteries such as Birr and Seirkieran, both in Co. Offaly. It was this key group of ecclesiastics who assisted in the realignment of west Munster political allegiances to facilitate the overall control of the province by the Eóganacht of Cashel and Emly, Co. Tipperary.[34] This rule was almost confederal in character, and did not seek the kind of territorial aggrandisement and lordship which characterized both the Uí Néill and Uí Briúin dynasties in the midlands and Connacht.

The beginnings of Christianity in Ireland may also have been located in the south and south-east of the island, reflecting perhaps its more intensive interaction with the Roman world of Gaul and south Britain. The original spread of Christianity into Ireland is a complex story, involving emigrants, immigrants, Irish mercenaries in the Roman army, reflux movements of Irish settlers from Britain's western fringes as well as traders, pirates and raiding parties.[35] The Christianizing process was clearly slow, piecemeal and regionally varied and there is no doubt that the energy and creativity of the early Christian culture owed much to deeper well-springs.[36] Byrne's map of churches and monasteries *c.* 900 demonstrates the pattern of its spread, identifying the territorial cores of Christian institutions in Ireland.[37] In the west, one such region stretched along an axis from Annaghdown, Co. Galway, to Mayo. A second comprised the Church of Columba and the Ards Peninsula and Strangford Lough region of Down which expanded outwards into the Irish Sea province centred on Iona. The historic core of Leinster churches from Kildare south to Leighlin, Co. Carlow, a region of magnificent high crosses, comprised a third cluster. But the most striking feature of Byrne's map is the evidence it presents for the core of Celtic Christianity, blossoming in the great concentration of monasteries that stretched west of Clonard and Kells in County Meath to Roscrea, Co. Tipperary, and Clonfert, Co. Galway. There are significant extensions of this Midland core, one north-westwards through Elphin in Roscommon to Drumcliff in Sligo, one north-eastwards through Armagh to north Ulster, and one trending southwards along the bogland boundary of Leinster and Munster to the 'gates' of Cashel. For once, the midlands occupied a core position in Irish culture.

As was shown in Chapter 1, these complex quasi-hierarchical networks of monasteries provided one basis for the transformation of economy and trade and eventually urbanization. For example, it would appear from aerial photographic, literary and other sources that Clonmacnoise, Co. Offaly, was one of the towns to emerge from this convergence of forces. The surrounding territory of Delbna Bethra was probably a small ecclesiastical state ruled by the Abbot of Clonmacnoise. In conjunction with the other subject properties and churches attached to the monastery, this gave it command of the surpluses of the region and made the Abbot a powerful monastic landlord.[38] But it must be remembered too that Clonmacnoise was also the centre of traffic and politics in the middle Shannon region, a place of international trade and the burial place of provincial kings from Connacht and Meath.

It was the overall wealth of such towns—not simply the treasures of the churches alone—which eventually drew the fleets of the Vikings. Driving southwards from the northern sea, they knifed through and dismantled the old Iona and Irish Sea province that stretched to Northumbria and beyond. Likewise, they consolidated their power base at Dublin and established significant rural settlements in its hinterland. They initiated the conquest of the already weakening core area of Ríocht na Mídhe, a process later decisively completed by the Anglo-Normans. They established ports at Wexford, Waterford, Limerick and Cork, thus decisively swinging economic and political power away from the Shannon and the Midlands and making the control of the southern and eastern coasts and associated seaways central to all Irish futures.

But the most decisive Viking contribution was to help reorientate the economy and the country outwards. For all their riches, the towns centred on ecclesiastical cores were, for the most part, inland and far more involved in the redistribution of local or regional surpluses than the import–export trade. The Irish word for market derived from the Old Norse *markadr* and likewise, the Irish words for coins and ships are of Scandinavian derivation.[39] It is clear that the most successful Irish elites of the period 900–1100 learned much from this engagement with the Vikings, particularly in the consolidation of polities. By the first half of the twelfth century, powerful over-kingdoms—the *mór-tuatha*—were emerging, often spatially coincident with the dioceses demarcated at the Synods of Ráthbreasail and Kells in 1111 and 1152 respectively (Fig. 12.4).[40] The present-day regional organization of dioceses was, for the most part, hammered out at this time to make for the most enduring of all territorial structures in all of Ireland's history. For example, the *mór-tuath* of the Ua Briain defined the medieval and modern diocese of Killaloe, while the diocese of Cork was essentially the territory of the Mac Cárrthaigs. The

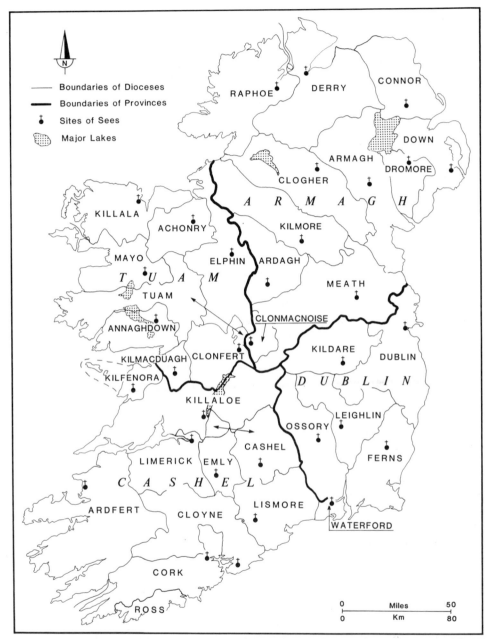

Fig. 12.4. The dioceses of Ireland, *c.* 1320 (after Ordnance Survey diocesan map and T. W. Moody et al (eds.), *New History of Ireland, IX; Maps, Genealogies, Lists,* (Oxford, 1984), map by F. J. Byrne, p. 27).

Hiberno-Norse kingdom of Dublin was a critical factor in shaping the diocese of Dublin and Glendalough, while the significance of the settled Christian Norse in Waterford is reflected in the dialectic between the city-focused diocese of that name and the Irish territories of the diocese of Lismore. However, it is unlikely that so many of these territorial structures could have been created and endured had their foundations not already been laid down in previous centuries, as the fuller integration of the Christian Church into Irish society was being achieved.

Thus, early medieval Ireland presents a paradoxical picture of considerable cultural unity coexisting with political fragmentation. At the same time, however, much larger provincial systems of territorial rule were becoming more effective in a society which—as we have seen in Chapter 1—was beginning to closely parallel the feudal conditions evolving elsewhere in Europe. Arguably, at the heart of this culture was the kinship system which, if it no longer served to integrate society as a whole, still defined particular groups within it. From *c.* 1000 onwards, the proliferation of Irish surnames began spreading from the key elite families downwards. Distinctive surnames were a boundary-making device, distinguishing the dynastic heirs from the disinherited edges of the kin group who acquired other surnames. Family names became embedded in specific landed properties, making for a complex mosaic of both small and large territorial lordships and the construction of a close-knit decentralized culture—problematic to interpret, even more difficult to conquer. All of this was paralleled by the wider scattering of institutions of rule, administration and ritual within a quasi-hierarchical system of landed organizations which stretched from the embryonic townland to the provincial kingdom and the archdiocese. While Evans has stressed the role of physically difficult areas such as the bogs and the mountains as the resilient 'refuge' areas for the survival of Irish culture,[41] it may be just as relevant to look to the powerful role of named and rooted kinship groups, observing strict rules about many things, including the non-alienation of family land.

The Legacy of the Middle Ages and the Long-term Cultural Impact of the Anglo-Normans

As we have seen in Chapter 2, the Anglo-Norman achievement in Ireland included the establishment of a durable urban and rural culture and an associated superstructure which became deeply embedded in over half the island. With this movement of settlers came a variety of new names, new ideas about towns, farming and commerce, new continental monastic orders and new territorial and governmental structures. These all led to the revitalization, elaboration and deepening of existing cultural and trading links within the varying parts of Ireland and between them and different parts of Britain. However, we need to recognize that the application of the ethnic label 'Anglo-Norman' to all subsequent developments in medieval Ireland obscures as much as it illuminates. Misleadingly, it infers the overwhelming importance of the spread of innovative settlers, as opposed to a recognition of the interaction between broader and more diverse currents of European life with the equally varied habitats and societies within Ireland. From the day the first Anglo-Normans landed in south Wexford, they were adapting, learning to survive and prosper in a new land and facing up to the possibilities and constraints offered by Ireland's locational considerations, environmental possibilities and above all by the resilience and skills of the populations they had come to conquer. But the latter too were to be irrevocably altered by the confrontation.

For the Anglo-Normans, Ireland's complicated distribution of mountains, hills and boglands brought many permanent difficulties. Even in the major zones of their penetration, upland refuge areas such as the Wicklow and Dublin Mountains still frowned down on the focal points of the colony. In particular, the complicated border zone of interlaced woods, bogs, lakes of the extensive drumlin and wet clay lands running across the north midlands and south Ulster, acted as a powerful barrier. Again the great midland bogs and woods acted as refuges for a resilient Gaelic-Irish culture. The Anglo-Normans did not like the wetlands; neither did their horses.[42] But the most profound ecological environment which they had to deal with was the grasslands and their associated mobile, flexible and pastoral society. The relative success or failure of the Anglo-Normans in a number of frontier regions within the island lay in the varied nature of their adjustments to this cultural world. The rich all-purpose grassland soils were characteristically fragmented and located in different parts of the lowlands, accentuating the importance of these various nuclear zones for regional sub-cultures. One does not understand the Anglo-Norman achievement in Ireland without recognizing how regionalized and fragmented its sub-cultures were.[43]

Finally and most relevant, the Anglo-Normans had to deal with the rooted Gaelic-Irish populations. Just as they were agents of change, the Anglo-Normans were also to borrow much from this culture, aptly described as 'cellular and decentralized', with its scattered institutions and mobile elites and the incompatibility of its cultural unity and political fragmentation.[44] The Anglo-Normans benefited from, exploited and deepened these patterns of political fragmentation. Heavily armed, well-drilled and land-hungry, they cut through the country like well-trained beagles, smelling out the good land.[45] However, we should not over-exaggerate their eye for country. Like the later Spanish conquistadors in Latin America, they went straight for the wealthy arable cores of the existing culture, understanding very early on the strategic centrality of the great monastic and secular centres. They appreciated, too, the crucial importance of labour supply for a society committed to tillage and the production of grain for the market.

The Anglo-Norman colonization had a powerful impact in the Dublin–Meath metropolitan core, and this must have involved a substantial displacement or integration of the older freeholder farmers and the reorganization of their territories (see the gap in the Dublin triangle apparent on Fig. 12.2). Elsewhere, it has been argued that the colonizers were, for the most part, constructing their manorial estates and associated parochial structures (centred around nucleated villages with castle, church and mill) within a territorial framework which was at least in part defined prior to their coming.[46] From the ploughlands/townlands through the manors and parishes right up to the cantred/baronial level, there was much dovetailing of older and newer units. Over-arching all these territorial structures was the twin system of the first centralized government ever established on the island. This pivoted around the castle and administration in Dublin and the local county/shire government, the latter in turn centred on the county court and the person of the sheriff. The beginnings of a county system of territorial administration represented a new and significant feature of the political geography of Ireland. By the middle of the thirteenth century, the imposition on the colony of the developing common law of England was well in hand, introducing into 'colonial ' Ireland a remarkably centralized legal system and a highly effective instrument for the extension of royal power.[47]

As we have seen in Chapter 2, underpinning all of these patterns was the development of towns and urban life, the central fulcrum of the Anglo-Norman colonial process. The late thirteenth- and early-fourteenth-century customs returns highlight the pre-eminence of the southern and south-eastern ports in the island (Fig. 2.9). All of these were Viking foundations except New Ross and Drogheda, which between them controlled the two richest grain-producing areas in the whole island, respectively along the Barrow and the Nore in the south-east and the Boyne. However, the later medieval period witnessed quite substantial changes in the port hierarchy, which hint at more profound transformations island-wide. These had been heralded by the great economic recessions and plagues of the fourteenth century, not to mention the contraction of the highly extended and loosely connected Anglo-Irish frontier. The so-called 'Gaelic Resurgence' included anchor points in south-west Munster, in much of Connacht, the Midlands, south Leinster and Ulster. In these regions, a more militant and effective system of Gaelic-Irish opposition could bring about a very rapid collapse in the Anglo-Irish settlement.[48]

Consequently, on the marches of the Anglo-Irish settlement, manorial villages and other settlements were abandoned or shrank in size. But—as we have seen in Chapter 3—it is doubtful if the Gaelic-Irish resurgence did actually overrun or obliterate either towns or well-established settler communities in the arable regions. Even allowing for the new plantation towns, as late as 1660 the urban pattern was still predominantly medieval in distribution and character. Most larger centres still maintained their defensive walls which marked the boundaries between the relatively privileged and now mainly English-speaking urban societies and the essentially rural worlds beyond their gates.[49] So in spite of the apparent disappearance or decline of some of the towns of the early Anglo-Norman frontiers, and the collapse of some centres in the other established settlement areas because of changing economic, political and physical conditions, the medieval urban pattern was for the most part a relatively enduring one. The majority of its towns remained in a position to benefit from the upswing in the economy from the late fourteenth century onwards.

Overall, the impression gained is that for most of the fifteenth and sixteenth centuries Irish towns and their 'Old English' merchants developed sophisticated regional and international trading links.[50] The further a port was from Britain, the deeper the involvement which it had in continental trade and fishing. Thus, the towns of Galway and Limerick and, to a lesser degree, Cork and Waterford acted with a degree of freedom from central government which the citizens of Bristol and London never dreamed of. Butlin compares the virtual 'city state' status of some Irish ports, particularly Galway with its rich Iberian trade, to the development of civic independence shown by the municipalities of Italy. Taking the analogy further, with the transformed trading patterns in Atlantic Europe and the shift in European trade away from the Mediterranean and towards the Atlantic, Ireland's position in the great ocean was akin to that of Italy in the Mediterranean; both formed bridgeheads between countries of different productive capacities.[51]

The importance of this mercantile economy in Ireland in the fifteenth and sixteenth centuries and the level of profit and prosperity accruing to the merchants is reflected in the striking tower houses cum town houses which they built for themselves (see Chapter 3). Conceivably, much of the literature about these tower houses has placed too much emphasis on their undoubtedly defensive function and far too little on their role as indicators of expanding wealth, a transformed class structure and a responsiveness to new fashions in buildings in the late medieval/ early modern transition in Ireland. There are very few references to tower houses in descriptions of local wars, but they are inevitably mentioned by owners in leases, wills, mortgages and family disputes.[52] Again, they were most numerous in the fertile heartlands of the great lordships where settled conditions prevailed, rather than in the more difficult border regions.

Unlike its likely predecessor—the medieval moated site—this new fortified residence does not appear to have defined a sharp cultural frontier between the Gaelic-Irish and Old English elites but rather a shared architectural tradition. Moreover, the tower house also points to a growing connection between the fortunes of town and countryside, as the sons of gentry entered the mercantile world and, as merchants, bought up or rented extensive estates in rural regions.[53] Thus the spread of the tower houses can be seen as symbolic of significant changes in Irish society and economy in the late medieval transition period. Their distribution suggests a strong relationship between towns, especially port towns, and the economic development of their rural hinterlands. It also implies a greater emphasis on commercialized mixed farming especially in sheep and cattle. The social stature of their builders— landowners, gentry and large leaseholders—suggests a break with the older feudal hierarchies and hints at the embryonic growth of a more independent breed of rural and urban capitalist entrepreneurs.

Such transformations involved new kinds of land management with large-scale production and a greater individualism in the ownership and occupation of land. They also led to a greater emphasis on sharecropping between large landowners and rural middlemen and the severely pressed sharecropping tenant and labouring classes.[54] These changes in economy and class structures may owe something to the territorial collapse of the 'colony' on the edge of the Anglo-Irish marchlands in the early fourteenth century. More probably, they also represented the cumulative consequences of the structural chaos that followed the Black Death and subsequent plagues and economic depressions in mid- and late-fourteenth-century Ireland. This altered trading patterns with Europe, occasioning a greater emphasis on exports dependent on pastoral rather than tillage regions. These changes also imply that the so-called 'Gaelic Resurgence' in its most mature and self-confident phase was a far more complex phenomenon involving significant internal, social and economic changes. Slow population recovery was also evident from the early fifteenth century onwards, and the population was to reach about one million by 1500 and to climb to about 1.4 million by 1600.

These developments seem to point to a new equilibrium between the several cultures in Ireland. A modified Anglo-Irish society had emerged which had obviously adjusted to the ecological possibilities and constraints of the Irish habitat and which had sometimes adopted Gaelic-Irish kinship strategies in dealing with the complex problems of both managing border territories and taking care of milch cattle. There were also other internal transformations within the Anglo-Irish lordships. On the other hand, the Gaelic-Irish societies, especially those of the south and west, had also been adjusting slowly to new modes of thought and production. A more parish-centred village culture was part of all of this as was the strength and self-confidence of its rural elites and middle classes. But as we have seen in Chapter 3, the most striking feature of fifteenth- and sixteenth-century Ireland was the expansion and consolidation of the great lordships into essentially autonomous regions. Each of these was dominated by key dynasties who developed their own spheres of administration and in some cases—as with the Butlers and the O'Reillys—their own regional legal codes as well. It was these lordships, displaying greater or lesser levels of disobedience to the Dublin and London administrations, which the Tudor administration set out to smash after 1530. The Tudor conquest may not have been a clash between a highly centralized absolutist state and a tribal society.[55] Rather, it was a long and bitter struggle between a modernizing centralized English state and a country where very large territorial entities had evolved. These were based on the forging of ambivalent links between the formal administrative regions of the lordships and the more dynamic functional regions pivoting around the ports.

Turning to the long-term cultural impact of the Anglo-Norman colonization, late medieval Ireland was clearly divided between regions of common law, regions of mixed law and areas where the flexible Brehon law prevailed.[56] Even more complex interactions occurred between different kinds of property systems, social and settlement structures, economy, population levels, the distribution of wealth and power and indeed the specific arrangement of family names within the Gaelic-Irish and the now Old English areas.[57] One can easily oversimplify the picture by stressing the polarities between a predominantly subsistence pastoral economy adjoining woodland, bog and mountain edges in the north, midlands and southwest, and the more stratified, densely populated rural village communities of the south and east. These lived within a more individually-based property system exposed to market conditions emanating from the local walled towns and major ports such as Waterford and Drogheda. In between were extensive hybrid zones where property systems were fluid but tended to private property structures, notably in the mixed farming pastoral belt that ran south from Roscommon and Westmeath through north Tipperary and Clare and on to north Cork.

Underneath this framework were the cumulative currents of more intangible cultural interactions, which came to be enshrined in townland, family and Christian names. Jones Hughes' work on Irish place-names has shown that only 14 per cent of Irish townland names derive from the medieval settlement.[58] The most critical of these incorporate the suffix 'town', combined usually with an Anglo-Norman surname. These place-names highlight the Old English property core of east Leinster in 1641. A secondary core area emerges in the Bargy and Forth region of south Wexford. In both these regions, the toponymic dominance of 'town' place-names suggests long-established English linguistic supremacy. Weaker core areas for the 'town' zone are found in County Kilkenny, south Tipperary, Limerick and east Cork, and here it is noticeable that a wide range of other hybrid Norman-Irish place-names such as Cloghkeating (Keating's castle) also appear. In other areas, hybrid place-names such as *baile* (bally) suggest an intermingling of Gaelic- and Anglo-Irish cultures, as in parts of Westmeath, east Connacht and east Leinster.[59]

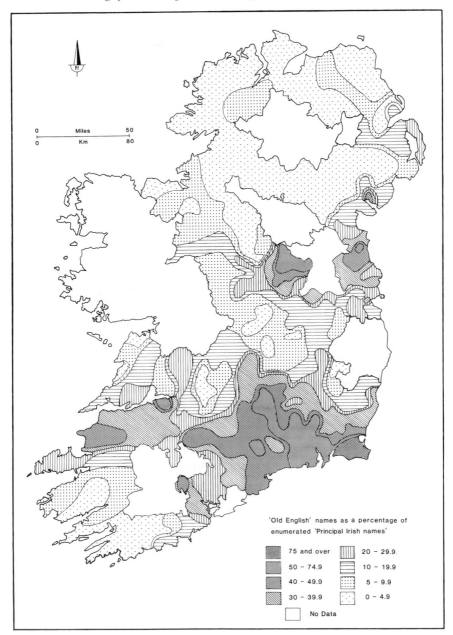

Fig. 12.5. The distribution of 'Old English' surnames as returned in the 1660 poll-tax.

Place-names provide us with a single layer of cultural accretions. The island-wide distribution of family names (as revealed in the 1660 poll-taxes) reflects more faithfully and more intimately the overall distribution of property and social systems and lordship boundaries (Fig. 12.5). For example, the scattering of more 'mobile' Old English names points to other forms of variation not revealed by the embedded place-names. The far greater impact of Anglo-Norman culture in the south of the island is here fully revealed, indicative of the great regional variations in the evolution of these names. In the Pale area, Old English surnames remained relatively unchanged, whereas in the far west—for example in the old Desmond Lordship—Anglo-Norman family names were markedly Gaelicized (Fig. 12.5).

Overall, the family name distribution strongly reinforces the view that it was in the southern half of the island that the great dialogue between Gaelic- and Anglo-Irish was most evenly balanced. It also hints at the importance of the much slower processes of colonization in the mixed upland and lowland topographies of the south. The rapid expansion of cultural groups along coasts and along the main river valleys did not necessarily involve much mutation of the dominant culture but the slow, ponderous and piecemeal expansion of settlement *overland* involved profound adaptations to local exigencies. This was evidently the situation in many parts of Munster and south Leinster. Such processes of adaptation and accultu-ration were more clearly accentuated in the great pastoral areas of east Connacht and the west Midlands.

Even more intimate levels of cultural exchange are revealed when we start to explore the use of characteristic Christian names amongst the Anglo-Norman and Gaelic-Irish populations.[60] The critical question here relates to the extent to which the Anglo- and Gaelic-Irish adopted Old Gaelic and Anglo-Norman Christian names respectively. Work published elsewhere on the changing distribution of Christian names highlights the consequences of the long processes of interaction between two peoples; of love-making, night-walking, made matches and daughters being beaten into church and into bed to satisfy the property alliances of the hardheaded Anglo- and Gaelic-Irish farmers.[61] The oscillations in the distri-bution of Anglo-Norman *vis-á-vis* Old Gaelic Christian names can be seen as a slow dance, orchestrated over the centuries as two societies engaged, retreated and advanced again. There were obviously other variables at work in shaping these naming patterns—the effect of different kinship and property inheritance systems on naming procedures, the effect of Church influences on naming fashions and a host of other imponderables. But even allowing for these, the gradations in Chris-tian naming patterns tells us much about the broader patterns of cultural interac-tion amongst the general population as well as amongst the elites. The island-wide pattern of Christian names cannot be fully reconstructed but the limited evidence suggests that the greatest changes in Gaelic-Irish naming patterns occurred in Leinster.[62] Conversely, the most resilient Gaelic-Irish naming patterns are in mid and west Ulster and south-west Munster. And again, as is often the case in Irish cultural history, east Munster, the Leinster–Ulster borderlands and east Connacht and Clare emerge as the great transitional areas.[63]

Thus the many-sided realities of the Anglo- and Gaelic-Irish interactions are revealed. As we have seen in Chapter 3, the use in the literature of the term, 'Gaelic Resurgence or Reconquest', requires qualification for it simplifies the complex processes taking place in late medieval Ireland. Such terms also obscure other cultural aspects. The Anglo-Irish adaptation of modified lineage systems, their use of excessive military exactions and elements of the Brehon law as well as a rich involvement in and patronage of the Irish language and literature did not mask a sharp sense of separate identity, particularly in the great lordships of the Anglo-

Irish dynasties. Equally, it would appear that these modified Old English cultural worlds exerted a profound influence on adjacent Gaelic-Irish regions. The interactions and adjustments between the two peoples depended on a wide range of factors—location, the relative size of the two populations locally, the degree of urbanization and market influence, the nature of the economy and the terrain, and the proximity or distance from major Anglicizing centres such as Kilkenny, Waterford and Dublin.[64] So for each region a different combination of circumstances was at work, all making for a great variety and a rich mosaic of traditions, naming patterns, dialects, styles of dress and leisure-time activities.

To take but one example, the Desmond lordship of south Munster, often rightly described as one of the most Gaelicized, was in terms of its material culture characteristic of the south-east of the country rather than the north-west. Its leaders were classic frontiersmen and astute politicians. While patronizing Gaelic-Irish poetry, literature and styles of living, nevertheless they ensured that sufficient territorial order prevailed to permit the efficient collection and export of the hides and woollen goods upon which the prosperity of the region depended. Despite frequent economic recessions and frontier conflict, the Anglo-Irish thus constructed a social and economic fabric that was resilient enough to facilitate interaction with Gaelic-Irish traditions, and yet strong enough to maintain a sufficiently distinct identity to allow them to dominate over half the island until the end of the Middle Ages and beyond.[65] Their hybrid character was most in evidence in the non-material areas of culture, in language, dress, literature and sport. Their narrower ethnic and political identity comes sharply into play when questions of property, legal status, privilege in church and government positions arose.

This issue of 'ethnic identity' had much more to do, perhaps, with the behaviour and attitudes of the elites than the population generally. The great source of ambivalence amongst the Old English elites lay in their feudal and political relationships with the English crown upon which their legal titles to land and other privileges were ultimately dependent. A succession of English monarchs and administrators used this feudal connection to regulate the degree of cultural integration that could take place in Ireland.[66] The Old English were fatally compromised by this ultimate dependence. They remained impaled on the cross of a fragmented identity until their material world was smashed and the basis for their separate identity appropriated by what one historian has described as 'the most catastrophic and far-reaching changes that took place anywhere in seventeenth-century Europe'—the Cromwellian conquest and settlement.[67] But the story does not end there. Each province, each county, each diocese and even each parish had its own lines of conflict, accommodation and assimilation between the Gaelic-Irish and the Old English. We have touched on some of the most enduring features of that engagement in our examination of tower house, village and town distributions and variations in property structures, as well as the regional variations in place-names, family names and Christian names. In trying to summarize what Ireland has inherited from the Middle Ages, one could perhaps turn to one final cultural index—in this case, a sporting one. The skilful field game of hurling is centred on the broad hybrid zone in the counties of the deep south (where the tower houses cluster most densely) and is also found in east Clare, south Galway, parts of Laois, Offaly, Meath, Dublin, Down and Antrim. This game was forbidden by the Statutes of Kilkenny in 1366. Yet nowhere is it played better than by the men and women of that county, half of whose teams invariably bear Norman-Welsh names. These hurlers can express in a much more economic and artistic way than I can the grace, dexterity, skill, toughness and persistence of this hybrid middle culture that comes down to us from the later Middle Ages. Such hurlers dance through history—mocking all official, exclusive and narrow definitions of identity.

Conquest and Assimilation: Ireland and the Creation of an English-speaking World

Within the broader framework of European cultural history, the Tudor, Cromwellian and Williamite military victories in Ireland during the sixteenth and seventeenth centuries completed a trinity of conquests or half-conquests of this island. This last conquest—that of the 'New English'—was to be the most complete, traumatic and comprehensive, rivalled only by the levels of political, linguistic and institutional supremacy achieved by the Celtic elites and their descendants. A brief examination of the cultural contrasts between Ireland c. 1530 and c. 1830 reveals the scale and rapidity of the transformations in the political, economic and social geographies of the island over this period. In 1530, Ireland was a land of locally or regionally powerful and relatively autonomous lordships: by the 1830s, an efficient and centralized administration was in the process of creating some of the most comprehensive and intimate of island-wide surveys. These included the production for both town and countryside of the detailed Six Inch Ordnance Survey Maps, the completion of Griffith's Valuation—an extraordinary inventory which purported to show the names of every household and every piece of property in the country—and the publication of what was in effect an exceptional 'social survey', the 1841 Census. And these three surveys were simply the pinnacle of a whole pyramid of Commission reports and 'state of the country' papers that engaged almost every aspect of Irish life in the first half of the nineteenth century.[68] In 1530, Irish language and literature, along with its patrons and practitioners—the local lords, brehons, poets and clerics—was still in the ascendancy. In the 1830s, the ultimate retreat of the Irish language to the remoter insular–peninsular edges of the western half of the island was still a few decades away. Nevertheless, already (and in some regions this had been so for a very long time) seven of the nine domains of language—the worlds of government and the civil service, the courts, the garrisons and the barracks, the fair and market, the print media, the church and the school—were dominated by English speech, words and images.[69] Only the domains of the home and the neighbourhood/street, and these only in very specific regions, were still Irish-speaking. Again, as discussed in Chapter 6, the single religious tradition of the sixteenth century had given way to a plurality of denominations by the nineteenth, each tending to occupy distinctly demarcated geographical areas. Towns and villages were relatively few and far between in the 1530s. Then, Ireland's economy comprised a series of relatively autonomous port-centred maritime regions, involved in some external trade. In contrast, the level of Ireland's economic development and especially the growth in its export trade in the intervening centuries is indicated by the fact that as late as 1800, Ireland was still not only second to Britain in economic importance within the wider British empire but was superior in trade and output to that of the now independent United States.[70] The latter boasted no cities remotely as large as Cork (70,000) or Dublin (200,000), which was the sixth largest city in the whole of Europe—surpassed only by London, Paris, Vienna, Naples and Amsterdam.[71]

The gap between the landscapes and environments of the 1530s and the 1830s was equally vast. Woodland remained a very significant element in the sixteenth-century environment; as late as 1640, it still occupied one-eighth of the land surface. Agricultural land uses were also more extensive than intensive. By the 1830s, the plough and the spade had colonized more arable land than ever before or since in Irish history. Apart from the absence of the now long denuded woodlands, perhaps a further one-quarter of Ireland, particularly land in difficult and marginal locations, had been colonized or recolonized for permanent settlement during the intervening centuries and especially from the 1760s onwards. Many of the colonizers were poor people—the ragged outer edges of a total population that had soared from around one million in 1500 to close on 8.5 million by 1845 (see Chapter 5).

The openness of the sixteenth-century landscape had also disappeared. As discussed in Chapter 7, by the 1830s both society and landscape had been regimented, regularized and reorganized. Compact widespread privatized farms and demesnes now dominated the rural landscape. These were served by a rapidly expanding cottier/labourer population living along the often newly created roadside edges. By 1830, Ireland had one of the densest road networks in the whole of Europe (second only to Belgium), linking even the remotest rural communities to the now almost ubiquitous market and fair towns. Cropping patterns had also been profoundly transformed everywhere across Ireland by the spread of the potato and by the massive intensification of flax production, particularly in the northern half of the island.

Class transformations were also marked in both scope and content. The highly compressed yet still elaborately stratified world of the sixteenth century had long since been extended upwards and downwards. At the top of the early-nineteenth-century social hierarchy were the rich privileged worlds of the great landowners and a small number of industrialists and merchants. Below these, a whole galaxy of new middle class positions had emerged in town and countryside. The skilled artisan classes had also been dramatically enlarged and diversified. At the other end of the class spectrum was the teeming and rapidly expanding impoverished and marginalized mass of the population, subsisting on roadside, bog, mountain and coastal edges or in the cabin suburbs of the cities and towns.

All of these changes intersected with a deeply fragmented society, characterized by complex political processes and divisions. Historians continue to debate the consequences of English, later British, policy in attempting either to assimilate the Irish population into the broader British body politic by peaceful strategies, or else establish an effective British hegemony by forceful and ruthless methods.[72] The ebb and flow of late-sixteenth- and especially seventeenth-century politics in Britain and Ireland resulted in the creation of a colonial system and society in Ireland. The new ruling elites, ethnically defined by their origins and especially by their religious conformity, took most of the glittering prizes and lived out their dream of ascendancy as the local, oftimes ambiguous, agents of the wider British

state. The losers defined as different and subservient by the ethnic marker of their
Catholic or Presbyterian beliefs—by their non-conformity—became involved in a
long and complex process of assimilation to new legal and cultural norms. Ireland
was to remain a deeply divided society which continued to produce a whole series
of hyphenated Irish men and women—the Scots-Irish, the Anglo-Irish, the Gaelic-
Irish and the Catholic-Irish.

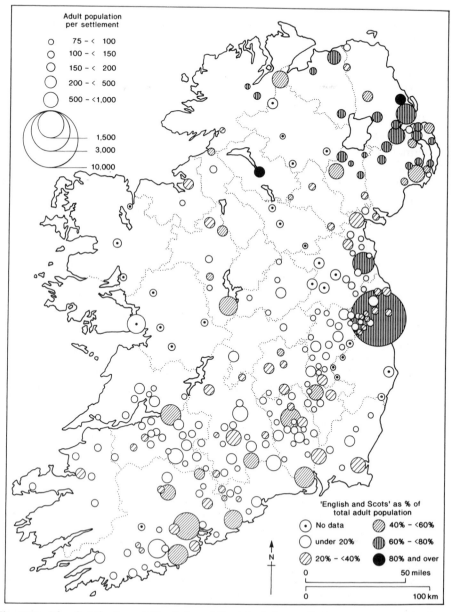

Fig. 12.6. The distribution of 'English and Scots' adult populations as returned in the 1660
poll-tax.

As seen in Chapter 4, we can begin a more detailed evaluation of the changing cultural geography of the island during this period by examining the distribution of immigrant communities in the country by 1660. In demonstrating the scale and regional impact of immigration, Fig. 12.6 highlights the revolutionary nature of seventeenth-century Irish demography for no other European country witnessed a comparable level of inward population movement. Possibly as many as 100,000 migrants came into Ireland between the 1590s and 1690s, almost as many as the total number of Spanish migrants to the whole of Latin America.[73] All these migrations powerfully affected the character of Irish society. There were three core areas of settlement. The largest and most enduring was in the north and northeast, and comprised significant Presbyterian as well as Anglican communities. A second Anglican core extended out from Dublin into the south midlands and along the east coast as far as north Wexford. In the long term the least enduring plantation region was in south Munster. But Fig. 12.6 also highlights the regions where planter settlement was not at all significant—over much of the still densely populated north Leinster plains, in extensive if fragmented belts of south Leinster and Munster and particularly over much of Connacht.

Both within and beyond the planted regions, perhaps the most critical transformation in early modern Ireland related to the ownership of property in town and countryside alike. In 1600 more than four-fifths of Ireland was still held by Catholic owners but by 1641 this figure had been reduced by plantation, intrigue and purchase to 59 per cent.[74] After the Cromwellian wars and settlement, Catholic ownership declined to 29 per cent and by 1703, only 14 per cent of the land remained in the hands of the old owners, a residual figure further reduced in the eighteenth century. No other European country witnessed such an upheaval in the composition of its landowning elites. However, it should be noted that these processes of displacement and dislocation were not uniform throughout the island. With the exception of pockets like Inishowen in Donegal or the Mourne country of Down, gentry dislocation was certainly a clear feature of that half of the island north of a line stretching from Drogheda, Co. Louth, to Ballina, Co. Mayo. In contrast much of south Connacht and Clare retained a significant proportion of old gentry families as did the Pale region of north Leinster. Munster and south Leinster reveal a classic dual structure characterized by a mosaic of old and new elites:

> a battleground of interests—areas where often the planters' more narrow political ascendancy is matched by both the residual class power and greater populations of an older society. Members of the latter society still held on to powerful hinge positions in urban and rural social hierarchies and ensured that the relative success of the new landlord inspired economy would both depend on and be mediated by them.[75]

In the cities and towns the process of displacement was generally more variable. In Dublin and the planted areas, the Old English merchant elites were usually replaced by the new immigrant middle class. Elsewhere, particularly in towns of medieval origin in Connacht and south Leinster, the Catholic merchants survived and prospered.

This colonial period also witnessed an enormously rapid transformation in the economy. Clearly a more commercially oriented market economy was already a feature of the long-urbanized lands of the south and east. However, the outward expansion of the British empire and Ireland's incorporation into a wider imperial and Atlantic economy meant that a rapid monetization and commercialization of the now island-wide economy began in the seventeenth century and was accentuated in the eighteenth. In the mid-sixteenth century, much of the surplus from the land was still being returned to the local lords in kind. Conversely, by the 1660s, it would appear that most rents were being paid in cash by a tenantry increasingly locked into a new landowning culture which had become solidly based on written contractual leaseholding arrangements.[76] One critical indicator of this nexus of trade and commerce was the rapid spread of fairs and markets throughout the whole island in the seventeenth century, followed by a further infilling of the fair network in more marginal locations during the eighteenth. At the centre of all these transformations were the towns, whether reconstructed or more often newly built, which must have given much of the seventeenth-century Irish landscape a dramatically novel appearance, especially in those regions so long dominated by essentially rural cultures. This is likely to have been true of Ulster, the Midlands, much of Connacht and west Munster and indeed pockets elsewhere, as in Wicklow and north Wexford.

In part, Ireland's growing economic integration via cities, towns, fairs and markets was a function of increasing regional specialization as the Irish economy became more and more subservient to the changing requirements of the British and Atlantic economies. Grain production remained solidly rooted in the old medieval arable cores of east and south Leinster and south-east Munster. Cattle farming, while widespread, became more strongly associated with the west Midlands, north Munster and in east Connacht where sheep farming also became conspicuous. Munster was the heartland of the dairying and provision industry, with parts of Ulster also playing a significant role in this sector of the economy as well as underpinning and acting as the diffusion centre for the now rapidly expanding rural-based flax and linen industry.

Economic and social interaction was also facilitated by the elaboration of the already solidly established road network from the 1720s onwards via the private turnpike trusts, and from the 1760s by the road-building activities of the Grand Juries.[77] The elaboration and multiplication of both the road and urban networks acted as a catalyst for the greater commercialization of local economies and also as a critical solvent of older agrarian structures—including the once dominant pattern of clustered townland settlements. Increasingly, the stronger farmers broke away from the older and more inhibiting townland structures and carved out their separate independent farms, often aligned along the new roads.[78] Other villagers came to live in roadside cabins, augmenting the by-now greatly enlarged agricultural and artisan classes which underpinned the society and the economy and literally built this whole new landscape of exploitation and commercialization. As Chapter 7 has shown, the development of a landlord culture across the island from the seventeenth century onwards created a new synthesis of territorial structures ranging from the townland farm through the estate, to the county Grand Jury. Eventually this extended to the island-wide administration centred on that 'committee of landlords', the eighteenth-century Irish Parliament, and onto the extensive connections with England and the Empire generally. This period was also what Flatrès has described as the Age of Pastoralism in Ireland.[79] The creation of large individual farms and the extension of enclosures right up to the edges of the

bogs and the mountains revolutionized the geography and structure of local societies. Some local families were privileged in the processes of landlord-led reform
and were allocated bigger townland farms, others slipped down the scale and
became smaller farmers within the townland or were banished to the margins of
the parish or the estate to create new 'colonial' farms.

The expansive culture of the eighteenth century also underpinned the diversification of rural classes, especially amongst the artisans. Carpenters, slaters, stone-
masons and master-builders all proliferated in this age of reconstruction. Likewise
there was a significant expansion in the composition of bureaucracy of many
landed estates, with their agents, stewards, nurserymen, foresters, horsebreakers,
coachdrivers, dairy women, and galaxy of house-servants. Landlords also encouraged the colonization of the still unenclosed marginal lands by land-hungry small
farmers and their brides by giving rent remissions and encouraging building.[80] The
more elaborate road system also facilitated the movement of manure, goods and
products to and from these former backward locations. Amongst the proliferating
rural labouring class, there were also internal subtleties and stratifications which
distinguished the relatively privileged occupants of the estate cottages from the
tied farm-labourers and the migrant labourers (or '*spailpíní fánacha*'). They, in turn,
symbolized the greater economic integration of the subsistence regions and
advanced farming regions, both within Ireland and between it and Britain. The
regular juxtaposition of bog, hill and poor land with rich lowland regions meant
that a whole mosaic of servant-exporting parishes coexisted alongside their ser-
vant-importing counterparts.[81] Arthur Young, despite his other agendas, managed
to capture some of the teeming diversity of this late-eighteenth-century culture and
comments on the high density of traffic on Irish roads compared to their French
equivalents.[82] In the more developed farming regions, other sons and daughters
were gravitating towards the expanding Irish towns and cities, while others were
already going further afield, smoothing—as we have seen in Chapters 10 and 11—
the later migrant pathways to Britain, North America and Australia. And bubbling
underneath all this buoyancy and bustle, there were gathering storms about
liberty, equality and fraternity, the Union, Catholic Emancipation, tenant rights
and church tithes. The decades from the 1780s to the 1820s were to be pivotal in
shaping the cultural and political geography of not only nineteenth-century but
also twentieth-century Ireland.

Symbolically, at the centre of this rapid social and economic transformation lay
the changing distribution of Irish and English speech. Recent work has allowed us
to move back into the crucial eighteenth century to get a picture of the changing
cultural regions of speechways, stories and songs.[83] An understanding of the
detailed geography of language change, brings us closer to an understanding of the
wider and deeper social, economic and cultural changes that enveloped Ireland
from the mid sixteenth century. There appear to have been three kinds of core
regions in the diffusion of English speech and images: the north-eastern region of
Scottish and English immigration and settlement; the Anglo-Irish cultural world
centred on Dublin and the midlands core; and the English-speaking worlds of the
major port-cities and towns elsewhere in the island. It was from these regions that
the battle was waged locally and regionally between an urbanizing, imperial, print-
based and aggressive English language and culture, and an Irish language and

culture that was rural-based, more oral and manuscript-centred. Crucially, it had already gone into decline, both socially and geographically, *before* mass communication, high levels of literacy and the forces for democratic social participation effectively developed across the island.

Already in the 1760s the north-eastern region stood out as the zone not only of dominant English speech but also the region with the highest levels of literacy on the island.[84] The north Leinster–south Ulster region was a contracting region of higher levels of Irish speech and illiteracy in English. It formed a buffer zone under pressure from both the literate north-east and the second growth zone of dominant English speech in the Dublin metropolitan region and the remainder of Leinster, with the exception of County Kilkenny. The latter together with Tipperary and Limerick formed part of a transitional zone, rapidly moving towards English speech dominance. This zone extended in a narrow belt through the east Connacht borderlands into east Donegal. South and west Munster, and even more emphatically the rest of Connacht as well as west Donegal, emerged in the mid-eighteenth century as the great bastions of the Irish language, their strong rural culture finding expression too in much Irish poetry and music.

Adams presents a compelling picture of changes in the pattern of language in Ulster.[85] From the north-eastern core of the long planted Scottish and English settlements, English spread southwards along the Lagan corridor. Adopted as a second language during the eighteenth century, it was established as the primary and finally as the only language by *c.* 1850. The core area of expansion extended southwards through Fermanagh and Sligo, essentially cutting off the rich literate Irish culture of south-east Ulster from the more oral-based Irish culture of the north-west. Irish language areas were becoming isolated islands within the island. Other major routeways carried people, trade and language in strong country carts through the lands between north Armagh and Newry, gradually eroding Irish speech as they did so. Likewise, by the mid-nineteenth century, the transverse route from Enniskillen, Co. Fermanagh, to Dublin through Kingscourt, Co. Cavan, had broken down and eroded long-standing areas of Irish speech. Even in the strongly Irish speaking areas of north Donegal, English was beginning to spread from the early nineteenth century onwards from Letterkenny through Kilmacrenan and Creeslough to Dunfanaghy. 'Leanann an Béarla and tearr'—'English follows the tarred roadway'—is how the local people described the interconnections between trade, mobility, better roads and changing speech patterns. Throughout southern Ulster, English speech was spreading northwards and westwards, reflecting the intensity of Dublin's trading interests in these regions. In Ulster, the Irish language declined most rapidly in the 1780s and again more especially after the 1820s, when the development of the national school system, the more exclusive orientation of the Irish economic and political life towards Britain, and emigration towards English speaking North America and other overseas territories all accelerated the drive to acquire English speech.[86] One can track similar language transformations all over the island. The extensive elaboration of the road network linking Dublin with Longford, Roscommon, Limerick and Cork, clearly enveloped inland Leinster and east Munster by the 1730s and 1740s and must have underpinned the early and relatively rapid erosion of Irish in these regions.[87] Likewise, maps of English and Irish speech and levels of literacy in the mid-nineteenth century illustrate the crucial long-term impact of the interactions between the port cities of Waterford, Limerick and Cork and their hinterlands.

Gender differences in levels of literacy are also highly informative. In Ulster, male literacy levels were already quite high in the 1760s and rose steadily to the 1820s. On the other hand there was at least a 20 per cent gap in female literacy rates in the 1760s, followed by a sharp upsurge in the 1780s and 1790s. Clearly women's roles and levels of mobility diversified and accelerated towards the end of the eighteenth century. By the 1820s gender differences in literacy levels in Ulster had been much reduced.[88] Leinster reveals rather similar patterns of development from a slightly lower overall base of literacy. A sharp surge in literacy levels for men occurred from the 1760s and for women from the 1770s and 1780s, with almost equal levels of literacy being achieved by each group by the 1820s. In Munster, male literacy levels rose steadily but not spectacularly up to the 1820s, whereas from the 1780s onwards, there again appear to have been very rapid literacy gains by women. The predominantly Irish-speaking province of Connacht was similar to Munster but with lower levels of literacy in the 1760s. Female literacy levels in English were less than 15 per cent. Again there was a steady rise in levels to the 1820s for both gender groups with a sharper surge after the 1780s. However, it should be noted that overall literacy levels in Connacht by the 1820s were no greater than the corresponding position for Leinster in the 1760s. Language and literacy therefore highlight the very different cultural regions coexisting in late-eighteenth- and early-nineteenth-century Ireland.

As with other cultural indicators, Ireland's language patterns reveal a nuanced and complex matrix of speech and customs which requires much greater analysis. What is clear is that by the mid-nineteenth century, Irish had become—except for some regions of south Munster and much of Connacht—the language of the poor. In the first instance, its areas of strength were confined to the more introverted village clusters of west Connacht. Elsewhere, it was most characteristic of areas with the lowest land values and the greatest levels of subsistence farming with little or no involvement in a commercial economy, plus those least affected by the landlord culture with its attendant construction of a dense network of roads and 'improved' towns and villages. The overall pattern suggests that by the early nineteenth century, Ireland was already divided into four different kinds of societies: a now receding oral-based Irish speaking culture, a modernizing increasingly literate English speaking culture which exhibited a complex and often confused amalgam of both intrusive and indigenous characteristics,[89] a still triumphant if rather brittle land-centred Anglo-Irish cultural elite which had already reached the zenith of its achievement, and—as discussed in Chapter 8—a burgeoning urban-industrial culture in the north-east, centred on the strongly Presbyterian city of Belfast.[90] This latter culture region had its roots in an older fully-fledged settler society which had become embedded in what was previously the most Gaelic and most resilient of all the Irish provinces—Ulster.

Decolonization and Division

More than a century later (*c.* 1940), the residue of Gaelic, or more properly, Irish-speaking Ireland had been assimilated as a symbol by the now dominant English-speaking Irish nationalist and mainly Catholic community. The political and economic power of the Anglo-Irish had dwindled, but in its twilight years, from Samuel Ferguson, George Petrie and Thomas Davis through to W. B. Yeats, Lady Gregory, Standish O'Grady and J. M. Synge, it had helped create a literature and cultural history transcending the old imperial order which with its excisions, reductions and derisions, invariably mocked the 'native' culture.[91] The Anglo-Irish writers and artists contributed to a new vision of Ireland, its history and prehistory, which was to profoundly affect Irish imagination, politics and art. Conversely, in the north, the predominantly Protestant Unionists were led by the Belfast Conservative industrial bourgeoisie in an alliance with the working classes and the rural tenant farmers. This outflanked the traditional leadership of the landed elites and eventually integrated the older Liberal tradition into a single powerful party machine.[92] It defeated a number of Liberal government attempts to establish Home Rule for all of Ireland and created the personnel and governing structures for the autonomous administration of Northern Ireland within the United Kingdom after the partitioning of the island in 1920/21.

The origins and geographical implications of these political and cultural transformations were equally complex. Events from the 1780s to the 1820s were decisive in shaping the Irelands of the future. Attempts to create a political movement which would have integrated 'Catholic, Protestant and Dissenter' in a reconstituted and more democratic Irish Parliament were ruthlessly crushed by the British state forces and the deliberately mobilized local militias. The Act of Union, which became law on 1 January, 1801, legally terminated the Irish Parliament, symbolizing the British government's lack of trust in the Anglo-Irish elite to manage the country effectively. After the Union, direct London-based state intervention in Irish affairs became a dominant feature of Irish life. The creation of island-wide police and national school systems, the establishment of a hierarchy of dispensaries, asylums, jails and poor law union workhouses, were all evidence of the state's attempts at social control in the nineteenth century, processes which often involved the main Churches (including the Catholic) as allies in this most turbulent of centuries.[93] The Union also meant the effective integration of Ireland's economy—mainly agrarian except in the north-east—into the expanding British industrial world. As we have seen in Chapter 9, this too was to profoundly affect local, regional and national economies and power structures in Ireland. With the introduction of better means of communications between the islands, the Union also led to Ireland being even more profoundly influenced by the wider political, economic and cultural influences flowing from Victorian England. These processes were to deepen the pathways of acculturation as witnessed by emigration to English and Scottish industrial cities, the more rapid spread of the English language in Ireland and the diffusion of English goods and fashions into Irish shops and communities. The same processes were also to stimulate further the legal and political skills necessary to undermine and subvert the whole process of political and cultural integration and help create an independent Ireland. And this latter movement, in turn, revealed the conditional defenders of the Union, the Unionists.

The resurgent Catholic Church is perhaps the most potent symbol of this transformation in the cultural, economic and political geography of the island. Figure 12.7 captures the spread of the territorial and organizational power of the Church

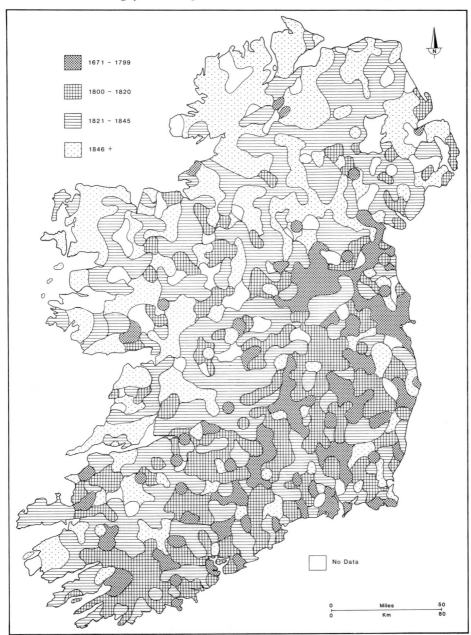

Fig. 12.7. The distribution of first surviving Catholic parish registers (based on National Library of Ireland index).

from the late seventeenth century to the 1880s. Clearly visible are the sharp contrasts between innovative, transitional and laggard regions in terms of Catholic mobilization and reform. Whelan has documented the existence of a core area of the reconstituted Catholic Church in the east and south-east which 'powered the establishment of Catholicism as a central force in the life of the nation'.[94] The cultural geography of the nineteenth-century Catholic Church reveals Ireland's transitional position between territorial and cultural forms of Catholicism in continental Europe and their more novel expressions overseas, particularly in the English speaking worlds of Australia and America where Irish-born priests and nuns played important organizational roles. As Chapter 6 has shown, the picture in Ireland is of a Church having to seek out and put down fresh parish structures and roots around the newly emerging axes of social and economic life. The colonial legacy made Ireland exceptional in western Europe in that a dual parish system emerged—one Anglican, one Catholic. But what this meant was that the Catholic Church was in a very good position to adapt to the rhythms and stresses of the emerging Ireland. While conscious of its medieval roots and territories, its flexible chapel- and parish-building strategies allowed the Catholic Church to adapt to the swift population movements of the cities and towns on the one hand and, if at a somewhat slower rate, to organize the newly populated remoter poorer regions into their respective parish and church communities.

This adaptation and reconstruction also saw the modern Catholic Church—like landlordism before it—launch an assault on archaic traditions and beliefs, as well as on the looser and more regionally diversified rural worlds that persisted well into the nineteenth century. The Catholic Church thus adjusted to and sought to shape the emerging dominant social formations in Irish society. It was part of a more commercialized, hybrid, thrifty, utilitarian English-speaking Ireland which was expanding its cultural space between the retreating and introverted Gaelic order on the one hand and an unsympathetic and weakening colonial world on the other. In this pivotal position, the Church became a crucial mobilizer of new energies, and in part, a creator of fresh images of Ireland. These greatly assisted the restoration of a feeling of dignity amongst individuals and groups and renewed a sense of cohesion in many communities, particularly those traumatized by the Famine and the great exodus associated with large-scale emigration. More particularly, in providing for a whole array of new central places in the countryside—the chapel-villages discussed in Chapter 6—the Church established a nationwide framework of meeting places for various local associations, organizations and movements. Ironically some such parish organizations were deeply frowned upon and opposed by the Catholic hierarchy.[95]

By the second half of the nineteenth century, a Roman-centred administrative framework of dioceses and parishes—underpinned by a now-completed urban and village hierarchy—had been constructed over the island by a mainly English-speaking Catholic clergy. The Church thus constructed an autonomous self-confident territorial hierarchy, a powerful instrument of acculturation, social control and group demarcation, which stretched downwards through a succession of levels to reach Catholic households and individuals alike. Thus, 'the big chapel' was an instrument of both decolonization and recolonization.

Arguably, the first real fusion of wider political, agrarian and Catholic agendas emerged with the Tithe War in the early 1830s. As Chapter 6 demonstrates, conflict over the payment of tithes to the established 'colonial' Church and its tithe proctors and farmers went back to at least the mid-eighteenth century. Then, it involved cross-denominational combinations and alliances between Protestant gentry and middlemen farmers, and varying strata in the Catholic population. By the late 1820s and early 1830s, however, the issue of tithes was no longer seen to be cross-denominational. The long drawn out battle for Catholic Emancipation, as well as related changes in the demographic and power structures of the late eighteenth and early nineteenth centuries, meant that polarization along ethnic/religious lines had deepened, affecting wider areas of Irish life. Therefore, the Tithe War was important for a number of reasons. It was probably the first agrarian cum political movement which originated in local and regional contexts yet grew sufficiently to embrace the whole island, in the process effectively utilizing the now well-established urban structures in addition to the maturing Catholic parochial and diocesan structures. It began in 1831 along the eastern borders of County Kilkenny, rapidly expanding from this old core area of resistance and long established 'counter-cultural' organizations into many adjacent counties. A second smaller epi-centre emerged further north along an axis from Louth to Longford. By 1833, this sophisticated and well orchestrated movement had embraced every county in the island (and emigrant cities in England), but with varying and interesting regional intensities. By 1833, the southern axis of this movement had swung westward to centre over Limerick, Tipperary and Cork, suggesting the merger of the essentially pacifist legal strategies of the more respectable middle class Catholic population with the coercive and violent methods of the turbulent labouring classes in this highly stratified region. The second epi-centre to the north had also expanded to embrace the counties north and east of Longford. This essentially Catholic protest movement against the excessive tithe impositions of what was now often described as a 'fat and colonial church' was weaker in three regions.[96] In the north-east, the divergence between the economic, political and cultural experiences of the now industrializing and mainly Protestant Belfast region in particular and the more agrarian and more Catholic south was growing and deepening. Again, the counties of the Dublin metropolitan region as well as those of the far west were somewhat less deeply committed to this protest.

All this changed with the final major agrarian/political assault on landlordism. In the so-called Land War of the late 1870s and early 1880s, the western counties— heretofore more silent, more remote, more passive—adopted a key leadership role. Crucial to this regional shift in mobilization and politicization was the great watershed of the Famine. Every aspect of modern Irish life would have been altered if that enormous and deeply traumatic transformation in population numbers, social structures, marriage patterns, beliefs and attitudes and languages spoken had not happened. What the Famine meant for the western counties was that the bitter memories of the horrors of those years would not be repeated in the recessionary and difficult years of 1877–79, when the potato crop was again threatened. Equally relevant, the west had been literally opened up to development in the immediate post-Famine decades through the relatively rapid spread of English speech and literacy, and the increased role of towns as centres of their hinterland communities. The latter was especially true of those served by the provincial newspapers and the expanding railway network (Fig. 7.4).[97] It should also be remembered that the final completion of the Catholic parish network in the west preceded this new mobilization (Fig. 12.7). Thus it was that the small struggling cattle farmers, their kin-connected townspeople and some of the returned emigrants of the west joined forces with the Parnell-led Irish Parliamentary Party to finally defeat landlordism in Ireland. In seventeenth-century England, the landlords had retained their ascendency over the peasantry; in nineteenth-century Ireland it was the tenant-farmers who defeated the landlords.[98] Rather like the experiences of the Old English of the mid-seventeenth century, the material basis of the Anglo-Irish was stripped away, their culture being marginalized in the making of the new Ireland. To paraphrase Standish O'Grady, the Protestant Anglo-Irish gentry, who had once owned Ireland from the centre to the sea, ended up on the edges, stranded between two cultures.[99]

The victory of the tenant farmer was followed in quick succession by the expansion of the cooperative dairying movement, the foundation of the Gaelic Athletic Association and the Gaelic League—the Irish language and cultural movement which established branches throughout the country. Thus the economic revolution of the 1880s led to a cultural revolution which, in turn, was followed in the early twentieth century by a political and military revolution. Eventually, these movements and other developments saw the older Irish nationalist parliamentary party replaced almost en bloc by the radical, exclusivist and introverted philosophy of Sinn Féin. A kind of Victorian 'Gaelic Reconquest' was set in motion—a mirror image, in part, of the limiting colonial nationalisms of the late eighteenth century. Yet the maps of parliamentary elections in Land League times and later in 1918 still showed the same gaps in nationalist representation in the north-east, already revealed on the maps of the Tithe War in the early 1830s. The north did not share in many of these developments and in most cases actually opposed their objectives. This region was to pursue a different cultural and political agenda.

In 1911, 62 per cent of the 577,000 Anglican or Episcopalian population of the island lived in the province of Ulster. Almost all of the 444,000 Presbyterians lived in the same nine Ulster counties.[100] The ethos of the northern ascendancy was predominantly Presbyterian, industrialization accentuating this pattern 'since it was the Presbyterians who were most strongly represented among the citizens who built the docks, and shipyards and linen mills on which Belfast rose to its precarious prosperity'.[101] The uncompromising Calvinism of Ulster Presbyterianism had its roots in the seventeenth-century plantations. In the nineteenth century (as in the later twentieth century), the battle between liberal and hard-line Presbyterianism ended in victory for the conservative evangelical wing of the movement. This helped underpin the extraordinary religious revival of 1859 which affected all denominations in the north but was primarily an Ulster Presbyterian phenomenon.[102] Again, in the bitter years of the late nineteenth century, the dormant and plebeian Orange Order was revitalized by gentry and industrialists to become more widely representative of the Protestant community. All of this reinforced a sectarian bigotry which was carried from the countryside into the towns and cities in the early and middle nineteenth century.

The Orange Order 'fostered a sense of community amongst Protestants and institutionalized the instinct of racial superiority over the conquered Catholics', thus augmenting the high degree of physical segregation which in turn reflected and reinforced physic segregation.[103] The political fracturing of the island between 1912 and 1922 nearly led to open war between the two parts of Ireland. These conflict-laden years confirmed northern Protestants in their hatred and fear of southern Republicanism. Northern Catholics were in turn locked into a position of non-co-operation and political inferiority. 'In both communities the already enhanced siege mentality was still further intensified.'[104] There thus developed a lack of congruence between the geographical reach of the new southern state and the *wider* geographical distribution of a population feeling a sense of belonging to this nationalist community; for the Unionists the problem has been that their distinctive sense of identity fails to extend even *as far* as the state boundary.

Conclusions

I have examined elsewhere the social and cultural geography of Ireland since the mid-nineteenth century and especially for this century.[105] Suffice to say here that the period from c. 1850 to c. 1950 could be described as a period of necessary 'closure' for much of the south as the struggle for political and cultural independence was both intensified and achieved. The striking stability of post-Famine southern society and its norms—determined especially by the ethos of the strong farmer which in turn was transferred into the Catholic Church and the towns—was built upon enormously high levels of emigration from the country as a whole. It was this kind of conservative society which put in place many of the essential institutions of an independent state and did so with some courage, ingenuity and tenacity. But there were severe and inevitable limitations to the ideology, imagination and capacities of the young state, cruelly exposed during the 1950s in a decade of fundamental adjustment and high emigration. Radical changes in the nature of the southern state and society took place in the 1960s as new economic, political and cultural policies were adopted, not least in terms of industrialization, the massive development of second and third level educational institutions and the radical transformation in levels of information and media influences. The Republic of Ireland in the late twentieth century is a more complex and secularized cultural world.

In part, the imaginative failure to assimilate the north to the early nationalist agendas reflects a failure to recognize that 'much history revolves around fears and prophecies'—especially the northern apprehensions that Home Rule would mean Rome Rule.[106] But at the beginning of the twentieth century, northern resistance also reflected the Unionists' determination to stay within the wider golden orbit of the then British Empire, so that the northern economy could benefit from the enlarged economies of scale. Since the United Kingdom and Ireland both joined the European Community in 1973, the wheel has come full circle. In recent decades, it is the Republic which has built and produced, however painfully, slowly and fitfully, the key state institutions and personnel to engage on an equal footing the countries and markets of an enlarged European and world community. In the north, deindustrialization, the expansion in miniature of a whole range of state functions, and direct rule from Westminster, have all made for a more dependent and provincial culture. The paramilitaries on both sides are scarcely forces of liberation but rather appear as reactionary voices and actors, locked into battles which belong more to the late nineteenth than the late twentieth century. A seemingly unimportant disagreement about the rendering of the place-name Doire/

Derry/Londonderry reveals both the nature and the depth of the division between these opposed Irish traditions. One ethnic group recognizes only a rendering which glorifies the pre-plantation past, the other the British-derived post-plantation heritage. Translated into the broader political framework, these differences indicate that the ultimate 'Republican' goal is to reverse both the Anglo-Norman and Tudor conquests. Conversely, for the 'Loyalist' community, the maintenance and assertion of their continued sense of superiority necessitates the retention of a British state apparatus and the non-recognition of the material and symbolic rights of the nationalist community.[107] Neither of these two positions is tenable, feasible, or desirable. That the situation in Ireland in 1992 is markedly different to that of 1892 is strongly suggested by a recent statement of the Managing Director of the Ulster Bank that the whole island of Ireland should be seen and treated as a single economy within the European Community.[108] The Anglo-Irish Agreement signed at Hillsborough represents one step in a unique, imaginative and *long-term* attempt to build structures on the island of Ireland, between Ireland and Britain, and between the two islands and the rest of the European Community which, hopefully, will bring about a process of recognition and general reconciliation between all the peoples and traditions north and south, and on both sides of the Irish Sea.

This chapter has addressed some of the complexities, nuances and faultlines of the many Irelands that have existed and still exist on this small diverse island. We need to explore the meanings and implications of these diversities as well as seeking to further understand the nature of the shared cultural heritage of all the peoples who have lived on this compact echo-chamber of an island. The old provincial structures are still relevant to understanding the deeper regional diversities that exist across Ireland. They also may be relevant to a longer-term and more fruitful collaboration between all its peoples.

References

1. James Joyce, *Portrait of the Artist as a Young Man*, (New York, 1966), p. 163.
2. Pierre Flatrès, *Géographie Rurale de Quatre Contrées Celtiques* (Rennes, 1957); E. Estyn Evans, 'The Atlantic ends of Europe', *Advancement of Science*, 58 (1958), pp. 1–8.
3. T. W. Moody, F. X. Martin and F. J. Byrne (eds.), *A New History of Ireland, III; Early Modern Ireland, 1534–1691*, (Oxford 1976), pp. 561–633; M. Richter, 'The European dimension of Irish history in the eleventh and twelfth centuries', *Peritia*, (1988), pp. 328–45; T. W. Moody, F. X. Martin and F. J. Byrne (eds.), *A New History of Ireland, IX; Maps, Genealogies, Lists*, (Oxford, 1984), Map 17, 'The Irish abroad c. 590–c. 1240; D. Whitelock, R. McKitterick and D. Dumville (eds.), *Ireland in Early Medieval Europe*, (Cambridge, 1982).
4. D. Moore (ed.), *The Irish Sea Province in Archaeology and History*, (Cardiff, 1970); M. Ryan (ed.), *Ireland and Insular Art, A.D. 500–1200*, (Dublin, 1987); C. E. Thomas (ed.), *The Iron Age in the Irish Sea Province*, (London, 1972).
5. W. J. Smyth, 'The western isle of Ireland and the eastern seaboard of America— England's first frontiers', *Irish Geography*, 9 (1978), pp. 1–22.
6. T. Jones Hughes, 'Society and settlement in nineteenth-century Ireland', *Irish Geography*, 5 (1965), pp. 79–96.
7. F. J. Byrne, *Irish Kings and High-Kings*, (London, 1973), pp. 202–29; T. F. O'Rahilly, *Early Irish History and Mythology*, (Dublin, 1946), pp. 280–4.
8. E. Estyn Evans, *The Personality of Ireland*, 2nd edn, (Belfast, 1981), pp. 18–41.

9. R. Warner, 'The earliest history of Ireland' in M. Ryan (ed.), *Illustrated Archaeology of Ireland*, (Dublin, 1991); L. Laing, 'The Romanization of Ireland in the fifth century', *Peritia*, **4** (1985), pp. 261–78.

10. D. A. Binchy, *The Linguistic and Historical Value of the Irish Law Tracts*, (Dublin, 1943).

11. A. and B. Rees, *Celtic Heritage*, (London, 1989), pp. 118–39; Evans, *Personality, op. cit.*, p. 25.

12. F. Mitchell, *The Irish Landscape*, (London, 1976), p. 94.

13. M. J. O'Kelly, *Early Ireland*, (Cambridge, 1989), pp. 33–67.

14. Mitchell, *Landscape, op. cit.*, p. 17. For America see J. Leighley (ed.), *Land and Life—A Selection of the Writings of Carl Ortwin Sauer*, (Berkeley, 1967).

15. Mitchell, *Landscape, op. cit.*, pp. 122–3.

16. D. Ó Corráin, 'Panorama 800', to be published in *New History of Ireland, I*, (Oxford, in press). My thanks to Professor Ó Corráin for providing me with a copy of this chapter in typescript. Page references are to this typescript copy.

17. Evans, *Personality, op. cit.*, pp. 44–6; B. Raftery, *La Tèene in Ireland: Problems of Origin and Chronology*, (Marburg, 1984); Idem, 'Barbarians to the West' in J. C. Barrett et al (eds.), *Barbarians and Romans in North-West Europe*, BAR International Series **471**, (Oxford, 1989), pp. 117–52.

18. Evans, *Personality, op. cit.*, p. 45.

19. *Ibid.*, pp. 1–17.

20. *Ibid.*, p. 43.

21. *Ibid.*, p. 50. See also Mitchell, *Landscape, op. cit.*, pp. 159–71.

22. E. Gwynn (ed.), *The Metrical Dinsenchas*, (Dublin, 1913). See also P. Sheeran, '*Genius Fabulae*: the Irish sense of place', *Irish University Review*, **18(2)** (1988), pp. 191–206.

23. For a general theoretical discussion on these issues see R. A. Dodgshon, *The European Past: Social Evolution and Spatial Order*, (London, 1987), especially pp. 55–105. For Ireland, see J. Hogan, 'The *tricha cét* and related land measures', *Proceedings of the Royal Irish Academy*, **38C** (1929), pp. 148–235; W. Reeves, 'On the townland distribution of Ireland', *Proceedings of the Royal Irish Academy*, **7** (1862), pp. 473–90; T. McErlean, 'The Irish townland scheme of landscape organisation' in T. Reeves Smyth and F. Hamond, *Landscape Archaeology in Ireland*, BAR British Series **116** (Oxford, 1983), pp. 315–39.

24. D. Ó Corráin, *Ireland Before the Normans*, (Dublin, 1972), pp. 52–61.

25. Ó Corráin, 'Panorama 800', *op. cit.*, pp. 20–1.

26. Hogan, 'The *tricha cét*', *op. cit.*, pp. 20–1.

27. Byrne, *Irish Kings, op. cit., passim.*

28. *Ibid.*, pp. 70–129.

29. G. MacNiocaill, *Ireland Before the Vikings*, (Dublin, 1972), pp. 1–41.

30. Byrne, *Irish Kings, op. cit.*, pp. 254–74.

31. A. P. Smyth, *Celtic Leinster: Towards a Historical Geography of Early Irish Civilisation, 500–1600*, (Dublin, 1982). See also, Byrne, *Irish Kings, op. cit.*, pp. 130–64; Ó Corráin, *Ireland, op. cit.*, pp. 23–7.

32. Byrne, *Irish Kings, op. cit.*, pp. 165–201. Rees, *Celtic Heritage, op. cit.*, pp. 126–39; Ó Corráin, *Ireland, op. cit.*, pp. 1–9.

33. Ó Corráin, *Ibid.*, pp. 6–7.

34. Byrne, *Irish Kings, op. cit.*, pp. 215–20.

35. H. Mytum, *The Origins of Eary Christian Ireland*, (London, 1992), pp. 21–52.

36. *Ibid.*, pp. 53–9; Evans, *Personality, op. cit.*, pp. 79–82; B. Ó Madagáin, 'Cultural continuity and regeneration', in G. Ó Tuathaigh (ed.), *Community, Culture and Conflict*, (Galway, 1986), pp. 17–30.

37. Moody et al (eds.), *New History of Ireland, IX*, pp. 23–7, esp. p. 23.

38. D. Dumville (ed.), *Church and Society in Ireland A.D. 400–1200*, (London, 1987), pp. 253–5; J. Ryan, *Clonmacnoise*, (Dublin, 1973).

39. C. Doherty, 'Some aspects of hagiography as a source for Irish economic history', *Peritia*, **1** (1982), pp. 300–28.

40. J. A. Watt, *The Church in Medieval Ireland*, (Dublin, 1972), pp. 1–27.

41. Evans, *Personality, op. cit.*, p. 25.

42. Mitchell, *Landscape, op. cit.*, pp. 183–91.
43. R. Frame, *Colonial Ireland, 1169–1369*, (Dublin, 1981), pp. 22–50.
44. P. MacCana, 'Early Irish ideology and the concept of unity', in R. Kearney (ed.), *The Irish Mind: Exploring Intellectual Traditions*, (Dublin, 1985), pp. 56–78.
45. F. Mitchell, *Landscape, op. cit.*, p. 185; M. G. Gardiner and T. Radford, *Soil Associations of Ireland and their Land Use Potential*, (Dublin, 1985), pp. 56–78.
46. I. Leister, *Peasant Open Field Farming and its Territorial Organisation in County Tipperary*, (Marburg, 1976), pp. 35–70; A. Simms, 'Continuity and change: settlement and society in medieval Ireland c. 500–1500' in W. Nolan (ed.), *The Shaping of Ireland—The Geographical Perspective*, (Dublin, 1986), pp. 44–65.
47. K. Nicholls, 'Anglo–French Ireland and after', *Peritia*, **1** (1982), pp. 370–403; see p. 371.
48. *Ibid.*, p. 372.
49. W. J. Smyth, 'Society and settlement in seventeenth century Ireland—the relevance of the "1659 Census"', in W. J. Smyth and K. Whelan (eds.), *Common Ground: Essays on the Historical Geography of Ireland*, (Cork, 1988), pp. 55–83; see pp. 76–9.
50. R. A. Butlin, 'Irish towns in the sixteenth and seventeenth centuries', in R. A. Butlin (ed.), *The Development of the Irish Town*, (London, 1977), pp. 61–100.
51. *Ibid.*, pp. 70–1.
52. C. Ó Danachair, 'Irish tower houses and their regional distribution', *Béaloideas*, **45(7)** (1977), pp. 158–63.
53. See, for example, B. Ó Bric, 'Landholding by Galway townsmen in Connacht 1585–1641', *Irish Economic and Social History*, **2** (1975), pp. 60–1.
54. K. Nicholls, *Land, Law and Society in Sixteenth-Century Ireland*, (N.U.I., O'Donnell Lecture, Cork, 1976).
55. R. Crotty, *Irish Agricultural Production: Its Volume and Structure*, (Cork, 1966). See Chapter 1.
56. K. Nicholls, *Gaelic and Gaelicised Ireland in the Late Middle Ages*, (Dublin, 1972), pp. 44–67.
57. See, for example, W. J. Smyth, 'Property, patronage and population—reconstructing the human geography of mid-seventeenth-century County Tipperary' in W. Nolan (ed.), *Tipperary: History and Society*, (Dublin, 1985), pp. 104–38; *Idem*, 'Territorial, social and settlement hierarchies in seventeenth-century County Kilkenny' in W. Nolan and K. Whelan (eds.), *Kilkenny: History and Society*, (Dublin, 1990), pp. 127–60.
58. T. Jones Hughes, 'Town and *baile* in Irish place-names', in N. Stephens and R. E. Glasscock (eds.), *Irish Geographical Studies in Honour of E. Estyn Evans*, (Belfast, 1970), pp. 244–58.
59. T. Jones Hughes, 'Historical geography of Ireland c. 1700' in G. L. Herries Davies (ed.), *Irish Geography Golden Jubilee, 1934–1984*, (Dublin, 1984), p. 151.
60. W. J. Smyth, 'Making the documents of conquest speak: the transformation of property, society and settlement in seventeenth century Counties Tipperary and Kilkenny', in P. Gulliver and M. Silverman (eds.), *Approaching the Past: Historical Anthropology Through Irish Case-Studies*, (New York, 1992), pp. 348–409.
61. *Ibid.*, pp. 362–3 and p. 369.
62. Based on a preliminary analysis of principal Irish surnames and gentry Christian names returned in S. Pender (ed.), *A Census of Ireland c. 1659*, (Dublin, 1939).
63. *Ibid.*
64. See Smyth, 'Tipperary', *op. cit.* and 'Kilkenny', *op. cit.* See also, *Idem*, 'Exploring the social and cultural topographies of sixteenth and seventeenth century County Dublin' in F. H. A. Aalen and K. Whelan (eds.), *Dublin City and County: From Prehistory to Present*, (Dublin, 1992), pp. 121–79.
65. Frame, *Colonial Ireland, op. cit.*, pp. 134–5; A. Clarke, *The Old English in Ireland 1625–42*, (London, 1966).
66. G. Ó Tuathaigh, unpublished lecture to Irish Adult Education Conference, Limerick, 1980.
67. T. W. Moody, 'Introduction', in Moody et al (eds.), *New History of Ireland, III op cit.*, pp. xiv–lxiii.

68. See, for example, J. H. Andrews, *A Paper Landscape, the Ordnance Survey in Nineteenth Century Ireland*, (Oxford, 1975); W. Nolan, *Tracing the Past: Sources for Local Studies in Ireland*, (Dublin, 1982), pp. 81–114; Jones Hughes, 'Historical Geography', *op. cit.*, pp. 149–51.

69. For a general analysis of domains of language see J. A. Fishman, 'Language mainten-ance and language shift as a field of enquiry', *Linguistics*, **9** (1964), pp. 32–70; *re* Irish situation, see R. Hindley, *The Death of the Irish Language*, (London, 1990), pp. 1–20; M. Daly and D. Dixon (eds.), *The Origins of Popular Literacy in Ireland: Language Change and Education Developments 1700–1920*, (Dublin, 1990).

70. F. E. James, *Ireland in the Empire 1688–1770*, (Harvard, 1973), pp. 1–3 and pp. 218–20.

71. L. M. Cullen, 'The growth of Dublin, 1600–1850' in Aalen and Whelan (eds.), *Dublin, op. cit.*, pp. 251–78.

72. See for example C. Brady and R. Gillespie (eds.), *Natives and Newcomers*, (Dublin, 1986); N. Canny, *From Reformation to Restoration: Ireland 1534–1660*, (Dublin, 1987); B. Brad-shaw, *The Irish Constitutional Revolution of the Sixteenth Century*, (Cambridge, 1979); H. Pawlish, *Sir John Davies and the Conquest of Ireland: A Study in Legal Imperialism*, (Cam-bridge, 1983); Moody et al (eds.), *New History of Ireland, III, op. cit.*

73. Smyth, 'Ireland and America—England's first frontiers', *op. cit.*, p. 8.

74. Clarke, *Old English, op. cit.*, pp. 235–7.

75. Smyth, '1659 Census', *op. cit.*, p. 72.

76. R. Gillespie, *The Transformation of the Irish Economy, 1550–1700*, (Dundalk, 1991), pp. 26–7.

77. J. H. Andrews, 'Road planning in Ireland before the railway age', *Irish Geography*, **15(1)** (1963), pp. 17–41.

78. L. M. Cullen, 'Man, landscape and roads—the changing eighteenth century', Nolan (ed.), *Shaping of Ireland, op. cit.*, pp. 123–36.

79. Flatrès, *Géographie Rurale, op. cit.*, pp. 210–50.

80. W. J. Smyth, 'Estate records and the making of the Irish landscape—an example from County Tipperary', *Irish Geography*, **8** (1976), pp. 39–49.

81. See for example, J. Bell, 'Hiring Fairs in Ulster', *Ulster Folklife*, **25** (1979), pp. 67–78; W. J. Smyth, 'Continuity and change in territorial organisations of Irish rural communi-ties', *Maynooth Review*, **1** (1975), pp. 51–73; J. H. Johnson, 'The two Irelands at the beginning of the nineteenth century', in Stephens and Glasscock (eds.), *Irish Geographi-cal Studies, op. cit.*, pp. 224–43. See also 1930 school manuscripts of the Irish Folklore Commission and the work of regional novelists and poets such as Peadar O'Connell and Patrick Kavanagh.

82. Arthur Young, *Touring Ireland*, A. W. Hutton (ed.), 2 vols, (London, 1892), **1**, p. 115.

83. Daly and Dickson, *Popular Literacy, op. cit.*; G. Fitzgerald, 'Estimates for baronies of minimum level of Irish speaking amongst successful decennial cohorts, 1771–1781 to 1861–1871', *Proceedings of the Royal Irish Academy*, **84C** (1984), pp. 3–155.

84. G. Kirkham, 'Literacy in north-west Ulster 1680–1860', in Daly and Dickson, (eds.), *op. cit.*, pp. 73–96; Introduction, Census of Ireland, 1841.

85. B. G. Adams, 'Language in Ulster, 1820–1850', *Ulster Folklife*, **19** (1973), pp. 50–5; 'The 1851 language Census in the north of Ireland', *Ulster Folklife*, **20** (1974), pp. 65–70.

86. Adams, 'Language', *op. cit.*, pp. 54–5.

87. Andrews, 'Road-planning', *op. cit.*, pp. 18–25 and especially Figure 3 on p. 23.

88. Based on an analysis of age-cohorts per county in the introductory section of the 1841 Census which deals with literacy levels.

89. L. M. Cullen, *The Emergence of Modern Ireland, 1600–1900*, (London, 1981), pp. 18–24.

90. J. C. Beckett and R. E. Glasscock (eds.), *Belfast: The Origin and Growth of an Industrial City*, (London, 1967), pp. 67–97.

91. E. W. Said, 'Yeats and decolonisation' in S. Deane (ed.), *Nationalism, Colonialism and Literature*, (Minneapolis, 1990), pp. 69–95.

92. See especially P. Gibbon, *The Origins of Ulster Unionism*, (Manchester, 1975), pp. 112–42.

93. O. MacDonagh, *Ireland Since the Union*, (2nd edn, London, 1979); M. Finnane, *Insanity*

and the Insane in Post-Famine Ireland, (London, 1981); D. M. Anderson and D. Killingray, *Policing the Empire: Government Authority and Control 1830–1940*, (Manchester, 1991), pp. 1–32; G. O'Brien, 'The new poor law in pre-Famine Ireland', *Irish Economic and Social History, XII*, (1985), pp. 33–49; G. Brocker, Rural Disorder and Police Reform in Ireland, 1812–36, (London, 1970).

94. K. Whelan, 'Catholic mobilisation 1750–1850', in P. Bergeron and L. M. Cullen, (eds.), *Comparative Aspects of Politicisation in Ireland and France*, (Paris, 1990).

95. See, for example, R. Comerford, *The Fenians in Context—Irish Politics and Society 1848–82*, (Dublin, 1985); S. J. Connolly, *Priests and People in Pre-Famine Ireland, 1780–1845*, (Dublin, 1982); S. Clarke and J. S. Donnelly, *Irish Peasants: Violence and Political Unrest, 1780–1914*, (Manchester, 1983), especially pp. 3–139; J. S. Donnelly, 'The Rightboy movement, 1785–8', *Studia Hibernica*, **17–18** (1977–8), pp. 120–202.

96. Based on an analysis of statistical tables presented in P. O'Donoghoe, 'Opposition to tithe payment in 1830–31' and 'Opposition to tithe payment in 1832–33', *Studia Hibernica*, **6** (1966), pp. 69–98 and **12** (1972), pp. 77–108.

97. S. Clark, *Social Origins of the Irish Land War*, (Princeton, 1979), pp. 65–104.

98. For the English situation, see especially J. Barrington Moore, Jr, *Social Origins of Dictatorship and Democracy*, (Boston, 1966), pp. 20–8.

99. Standish O'Grady, quoted by F. S. Lyons, *Culture and Anarchy in Ireland, 1890–1939*, (Oxford, 1979), p. 180.

100. *Ibid.*, pp. 23–4.

101. *Ibid.*, pp. 24–5.

102. Gibbon, *Origins of Ulster Unionism, op. cit.*, pp. 44–66.

103. J. J. Lee, *Ireland 1912–1985: Politics and Society*, (Cambridge, 1990), pp. 2–3.

104. Lyons, *Culture and Anarchy, op. cit.*, pp. 104–5.

105. W. J. Smyth, 'Social geography of rural Ireland—inventory and prospect' in Herries Davies (ed.), *Irish Geography Jubilee Volume, op. cit.*, pp. 204–36; *Idem*, 'Explorations of place' in J. J. Lee, *Ireland: Towards a Sense of Place*, (Cork, 1985), pp. 1–20; *Idem*, 'Continuity and change in the territorial organisation of Irish rural communities, Part II', *Maynooth Review*, **1(2)** (1975), pp. 152–180; *Idem*, 'The cultural geography of rural Ireland in the twentieth century' in Nolan (ed.), *Shaping of Ireland, op. cit.*, pp. 165–75.

106. Lee, *Ireland, op. cit.*, p. 19. For a comprehensive survey and analysis of the vast literature on one of the most heavily researched areas in the world, see J. Whyte, *Interpreting Northern Ireland*, (Oxford, 1991).

107. Smyth, 'Social Geography', *op. cit.*, p. 227.

108. *Irish Times*, 23 March, 1992.

Index